John Hawkins

A General History of the Science and Practice of Music in Five

Volimes

John Hawkins

A General History of the Science and Practice of Music in Five Volimes

ISBN/EAN: 9783741136467

Manufactured in Europe, USA, Canada, Australia, Japa

Cover: Foto ©Angelika Wolter / pixelio.de

Manufactured and distributed by brebook publishing software
(www.brebook.com)

John Hawkins

A General History of the Science and Practice of Music in Five

Volimes

TO

GEORGE THE THIRD,

KING OF GREAT BRITAIN, ETC.

A PRINCE

NOT MORE DISTINGUISHED

BY HIS PATRONAGE OF THOSE ELEGANT ARTS

WHICH EXALT HUMANITY

AND ADMINISTER TO THE IMAGINATIVE FACULTIES

THE PUREST DELIGHTS,

THAN

HONOURED AND BELOVED

FOR HIS REGAL AND PRIVATE VIRTUES,

THE FOLLOWING HISTORY IS,

WITH ALL DUE REVERENCE

AND GRATITUDE,

DEDICATED

BY HIM WHO ESTEEMS IT

EQUALLY AN HONOUR AND A FELICITY

TO SUBSCRIBE HIMSELF

HIS MAJESTY's FAITHFUL AND DEVOTED

SUBJECT AND SERVANT,

THE AUTHOR..

P R E F A C E.

A HISTORY of Mufic by any but a profeffor of the fcience, may poffibly be looked on as a bold undertaking; and it may appear not a little ftrange that one, who is perhaps better known to the world as occupying a public ftation, than as a writer, fhould choofe to be the author of a work of this kind, and for which the courfe of his ftudies can hardly be fuppofed to have in any degree qualified him.

In juftification of the attempt, and to account for this feeming inconfiftency, the reader is to know, that the author having entertained an early love of mufic, and having in his more advanced age not only become fenfible of its worth, but arrived at a full conviction that it was intended by the Almighty for the delight and edification of his rational creatures, had formed a defign of fome fuch work as this many years ago, but faw reafon to defer the execution thereof to a future period.

About the year 1759, he found himfelf in a fituation that left his employments, his ftudies, and his amufements in a great meafure to his own choice; and having in a courfe of years been as induftrious in making collections for the purpofe as could well confift with the exercife of a laborious profeffion, he, with a copious fund of materials, began the work: But before any confiderable progrefs could be made therein, he was interrupted by a call to prefide in the magiftracy of the county of his refidence, which, though unfolicited on his part, he could not decline without betraying an indifference to the interefts of fociety, and the prefervation of public order, or fuch an averfion to the occupations of an active life, as in few cafes is excufable, and in many reproachful.

Deter-

PREFACE.

Determining, however, to avail himself of those intervals of leisure which the stated recesses from the exercise of his office afforded, and which seemed too precious to be wasted either in sloth and indolence, or those fashionable recreations and amusements, to which he was ever disposed to prefer the pursuit of literature, he re-assumed his work; and with the blessing of health, scarcely interrupted for a series of years, has been able to present it to the world in the condition in which it now comes forth.

What the reader is to expect from it, and as the fruit of many years study and labour, is the history of a science deservedly ranked among those, which, in contradistinction to the manual arts, and others of lower importance, have long been dignified with the characteristic of liberal; and as the utility of Music is presupposed in the very attempt to trace its progress, an enumeration of its various excellencies will scarcely be thought necessary; the rather perhaps as its praises, and the power it exercises over the human mind, have been celebrated by the ablest panegyrists.

Farther than the circumstances attending the peculiar situation of the author and the work may be allowed to entitle him to it, the favour or indulgence, or whatever else it is the practice of writers to crave of the public, is not here sued for, either on the ground of want of leisure, inadvertence, or other pretences; for this reason, that there can be no valid excuse for a publication wittingly imperfect: And it is but a sorry compliment that an author makes to his reader, when he tenders him a work less worthy regard than it was in his power to make it.

To be short, the ensuing volumes are the produce of sixteen years labour, and are compiled from materials which were not collected in double that time. The motives to the undertaking were genuine, and the prosecution of it has been as animated as the love of the art, and a total blindness to lucrative views, could render it. And perhaps the best excuse the author can make for the defects and errors that may be found to have escaped him, must be drawn from the novelty of his subject, the variety of his matter, and

the

the necessity he was under of marking out himself the road which he was to travel.

It may perhaps be objected that music is a mere recreation, and an amusement for vacant hours, conducing but little to the benefit of mankind, and therefore to be numbered among those vanities which it is wisdom to contemn. To this it may be answered, that, as a source of intellectual pleasure, music has greatly the advantage of most other recreations; and as to the other branch of the objection, let it be remembered that all our desires, all our pursuits, our occupations, and enjoyments are vain. What are stately palaces, beautiful and extensive gardens, costly furniture, sculptures, and pictures, but vanities? and yet there are few men so vain as that they had rather be without than possess them. Nay, if these be denied us, where are we to seek for amusements, for relief from the cares, the anxieties and troubles of life, how support ourselves in solitude, or under the pressure of affliction, or how preserve that equanimity, which is necessary to keep us in good humour with ourselves and mankind? As to the abuses of this excellent gift, enough it is presumed is said in the ensuing work by way of caution against them, and even to demonstrate that as there is no science or faculty whatever that more improves the tempers of men, rendering them grave, discreet, mild, and placid, so is there none that affords greater scope for folly, impertinence, and affectation.

The end proposed in this undertaking is the investigation of the principles, and a deduction of the progress of a science, which, though intimately connected with civil life, has scarce ever been so well understood by the generality, as to be thought a fit subject, not to say of criticism, but of sober discussion: Instead of exercising the powers of reason, it has in general engaged only that faculty of the mind, which, for want of a better word to express it by, we call Taste; and which alone, and without some principle to direct and controul it, must ever be deemed a capricious arbiter. Another end of this work is the settling music upon somewhat like a footing of equality with those, which, for other reasons than that,

P R E F A C E.

like music, they contribute to the delight of mankind, are termed the sister arts; to reprobate the vulgar notion that its ultimate end is merely to excite mirth; and, above all, to demonstrate that its principles are founded in certain general and universal laws, into which all that we discover in the material world, of harmony, symmetry, proportion and order, seems to be resolvable.

The method pursued for these purposes will be found to consist in an explanation of fundamental doctrines, and a narration of important events and historical facts, in a chronological series, with such occasional remarks and evidences, as might serve to illustrate the one and authenticate the other. With these are intermixed a variety of musical compositions, tending as well to exemplify that diversity of styles which is common both to music and speech or written language, as to manifest the gradual improvements in the art of combining musical sounds, The materials which have furnished this intelligence must necessarily be supposed to be very miscellaneous in their nature, and abundant in quantity: To speak alone of the treatises for the purpose, the author may with no less propriety than truth assert, that the selection of them was an exercise of deep skill, the result of much erudition, and the effect of great labour, as having been for a great part of his life the employment of that excellent theorist in the science, Dr. Pepusch. These have been accumulating and encreasing for a series of years past: For others of a different kind recourse has been had to the Bodleian library and the college libraries in both universities; to that in the music-school at Oxford; to the British Museum, and to the public libraries and repositories of records and public papers in London and Westminster; and, for the purpose of ascertaining facts by dates, to cemeteries and other places of sepulture; and to him that shall object that these sources are inadequate to the end of such an undertaking as this, it may be answered, that he knows not the riches of this country.

A correspondence with learned foreigners, and such communications from abroad as suit with the liberal sentiments and disposition of the pre-

sent

P R E F A C E.

sent age, together with a great variety of oral intelligence respecting persons and facts yet remembered, have contributed in some degree to the melioration of the work, and to justify the title it bears of A General History; which yet it may be thought would have been more properly its due, had the plan of the work been still more extensive, and comprehended the state of music in countries where the approaches to refinement have as yet been but small.

It must be confessed that in some instances, particularly in the discussion of the first principles of morality, and the origin of human manners, the researches of learned men have been extended to nations, or tribes of people, among whom the simple dictates of nature seemed to be the only rule of action; but the subjects here treated of are science, and the scientific practice of music: Now the best music of barbarians is said to be hideous and astonishing sounds*. Of what importance then can it be to enquire into a practice that has not its foundation in science or system, or to know what are the sounds that most delight an Hottentot, a wild American, or even a more refined Chinese?

For the style, it will be found to be uniformly narratory; as little incumbered with technical terms, and as free from didactic forms of speech, as could consist with the design of explaining doctrines and systems; and it may also be said that care has been taken not to degrade the work by the use of fantastical phrases and modes of expression, that, comparatively speaking, were invented yesterday, and will die to-morrow; these make no part of any language, they conduce nothing to information, and are in truth nonsense sublimated.

For the insertion of biographical memoirs and characters of eminent musicians, it may be given as a reason, that, having benefited mankind by their studies, it is but just that their memories should live: Cicero, after Demosthenes, says that 'bona fama propria possessio defunctorum;' and

---

* Characteristics, vol. I. page 242.

for

P R E F A C E.

for bestowing it on men of this faculty, we have the authority of that scripture which exhorts us to praise 'such as found out musical tunes, and ' recited verses in writing' * : Besides which it may be observed, that in various instances the lives of the professors of arts are in some sort a history of the arts themselves. For digressions from his subject, the insertion of anecdotes that have but a remote relation to it, or that describe ancient modes or customs of living, the author has less to say; these must be left to the judgment of his readers, who cannot be supposed to be unanimous in their opinions about them.

It remains now that due acknowledgement be made of the assistance with which the author has been favoured and honoured in the course of his work; but as this cannot be done without an enumeration of names, for which he has obtained no permission, he is necessitated to declare his sense of the obligation in general terms, with this exception, that having need of assistance in the correction of the music plates, he was in sundry instances eased of that trouble by the kind offices of one, who is both an honour to his profession and his country, Dr. William Boyce ; and of the difficulty of deciphering, as it were, and rendering in modern characters the compositions of greatest antiquity among those which he found it necessary to insert, by the learning and ingenuity of Dr. Cooke, of Westminster-abbey, Mr. Marmaduke Overend, organist of Isleworth in Middlesex, and Mr. John Stafford Smith, of the royal chapel.

* Wisdom, chap. xliv. verse 5.

Hatton Garden,
24th Aug. 1776.

PRELIMINARY

(1)

PRELIMINARY

D I S C O U R S E.

THE powers of the imagination, with great appearance of reafon, are faid to hold a middle place between the organs of bodily fenfe and the faculties of moral perception; the fubjects on which they are feverally exercifed are common to the fenfes of feeing and hearing, the office of which is fimply perception; all pleafure thence arifing being referred to the imagination.

The arts which adminifter to the imaginative faculty the greateft delight, are confeffedly poetry, painting, and mufic; the two former exhibiting to the mind by their refpective media, either natural or artificial *, the refemblances of whatever in the works of nature is comprehended under the general divifion of great, new, and beautiful; the latter as operating upon the mind by the power of that harmony which refults from the concord of founds, and exciting in the mind thofe ideas which correfpond with our tendereft and moft delightful affections.

Thefe, it muft be obferved, conftitute one fource of pleafure; but each of the above arts may in a different degree be faid to afford another, namely, that which confifts in a comparifon of the images by them feverally and occafionally excited in the mind, with their architypes; thus, for inftance, in poetry, in comparing a defcription with the thing defcribed; in painting, a landfcape and the fcene reprefented by it, or a portrait and its original; and in mufic, where imitation is intended, as in the fongs of birds, or in the expreffion of thofe various in-

* The natural media feem to confift only in colour and figure, and refer folely to painting: the artificial are words, which are fymbols by compact of ideas, as are alfo, in a limited fenfe, mufical founds, including in the term the accident of time or durat'on.

Vol. I.   a   flexions

flexions of the voice which accompany paffion or exclamation, weeping, laughing, and other of the human affections, the found and the thing fignified.

It is eafy to difcover that the pleafures above defcribed are of two diftinct kinds, the one original and abfolute, the other relative; for the one we can give no reafon other than the will of God, who in the formation of the univerfe and the organization of our bodies, has eftablifhed fuch a relation as is difcoverable between man and his works; the other is to be accounted for by that love of truth which is implanted in the human mind *. In poetry and painting therefore we fpeak, and with propriety, of abfolute and relative beauty; as alfo of mufic merely imitative; for as to harmony, it is evident that the attribute of relation belongs not to it, as will appear by a comparifon of each with the others †.

* In this fentiment liberty has been taken to differ from Mr. Harris, who with his ufual accuracy, has analyfed this principle of the human mind in the following note on a paffage in the fecond of his Three celebrated Treatifes.

' That there is an eminent delight in this very recognition itfelf, abftract from
' any thing pleafing in the fubject recognized, is evident from hence———that, in
' all the mimetic arts, we can be highly charmed with imitations, at whofe origi-
' nals in nature we are fhocked and terrified. Such, for inftance, as dead bodies,
' wild beafts, and the like.

' The caufe affigned for this, feems to be of the following kind: We have a
' joy, not only in the fanity and perfection, but alfo in the juft and natural ener-
' gies of our feveral limbs and faculties. And hence, among others, the joy in
' reafoning, as being the energy of that principal faculty, our intellect or under-
' ftanding. This joy extends, not only to the wife, but to the multitude. For
' all men have an averfion to ignorance and error; and in fome degree, however
' moderate, are glad to learn and to inform themfelves.

' Hence therefore the delight arifing from thefe imitations; as we are enabled
' in each of them to exercife the reafoning faculty; and, by comparing the copy
' with the architype in our minds, to infer that this is fuch a thing, and that an-
' other; a fact remarkable among children, even in their firft and earlieft days.'

† Neverthelefs there have not been wanting thofe, who, not contemplating the intrinfic excellence of harmony, have refolved the efficacy of mufic into the power of imitation; and to gratify fuch, fubjects have been introduced into practice, that to injudicious ears have afforded no fmall delight; fuch, for inftance, as the noife of thunder, the roaring of the winds, the fhouts and acclamations of multitudes, the wail-

ings,

With regard to poetry, it may be said to resemble painting in many respects, as in the description of external objects, and the works of nature ; and so far it must be considered as an imitative art ; but its greatest excellence seems to be its power of exhibiting the internal constitution of man, and of making us acquainted with characters, manners, and sentiments, and working upon the passions of terror, pity, and various others. Painting is professedly an imitative art ; for, setting aside the harmony of colouring, and the delineation of beautiful forms, the pleasure we receive from it, great as it is, consists in the truth of the representation.

But in music there is little beyond itself to which we need, or indeed can, refer to heighten its charms. If we investigate the princi-

ings of grief and anguish in the human mind ; the song of the cuckow, the whooting of the screech-owl, the cackling of the hen, the notes of singing-birds, not excepting those of the lark and nightingale. Attempts also have been made to imitate motion by musical sounds ; and some have undertaken in like manner to relate histories, and to describe the various seasons of the year. Thus, for example, Froberger, organist to the emperor Ferdinand III. is said to have in an allemand represented the passage of Count Thurn over the Rhine, and the danger he and his army were in, by twenty-six cataracts or falls in notes. See vol. IV. page 183. Kuhnau, another celebrated musician, composed six sonatas, entitled Biblische Historien, wherein, as it is said, is a lively representation in musical notes of David manfully combating Goliah. Vol. IV. page 281, in not. Buxtehude of Lubec also composed suites of lessons for the harpsichord, representing the nature of the planets. Vol. V. page 251. Vivaldi, in two books of concertos, has striven to describe the four seasons of the year. Vol. V. page 214. Geminiani has translated a whole episode of Tasso's Jerusalem into musical notes. Vol. V. page 423. And Mr. Handel himself, in his Israel in Egypt, has undertaken to represent two of the ten plagues of Egypt by notes, intended to imitate the buzzing of flies and the hopping of frogs.

But these powers of imitation, admitting them to exist in all the various instances above enumerated, constitute but a very small part of the excellence of music ; wherefore we cannot but applaud that shrewd answer of Agesilaus, king of Sparta, recorded in Plutarch, to one who requested him to hear a man sing that could imitate the nightingale, ' I have heard the nightingale herself.' The truth is, that imitation belongs more properly to the arts of poetry and painting than to music ; for which reason Mr. Harris has not scrupled to pronounce of musical imitation, that at best it is but an imperfect thing. See his Discourse on Music, Painting, and Poetry, pag. 69.

a 2 ples

ples of harmony, we learn that they are general and univerfal; and
of harmony itfelf, that the proportions in which it confifts are to be
found in thofe material forms, which are beheld with the greateft
pleafure, the fphere, the cube, and the cone, for inftance, and conftitute what we call fymmetry, beauty, and regularity; but the imagination receives no additional delight; our reafon is exercifed in the
operation, and that faculty alone is thereby gratified. In fhort, there
are few things in nature which mufic is capable of imitating, and
thofe are of a kind fo uninterefting, that we may venture to pronounce, that as its principles are founded in geometrical truth, and
feem to refult from fome general and univerfal law of nature, fo its
excellence is intrinfic, abfolute, and inherent, and, in fhort, refolvable
only into his will, who has ordered all things in number, weight,
and meafure *.

Seeing therefore that mufic has its foundation in nature, and that
reafon recognizes what the fenfe approves, what wonder is it, that in
all ages, and even by the leaft enlightened of mankind, its efficacy
fhould be acknowledged; or that, as well by thofe who are capable
of reafon and reflection, as thofe who feek for no other gratifications
than what are obvious to the fenfes, it fhould be confidered as a
genuine and natural fource of delight? The wonder is, that lefs
of that curiofity, which leads men to enquire into the hiftory and
progrefs of arts, and their gradual advances towards perfection, has
been exercifed in the inftance now before us, than in any other of
equal importance.

If we take a view of thofe authors who have written on mufic, we
fhall find them comprehended under three claffes, confifting of thofe
who have refolved the principles of the fcience into certain mathematical proportions; of others who have treated it fyftematically, and
with a view to practice; and of a third, who, confidering found as a
branch of phyfics, have from various phenomena explained the manner in which it is generated and communicated to the auditory fa-

* Wifdom, xi. 20.

culty.

culty.   But to whom we are indebted for the gradual improvements of the art, at what periods it flourifhed, what checks and obftructions it has at times met with, who have been its patrons or its enemies, what have been the characteriftics of its moft eminent profeffors, few are able to tell.   Nor has the knowledge of its precepts been communicated in fuch a manner as to enable any but fuch as have devoted themfelves to the ftudy of the fcience to underftand them.   Hence it is that men of learning have been betrayed into numberlefs errors refpecting mufic ; and when they have prefumed to talk about it, have difcovered the groffeft ignorance.   When Strada, in the perfon of Claudian, recites the fable of the Nightingale and the Lyrift, how does his invention labour to defcribe the conteft, and how does he err in the confufion of the terms melody and harmony; and in giving to mufic either attributes that belong not to it, or which are its leaft excellence ! and what is his whole poem but a vain attempt to excite ideas for which no correfpondent words are to be found in any language ?   Nor does he, who talks of the genius of the world, of the firft beauty, and of univerfal harmony, fymmetry, and order, the fublime author of the Characteriftics, difcover much knowledge of his fubject, when after afferting with the utmoft confidence that the ancients were acquainted with parts and fymphony, he makes it the teft of a good judge in mufic ' that he underftand a fiddle *.'

Sir William Temple fpeaking of mufic in his Effay upon the ancient and modern Learning, has betrayed his ignorance of the fubject in a comparifon of the modern mufic with the ancient ; wherein, notwithftanding that Paleftrina, Bird, and Gibbons lived in the fame century with himfelf, and that the writings of Shakefpeare, and the Paradife Loft were then extant, he fcruples not to affert that ' the ' fcience is wholly loft in the world, and that in the room of mufic ' and poetry we have nothing left but fiddling and rhyming.'

Mr. Dryden, in thofe two admirable poems, Alexander's Feaft, and his leffer Ode for St. Cecilia's day, and in his Elegy on the death

* Vide Characteriftics, vol. III. page 263, in not. 269.

of Purcell, with great judgment gives to the several instruments mentioned by him their proper attributes; and recurring perhaps to the numerous common places in his memory respecting music, has described its effects in adequate terms; but when in the prefaces to his operas he speaks of recitative, of song, and the comparative merit of the Italian, the French, and the English composers, his notions are so vague and indeterminate, as to convince us that he was not master of his subject, and does little else than talk by rote.

Mr. Addison, in those singularly humorous papers in the Spectator, intended to ridicule the Italian opera, is necessitated to speak of music, but he does it in such terms, as plainly indicate that he had no judgment of his own to direct him. In the paper, Numb 18, the highest encomium he can vouchsafe music is, that it is an agreeable entertainment; and a little after he complains of our fondness for the foreign music, not caring whether it be Italian, French, or High Dutch, by which latter we may suppose the author meant the music of Mynheer Hendel, as he calls him.

In another paper, viz. Numb. 29, the same person delivers these sentiments at large respecting Recitative: ‘ However the *Italian* ‘ method of acting in *Recitativo* might appear at first hearing, I ‘ cannot but think it more just than that which prevailed in our ‘ *English* Opera before this Innovation; the Transition from an air ‘ to Recitative Musick being more natural than the passing from a ‘ Song to plain and ordinary Speaking, which was the common ‘ Method in *Purcell's* operas.

‘ The only Fault I find in our present Practice, is the making use ‘ of the *Italian Recitativo* with *English* words.

‘ To go to the Bottom of this Matter, I must observe that the ‘ Tone, or, as the *French* call it, the Accent of every Nation in ‘ their ordinary Speech is altogether different from that of every ‘ other People, as we may see even in the Welsh and Scotch, who ‘ border so near upon us. By the Tone or Accent I do not mean ‘ the Pronunciation of each particular Word, but the Sound of the ‘ whole

' 'whole Sentence. Thus it is very common for an English gentle-
'·man, when he hears a French Tragedy, to complain that the Actors
' all of them speak in a Tone; and therefore he very wisely prefers
' his own Countrymen, not considering that a Foreigner complains
' of the same Tone in an English Actor.

' For this Reason, the Recitative Music in every Language should
' be as different as the Tone or Accent of each Language; for other-
' wise what may properly express a Passion in one Language, will
' not do it in another. Every one that has been long in Italy knows
' very well that the Cadences in the Recitativo bear a remote Affinity
' to the Tone of their Voices in ordinary Conversation; or, to speak
' more properly, are only the Accents of their Language made more
' Musical and Tuneful.

' Thus the Notes of Interrogation or Admiration in the Italian
' Musick, (if one may so call them) which resemble their Accents in
' Discourse on such Occasions, are not unlike the ordinary Tones of an
' English Voice when we are angry; insomuch that I have often seen
' our Audiences extreamly mistaken as to what has been doing upon
' the Stage, and expecting to see the Hero knock down his Mes-
' senger when he has been asking him a question; or fancying that
' he quarrels with his Friend when he only bids him Good-morrow.

' For this Reason the Italian artists cannot agree with our English
' musicians in admiring Purcell's Compositions, and thinking his Tunes
' so wonderfully adapted to his words, because both Nations do not
' always express the same Passions by the same Sounds.

' I am therefore humbly of opinion that an English Composer
' should not follow the Italian Recitative too servilely, but make
' use of many gentle Deviations from it in Compliance with his own
' Native Language. He may copy out of it all the lulling Softness
' and Dying Falls, (as Shakespeare calls them) but should still re-
' member that he ought to accommodate himself to an English Au-
' dience, and by humouring the Tone of our Voices in ordinary
' Conversation, have the same Regard to the Accent of his own
' Lan-·

' Language, as thofe Perfons had to theirs whom he profeffes to
' imitate. It is obferved that feveral of the finging Birds of our own
' Country learn to fweeten their Voices, and mellow the Harfhnefs
' of their natural Notes by practifing under thofe that come from
' warmer Climates. In the fame manner I would allow the Italian
' Opera to lend our Englifh Mufick as much as may grace and foften
' it, but never entirely to annihilate and deftroy it. Let the Infu-
' fion be as ftrong as you pleafe, but ftill let the Subject Matter of
' it be Englifh.

' A Compofer fhould fit his Mufick to the Genius of the People,
' and confider that the Delicacy of Hearing and Tafte of Harmony
' has been formed upon thofe Sounds which every Country abounds
' with. In fhort, that Mufick is of a relative Nature, and what is
' Harmony to one Ear may be Diffonance to another.'

Whoever reflects on thefe fentiments muft be inclined to queftion
as well the goodnefs of the author's ear as his knowledge of
fubject. The principle on which his reafoning is founded, is
clearly that the powers of mufic are local ; deriving their efficacy from habit, cuftom, and whatever elfe we are to underftand by
the genius of a people ; a pofition as repugnant to reafon and experience as that which concludes his difquifition, viz. that ' what is
harmony to one ear may be diffonance to another ;' whence as a corollary it muft neceffarily follow, that the fame harmony or the fame
fucceffion of founds may produce different effects on different perfons ; and that one may be excited to mirth by an air that has drawn
tears from another.

A late writer, in a ftrain of criticifm not lefs erroneous than af-
fectedly refined, forgetting the energy of harmony, independent of
the adventitious circumftances of loudnefs or foftnefs that accompany
the utterance of it ; or perhaps not knowing that certain modulations
or combinations of founds have a neceffary tendency to infpire grand
and fublime fentiments, fuch, for inftance, as we hear in the Exal-
tabo of Paleftrina, the Hofanna of Gibbons, the opening of the firft
con-

concerto of Corelli, and many of Mr. Handel's anthems, afcribes to the *burfti*, as he calls them, of Boranello [*], and the fymphonies of Yeomelli [†] the power of dilating, agitating, and rouzing the foul like the paintings of Timomachus and Arifiides [‡], whofe works by the way no man living ever faw, and of whofe very names we fhould be ignorant, did they not occur, the one in Pliny, the other in fome of the epigrams in the Greek Anthologia.

In a manner widely different do thofe poets and philofophers treat mufic, who, being fufceptible of its charms, and confidering it as worthy the moft abftract fpeculation, have made themfelves acquainted with its principles. Milton, whenever he fpeaks of the fubject, and there are many paffages in the Paradife Loft and and his other poems, where he has taken occafion to introduce it, befides expreffing an enthufiaftic fondnefs for mufic, talks the language of a mafter.

His ideas of the joint efficacy of mufic and poetry, and of the nature of harmony, are manifefted in the following well-known paffage:

> And ever againft eating cares
> Lap me in foft Lydian aires ;
> Married to immortal verfe,
> Such as the meeting foul may pierce
> In notes, with many a winding bout
> Of linked fweetnefs long drawn out,
> With wanton heed, and giddy cunning,
> The melting voice through mazes running ;
> Untwifting all the chains, that tye
> The hidden foul of harmony.

Cathedral mufic and choral fervice he defcribes in terms that fuf-

* i. e. Buranello, a difciple of Lotti.

† Nicola Iomelli, a celebrated compofer now living at Naples.

‡ See an Inquiry into the Beauties of Painting by Daniel Webb, Efq. 8vo, 1769, page 167.

ficiently declare his abilities to judge of it, and its effects on his own
mind:

> There let the pealing organ blow,
> To the full-voic'd choir below,
> In fervice high, and anthems clear,
> As may with fweetnefs through mine ear
> Diffolve me into extafies,
> And bring all heav'n before mine eyes.

The following fonnet, addreffed to his friend Mr. Henry Lawes,
points out one of the great excellencies in the compofition of mufic
to words:

> Harry, whofe tuneful and well-meafur'd fong
>   Firft taught our Englifh mufic how to fpan
>   Words with juft note and accent, not to fcan
> With Midas' ears, committing fhort and long;
> Thy worth and fkill exempt thee from the throng,
>   With praife enough for envy to look wan;
>   To after-age thou fhalt be writ the man,
> That with fmooth air could humour beft our tongue.
>   Thou honour'ft verfe, and verfe muft lend her wing
>   To honour thee, the prieft of Phœbus' choir,
> That tun'ft their happieft lines in hymn, or ftory.
>   Dante fhall give Fame leave to fet thee higher
>   Than his Cafella, whom he woo'd to fing,
> Met in the milder fhades of Purgatory.

His fonnet to Mr. Lawrence Hyde conveys his fenfe of the delights of a mufical evening.

> Lawrence, of virtuous father virtuous fon,
>   Now that the fields are dank, and ways are mire,
>   Where fhall we fometimes meet, and by the fire
> Help wafte a fullen day; what may be won
> From the hard feafon gaining? time will run

On fmoother, till Favonius re-infpire
The frozen earth; and cloath in frefh attire
The lilie and the rofe, that neither fow'd nor fpun.
What neat repaft fhall feaft us, light and choice,
Of Attic tafte, with wine; whence we may rife
To hear the lute well toucht, or artful voice
Warble immortal notes and Tufcan air?
He, who of thofe delights can judge, and fpare
To interpofe them oft is not unwife.

And in his tractate on Education, he recommends the practice of mufic in terms that befpeak his fkill in the fcience. ' The interim ' of unfweating themfelves regularly, and convenient reft before meat, ' may both with profit and delight be taken up in recreating and ' compofing their travail'd fpirits with the folemn and divine harmo- ' nies of mufick heard or learnt; either while the fkilful organift plies ' his grave and fancied defcant, in lofty fugues,or the whole fymphony ' with artful and unimaginable touches adorn and grace the well- ' ftudied chords of fome choice compofer; fometimes the lute, or foft ' organ-ftop waiting on elegant voices either to religious, martial, ' or civil ditties; which, if wife men and prophets be not extremely ' out, have a great power over difpofitions and manners, to fmooth ' and make them gentle from ruftick harfhnefs and diftempered ' paffions.'

Lord Bacon, in his Natural Hiftory, has given a great variety of experiments touching mufic, that fhew him to have been not barely a philofopher, an enquirer into the phenomena of found, but a mafter of the fcience of harmony, and very intimately acquaint- ed with the precepts of mufical compofition.

That we have fo few inftances of this kind is greatly to be won- dered at, feeing that in poetry and painting the cafe is far otherwife: In the courfe of a claffical education men acquire not only a tafte of the beauties of the Greek and Roman poets, but a nice and difcrimi-

nating

nating faculty, that enables them to difcern their excellencies and
defects; and in painting, an attentive perufal of the works of eminent artifts, aided by a found judgment, will go near to form the
character of a connoiffeur, and render the poffeffor of it fufceptible
of all that delight which the art is capable of affording; and this we
fee exemplified in numberlefs inftances, where perfons unfkilled in
the practice of painting become enabled to diftinguifh hands, to
compare ftyles, and to mark the beauties of compofition, character,
drawing, and colouring, with a degree of accuracy and precifion
equal to that of mafters. But few, except the mafters of the fcience,
are poffeffed of knowledge fufficient to enable them to difcourfe with
propriety on mufic; nor indeed do many attend to that which is its
greateft excellence, its influence on the human mind, or thofe irrefiftible
charms which render the paffions fubfervient to the power of well
modulated founds, and infpire the mind with the moft exalted fentiments. One admires a fine voice, another a delicate touch, another what he calls a brilliant finger; and many are pleafed with
that mufic which appears moft difficult in the execution, and in judging of their own feelings, miftake wonder for delight.

To remove the numberlefs prejudices refpecting mufic, which thofe
only entertain who are ignorant of the fcience, or are miftaken in its
nature and end; to point out its various excellencies, and to affert
its dignity, as a fcience worthy the exercife of our rational as well as
audible faculties, the only effectual way feems to be to inveftigate its
principles, as founded in general and invariable laws, and to trace the
improvements therein which have refulted from the accumulated
ftudies and experience of a long fucceffion of ages, fuch a detail is
neceffary to reduce the fcience to a certainty, and to furnifh a ground
for criticifm; and may be confidered as a branch of literary hiftory,
of the deficiency whereof Lord Bacon has declared his fentiments in
the following emphatical terms:

'Hiftory is Natural, Civil, Ecclefiaftical, and Literary; whereof
'the three firft I allow as extant, the fourth I note as deficient. For

* no

‘ no man hath propounded to himſelf the general ſtate of learning to
‘ be deſcribed and repreſented from age to age, as many have done
‘ the works of nature, and the ſtate civil and eccleſiaſtical ; without
‘ which the hiſtory of the world ſeemeth to me to be as the ſtatue of
‘ Polyphemus with his eye out, that part being wanting which doth
‘ moſt ſhew the ſpirit and life of the perſon. And yet I am not ig-
‘ norant, that in divers particular ſciences, as of the juriſconſults, the
‘ mathematicians, the rhetoricians, the philoſophers, there are ſet
‘ down ſome ſmall memorials of the ſchools, authors, and books; and
‘ ſo likewiſe ſome barren relations touching the invention of arts or
‘ uſages.

‘ But a juſt ſtory of learning, containing the antiquities and ori-
‘ ginals of knowledges and their ſects, their inventions, their tra-
‘ ditions, their diverſe adminiſtrations and managings, their flouriſh-
‘ ings, their oppoſitions, decays, depreſſions, oblivions, removes,
‘ with the cauſes and occaſions of them, and all other events concern-
‘ ing learning, throughout the ages of the world, I may truly affirm
‘ to be wanting *.’

If any thing can be neceſſary to enforce arguments ſo weighty
as are contained in the above paſſage, it muſt be inſtances of
error, reſulting from the want of that intelligence which it is the
buſineſs of hiſtory to communicate ; and it is greatly to be lamented
that muſic affords more examples of this kind than perhaps any ſcience
whatever : for, not to remark on thoſe uncertain and contradictory
accounts which are given of the diſcovery of the conſonances, ſome
writers attributing it to Pythagoras, others to Diocles, that relation
of the fact which has gained moſt credit with mankind, as deriving
its authority from the Pythagorean ſchool, is demonſtrably falſe and
erroneous †. Again, as to the invention of ſymphoniac harmony, or,
as we now call it, muſic in parts, many aſcribe it to the ancients,
and ſay that it was in uſe among the Greeks, though no evidence of

* Of the Advancement of Learning, book II.
† Vide infra, vol. 1. page 29, et ſeq.

the

the fact can be drawn from their writings now extant. Others affert it to be a modern improvement, but to whom it is due no one has yet been able to discover.

As to the modern system, there is the irrefragable evidence of his own writings extant, though not in print, that it was settled by Guido Aretinus, a Benedictine monk of the monastery of Pomposa in Tuscany, who flourished about the year 1028; yet this fact, which is also related as an important event in the Annales Ecclefiastici of Cardinal Baronius, has been rendered doubtful by an affertion of a writer now living, Signor Martinelli, that one of the same name and place, Fra Guittone d'Arezzo, an Italian poet of great eminence, and who lived about two hundred years after, adjusted that musical scale by which we now sing *; and further that the same Fra Guittone was the inventor of counterpoint. Again, those who give the invention of the modern system, and the application thereto of the syllables used in solmisation to the true author, ascribe also to him the invention of music in consonance, and also of the Clavicembalum or harpsichord; whereas the harpsichord is an improvement of the Clavicitherium, an instrument known in England in Gower's time by the name of the Citole, from CISTELLA, a little chest. Another writer afferts, on what authority we are not told, that counterpoint, which implies music in consonance, was invented by John of Dunstable, who flourished anno 1400; and another †, mistaking the name,

* ' Fra Guittone d'Arezzo, celebre per i fuoi scritta sopra la musica, inventore ' del contrappunto, e dal quale furono fissati i tuoni, che presentemente si cantano.' Lettere familiari e critiche di Vincenzio Martinelli, Londra, 1758. Prefazione, pag. viii. This person had undertaken to write a history of music. See his letters above cited, pag. 164, containing an apology for his not having published it.

Of this Fra Guittone an account may be seen in the Istoria della volgar Poesia of Crescimbeni, lib. II. pag. 84. He flourished about 1250, and is celebrated among the best of the ancient Tuscan poets. In the same work, lib. III. pag. 176, is a sonnet of his writing; and in Mr. Baretti's History of the Italian Tongue, prefixed to his Italian library, page ix. is a fable of Fra Guittone, which Baretti says might be taken for a composition of yesterday.

† Wolfgang Caspar Printz, in his History of Music, written in the German language, and published at Dresden in the year 1690, who has given a relation

pur-

attributes it to St. Dunstan, archbishop of Canterbury. Mr. Marpourg of Berlin, a person now living, has taken up this relation, groundless as it is, and in a book of his writing, entititled 'Traité de 'la Fugue et du Counterpoint,' has done little less than assert that St. Dunstan invented counterpoint, by reducing into order the rules for composition in four parts, and not a few give credit to his testimony *.

Again we are told, that whereas the Greeks signified the several sounds in their scale by the letters of their alphabet, or by characters derived from them, Guido invented a more compendious method of notation, by points stationed on a stave of five lines, and occupying both the lines and the spaces. This assertion is true but in part; for the stave, and that of many lines, was in use near half a century before Guido was born; and all that can be ascribed to him is the placing points as well in the spaces as on the lines, which it must be owned is an ingenious and useful contrivance.

To assist the memory and facilitate the practice of solmisation, it is also said that Guido made use of the left hand, giving to the top of the thumb the note ΓAM UT, to the joint below it A RE, to the next B MI, and so on, placing the highest note of his system, E LA, at the extremity of the hand, viz. the tip of the middle finger; but nothing of this kind is to be found, or indeed is mentioned, or even hinted at, in any of his writings, and we may therefore conclude that the whole is an invention of some other person.

purporting that ' In the year of our Lord 940, Dunstan, otherwise Dunstaphus, 'an Englishman, being very young, betook himself to the study of music, and 'thereby acquired immortal fame. He was the first that composed songs of dif- 'ferent parts, that is to say, Base, Tenor, Descant, and Vagant or Alt,' pag. 104, sect. 23. The whole relation is an error, arising from a mistaken sense of a passage in the Praeceptiones Musicae Poeticae of Johannes Nucius, a writer on music in the year 1613. Vide infra, vol. II. page 18, n. 298, n. vol. IV. 248, n.

* ' Dunstan, Archevêque de Canterbory, qui vivoit dans le dixième siècle, a tou- 'jours eu l'honneur d'avoir commencé, ainsi que d'avoir frayé le chemin aux autres. 'Il redigea en ordre le regles de la composition à quatre parties & par là donna 'une nouvelle époque à la musique.' Partie II. pag. vi.

Little

Litt'e lefs confufion attends the relations extant refpecting the invention of the Cantus Menfurabilis, and thofe marks or characters ufed to fignify the feveral lengths or durations of notes. The vulgar tale is, that John de Muris, a Norman, and a doctor of the Sorbonne about the year 1330, invented eight mufical characters, namely, the Maxima, or as we call it, the Large, the Long, the Breve, Semibreve, Minim, Semiminim or Crotchet, Chroma or Quaver, and the Semichroma, affigning to each a feveral length in refpect of time or duration *. Now upon the face of the relation there is great reafon to conclude, that in the original inftitution of the Cantus Menfurabilis, the femibreve was the fhorteft note; but there is undeniable evidence that as well the minim as the notes in fucceffion after it, were of comparatively late invention.

But this is not all; De Muris was not a Norman, but an Englifhman: He was not the inventor of the Cantus Menfurabilis: Not he, but a perfon of the name of Franco, a fcholaftic, as he is called, of Liege, about the middle of the eleventh century invented certain characters to fignify the duration of founds †, that is to fay, the four firft abovementioned.

Another prevailing error refpecting mufic has got poffeffion of the minds of many people, viz. that thofe fingularly fweet and pathetic melodies with which the Scots mufic abounds, were introduced into it by David Rizzio, an Italian mufician, and a favourite of Mary queen of Scots: The reverfe is the truth of the matter, and that by the teftimony of Italians themfelves; the Scots tunes are the genuine produce of Scotland; thofe of greateft merit among them are compofitions of a king of that country; and of thefe fome of the moft celebrated madrigals of one of the greateft of the Italian compofers are avowed imitations ‡.

* Nicola Vicentino, a writer of the fixteenth century, with fome degree of ingenuity, attempts to fhew that thefe characters are but different modifications of the round and fquare b, which had been introduced into Guido's fcale for another purpofe.

† Vide infra, vol. II. pag. 140, 150, 237.   ‡ Vol. IV. page 5.

Again,

Again, few are fufficiently acquainted with the hiftory of the fcience, and in particular how long the feveral mufical inftruments now known by us have been in ufe, to prevent being impofed on by pretended new inventions: The harp of Æolus, as it is called, on which fo much has been lately faid and wrote, was conftructed by Kircher above a century ago, and is accurately defcribed in his Mufurgia; as is alfo the perpendicular harpfichord, and an inftrument fo contrived as to produce found by the friction of wheels, from which the modern lyrichord is manifeftly taken. The new fyftem, as it is called, of the flute abec, propofed about forty years ago by the younger Stanefby, is in truth the old and original fyftem of that inftrument, and is to be found in Merfennus; and the clarinet, an inftrument unknown in England till within thefe laft twenty years, was invented by John Chriftopher Denner, a wind mufical inftrument maker of Leipfic above a century ago *.

Farther, it has for the honour of this our native country been faid of Purcell, that his mufic was very different from the Italian; that it was entirely Englifh, that it was mafculine †. Againft the two firft of thefe affertions we have his own teftimony in the preface to one of his works, wherein he fays that he has endeavoured at a juft imitation of the moft famed Italian mafters, with a view, as he adds, to bring the gravity and ferioufnefs of that fort of mufic into vogue ‡. As to the third, the judicious perufer of his compofitions will find that they are ever fuited to the occafion, and are equally calculated to excite tender, and robuft or manly affections.

Laftly, of the many who at this time profefs to love mufic, few are acquainted with the characters, and even the names of thofe many eminent perfons celebrated for their fkill and great attainments in the fcience, and who flourifhed under the patronage of the greateft potentates, previous to the commencement of the prefent century; and,

* Vide infra vol. IV. page 249.
† Granger's Biographical Hiftory of England, as it is called, vol. II. part II. clafs X. tit. MUSICIANS, art. HENRICUS PURCELL.
‡ Vide infra vol. IV. page 497.

with

with refpect to thofe of our own country, it is true there is fcarce a boy in any of the choirs in the kingdom but knows that Tallis and Bird compofed anthems, and Child, Batten, Rogers, and Aldrich fervices; but of their compofitions at large, and in what particulars they excelled, even their teachers are ignorant.

Under a thorough conviction of the benefits that muft refult from the kind of intelligence here recommended, attempts have been made at different periods to trace the rife and progrefs of mufic in a courfe of hiftorical narration; and let it not be deemed an invidious office, if thofe defects in the attempts of others are pointed out, which alone can juftify the prefent undertaking.

In the Menagiana, tome I. page 303, mention is made of a canon of Tours of the name of Ouvard, who wrote a hiftory of mufic; Matthefon, in his Vollkommenen Capellmeifter, takes notice of this work, and fays that it comes down to the end of the feventeenth century, and is perhaps extant in MS. in fome library at Paris. But the firft attempt of this kind in print is a treatife of Johannes Albertus Bannius, ' De Muficæ origine, progreffu et denique ftudio bene in- ' ftituendo,' publifhed in 1637, in octavo.

Next to this, in point of time, is the Hiftory of Mufic of Wolfgang Cafpar Printz, chapel-mafter and director of the choir of the church of Sorau, printed at Drefden in the year 1690, in a fmall quarto volume, with the title of ' Hiftoriche Befchreibung der Edelen Sing- ' und Klingkunft.' Neither of the two latter works can be confidered as a hiftory of the fcience; the firft of them is a very fmall volume, and the other not a large one, containing little more than a lift of writers on mufic difpofed in chronological order.

The appendix of Dr. Wallis to his edition of Ptolemy, publifhed in 1682, though not a hiftory of the fcience, contains many hiftorical particulars refpecting mufic, befides that in fundry inftances it renders intelligible the doctrines of the ancient writers. It is written with great accuracy and perfpicuity, and abounds with inftances of that acutenefs and penetration for which the author is celebrated.

In

In 1683, the Sieur Gabriel Guillaume Nivers, organist of the chapel of Lewis XIV. publifhed ' Differtation fur le Chant Gregorien,' a fmall octavo volume, but in effect a hiftory of ecclefiaftical mufic, with a relation of the many corruptions it has undergone. In it are many curious paffages relating to the fubject, extracted from the fathers and the ritualifts, with the obfervations of the author, who appears to have been a learned man in his profeffion.

In 1695 Gio. Andrea Angelini Bontempi, of Perugia, publifhed in a thin folio volume a work of fome merit, entitled ' Hiftoria Mufica.' Berardi mentions a work of one Pietro Arragona, a Florentine, entitled ' Moria Armonica.' but Broffard doubts the exiftence of it *.

A hiftory of the pontifical chapel, and of the college of fingers thereto belonging, is contained in a work entitled ' Offervazioni per ' ben regolare il Coro de i Cantori della Cappella Pontificia, tanto 'nelle Funzioni ordinarie, che ftraordinarie,' by Andrea Adami da Bolfena, Maeftro della Cappella Pontificia, publifhed at Rome in 1711, in a quarto volume. In this book are many curious particulars.

There is alfo extant in two volumes duodecimo, but divided into four, a book entitled ' Hiftoire de la Mufique et de fes Effets,' printed firft at Paris in 1715, and afterwards at Amfterdam in 1725. The materials for this publication were certain papers found in the ftudy of the Abbé Bourdelot, and others of his nephew Bonnet Bourdelot, phyfieian to the king of France, the letters of the Abbé Raguenet and others, on the comparative merits of the Italian and French opera and mufic, together with fundry other papers on the fame fubject. The publifher was Bonnet, a nephew of the Abbé Bourdelot; and the beft that can be faid of the work is, that the whole is a confufed jumble of intelligence and controverfy ; and, faving that it contains fome curious memoirs of Lully and a few other of the French muficians, has very little claim to attention.

* Catalogue of writers on mufic at the end of his ' Dictionnaire de Mufique,' octavo, page 369.

John

About the year 1730, Mr. Peter Prelleur, an able mufician and organift, publifhed a work entitled ' The modern Mufic-mafter, contain-' ing an introduction to finging, and inftructions for moft of the in-' ftruments in ufe.' At the end of this book is a brief hiftory of mufic, in which are fundry particulars worth noting : it has no name to it, but was neverthelefs compiled by the above perfon.

John Godfrey Walther, a profeffor of mufic, and organift of the church of St. Peter and Paul at Weimar, publifhed in 1732 a mufical Lexicon or Bibliotheque, wherein is a great variety of information refpecting mufic and muficians of all countries and ages. Matthefon of Hamburg, in his ' Critica Mufica,' his ' Orcheftre,' and a work entitled ' Vollkommenen Capellmeifter,' i. e. the perfect Chapelmafter, has brought together many particulars of the like kind ; but the want of method renders thefe compofitions, in an hiftorical view, of little ufe.

In the year 1740, an ingenious young man of the name of Graffineau *, publifhed a Dictionary of Mufic in one octavo volume, with a recommendation of the work by Dr. Pepufch, Dr. Greene, and Mr. Galliard. The book had the appearance of a learned work, and all men wondered who the author could be : It feems he had been an amanuenfis of the former of thefe perfons. The foundation of this dictionary is a tranflation of that of Sebaftian Broffard ; the additions include all the mufical articles contained in the two volumes of Chambers's Dictionary, with perhaps a few hints and emendations furnifhed by Dr. Pepufch. The book neverthelefs abounds with errors, and, though a ufeful and entertaining publication, is not to be relied on.

In 1756, Fr. Wilhelm Marpourg, a mufician of Berlin, publifhed in a thin quarto volume, ' Traite de la Fugue et du Contrepoint,' the the fecond part whereof is a brief hiftory of counterpoint and fugue. The fame perfon is alfo the author of a work entitled ' Critifche ' Einleitung in die Gefchichte und Lehrfake der alten und neuen Mufck,' printed at Berlin in 1759. It is part of a larger work, and the remainder is not yet publifhed.

* See an account of him vol. I. page 86, in the notes.

The

The 'Storia della Musica' of Padre Martini of Bologna, of which as yet only two volumes have been published, and those at the distance of thirteen years from each other, is a learned and curious work; but the great study and labour bestowed by the author in compiling it, make us despair of ever seeing it completed.

The 'Histoire generale, critique, et philologique de la Musique,' of Monsf. De Blainville, printed at Paris in 1767, in a thin quarto volume, has very little pretence to the title it bears: Like some other works of the kind, it is diffuse where it ought to be succinct, and brief where one would wish to find it copious.

A character very different is due to a work in two volumes, quarto, entitled ' De Cantu et Musica sacra, a prima Ecclesiæ Ætate usque ad ' præsens Tempus; Auctore Martino Gerberto, Monasterii et Congre- ' gationis Sancti Blasii in Silva Nigra Abbate, Sacrique Romani Impe- ' rii Princeps. Typis San-Blasianis, 1774.' In this most valuable work the author has with great learning, judgment, and candour given the history of ecclesiastical music; and the author of the present work felicitates himself on the finding his sentiments on the subject, particularly of the church composers, and the corruptions of the church style, confirmed by the testimony of so able a writer. He is farther happy to see that without any communication with this illustrious dignitary, and without having perused his book, by the help of materials, which this country alone has furnished, he has been able to pursue a similar track of narration, and to relate and authenticate many facts contained therein *.

At the beginning of this present year 1776, the musical world were favoured with the first volume of a work entitled ' A General ' History of Music from the earliest Ages to the present Period, with ' a Dissertation on the Music of the Ancients, by Charles Burney, ' Mus. D. F. R. S.' The author in the proposals for his subscription.

* The fact is, that the fifth volume of this work was printed off in July in the present year, and the former ones in succession in the years preceding, and the two volumes of the Abbot Gerbert's work came to hand in the month immediately following.

has

has given affurances of the publication of a fecond, which we doubt not he will make good.

From thofe who have thus taken upon them to trace the rife and progrefs of mufic in a courfe of hiftorical deduction, we pafs to others who appear to have made collections for the like purpofe, but were defeated in their intentions of benefiting the fcience by their labours.

And firft Anthony Wood, who himfelf was a proficient in mufic, and entertained an enthufiaftic fondnefs for the art, had it feems meditated a hiftory of muficians, a work which his curiofity and unwearied induftry rendered him very fit for : To this end he made a collection of memoirs, which is extant, in his own hand-writing, among the manufcripts in the Afhmolean Mufeum ; and in the printed catalogue thereof is thus numbered and defcribed : ' 8568. 106. Some ' materials toward a hiftory of the lives and compofitions of all Eng-' lifh muficians ; drawn up according to alphabetical order in 210 ' pages by A. W.' Of thefe materials he feems to have availed himfelf in the Fafti Oxonienfes, wherein are contained a great number of memoirs of eminent Englifh muficians, equally curious and fatisfactory, the perufal whereof in the original MS. has contributed to render this work fomewhat lefs imperfect than it muft have been without fuch information as they afford.

Dr. Henry Aldrich, dean of Chrift Church, an excellent fcholar, and of fuch fkill in mufic, that he holds a place among the moft eminent of our Englifh church muficians, had formed a defign of a hiftory of mufic on a moft extenfive plan. His papers in the library of 'Chrift Church college, Oxford, have been carefully perufed : Among them are a great number of loofe notes, hints, and memoranda relating to mufic and the profeffors of the fcience ; in the collection whereof he feems to have purfued the courfe recommended by Broffard in the catalogue of writers on mufic at the end of his Dictionnaire de Mufique, page 367 ; but among a great multitude of papers in his own hand-writing there are none to be found from whence it can with certainty be concluded that he had made any progrefs in the work.

Nicola

Nicola Francefco Haym, a mufician, and a man of fome literature, publifhed, above forty years ago, propofals, containing the plan of a hiftory of mufic written by himfelf, but, meeting with little encouragement, he defifted from his defign of printing it.

Much intelligence refpecting mufic might have been hoped for from the abilities and induftry of Afhmole, Dr. Hooke, and Sir William Petty, the two former of whom had been chorifters, the one in the cathedral of Litchfield, the other of Chrift Church, Oxford: The latter of the three was profeffor of mufic at Grefham college; but thefe perfons abandoning the faculty in which they had been inftituted, betook themfelves to ftudies of a different kind: Afhmole, at firft a folicitor in Chancery, became an antiquary, a herald, a virtuofo, a naturalift, and an Hermetic philofopher: Hooke took to the ftudy of natural philofophy, mechanics, and architecture, and attained to great fkill in all *: And Petty, choofing the better part, laid the foundation

* It is faid by Anthony Wood of Dr. Hooke, that, being at Weftminfter-fchool, he lodged and dined in the houfe of Mr. Bufby, the mafter, and that there, of his own accord, he learned to play twenty leffons on the organ, and invented thirty feveral ways of flying. Athen. Oxon. vol. II. col. 1039. The latter of thefe facts muft ftand on the authority of the relator, or rather his authors, Dr. Bufby and the great Dr. Wilkins of Wadham college; but the former is rendered highly probable by the following anecdote refpecting Dr. Bufby, the communication whereof we owe to Dr. Wetenhall, one of Bufby's fcholars, and afterwards bifhop of Cork and Rofs, viz. that ' the firft organ he ever faw or heard was in his, Dr. ' Bufby's, houfe; and that the fame was kept for facred ufe, and that even when ' it was interdicted.' Dedication of a treatife entitled ' Of Gifts and Offices in ' the publie Worfhip of God, by Edward Wetenhall, D. D. Chanter of Chrift ' Church, Dublin, 8vo. 1679.' That he was alfo eminently fkilled in architecture, may be inferred from an affertion of Dr. Ward, in his life of Sir Chriftopher Wren, among the Grefham profeffors, viz. that he greatly affifted Sir Chriftopher in rebuilding the publie edifices. Wood goes fo far as to fay that Hooke defigned New Bedlam, Montague-houfe, the college of phyficians, and the pillar on Fifh-ftreet Hill; but the erection of the latter of thefe edifices is afcribed to Sir Chriftopher Wren. As to Montague-houfe and the College of Ph.ficians, there are in Moxon's Mechanic Exercifes, under the head of Bricklayer's Work, intimations that they were both defigned by Hooke; and Stryps, in his edition of Stowe's Survey of London, fpeaking of Afhe's hofpital at Hoxton, fays it was built after a modern defign of Dr. Hooke,

Of

of an immenfe eſtate by a various exertion of his very great talents, and was ſucceſſively a phyſician, a mathematician, a mechanic, a projeſtor, a contraſtor with the government, and an improver of land.

Enough it is preſumed has been ſaid to prove the utility, and even the neceſſity, in order to a competent knowledge of the ſcience, of a Hiſtory of Muſic, in the deduſtion whereof the firſt objeſt that preſents itſelf to view is the ſyſtem of the ancient Greeks, adjuſted, it muſt be confeſſed, with great art and ingenuity, but labouring under many defeſts, which, if we are not greatly deceived, are remedied in that of the moderns. Of the origin of this ſyſtem we have ſuch authentic intelligence as leaves little room to doubt that it was invented by Pythagoras, a name ſufficiently known and revered, and the ſubſequent deduſtion of the progreſs of the ſcience, involving in it the names and improvements of men well known, ſuch as Philolaus, Archytas of Tarentum, Ariſtoxenus, Euclid, Nicomachus, Ptolemy, and many others, may truly be called hiſtory, as being founded in truth; and the utility and certainty of their relations will teach us to diſtinguiſh between faſt and fable.

It is much to be lamented that the greater part of what we believe touching muſic, is founded on no better authority than the fiſtions of poets and mythologiſts, whoſe relations are in moſt inſtances merely typical and figurative; ſuch muſt the ſtories of Orpheus and Amphion appear to be, as having no foundation in truth, but being calculated ſolely for the purpoſe of moral inſtruſtion.

And with regard to faſts themſelves, a diſtinſtion is to be made between ſuch as are in their own nature intereſting, and thoſe that tend only to gratify an idle curioſity: To inſtance in the latter, what

Of this latter perſon it may be ſaid, that he was perhaps one of the greateſt proficients in the art of thriving of his time: By places, by projeſts, and by grants, ſome to himſelf, and others to his wife, he acquired eſtates, real and perſonal, to the annual amount of 15,000l. to the accumulation of which wealth we may well ſuppoſe that the virtue of parſimony contributed not a little, and the rather as he ſuffered a natural daughter of his to be an aſtreſs on the ſtage under Sir William D'Avenant at the Duke's theatre in Dorſet-Garden.

ſatis-fatisfaction does the mind receive from the recital of the names of those who are said to have increased the chords of the primitive lyre from four to seven, Chorebus, Hyagnia, and Terpander; or when we are told that Olympus invented the enarmonic genus, as also the Harmatian mood; or that Eumolpus and Melampus were excellent muficians, and Pronomus, Antigenides, and Lamia celebrated players on the flute? In all these instances, where there are no circumstances that constitute a character, and familiarize to us the person spoken of, we naturally enquire who he is; and, for want of farther information, become indifferent as to what is recorded of him.

Mr. Wollaston has a remark upon the nature of fame that seems to illustrate the above obfervation, and indeed goes far beyond the cafe here put, irafmuch as the perfons by him fpoken of, are become well known characters: his words are these: ' When it is faid that ' Julius Cæfar fubdued Gaul, beat Pompey, changed the Roman ' commonwealth into a monarchy, &c. it is the fame thing as to fay, ' the conqueror of Pompey was Cæfar; that is, Cæfar and the con- ' queror of Pompey are the fame thing; and Cæfar is as much known ' by one defignation as the other. The amount then is only this: ' That the conqueror of Pompey conquered Pompey; or fomebody ' conquered Pompey; or rather, fince Pompey is as little known as ' Cæfar, fomebody conquered fomebody *.'

That memorials of perfons, who at this diftance of time muft appear thus indifferent to us, fhould be tranfmitted down to pofterity, together with thofe events that make a part of mufical hiftory, is not to be wondered at; and Plutarch could never have recorded the facts mentioned by him in his Dialogue on Mufic, had he not alfo given the names of thofe perfons to whom they are feverally afcribed; and if they now appear uninterefting we may reject them: But the cafe is far otherwife with refpect to what is told us of the marvellous power and efficacy of the ancient mufic. Ariftoxenus exprefsly af-

* Religion of Nature delineated, page 117.

ferts that the foundation of ingenuous manners, and a regular and decent difcharge of the offices of civil life, are laid in a mufical education; and Plutarch, fpeaking of the education of Achilles, and relating that the moſt wife Chiron was careful to inſtruct him in mufic, fays, that whoever ſhall in his youth addict himfelf to the ſtudy of mufic, if he be properly inſtructed therein, ſhall not fail to applaud and practiſe that which is noble and generous, and deteſt and ſhun their contraries: Mufic teaching thofe that purfue it to obferve decorum, temperance, and regularity; for which reafon he adds, that in thofe cities which were governed by the beſt laws, the greateſt care was taken that their youth ſhould be taught mufic. Plato, in his treatiſe De Legibus, lib. II. infiſts largely on the utility of this practice; and Polybius, lib. IV. cap. iii. ſcruples not to attribute the misfortunes of the Cynetheans, a people of Arcadia, and that general corruption of their manners, by him defcribed, to the neglect of the difcipline and exercife of mufic; which he fays the ancient Arcadians were fo induſtrious to cultivate, that they incorporated it into, and made it the very eſſence of, their government; obliging not their children only, but the young men till they attained the age of thirty, to perfiſt in the ſtudy and practice of it. Innumerable alfo are the paſſages in the ancient writers on harmonics wherein the power of determining the minds of men to virtue or vice is afcribed to mufic with as little doubt of its efficacy in this refpect, as if the human mind was poſſeſſed of no fuch power as the will, or was totally diveſted of thofe paſſions, inclinations, and habits, which conſtitute a moral character.

Now, forafmuch as we at this day are incapable of difcovering any fuch power as is here attributed to mere mufical founds, we feem to be warranted in withholding our aſſent to thefe relations, till the evidence on which they are grounded becomes more particular and explicit; or it ſhall be ſhewn that they are not, what fome men conceive them to be, hyperbolical forms of fpeech, in which the literal is as far from the true fenfe, as it is in the ſtories of the effects of mufic

on

on inanimate beings : If indeed by mufic we are to underfland mufical founds jointly operating with poetry, for this reafon that mufic is
ever fpoken of by the ancients as infeparably united with poetry; and
farther, becaufe we are told that the ancient poets, for inftance, Demodocus, Thaletas of Crete, Pindar, and others, not only compofed the
words, but alfo the mufic to their odes and pæans, and fung them to
the lyre, a degree of efficacy muft be allowed it, proportioned to the
advantages which it could not but derive from fuch an union * : But

* Quintilian has elegantly exprefled his fenfe of the joint efficacy of mufic
and poetry in the following paffage : ' Namque et voce et modulatione grandia
' elate, jucunda dulciter, moderata leniter canit, totáque arte confentit cum eorum,
' quæ dicuntur, affectibus.' Inft. Orat. lib. I. cap. x.

But, notwithftanding this obfervation, which, as far as it goes, muft be allowed
to be juft, the powers of mufic will be found inadequate to the expreffion of many
of thofe fentiments in poetry which are comprehended in the ideas of the beautiful
and the fublime ; fuch, for inftance, as thefe :

Where glowing embers round the room
Teach light to counterfeit a gloom.

Where I may oft outwatch the bear,
With thrice great Hermes, and unfphere
The fpirit of Plato to unfold
What worlds or what vaft regions hold
The immortal mind.

Sentiments that defy the utmoft powers of mufic to fuit them with correfpondent
founds.

Nor will it be found that the melody or the cadence of founds are either of them
fo peculiarly appropriated to particular paffions or defcriptions, as to rank the faculty
of expreffion among the principal excellencies of mufic. And in proof of this affertion fome examples might be given that would ftagger an infidel in thefe matters. The late Dr. Brown, when he had wrote his ode entitled the Cure of Saul,
for the mufic to it made a felection from the works of the moft celebrated compofers,
of fuch favourite movements as he thought would beft exprefs the fenfe of the
words ; in particular he took the faraband in the eighth fonata of Corelli's fecond
opera for a folo air ; and that moft divine movement in Purcell's ' O give thanks,'
' Remember me O Lord,' for a chorus ; and any ftranger would have thought that
the mufic had been originally compofed to the words : The mufic to that admired

d 2   fong

here a difficulty will arife, which, though it does not deftroy the credit of thefe reports, as they ftand on the footing of other hiftorical
facts, would incline us to fufpect that the mufic here fpoken of was
of a kind very different from what it is in general conceived to be,
and that for the following reafon:

We know by experience that there is no neceffary connexion between mufic and poetry; and fuch as are competent judges of either,
know alfo that though the powers of each are in fome inftances con-
current, each is a feparate and diftinct language: The poet affects
the paffions by images excited in the mind, or by the forcible impreffion of moral fentiments; the mufician by founds either fimple,
and harmonical only in fucceffion, or combined: Thefe the mind,
from its particular conftitution, fuppofing it endued with that fenfe
which is the perfection of the auditory faculty, without referring to
any other fubject or medium, recognizes as the language of nature;
and the affections of joy, grief, and a thoufand namelefs fenfations,
become fubfervient to their call.

As the powers of mufic and poetry are thus different, it neceffarily follows that they may exift independent of each other; and the
inftances are as numerous of poets incapable of articulating mufical
founds, as of muficians unpoffeffed of a talent for poetry.

If then the poets of the ancients were only fuch as to the harmony
of their verfe were capable of joining that of mufic, by compofing
mufical airs, and alfo finging them, and that to an audience grounded and well inftructed in mufic, what can we fuppofe the mufic of
their odes to have been? Perhaps little elfe than bare recitation; not

fong in Samfon, ' Return O God of hofts,' was taken from an Italian cantata of
Mr. Handel, compofed in his youth; as was alfo the mufic to the other, ' Then
' long eternity,' in the fame oratorio: Farther, the chorus in Alexander's Feaft,
' Let old Timotheus yield the prize,' faving the addition of one of the interior parts,
was originally an Italian trio; as was alfo that in the Il Penfrofo, ' Thefe
' pleafures melancholy give.' Finally, a great part of the mufic to Mr. Dryden's
leffer ode for St. Cecilia's Day was originally compofed by Mr. Handel for an opera
entitled Alcefte, written by Dr. Smollet, but never performed.

in true mufical intervals, but with fuch inflexions of the voice as accompany fpeech when calculated to make a forcible impreffion on the
hearers.

As to the relations of the effects of mufic in former ages on the
paffions of men, and of its provoking them to acts of defperation, it
may be faid that they afford no greater proofs of its influence on the
paffions than modern hiftory is capable of furnithing *. But there

* Vide infra, vol. 1. page 317, 318, n. and Plutarch relates that Antigenides,
the tibieinift, playing before Alexander the Great, in a meafure of time diftinguifhed by the name of the Harmatian mood, enflamed the hero to fuch a degree, that,
leaping from his feat, and drawing his fword, he in a frenzy of courage affailed
thofe who were neareft him. In Orat. II. De Fortun. vel. Virtut. Alexandr:
Magn..

To thefe inflances may be oppofed the following, which modern hiftory affords:
The firft is related of Ericus, king of Denmark, furnamed the Good, who reigned
about 1130, and is to the following purport. When Ericus was returned into his
kingdom, and held the yearly affembly, he was greatly pleafed with the induftry
both of his foldiers and artificers. Among other of his attendants was a mufician,
who afferted that by the power of his art he was able to excite in men whatfoever
affections he thought proper; and to make the fad chearful, the chearful fad, the
angry placid, and fuch as were pleafed difcontented, and even drive them into a
raging madnefs; and the more he infifted on his abilities the greater was the king's
defire to try them. The artift now began to repent his having thus magnified his
talent, forefeeing the danger of making fuch experiments on a king, and he was
afraid that if he failed in the performance of what he had undertaken, he fhould be
efteemed a liar; he therefore entreated all who had any influence over the king to
endeavour to divert him from his intention to make proof of his art; but all without effect, for the more defirous he was to evade the trial of his fkill, the more the.
king infifted on it. When the mufician perceived that he could not be excufed,
he begged that all weapons capable of doing mifchief might be removed, and took
care that fome perfons fhould be placed out of the hearing of the Cithara, who
might be called in to his affiftance, and were, if neceffity required it, to fnatch the
inftrument from his hands, and break it on his head. Every thing being thus.
prepared, the citharift began to make proof of his art on the king, who fat with
fome few about him in an open hall; firft, by a grave mode, he threw a certain melancholy into the minds of the auditors; but, changing it into one more chearful,.
he converted their fadnefs into mirth that almoft incited his hearers to dancing;
then varying his modulation, on the fudden he infpired the king with fury and.
indignation, which he continued to work up in him till it was eafy to fee he was
approach-

are others that stagger human belief, and leave us in doubt whether
to give or refuse credit to them ; such, for instance, are the stories of
the cure of diseases, namely the sciatica, epilepsy, fevers, the bites of
vipers, and even pestilences, by the power of harmony.

What an implicit assent has been given to the reports of the sove-
reign efficacy of music in the cure of the frenzy occasioned by the bite
of the Tarantula! Baglivi, an eminent physician, a native of Apu-
lia, the country where the Tarantula, a kind of spider, is produced, has given the natural history of this supposed noxious in-
sect, and a variety of cases of persons rendered frantic by its bite, and
restored to sanity and the use of their reason; and in Kircher's Musurgia
we have the very air or tune by which the cure is said to be effected.
Sir Thomas Brown, that industrious exploder of vulgar errors, has let

approaching to frenzy. The sign was then given for those who were in waiting to
enter, they first broke the Cithara according to their directions, and then seized on
the king ; but such was his strength, that he killed some of them with his fist, being
afterwards overwhelmed with several beds, his fury became pacified, and, recover-
ing his reason, he was grievously afflicted that he had turned his wrath against his
friends. Saxo Grammaticus, in Hist. Danicæ, edit. Basil, lib. XII. pag. 123. The
same author adds, that he broke open the doors of a chamber, and, snatching up a
sword, ran four men through the body ; and that when he returned to his senses
he made a pilgrimage to Jerusalem as an expiation of his crime. Olaus Magnus,
who tells the same story, says that he afterwards died in the island of Cyprus. Vide
Olaus Magnus, in Hist. Gent. Sept. lib. XV. cap. xxviii, and Krantsius, in
Chron. Regn. Daniæ, Sueciæ, et Norvegiæ.

　　Hieronymus Magius gives the following relation of a fact recent in memory in
the year 1564 : Cardinal Hippolyto de Medicis, being a legate in the army at Pan-
nonia, the troops being about to engage, upon sounding the alarm by the trumpets
and drums, was so enflamed with a martial ardour, that, girding on his sword, he
mounted his horse, and could not be restrained from charging the enemy at the head
of those whose duty it was to make the onset. Var. Lect. seu Miscell. Venet. 1564,
lib. IV. cap. xiii.

　　And, lastly, it is related, that at the celebration of the marriage of the duke of
Joyeuse, a gentleman was so transported with the music of Claude le Jeune, performed at that solemnity, that he seized his sword, and swore that, unless prevented,
he must fight with some one present ; but that a sudden change in the music calmed
him. Bayle, art. Goudimel, in not. Vide infra, vol. III. page 205.

　　　　　　　　　　　　　　　　　　　　　　　　　　　　　this,

this, perhaps the moft egregious of any that he has animadverted on, pafs as a fact not to be controverted; and Dr. Mead has ftrengthened the belief of it by his reafoning on the nature of poifons. After all the whole comes out to be a fable, an impofture calculated to deceive the credulous, and ferve the ends of defigning people inhabiting the country *.

The natural tendency of thefe reflections is to draw on a comparifon of the ancient with modern mufic; which latter, as it pretends to no fuch miraculous powers, has been thought by the ignorant to be fo greatly inferior to the former, as fcarce to deferve the name. In like manner do they judge of the characters of men, and the ftate of human manners at remote periods, when they compare the events of ancient hiftory, the actions of heroes, and the wifdom of legiflators, with thofe of modern times, inferring from thence a depravity in mankind, of which not the leaft trace is difcernible.

This miftaken notion feems to be but the neceffary confequence of that fyftem of education which directs the attention of young minds to the difcoveries and tranfactions of the more early times; affigning, as the rule of civil policy, and the ftandard of moral perfection and excellence in arts, the conduct, the lives and works of men whofe greateft atchievements are only wonderful as they were rare; whofe valour was brutality, and whofe policy was in general fraud, or at beft craft; and whofe inventions and difcoveries have in numberlefs inftances been fuperfeded by thofe of later times. To thefe, which we may call claffical prejudices, we are to impute thofe numerous and reiterated complaints which we meet with of the degeneracy of modern times; and when they are once imbibed, complaints of the declenfion of fome arts, and of the lofs of others, as alfo of the corruption of manners, appear to be but of courfe. Whether therefore our reverence for antiquity has not been carried too far both as to matters of fcience and morality, comprehending in the latter the virtue of juftice, and the qualities of perfonal courage, general benevolence, and refined humanity, of which the examples

* Vide infra, vol. IV. page 256, a.

are

are not lefs numerous and confpicuous in modern than in ancient hiftory, is a queftion well worthy confideration *.

* In a book, which few readers at this day think worth looking into, Dr. Hakewill's Apologie for the Power and Providence of God, are the following fentiments touching the reverence due to antiquity. 'Antiquity I unfeignedly honour
' and reverence; but why I fhould reverence the ruft and refufe, the drofs and
' dregs, the warts and wens thereof, I am yet to feek.——As in the little, fo in
' the great world, reafon will tell you that old age or antiquity is to be accounted
' by the farther diftance from the beginning, and the nearer approach to the end;
' and as grey beards are for wifdom and judgment to be preferred before young
' green heads, becaufe they have more experience in affairs; fo likewife for the
' fame caufe the prefent times are to be preferred before the infancy or youth of the
' world, we having the hiftory and practice of former ages to inform us, which they
' wanted.——In difgracing the prefent times you difgrace antiquity properly fo
' called.' Book V. page 133.
Farther to this purpofe the learned and fagacious Sir Thomas Brown delivers his fentiments in the following terms: ' The mortalleft enemy unto knowledge, and
' that which hath done the greateft execution upon truth, hath been a peremptory
' adhefion unto authority; and more efpecially the eftablifhing of our belief upon
' the dictates of antiquity. For, (as every capacity may obferve) moft men of ages
' prefent, fo fuperftitioufly do look upon ages paft, that the authorities of the one
' exceed the reafons of the other: Whofe perfons indeed being far removed from our
' times, their works, which feldom with us pafs uncontrouled, either by contempo-
' raries, or immediate fucceffors, are now become out of the diftance of envies:
' And the farther removed from prefent times, are conceived to approach the nearer
' unto truth itfelf. Now hereby methinks we manifeftly delude ourfelves, and wide-
' ly walk out of the track of truth.

' For, firft, men hereby impofe a thraldom on their times, which the ingenuity of
' no age fhould endure, or indeed the prefumption of any did ever yet enjoin.
' Thus Hippocrates, about two thoufand years ago, conceived it no injuftice either
' to examine or refute the doctrines of his predeceffors: Galen the like, and Ariftotle
' the moft of any. Yet did not any of thefe conceive themfelves infallible, or fet
' down their dictates as verities irrefragable: But when they either deliver their own
' Inventions, or reject other men's opinions, they proceed with judgment and in-
' genuity: eftablifhing their affertions, not only with great folidity, but fubmitting
' them alfo unto the correction of future difcovery.

' Secondly, men that adore times paft, confider not that thofe times were once
' prefent, that is, as our own are at this inftant; and we ourfelves unto thofe to
' come, as they unto us at prefent: As we rely on them, even fo will thofe on us,
' and

Of the loss of many arts, that contribute as well to the benefit as delight of mankind, much has been said; and there is extant a large volume, written in Latin by Guido Pancirollus, a lawyer of Padua, entitled ‘ De rebus memorabilibus deperditis et noviter inventis,’ which has not escaped censure for the mistakes and puerilities with which it abounds, the tendency thereof being to shew that many arts known to the ancients are either totally lost, or so greatly depraved, that they can scarcely be said to have an existence among us *. In

* and magnifie us hereafter, who at present condemn ourselves. Which very ab-
‘ surdity is daily committed amongst us, even in the esteem and censure of our own
‘ times. And, to speak impartially, old men, from whom we should expect the
‘ greatest example of wisdom, do most exceed in this point of folly ; commending
‘ the dayes of their youth, which they scarce remember, as least well understood not ;
‘ extolling those times their younger years have heard their fathers condemn, and
‘ condemning those times the gray heads of their posterity shall commend. And
‘ thus is it the humour of many heads to extol the dayes of their fore-fathers, and de-
‘ claim against the wickedness of times present. Which, notwithstanding they can-
‘ not handsomly do, without the borrowed help and satyrs of times past, condemn-
‘ ing the vices of their own times, by the expressions of vices in times which they
‘ commend ; which cannot but argue the community of vice in both. Horace,
‘ therefore, Juvenal, and Persius were no prophets, although their lines did seem to
‘ indigitate and point at our times. There is a certain list of vices committed in
‘ all ages, and declaimed against by all authors, which will last as long as humane
‘ nature ; which, digested into common places, may serve for any theme, and never
‘ be out of date until Doom’s-day.’ Enquiries into Vulgar and Common Errours,
Book I, Chap. vi.

* Of the many instances of arts or inventions lost, or in a state of depravity at
this time, there are very few, if any, of which evidence can be found, or at least
that have not been succeeded by others tending to the same purpose, and of far
greater utility. To instance in a few particulars, instead of the papyrus of the ancients, prepared from the leaves of a certain bulrush, we have the paper of the moderns ; in the room of their specular stones, glass ; and of clepsydræ, instruments that measured time by the dropping of water, or the falling of sand, clocks
and watches. As to the art of staining or painting glass, which ceased to be
practised about the Reformation, and has almost ever since been deplored as a lost
invention, it is effected by chemical means, and is at this day in as great perfection as ever. Vide Chambers’s Dict. voce GLASS, Anecdotes of Painting in
England by Mr. Horace Walpole, vol. II. page 15.

VOL. I.   e   this

this book, which has proved a plentiful source of intelligence to such as have laboured to depreciate all modern attainments, it is roundly asserted of music, which was anciently a science, that there are not the least footsteps remaining: and further, that the Cardinal of Ferrara, by whom it is supposed is meant Hippolyto de Esse, the patron of Vicentino took great pains to recover it, but all to no purpose *.

Such as seem to have adopted the opinion of Pancirollus with respect to music, for example, Dr. Pepusch, and a few of his disciples, have asserted as an instance in support of it, that the chromatic and enarmonic genera are now neither practised nor accurately known. Farther they add, that of the various modes of the ancients, only two are remaining, viz. those which answer to the keys A and C; for, say they, the ancients took the tones and semitones in order as they naturally arise in the diapason system, and, without any dislocation of either, considered the progression from any fundamental chord as a mode or key, and formed their melodies accordingly.

With regard to the enarmonic genus, it will in the ensuing volumes be shewn that the ancients themselves suffered it to grow into disuse by reason of its intricacy; and therefore it cannot so properly be said to have been lost, as that it is rejected, and the rather as we are assured that Salinas and others have accurately determined it †: Of the chromatic as much seems to have been retained as is necessary to the perfection of the diatonic; and as to the modes, it will also be shewn that there never was, nor can there in nature be more, or any other than the two abovementioned; and consequently that in this respect music has sustained no injury at all.

The loss of arts is a plausible topic of declamation, but the possibility of such a calamity by other means than a second deluge, or the

---

* A like attempt was made in France in the year 1570, by the establishment of an academy under the direction of Jean-Antoine Baïf and Joachim Theobalde de Courville, but through envy, as it is said, the design failed. Merkenous in Quest. et Explic. in Genesis. art. XV. pag. 1683. Walth. Musicalisches Lexicon, voce ACADEMIE ROYALE DE MUSIQUE.

† Vide infra, vol. I. page 110.

inter-

interpofition of any lefs powerful agent than G xl himfelf, is a matter of doubt; and when appearances every where around us favour
the opinion of our improvement not only in literature, but in the fciences
and all the manual arts, it is wonderful that the contrary notion
fhould ever have got footing among mankind.

As to the general prejudices in behalf of antiquity, it has been hinted above that a reafon for them is to be found in that implicit belief
which the courfe of modern education difpofes us to entertain of the
fuperior virtue, wifdom, and ingenuity of thofe, who in all thefe inftances we are taught to look on as patterns the moft worthy of imitation; but it can never be deemed an excufe of fome writers for
complimenting nations lefs enlightened than ourfelves with the poffeffion or enjoyment of arts which it is pretended we have loft; as
they do when they magnify the attainments of nations comparatively
barbarous, and making thofe countries on which the beams of knowledge can fcarcely be faid to have yet dawned the theatres of virtue
and the fchools of fcience, recommend them as fit exemplars for our
imitation.

Of this clafs of authors, Sir William Temple and Ifaac Voffius feem
to be the chief; the one a ftatefman retired from bufinefs, an ingenious
writer, but poffeffed of little learning, other than what he acquired in
his later years, and which it is fufpected was not drawn from the
pureft fources; the other a man of great erudition, but little judgment, the weaknefs whereof he manifefted in a childifh credulity, and
a difpofition to believe things incredible. Thefe men, upon little better
evidence than the reports of travellers, and the relations of miffionaries,
who might have purpofes of their own to ferve, have celebrated the policy, the morality, and the learning of the Chinefe, and done little lefs
than propofed them as examples of all that is excellent in human
nature *.

* As an inftance of their fuperior fkill in the fcience of medicine, he fays that
their phyficians pretend that they are able, not only to tell by the pulfe how many
hours or days a fick man can laft, but how many years a man in perfect feeming
e 2   health

The topics infifted on by Sir William Temple, in that part of his Effay on Heroic Virtue, where he takes occafion to fpeak of the Chinefe, are their wifdom, their knowledge, their wit, their learning, ingenuity, and civility, on which he beftows the moft extravagant encomiums.

Voffius is more particular, and fays that ' the Chinefe deplore ' the lofs of their mufic, the fuperior merit whereof may be in- ' ferred from the relics of it yet remaining, which are fo excel- ' lent, that for their perfection in the art, the Chinefe may impofe ' filence on all Europe.' Farther he fays of their pantomimes, or theatrical reprefentations by mute perfons, in which the fentiments are expreffed by gefticulations, and even nods, that ' thefe declare their

health may live, in cafe of no accident or vio'ence. Effay of Heroic Virtue, fect. II.

The following fummary of Chinefe knowledge may ferve to fhew how well they are entitled to the exaggerated encomiums of fuch writers. They carry their hiftory back to many ages before the time of the creation. Hearne's Duct. Hiftorie. vol. I. page 16. Their notion of an eclipfe is, that there is in heaven a dragon of an immenfe bignefs, ready at all times to eat up the fun or moon, which he likes beft; when an eclipfe of either happens, they fuppofe he has got the planet between his teeth, and, to make him quit his hold, they beat drums and brafs kettles. Le Comte's Memoirs of China, edit. 1738, pag. 70, 468. In the judgment of Caffini, and other great aftronomers, they err in their accounts of fundry conjunctions of the planets; in fome of them not lefs than five hundred years. Jenkin on the Reafonablenefs and Certainty of the Chriftian Religion, vol. I. p. 339. They are fo little fkilled in mechanics, that they took a watch, brought into their country by a Jefuit, for an animal. They are ftrangers to the ufe of letters as the elements of words; and have even at this day no alphabet. Ibid. Moreover they pretend to be the inventors of mufic, notwithftanding that in the opinion of Father Le Comte they have nothing among them that deferves the name. See his Memoirs, page 214.

Of their propenfity to fraud and deceit in their dealings, there are abundant examples in Le Comte and Lord Anfon's voyage; and of their morality and civil policy, which are fo highly extolled, any one may judge, when he is told that in Pekin and other large cities there is an officer, whofe duty it is every morning to deftroy the numerous infants that have been expofed in the ftreets in the preceding night. Mod. Univ. Hift. fol. vol. I. page 173.

' fkill

' skill in the rythmus, which is the soul of music *.' Elsewhere he takes occasion to celebrate this people for their skill on the tibia, and bestows on their performance the following enthusiastic encomium : ' The tibia, by far to be preferred to the stringed instruments of every ' kind, is now silenced, so that, excepting the Chinese, who alone ' excel on it, scarce any are to be found that are able to please even ' an ordinary hearer †.'

Another writer is more particular, and gives us for history this nonsense; that Fou-Hi, the first of the emperors and legislators of China, delivered the precepts of music, and having invented fishing. composed a song for those who exercised the art; and to banish all impurity from the heart, made a lyre with strings of silk ; and farther that Chin-Nong, a succeeding emperor, celebrated the fertility of the earth in songs of his own composing, and made a beautiful lyre and a guitar enriched with precious stones, which produced a noble harmony, curbed the passions, and elevated many to virtue and heavenly truth ‡.

These are the opinions of men who have acquired no small reputation in the world of letters ; and therefore that error might not derive a sanction from authority, it seemed necessary to enquire into the evidence in support of them ; of what sort it is, the passages above cited may serve to shew. It remains now to make the comparison above proposed of the modern with the ancient music.

The method hitherto pursued by those writers who have attempted to draw a parallel between the ancient and modern music, has been to bring together into one point of view the testimonies in favour of the former, and to strengthen them by their own suffrages, which upon examination will be found to amount to just nothing ; for these testimonies being no more than verbal declarations or descriptions, every

* De poemat. cant. et virib. Rythmi, pag. 95.
† Ibid. pag. 107.
‡ Extrait des Hist. Chinois, published by Monf. Goguet, pag. 567, 572. Differt. on the Union, &c. of Poetry and Music, page 167.

reader is at liberty to fupply them by ideas of his own; ideas which can only have been excited by that mufic which he has actually heard, or at leaft perufed and contemplated. An inftance borrowed from the practice of fome critics in painting, may poffibly illuftrate this fentiment : The works of Apelles, Parrhafius, Zeuxis, and Protogenes, together with thofe of other artifts lefs known, fuch as Bularchus, Euphranor, Timanthes, Polygnotus, Polycletes, and Ariftides, all famous painters, have been celebrated in terms of high applaufe by Ariftole, Philoftratus, Pliny, and the poets ; and thofe who attend to their defcriptions of them, affociate to each fubject ideas of excellence as perfect as their imaginations can fuggeft, which can only be derived from fuch works of later artifts as they have feen; in like manner as we affift the defcriptions of Helen in Homer and of Eve in Milton, with ideas of female beauty, grace, and elegance, drawn from our own obfervation * : The refult of fuch a comparifon in the cafe of painting, has frequently been a determination to the prejudice of modern artifts ; and the works of Raphael, Domenichino, and Guido have been condemned as not anfwering to thofe characters of fublime and beautiful, which are given to the productions of the ancient ar-

* Mr. Harris to this purpofe has given his fentiments in the following judicious obfervation : ' When we read in Milton of Eve, that

' Grace was in all her fteps, heav'n in her eye,
' In ev'ry gefture dignity and love ;

' we have an image not of that Eve which Milton conceived, but of fuch an Eve
' only as every one by his own proper genius is able to reprefent from reflecting on
' thofe ideas which he has annexed to thofe feveral founds. The greater part in the
' mean time have never perhaps beftowed one accurate thought upon what Grace,
' Heaven, Love, and Dignity mean; or ever enriched the mind with ideas of
' beauty, or afked whence they are to be acquired, and by what proportions they are
' conftituted. On the contrary, when we view Eve as painted by an able painter,
' we labour under no fuch difficulty ; becaufe we have exhibited before us the bet-
' ter conceptions of an artift, the genuine ideas of perhaps a Titian or a Raphael.'
Difc. on Mufic, Painting, and Poetry, page 77, in not.

tifts.

tiſts *. In like manner to ſpeak of muſic, we can form ideas of the perfection of harmony and melody, and of the general effect reſulting from the artful combination of muſical ſounds, from that muſic alone which we have actually heard; and when we read of the muſic of Timotheus or Antigenides, we muſt either reſemble it to that of the moſt excellent of the modern artiſts, or forbear to judge about it; and if in the compariſon ſuch critics as Iſaac Voſſius, Sir William Temple, and ſome others, reject the muſic of the moderns as unworthy of attention or notice, how egregiouſly are they deceived, and what do they but forego the ſubſtance for the ſhadow?

Other writers have taken a different courſe, and endeavoured to prove the inferiority of the modern muſic to the ancient, by a compariſon of the powers of each in depriving men of the exerciſe of their rational faculties, and by impelling them to acts of violence. To theſe it may be ſaid, that, admitting ſuch a power in muſic, it ſeems to be common in ſome degree to that of all ages and countries, even the moſt ſavage; but the fact is, that theſe effects are adventitious, and in all the inſtances produced will be found to have followed from ſome prediſpoſition of the mind of the hearer, or peculiar coincidence of circumſtances, for that in truth muſic pretends not to the power of working miracles, nor is it the more to be eſteemed for exciting men to frenzy: Thoſe who contemplate it in a philoſophical and rational manner, and attend to its genuine operation on the human affections, are abundantly ſatisfied of its efficacy, when they diſcover that it has a tendency to exhilarate the mind, to calm the paſſions, to aſſuage the pangs of affliction †, to aſſiſt devotion, and to inſpire the mind with the moſt noble and exalted ſentiments.

* Vide Inquiry into the Beauties of Painting, by Daniel Webb, Eſq. paſſim.

† To this purpoſe we meet in Procopius with the following affecting relation, viz. that Gelimer, king of the Vandals, being at war with the emperor Juſtinian, and having been driven to the mountains by Beliſarius, his general, and reduced to great ſtraits, was adviſed in a letter by a friend of his named Pharas to make terms with the enemy; but in the greatneſs of his ſpirit diſdaining ſubmiſſion, he return-

ed

Others, despairing of the evidence of facts, have recourse to argument, contending that the same superiority with respect to music is to be yielded to the ancients as we allow them in the arts that afford delight to the imagination ; poetry, eloquence, and sculpture, for instance, of which say they, their works bear luculent testimony. To this it may be answered, that the evidence of works or productions now existing is irrefragable, but in a question of this kind there is no reasoning by analogy; and farther, that in the case of music, proof of the superiority of the ancients is not only wanting, but the weight of the argument lies on the other side ; for where are those productions of the ancients that must decide the question? Lost, it will be said, in the general wreck of literature and the arts : If so, they cease to be evidence. Appeal we then to those remaining monuments that exhibit to us the forms of their instruments, of which the lyre and the tibia

ed this answer : ‘ Quod mihi consilium dedisti, magnam habeo tibi gratiam, ut etiam hosti injusto serviam ; id vero mihi intolerandum videtur. Si Deus faveret, repetere poenas ab eo vellem, qui à me nunquam nec facto violatus nec verbo, bello, cujus nulla est causa legitima, praetextum praebuit, meque in hunc statum redegit, arcito, nescio unde, immiscuique Belisario. Non improbabile esse sciat, passurum ipsum, tanquam hominem ac principem, eorum aliquid, unde abhorrit. Nequit ultra progredi stylus, auferente mentem calamitate, quae me circumvenit. Vale, amice Phara, et mihi quod te oro, citharam, panem unum ac spongiam mitte.’ Procopius Caesariensis de Bello Vandalico, vol. I, lib. II. cap. vi, pag. 740, edit. Paris, 1662: which we thus render : I esteem it a great kindness that you vouchsafe me your advice, recommending a submission to my enemy, unjust as he has been to me, but the thought thereof is intolerable. If it please God I am prepared to suffer the worst from him, who having never been injured by me, has found a pretext for a war, for which no justifiable reason can be assigned ; and has let loose upon me Belisarius, who has reduced me to this extremity. Let him know that he is a man, and, though a prince, that he is not beyond the reach of misfortune. I can proceed no farther, the calamities which surround me depriving me of my reason. Farewell my friend Phara, and send to me an harp, a loaf of bread, and a spunge. The historian adds, that the harp was to console him in his affliction, the loaf to satisfy his hunger, he not having seen bread for a long time, and the spunge to dry up his tears.

are

are the most celebrated; and that these are greatly excelled by the instruments of the moderns will not bear a question. As to the lyre,
considered as a musical instrument, it is a very artless invention,
consisting merely of a few chords of equal length but unequal
tensions, in such a situation, and so disposed, as, without any contrivance to prolong or reverberate the sound, to vibrate in the empty air.
The tibia, allowing it the perfection to which the flute of the moderns
is arrived, could at best be but an imperfect instrument *; and yet we
are told it was in such estimation among the ancients, that at Corinth
the sum of three, some say seven, talents was given by Ismenias, a
musician, for a flute.

But a weightier argument in favour of modern music, at least so far
as regards the improvements in theory and practice that necessarily
result from the investigation of new principles and the discovery of
new combinations, may be drawn from the natural course and order
of things, which is ever towards perfection, as is seen in other sciences,
physics and mathematics, for instance; so that of music it may be
said, that the discoveries of one age have served but as a foundation
for improvements in the next; the consequence whereof is, that the
fund of harmony is ever encreasing. What advantages must accrue to
music from this circumstance, may be discerned if we enquire a little
into those powers which are chiefly exercised in practical composition: The art of invention is made one of the heads among the precepts of rhetoric, to which music in this and sundry instances bears a
near resemblance; the end of persuasion, or affecting the passions,
being common to both. This faculty consists in the enumeration of
common places, which are revolved over in the mind, and requires

* The imperfection of the flute consists in the impossibility of attempering its
tones, there being no rule or canon by which it can be tuned; to which we
may add, that the tones in the upper octave are as dissimilar, in respect of sound,
as those of the human voice in those persons who have what is called the falsetto.
In the flute also the difference is discernible in the double shake, which is made on
a note that divides the two systems of the natural and artificial tones.

both an ample ſtore of knowledge in the ſubject upon which it is exerciſed, and a power of applying that knowledge as occaſion may require. It differs from memory in this reſpect, that whereas memory does but recall to the mind the images or remembrance of things as they were firſt perceived, the faculty of invention divides complex ideas into thoſe whereof they are compoſed, and recompounds them again after different faſhions, thereby creating variety of new objects and conceptions: Now the greater the fund of knowledge above ſpoken of is, the greater is the ſource from whence the invention of the artiſt or compoſer is ſupplied; and the benefits thereof are ſeen in new combinations and phraſes capable of variety and permutation without end. And thus much muſt ſerve at preſent touching the comparative merits of the ancient and modern muſic.

In tracing the progreſs of muſic, it will be obſerved, that it naturally divides itſelf into the two branches of ſpeculation and practice, and that each of theſe requires a diſtinct and ſeparate conſideration *. Of the dignity and importance of the former Ptolemy, lib. I. cap. ii. has delivered his ſentiments to the following purpoſe: ' It is in all things the ' buſineſs of contemplation and ſcience to ſhew that the works of nature, ' well regulated as they are, were conſtituted according to reaſon, and to ' anſwer ſome end; and that nothing has been done by her without ' conſideration, or as it were by chance; more eſpecially in thoſe that ' are deemed the fineſt of her works, as participating of reaſon in the ' greateſt degree, the ſenſes of ſight and hearing.' And Sir Iſaac New-

---

* There are but few inſtances of muſicians that have been eminently diſtinguiſhed for ſkill both in the theory and practice of muſic, Zarlino, Tartini, and Rameau excepted: The two branches of the ſcience have certainly no connection with each other, as may be gathered from the following ſentiment of an ingenious writer on the ſubject: ' The delights of practical muſic enter the ear without acquainting the ' underſtanding from what proportions they ariſe, or even ſo much as that proportion ' is the cauſe of them; This the philoſopher obſerves from reaſon and experience, ' and the mechanic muſt be taught, for the framing inſtruments; but the practiſer ' has no neceſſity to ſtudy, except he deſires the learning as well as the pleaſure of ' his art.' Propoſal to perform Muſic in perfect and mathematical Proportions, by Tho Salmon, 4to. Lond. 1688.

ton, fpeaking of the examination of thofe ratios that afford pleafure to the eye in architectural defigns, fays it tends to exemplify the fimplicity in all the works of the Creator. And farther he gives it as his opinion, ' that fome general laws of the Creator prevail with ref- ' pect to the agreeable or unpleafing affections of all our fenfes *.' By practical mufic we are to underftand the art of compofition as founded in the laws of harmony, and deriving its grace, elegance, and power of affecting the paffions from the genius and invention of the artift or compofer; in the exercife of which faculty it may be obferved, that the precepts for combining and affociating founds are as it were the fyntax of his art, and are drawn out of it, as the rules of grammar are from fpeech †.

In mufical hiftory the feveral events moft worthy of attention feem to be thofe of the firft eftablifhment of a fyftem, the introduction of mufic into the church fervice, the rife of dramatic mufic; under thefe feveral heads all that intelligence which to us is the moft interefting may be comprehended. As touching the firft, it is certain that we owe it to the Greeks, and there is nothing that at this diftance of time can be fuperadded to the relations of the ancient writers on the fubject; nor can it be fafe to deviate, either in refpect of form or manner, from the accounts from them tranfmitted to us of the original conftitution of the lyre, or of the invention and fucceffive progrefs of a mufical fcale; much lefs can we be warranted in fpeaking of the ancient practice, and the more abftrufe parts of the fcience, namely the genera and the modes, in any other terms than themfelves make ufe of: Were a liberty to do otherwife allowed, the fame mifchief would follow that attends the multiplication of the copies of a manufcript, or a tranflation through the medium of divers languages, where a new fenfe may be impofed upon the text by

* Vide Infra, vol. III. page 142, 143, in not.

† ' The art by which language fhould be regulated, viz. Grammar, is of much ' later invention than languages themfelves, being adapted to what was already in ' being, rather than the rule of making it fo.' Bifhop Wilkins's Effay towards a real Character, pag. 19.

different

different tranfcribers and tranflators in fuccefſion, till the meaning of the original becomes totally obfcured.

Vitruvius, in his treatiſe De ArchiteCtura, has a chapter on muſic, wherein he laments the want of words in the Roman language equivalent to the Greek muſical terms; the ſame difficulty is experienced in a greater or leſs degree by all who take occaſion to ſpeak of the ancient muſic, whether of the Hebrews or the Greeks. The Engliſh tranſlators of the Bible were necefſitated to render the words כנור Kinnor and עוגב Gnugab, by harp and organ; and a tranſlator of muſical appellatives will in many inſtances be reduced to as great difficulty as the Laplander, who in rendering a paſſage in the Canticles, ' He looketh forth at the windows, ſhewing himſelf through 'the lattice,' could find no nearer a reſemblance to a lattice than a ſnow-ſhoe, a thing like a racket uſed in the game of tennis, and tranflated it accordingly.

The complaint of Vitruvius above mentioned furniſhes an occaſion of enquiry into the ſtate of muſic among the Romans; and this will appear, even in their moſt flouriſhing condition, to have been, both in theory and practice, very low, there being no author to be found till after the deſtruction of the commonwealth who has written on the ſubject; and of thoſe that lived in the time of Auguſtus and afterwards, the number is ſo ſmall, and, if we except Boetius, their writings are ſo inconfiderable, as ſcarce to deſerve notice. Vitruvius wrote not profeſſedly on muſic; all that he ſays of it is contained in the third, fourth, and fifth chapters of the third book of his treatiſe De ArchiteCtura; wherein laying down the rules for the conſtruction of theatres, he ſpeaks of harmony in general terms, and afterwards of certain hollow veſſels diſpoſed in niches for the purpoſe of reverberating the voice of the ſingers or actors; and thence takes occaſion to mention the genera of the ancients, which he illuſtrates by a ſcale or diagram, compoſed, as he ſays, by Ariſtoxenus himſelf, though it does not occur in the valuable edition of that author publiſhed by Meibomius. In the ſame.

work,

work, lib. X. cap. ii. entitled De Hydraulicis, he defcribes the hy-draulic organ of the ancients, but in fuch terms, that no one has been able fatisfactorily to afcertain either its figure or the ufe of its parts.

Of Cenforinus, Macrobius, Martianus Capella, and Caffiodorus, it was never pretended that they had made any new difcoveries, or contributed in the leaft to the improvement of mufic. Boetius indeed with great induftry and judgment, collected the fenfe of the ancient Greek writers on Harmonics, and from the feveral works of Arifto-xenus, Euclid, Nicomachus, Alypius, Ptolemy, and others whofe difcourfes are now loft, compiled his moft excellent treatife De Mu-fica. In this he delivers the doctrines of the authors above mention-ed, illuftrated by numerical calculations and diagrams of his own in-vention; therein manifefting a thorough knowledge of the fubject. Hence, and becaufe of his great accuracy and precifion, this work of Boetius, notwithftanding it contains little that can be faid to be new, has ever been looked upon as a valuable repofitory of mufical eru-dition *.

Long before the time of Boetius, the enarmonic and chromatic ge-nera had grown into difufe; the diatonic genus only remaining, the mufical characters were greatly reduced in number; and the notation of mufic became fo fimple, that the Romans were able to reprefent the whole feries of founds contained in the fyftem of a double octave, or the bifdiapafon, by fifteen characters; rejecting therefore the cha-racters ufed by the Greeks for the purpofe, they affumed the firft fif-teen letters of their own alphabet; and this is the only improvement or innovation in mufic that we know of that can be afcribed to the Romans.

As to the practice of mufic, it feems to have been carried to no very great degree of perfection by the Romans; the tibia and the lyre feem

* The works of Boetius were publifhed in a folio volume at Venice in the year 1499, and at Bafil by Glareanus, in 1570. In the treatife De Mufica are fundry diagrams invented by the editor, which tend greatly to the illuftration of his author.

to have been the only inftruments in ufe among them ; and on thefe there were no performers of fuch diftinguifhed merit as to render them worthy the notice of pofterity, which perhaps is the reafon that the names of but few of them are recorded.

Cafpar Bartholinus has written a treatife ‘ De Tibiis veterum et ‘ earum antiquo ufu,' in which he has brought together a great variety of intelligence refpecting the flutes of the ancients : In this tract is a chapter entitled ‘ Tibia in Ludis Spectaculis atque Comediis,' wherein the author takes occafion to fpeak of the tibiæ pares et impares, and alfo of the tibiæ dextræ et finiftræ, ufed in the reprefentation of the comedies of Terence, which he illuftrates by plates reprefenting the forms of them feverally, as alfo the manner of inflating them, taken from coins and other authentic memorials. In particular he gives an engraving from a manufcript in the Vatican library, of a fcene in an ancient comedy, in which a tibicinift is delineated ftanding on the ftage, and blowing on two equal flutes: What relation his mufic has to the action we are to feek. He alfo gives from a marble at Rome the figure of a man with an inflected horn near him, thus infcribed, M. IULIUS VICTOR EX COLLEGIO LITICINUM CORNICINUM.

It appears from a paffage in Valerius Maximus, that there was at Rome a college of tibicinifts or players on the flute, who we may fuppofe were favoured with fome fpecial privileges and immunities. Thefe feem to have been a diftinct order of muficians from the former, at leaft there are fundry infcriptions in Gruter purporting that there was at Rome a college comprehending both tibicinifts and fidicinifts ; which latter feem to have been no other than lyrifts, a kind of muficians of lefs account among the Romans than the players on their favourite inftrument the flute. Valerius Maximus, lib. II. cap. v. relates of the tibicinifts that they were wont to play on their inftruments in the forum, with their heads covered, and in party-coloured garments.

That the tibicinifts were greatly indulged by the Romans, may be inferred from the nature of their office, which required their attendance

PRELIMINARY DISCOURSE. xlvii

dance at triumphs, at facrifices, and indeed all public folemnities; at
leaft the fenfe of their importance and ufefulnefs to the ftate is the
only reafon that can be fuggefted for their intemperance, and that in-
folence for which they were remarkable, and which both Livy and
Valerius Maximus have recorded in a narration to the following purpofe. ‘ The cenfors had refufed to permit the tibicines to eat in the
‘ temple of Jupiter, a privilege which they claimed as founded on an-
‘ cient cuftom; whereupon the tibicines withdrew to Tibur, a town
‘ in the neighbourhood of Rome, now Tivoli. As the tibicines were
‘ neceffary attendants on the facrifices, the magiftrates were at a lofs
‘ how to perform thofe folemnities in their abfence; the fenate there-
‘ fore fent embaffadors to the Tiburtines, requefting them to deliver
‘ them up as officers of the ftate who had fled from their duty: At
‘ firft perfuafions were tried, but thefe proving ineffectual, the Tibur-
‘ tines had recourfe to ftratagem; they appointed a public feaft, and
‘ inviting the tibicines to affift at it, plied them with wine till they be-
‘ came intoxicated, and, while they were afleep, put them into carts,
‘ which conveyed them to Rome. The next day, having in fome de-
‘ gree recovered their reafon, the tibicines were prevailed on to ftay in
‘ the city, and were not only reftored to the privilege of eating in the
‘ temple, but were permitted annually to celebrate the day of their
‘ return, though attended with circumftances fo infamous to their
‘ office, by proceffions in which the moft licentious exceffes were
‘ allowed *.’

The feceffion of the tibicinifts was in the confulate of Caius Junius
Bubulcus and Quintus Æmilius Barbula; that is to fay in the year of
the world 3640, three hundred and eight years before Chrift; and
ferves to fhew the extreme licentioufnefs of Roman manners at that
period, as alfo the low ftate of their mufic, when the beft inftruments
they could find to celebrate the praifes of their deities were a few

* Livy, lib. IX. cap. xxx. See alfo Valerius Maximus, lib. II. cap. v. The
fame ftory is related by Ovid, Fafti, lib. VI. who adds that the thirteenth day of
June was celebrated as the anniverfary.

forty

forry pipes, little better than thofe which now ferve as playthings
for children.

But, leaving the tibicines and their pipes to their admirers, if we
proceed to enquire into the ftate of mufic among the Romans at any
given period of their hiftory, we fhall find, that as a fcience
they held it in fmall eftimation: And to this fact Cornelius Nepos
bears the fulleft teftimony, for relating in his life of Epaminondas
that he could dance, play on the harp and flute, he adds, that in
Greece thefe accomplifhments were greatly efteemed, but by the
Romans they were little regarded. And Cicero, in his Tufculan
Queftions, lib. I. cap. i. to the fame purpofe, obferves that the ancient
Romans, addicting themfelves to the ftudy of ethics and politics, left
mufic and the politer arts to the Greeks.   Farther we may venture to
affert, that neither their religious folemnities, nor their triumphs, their
fhews or theatrical reprefentations, fplendid as they were, contributed
in the leaft to the improvement of mufic either in theory or practice :
To fay the truth, they feemed fcarcely to have confidered it as a fubject of fpeculation; and it was not until it received a fanction from
the primitive fathers of the church, that the fcience began to recover
its ancient dignity.

The introduction of mufic into the fervice of the church affords
ample fcope for reflection, and comprehends in its hiftory a great
part of what we know of modern mufic. All that need be mentioned in this place refpecting that important event is, that after the example of the Jews, and upon the authority of fundry paffages in fcripture, and more efpecially in compliance with the exhortation of St.
Paul in his Epiftles, St. Bafil, St. Ambrofe and St. Chryfoftom about
the middle of the fourth century inftituted antiphonal finging in their
refpective churches of Cefarea in Cappadocia, Milan, and Conftantinople. St. Ambrofe, who muft be fuppofed to have been eminently
fkilled in the fcience, prefcribed a formula of finging in a feries of
melodies called the ecclefiaftical tones, apparently borrowed from the
modes of the ancient Greeks ; thefe, as conftituted by him, were in
number

number only four, and are meant when we speak of the Cantus Ambrosianus ; but St. Gregory, near two centuries after, increased them to eight. The same father drew up a number of precepts respecting the limits of the melodies, the fundamental note, and the succession of tones and semitones in each ; and, with a view to the establishment of a settled and uniform musical science, that would apply to all the several offices at that time used in divine worship, founded and endowed a school for the instruction of youth in the rudiments of music, as contained in this formula, which was distinguished by the appellation of the Cantus Ecclesiasticus, and in later times by that of the Cantus Gregorianus.

 Before this time music had ceased to be a subject of speculation: Ptolemy was the last of the philosophers that had written professedly on it ; and though it may be said that his three books of Harmonics, as also those of Aristoxenus, Euclid, Nicomachus, Aristides Quintilianus, and others, being extant, music was in a way of improvement from the studies of men no less disposed to think and reflect than themselves ; yet the fact is, that among the Romans the science not only had made no progress at all, but even before the dissolution of the commonwealth, with them it seemed to be extinct. Nor let the supposition be thought groundless, that during some of the succeeding ages the books, the very repositories of what we call musical science, might be lost ; the history of the lower empire furnishing an instance, the more remarkable, as it relates to their own, the Roman civil law, which proves at least the possibility of such a misfortune *.

 To these causes, and the zeal of the fathers abovementioned, and more especially of St. Gregory, to disseminate its precepts, it is to be ascribed that the cultivation of music became the peculiar care of the clergy. But here a distinction is to be noted between the study and the practice of the science ; for we find that at the time of the institution of the Cantus Ambrosianus, an order of clergy was also established, whose employment it was to perform such parts of the service as were

* See the relation of the discovery of the Litera Pisana in vol. II. page 28.

required

required to be fung: Thefe were called Pfalmiftæ; and though by Bellarmine and a few other writers they are confounded with the Lectors, yet were they by the canonifts accounted a feparate and diftinct order. The reafon for their inftitution was, that whereas in the apoftolical age the whole congregation fang in divine fervice, and great confufion and diforder followed therefrom, it was found neceffary to fettle what the church calls a regular and decent fong, which, as it was framed by rule, and founded in the principles of harmony, required fkill in the performance; and accordingly we find a canon of the council of Laodicea held as early as the beginning of the fourth century, forbidding all excepting the canonical fingers, that is to fay, thofe who were ftationed in the Ambo, where the finging-defk was placed, and who fang out of a book or parchment, to join in the pfalms, hymns, and other parts of mufical divine fervice. We may well fuppofe that this order of men were endowed with all the requifites for the difcharge of their function; and that that peculiar form which the council of Carthage directs to be ufed for the ordination of Pfalmiftæ or fingers *, was in effect a recognition of their fkill and abilities.

The order of men abovementioned can be confidered in no other view than as mere practical muficians, the principal object of whofe attention was to make themfelves acquainted with the fongs of the church, and to utter them with that decency and gravity, and in fuch a manner as tended moft to edification: From the frequent repetition of the fame offices it muft be fuppofed that in general they fang by rote; at leaft we have no better reafon to affign than that they muft have fo done, for the eftablifhment of a fchool by St. Gregory for the inftruction of youth in the Cantus Ecclefiafticus, as reformed by himfelf, and for that fedulous attention to their improvement in it which he manifefted in fundry inftances.

At the fame time that we applaud the zeal of this father of the church, we cannot but wonder at that of his predeceffors, which is not more apparent in their commendations of mufic, as affociated with

* See it in vol. I. page 284, n.

reli-

religious worſhip, than in their ſevere cenſures of that which was calculated for private recreation: As to the ſong's of the ſtage in the ages
immediately ſucceeding the Chriſtian era, we know little more of
them than in general that they were ſuited to the corrupt manners of
the times; and theſe, by reaſon of their lewdneſs, and perhaps impiety
of ſentiment, might be a juſt ſubject of reprehenſion; but againſt the
muſic, the ſounds to which they were uttered, or the particular inſtruments that aſſiſted the voice in ſinging them, an objection can ſcarce
be thought of, and yet ſo frequent and ſo bitter are the invectives of
the primitive fathers, namely, Clemens Alexandrinus, Tertullian,
St. Cyprian, Lactantius, Epiphanius, Gregory Nazianzen, and of St.
Baſil, St. Auguſtine, and St. Chryſoſtom, who were lovers and pro-
moters of the practice of muſic, againſt wicked meaſures and effeminate melodies, the noiſe of flutes, cymbals, harps, and other inſtruments of deceit, ſeducing the bearers to intemperance, and even idolatry, that if credit be given to their opinions of the nature and tendency of ſecular muſic, we muſt be inclined to believe, as they in
good earneſt profeſs to have done, that it was an invention of the
Devil.

The cultivation of muſic as a ſcience was the employment of a ſet
of men, in whom all the learning of the times may then be ſaid to
have centered; theſe were the regular clergy, of ſuch of whom as
flouriſhed in the eleventh century and afterwards, it muſt in juſtice be
ſaid, that what they wanted in knowledge, they made up in induſtry;
and that thoſe frequent barbariſms which occur in their writings,
were in no ſmall degree atoned for by the clearneſs and preciſion *
with which on every occaſion they delivered their ſentiments. Nor

* Theſe qualities ſeem to be but the neceſſary reſult of the old ſcholaſtic method
of inſtitution, in which logic made a conſiderable part, and are in no inſtance
more manifeſt than in the ancient forms of judicial proceedings, ſuch as writs and
pleadings; of which Sir Matthew Hale, in his Hiſtory of the Law, chap. 7, remarks that they were very ſhort, but very clear and conſpicuous, orderly digeſted,
pithy, clear, and rational. The ſame may be ſaid in general of the more ancient
ſtatutes.

was

was the concisenefs and method of the monkifh treatifes on mufic a lefs recommendation of them than their perfpicuity : They confifted either of fuch maxims as were deemed of greateft importance in the ftudy of the fcience, or of familiar colloquies between a mafter and his difciple, in which in an orderly courfe of gradation, firft the elements, and then the precepts of the art were delivered and illuftrated. To enumerate the inftances of this kind which have occurred in the courfe of this work, would be an endlefs tafk; let it fuffice to fay that the Hiftoire Litteraire de France, and the Memoirs of Bale, Pits, and the Bibliotheca of Tanner abound with references to a variety of manufcript tracts depofited in the public and other libraries, that abundantly prove the mode of mufical inftruction to have been fuch as is above defcribed.

Before the period above fpoken of, mufic had for very good reafons been admitted into the number of the liberal fciences ; and accordingly in the fcholaftic divifion of the arts into the trivium and quadrivium, it held a place in the latter : Neverthelefs, till the Greek literature began to revive in Europe, faving the fummary of harmonics contained in the treatife De Mufica of Boetius, the ftudents in that faculty had fcarce any fource of intelligence ; and to this it muft be attributed that in none of the many tracts written by the monks of thofe times, and afterwards by the profeffors or fcholaftics as they were called, do we meet with any of thofe profound difquifitions on harmony and the proportions which refolve the principles of mufic into geometry; nor any of thofe nice calculations and comparifons of ratios, or fubtile diftinctions between the confonances of one kind and thofe of another, which abound in the writings of the ancient Greeks; fo, that were we to judge from the many difcourfes written during that dark period, and bearing the titles of Micrologus, Metrologus, and others of the like import, we fhould conclude that the fcience of harmonics had fcarce any exiftence among mankind. Nor could any great advantages refult from the writings of Boetius, feeing that there wanted light to read them by ; and this was not obtained till Franchinus introduced

troduced it, by procuring tranflations of thofe authors from whofe
writings Boetius had compiled his work.

That the ftudies of the monkifh muficians muft have been confined
to the Cantus Gregorianus is evident from this confideration, that
they were ftrangers to mufic of every other kind; an affertion which
will be the more readily credited when we are told that till the middle
of the eleventh century rythmic or menfurable mufic was not known:
Their method of teaching it was by the monochord, without which
they had no method of determining the progreffion of tones and femitones in the oflave, nor confequently of meafuring by the voice any
of the intervals contained in it.

The reformation of the fcale by Guido Aretinus, and more efpecially his invention of a method of finging by certain fyllables adapted to the notes, facilitated the practice of finging to fuch a degree,
that, as himfelf relates, the boys of his monaflery were rendered capable in a month's time of finging in a regular and orderly fucceffion
the feveral intervals with the utmoft accuracy and precifion*.   We are
told, though not by himfelf, that he alfo by an ingenious contrivance transferred the notes of his fcale to the left hand, making a feveral joint of each of the fingers the pofition of a note.   Whether this
invention is to be aſcribed to him or not, it is pretty certain that it followed foon after the reformation of the fcale ; and that it gave rife
to a diftinction of mufic into manual and tonal, the firft comprehending the precepts of finging by the fyllables, the other the Cantus Ecclefiafticus, as inftituted in the formula of St. Gregory.

At this time the world were ftrangers to what we call rythmic mufic, the practice of finging, and thereby of affociating mufic with
poetry, which till then had univerfally prevailed, rendering any fuch
invention unneceffary :. Neverthelefs there were fome writers who had
entertained an idea of transferring the profody of poetry to mufic ;
and a few fcattered hints of this kind, which occur in the writings of
St. Auguftine and our countryman Bede on the fubject of metre, fug-

* Vide infra, vol. I. pag. 448.

gefted!

gested the formation of a system of metrical laws, such as would not only enable music to subsist of itself, but aid the powers of melody with that force and energy which it is observed to derive from the regular commixture and interchange of long and short quantities.

This improvement was effected in the institution of what is called the Cantus Mensurabilis; a branch of musical science which subjected the duration of musical sounds to rule and measure, by assigning to those of the flowest progression certain given portions of time, and to the next in succession a less, in a regular gradation; and which taught a method of signifying by characters, varying in form and colour, the radical notes, with their several ramifications, terminating in those of the smallest value, i. e. of the shortest duration.

An invention of this kind was all that could then be thought wanting to the perfection of instrumental music; and from this period we may observe that it began to flourish: It is true that the state of the mechanic arts was then very low, and that the instruments in common use were so rudely constructed, as to be scarcely capable of yielding musical sounds. Bartholomeus, in his book De Proprietatibus Rerum, in an enumeration of the musical instruments of his time, has described the flute as made of the boughs of an elder-tree hollowed; and an instrument called the Symphonia, as made of a hollow tree, closed in leather on either side, which he says is beaten of minstrels with sticks, and that ' by accord of hyghe and lowe thereof comyth full ' swete notes:' And again, describing the Psalterium or Sawtrie, he says it differs from the harp, for that it is made of an hollow tree, and that ' the fowne comythe upwarde, the strynges being smytte ' downwarde; whereas in the harpe the holowneffe of the tre is by- ' nethe.' These descriptions, and others of the like kind which are elsewhere to be met with, are evidence of the inartificial construction of musical instruments in those days, and leave it a question what kind of a harp or other instrument that could be on which king Alfred had attained to such a degree of excellence as to rival the musicians of his time.

Never-

Neverthelefs it appears that there were certain inftruments, perhaps not in common ufe, better calculated to produce melody than thofe abovementioned, namely, thofe of the viol kind; the fpecific difference between which and other ftringed inftruments is, that in the former the found is produced by the action of a plectrum or bow of hair on the ftrings: Of thefe the mention is not only exprefs, but frequent in Chaucer, by the names of the Fithel, Getron, Ribible, and other appellations, clearly fynonymous: The invention of this clafs of inftruments is by fome, who make the viol the prototype of it, afcribed to the French; but there are other writers who derive the viol itfelf from the Arabian Rebab, from whence perhaps Ribible and Rebec, the ufe whereof it is faid the Chriftians learned from the Saracens in the time of the Crufades; but it is more probable, by reafon of its antiquity, that it was brought into Spain by the Moors.

To afcertain the degree of perfection to which the practice of inftrumental mufic had attained at any period before the fixteenth century, would be very difficult. The Provençal fongs, as being mere vocal compofitions, afford no ground on which a conjecture might be formed; and as to their popular tunes, the airs of the Mufars and Violers, befides that they feem to have been mere melodies, for the moft part the effufions of fancy, and not regulated by harmonical precepts, the impreffion of them can hardly be fuppofed to have been either deep or lafting; and this may be the chief reafon that the knowledge of them has not reached pofterity.

That the practice of inftrumental mufic was become familiar with fuch young perfons of both fexes as had received the benefit of a good education, is clearly intimated by the old poets. Not only the Squire, but the Clerk, Abfolon, in Chaucer, are by him defcribed, the one as floyting, i. e. fluting all the day, the other as playing fongs on a fmall Ribible, and elfewhere on the Geterne *; and in the Confeffio Aman-

* See the character of the Squire among the Prologues to the Canterbury Tales, as alfo the Miller's Tale paffim.

tie-tis of Gower, fol. 178, b. is a plain intimation that the Citole, an inflrument nearly refembling the virginal, was in his time the recreation of well educated young women *.

We are alfo told by Boccace, in his Account of the Plague at Florence in 1348, that the ladies and gentlemen who retired from that city, and are the relators of the feveral ftories contained in his Decameron, among other recreations in the intervals of their difcourfes, intermixed mufic ; and that fundry of the perfons whofe names he mentions played on the lute and the viol. They alfo danced to the mufic of the Cornamufa or bagpipe, an inflrument which we may infer to have been held in but ordinary eftimation from this circumftance, that it is put into the hands of Tindarus, a domeflic of one of the ladies; befides that Chaucer in characterizing his Miller fays,

   ' A baggepipe well couth he blowe and foune.'

Of vocal concerts, as they ftood about the year 1550, or perhaps earlier, a judgment may be formed from the madrigals of that time, which abound with all the graces of harmony. Concerts of inflruments alone feem to be of later invention, at leaft there is no clear evidence of the form in which they exifted, other than treatifes and compofitions for concerts of viols called Fantafias, few whereof were publifhed till thirty years after †.

Gio. Maria Artufi, an ecclefiaftic of Bologna, and a writer on mufic about the year 1600, defcribes the concerts of his time as abounding in fweetnefs of harmony, and confifting of cornets, trumpets,

---

* Vide infra, vol. II, page 106.

† The earlieft of which we can fpeak with certainty, is a treatife in folio by Thomas à Sancta Maria, a Spanifh Dominican, publifhed at Valladolid in 1570, entitled ' Arte de tanner fantafia para tecla, viguela, y todo inflrumendo de tres o ' quatro ordenes,' which carries the antiquity of concerts for viols, and thofe compofitions called Fantafias, back to that time, but leaves us at a lofs as to other inflrumental concerts.

violins,

violins, viols, harps, lutes, flutes, and harpsichords: These, as also organs, regals, and guitars, are enumerated in the catalogue of instruments prefixed to the opera, L'Orfeo, composed by Claudio Monteverde, and represented at Mantua in 1607. Tom Coryat speaks also of a performance at Venice, chiefly of instrumental music, which he protests he would have travelled an hundred miles on foot to hear, but without any such particular description as can enable us to compare it with the concerts of more modern times.

As touching the theory of the science, it has above been said to have consisted in manual, tonal, and mensurable music, with this farther remark, that, as it was included in the very nature of their profession, and besides required some degree of literature, the great cultivators of it were the regular clergy. These men contented themselves with that small portion of knowledge which was to be attained by the perusal of Boetius, Cassiodorus, Guido, and a few others, who wrote in the Latin tongue; the little they knew they freely communicated; and it was not till the beginning of the fourteenth century that men began to suspect that the science was capable of farther improvement.

About this time Johannes De Muris improved the Cantus Mensurabilis, by reducing it to form and demonstrating that the measures thereof, like the ratios of the consonances, were founded in number and proportion: From the rules laid down by him in a treatise entitled Practica Mensurabilis Cantûs, are derived the distinctions of duple and triple proportion, as they respect the duration of sounds, with all the various modifications thereof. On this tract Prosdocimus Beldimandis wrote a commentary, and farther illustrated the doctrines contained therein in sundry discourses on the subjects of plain and mensurable music. It appears that both these persons were philosophers at large, and eminently skilled in the mathematics; and the liberal manner in which they wrote on music, treating it as a subject of deep speculation, was an inducement with many learned men, who lived under no ecclesiastical rule, to enter into an investigation of its principles. Some of these assumed the character of professors of the science, and undertook by public lectures to disseminate its principles. The most eminent of these persons were Marchettus of Padua, Johannes Tinctor, Gulielmus Garnerius, and Antonius Suarcialupus, to whom we may add Politian, whose skill in music is manifested in a discourse De Musica, contained in his Panepistemon or Prælectiones, extant in print. But notwithstanding the pains thus taken to revive the science, the improvement of it went on very slowly; whatever advances were made in practice, the theoretical topics of disquisition were soon exhausted, and the science of harmonics may be said to have been for some ages at a stand.

At length the beams of learning began to dawn on the western empire : The city of Conflantinople had been the seat of literature for some ages, but the sack of it by the Turks in the year 1453, had driven a great number of learned Greeks thence, who bringing with them an immense treasure of manuscripts, took refuge in Italy. Being settled there, they opened their stores, took possession of the public schools, and became the professors and teachers of the mathematical and other sciences, and indeed of philosophy, eloquence, and literature in general, in all the great cities. Of the many valuable books of Harmonics that are known to have been written by the mathematicians and other ancient Greeks, some had escaped that fate which learning is sure to experience from the ravages of conquest*, and the contents of these being made public, the principles of the science began to be known and understood by many, who till then were scarcely sensible that it had any principles at all.

This communication of intelligence was very propitious to music, as it determined many persons to the study of the science of harmony. The tonal laws and the Cantus Mensurabilis were left to those whose duty it was to understand them ; the ratios of sounds, and the nature of consonance were considered as essentials in music, and the investi-

* Laurus Quirinus of Venice was told by Cardinal Ruthen that upwards of one hundred and twenty thousand volumes were destroyed. Hody, De Græcis illustr. lib. II. cap. 1.

gation

gation of thefe was the chief purfuit of fuch as were fenfible of the value of that kind of learning.

Of the many who had profited in this new fcience, as it may be called, one was Franchinus Gaffurius, a native of Lodi, who having quitted the tuition of a Carmelite monk, who had been his inftructor, became foon diftinguifhed for fkill in thofe theoretic principles, the knowledge whereof he had derived from an attendance on the Greek teachers. And having procured copies of the treatifes on harmonics of Ariftides Quintilianus, Ptolemy, Manuel Bryennius, and Bacchius fenior, he caufed them to be tranflated into Latin; and, befides difcharging the duty of a public profeffor of mufic in the feveral cities of Italy, became the revivor of mufical erudition; and that as well pofterity, as thofe of his own time, might profit by his labours, he digefted the fubftance of his lectures into diftinct treatifes, and gave them to the world.

The writings of Franchinus, as they were replete with learning drawn from the genuine fource of antiquity, and contained the cleareft demonftrations of the principles of harmony, were fo generally ftudied, that mufic began now to affume the character of a fecular profeffion. The precepts therein delivered afforded a greater latitude to the inventive faculty than the tonal laws allowed of; and emancipating the fcience from the bondage thereof, many who had no relation to the church fet themfelves to frame compofitions for its fervice, in which the powers both of harmony and melody were united. And hence we may at leaft with a fhew of probability date the origin of an office that yet fubfifts in the choral eftablifhments of Italy, namely, that of Maeftro di Cappella; the duty whereof feems uniformly to have been not only that the perfon appointed to it fhould as precentor regulate the choir, but alfo adapt to mufic the offices performed both on ordinary and folemn occafions. Of the dignity and importance of the office of Maeftro di Cappella a judgment may be formed from this circumftance, that the perfons elected to it for fome centuries paft appear to have been of diftinguifhed emi-

h 2   nence;

nence[*]; and of its neceffity and utility no ftronger argument can
be offered, than that among the Germans, to whom the knowledge of mufie was very foon communicated after its revival in
Italy, the office was recognized by the appointment of a director
of the choir in the principal churches of all the provinces and cities.

The fame fenfe of the importance of this office appears to have
been entertained by the proteftants, who at the time of the Reformation we find to have been no lefs fedulous in the cultivation of mufie
with a view to religious worfhip, than the church that had eftablifhed
it. It is true that Calvin was for fome time in doubt whether to adopt
the folemn choral fervice, or that plain metrical pfalmody which is
recommended by St. Paul to the Coloffians, as an incentive to fuch
mirth as was confiftent with the Chriftian profeffion, and at length
determined on the latter.

But Luther, who was excellently fkilled in mufie, confidered it not
merely as a relief under trouble and anxiety, but as the voice of
praife, and as having a tendency to excite and encourage devout affections, befides that he had tranflated into the German language the
Te Deum, and compofed fundry hymns, as alfo tunes to fome of the
German pfalms [†], he, with the approbation of Melancthon, received into
his church a folemn fervice, which included anthems, hymns, and certain fweet motetæ, of which he fpeaks very feelingly. and of mufie in
general he gives his opinion in thefe words: ' Scimus muficam dæmo-
' nibus etiam invifam et intolerabilem effe [‡].' That the office of a

---

* Andrea Adami Bolfena, in the hiftorical preface to his ' Offervazioni per ben
' regolare il Coro de l Cantori delle Cappella Pontificia,' afferts that anciently in
the college of pontifeal fingers the maeftro di cappella was a bifhop.

† Melchior Adamus, in his life of Luther, has inferted a letter from him to Spalatinus, written anno 1524, wherein he fays he is looking out for poets to tranflate
the whole of the Pfalms into the German tongue, and requefts of Spalatinus his affiftance therein. This was fome years before Marot tranflated the Pfalms into French.

‡ In an epiftle to Senfelius, Muficus, cited by Dr. Wetenhall from Sethus Calvifius, in his Gifts and Offices in the public Worfhip of God, page 434, but without reference to any work of Calvifius. This epiftle, wherever it is, and the above-
cited paffage is alfo noticed by Butler in his Principles of Mufic, page 115. Dr.
Weten-

chapel-mafter was recognized by the proteflants in the manner abovementioned is hardly to be doubted, feeing that it was exercifed at Bavaria by Ludovicus Senfelius, a difciple of Henry Ifaac, and an intimate friend and correfpondent of Luther [*], and fubfifts in Germany to this day.

For the reafons above affigned, we may without fcruple attribute to Franchinus a fhare of that merit which is afcribed to the revivors of literature in the fifteenth century ; and the rather as his writings, and the feveral tranflations of ancient treatifes on harmonics which he procured to be made, furnifhed the fludents in the fcience with fuch a copious fund of information, as enabled them not only to reafon juftly on its principles, but to extend the narrow bounds of harmony, and lay a foundation for thofe improvements, which it has been the felicity of later times to experience : And it is not a groundlefs fuppofition that the reputation of his writings was a powerful incentive to the publication of thofe numerous difcourfes on mufic of which the enfuing work contains a detail. Indeed fo general was the propenfity in the profeffors of the fcience in Italy, and in Germany more efpecially, to the compilation of mufical inftitutes, dialogues, and difcourfes in various forms, that the fcience was for fome time rather hurt by the repetition of the fame precepts, than benefited by any intelligence that could in ftrictnefs be faid to be new. The writings of Zarlino and Salinas are replete with erudition ; the fame, though in a lefs eminent degree, may be faid of thofe of Glareanus and the elder Galilei ; but of the generality of the Introductions, the Enchiridions, and the Erotemata publifhed in Italy and Germany from about the year 1550 to the middle of the next century, the perfpicuity of them is their beft praife.

As the revival of the theory of mufic is to be afcribed to the Italians, fo alfo are thofe improvements in the practice of it that have

Wetenhall applies this paffage to the mufic of our church, and on the authority thereof pronounces it to be fuch as no Devil can ftand againft.

[*] Some motets of his compofition are extant in the Dodecachordon of Glareanus.

brought

brought it to the state of perfection in which we behold it at this day. It is true that in the practice of particular instruments the masters of other countries have been eminently distinguished, as namely, those of Germany for skill on the organ; the French for the lute and harpsichord; and we are indebted for many valuable discoveries touching the nature and properties of found, of consonance and dissonance, the method of constructing the various kinds of musical instruments, and, above all, for a nice and accurate investigation of the principles of harmonics, to the learning and industry of Mersennus, a Frenchman; but in the science of composition the musicians of Italy have uniformly been the instructors of all Europe.

To relate the subsequent instances of improvement in music, or to enumerate the many persons of distinguished eminence that have excelled in the theory and practice thereof, would be to anticipate that information, which it is the end of history to communicate; and to animadvert on the numberless defects of the ancient music, may seem unnecessary, seeing that as well the paucity as the structure of the ancient instruments affords abundant evidence of a great disproportion between their practice and their theory; it is nevertheless worthy of remark, that they who were so skilful and accurate in the invention of characters and symbols, the types not only of things but of images or ideas, as the Greeks are allowed to have been, have, in the instance of music, manifested a great want of that faculty, inasmuch as there is not to be found in any of the characters in the ancient musical notation, the least analogy or relation between the sign and the found or thing signified; a perfection so obvious in the practice of the moderns, that we contemplate it with astonishment, there being no possible arrangement or disposition of musical sounds, nor no series or succession of equal or unequal, similar or dissimilar measures, but may with the greatest accuracy be described by the stave of Guido, and the forms of notes with their adjuncts, as directed by the rules of the Cantus Mensurabilis; insomuch that the modern system of notation, comprehending in it the types or symbols of things, and

not

not of notions or ideas, may be said to possess all the advantages of a real character.

To celebrate formally the praises of music in a work, the design whereof is to display its excellencies, may seem unnecessary; and the rather, as it has from the infancy of the world, with historians, orators, and poets, been a subject of panegyric: Besides the power and effect of musical sounds to assuage grief and awaken the mind to the enjoyment of its faculties, is acknowledged by the most intelligent of mankind; and, were it necessary, to prove that the love of music is implanted in us, and not the effect of refinement, examples thereof might be produced from the practice of those, who, from their particular situation of country, or circumstances of life, are presumed to approach nearly to that state in which the natural and genuine suggestions of the will are supposed to be most clearly discernible. To say nothing of the Turks, who are avowed enemies of literature, or of the Chinese, who, as has been shewn, notwithstanding all that is asserted of them, are so circumstanced, as seemingly never to be able to attain to any degree of excellence, nations the most savage and barbarous profess to admit music into their solemnities, such as they are, their rejoicings, their triumphs for victories, the meetings of their tribes, their feasts and their marriages; and to use it for their recreation and private solace [*]. St. Chrysostom, in his Homily on

[*] Father Lafitau, in his *Mœurs des Sauvages*, tome II. page 213, et seq. has given a full description of the festal solemnities, accompanied with music, of the Iroquois, Hurons, and other tribes of American savages; and in the Royal Commentaries of Peru, book II. chap. xiv. the author, Garcilasso de la Vega, besides informing us that their fabulous songs were innumerable, and carried in them the evidence of a savage spirit, speaks thus particularly of their music: ‘ In music they arrived to a certain ‘ harmony, in which the Indians of Colla did more particularly excell, having been ‘ the inventors of a certain pipe made of canes glued together, every one of which ‘ having a different note of higher and lower, in the manner of organs, made a ‘ pleasing musick by the dissonancy of sounds, the treble, tenor and base exactly ‘ corresponding and answering each to other; with these pipes they often plaid ‘ in consort, and made tolerable musick, though they wanted the quavers, semi- ‘ quavers, aires, and many voices, which perfect the harmony amongst us. They ‘ had

pſalm xlі. eſtimates the importance of muſic by its univerſality, and, in a ſtrain of ſimplicity, correſponding with the manners of the times in which he lived, ſays that human nature is ſo delighted with can-ticles and poems, that by them infants at the breaſt when they are froward or in pain, are lulled to reſt; that travellers in the heat of noon, driving their beaſts, ſuch as are occupied in rural labours, as treading or preſſing grapes, or bringing home the vintage; and even mariners labouring at the oar, as alſo women at their diſtaff, deceive

' had alſo other pipes, which were flutes with four or five ſtops, like the pipes of
' ſhepherds; with theſe they played not in conſort, but ſingly, and tuned them to
' ſonnets, which they compoſed in metre, the ſubject of which was love, and the
' paſſions which ariſe from the favours or diſpleaſures of a miſtreſs. Theſe muſi-
' cians were Indians trained up in that art for divertiſement of the Incas, and the
' Curacas, who were his nobles, which, as ruſtical and barbarous as it was, it was
' not common, but acquired with great induſtry and ſtudy.'

' Every ſong was ſet to its proper tune; for two ſongs of different ſubjects
' could not correſpond with the ſame aire, by reaſon that the muſick which the
' gallant made on his flute, was deſigned to expreſs the ſatisfaction or diſcontent of
' his mind, which were not ſo intelligible perhaps by the words, as by the melan-
' choly or chearfulneſs of the tune which he plaid. A certain Spaniard one night
' late encountered an Indian woman in the ſtreets of Cozco, and would have
' brought her back to his lodgings; but ſhe cryed out, " For God's ſake, Sir, let
" me go, for that pipe which you hear in yonder tower calls me with great paſſion,
" and I cannot refuſe the ſummons, for love conſtrains me to go, that I may be
" his wife and be my huſband."

' The ſongs which they compoſed of their wars and grand atchievements were
' never ſet to the aires of their flutes, being too grave and ſerious to be intermixed
' with the pleaſures and ſoftneſſes of love; for thoſe were onely ſung at their prin-
' cipal feſtivals, when they commemorated their victories and triumphs. When I
' came from Peru, which was in the year 1560, there were then five Indians reſiding
' at Cozco, who were great maſters on the flute, and could play readily by book any
' tune that was laid before them; they belonged to one Juan Rodriguez, who
' lived at a village called Labos, not far from the city: And now at this time,
' being the year 1602, 'tis reported that the Indians are ſo well improved in muſick,
' that it was a common thing for a man to found divers kinds of inſtruments; but
' vocal muſick was not ſo uſual in my time, perhaps becauſe they did not much practiſe
' their voices, though the mongrils, or ſuch as came of a mixture of Spaniſh and
' Indian blood, had the faculty to ſing with a tunable and a ſweet voice.'

the

the time, and mitigate the feverity of their labour by fongs adapted to their feveral employments or peculiar conditions. Clearchus relates that at Lefbos the people had a fong which they fung while they were grinding corn, and for that reafon called ἐπιμύλιον; and Thales affirms that he had heard a female flave of that country finging it, turning the mill: It began ' Mole piftrinum mole, nam et Pittacus molit rex ' magnæ Mitylenæ,' and alluded to the practice of that king, who was ufed to grind corn with a hand-mill, efteeming it a healthy exercife.

Other writers go farther, and affect to difcern the principles of mu-fic not only in the fongs, but the occupations and exercifes of artificers and even labourers; one of thefe in a vein of enthufiafm, perhaps more humorous and fingular than perfuafive, fays, ' What fhall I ' fpeak of that pettie and counterfeit mufic which carters make with ' their whips, hempknockers with their beetels, fpinners with their ' wheels, barbers with their fizzers, fmithes with their hammers? ' where methinkes the mafter-fmith with his treble hammer fings ' defkant whileft the greater buz upon the plainfong: Who doth not ' ftraitwaies imagin upon mufick when he hears his maids either at ' the woolhurdle or the milking pail? good God, what diftinct inten-' tion and remiffion is there of their ftrokes? what orderly dividing of ' their ftraines? what artificial pitching of their flops *?'

But befides the pleafure that men derive from mufic, this fatisfac-tion arifes from the ftudy of it, that its principles are founded in the very frame and conftitution of the univerfe, and are as clearly demon-ftrable as mathematical truth and certainty can render them; and in this refpect mufic may be faid to have an advantage over many fciences

* The Praife of Muficke, 8vo. printed anno 1586, n Oxford, for Jofeph Barnes, but conjectured to have been written by Dr. John Cafe, page 76. Of this perfon there is a curious account in Athen. Oxon, col, 299. Thomas Raven-fcroft, in the Apologie prefixed to his difcourfe on the true charactering of mufic, publifhed in 1614, cites it as a work of Dr. Cafe, whom he ftyles a ' Mæcenas of ' muficke.'

and faculties in the pursuit whereof the attention of mankind has
at different periods been deeply engaged: To say nothing of school
divinity, which, happily for the world, has given place to rational
theology, what can be said of law in general, other than that it is
mere human invention? a fabric of science erected it is true on the basis
of a few uncontrovertible principles of morality, and of that which
we call natural justice, but so accommodated to particular circumstances,
to the genius, situation, temper, and capacities of those who are the
objects of it, as that what is permitted and encouraged in one country, poligamy, for instance, shall be punished in another. In some
constitutions a difference of sex shall aggravate the guilt of the same
offence; and custom and usage shall preserve the inheritance of the
parent for the benefit of the eldest of his male descendants with the
same pretence to justice as the law of nature and reason distributes
it among them all. Finally, what shall we say to that system of ju-
risprudence, which, being allowed to be imperfect, craves the aid of
equity to regulate its operation, and mitigate its rigours? or of those
glosses and comments which in the civil and canon law are of little
less authority than the laws themselves?

As to medicine, setting aside the knowledge of the human frame,
and the uses of its constituent parts, a noble subject of speculation it
must be confessed, the wiser part of men, rejecting theory as vain and
delusive, resolve the whole of the science into observation and practice;
thereby confessing that its principles are either very few, or so void
of certainty, as not with safety to be relied on.

Of other liberal arts, such as grammar, logic, and rhetoric, it must
be allowed that they are of singular use; but, as being the mere inventions of men, and at best auxiliaries to other arts or faculties, they
are in their nature subordinate, and in that respect do but resemble the
art of memory, which all men know to be founded on principles not
existing in nature, but assumed by ourselves, widely differing from
those which are the basis as well of musical as mathematical science.

From

From this view of the comparative excellence of mufic, and its pre-eminence over many other fciences and faculties, we become convinced of the ftability of its principles, and are therefore at a lofs for the reafons why, in thefe later times at leaft, novelty in mufic fhould be its beft recommendation ; or that the love of variety fhould fo poffefs the generality of hearers, as almoft to leave it a queftion whether or no it has any principles at all.

To fatisfy thefe doubts, it may be fufficient to obferve that the principles of harmony allow, as it is fit they fhould, great fcope for the exercife of the invention ; and though few pretend to fkill in the arts without being in fome degree or other poffeffed of it, yet as all the imaginative arts prefuppofe a difpofition in mankind to receive their impreffions, all claim a right, and many the ability, to judge of works of invention and fancy.

The epic poet, trufting that the mind of his reader is co-extenfive with his own, endeavours to excite in him the ideas of fublimity and beauty ; the dramatic writer hopes to move the affections of his audience to terror and pity by the reprefentation of actions, the reflection on which infpired his mind with thofe paffions; and the painter, giving form to thofe ideas of grace, greatnefs, and character which occupy his mind, or felecting the beauties of nature, and transferring them to canvas, or at other times contenting himfelf with fimple imitation, in all thefe exercifes of imagination and art, expects from the judgment of the well-informed connoiffeur the approbation of his work.

Now in the feveral inftances above adduced, notwithftanding the conceffions made to them, we may difcern in the generality of men the want of that fenfe to which the appeal is made; for, with refpect to the epic poem, few are endowed with an imagination fufficiently capacious to difcover its beauties ; and as to dramatic reprefentation, the moft favourite of all public entertainments, although all men pretend to be judges of nature, and the cant of theatres has perfuaded moft that they are fo, few are acquainted with

ber

her operations in the various inflances exhibited on the flage, or know with any kind of certainty in what manner the actor is to fpeak, what tones or inflexions of the voice are appropriated to different paffions, or what are the proper gefticulations to exprefs or accompany the fentiment which he is to utter. How many individuals among thofe numerous audiences, who for a feries of years paft have affected to admire our great dramatic poet, may we fuppofe capable of difcerning his fenfe, delivered in a ftyle of dialogue very little refembling that of the prefent day, or of relifhing thofe high philofophical fentiments with which his compofitions and thofe of Milton abound ? * The anfwer muft be very few : Even humour, a talent which lies level with the obfervation of the many, is not alike intelligible to all; and fome are difgufted with thofe delineations of low manners, however juft and natural, that afford delight to others, as exhibiting to view the human mind in the fimplicity of nature, and free from thofe reftraints which are impofed on it by education and refinement.

The painter, in like manner, fubmitting his work to the public cenfure, fhall find for one that will applaud the grandeur of the defign, the finenefs of the compofition, or the correctnefs of the drawing, a hundred that would have difpenfed with all thefe excellencies for a greater glare of colouring, and attitudes fuited to their own ideas. of grace and elegance.

---

* The mafque of Comus, written for the entertainment of a noble family, and a company of chofen fpectators, which within thefe few years was introduced on the public ftage, may feem to contradict this obfervation, for this reafon, that although the fentiments contained in it are well known to be drawn from the Platonic, the fublimeft of all philofophy ; and the imagery has an immediate and uniform reference to the fictions of mythology, it afforded great entertainment to the upper gallery ; and the performance gave rife to fundry meetings for the purpofe of drinking and finging, fome of which were dignified with the name of Comus's Court. Neverthelefs it may be fuppofed that the mirth of the enchanter and his crew were more fenfibly felt by the multitude than the charms of divine philofophy, which the author endeavours to difplay, or the reliance on divine providence, which it is the end of the poem to inculcate.

The

The case is the same in sculpture and architecture; to speak of the first: In Roubiliac's statue of Mr. Handel at Vauxhall, few are struck with the ease and gracefulness of the attitude, the dignity of the figure, the artful disposition of the drapery, or the manly plumpness and rotundity of the limbs, but all admire how naturally the slipper depends from the left foot. In works of architecture we look for elegance joined with stability; for symmetry, harmony of parts, and a judicious and beautiful arrangement of pleasing forms; but to these a vulgar eye is blind; whatever is great or massy, it rejects as heavy and clumsey: Such judges as these prefer for its lightness a Chinese to a Palladian bridge; and are pleased with a diagonal view of the towers at the west end of St. Paul's cathedral, for the same reason as they are with a bird cage.

Finally, with respect to music, it must necessarily be, that the operation of its intrinsic powers can extend no farther than to those whom nature has endowed with the faculty which it is calculated to delight; and that a privation of that sense, which, superadded to the hearing, is ultimately affected by the harmony of musical sounds, must disable many, and, as some compute, not fewer than nine out of ten, from receiving that gratification in music which others experience. Such hearers as these are insensible of its charms, which yet they labour to persuade themselves are very powerful; but finding little effect from them, they seek for that gratification in novelty which novelty will not afford; and hence arises that incessant demand for variety which has induced some to imagine that music is in its very nature as mutable as fashion itself. It may be sufficient in this place to have pointed out the reasons or causes of this erroneous opinion of the nature and end of music, the effects and operation thereof will be the subject of future disquisition.

In the interim it must be confessed that there is somewhat humiliating in a discrimination of mankind, that tends to exclude the greater number of them from the enjoyment of those elegant and refined pleasures which the works of genius and invention afford; but this condition

of

of human nature is capable of proof, and is juſtified by that partial diſpenſation of thoſe faculties and endowments which we are taught to conſider as bleſſings, and which no one without impiety can cenſure. Seeing this to be the caſe, it may be aſked how comes it to paſs that a ſenſe of what is true, juſt, elegant, and beautiful in any of the abovementioned arts, exiſts as it does at this day? or that there are any works of genius which men with one common conſent profeſs to applaud and admire as the ſtandards of perfection? To this it may be anſwered, that although the right of private judgment is in ſome degree exerciſed by all, it is controuled by the few; and it is the uniform teſtimony of men of diſcernment alone that ſtamps a character on the productions of genius, and conſigns them either to oblivion or immortality.

It is beſide the purpoſe of the preſent diſcourſe to enter into a minute inveſtigation of any particular branch of the ſcience of which this work is the hiſtory; what is here propoſed is the communication of that intelligence which ſeemed but the prerequiſite to the underſtanding of what will hereafter be ſaid on the ſubject. This was the inducement to the above obſervations on Taſte, and the motives that influence it; and this muſt be the apology for a further examen, a pretty free one it may be ſaid, of thoſe muſical entertainments, and that kind of muſical performance which the public are at preſent moſt diſpoſed to favour.

The preſent great ſource of muſical delight throughout Europe, is the opera, or, as the French call it, the muſical tragedy, concerning which it is to be known, that, if regard be due to the opinions of ſome writers, who yet are no friends to this entertainment, it is a revival of the old Roman tragedy; and it ſeems that the inventors of the modern recitative, Jacopo Peri and Giulio Caccini wiſhed to have it thought ſo; foraſmuch as they profeſſed in this ſpecies of muſical intonation to imitate the practice of the ancients, remarking with great accuracy the ſeveral modes of pronunciation, and the notes and accents proper to expreſs grief, joy, and the other affections of the human
man

man mind; but by what exemplars they regulated their imitation we are no where told; and it is to be conjectured that those general directions for pronunciation, which are to be found in many discourses on the subject of oratory, were the chief sources whence their intelligence was derived.

In what other respects the musical representations of the ancients and moderns bear a resemblance to each other it is not necessary here to enquire; it may suffice to say of the modern opera, that by the sober and judicious part of mankind it has ever been considered as the mere offspring of luxury; and those who have examined it with a critical eye, scruple not to pronounce that it is of all entertainments the most unnatural and absurd. To descend to particulars in proof of this assertion, would be but to repeat arguments which have already been urged, with little success it is true, but with great force of reason, aided by all the powers of wit and humour.

The principal objections against the opera are summed up by an author, who, though a professed lover of music, has shewn his candour in describing the genuine effect of representations of this kind on an unprejudiced ear. The person here spoken of is Monf. St. Evremond, and the following are his sentiments.

' I am no great admirer of comedies in music *, such as now-a-
' days are in request. I confess I am not displeased with their mag-
' nificence; the machines have something that is surprising; the
' musick, in some places, is charming, the whole together seems won-
' derful: But it must be granted me also, that this wonderful is very
' tedious; for where the mind has so little to do, there the senses must
' of necessity languish. After the first pleasure that surprize gives us,
' the eyes are taken up, and at length grow weary of being conti-

* The word COMEDIE in French comprehends every kind of theatrical representation; a truer designation of an opera is the term Tragedie en Musique; those of
Lully are in general so called in the title-page; and it is plain by the context that
the author means not the comic but the tragic opera.

* nually

' nually fixed upon the fame object. In the beginning of the con-
' forts we obferve the juftnefs of the concords; and amidft all the va-
' rieties that unite to make the fweetnefs of the harmony, nothing
' efcapes us. But 'tis not long before the inftruments ftun us, and the
' mufick is nothing elfe to our ears but a confufed found that fuffers
' nothing to be diftinguifhed. Now how is it poffible to avoid being
' tired with the Recitativo, which has neither the charm of finging,
' nor the agreeable energy of fpeech? The foul fatigued by a long
' attention, wherein it finds nothing to affect it, feeks fome relief
' within itfelf; and the mind, which in vain expected to be enter-
' tained with the fhow, either gives way to idle mufing, or is diffatis-
' fied that it has nothing to employ it. In a word, the fatigue is fo
' univerfal, that every one wifhes himfelf out of the houfe, and the
' only comfort that is left to the poor fpectators, is the hopes that the
' fhow will foon be over.

' The reafon why, commonly, I foon grow weary at operas is, that
' I never yet faw any which appeared not to me defpicable, both as to
' the contrivance of the fubject, and the poetry. Now it is in vain to
' charm the ears, or gratify the eyes, if the mind be not fatisfied; for
' my foul being in better intelligence with my mind than with my
' fenfes, ftruggles againft the impreffions which it may receive, or at
' leaft does not give an agreeable confent to them, without which even
' the moft delightful objects can never afford me any great pleafure.
' An extravagance, fet off with mufick, dances, machines, and fine
' fcenes, is a pompous piece of folly, but 'tis ftill a folly. Tho' the
' embroidery is rich, yet the ground it is wrought upon is fuch
' wretched ftuff, that it offends the fight.

' There is another thing in operas fo contrary to nature, that I can-
' not be reconciled to it, and that is the finging of the whole piece,
' from beginning to end, as if the perfons reprefented were ridiculoufly
' matched, and had agreed to treat in mufick both the moft common,
' and moft important affairs of life. Is it to be imagined that a mafter
' calls his fervant, or fends him on an errand, finging; that one friend
                                                ' imparts

' imparts a fecret to another, finging ; that men deliberate in council
' finging ; that orders in time of battle are given finging; and that
' men are melodioufly kill'd with fwords and darts. This is the
' downright way to lofe the life of reprefentation, which without
' doubt is preferable to that of harmony; for harmony ought to be
' no more than a bare attendant, and the great mafters of the ftage
' have introduced it as pleafing, not as neceffary, after they have per-
' form'd all that relates to the fubject and difcourfe. Neverthelefs
' our thoughts run more upon the mufician than the hero in the
' opera ; Luigi, Cavallo, and Cefti, are ftill prefent to our imagina-
' tion. The mind not being able to conceive a hero that fings, thinks
' of the compofer that fet the fong ; and I don't queftion but that in
' the operas at the Palace Royal, Baptift is an hundred times more
' thought of than Thefeus or Cadmus *.'

The fame author, fpeaking of recitative, particularly that of the
Venetian opera, fays that it is neither finging nor reciting †, but

* Works of Monf. St. Evremond, vol. II. page 84, in a letter to Villiers,
duke of Buckingham.

† This remark upon examination will be found to be but too true, notwithftanding the arguments in favour of recitative, which amount in fubftance to this,
that it is a kind of profe in mufic, that its beauty confifts in coming near nature,
and in improving the natural accents of words by more pathetic or emphatical tones.
Preface to the opera of Semele by Mr. Congreve. Mr. Hughes, to the fame purpofe,
delivers thefe as his fentiments : ' The recitative ftyle in compofition is founded on
' that variety of accent which pleafes in the pronunciation of a good orator, with as
' little deviation from it as poffible. The different tones of the voice in aftonifhment,
' joy, forrow, rage, tendernefs, in affirmations, apoftrophes, interrogations, and all
' the other varieties of fpeech, make a fort of natural mufick which is very agree-
' able ; and this is what is intended to be imitated, with fome helps, by the compo-
' fer, but without approaching to what we call a tune or air; fo that it is but a
' kind of improved elocution.' Preface to Mr. Hughes's Cantatas in the firft volume of his Poems.

Upon thefe feveral paffages it may be remarked, that in the expreffion of the paffions nature doth not offer mufical founds to the human ear : For though the natural tones of grief and joy, the two paffions which are moft effectually expreffed by
mufic, approach nearer to mufical precifion than any other, yet ftill they are in-

Vol. I.   k   concinnous

somewhat unknown to the ancients, which may be defined to be an aukward ufe of mufic and fpeech [a].

It may perhaps be faid that mufic owes much of its late improvement to the theatre, and to that emulation which it has a tendency to excite, as well in compofers as performers; but who will pretend to fay what direction the ftudies of the moft eminent muficians of late years would have taken, had they been left to themfelves; it being moft certain that every one of that character has two taftes, the

concinnous and unmufical. Farther, that the founds of the voice in fpeech are immufical is afferted by Lord Bacon in the following paffage: " All founds ' are either mufical founds, which we call tones, whereunto there may be an ' harmony; which founds are ever equal, as finging, the founds of ftringed and ' wind inftruments, the ringing of bells, &c. or immufical founds, which are ever ' unequal; fuch as are the voice in fpeaking, all whifperings, all voices of beafts ' and birds, except they be finging-birds, all percuffions of ftones, wood, parchment, ' fkins, as in drums, and infinite others.' Nat. Hift. cent. II. fect. 101.

The conclufion from thefe premifes muft be, that mufical founds do not imitate common fpeech; and therefore that recitative can in no degree be faid to be an improvement of elocution.

But admitting the contrary to be the cafe, and that the founds of fpeech were equally mufical with thofe employed in recitative, the inflexions of the voice are too minute to fall in with the divifion of the fcale, allowing even the enarmonic diefis, or the comma, the fmalleft of all fenfible intervals, to make a part of it; and of this opinion is Monf. Duclos, who, in the Encyclopedia, art. Declamation des Anciens, for this reafon denies the poffibility of a notation for fpeech.

Upon the whole, the beauties of the recitative ftyle in mufic confift not in the power of imitating the tones, much lefs the various inflexions of the voice in fpeech, but in the varieties of accent and melody, which follow from its not being fubject to metrical laws: In fhort, what has been faid and infifted on in this difcourfe of mufic in general, may be applied to recitative, viz. that its mimetic powers are very inconfiderable, and that whatever charms it poffeffes are abfolute and inherent.

[a] Thefe obfervations of St. Evremond refpect the mufical tragedy, but the Italians have alfo a mufical comedy called a Burletta, which has been lately introduced into England, and given rife to the diftinction in the advertifements for fubfcriptions of firft, fecond, &c. ferious man or woman. This entertainment affords additional proof how little mufic, as fuch, is able to fupport itfelf: In the tragic opera it borrows aid from the fublimity of the poetry; in the comic, from the powers of ridicule, to which mufic has not the leaft relation.

one for himself, and the other for the public? Purcell has given a plain
indication of his own, in a declaration that the gravity and seriousness
of the Italian music were by him thought worthy of imitation * :
The studies of Stradella, Scarlatti, and Bononcini for their own delight were not songs or airs calculated to astonish the hearers with
the tricks of the finger, but cantatas and duets, in which the sweetness of the melody, and the just expression of fine poetical sentiments, were their chief praise; or madrigals for four or more voices,
wherein the various excellencies of melody and harmony were united,
so as to leave a lasting impression on the mind. The same may be
said of Mr. Handel, who, to go no farther, has given a specimen of
the style he most affected in a volume of lessons for the harpsichord,
with which no one will say that any modern compositions of the kind
can stand in competition. These, as they were made for the practice of an illustrious personage, as happy in an exquisite taste and correct judgment as a fine hand, may be supposed to be, and were in fact
compositions con amore. In other instances this great musician compounded the matter with the public, alternately pursuing the suggestions of his fancy, and gratifying a taste which he held in contempt †.

Whoever is curious to know what that taste could be, to which so
great a master as Mr. Handel was compelled occasionally to conform,
in prejudice to his own, will find it to have been no other than that which
is common to every promiscuous auditory, with whom it is a notion that
the right, and as some may think, the ability to judge, to applaud and
condemn is purchased by the price of admittance; a taste that leads all

* It is worth remarking that the poets, who of all writers seem the most sensible
of the efficacy of music, appear uniformly to consider it as an intellectual, and consequently a serious pleasure, engaging not only the attention of the ear, but the powers
and faculties of the soul. To this end, and not for the purpose of exciting mirth,
it is in numberless instances introduced by Shakespeare, and among the poems of
Milton is one entitled ' At a solemn Music.'

† An intimate friend of Mr. Handel, looking over the score of an opera newly
composed by him, observed of some of the songs that they were excellent: You
may think so, says Mr. Handel, but it is not to them, but to these, turning to
others of a vulgar cast, that I trust for the success of the opera.

k 2   who

who poſſeſs it to prefer light and trivial airs, and ſuch as are eaſily retained in memory, to the fineſt harmony and modulation; and to be better
pleaſed with the licentious exceſſes of a ſinger, than the true and juſt
intonation of the ſweeteſt and moſt pathetic melodies, adorned with
all the graces and elegancies that art can ſuggeſt. Such critics as
theſe, in their judgment of inſtrumental performance, uniformly determine in favour of whatever is moſt difficult in the execution, and, like
the ſpectators of a rope-dance, are never more delighted than when
the artiſt is in ſuch a ſituation as to render it doubtful whether he
ſhall incur or eſcape diſgrace.

To ſuch a propenſity as this, the gratifications whereof are of neceſſity but momentary, leaving no impreſſion upon the mind, we may
refer the ardent thirſt of novelty in muſic, and that almoſt general re-
probation of whatever is old, againſt the ſenſe of the poet:

> Now, good Ceſario, but that piece of ſong,
> That old and antique ſong we had laſt night,
> Methought it did relieve my paſſion much ;
> More than light airs, and recollected terms
> Of theſe moſt briſk and giddy-paced times.
>   TWELFTH-NIGHT, Act II. Scene iv.

But to account for it is in no ſmall degree difficult : To juſtify it, it is
ſaid that there is a natural viciſſitude of things, and that it were vain
to expect that muſic ſhould be permanent in a world where change
ſeems to predominate.

But it may here be obſerved, that there are certain laws of nature
that are immutable and independent on time or place, the precepts of
morality and axioms in phyſics for inſtance ; there never was ſince the
creation a time when there did not exiſt an irreconcileable difference
between truth and falſehood ; or when two things, each equal to the
ſame third, were unequal one to the other ; or, to carry the argument
farther, when conſonance and diſſonance were not as eſſentially diſtinguiſhed from each other, both in their ratios and by their effects, as
                                                                    they

they are at this day; or when certain interchanges of colours, or forms and arrangements of bodies were less pleasing to the eye than the same are now; from whence it should seem that there are some subjects on which this principle of mutation does not operate: And, to speak of music alone, that, to justify the love of that novelty which seems capable of recommending almost any production, some other reasons must be resorted to than those above.

But, declining all farther research into the reason or causes of this principle, let us attend to its effects; and these are visible in the almost total ignorance which prevails of the merits of most of the many excellent artists who flourished in the ages preceding our own: Of Tye, of Redford, Shephard, Douland, Weelkes, Wilbye, Est, Bateson, Hilton, and Brewer, we know little more than their names; these men composed volumes which are now dispersed and irretrievably lost, yet did their compositions suggest those ideas of the power and efficacy of music, and those descriptions of its manifold charms that occur in the verses of our best poets. To say that these and the compositions of their successors Blow, Purcell, Humphrey, Wise, Weldon, and others were admired merely because they were new, is begging a question that will be best decided by a comparison, which some of the greatest among the professors of the art at this day would shrink from.

Upwards of two hundred years have elapsed since the anthem of Dr. Tye, 'I will exalt thee,' was composed; and near as long a time since Tallis composed the motet 'O sacrum convivium,' which is now sung as an anthem to the words 'I call and cry to thee, O Lord;' and it is comparatively but a few years since Geminiani was heard to exclaim in a rapture that the author of it was inspired *. Amidst all the va-

* To this testimony we may add that of a foreigner respecting the church-music of queen Elizabeth's days, thus recorded by Strype in his Annals of the Reformation, vol. II. page 314.

* In her [the queen's] passing, (I say) she visited Canterbury; how magnificently she was received and entertained here by archbishop Parker, I have related elsewhere. This I only add, that while she was here, the French ambassador came

* to

rieties of compofition in canon, which the learning and ingenuity of
the ablest muficians have produced, that of Bird, compofed in the
reign of his miftrefs Elizabeth, is confidered as a model of perfection.
Dr. Blow's fong, ' Go, perjured man,' was compofed at the command
of king Charles the Second, and Purcell's ' Sing all ye Mufes,' in the
reign of his fucceffor; but no man has as yet been bold enough to attempt to rival either of thefe compofitions. Nor is there any of the vocal
kind, confifting of recitative and air, which can ftand a competition
with thofe two cantatas, for fo we may venture to call them, ' From
' rofy bowers,' and ' From filent fhades.'

Of poetry, painting, and fculpture, it has been obferved that they
have at different periods flourifhed and declined; and that there have
been times when each of thofe arts has been at greater perfection than
now, is to be attributed to that viciffitude of things which gave rife to
the prefent enquiry, and is implied in an obfervation of Lord Bacon,
that in the youth of a ftate arms do flourifh, in its middle age
learning, and in its decline mechanical arts and merchandize [*]. And
if this obfervation on the various fates of poetry, painting, and
fculpture be true, why is it to be affumed of mufic that it is continually improving, or that every innovation in it muft be for the
better? That the mufic of the church has degenerated and been
greatly corrupted by an intermixture of the theatric ftyle, has long
been a fubject of complaint; the Abbat Gerbert laments this and other
innovations in terms the moft affecting [†]; and indeed the evidence of
this corruption muft be apparent to every one that reflects on the ftyle

' to her. Who hearing the excellent mufic in the cathedral church, extolled it up
' to the fky, and brake out into thefe words : " O God, I think no prince befide in
" all Europe ever heard the like, no, not our Holy Father the Pope himfelf." A
' young gentleman that ftood by him replied, " Ah, do you compare our queen to
" the knave of Rome, or rather prefer him before her?" Whereat the ambaffador
' was highly angred, and told it to fome of the councillors. They bade him be
' quiet, and take it patiently, for the boys, faid they, with us do fo call him and
' the Roman Antichrift too.'
  [*] Effay of Viciffitude of Things.
  [†] De Cantu et Mufica Sacra, tom. II. pag. 375.

and -

and ftructure of thofe compofitions for the church that are now moft
celebrated abroad, even thofe of Pergolefi, his maffes, for inftance,
and thofe of Iomelli and Perez, have nothing that diftinguifhes them
but the want of action and fcenic decoration, from dramatic reprefentations: Like them they abound in fymphony and the accompanyment of various inftruments, no regard is paid to the fenfe of the
words, or care taken to fuit it with correfpondent founds; the claufes
Kyrie Eleifon and Chrifte Eleifon, and Miferere mei and Amen are
uttered in dancing metres; and the former not feldom in that of a mi-
nuet or a jig. Even the funeral fervice of Perez, lately publifhed in
London, fo far as regards the meafures of the feveral airs, and the inftrumental aids to the voice-parts, differs as far from a facred and folemn compofure as a burletta does from an opera or mufical tragedy.

From thefe premifes it may be allowed to follow, that a retrofpect
to the mufical productions of paft ages is no fuch abfurdity, as that a
curious enquirer need decline it. No man fcruples to do the like in
painting; the connoiffeurs are as free in remarking the excellencies of
Raphael, Titian, Domenichino, and Guido, as in comparing fucceeding artifts with them; and very confiderable benefits are found to
refult from this practice: Our prefent ignorance with refpect to mufic may betray us into a confufion of times and characters, but it is
to be avoided by an attention to thofe particular circumftances that
mark the feveral periods of its progrefs, its perfection and its decline.

Of the monkifh mufic, that is to fay the Cantus Ecclefiafticus,
little can be faid, other than that it was folemn and devout : After the
introduction into the church fervice of mufic in confonance, great
fkill and learning were exercifed in the compofition of motets; but
the elaborate contexture, and, above all, the affectation of mufical
and arithmetical fubtilties in thefe compofitions, as they conduced but
little to the ends of divine worfhip, fubjected them to cenfure, and
gave rife to a ftyle, which, for its fimplicity and grandeur many look
up to as the perfection of ecclefiaftical harmony ; and they are not a
few who think that at the end of the fixteenth century the Romifh
church-

church-mufic was at its height, as alfo that with us of the reformed church its moft flourifhing ftate was during the reign of Elizabeth ; though others poftpone it to the time of Charles II. grounding their opinion on the anthems of Blow, Humphrey, and Purcell, who received their firft notions of fine melody from the works of Cariffimi, Cefti, Stradella, and others of the Italians.

For the perfection of vocal harmony we muft refer to a period of about fifty years, commencing at the year 1560, during which were compofed madrigals for private recreation in abundance, that are the models of excellence in their kind; and in this fpecies of mufic the compofers of our own country appear to be inferior to none. The improvement of melody is undoubtedly owing to the drama; and its union with harmony and an affemblage of all the graces and elegancies of both we may behold in the madrigals of Stradella and Bononcini, and the choruffes and anthems of Handel; and among the compofitions for private practice in the duets of Steffani and Handel. As to the harmony of inftruments, it is the leaft praife that can be beftowed on the works of Corelli, Geminiani, and Martini, to fay that through all the viciffitudes and fluctuations of caprice and fancy, they retain their primitive power of engaging the affections, and recommending themfelves to all fober and judicious hearers *.

* Of the inftrumental mufic of the prefent day, notwithftanding the learning and abilities of many compofers, the characteriftics of it are noife without harmony, exemplified in the frittering of paffages into notes, requiring fuch an inftantaneous utterance, that thirty-two of them are frequently heard in the time which it would take moderately to count four ; and of this caft are the Symphonies, Periodical Overtures, Quartettos, Quintettos, and the reft of the trafh daily obtruded on the world.

Of folos for the violin, an elegant fpecies of compofition, as is evident in thofe moft excellent ones of Corelli and Geminiani, and in many of thofe of Le Clair, Carbonelli, Feftiog, and Tartini, few have of late been publifhed that will bear twice hearing ; in general, the fole end of them is to difplay the powers of execution in prejudice to thofe talents which are an artift's greateft praife.

The leffons for the harpfichord of Mr. Handel, abounding with fugues of the fineft contexture, and the moft pathetic airs, are an inexhauftible fund of delight ; thofe of the prefent time have no other tendency than to degrade an inftrument invented

for

To music of such acknowledged excellence as this, the preference of another kind, merely on the score of its novelty, is surely absurd; at least the arguments in favour of it seem to be no better than those of Mr. Bayes in behalf of what he calls the new way of dramatic writing; which however were not found to be of such strength as to withstand the force of that ridicule, which was very seasonably employed in restoring the people to their wits.

The performance on the organ is for the most part unpremeditated, as the term Voluntary, which is appropriated to that instrument, imports; we may therefore look on this practice as extemporary composition; and it is not enough to be regretted how much the applauses bestowed on the mere powers of execution have contributed to degrade it. Bird and Blow, as organists, are celebrated not so much for an exquisite hand, as for their skill, and that fullness of harmony which distinguished their performance, and which this noble instrument alone is calculated to exhibit *. The canzones of Frescobaldi, Kerl, Krieger, and Thiel, and above all, the fugues of Mr. Handel, including those in his lessons, shew us what is the true organ style, and leave us to lament that the idea of a voluntary on the organ is lost in those Capriccios on a single stop, which, as well in our parochial as cathedral service, follow the psalms. As to what is called a concerto on the organ, it is a kind of composition consisting chiefly of solo passages, contrived to display what in modern musical phrase is termed a brilliant finger; and which, if attended to, will, amidst the clamour of the accompanyment, in fact be found instead of four, to consist of but two parts.

for the elegant recreation of the youthful of the other sex, and to render it what at best it now appears to be, and may as truly as emphatically be termed, a tinkling cymbal.

* Old Mr. Arthur Bedford, chaplain to Aske's Hospital at Hoxton, and who died not many years ago, was acquainted with Dr. Blow, and says of him that he was reckoned the greatest master in the world for playing most gravely and seriously in his voluntaries. The Great Abuse of Musick, by Arthur Bedford, M. A. Lond. 8vo. 1711, page 248.

But of all the abuses of inftrumental performance, none is more in-
jurious to mufic than the practice of fingle inftruments, exemplified
in folos and folo concertos, originally intended for private recreation,
but which are now confidered as an effential part of a mufical entertainment. Mufic compofed for a fingle inftrument, as confifting of
the mere melody of one part, is lefs complicated than that which is
contrived for many; and melody is ever more pleafing to an unlearned
ear than the harmony of different parts. The uniformity of a mi-
nuet, confifting of a determined number of bars, the emphafis of each
whereof returns in an orderly fucceffion of meafures or times, correfponds with fome ideas of metrical regularity which are common to
all minds, and affords a reafon for that delight which the ear receives
from the pulfatile inftruments. Hence it is eafy to account for the
obtrufion of fuch compofitions on the public ear as furnifh opportunities of difplaying mere manual proficiency in the artift; a folo
or a concerto on the violin, the violoncello, the hautboy, or fome
other fuch inftrument, does this, and gives fcope for that exercife of
a wild and exuberant fancy which diftinguifhes, or rather difgraces,
the inftrumental performance of this day.

The firft effays of this kind were folos for the violin, the defign
whereof was to affect the hearer by the tone of the inftrument, and
thofe graces of expreffion which are its known characteriftic; but it
was no fooner found that the merit of thefe compofitions was efti-
mated by the difficulty of performing them, than the plaudits of the
auditory became an irrefiftible temptation to every kind of extravagance: Thefe have been fucceeded by compofitions of a like kind,
but framed with a very different view, Solos and Concertos, containing paffages that carried the melody beyond the utmoft limits
of the fcale, indeed fo high on the inftrument, that the notes could
not be diftinctly articulated, in violation of a rule that Lord Bacon
has laid down, that the mean tones of all inftruments, as being the
moft fweet, are to be preferred to thofe at either extremity of either

the

the voice or inſtrument [*]. The laſt improvement of licentious practice
has been the imitation of tones diſſimilar to thoſe of the violin, the
flute, for inſtance, and thoſe that reſemble the whiſtling of birds; and
the ſame tricks are played with the violoncello. To what farther
lengths theſe extravagancies will be carried, time only can diſcover.

Amidſt that ſtupor of the auditory faculties, which leads to the
admiration of whatever is wild and irregular in muſic, a judicious
hearer is neceſſitated to ſeek for delight in thoſe compoſitions, which,
as owing their preſent exiſtence ſolely to their merit, muſt, like the
writings of the claſſic authors, be looked on as the ſtandards of perfection; in the grave and ſolemn ſtrains of the moſt celebrated com-
poſers for the church, including thoſe of our own country, who in
the opinion of the beſt judges are inferior to none[†]; or in the gayer

---

[*] Nat. Hiſt. cent. II. ſect. 173. The Sylva Sylvarum, or Natural Hiſtory of
Lord Bacon, contains a great variety of experiments and obſervations tending to explain the properties of ſound and the nature of harmony. The following judicious
remark may ſerve as a ſpecimen of the author's ſkill in his ſubject, and at the ſame
time ſhew his ſentiments of harmony, and in what he conceived the perfection
thereof to conſiſt. 'The ſweeteſt and beſt harmony is, when every part or inſtru-
' ment is not heard by itſelf, but a confuſion of them all; which requireth to
' ſtand ſome diſtance off, even as it is in the mixture of perfumes, or the taking of
' the ſmells of ſeveral flowers in the air.' Cent. III. ſect. 225.

† Such muſic as this has been the delight of the wiſeſt men in all ages. Luther,
who was ſo great an admirer of muſic, that he ſcrupled not, as a ſcience, to rank it
next to theology, which is ſtyled the queen of the ſciences, was often uſed to be re-
created with the ſinging of motets. Biſhop Williams, while he was lord keeper,
choſe to retain the deanery of Weſtminſter for the ſake of the choral ſervice performed there: 'He was loath,' ſays his hiſtorian, ' to ſtir from that ſeat where he
' had the command of ſuch exquiſite muſic:' And in a more particular manner the
ſame perſon ſpeaks of the love which that great prelate bore to muſic, for, ſays he,
' that God might be praiſed with a chearful noiſe in his ſanctuary, he procured
' the ſweeteſt muſic both for the organ and voices of all parts that ever was heard
' in an Engliſh quire. In thoſe days that abbey and the Jeruſalem Chamber, where
' he gave entertainment, were the volaries of the choiceſt ſingers that the land had
' bred.' Life of the Lord Keeper Williams by Hackett, Biſhop of Litchfield and Coventry, pag. 62, 46. Milton has been very explicit in declaring
                                                                    what

and more elegant compositions, as well instrumental as vocal, of others contrived for the recreation and solace, in private assemblies and select companies, of persons competently skilled in the science.

How far remote that period may be when music of this kind shall become the object of the public choice, no one can pretend to tell: To speak of music for instruments, the modern refinements in practice, and the late improvements in the powers of execution have placed it beyond the reach of view: and it affords but small satisfaction to a lover of the art to reflect that the world is in possession of such instrumental compositions as those of Corelli, Bononcini, Geminiani, and Handel, when not one principal performer in ten has any relish of their excellencies, or can be prevailed on to execute them but with such a degree of unfeeling rapidity, as to destroy their effect, and utterly to defeat the intention of the author. In such kind of performance, wherein not the least regard is paid to harmony or expression, we seek in vain for that most excellent attribute of music, its power to move the passions, without which this divine science must be considered in no better a view than as the means of recreation to a gaping crowd, insensible of its charms, and ignorant of its worth.

what kind of music delighted him most, in the verses entitled ' At a solemn music.' Dr. Busby, the master of Westminster-school had an organ, and music of the most solemn kind in his house at the time when choral service was throughout the kingdom forbidden to be performed. Vide ante, pag. xxiii. in not.

A

GENERAL HISTORY

OF THE

SCIENCE and PRACTICE

OF

MUSIC.

BOOK I. CHAP. I.

THERE is fcarce any confideration that affords greater occafion to lament the inevitable viciffitude of things, than the
obfcurity in which it involves, not only the hiftory and real
characters, but even the difcoveries of men. When we confider the
various purfuits of mankind, that fome refpect merely the intereft of
individuals, and terminate with themfelves, while others have for
their object the inveftigation of truth, the attainment and communication of knowledge, or the improvement of ufeful arts ; we applaud
the latter, and reckon upon the advantages that pofterity muft
derive from them: but this it feems is in fome degree a falla-
cious hope ; and, notwithftanding the prefent improved ftate of learning in the world, we have reafon to deplore the want of what is loft
to us, at the fame time that we rejoice in that portion of knowledge
which we poffefs.

Whoever is inclined to try the truth of this obfervation on the
fubject of the prefent work, if he does not fee caufe to acquiefce in it,
will at leaft be under great difficulties to fatisfy himfelf how it comes
to pafs, that feeing what miraculous effects have been afcribed to the
mufic of the ancients, we know fo little concerning it, as not only to
be ignorant of the ufe and application of moft of their inftruments,
but even in a great meafure of their fyftem itfelf.

VOL. I.   B   To

To say that in the general deluge of learning, when the irruptions of barbarous nations into civilized countries, the seats and nurseries of science, became frequent, music, as holding no sympathy with minds actuated by ambition and the lust of empire, was neceffarily overwhelmed, is not folving the difficulty; for though barbarifm might check, as it did, the growth of this as well as other arts, the utter extirpation of it feems to have been as much then, as it is now, impoffible. That conqueft did not produce the fame effect on the other arts is certain ; the architecture, the fculpture, and the poetry of ancient Greece and Rome, though they withdrew for a time, were yet not loft, but after a retirement of fome centuries appeared again. But what became of their music is ftill a queftion : the pyramids, the Pantheon, the Hercules of Glycon, the Grecian Venus, the writings of Homer, of Plato, of Ariftotle, and other ancients, are ftill in being; but who ever faw, or where are depofited, the compofitions of Terpander, Timotheus, or Phrynis ? Did the music of thefe, and many other men whom we read of, confift of mere Energy, in the extemporary prolation, of folitary or accordant founds ; or had they, in thofe very early ages, any method of notation, whereby their ideas of found, like thofe of other fenfible objects, were rendered capable of communication ? It is hard to conceive that they had not, when we reflect on the very great antiquity of the invention of letters; and yet before the time of Alypius, who lived A. C. 115, there are no remaining evidences of any fuch thing.

The writers in that famous controverfy fet on foot by Sir William Temple, towards the clofe of the laft century, about the comparative excellence of the ancient and modern learning, at leaft thofe who fided with the ancients, feem not to have been aware of the difficulty they had to encounter, when they undertook, as fome of them did, to maintain the fuperiority of the ancient over the modern music, a difficulty arifing not more from the fuppofed weight on the other fide of the argument, than from the want of fufficient Data on their own. In the comparifon of ancient with modern music, it was reafonable to expect that the advocates for the former fhould at leaft have been able to define it; but Sir William Temple, who contends for its fuperiority, makes no fcruple to confefs his utter incapacity to judge about it : ‘ What, fays he, are become of the charms of music, ‘ by which men and beafts, fifhes, fowls, and ferpents were fo fre-
‘ quently

' quently enchanted, and their very natures changed ; by which the
' paffions of men are raifed to the greateſt height and violence ; and
' then fo fuddenly appeafed, fo as they might be juſtly ſaid to be
' turned into lions or lambs, into wolves or into harts, by the powers
' and charms of this admirable art ?   'Tis agreed of all the learned
' that the fcience of mufic, fo admired by the ancients, is wholly loſt
' in the world, and that what we have now is made up of certain
' notes that fell into the fancy or obfervation of a *poor friar* in chant-
' ing his mattins : fo as thofe two divine excellencies of mufic and
' poetry are grown in a manner to be little more but the one *fiddling*,
' and the other rhyming, and are indeed very worthy the ignorance
' of the friar, and the barbaroufnefs of the Goths that introduced
' them among us *.'

Whatever are the powers and charms of this admirable art, there
needs no farther proof than the paffage above-cited, that the author
of it was not very fufceptible of them ; for either the learned of thefe
later times are ſtrangely miſtaken, or thofe *certain notes*, which he
fpeaks fo contemptuouſly of, have, under the management of ſkilful
artiſts, produced effects not much lefs wonderful than thofe attributed
to the ancient mufic.   And it is not to be imagined but that Sir William Temple, in the courfe of a life fpent among foreigners of the
firſt rank, and at a time when Europe abounded with excellent maſters,
muſt have heard fuch mufic, as, had he had any ear to appeal to,
would have convinced him that the art had ſtill its charms, and
thofe very potent ones too.

But, not to follow the example of an author, whofe zeal for a favourite hypothefis had led him to write on a fubject he did not underſtand, we will proceed to trace the various progrefs of this art : its
progrefs, it is faid, for the many accounts of the time of the invention, as well as of the inventors of mufic, leave us in great uncertainty as to its rife.   The authority of poets is not very refpectable in
matters of hiſtory ; and there is hardly any other for thofe common
opinions that we owe the invention of mufic to Orpheus, to Amphion,
Linus, and many others ; unlefs we except that venerable doctor and
fchoolman Thomas Aquinas, who afferts, that not mufic alone, but
every other fcience, was underſtood, and that by immediate revela-

* Eſſay on the ancient and modern learning.

tion from above, by the firſt of the human race. However, it may not be amiſs to mention the general opinions as to the invention of muſic, with this remark, that no greater deference is due to many of them than is paid to other fables of the ancient poets and mythologiſts.

There can be no doubt but that vocal muſic is more ancient than inſtrumental, ſince mankind were endowed with voices before the invention of inſtruments ; but the great queſtion is, at what time they began to frame a ſyſtem, and this naturally leads to an enquiry into the time of the invention of inſtruments; for if we conſider the evaneſcence of ſound uttered by the human voice, the notion of a ſyſtem without, is at this day not very intelligible.

But previous to any ſuch enquiry, we may very reaſonably be allowed the liberty of conjecture, in which if we indulge ourſelves, we cannot ſuppoſe but that an art ſo ſuited to our natures, and adapted to our organs, as muſic is, muſt be nearly as ancient as thoſe of Agriculture, Navigation, and numberleſs other inventions, which the neceſſities of mankind ſuggeſted, and impelled them to purſue : the deſire of the conveniences, the comforts, the pleaſures of life, is a principle little leſs active than that which leads us to provide for its wants; and perhaps it might be even before they had learned to ' go down to the ſea in ſhips' that men began to ' handle the harp and organ,' which it cannot be ſuppoſed they could do to any delightful purpoſe, without ſome knowledge of thoſe harmonical relations and coincidences of ſound, which are the eſſence of the art. Such a knowledge as this we may eaſily conceive was ſoon attained by even the earlieſt inhabitants of the earth. The voices of animals, the whiſtling of the winds, the fall of waters, the concuſſion of bodies of various kinds, not to mention the melody of birds, as they all contain in them the rudiments of harmony, may eaſily be ſuppoſed to have furniſhed the minds of intelligent creatures with ſuch ideas of ſound, as time, and the accumulated obſervation of ſucceeding ages, could not fail to improve into a ſyſtem *.

---

* Lucretius ſuppoſes that mankind took their firſt notions of muſic from the ſinging of birds.

    At liquidas avium voces imitarier ore
    Ante fuit multò, quam lævia carmina cantu
    Concelebrare homines poſſent, aureiſque juvare. Lib. V.

And

A reafon has already been given to fhew that the notion of a mufical fyftem does neceffarily prefuppofe mufical inftruments; it

And the fame poet has in fome fort afcertained the origin of wind inftruments in the
following elegant verfes.

> Et zephyri cava per calamorum fibila primum
> Agreftes docuere cavas inflare cicutas,
> Inde minutatim dulces didicere querelas,
> Tibia quas fundit digitis pulfata canentum.   Ibid.

> Thro' all the woods they heard the charming noife
> Of chirping birds, and try'd to frame their voice
> And imitate. Thus birds inftructed man,
> And taught them fongs before their art began ;
> And whilft foft evening gales blew o'er the plains,
> And fhook the founding reeds, they taught the fwains,
> And thus the pipe was fram'd and tuneful reed.   CREECH.

Part of the natural fong of the black-bird confifts of true diatonic intervals, and is
thus to be expreffed in mufical notes.

That of the cuckow is well known to be this :

Cu cu,   Cu cu,   Cu cu.

And Kircher, Mufurg. lib. I. cap. xiv. has given the fongs of other birds, which with
great ingenuity and induftry he had inveftigated, as namely that of the nightingale, the
quail, the parrot, the cock and hen, in the common characters of mufical notation.
Though that which he gives of the common dunghill cock feems to be erroneous, and is
thus to be expreffed :

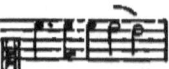

And it may be obferved that between the dunghill and bantam cock there is a difference, for the latter intonates the following founds, which conftitute the interval of a
true fifth.

The fong of the hen at the time of her laying, is thus defcribed by him :

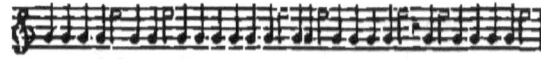

and clearly appears to be an intonation of a major fixth.

therefore becomes neceſſary to trace the invention of ſuch inſtruments as are diſtinguiſhed by the ſimplicity of their conſtruction, and whoſe forms and properties at this diſtance of time are moſt eaſily to be conceived of, and theſe clearly ſeem to be reduced to two, the lyre and the pipe.

The ſame author aſſerts that other animals, and even quadrupeds, articulate different ſounds that have a muſical ratio to each other, as an inſtance whereof he mentions an animal produced in America called the *Pigritia*, or Sloth, of which he gives the following curious account.

‘ Before I ſpeak of his voice I will give a deſcription of this whole animal, which this
‘ very year I received from the mouth of father Johannes Torus, procurator of the pro-
‘ vince of the new kingdom in America, who had ſome of theſe animals in his poſſeſſion,
‘ and made ſeveral trials of their natures and properties. The figure of this animal is
‘ uncommon, they call it *Pigritia*, on account of the ſlowneſs of its motions. It is of
‘ the ſize of a cat, has an ugly countenance, and claws projecting in the likeneſs of fin-
‘ gers: it has hair on the back part of its head, which covers its neck; it bruſhes the very
‘ ground with its fat belly. It never riſes upon its feet, but moves forward ſo ſlowly, that
‘ it ſcarce in a continued ſpace advances above the caſt of a dart in even fifteen days. No
‘ one knows what meat it feeds on, nor are they ſeen to eat; they for the moſt part keep on
‘ the tops of trees, and are two days aſcending and as many in deſcending. Moreover, na-
‘ ture ſeems to have furniſhed them with two kinds of arms or weapons againſt other beaſts
‘ and animals their enemies. Firſt their feet, in which they have ſuch ſtrength, that what-
‘ ſoever animal they lay hold on they keep it ſo faſt, that it is never after able to free itſelf
‘ from their nails, but it is compelled to die through hunger: the other is, that this beaſt
‘ ſo greatly affects the men that are coming towards it by its countenance, that in pure
‘ compaſſion they refrain from moleſting it, and eaſily perſuade themſelves not to be ſoli-
‘ citous about that which nature has ſubjected to ſo defenceleſs and miſerable a ſtate of body.
‘ The above-mentioned father, in order to make a trial of this, procured one of theſe ani-
‘ mals to be brought to the college of our ſociety at Carthagena of the new kingdom, and
‘ threw a long pole under its feet, which he immediately graſped ſo tenaciouſly, that it
‘ would by no means let it go; the animal thus bound by a voluntary ſuſpenſion, was
‘ placed between two beams, where he ſtuck thus ſuſpended for forty days together, with-
‘ out either meat, drink, or ſleep, having his eyes continually fixed on thoſe that looked
‘ on him, whom he affected ſo with his ſorrowful aſpect, that there was ſcarce any one that
‘ was not touched with pity for him. Being at length freed from this long ſuſpenſion, a
‘ dog was thrown to him, which he immediately ſeized with his feet, and forcibly detained
‘ for the ſpace of four days, at the end whereof the miſerable creature expired, being
‘ famiſhed through hunger. This I had from the mouth of the above father.’

They add moreover (to return to the purpoſe) that this beaſt makes no noiſe or cry but in the night, and that with a voice interrupted only by the duration of a ſigh or ſemi-pauſe. It perfectly intonates, as learners do, the firſt elements of muſic, *ut, re, mi, fa, ſol la, la, ſol, fa, mi, re, ut.* aſcending and deſcending through the common intervals of the ſix degrees, inſomuch that the Spaniards, when they firſt took poſſeſſion of theſe coaſts, and perceived ſuch a kind of vociferation in the night, thought they heard men accuſtomed to the rules of muſic. It is called by the inhabitants *Hant*, for no other reaſon than that it repeats through every degree of the interval of a ſixth the ſound ha, ha, ha, ha, ha, ha, &c.

ha,   ha,   ha,   ha,   ha,   ha,   ha,   ha,   ha,   ha,   ha.

The

The lyre, the moft confiderable of the two, and the prototype of the *fidicinal* or ftringed fpecies, is faid to have been invented about the year of the world 2000, by Mercury, who finding on the bank of the river Nile a fhell-fifh of the tortoife kind, which an inundation of that river had depofited there, and obferving that the flefh was already confumed, he took up the back fhell, and hollowing it, applied ftrings to it [*]; though concerning the number of ftrings there is great controverfy, fome afferting it to be only three, and that the founds of the two remote were acute and grave, and that of the intermediate one a mean between thofe two extremes: that Mercury refembled thofe three chords to as many feafons of the year, which were all that the Greeks reckoned, namely, Summer, Winter, and Spring, affigning the acute to the firft, the grave to the fecond, and the mean to the third.

Others affert that the lyre had *four* ftrings; that the interval between the firft and fourth was an octave; that the fecond was a fourth + from the firft, and the fourth the fame diftance from the third, and that from the fecond to the third was a tone ‡.

Another clafs of writers contend that the lyre of Mercury had *feven* ftrings: Nicomachus, a follower of Pythagoras, and the chief of them, gives the following account of the matter : ‘ The lyre made ‘ of the fhell was invented by Mercury, and the knowledge of it, as ‘ it was conftructed by him of feven ftrings was tranfmitted to Or- ‘ pheus; Orpheus taught the ufe of it to Thamyris and Linus, the ‘ latter of whom taught it to Hercules, who communicated it to ‘ Amphion the Theban, who built the feven gates of Thebes to the ‘ feven ftrings of the lyre.’ The fame author proceeds to relate ‘ that ‘ Orpheus was afterwards killed by the Thracian women, and that ‘ they are reported to have caft his lyre into the fea, which was after-

---

[*] Nicomachi Harmonices Manualis, lib. II. ea verf. Meibom. p. 29.

[†] In this and all other inftances, where the meafures of intervals are affigned, it is to be obferved that they include the two extreme terms, in which refpect the phrafes of mufic and phyfic agree; to this purpofe a very whimfical but ingenious and learned writer on mufic and many other fubjects, in the laft century, namely Charles Butler, thus fpeaks : ‘ As phyficians fay a tertian ague, which yet cometh but every fecond day, and a quar- ‘ tan, whofe accefs is every third day, (becaufe they count the firft fit-day for one) fo do ‘ muficians call a third, a fourth, and a fifth (which yet are but two, three, and four notes ‘ from the ground) becaufe they account the ground itfelf for one.’ Principles of Mufic, by Charles Butler. quarto, London 1636, pag. 52, in not.

[‡] Boetius de Mufica, lib. I. pag. 29.

4 wards

' wards thrown up at Antiſſa, a city of Leſbos; that certain fiſhers
' finding it, they brought it to Terpander, who carried it to Egypt, ex-
' quiſitely improved, and ſhewing it to the Egyptian prieſts, aſſumed
' to himſelf the honour of its invention *.'

And with reſpect to the form of the ancient lyre, as little agreement is to be found among authors as about the number of ſtrings;
the beſt evidences concerning it are the repreſentations of that inſtrument in the hands of ancient ſtatues of Apollo, Orpheus, and others,
on bas reliefs, antique marbles, medals and gems †; but of theſe
it muſt be confeſſed that they do not all favour the ſuppoſition
that it was originally formed of a tortoiſe ſhell; though on the other
hand it may be ſaid, that as none of thoſe monuments can pretend
to ſo high an antiquity as the times to which we aſſign the invention
of the lyre, they are to be conſidered as exhibitions of that inſtrument in a ſtate of improvement, and therefore are no evidence of
its original form.   Galilei mentions a ſtatue of Orpheus in the
Palazzo de Medici, made by the Cavalier Bandinelli, in the left hand
whereof is a lyre of this figure ‡.

* Nicom. lib. II. pag. 29.
† Merſenous de Inſtrumentis Harmonicis, lib. 1. pag. 7. Vincenzio Galilei Dialogo
della Muſica Antica e Moderna, pag. 125. Athanaſius Kircher Muſurgia univerſalis, lib. II.
cap. vi. § iii.
‡ Galilei, 129.

                                                                    He

He also cites a paffage from Philoſtratus, importing that the lyre was made of the horns of a goat, from which Hyginius undertook thus to delineate it.

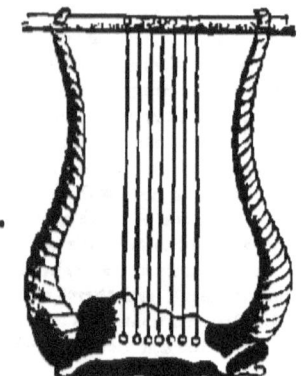

Merfennus fays that by means of his friends Naudè and Gaffarel, he had obtained from Rome, and other parts of Italy, drawings of fundry ancient inſtruments from coins and marbles; among many which he has given, are thefe of the lyre: the firſt is apparently a part of a tortoife-ſhell, the other he fays is part of the head with the horns of a bull.

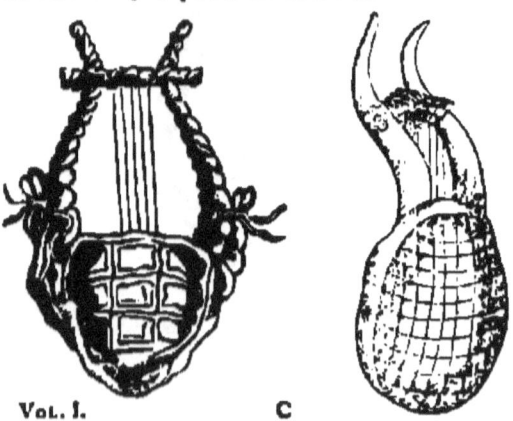

VOL. I.   C

The above-cited authors mention also a *Plectrum*, of about a span in length, made of the lower joint of a goat's leg; the use whereof was to touch the strings of the lyre, as appeared to Galilei by several ancient bass-reliefs and other sculptures discovered at Rome in his time.

Kircher has prefixed as a frontispiece to the second tome of the Musurgia, a representation of a statue in the Matthei garden near Rome, of Apollo standing on a circular pedestal, whereon are carved in basso relievo a great variety of ancient musical instruments. But the most perfect representation of the lyre is the instrument in the hand of the above statue, which is of the form in which the lyre is most usually delineated. Vide Musurg. tom. I. pag. 536 *.

The Pipe, the original and most simple of wind instruments, is said to have been formed of the shank-bone of a crane, and the invention thereof is ascribed to Apollo, Pan, Orpheus, Linus, and many others. Marsyas, or as others say, Silenus, was the first that joined pipes of different lengths together with wax; but Virgil says,

* Isaac Vossius, a bigotted admirer of the ancients, de Poemat. cant. et viribus. Rythm. pag. 97, contends that hardly any of these remaining monuments of antiquity are in such a state as to warrant any opinion touching the form of the ancient lyre. He speaks indeed of two statues of Apollo in the garden of his Britannic majesty at London, in the year 1673, (probably the Privy Garden behind the then palace of Whitehall) each holding a lyre; and as neither of these instruments was then in the least mutilated, he considers them as true and perfect representations of the ancient cythara or lyre, in two forms, and has thus delineated and described them.

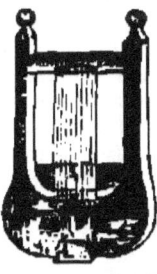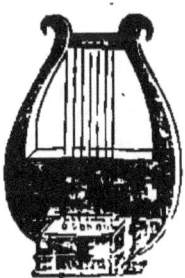

A The bridge over which the chords are stretched.
B The chordotonum, from which the chords proceed.
C C The echei, made of brass, and affixed to the bridge to encrease the sound.
D The bridge as in the former figure.

Pan primos calamos cera conjungere plures
Inſtituit. *

forming thereby an inſtrument, to which Iſidore, biſhop of Seville
gives the name of Pandorium, and others that of Syringa, and which
is frequently repreſented in collections of antiquities †.

As to the inſtruments of the pulſatile kind, ſuch as are the Drum,
and many others, they can hardly be ranked in the number of muſical inſtruments; inaſmuch as the ſounds they produce are not reducible to any ſyſtem, though the meaſure and duration or ſucceſſion
of thoſe ſounds is; which is no more than may be ſaid of many
ſounds, which yet are not deemed muſical.

Such are the accounts that are left us of the invention of the inſtruments above-mentioned, which it is neceſſary to make the baſis
of an enquiry into the origin of a ſyſtem, rather than the Harp, the
Organ, and many others mentioned in ſacred writ, whoſe invention
was earlier than the times above referred to, becauſe their reſpective
forms are known even at this time of day to a tolerable degree of
preciſion : a lyre conſiſting of ſtrings extended over the concave of a
ſhell, or a pipe with a few equidiſtant perforations in it, are inſtruments we can eaſily conceive of; and indeed the many remaining monuments of antiquity leave us in very little doubt about them ; but there
is no medium through which we can deduce the figure or conſtruction of any of the inſtruments mentioned either in the Pentateuch, or
the leſs ancient parts of ſacred hiſtory; and doubtleſs the tranſlators
of thoſe paſſages of the Old Teſtament, where the names of muſical
inſtruments occur, after due deliberation on the context, found themſelves reduced to the neceſſity of rendering thoſe names by ſuch terms
as would go the neareſt to excite a correſpondent idea in their readers :
ſo that they would be groſsly miſtaken who ſhould imagine that the
organ, handled by thoſe of whom Jubal is ſaid to have been the
father ‡, any way reſembled the inſtrument now known among us
by that name.

Thoſe accounts which give the invention of the lyre to Mercury,
agree alſo in aſcribing to him a ſyſtem adapted to it ; though with

* Eclog. II. ver. 32.
† Vide Merſen. de Inſtrum. Harmon. lib. II. pag. 73.
‡ Geneſis, ch. iv. ver. 21.

reſpect

refpect to the nature of that fyftem, as alfo to the number of ftrings of which the lyre confifted, there is a great diverfity of opinions; and indeed the fettling the firft of thefe queftions would go near to determine the other. Boetius inclines to the opinion that the lyre of Mercury had only four ftrings; and adds, that the firft and the fourth made a diapafon; that the middle diftance was a tone, and the extremes a diapente *.

Zarlino, following Boetius, adopts his notion of a tetrachord, and is more particular in the explanation of it †; his words are as follow: ' From the firft ftring to the fecond was a diateffe-
' ron or a fourth; from the fecond to the third was a tone; and
' from the third to the fourth was a diateffcron; fo that the firft with
' the fecond, and the third with the fourth, contained a diateffcron;
' the firft with the third, and the fecond with the fourth, a dia-
' pente or fifth.' Admitting all which, it is clear that the firft and fourth ftrings muft have conftituted a diapafon.

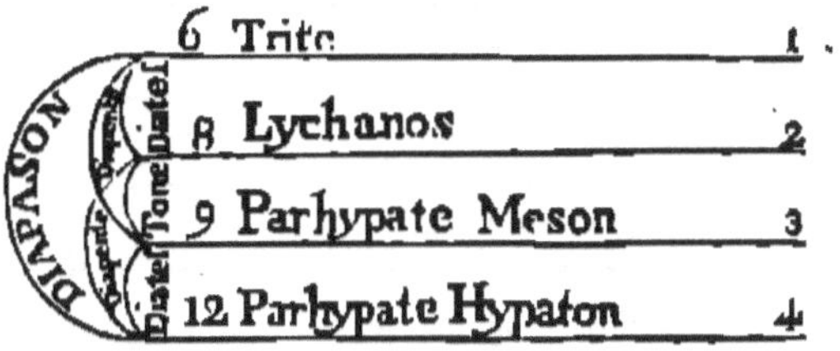

It is to be obferved that the above diagram is ufed by Boetius, and is adopted by Zarlino, Kircher, and many other writers ‡; but that though the application of the letters C. G. F. C. in one edition of Boetius, is plainly intended to fhew that the ftrings immediately below them were fuppofed to correfpond with thofe notes in our fyftem, yet the authors who follow Boetius have not ventured to make ufe of them; and indeed there is great reafon to reject them; for in the earlier editions of Boetius de Mufica, the diagram above given is without letters. It feems as if

* De Mufica, lib. I. cap. 20. Bontempi, 48.
† Iftitutioni Harmoniche, pag. 72.
‡ Vide Boe.ius de Mufica, lib. I. cap. 20. Kircher, Mufurgia univerfalis, tom. I. lib. ii. cap. 6. Zarlino Iftit. Harmon. pag. 73, 75.

Clareanus,

Glareanus, who affifted in the publication of the Bafil edition of that author, in 1570, thought he fhould make the fyftem more intelligible by the addition of thofe letters ; but there is no ground to fuppofe that the Mercurian lyre, admitting it to confift of four ftrings, was fo conftructed.

Bontempi, an author of great credit, relying on Nicomachus fufpects the relation of Boetius, as to the number of the ftrings of the Mercurian lyre ; and farther doubts whether the fyftem of a diapafon, as it is above made out, did really belong to it or not ; and indeed his fufpicions feem to be well grounded ; for, fpeaking of this fyftem, he fays that none of the Greek writers fay any thing about it, and that the notion of its formation feems to be founded on a difcovery made by Pythagoras, who lived about 500 years before Chrift, of which a very particular relation will be given in its proper place ; and farther to fhew how queftionable this notion is, he quotes the very words of Nicomachus before-cited, concluding with a modeft interpofition of his own opinion, which is that the lyre of Mercury had *three* ftrings only, and was thus conftituted *.

————————————————————— G
Interval of a tone.
————————————————————— F
Interval of a hemitone.
————————————————————— E

However, notwithftanding the reafons of the above author, the received opinion feems to have been that the lyre confifted of four ftrings, tuned to certain concordant intervals, which intervals were undoubtedly at firft adjufted by the ear ; but neverthelefs had their foundation in principles which the inventor was not aware of, though what that tuning was, is another fubject of controverfy. Succeeding muficians are faid to have given a name to each of thefe four ftrings, which names, though they are not expreffive of the intervals, are to be adopted in our enquiry after a fyftem: to the firft or moft grave was given the name of Hypate, or principal ; the fecond was called Parhypate, viz. next to Hypate ; the third was called Paranete, and the fourth Nete, which fignifies loweft ; it is obfervable here, that

* Hift. Mufic. pag. 49.

it

it feems to have been the practice of the ancients to give the more grave tones the uppermoft place in the fcale, contrary to the moderns, by whom we are to underftand all who fucceeded the grand reformation of mufic by Guido, in the eleventh century, of which there will be abundant occafion to fpeak hereafter.

The feveral names above-mentioned exhibit the lyre in a very fimple flate, viz. as confifting of four ftrings, having names from whence neither terms nor intervals can be inferred.

Thofe who fpeak of the lyre in the manner above-mentioned, feem to imagine that its compafs included two diatefferons or fourths, which being conjoined, extended to a feventh, differing from that of Boetius, in that his diatefferons, being feparated by a tone, took in the extent of an octave, and thereby formed a diapafon. They proceed to relate farther, that Chorebus, the fon of Atys king of Lydia, added a fifth ftring, which he placed between Parhypate and Paranete, calling it, from its middle fituation, Mefe, that Hyagnis, a Phrygian, added a fixth, which he placed between Mefe and Parhypate; this ftring he called Lychanos, a word fignifying the indicial finger, viz. that on the left hand, next the thumb: and laftly fay thefe writers, Terpander added a feventh ftring, which he placed between Mefe and Paranete, and called Paramefe: the lyre, thus improved, included a feptenary, or fyftem of feven terms, difpofed in the following order.

CHAP.

C H A P.   II.

THE fyftem above exhibited was the Heptachord Synemmenon of the Greeks; it confifted of two tetrachords or fourths, conjoined, that is to fay, the middle term was the end of the one, and the beginning of the other; and as the laft ftring was added by Terpander, the fyftem was diftinguiſhed by his name, and confidered as the fecond ftate of the lyre.

Here then we may difcern the foundation of a fyftem, viz. a fucceffion of feven founds, including two tetrachords, conjoined, by having the Mefe or middle term common to both, thus reprefented by Glareanus in his edition of Boetius, lib. i. cap. 20.

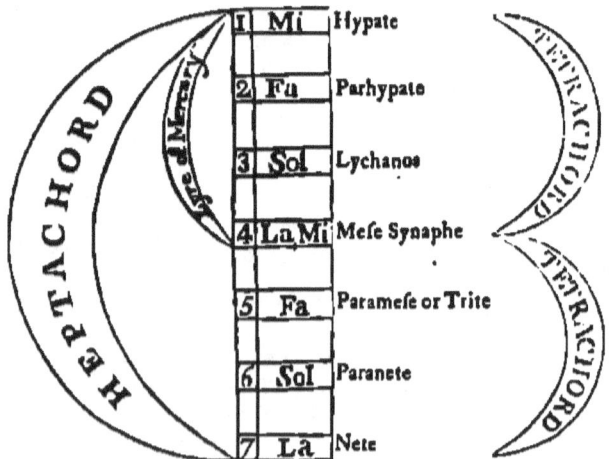

1	Mi	Hypate
2	Fa	Parhypate
3	Sol	Lychanos
4	La Mi	Mefe Synaphe
5	Fa	Paramefe or Trite
6	Sol	Paranete
7	La	Nete

The feeming perfection of this fyftem, as alfo the confideration that in mufical progreffion every eighth found is but the replicate of its unifon, has ferved to confirm an opinion that there is fomewhat myfterious in the number feven; to fay the truth, for different reafons

an

an equal degree of perfection has been ascribed to almost every other of the digits: the number four was greatly reverenced by Pythagoras and his disciples, as that of three is at this day by many Christians. Seven and nine multiplied into themselves make sixty-three commonly esteemed the grand climacteric of our lives; the ground of superstitious fears in persons of middle age, and the subject of much learned disquisition: and there is now extant a treatise in folio, intituled, *Mystica numerorum significationis*, written by one Peter Bongus, and published at Bergamo, in the year 1585; the sole end whereof is to unfold the mysteries, and explain the properties of certain numbers; and whoever has the curiosity to search after so insignificant a work, will find that in the judgment of its author this of Seven is intituled to a kind of pre-eminence over almost every other number.

Had these opinions of numerical mystery no better a foundation than the suffrage of astrologers, they would hardly deserve confutation, even though perhaps in the case of errors so glaring, to expose is to detect them; but when we find them maintained not only by men of sound understandings, but by the gravest philosophers, they become matter of importance; at least there is somewhat of curiosity in observing the extravagancies of an heated imagination, and marking the absurdities that a favourite hypothesis will frequently lead men into.

There is not perhaps a more pregnant instance of this kind, or of the misapplication of learned industry, than the work above-mentioned; as a proof whereof the following chapter is selected, as well by way of specimen of the manner of reasoning usual among writers of his class, as to explain the properties of the number seven, the only one which we are here concerned to enquire about. If the arguments in favour of its perfection are not so conclusive as might be expected, the reader may rest assured that they are some of the best that have yet been adduced for the purpose.

' The number Seven,' says this learned author, ' has a wonder-
' ful property, for it neither begets nor is begotten, as the rest are,
' by any of the numbers within ten, wherefore philosophers resemble
' it to the ruler or governor of all things, who neither moves nor is
' moved. Philolaus the Pythagorean, no ignoble author, testifies
' thus, and writes that the eternal God is permanent, void of mo-
' tion, similar to himself, and different from others; and Boetius has

6   ' a pas-

' a paſſage much to the ſame purpoſe. The idea of virginity had
' ſuch a relation to the number Seven, that it was alſo named Pallas ;
' and the Pythagoreans, initiated in her rites, compare the virgin
' Minerva to that number, ſeeing ſhe was not born, but ſprung from
' the head of Jupiter. God reſted on the Seventh day, wherefore it is
' named Sabbath, a word ſignifying reſt. The Seventh petition of
' the Lord's Prayer is, deliver us from evil ; becauſe the number
' Seven denotes reſt, and all evil being removed from man, he reſts
' in good ; and farther, the ſeventh day or ſabbath repreſents death,
' or the reſt of the ſoul from worldly labours. In Seven days after
' Noah entered the ark the flood began : in the Apocalypſe Seven
' trumpets are mentioned : Job ſpeaks of the viſitation of ſix tribu-
' lations, which ſix ſucceeding days brought on him, but on the
' Seventh no harm could touch the juſt : God bleſſed only the
' Seventh day, wherefore the number Seven is attributed to the
' Holy Ghoſt, without whom there is no bleſſing. This St. John
' proves, when in the Apocalypſe he calls the Seven horns and the
' Seven eyes the Seven ſpirits of God. The fever left the ſon of Re-
' gulus, according to St. John, at the Seventh hour. Eliſha breathed
' Seven times on the dead man. Chriſt after his reſurrection feaſted
' with Seven diſciples ; and Seven brothers were ſent to baptize
' Cornelius. The Seven hairs of Sampſon ; Seven golden candle-
' ſticks : and in Leviticus command was given to ſprinkle the blood,
' and oil Seven times. The Seven ſtars in the bear ; the Seven prin-
' cipal angels who rule the world under God, and have charge of the
' Seven planets, as namely, Horophiel the ſpirit of Saturn, Anael the
' ſpirit of Venus, Zachariel of Jupiter, Raphael of Mercury, Samael
' of Mars, Gabriel of the moon, and Michael the ſpirit of the ſun.
' The moon changes its form Seven times, and completes its courſe
' in twenty-eight days, which is the ſum of the number Seven, and
' all the numbers under it. Joſephus writes that a certain river in
' Syria is dry for ſix days, and full on the Seventh. Farther, the great
' artiſt did not only dignify the heavens, but he alſo adorned
' with the number Seven his favourite creature man, who has
' ſeven inward parts, or bowels, ſtomach, heart, lungs, milt, liver,
' reins, and bladder ; and ſeven exterior, as head, back, belly,
' two hands, and two feet. There are Seven objects of ſight, as
' body, diſtance, figure, magnitude, colour, motion, and reſt : and

Vol. I.   D   ' Seven

' Seven fpecies of colour, taking in the two extremes of white and
' black, viz. yellow, fky-blue, green, purple, and red. No one
' can without eating live after the Seventh day.   Phyficians-reckon
' ten times Seven years to be the period of human life, which Hippo-
' crates divides into Seven ftages.   The ancient lyre, ufed both by
' Orpheus and Amphion, had only Seven chords, anfwering, as it is
' faid, to the Seven gates of Thebes.   Every Seventh daughter, no
' fon coming between, hath, by virtue of the number Seven as I
' imagine, a great power in eafing the pains of child-birth : and
' every Seventh fon, no daughter coming between, has the power of
' curing the fcurvy and leprofy by the bare touch ; fo that difeafes;
' incurable by phyficians, are curable by the virtue contained in the
' number Seven. A right-angled triangle is conftituted of the fides three,
' four, five, but three and four contain the right angle, which is perfec-
' tion itfelf, and therefore their fum feven, muft as a number be moft
' perfect.   Every active body has three dimenfions, length, breadth;
' and thicknefs, and thefe have four extremes, point, line, furface;
' and folid, and thefe together make up the number Seven.'
By fuch arguments as thefe do many of the mufical writers endeavour to excite a myfterious reverence for that number which is confeffedly the limits of a fyftem, as far as it goes, perfect in its kind; in
anfwer to which it may be faid, that this fuperftitious regard for certain
numbers feems to be very defervedly ranked among thofe vulgar and
common errors, which it is profeffedly the end of a very learned and
juftly celebrated publication of the laft century to refute, wherein it
is faid, that ' with refpect to any extraordinary power or fecret virtue
' attending the number fixty-three, or any other, a ferious reader will
' hardly find any thing that may convince his judgment, or any far-
' ther perfuade than the lenity of his belief, or pre-judgment of rea-
' fon inclineth *.'
But to return from this digreffion : the rudiments of the prefent
greater mufical fyftem are difcernible in that of a feptenary, adjufted,
as we are told, by Terpander, in the form above declared; and as to
the intervals of which it was conftituted, modern authors have not
fcrupled to affert that they were precifely the fame as thofe contained
in a double diatefferon, according to the prefent practice; the con-

* Sir Thomas Browne's Enquiry into Vulgar Errors, 173.

fequence

fequence whereof muft be, that each of the two tetrachords, of which the above fyftem is fuppofed to have been formed, confifted of a hemitone and two tones; which will be readily conceived by fuch as reflect, that in the paffage either upwards or downwards from any given note to its fourth, in that progreffion which is moft grateful to the ear, thofe intervals muft neceffarily occur. Perfuaded of the truth of this fuppofition, fucceeding muficians have ventured to apply the modern method of notation to the terms of the ancients, and are pretty well agreed that the term Mefe anfwered to a, or LA, in our fcale. Taking this for granted, the fyftem of Terpander will appear in the following form.

SYSTEM of TERPANDER.

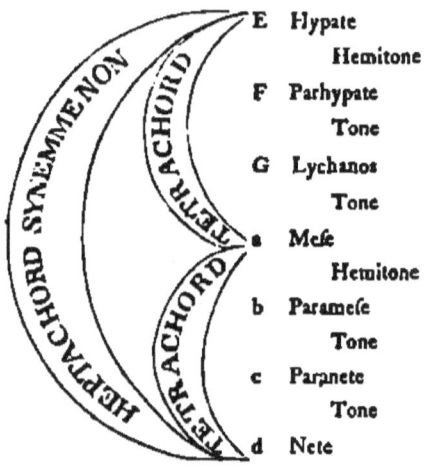

E	Hypate
	Hemitone
F	Parhypate
	Tone
G	Lychanos
	Tone
a	Mefe
	Hemitone
b	Paramefe
	Tone
c	Paranete
	Tone
d	Nete

But here it is neceffary to obferve, that though, as has been faid, it was the practice with the ancients to give the grave tones the uppermoft, and the more acute the lowermoft place in their fcale *, which they might very properly do, if, as there is the greateft reafon

* Vincentio Galilei, Dialog. della Mufica, pag. 113. Francifcus Salinas de Mufica, lib. iii. cap. 4.

to believe, their mufic was folitary, and they were ftrangers to the art of combining founds in confonance. Yet the moderns, immediately on the making that moft important difcovery, found it neceffary to differ from them, and accordingly we now place the grave tones at the bottom, and the acute at the top of our fcale * ; the confequence of this diverfity has been, that whenever any of the modern authors have taken occafion to exhibit the whole or any part of the ancient Greek fcale, they have done it in their own way, placing Hypate at the bottom of the diagram ; and this will be the method we fhall obferve for the future.

Great confufion has arifen among the writers on mufic, in refpect to the order of the feveral additions to the fyftem of Terpander. That it was perfected by Pythagoras will be related in due time ; but the eagernefs of moft authors to explain the improvements made by him, has betrayed them into the error of confounding the two fyftems together, whereby they have rendered their accounts unintelligible. Boetius has erred in this refpect ; and Bontempi, a modern Italian, notwithftanding he profeffes to have followed the Greek writers, more particularly Nicomachus, has made the fame miftake ; for in every one of the reprefentations of the improved fyftem of Terpander which he has given, is contained an exhibition of the Synemmenon or conjunct tetrachord, which before the invention of the Diezeugmenon or disjunct tetrachord by Pythagoras, could have no exiftence. He indeed confeffes as much when he admits that the diftinction imported by its name was rather *potential* than *actual*; or, as we perhaps fhould fay, rather *contingent* than *abfolute*. To refute this error it is neceffary in fome fort to adopt it, and proceed after Bontempi to defcribe what he calls the firft addition to the fyftem of Terpander. His words are nearly thefe.

‘ To the lyre of feven ftrings, forming a conjunct tetrachord, were
‘ added two tetrachords ; the moft grave was joined to that tetrachord,
‘ which for its graveft, or, to ufe the modern method of pofition, its
‘ loweft found, had Hypate, and the moft acute tetrachord was
‘ joined to that which for its moft acute found had Nete: the acuter
‘ of thefe two additional tetrachords, from its fituation named hyper-
‘ boleon, proceeded from Nete by three other terms, viz. Trite, Para-
‘ nete, and Nete, to each whereof was given the epithet Hyperbo-

* Bontemp. 51, 52.

‘ leon,

' leon, to diſtinguiſh them from the ſounds denoted by the ſame
' names in the primitive ſeptenary. The other of the additional
' tetrachords, which began from Meſe, was called Synemmenon or
' conjunct, and proceeded likewiſe by the ſame terms of Trite, Para-
' nete, and Nete; and each of theſe had, for the reaſon juſt given,
' the epithet of Synemmenon, as in the following figure appears.'

ADDITION I. to the SYSTEM of TERPANDER.

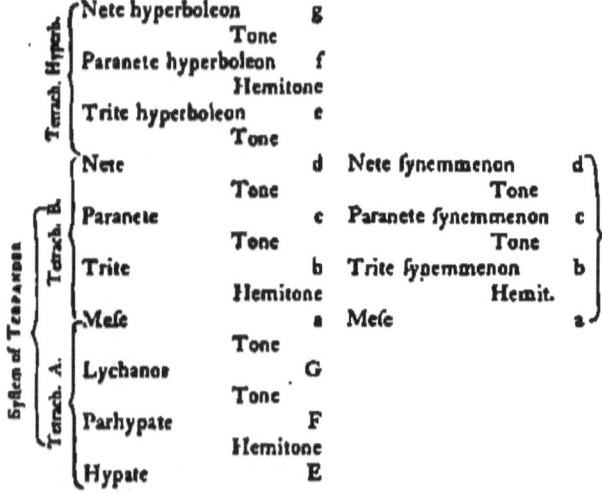

It is obſervable in the above ſcheme, that between the Synemmenon tetrachord and that marked B, which was originally a part of the
ſyſtem of Terpander, there is not the leaſt difference : the interval
of a hemitone between a and b being common to both ; of what uſe
then this auxiliary tetrachord was, or how it became neceſſary to diftinguiſh it by the epithet Synemmenon or conjoined, from that
which as yet had never been disjoined, is hard to conceive ; the only
addition therefore that we conſider is that of the Hyperboleon tetrachord, which increaſed the number of terms to ten, as above is
ſhewn : however, after all, as the lyre thus limited to the compaſs
of a muſical tenth, reaching from E to g, was not commenſurate in
general

general to the human voice, a farther extension of it was found necessary; and another tetrachord was added to this, which began at
Hypate in the former system, and proceeded by a repetition of the
same terms as that did, with the addition of hypaton. This addition
begat also a distinction in the terms of the tetrachord, to which it
had been joined; which, to shew their relation to the Mese, had each
of them the adjunct of meson, and the tetrachord to which they belonged was thence called the tetrachord meson. This last addition
of the tetrachord Hypaton increased the number of terms to thirteen,
in which were included four conjunct tetrachords, the Mese being
the seventh from each extreme, and carried the system down to B;
though to shew that hypate Hypaton was a hemitone below Parhypate or C, the Italians generally denote it by the character ♭.

ADDITION II. to the SYSTEM of TERPANDER.

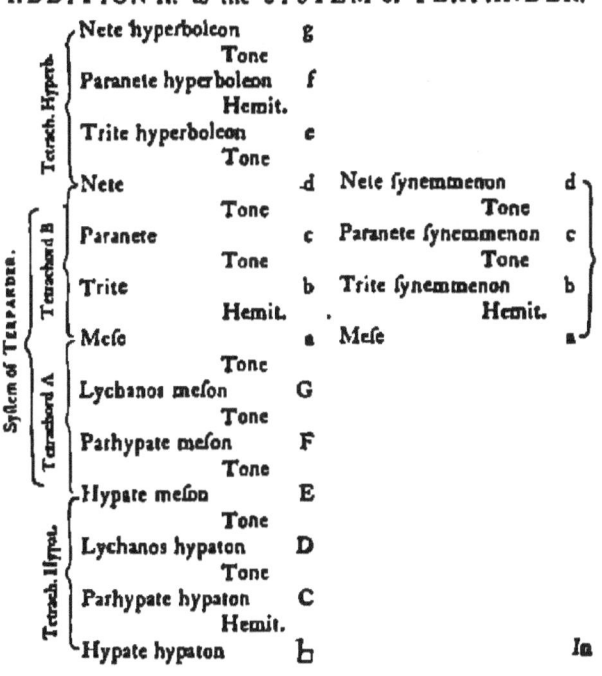

	Nete hyperboleon	g	
	Tone		
Tetrach. Hyperb.	Paranete hyperboleon	f	
	Hemit.		
	Trite hyperboleon	e	
	Tone		
	Nete	d	Nete fynemmenon	d
Tetrachord B	Tone		Tone
	Paranete	c	Paranete fynemmenon	c
	Tone		Tone
	Trite	b	Trite fynemmenon	b
	Hemit.		Hemit.
	Mefe	a	Mefe	a
Tetrachord A	Tone		
	Lychanos meson	G	
	Tone		
	Parhypate meson	F	
	Tone		
	Hypate meson	E	
Tetrach. Hypat.	Tone		
	Lychanos hypaton	D	
	Tone		
	Parhypate hypaton	C	
	Hemit.		
	Hypate hypaton	♭	

System of Terpander.

In

In this diagram alfo the Synemmenon Tetrachord is inferted : we forbear to repeat the reafons againft connecting it with the fyftem of Terpander, with which it feems abfolutely incompatible, and fhall hereafter endeavour to fhew when and how the invention of it became neceffary, and what particular ends it feems calculated to anfwer. In order to this it muft be obferved, that the fyftem, improved even to the degree above related, wanted much of perfection: it is evident that the lower found Hypate hypaton, or as we fhould now call it, B ♭, was a hemitone below C, and that b, which in the order of fucceffion upwards was the eighth term, was a whole tone below the term next above it, confequently it was a hemitone fhort of a complete mufical octave or diapafon ; to remedy this defect, as alfo for divers other reafons, Pythagoras is faid to have reverted to the primitive fyftem of a feptenary, and with admirable fagacity, by interpofing a tone in the middle of the double tetrachord, to have formed the fyftem of a Diapafon or Octochord.

But before we proceed to relate the particulars of this and other improvements of Pythagoras in mufic, and the wonderful difcovery made by him of the proportions of mufical founds, it may be proper to take notice of two variations in the feptenary, introduced by a philofopher, and a difciple of Pythagoras, named Philolaus ; the one whereof, for ought we can difcover, feems to have been but very inconfiderable, that is to fay, no more than an alteration of the term Mefe, which, becaufe that found war a third diftant from Nete, he called Trite ; the other confifted in an extenfion of the diatefferon included between the Mefe and Nete to a diapente, by the infertion of a trihemitone between Paramefe, or as he termed it, Trite and Paranete ; by which the fyftem, though it laboured under the inconvevience of an Hiatus, comprehended the interval of a diapafon, the extreme terms whereof formed a confonance much more grateful to the ear than any of thofe contained in that of Terpander. Nicomachus fpeaks more than once of Philolaus, and fays that he was the firft who called that Trite, which before was named Paramefe, as being a diatefferon diftant from Nete. But although it is certain that he was a contemporary of Pythagoras, we muft fuppofe this improvement of his to be prior to that of Pythagoras above hinted at ; for the latter adopted the appellation of Trite, though by reftoring the ancient name Paramefe, which he gave to the inferted tone, he altered the fituation of it, as will be fhewn hereafter.

SYSTEM

SYSTEM of PHILOLAUS.

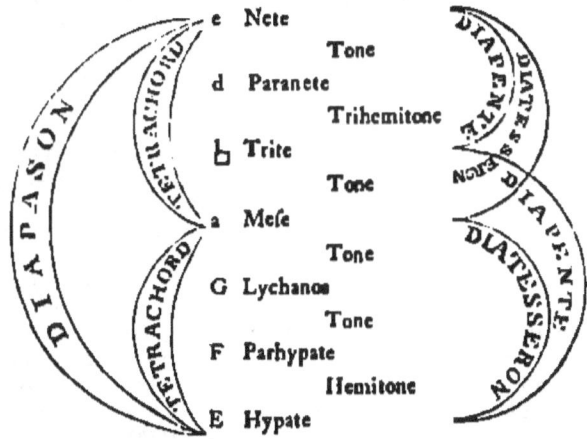

The gradual improvements of this fyftem from the time of Terpander to that of Philolaus having been feverally enumerated, and
its imperfection noted, we are now to fpeak of thofe made by
Pythagoras. His regulation of the octave by the infertion of a tone
has been juft hinted, and it will be neceffary to be more particular; but previous to this it is requifite to mention that difcovery of
his, which though merely accidental, enabled him to inveftigate the
ratios of the confonances, and to demonftrate that the foundations of
mufical harmony lay deeper than had ever before his time been
imagined.

Of the manner of this difcovery Nicomachus has given a relation,
which Mr. Stanley has inferted in his Hiftory of Philofophy in
nearly the following terms.

‘ Pythagoras being in an intenfe thought whether he might invent
‘ any inftrumental help to the ear, folid and infallible, fuch as the
‘ fight hath by a compafs and a rule, and by a Dioptre; or the
‘ touch, or by a balance, or by the invention of meafures; as he
‘ paffed by a fmith’s fhop by a happy chance he heard the iron ham-
6   ‘ mers

' mers ftriking on the anvil, and rendering founds moft confonant
' to one another in all combinations except one. He obferved in
' them thefe three concords, the diapafon, the diapente, and the
' diatefferon ; but that which was between the diatefferon and the
' diapente he found to be a difcord in itfelf, though otherwife ufe-
' ful for the making up of the greater of them, the diapente. Ap-
' prehending this came to him from God, as a moft happy thing,
' he haftened into the fhop, and by various trials finding the diffe-
' rence of the founds to be according to the weight of the hammers,
' and not according to the force of thofe who ftruck, nor according
' to the fafhion of the hammers, nor according to the turning of the
' iron which was in beating out: having taken exactly the weight
' of the hammers, he went ftraightway home, and to one beam
' faftened to the walls, crofs from one corner of the room to the
' other, left any difference might arife from thence, or be fufpect-
' ed to arife from the properties of feveral beams, tying four ftrings
' of the fame fubftance, length, and twift, upon each of them he
' hung a feveral weight, faftening it at the lower end, and making
' the length of the ftrings altogether equal ; then ftriking the ftrings
' by two at a time interchangeably, he found out the aforefaid con-
' cords, each in its own combination ; for that which was ftretched
' by the greateft weight, in refpect of that which was ftretched by
' the leaft weight, he found to found a Diapafon. The greateft
' weight was of twelve pounds, the leaft of fix ; thence he deter-
' mined that the diapafon did confift in double proportion, which
' the weights themfelves did fhew. Next he found that the
' greateft to the leaft but one, which was of eight pounds, founded
' a Diapente ; whence he inferred this to confift in the proportion
' called Sefquialtera, in which proportion the weights were to one
' another ; but unto that which was lefs than itfelf in weight, yet
' greater than the reft, being of nine pounds, he found it to found a
' Diatefferon ; and difcovered that, proportionably to the weights,
' this concord was Sefquitertia ; which ftring of nine pounds is natu-
' rally Sefquialtera to the leaft ; for nine to fix is fo, viz. Sefquialtera,
' as the leaft but one, which is eight, was to that which had the
' weight fix, in proportion Sefquitertia ; and twelve to eight is Sef-
' quialtera ; and that which is in the middle, between Diapente and
' Diatefferon, whereby Diapente exceeds Diatefferon, is confirmed

‘ to be in Sefquioftava proportion, in which nine is to eight. The
‘ fyftem of both was called Diapafon *, that is both of the Diapente
‘ and Diatefferon joined together, as duple proportion is compound-
‘ ed of Sefquialtera and Sefquitertia ; fuch as are twelve, eight, fix,
‘ or on the contrary, of Diatefferon and Diapente, as duple propor-
‘ tion is compounded of Sefquitertia and Sefquialtera, as twelve, nine,
‘ fix, being taken in that order.

‘ Applying both his hand and ear to the weights which he had
‘ hung on, and by them confirming the proportion of the relations,
‘ he ingenioufly transferred the common refult of the ftrings upon
‘ the crefs beam to the bridge of an inftrument, which he called
‘ Χορδτόνος, Chordotonos ; and for ftretching them proportionably to
‘ the weights, he invented pegs, by the turning whereof he diftend-
‘ ed or relaxed them at pleafure. Making ufe of this foundation as
‘ an infallible rule, he extended the experiment to many kinds of
‘ inftruments, as well pipes and flutes, as thofe which have ftrings † ;
‘ and he found that this conclufion made by numbers was confonant
‘ without variation in all. That found which proceeded from the
‘ number fix he named Hypate ; that from eight Mefe, being Sef-
‘ quitertia to the other; that from nine Paramefe, it being one tone
‘ more acute, and fefquioctave to the Mefe ; that from twelve he
‘ termed Nete ; and fupplying the middle fpaces with proportionable
‘ founds, according to the diatonic genus, he fo ordered the octo-
‘ chord with convenient numbers, Duple, Sefquialtera, Sefquitertia,
‘ and the difference of the two laft, Sefquioctava.

‘ Thus by a kind of natural neceffity he found the progrefs from
‘ the loweft to the higheft, according to the diatonic genus ; and
‘ from thence he proceeded to declare the chromatic and enarmonic
‘ kinds ‡’. Hift. of Philofophy, pag. 587. folio edit. 1701.

* i. e. per omnes.
† This feems difficult to conceive, for the tuning of pipes and flutes is regulated by
the fize and diftance of the apertures for the emiffion of the wind or breath ; and to thefe
the proportions of fix, eight, nine, twelve, are in no way whatever applicable.
‡ The refult of this difcovery is, that confonancy is founded on geometrical principles,
the contemplation whereof, and the making them the teft of beauty and harmony, is a
pleafure feparate and diftinct from that which we receive by the fenfes. This geometrical relation of the confonances has been farther illuftrated by Archimedes, who has demonftrated that the proportions of certain folid bodies are the fame with thofe of the mufical confonances; to fpeak firft of the diapafon.
By a corollary from the thirty-fourth propofition of Archimedes it is fhewn, that the
proportion of the octave is as the whole fuperficies of a right cylinder defcribed about a
fphere,

Other writers attribute the discovery of the consonances to another, namely Diocles, who, say they, passing by a potter's shop, chanced to strike his stick against some empty vessels which were standing there; that observing the sounds of grave and acute resulting from the strokes on vessels of different magnitudes, he investigated the proportions of music, and found them to be as above related †; notwithstanding which testimony, the uniform opinion of

sphere, is to the whole superficies of an equilateral cylinder inscribed, that is to say, as 2 is to 1. For the circumscribed is to the spheric superficies as 12 is to 8; but the spheric is to the inscribed as 8 is to 6; therefore the circumscribed is to the inscribed as 12 is to 6, or 2 to 1. Vide Theorems selected out of Archimedes by Andrew Tacquet, printed at the end of Whiston's Euclid.

As to the diatessaron, the proportion of it is precisely the same with that which subsists between the superficies of a sphere and the whole superficies of a square cylinder inscribed therein, viz. 4 to 3. Ibid. Prop. xxxiv.

But which is admirable, the sesquialteral proportion of the diapente, and of the same interval continued, is demonstrated by Tacquet himself, by a sphere, a right cylinder, and an equilateral cone thus disposed:

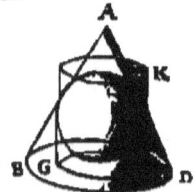

His words are these: ' An equilateral cone circumscribed about a sphere, and a right cylinder in like manner circumscribed about the same sphere, and the same sphere itself continue the same proportion; to wit, the sesquialteral, as well as in respect of the solidity as of the whole superficies.

' For by 32 of this book, the right cylinder G K encompassing the sphere, is to the sphere, as well in respect of solidity, as of the whole superficies, as 3 is to 2 or as 6 to 4. But by the foregoing, the equilateral cone B A D circumscribed about the sphere, is to the sphere, in both the said respects, as 9 is to 4. Therefore the same cone is to the cylinder, both in respect of solidity and surface, as nine is to six: wherefore these three bodies, a cone, a cylinder, and sphere, are betwixt themselves as the numbers 9, 6, 4; and consequently continue the sesquialteral proportion.' Q. E. D. Prop. xlv. at the conclusion of the Theorems of Archimedes by Tacquet.

Further the same author shews, that the same sesquialteral proportion holds betwixt an equilateral cone and cylinder circumscribed about the same sphere, in respect of their whole surfaces, their simple surfaces, their solidities, altitudes, and bases.

Archimedes was so delighted with the thirty-second of his propositions, above referred to, that he left it in charge to his friends to erect on his tomb a sphere included in a cylinder, and Tacquet seems to have been little less pleased with his improvement on it, for he has given the figure referred to in the demonstration of it, in the title page of his Theorems selected from Archimedes.

† Vincent. Galilei, Dial. della Musica, pag. 127.

mankind

mankind has been, that we owe this invention to Pythagoras; the result whereof may be conceived by means of the following diagram.

It is obfervable that there is nothing in this account to authorife the fuppofition that the lyre of Mercury was tuned in any of thofe proportions which this difcovery had fhewn to be confonant. Bontempi, who, as we have hinted before, had his doubts about it, fays exprefsly that none of the Greek writers affert any fuch matter; and Zarlino, though he adopts the relation of Boetius, does it in fuch a way as fufficiently fhews it fluck with him: we may therefore juftly refpect that Boetius went too far in affigning to the ftrings of the Mercurian lyre the proportions of fix, eight, nine, twelve.

CHAP.

C H A P. III.

IF we confider the amount of this difcovery, it will appear to be, that certain founds, which the human ear had previoufly recognized as grateful and harmonious, were, by the fagacity of Pythagoras, found to have a wonderful relation to each other in certain proportions; that thofe proportions do really fubfift between the mufical concords above-mentioned is demonftrated by Ptolemy, and will be fhewn hereafter; but then it has been by experiments of a different kind from that of ftrings diftended by hammers or other weights in the proportions of fix, eight, nine, twelve, and fuch as prove a moft egregious error in thofe faid to be made by Pythagoras; fo that though his title to the difcovery of the proportions above-mentioned is not contefted; yet that it was the refult of the experiment above related to have been made by him, is demonftrably falfe.

For fuppofe, as will be fhewn hereafter, that the founds of four ftrings, in every other refpect alike, and in length as thefe numbers, fix, eight, nine, twelve, will make the intervals above-mentioned, viz. a fourth, fifth, and octave; yet let weights in thefe proportions be hung to ftrings of equal length and thicknefs, and the intervals between the founds produced by ftrings thus diftended will be far different from thofe above-mentioned.

It is faid that we owe the detection of this error to the penetration and induftry of Galileo Galilei, whofe merits as well as fufferings are fufficiently known. He was the natural fon of a noble Florentine named Vincentio Galilei, the author of a moft learned and valuable work, intitled Dialogo della Mufica antica e moderna, printed at Florence in 1581 and 1602; and alfo of a tract, intitled Difcorfo intorno all' Opere del Zarlino; and of his father, who was an admirable performer on the lute, learned both the theory and practice of mufic; in the latter whereof he is faid to have been fuch a proficient, as to be able to perform to a great degree of excellence on a variety of inftruments; however, notwithftanding this his propenfity to mufic, his chief purfuits were natural philofophy and the mathematics.

The

The inquifitivenefs of his temper leading him to the making experiments, in the courfe thereof he made many noble difcoveries; that of the telefcope feems to be univerfally attributed to him; his firft effay towards an inftrument for viewing the planets was an organ-pipe with glaffes fixed therein; and it was he that firft inveftigated thofe laws of pendulums, which Mr. Huygens afterwards improved into a regular and confiftent theory.

In a work of the younger Galilei, intitled Difcorfi e Dimoftrazioni Matematiche intorno à due nuove Scienze, attenenti alla Mecanica, & i Movimenti locali, is contained a detection of that error, which it is here propofed to refute.

It is true fome writers refer this difcovery to Vincentio Galilei; and firft Bontempi fays, that in his difcourfe on the works of Zarlino, he affirms, that in order ' to find the confonances by weights ' hung to chords, the weight to produce the diapafon ought to be ' in quadruple proportion; that to produce the diapente ought to ' be in dopla fefquiquarta; for the diatefferon in fefquifettima par-' tientenono and for the tone in fefquifettima partiente 64 *.

Malcolm alfo, fpeaking of the difcovery of the confonances by Pythagoras, makes ufe of thefe words: ' But we have found an ' error in this account, which Vincenzo Galileo, in his Dialogues of ' the ancient and modern Mufic, is, for what I know, the firft who ' obferves; and from him Meibomius repeats it in his notes upon ' Nicomachus †.'

Here it may be obferved, that this author Malcolm has himfelf been guilty of two miftakes; for firft, it is not in his notes on Nicomachus, but in thofe on Gaudentius that Meibomius mentions the error now under confideration: and farther, in the paffage of Meibomius, which Malcolm meant to refer to, the difcovery is not af-cribed to Vincentio Galilei, but to Galileo Galilei his fon.   To take the whole together, Gaudentius, fpeaking of the experiment of Pythagoras, and afferting, that if two equal chords be diftended by weights in the fame proportion to each other as the terms of the ratio, containing any interval, thofe chords when ftruck will give that interval.   Meibomius upon this paffage remarks in the following words: ' Mirandum fane, hanc experientiam, tot graviffimorum aucto-

' rum

' ruin adfertione confirmatam, noftro primum feculo deprehenfam
' effe falfam. Inventionis gloriam debemus nobiliffimo mathematico
' Galileo Galilei, quem vide pag. 100. Tractatus qui infcribitur: Dif-
' corfi e Dimoftrazioni Matematiche intorno à due nuove Scienze *'.

But notwithftanding Bontempi has given from the elder Galilei a
paffage which feems to lead to a difcovery of the error of Pythagoras,
yet he himfelf acquiefces in the opinion of Meibomius, that the
honour of a formal refutation of it is due to the younger, and is contained in the paffage above referred to, which tranflated is as follows.

' I ftood a long time in doubt concerning the forms of confonance,
' not thinking the reafons commonly brought by the learned authors
' who have hitherto wrote of mufic fufficiently demouftrative. They
' tell us that the diapafon, that is the octave, is contained by the
' double; and that the diapente, which we call the fifth, is contained by
' the fefquialter: for if a ftring, ftretched upon the monochord, be
' founded open, and afterwards placing a bridge under the midft of
' it, its half only be founded, you will hear an eighth ; and if the
' bridge be placed under one third of the ftring, and you then ftrike
' the two thirds open, it will found a fifth to that of the whole ftring
' ftruck when open ; whereupon they infer that the eighth is con-
' tained between two and one, and the fifth between three and two.
' But I do not think we can conclude from hence that the double
' and fefquialteral can naturally affign the forms of the diapafon and
' diapente ; and my reafon for it is this : there are three ways by
' which we may fharpen the tone of a ftring, viz. by fhortening it,
' by ftretching it, or by making it thinner : if now, retaining the
' fame tenfion and thicknefs, we would hear an eighth, we muft
' make it fhorter by half; i. e. we muft firft found the whole ftring,
' and then its half. But if, keeping the fame length and thicknefs,
' we would have it rife to an eighth from its prefent tone, by ftretch-
' ing it, or fcrewing it higher, it is not fufficient to ftretch it with a
' double, but with four times the force: thus, if at firft it was dif-
' tended by a weight, fuppofe of one pound, we muft hang a four-
' pound weight to it, in order to raife its tone to an eighth. And
' laftly, if, keeping the fame length and tenfion, we would have a
' ftring to found an eighth, this ftring muft be but one fourth of the
' thick-

* Meibom. Not. in Gaudent. pag. 37.

' thickneſs of that which it muſt ſound an eighth to *. And this
' that I ſay of the eighth, I would have underſtood of all other muſi-
' cal intervals. To give an inſtance of the fifth, if we would pro-
' duce it by tenſion, and in order thereto hang to the grave ſtring a
' four-pound weight ; we muſt hang to the acute, not one of ſix,
' which yet is in ſeſquialtera proportion to four, viz. three to two,
' but one of nine pounds. And to produce the above intervals by
' ſtrings of the ſame length, but different thickneſs, the proportion
' between the grave and the acute ſtring muſt be that of nine to four.
' Theſe things being really ſo in fact, I ſaw no reaſon why theſe ſage
' philoſophers ſhould rather conſtitute the form of the eighth double
' than quadruple, and that of the fifth rather in ſeſquialtera than in
' double ſeſquiquarta, &c.' † Diſcorſi e Dimoſtrazioni Matematiche
del Galileo Galilei, pag. 75.

To give yet farther weight to the above objection, it may be neceſſary here briefly to explain a doctrine yet unknown to the ancients,
viz. that of pendulums, between the vibrations whereof, and thoſe
of muſical chords, there is an exact coincidence.

* Iſaac Voſſius ſays that in this paſſage the author has erred, and with his uſual temerity
aſſerts, that, cæteris paribus, the thicker the chord, the acuter the ſound. De Poemat.
Cant. et Viribus Rythmi, pag. 113. And this, even though he confeſſes that both Des
Cartes and Merſennus were of opinion with Galilei in this reſpect. The only appeal in
ſuch a caſe as this muſt be to experiment, and whoever will make one for the purpoſe will
find the converſe of this propoſition to be true, and that, as Galilei has ſaid, chords comparatively thin render acute, and not grave ſounds.
† The reaſon of theſe ſage philoſophers for doing thus, notwithſtanding that Galilei
could not diſcover it, ſeems to be very obvious: they conſtituted the form of the eighth
double becauſe they found it to ariſe from the diviſion of a chord into two equal parts; and
the fifth they found to ariſe from the diviſion of a chord into five parts, three whereof
ſtruck againſt the remaining two produced that interval: therefore they aſſigned to it the
ſeſquialtera proportion, 3 to 2. And certainly there needs no better reaſon for the
Pythagorean conſtitution of the conſonances, than that it is founded in the actual diviſion
of a chord; and had the followers of Pythagoras reſted the matter there, their tenets would
have eſcaped reprehenſion.
But they ſay of him that he produced the conſonances by chords of equal length and
thickneſs, diſtended by weights of ſix, eight, nine, and twelve pounds: Galilei has ſhewn
that this could not be; and from the principles laid down by writers ſince his time, as alſo
by experiments, it moſt evidently appears, that to produce the conſonances, from chords
thus conditioned, weights muſt be uſed of a very different proportion from thoſe ſaid to
have been taken by Pythagoras.
As to the proportions, there can be no doubt but that they are as above-ſtated; but the
error chargeable on the Pythagoreans is the making the diſcovery of them the reſult of an
experiment, which muſt have produced, inſtead of conſonances, diſſonances of the moſt
offenſive kind.

Sound is produced by the tremulation of the air, excited by the infenfible vibrations of fome elaftic, fonorous body; and it has been
manifefted by repeated experiments, that of mufical founds the acute
are produced by fwift, and the grave by comparatively flow vibrations [*]. A chord diftended by a weight or otherwife, is, with refpect to the vibrations made between its two extremities, to be confidered as a double pendulum [†], and as fubject to the fame laws.

The proportions between the lengths of pendulums, and the number of vibrations made by them, are in an inverfe duplicate ratio;
fo that if the length be quadrupled, the vibrations will be fubdupled;
on the contrary, if the length be fubquadrupled, the vibrations will
be dupled [‡].

The fame proportions hold alfo with refpect to a chord, but with
this difference, that in the cafe of pendulums the ratios are inverfe,
the greater length giving the fewer vibrations; whereas in that of
chords they are direct, the greater tenfion giving the greater number
of vibrations: thus if the tenfive power be as one, if that be quadrupled, the number of vibrations. is dupled; and the found produced by the greater power will be duple in acumen to that produced by the leffer. In a word, the fame ratios that fubfift between
the vibrations of pendulums and their refpective lengths, are to be
found inverfely between the vibrations of chords and the powers that
diftend them: what thofe ratios are, fo far as they refpect the acutenefs or gravity of found, will fhortly be made appear.

In order to apply the doctrine of tenfive powers to the queftion in
debate, it is neceffary to ftate the ratios of the feveral confonances,
and thofe are demonftrated to be as follows, viz. that of the diapente 3 to 2, and of the diateffaron 4 to 3, that of the diapafon 2 to 1, and that of the tone 9 to 8; or in other words,
a chord being divided into five parts, the found produced at three
of thefe parts will be a diapente to that produced at two; if
divided into feven parts, four of them will found a diateffaron againft
the remaining three; and if divided into three parts, two of them

[*] Treatife on the natural Grounds and Principles of Harmony, by William Holder.
Paffim.
[†] Ibid. xi. 43.
[‡] Ibid. 16.

make

make a diapason againſt the other one: farther, if the chord be divided into ſeventeen parts, nine of them on one ſide will ſound a ſeſquioctave tone to the eight remaining on the other. Theſe are principles in harmonics which we may ſafely aſſume, and the demonſtrations may be ſeen in Ptolemy's deſcription of the nature and uſe of the Harmonic Canon *.

It is equally certain, and is deducible from the doctrine of pendulums, that if two chords, of equal lengths, A D be ſo diſtended as that their vibrations ſhall be as three to two, that is, that A ſhall make three vibrations while B is making two, the conſonance produced by ſtriking them together will be a diapente.

If the vibrations be as four to three, the conſonance will be a diateſſaron.

If the vibrations be as two to one, the conſonance will be a diapaſon; and laſtly,

If the vibrations be as nine to eight, the interval will be a ſeſquioctave tone.

We are now to enquire what are the degrees of tenſive power requiſite to produce the vibrations above-mentioned; and here we muſt recur to the principle above laid down, that the ſquares of the vibrations of equal chords are to each other as their reſpective tenſions: if then we ſuppoſe a given ſound to be the effect of a tenſion by a weight of ſix pounds, and would know the weight neceſſary to produce the diapente, which has a ratio to its uniſon of 3 to 2, we muſt take the ſquare of thoſe numbers 9 to 4, and ſeek a number that bears the ſame ratio to ſix, as nine does to four, and this can be no whole number, but is thirteen and a half.

By the ſame rule we adjuſt the weight for the diateſſaron, 4 to 3, which numbers ſquared are ſixteen and nine, and as 16 is to 9, ſo is 10⅔ to 6.

For the diapaſon 2 to 1, which numbers ſquared are 4 to 1, the weight muſt be twenty-four; for as 4 is to 1, ſo is 24 to 6.

* Merſennus recommends for the purpoſe of making theſe experiments, the uſe of two chords rather than one, for this reaſon, that where one only is taken, only one ſound can be heard at a time; whereas when two are uſed, both ſounds are heard at the ſame inſtant, and thereby the conſonance is perceived. Harmonic univerſelle, Traité des Inſtrumens, Prop. v.

The

The several weights above adjusted, have a reference to the unison expressed in the scheme of Pythagoras, by the number six, supposed to result from a tension of six pounds. But the sesquioctave tone, as it is the difference between the diapente and diatessaron, takes its ratio from the sound expressed by the number eight, as the diapente does from that expressed by nine, in order then to adjust the weight for this interval, we must square those numbers; and as 81 is to 64, so is 13½ to 10⅔.

Whoever is disposed to prove the truth of these positions, and doubts the certainty of numerical calculation, may have recourse to experiment; in which however this caution is to be observed, that in the making it the utmost degree of accuracy is necessary; for it should seem that one of the authors above-cited failed in an attempt of this sort, which is not to be wondered at, if we consider the nature of the subject.

The author here meant is Bontempi; who, after citing the authority of Vincentio and Galileo Galilei, adds, that, ' prompted by cu-
' riosity, he made an experiment by hanging weights to strings of
' equal lengths and thickness, the result whereof was, that the
' first and second strings, having weights of 12 and 9, produced
' not the diatessaron, but the trihemitone; the first and third 12,
' 8, not the diapente but the ditone; the first and fourth, 12,
' 6, not the diapason but the tritone; the second and the third, 9,
' 8, not the tone, but the defective or incomplete hemitone; the
' second and fourth, 9, 6, not the diapente, but the semidi-
' tone; and the third and fourth 8, 6, not the diatessaron, but the
' distended or excessive tone, as the following figure demonstrates *.

* Egli è cosa da restar confuso, e formare un cumulo di maraviglie, che questo sperimento, confermato da gravissimi autori, e tenuto tanti secoli per vero sia stato finalmente
scoperto esser falso da Galileo Galilei, siccome riferisce ne' suoi Discorsi e Dimostrazioni
Mathematiche, e Vincenzo Galilei nel discorso intorno all' opere del Zarlino afferma,
che per ritrovare co' pesi attaccati alle corde le consonanze de Martelli; per la diapason
debbono costituirsi i pesi in quadrupla proportione; per la diapente, in dupla sesquiquarta;
per la diatessaron, in sesqui 7 partiente 9; e pel tuono, in sesqui 7 partiente 64. E noi,
spinti dalla curiosità messo in opera questo sperimento co' pesi de Martelli, habbiamo ritrovato
che il primo et il secondo 12, 9, partorisono non la diatessaron: ma il trihemituono; il
primo ed il terzo 12, 8, non la diapente: ma il ditono; il primo e'l quarto 12, 6, non la
diapason; ma il tritono; il secondo e'l terzo 9, 8, non il tuono: ma l'hemituono rimesso
o mancante; il secondo e'l quarto 9, 6, non la diapente: ma il semidituono; ed il terzo
e'l quarto 8, 6, non la diatessaron: ma il tuono disteso overo eccedente, siccome la sotto-
posta figura dimostra. Bontempi, pa. 54.

F 2 Ptolemy

TRITONE.

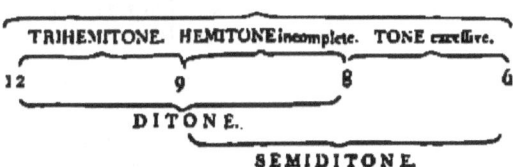

But that the proportions of a diateſſaron tone and diateſſaron would reſult from an experiment made by ſtrings of the ſeveral lengths of twelve, nine, eight, ſix; or rather by a diviſion of the monochord, according to that rule, is demonſtrable. This invention of Pythagoras, as it regarded only the proportions or ratios of ſounds, was applicable to no one ſyſtem in particular; however it produced a diſcovery, which enabled him at once to ſupply a defect in even the improved ſyſtem of Terpander, and lay a foundation for that more enlarged one, which is diſtinguiſhed by his name, and has never ſince his time been capable of any ſubſtantial improvement. We are here to remember that the diapaſon or octave had been found to conſiſt in duple proportion, or in the ratio of 12 to 6; and that the interval between the diateſſaron twelve, nine, and that other eight, ſix, viz. nine, eight, was a complete tone, or ſeſquioctave ratio. Pythagoras, in conſequence of this diſcovery recurring to the antient ſeptenary, found that its extremes were diſcordant, and that there wanted but little to produce that ſupremely ſweet concord the diapaſon, which the means above had enabled him to inveſtigate. Obſerving farther that in the ſeptenary the interval between Meſe and Parameſe was but a hemitone, he immediately interpoſed between them a whole tone, and thereby completed the diapaſon.

Ptolemy obſerves, that it is extremely difficult to find chords perfectly equal in reſpect of craſſitude, denſity, and other qualities that determine their ſeveral ſounds; and farther he ſays, that the ſame chord diſtended by the ſame weight, will at different times yield different ſounds. Ptolem. Harmonicor. lib. I. cap. 8. Ex verſ. Wallis. Merſenn. Harm. univerſelle, Traite des Inſtrumens, Prop. iv. So that the ſucceſs of experiments for inveſtigating the conſonances, by the means of weights hung to chords, muſt be very precarious, and is little to be depended on.

It

It muſt be confeſſed that ſome authors have in general terms
aſcribed the addition of an eighth ſtring to the heptachord lyre to
others; Boetius gives it to Licaon, and Pliny to Simonides; but
Nicomachus, from whom the following relation is taken, does moſt
expreſsly attribute it to Pythagoras.

Hiſtory has alſo tranſmitted to us the bare names of ſundry perſons, by whom at different times the ſtrings of the lyre are ſaid to
have been encreaſed to eighteen in number; as Theophraſtus, who
added a ninth; Heſtius, who added a tenth, and ſo on *; but as to
the ratio ſubſiſting between them, or any ſyſtem to which they could
be ſaid to be adapted, there is a total ſilence.   Indeed we have the
greateſt reaſon to think that theſe additions were not made in any
ratio whatever, but ſerved only to increaſe the variety of ſounds ‡.
That innovations were made in the heptachord is certain; and when
we are informed that Timotheus, for his preſumption in adding to
the ſtrings of the ancient lyre, had a fine impoſed on him by the
magiſtracy, we may fairly conclude that thoſe innovations tended
rather to the corruption than the improvement of muſic.

But the caſe is different with reſpect to him of whom we are now
ſpeaking; the ſyſtem of Pythagoras had its foundation in nature : the
improvement of an inſtrument was not his care; he was a philoſopher and a muſician in the genuine ſenſe of the word, and propoſed
nothing leſs than the eſtabliſhment of a theory to which the practice
of ſucceeding ages ſhould be accommodated.   His motives for attempting it, and in what manner he effected this great purpoſe, ſhall
now be given in the words of his learned biographer.

‘ Pythagoras, left the middle ſound by conjunction being com-
‘ pared to the two extremes, ſhould render the diateſſaron concent
‘ both to the Nete and the Hypate; and that we might have a greater
‘ variety, the two extremes making the fulleſt concord each to other,
‘ that is to ſay, a diapaſon, which conſiſts in duple proportion, in-
‘ ſerted an eighth ſound between the Meſe and the Parameſe, pla-
‘ cing it from the Meſe a whole tone, and from the Parameſe a ſemi-
‘ tone; ſo that what was formerly the Parameſe in the heptachord,

* Boetius de Muſica, lib. ii. cap. 20. Vincen. Galilei, Dial. della Muſica, pag. 116.
‡ Nicom. lib. ii. Boet. lib. i. cap. 20. Kunt. pag. 71.

‘ is

' is still the third from the Nete, both in name and place; but that
' now inserted is the fourth from the Nete, and hath a concent to it
' of diatessaron, which before the Mese had to the Hypate: but the
' tone between them, that is the Mese, and the tone inserted, called
' the Paramese, instead of the former, to whichsoever tetrachord it
' be added, whether to that which is at the Hypate, being the
' lower, or to that of the Nete, being the higher, will render the
' concord of diapente; which is either way a system, consisting both of
' the tetrachord itself, and of the additional tone: And as the diapente
' proportion, viz. sesquialtera, is found to be a system of sesquitertia
' and sesquioctava, the tone therefore is sesquioctava. Thus the in-
' terval of four chords, and of five, and of both conjoined together,
' called diapason, with the tone inserted between the two tetra-
' chords, completed the octochord *."

* Stanl. Hist. of Philosophy, pag. 386, from Nicom. lib. i.

SYSTEM

SYSTEM of PYTHAGORAS.

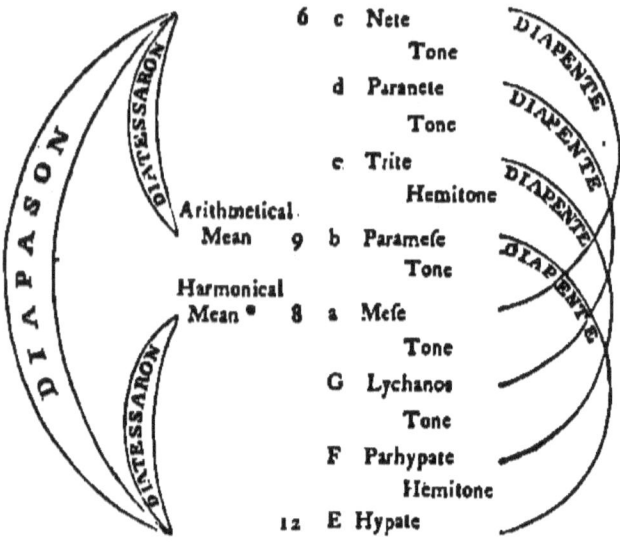

It remains now to enquire what this variation of and addition to the septenary led to. Pythagoras immediately after he had adjusted his system of the octochord in the manner above related, transferred to it the additions which had been made to that of Terpander; and first he connected with it the tetrachord hypaton, which carried the system down to B, and placing at the other extremity the hyperboleon tetrachord, he continued it up to a a, as here is shewn.

* The difference between the arithmetical and harmonical division of the diapason is explained in a subsequent chapter. But as this division is frequently occurring, it may not be improper here to remark in general that the numbers 9, 6, 12, express the arithmetical, and 12, 8, 6, the harmonical division.

GREAT

GREAT SYSTEM of PYTHAGORAS.

Nete hyperboleon		aa
	Tone	
Paranete hyperboleon		g
	Tone	
Trite hyperboleon		f
	Hemit.	
Nete diezeugmenon		e
	Tone	
Paranete diezeugmenon		d
	Tone	
Trite diezeugmenon		e
	Hemit.	
Paramese		♮
	Tone	
Mese		a
	Tone	
Lychanos meson		G
	Tone	
Parhypate meson		F
	Hemit.	
Hypate meson		E
	Tone	
Lychanos hypaton		D
	Tone	
Parhypate hypaton		C
	Hemit.	
Hypate hypaton		♮

In confequence of the feparation in the fyftem of the octochord above noted, we fee that in the above diagram the tetrachord B is feparated from the tetrachord A by a whole tone : this difunion of the one diateffaron from the other, gave rife to the epithet of Diezeug-menon or disjunct, whereby the former of the two tetrachords is diftinguifhed : we are therefore now to look for the invention of that other tetrachord, which hitherto has been reprefented as part of a fyftem, to which it could never with any propriety be applied.

No

No one in the least acquainted with the principles of harmony need be told, that that relation which modern muficians denominate a Tritonus, can have no place in any regular feries of progreffion, either afcending or defcending ; for of the effects of founds produced at the fame inftant we are not now fpeaking : that fuch a relation immediately arofe from the feparation of the Diezeugmenon and Mefon tetrachords, will appear by obferving that in the progreffion upwards through the Mefon tetrachord, beginning at Parhypate Mefon, and proceeding to Paramefe, that interval which fhould be a diateffaron, and confift of two tones and a hemitone, will contain three tones, and have for its ultimate found what in this place is to be confidered as an exceffive fourth *. The confequence of this was, that the lower found could never be ufed as a fundamental ; and fo far the fyftem muft be faid to have been imperfect. To remedy this defect in part, collateral or auxiliary tetrachord was with great ingenuity conftituted, in which the founds followed in the order of hemitone, tone, and tone, a fucceffion which a true and perfect diateffaron requires.

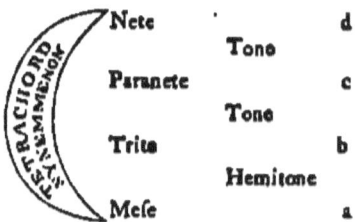

Nete		d
	Tone	
Paranete		c
	Tone	
Trite		b
	Hemitone	
Mefe		a

The intervals that compofe this fyftem will appear upon comparifon to be precifely the fame with thofe of the tetrachord B, in the conjunct fyftem ; whereas between the tetrachord B, in the disjunct fyftem, and that at prefent under confideration, this difference is apparent ; in the former the diftance between a and b is a whole tone, in the latter it is a hemitone : if therefore this queftion fhould be afked, Wherein did the merit of the improvements made by Py-

* Some writers have given the name of Tritonus to the defective fifth, ♭ f, for this reafon, that it is an interval compounded of hemitone, tone, tone, and hemitone, the fum whereof is three tones. But in this they are miftaken, for the ratio of the tritonus or exceffive fourth, and the femidiapente or defective fifth are different, the one being 45 to 32, the other 64 to 45. Vide Merfennus Harmonic, De Diffonantiis, pag. 75. Holder on the natural Grounds and Principles of Harmony, pag. 128.

thagoras to the ancient fyftem confift? the anfwer would be, firft, in the invention of the disjunct fyftém, and the confequent completion of the octochord; next in the introduction of the octochord into the fyftem of Terpander; and laftly, in fuch a difpofition of the disjunct tetrachord as was yet confiftent with the re-admiffion of that part of the fyftem which it feems to exclude whenever the perfection of the harmony fhould require it. After what has been faid it will be need-lefs to add that this collateral tetrachord was diftinguifhed by the epithet of Synemmenon or conjunct. With thefe improvements the, Pythagorean fyftem affumed the following form.

ADDITION to the Great Syftem of PYTHAGORAS,.

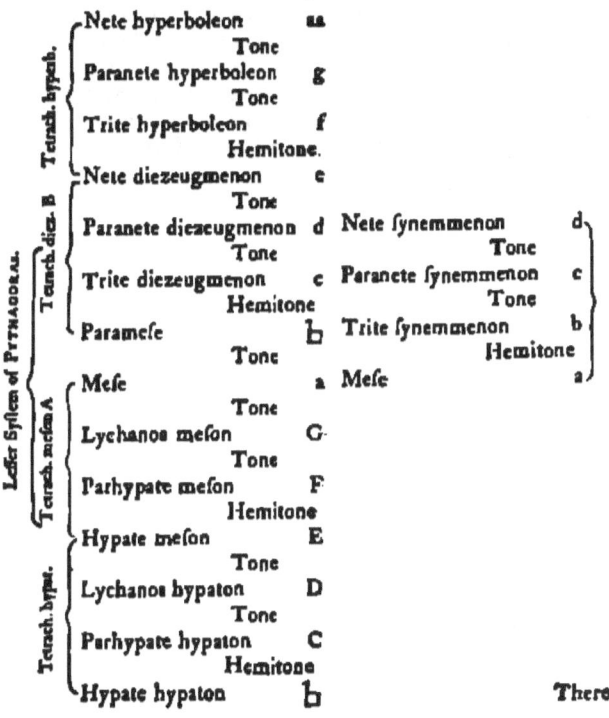

There

There were two reafons that feemed to fuggeft a ftill farther improvement; the one was that by the feparation of the Diezeugmenon and Mefon tetrachords there followed an unequal divifion of the
fyftem; for, afcending from Mefe to Nete Hyperboleon, the diftance
was a complete Octave; whereas defcending to Hypate Hypaton it
was only a Seventh: from hence arofe another inconvenience, a falfe
relation between Hypate Hypaton and Parhypate Mefon, which
though to appearance a fifth, was in truth an interval of only two tones
and two hemitones, conftituting together the very difcordant relation
of a defective fifth. To fupply this defect nothing more was required
than the addition of a tone at the lower extremity of the fyftem:
Pythagoras accordingly placed another chord at the diftance of a tone
below Hypate Hypaton, which he named Proflambanomenos, a
word fignifying additional or fupernumerary, it not being includable
in the divifion of the fyftem by tetrachords; and thus was completed
that fyftem of a Bifdiapafon or double octave, which the Italians diftinguifh by the feveral appellations of Syftema immutabile, Syftema
diatonico, Syftema Pitagorico, and Syftema maffimo.

IMMUTABLE Syſtem of PYTHAGORAS.

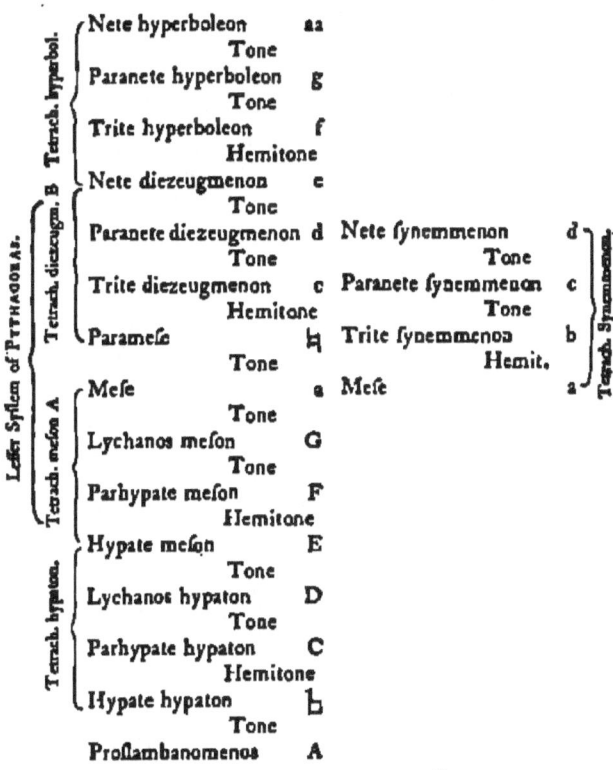

Nete hyperboleon	aa	
Tone		
Paranete hyperboleon	g	
Tone		
Trite hyperboleon	f	
Hemitone		
Nete diezeugmenon	e	
Tone		
Paranete diezeugmenon	d	Nete ſynemmenon d
Tone		Tone
Trite diezeugmenon	c	Paranete ſynemmenon c
Hemitone		Tone
Parameſe	♮	Trite ſynemmenon b
Tone		Hemit.
Meſe	a	Meſe a
Tone		
Lychanos meſon	G	
Tone		
Parhypate meſon	F	
Hemitone		
Hypate meſon	E	
Tone		
Lychanos hypaton	D	
Tone		
Parhypate hypaton	C	
Hemitone		
Hypate hypaton	♭	
Tone		
Proſlambanomenos	A	

Here it is to be obſerved, that although in this and the preceeding
ſcale the Synemmenon tetrachord is given at large, yet the generality of writers either inſert it entire in its place, immediately above
the Meſon tetrachord, placing the Diezeugmenon tetrachord above
it, as Kircher in his Muſurgia, tom. I. lib. III. cap. xiii. or elſe,
                         follow-

following perhaps the example of Guido, whose reformation of the scale might suggest this latter method as the most concise, they have borrowed from the Synemmenon tetrachord one only of its terms, Trite, and inserted it immediately after Mese, with Paramese next above it; thereby leaving it to the imagination to select which of the two sounds the nature of the progression might require; however, the better to explain its construction and use, it was here thought proper to exhibit the Synemmenon tetrachord in that detached situation which seems most agreeable to its original formation *.

C H A P.   IV.

BUT here it may very naturally be asked what were the marks or characters whereby the ancients expressed the different positions or powers of their musical sounds? An answer to this question may be produced from an author of undoubted credit, Boetius, and also Alypius, an ancient Greek, of whose writings we shall have occasion to speak more particularly, and these inform us that the only characters in use among the Greeks to denote the sounds in music, were the letters of their alphabet, a kind of Brachygraphy totally devoid of analogy or resemblance between the sign and the thing signified. Boetius de Musica, lib. IV. cap. iii. gives an account of the ancient method of notation in the following words. ' The ancient musicians, to avoid the necessity of always ' writing them at length, invented certain characters to express the ' names of the chords in their several genera and modes; this short ' method was the more eagerly embraced, that in case a musician ' should be inclined to adapt music to any poem, he might, by means ' of these characters, in the same manner as the words of the poem ' were expressed by letters, express the music, and transmit it to ' posterity. Out of all these modes we shall only specify the Lydian.' This description of the sounds consisted in the different application of the Greek letters to each of them; Boetius proceeds thus: ' To ex- ' press Proslambanomenos, which may be called Acquisitus, was used

* Merſenn. Harmon. lib. vi. De Generibus et Modis, pag. 100.

' Z im-

' z imperfect, and tau lying ⊣· Hypate hypaton, Γ reverſed and Γ right
' Π. Parhypate hypaton, в imperfect Γ ſupine, ⸢B⸣ Hypaton enarmo-
' nios, V ſupine and Γ reverſed, having a ſtroke ∮ Hypaton chromatice,
' v, having a line and Γ reverſed, having two lines ⸢V⸣ Hypaton dia-
' tonos, φ Greek, and digamma ⸢φ⸣. Hypate meſon C and C, ⸢C⸣. Par-
' hypate meſon P and C ſupine ⸢P⸣· Meſon enarmonios, Π Greek and C
' reverſed ⸢Π⸣· Meſon chromatice, Π having a ſtroke, and C reverſed,
' having a ſtroke through the middle ᓫ. Meſon diatonos, M Greek
' and Π drawn open ⸢M⸣. Meſe, I and Λ lying ⸢I⸣. Trite ſynemmenon,
' Θ and Λ ſupine ⸢Θ⸣. Synemmenon enarmonios, H Greek and Λ lying,
' with a ſtroke through the middle, ⸢≤⸣· Synemmenon chromatice, H
' Greek and Λ reverſed with a ſtroke ⸢Λ⸣. Synemmenon diatonos, Γ
' and N ⸢N⸣. Nete ſynemmenon, Ω ſupine and z, ⸢z⸣· Parameſe, Z and
' Γ Greek lying ⸢Γ⸣. Trite diezeugmenon, Σ ſquare and Γ ſupine ⸢Σ⸣
' Diezeugmenon enarmonios, Δ and Γ Greek lying reverſed ⸢Δ⸣. Die-
' zeugmenon chromatice, Δ with a ſtroke, and Π Greek lying reverſed
' with an angular line ⸢Δ⸣. Diezeugmenon diatonos, Ω ſquare and z, ⸢z⸣
' Nete diezeugmenon, φ lying and N inverted drawn open ⸢φ⸣. Trite
' hyperboleon, Γ looking downwards to the right, and half Λ to the
' left ⸢L⸣. Hyperboleon enarmonios, T ſupine and half A to the right
' ſupine, ⸢T⸣. Hyperboleon chromatice, T ſupine, having a line and
' half A to the right ſupine, having a line drawn backward ⸢Z⸣. Hy-
' perboleon, diatonos M Greek having an acute, and Γ having an acute
' ⸢M⸣. Nete hyperboleon, I having an acute, and Λ lying, having an
' acute alſo ⸢Γ⸣.

* Boetius as he goes along gives the Latin ſignification of the Greek names, which it
was thought proper to omit in order to make room for an extract from Kircher to the ſame
purpose.

Here it is to be remarked, that although the above passage of Boetius is given, not from any of the printed copies of his works, but from a very ancient manuscript, which Mr. Selden collated, and is prefixed to Meibomius's version of Alypius : there occur in it some instances of disagreement between the verbal description of the character and the character itself; some of these Meibomius in his notes has remarked, and others have escaped him; nevertheless it was not thought adviseable to vary the representation which Boetius has given, and therefore the following scheme of the ancient musical characters is inserted, as he has delivered it in lib. IV. cap. iii. of his book De Musica.

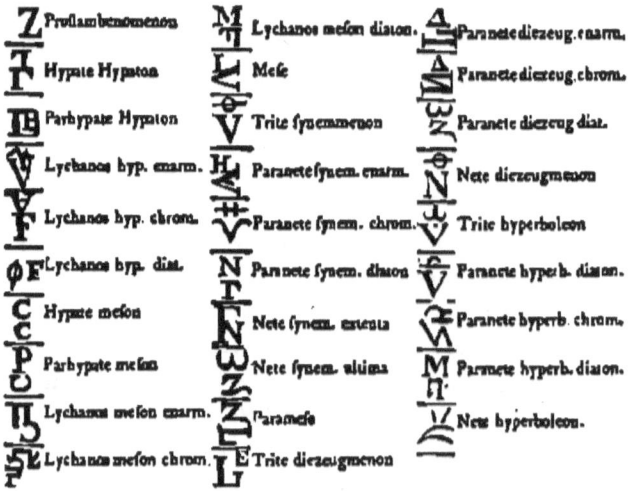

There is this remarkable difference between the method of notation practised by the ancients, and that now in use, that the charac-

purpose, wherein the Latin are opposed to the Greek names in the order in which they arise in the several tetrachords.

Tetrachordon Neton	aa	Nete hyperboleon, five ultima acutarum.
	g	Paranete hyperboleon, five secunda acutarum.
	f	Trite hyperboleon five, tertia acutarum.

c

ters used by the former were arbitrary, totally destitute of analogy, and no way expressive of those essential properties of sound, gravity and acuteness; which is the more to be wondered at, seeing that in the writings of the ancients the terms Acumen and Gravitas are perpetually occuring, whereas the modern scale is so adjusted, that those sounds, which in their own nature are comparatively grave or acute, have such a situation in it, as does most precisely distinguish them according to their several degrees of each; so that the graver sounds have the lowest, and the acuter the highest place in our scale. But here it may be asked, does this distinction of high and low properly belong to sound, or do we not borrow those epithets from the scale in which we see them so posited? It should seem that we do not; for if we attend to the formation of sounds by the animal organs, we shall find that the more grave are produced from the lower part of the larynx, as the more acute are from the higher; so that the difference between the one and the other seems to be more than ideal, and to have its foundation in nature: the modern musicians seem however to pay a greater regard to this diversity than is either requisite or proper; for where is the necessity that in a vocal composition such a sentiment as this ' They that go down to the sea in ships,' &c. should be expressed by such sounds, as for the degree of gravity few voices can reach? much less can we see the reasonableness of that precept which directs that the words Hell, Heaven, are invariably to be expressed, the one by a very grave, and the other by a very acute sound. Those who affect to be severely critical on the compositions of this la-

Tetrachordon Diezeugm.	a	Nete, sive ultima disjunctarum.
	d	Paranete diezeugmenon, sive secunda disjunctarum.
	c	Trite diezeugmenon, sive tertia disjunctarum.
Tetrachordon Synemmen.	b	Paranete, sive vicina mediis.
	d	Nete synemmenon, sive ultima conjunctarum.
	c	Paranete synemmenon, sive secunda conjunctarum.
	b	Trite synemmenon, sive tertia conjunctarum.
Tetrachordon Mefon.	a	Mese, id est media.
	G	Lychanos mefon, sive index mediarum.
	F	Parhypate mefon, sive secunda mediarum.
Tetrachordon Hypaton	E	Hypate mefon, sive gravis mediarum.
	D	Lychanos hypaton, sive index gravium.
	C	Parhypate hypaton, sive secunda gravium.
	B	Hypate hypaton, sive gravia gravium.
	A	Proslambanomenos, sive vox assumpta.

ter age, allow no greater merit to this fort of analogy than is due to a
pun, and their cenfure feems to be no more than the error will warrant.
The defcription above given of the ancient mufical characters,
is derived, through Boetius, from Alypius, the moft copious
and intelligible of all the Greek writers on this branch of mufic:
his authority, fo far as it goes, has been implicitly acquiefced
in ; and indeed from his teftimony there can lye no appeal.
The reader will naturally expect to be informed of the method by
which the ancients denoted the different degrees in the length or
duration of their mufical founds; but it feems they were ftrangers to
mufic merely inftrumental : the lyre, and other inftruments in ufe
among them, was applied in aid of the voice ; and the ode, or
hymn, or pean, or whatever elfe the mufician fung, determined by
its meafure, and the feet of the verfe the length of the founds adapted to it, and took away the neceffity for fuch marks or characters of
diftinction in this refpect as are ufed by the moderns.   Nor need we
any farther proof of this affertion, than the abfolute filence of the
Greek writers as to any method of denoting what we now underftand by the Time or meafure of founds.   It is true that thofe among
the learned who have undertaken a tranflation of fome few remaining fragments of ancient mufic into modern notes, have, in particular inftances, ventured to render the characters in the original by
notes of different lengths ; but it is to be prefumed they were determined fo to do rather by the cadence of the verfe, than by any ryth-
mical defignation obfervable in any of thofe characters.   Mr. Chilmead, the publifher of the Oxford edition of Aratus, and of Eratofthenes de Aftris, in octavo, 1672, has given at the end of it three
hymns or odes of a Greek poet named Dionyfius, with the ancient
mufical characters, which he has rendered by breves only; but
Kircher, in his Mufurgia, tom. I. pag. 541, from a manufcript in
the library of the monaftery of St. Salvator, near the gate of Meffana
in Sicily, has inferted an ancient fragment of Pindar, with the mufical notes, which he has explained by the different figns of a breve,
femibreve, crotchet, and quaver, as underftood by us moderns.
Meibomius alfo has given from an ancient manufcript a Te Deum,
with the Greek characters, and in modern notes, the former of
which appear to be more fimple and lefs combined than thofe defcribed by Boetius ; which is the lefs to be wondered at confidering

that St. Ambrofe, who is faid to have been the author of that hymn*, was confecrated bifhop of Milan, A. C. 374, and Bootius flourifhed not till about the year 500; fo that there is a period of more than one hundred years, during which every kind of literature fuffered from the rage of conquefl that prevailed throughout all Europe, to induce a fufpicion that the Greek characters were not tranfmitted down to the time of Boetius uncorrupted. In the tranflation of thefe mufical characters of the above-mentioned Te Deum, Meibomius has made ufe of the breve, the femibreve, and minim: upon what authority thofe feveral modes of tranflation is founded we do not pretend to determine; it feems that nothing is wanting to enable us to judge with certainty in this matter but a perfect knowledge of the powers of the ancient characters, with refpect to the founds which they were intended to fignify; and concerning thefe Kircher feems to have entertained no kind of doubt: he had accefs to two manu-fcripts of great antiquity, and his judgment of their authority, and the ufe that may be made of them he has given in the following words:

' The ancient mufical characters were no way fimilar to thofe of the
' moderns; for they were certain letters, not indeed the pure Greek
' ones, but thofe fometimes right, fometimes inverted, and at others
' mutilated and compounded in various manners, each of which cha-
' racters anfwered to one of the chords in the mufical fyflem. I
' laid my hands on two manufcripts, which by God's mercy, were
' preferved from the injuries of time, the one in the Vatican library,
' the other in ours of the Roman college: the author is Alypius; he,
' in order to give the harmonical characters of the ancients in great
' perfection, has exhibited with wonderful care every tone in the
' Octodecachord, according to the different genera. He keeps a
' twofold order in thefe feveral characters; the firft as they were
' ufed in the Cantus; the fecond as adapted to inftruments, differing
' from the former almoft after the fame manner as at this day the
' notes of vocal mufic do from thofe characters called by us the Tab-
' lature, which are ufed only in inftrumental mufic. Several writers,

* The Te Deum is commonly filled the Song of St. Ambrofe, and it is faid that it was compofed jointly by him and St. Auguftine, upon occafion of the baptifm of the latter by St. Ambrofe Alliance of Divine Offices, by Hamon L'Eftrange, folio, 1690, pag. 79. But archbifhop Ufher afcribes it to Nicetius, and fuppofes it not to have been compofed till about the year 500, which was long after the time of Ambrofe and Auguf-tine. Ibid.

' not underſtanding this order of Alypius, have conſidered this two-
' fold ſeries as a ſingle one : among theſe are Liardus, and Solomon
' de Caux, who has followed him, both of whom have given to the
' world moſt falſe and corrupted ſpecimens of antient muſic. Aly-
' pius wrote an entire volume on the muſical characters or notes,
' which, together with other manuſcripts of the old Greek muſicians,
' remain preſerved in the library of the Roman college : a tranſlation
' of this volume into the Latin language, I will, with the permiſſion
' of God, at a convenient opportunity give to the learned world ; in
' the interim I truſt I ſhall do a favour to poſterity by exhibiting a
' ſpecimen of the characters in the order in which they lie in the
' manuſcript, correcting from the interpretations thereto annexed
' ſuch errors as I found required it *.'

The ſpecimen, the whole of which ſeems by his account to be
taken from Alypius, contains the characters through all the fifteen
tones in the diatonic and chromatic genera in two ſeparate tables, and
is as follows.

* It ſeems by this that Alypius had not been publiſhed in Kircher's time ; and though
he here promiſes to give the world a tranſlation of it, there is no other extant than that
very correct one of Meibomius Kircher expreſſes a confidence that by publiſhing theſe
characters he ſhould confer an obligation on the learned world, but the manner in which
he has done it furniſhed a ground of cenſure to Meibomius, which he delivers in very
bitter terms in the preface to his edition of the Greek writers.

Nomina et Charactères musici veterum iuxta Diatonum Genus	Charact. Toni Lydij		Charact. Toni Hyperlydij		Charact. Toni Hyperlydij		Charact. Toni Eolij		Charact. Toni Ionici		Charact. Toni Ionici		Charact. Toni Hypoæol.		Charact. Toni Phrygij		Charact. Toni Hypophrygij		Charact. Toni Hypophrygij		Charact. Toni Eolij		Charact. Toni Hypoeol.		Charact. Toni Hypœol.		Charact. Toni Dorij		Charact. Toni Hypodor.		Charact. Toni Hyperdor.	
	Vox infer	Vox infer	Vox infer	Vox infer	Vox infer	Vox infer	Vox infer	Vox infer	Vox infer	Vox infer	Vox infer	Vox infer	Vox infer	Vox infer	Vox infer	Vox infer
aa Nete Hyperbolæon	I λ	θ N	ʊ ʒ	κ ʍ	ʒ ⊏	α \	м η	ʊ ʒ	Γ N	O K	α \	ʒ ⊏	⊥ ⌐	Γ N	н Y
g Paranete Hyperbolæon diaton	м η	ʊ ʒ	Γ N	O K	ж λ	ʒ ⊏	⊥ Y	Γ N	н λ	θ η	ʒ ⊏	I ⊏	B /	н λ	κ λ
f Trite Hyperbolæon	∧ Ɣ	E ʍ	θ ⊀	θ н	∂ \	I ⊀	∧ ∧	θ ⊀	λ o	ʊ ʒ	I ⊏	ξ ʍ	Γ N	λ ⊏	ỏ K
e Nete Diezeugmenon	θ н	ʒ ⊏	I ⊏	x λ	н Y	κ λ	ʊ ʒ	I ⊀	⊥ o	α \	R \	o ⊀	н ⊏	м η	⊥ ⊏
d Paranete Diezeugmenon diaton	ʊ ʒ	I ⊀	м η	⊀ \	κ λ	O K	Γ N	ʍ η	м η	ʒ ⊏	o K	θ н	λ ⊏	π ⊐	ж λ
c Trite Diezeugmenon	E ʍ	ξ ʍ	π ⊏	ʒ ⊏	O K	θ н	θ λ	ʒ O	⊥ ʊ	I ⊏	⊏ ⊏	ʊ ʒ	м η	ʊ ʍ	B /
♮ Paramese	ʒ ⊏	O K	θ н	н Y	η ⊐	ж λ			⊏ ⊏	ʊ ʒ	κ λ	τ η	α /	н ⊅	φ F	Γ N
c Nete Synemmenon	ʊ ʒ	I ⊀	м η	α \	κ ʍ	O K	Γ ʍ	ʍ η		ʒ ⊏	⊏ ⊏	θ η	κ ⊏	π ⊐	ж λ
♭ Paranete Synemmenon diaton	Γ N	м η	⊥ ⊏	ʒ ⊏	O K	θ η	н ⊏	ʊ ⊐	ж λ	I ⊏	φ F	ʊ ʒ	o K	τ F	α \
b Trite Synemmenon	θ ⊀	ʒ ʊ	ʌ ⊏	I ⊀	⊏ ⊏	ʊ ʒ	λ ⊏	ʊ ʍ	B /	ξ ʍ	x ʊ	E ʍ	η ⊐	⊐	ʒ ⊏
a Mese	I ⊀	⊏ ⊏	ʊ ʒ	κ ỏ	τ ꓶ	α \	м η	φ F	Γ N	O K	ξ ʍ	ʒ ⊏	τ ꓶ	ʊ ʍ	н ⊅
G Mese diatonos	м η	φ F	Γ N	O K	x ʊ	ʒ ⊏	π ⊐	ʊ ʍ	м >	⊏ ⊏	τ Γ	I ⊀	Ψ ⊐	ʁ ꓶ	κ λ
F Lichanos meson	ʒ ʊ	ʁ ⌐	θ ⊀	⊏ ⊏	τ Γ	I ⊀	ʊ ʍ	F ⊥	λ ꓶ	φ F	ʒ ꓶ	ξ ʍ	ʊ ʍ	τ ʊ	O K
E Hypate meson	⊏ ⊏	τ Γ	I ⊀	τ ꓶ	ʁ ꓶ	κ ꓶ φ F	ʒ ꓶ	м η	x ʊ	ʍ ꓱ	O K	ʁ ꓶ	\ E	π ⊐
D Lichanos hypaton diatonos	φ F	ξ ꓶ	ꓶ м η	x й	ꓶ ꓱ	O K	ʊ ʍ	\ E	π ⊐	τ Γ	w h	⊏ ⊏	⊥ ʊ	н ꓞ	τ ꓶ
C Parhypate hypaton	ʁ L	ʊ I	ʒ ʊ	ꓶ Γ	w н	⊏ ⊏	F ⊥	ʍ н ʊ ʍ	ʒ ꓶ	φ н	φ F	ʁ ⊏	δ ʊ	Ψ ⊥
♮ Hypate hypaton	ꓶ Γ	w н	⊏ ⊏	ʁ ꓶ	н ꓞ	τ F	⊀ ꓶ	φ н	φ F	н ꓱ	⊏ ʒ	x ʊ	\ E	ʒ ξ	ʊ ʊ
A Proslambanomenos	ʒ ꓶ	φ н	φ F	н ꓱ	ʊ ʒ	I ʊ	ʒ E	ʒ ξ	w ʊ	w ʍ	ꓶ τ	ꓶ Γ	н ꓱ	∂∂	ʁ ꓶ

Notæ et Characteres musici veterum iuxta Boeten Canones	Charact. Toni Lydij	Charact. Toni Hypolydi	Charact. Toni Hyporlydi	Charact. Toni Æolij	Charact. Toni Hyperæol.	Charact. Toni Hyporæol.	Charact. Toni Phrygij	Charact. Toni Hypophrygij	Charact. Toni Iastij	Charact. Toni Iastij	Charact. Toni Hypoiast	Charact. Toni Hypat	Charact. Toni Dorij	Charact. Toni Hypodor	Charact. Toni Hyperdor
Proslambanomenos	℟⋌	ΘΗ	ʋʒ	ΝΧ	Χᛏ	ᾱⅽ	ᴍᛂ	ᴨᴑʒ	ΓΝ	ΟΚ	αⅼ	ʒˊ ʒˊ	⊥ʋ	ᴜΓΝ	ᴨℾ
Hypate hypaton	⊂⋌	ΔⅼΧ	ɲɔ	ᒪᛐ	ᴧᴢᴧ	⊁ʍ	ᴋᴧ	ɟʼʒ	ᴋᴜ	ᴧᴧ	ᴨʒ	ᴧⁱᴧ	αⅼʋ	ᴋᴧᴧ	ᴋᴧ
Parhypate hypaton	ᴀʏℂ	ᛣⱲ	θˊⱺ	θ⋀	ᴤ⅁ᴨ	ᴣ⁊⋖	⋌ᴧℭᴧ	ᴧⱱ	ᴧᴑ	ʋʒ	ⅼ⌄	ʒⁱᴈᴋ	ᴃⅰ	ᴧᴈ	οᴋ
Lychanos hypaton	θΗ	ᴫᛣⅇ	Ⴒᴧ	⋆⋆ʒ	ᴎⱭⅰ	ᴧᴎʒ	ᴧⱱⱺᴢ	ᛃ∔⊓	ᴍᴨ	αⅼ	ᴎᴧ	Οᴋ	Γᴎ	ᴧᴧⅼ	⊥ᴧ
Hypate meson	⊇ᴧ	ⅼᴎℨ	Ⴆᴧ	ᴧ∔	ᴧᴧ	ℷᴧᴨ	ᴨᴅⴲᴧ	ᴧ	ᴫ⁊	ᴨⴰ	ᴧᴧ		⊤⋾	αⅼ	
Parhypate meson	ᴇᴧⅼ	ᴫⅹⵘ	ʒⱱ	ʒℭ	ᴘᴎᴧ	ⴼⱭᴧⵘ	ᴧᴤᴧ	ᴅⱭⅹ	ᴖⅰᴠ	ℭℭ	ʋʒ	ᴋ⌄	ᴜᴧ	θᴜ	ᴃⅰ
Lychanos meson	ᴧᴈ	ᴑᴧ	θᴎ	ᴎʒ	Ɑᴦⅼ	ᴧᴧ	ⅰᴎ	ᴤᴈ	ᴋᴧ	ᴧᴊᴦ	αⅼʋ	ᴜᴧ	θᴜ	Γᴎ	
Mese	Ɑⴟ	ᴵ∟	ᴍᴨ	ᴧᴜ	ᴧ	ᴋᴦᴎ	ᴍ⊕	ʒⅽ	ʒℭ	Οᴋᴋⅼ	θᴎ	ᴎʒ	ᴨᴈ	ᴧᴧ	ᴧⅹ
Paramese	ᴧⱭ	ᴨᴢ⁊	ᴧᴧ	ᴧ⁒ᴧ	ᴧ⅁ᴧ	ᴋⱭ	⊤᧞ᴘ	ᴳᴧᴎ	ᴎᴋ	ᴧᴈ	ᴅᴈᴎᴋ	ᴧᴅᴈ	ᴎᴋ	ᴧⱭⱱ	ℭᴅ
Trite diezeugmenon	Ɑᴦ	ᴎⱭ	ᴧⱭᴎᴧ	ⁱˊᴧⱭ	ᴔ⁊⅁ʒ	ᴧᴃ	ᴪᴧᴜᴧᴧ	ᴧⱭᴧᴠ	⁒ⅹ	Φᖲ	Εᴜ	Οᴧ	⊥⅁∔	ʒⱭ	ℭ
Paranete diezeugmenon	ⅼᴧ	ℭℭ	ʋʒ	ᴋ⋀ᴧ	ᴦⅼᴧⱺ	ⱱᴎᴦ	θᴧ	Γᴍ	Οᴋ	ᴪⱽ	ʒℭ	ᴨᴑ	ⱳᴜ	ᴧᴎ	ⅼʒᴠ
Nete diezeugmenon	ᴨ⅌ᴧ	ℷᴎ	ᴄ	ᴎᵷⅼᴡ	ᴎᴧᴧᴧ	ᴧᴜ⁊	⊤⊤⋋ʒ	ᴧ⁊ʒ	ᴋᴧ	⊤ʒ	⥾ᴧᴧ	ᴎᴋ	ᴧᴧᴜ	ᴋᴎᴧ	ᴋᴎ
Paranete hyperbolaion	ᴦⱭᴜ	ᴜᴧᴧ	θᴦ	ℭℭⅹ	ᛐ⁊ᴧ	ⅰᴏⅼ	ʒᴜᴜ	ᴧⅰ	ᴧᴧ	Φᖲ	ʒ∔	⥾ᴌ	ᴧʒⅿ	⊤ⱳ	ᴏᴋ
Nete hyperbolaion	ℭᴇ	ⅼᴧⱭ	ᴵⅰˊⱱ	ᴵⱶᴧⱭ	ᴦᴧⱭᴧ	ᴧᴃⱭᴋ	ʒᴧ∔	ᴩ⁊	ΧⱲ	ΕΝ	Οᴋᴦ	ⱳᴜᴼ	ᴎᴇᴧ	ℭᴨⱳ	ℭℭ
Lychanos hypaton	ᴧᴇ	ᴋⱭᴎ	ᴨℭ	ᴦᴦ	ᴧᴧ⁊Ⅎ	ʒ⅀ᴧ	⊤ᴦᴧ	⊤ᴀ	ᴧᴢᴎ	⊤ᴋ	ᴎᴎᴧ	⊤ʒ	ᴎᴇ	ᴊᵶʒ	ᴧᴡ
Parhypate hypaton	ℬ⋁ˣᴈ	⅌ℭ	ℬℭ	ᴦᴦ	ᴦᴡᴎ	ℭℭ	℻	⌶ᴀᴅⱱ	ⱳᴜ	ʒ⌄	ᴩⱵᴎ	Φᖲ	⅃ᴡ		⊁Ƴ
Hypate hypaton	ᴦᴦ	ⱳᴎ	ℭℭ	δᴧⱶᴧ	ᴎᴧ	⊤ʒ	ᴧ⊥ᴧ	Ⱶᴩᴎ	Φᖲ	ᴪʒ	ᴎʒ	Χᴜ	⅃ᴇ	ᴃⱳᴎⱳᴎ	ⱳᴎᴧ
Proslambanomenos	⌄⊤	Ⱶᴩᴎ	Φᖲ	ᴎʒ	ᴜʒ	Χᴜ	ⱽᴧ	Εʒᴈ	ℭᴡᴎ	ⱳᴎ	ⅰ⊤⊤	Γᴦ	ᴎᴦᴇ	ℭℭ⁊	⊽ᴧⱼ

Kircher gives the following explanation of the above characters.
The top of the plate contains the names of the fifteen tones or
modes : the side exhibits eighteen chords, anfwering to every tone,
and expreffed by their Greek names, to each of which the Guidonian keys now ufed by the Latins anfwer, in the firft column. To
know therefore for inftance by what characters the ancients expreffed
the Mefe in the Phrygian tone, we muft look in the fide for the
chord Mefe, and on the top for Tonus Phrygius, and where they
meet we fhall find the character fought for, and fo for the reft.

Having exhibited this key to the ancient characters, Kircher gives
the fragment of Pindar above-mentioned in the Greek notes, and
alfo in thofe of the modern fcale, as here under is reprefented.

And the table herein before given from him feems to have been his authority for rendering the ancient characters in modern notes, as above is fhewn. By way of illuftration he adds, that the Chorus vocalis above contains the characters written over each word; and that the Chorus inftrumentalis, which is nothing elfe but the antiftrophe to the former, was played according to the ftrophe, on the cythara or the pipe. As the characters agree with thofe of Alypius, he fays he has no doubt about their meaning; and as to the time, he is clear that it was given by the meafures of the fyllables, and not by the characters.

The feveral variations of the fyftem of mufic have been traced with as much accuracy as the nature of the fubject would allow of: the improvements made by Terpander and others, more efpecially Pythagoras, have been diftinctly enumerated, we are therefore now to proceed in our narration.

Pythagoras having, as has been related, inveftigated the proportions of founds, and extended the narrow limits of the ancient fyftem, and alfo demonftrated, not merely the affinity of founds, but that a harmony, analogous to that of mufic, was to be found in other fubjects wherein number and proportion were concerned; and that the coincidences of founds were a phyfical demonftration of thofe proportions which arithmetic and the higher geometry had till then enabled mankind only to fpeculate, it followed that mufic from thenceforth became a fubject of philofophical contemplation. Ariftotle, by feveral paffages in his writings now extant, appears to have confidered it in this view: it is even faid that he wrote a treatife profeffedly on the fubject of mufic, but that it is now loft.

Fabricius has given a catalogue of fundry writers, as namely, Jades, Lafus Hermionenfis, Mintanor, Diocles, Hagiopolites, Agatho, and many others, whofe works are loft; and in the writings of Ariftoxenus, Nicomachus, Ptolemy, Porphyry, Manuel Bryennius, and other ancient authors, we meet with the names of Philolaus, Eratofthenes, Archytas of Tarentum, and Didymus of Alexandria, who feem moftly to have been philofophers; but as they are alfo enumerated among the fcriptores perditi, nothing can be faid about them. In thofe early times the principles of learning were very flowly diffeminated among mankind; and it does not appear, that from the time of Pythagoras, to that of Ariftoxenus, which included a period of near three

hundred

hundred years, the mufic of the ancients underwent any very confiderable alteration, unlefs we except that new arrangement and fubdivifion of the parts of the great fyftem, which conftituted the Genera,
and thofe diffimilar progreffions from every found to its diapafon,
which are diftinguifhed by the name of Modes. Of thefe it is neceffary now to fpeak ; and firft of the Genera.

Till the time of Pythagoras, the progreffion of founds was in that
order, which as well the modern as the ancient writers term the diatonic, as proceeding by tones, a progreffion from the unifon to its
fourth by two tones and a hemitone, which we fhould now exprefs
by the fyllables DO, RE, MI, FA, confeffedly very natural and extremely grateful to the ear; though it feems not fo much fo as to hinder fucceeding muficians from feeking after other kinds of progreffion;
and accordingly by a different divifion of the integral parts of each of
the tetrachords, they formed another feries of progreffion, to which,
from the flexibility of its nature they gave the epithet of Chromatic,
from Chroma, a word fignifying colour; and to this they added another, which was termed enarmonic; befides this they invented a
fubvariation of each progreffion, and to diftinguifh the one from the
other they made ufe of the common logical term genus, by which
we are to underftand, as Kircher tells us, tom. I. lib. III. cap. xiii.
a certain conftitution of thofe founds that compofe a diateffaron, or
mufical fourth; or, in other words, a certain relation which the
four chords of any given tetrachord bear to each other. The Genera
are elfewhere defined, certain kinds of modulation arifing from the
different difpofition of the founds in a tetrachord : every Cantus or
compofition, fays Ariftoxenus *, is either Diatonic, Chromatic, or
Enarmonic; or it may be mixed, and include a community of the
genera. Ariftoxenus, for ought now difcoverable, is the firft that
has written profeffedly, though obfcurely, on this part of mufic.
Ptolemy, as he is in general the moft accurate and methodical of all
the ancient writers, fo is he more copious in his explanation of the
Genera. Nicomachus has mentioned them, but in a very fuperficial
manner; and as to the latter authors, we are not to wonder if they
have contented themfelves with the bare enumeration of them; fince
before the times in which the greater number of them wrote, the
Diatonic was the only one of the three genera in common ufe.

* Lib. II. pag. 44. ex Verf. Meibom.

6

Nor

Nor does it any where appear, that even of the five Species, into which that Genus was divided, any more than one, namely, the syntonous or intense of Ptolemy, was in general estimation. It must be confessed that no part of the musical science has so much divided the writers on it as this of the genera; Ptolemy has exhibited no fewer than five different systems of generical harmony, and, after all, the doctrine on this subject is almost inscrutable: however, the substance of what these and other authors have related concerning the nature of it, is here, as in its proper place, referred to the consideration of such as are desirous to know the essential difference between the music of this and the more early ages.

But before this doctrine of the Genera can be rendered to any degree intelligible, it is necessary to observe, that hitherto we have spoken only of the more common and obvious musical intervals, the tone and hemitone; for the system of Pythagoras is formed of these only; and a more minute division of it was not till after his time thought on, nevertheless it is to be noted, that in order to the completion of his system, it was found requisite to institute a method of calculation that should as it were resolve the intervals into their elements, and adjust the ratios of such sounds as were not determinable by the division of a chord in the manner herein before-mentioned. That division was sufficient, and it answered to the greatest degree of mathematic exactness for ascertaining the ratios of the diatessaron, the diapente, and the tone: and, agreeable to what has been already laid down concerning the investigation of the consonances by Pythagoras, it will most evidently appear upon experiment, that if a chord be divided into twelve equal parts, six of those parts will give an octave to that sound which would have been produced by the same chord, if struck before such division; from whence it appears, that the ratio subsisting between the unison and its octave is duple: again, that eight parts of the twelve will give a diatessaron, which bears to the unison six a ratio of 4 to 3; and that nine parts, according to the same division, will produce the diapente, which bears to the unison six a ratio of 3 to 2; and lastly, that the sound produced at the ninth part will be distant from that at the eighth, and so reciprocally; a tone, in the ratio of 9 to 8, called a Sesquioctave, and often the Diezeuctic tone, which furnished the ear at least with a common measure for the greater intervals.

But we are to note, that the fyftem of Pythagoras was not completed, till, by the very artful contrivance of two tetrachords, to be ufed alternately, as the nature of the melody might require, a divifion of the tone between a and ♮ was effected. By this an interval of a Hemitone was introduced into the fyftem, with which no one fection of the chord, fuppofing it to be divided into twelve parts, would by any means coincide: with great ingenuity therefore did Euclid invent that famous divifion the Sectio Canonis, by means whereof not only the pofitions of the feveral founds on a fuppofed chord are precifely afcertained, but a method is fuggefted for bringing out thofe larger numbers, which alone can fhew the ratios of the fmaller intervals, and which therefore make a part of every reprefentation that fucceeding writers have given of the immutable fyftem.

The Sectio Canonis of Euclid is a kind of appendix to his Ifagoge, or Introductio Harmonica, containing twenty theorems in harmonics. Neverthelefs the title of Sectio Canonis was by him given to the following fcheme of a fuppofed chord, divided for the purpofe of demonftrating the ratios of the feveral intervals thereby difcriminated, which fcheme is inferted at the end of his work.

SECTIO.

SECTIO CANONIS OF EUCLID.

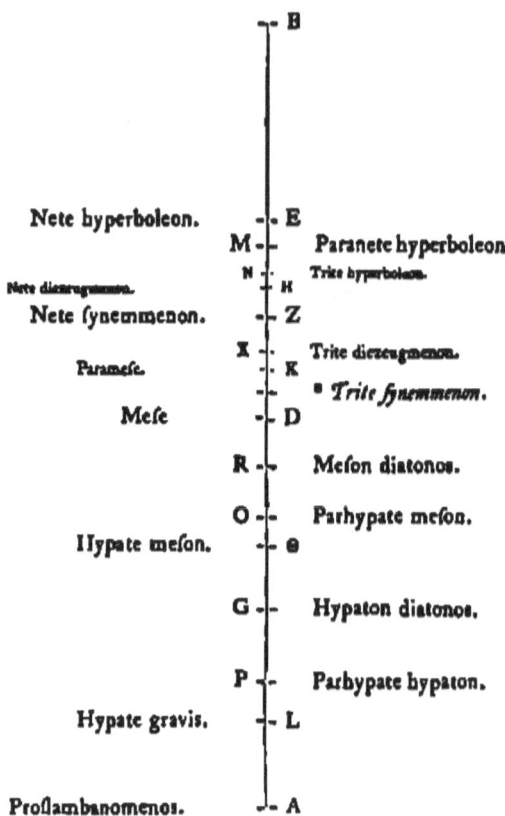

The foregoing canon or scheme of a division is introduced by a series
of theorems, preparatory to an explanation of it, which explanation is

I 2   contained

contained in Theorems XIX. and XX. the firft of thefe refers to the immoveable founds, that is to fay, Proſlambanomenos, and the other founds to the left of the line, and the latter to the moveable, which are Parhypate and the reft on the right thereof; the fum of which two fpecies compofed the great or immutable fyſtem.

Theorem XIX. directs the adjuſtment of the canon for the Stabiles or immoveable founds, and that in the manner following.

' Let the length of the canon be A B, and let it be divided into four ' equal parts at G D E, therefore D A, as it will be the graveft found, ' will be the fonus bombus. Farther, A B is fupertertius of G B, there- ' fore G B will found a diateſſaron to A B, towards the acumen, and ' A B is Proſlambanomenos ; wherefore G B will be Hypaton Diato- ' nos. Again, becaufe A B is duple of B D, the former will found a ' diapafon to the latter, and B D will be Mefe. Again, becaufe A B ' is quadruple of E B, E B will be Nete Hyperboleon ; therefore G B ' is divided twofold in Z, and G B will be duple of Z B, fo as G B ' will found to Z B the interval of a diapafon, wherefore Z B is Nete ' Synemmenon. Cut off from D B a third part D H, and D B will be ' fefquialtera to H B, fo as for this reafon D B will found to H B the ' interval of a diapente, therefore H B will be Nete diezeugmenon. ' Farther, make H Θ equal to H B, therefore Θ B will found a diapafon ' to H B, fo that Θ B will be Hypate mefon. Again, take the third ' part of Θ B, Θ K, and then Θ B will be fefquialtera to K B, fo that ' K B will be Paramefe. Laftly, cut off L K equal to K B, and then ' L B will be Hypate the moft grave, and thus all the immoveable ' founds will be taken in the canon.'

Theorem XX contains the following directions refpecting the Mo- biles or moveable founds.

' Divide E B into eight parts, of which make E M equal to one, ' fo as M B may be fuperoctave of E B. And again, divide M B into ' eight equal parts, and make one of them equal to N M, therefore ' N B will be a tone more grave than B M, and M B will be a tone · graver than B E ; fo as N B will be Trite hyperboleon, and M B will ' be Paranete hyperboleon diatonos. Farther, divide N B into three ' parts, and make N X equal to one of them, fo as X B will be fu- ' pertertius of N B, and the diateſſaron will be produced towards the ' grave, and X B will be Trite diezeugmenon. Again, taking half of ' X B, make X O equal to it, fo as for this reafon O B will give a
' diapente

' diapente to X B, wherefore O B will be Parhypate mefon; then
' make O P equal to O B *, fo as P B will be Parhypate hypaton.
' Laftly, take the fourth part of G B, G R, and R B will be Mefon
' diatonos.

CHAP.   V.

THE Sectio Canonis of Euclid, in the judgment of the moft
eminent writers on harmonics, was the firft effay towards a
determination of the ratios by the fuppofed divifion of a chord ; and,
affuming the proportions of the diapafon, diapente, diateffaron, diezeuctic tone, and limma, as laid down by the Pythagoreans, the divifion will be found to anfwer to the ratios : yet this does not appear
by a bare infpection, but can only be proved by an actual admeafurement of the feveral intervals contained in the canon.   Now as whatever is geometrically divifible, is alfo divifible by numbers, fucceeding writers in affigning the ratios of the intervals have taken the aid
of the latter, and have applied the numbers to each of the founds,
as they relult from a divifion of the canon.   How they are brought
out will hereafter be made appear.

But here it is neceffary to add, that the Sectio Canonis of Euclid,
perfect in its kind as it may feem, is fuppofed to have received fome
improvement from Ariftides Quintilianus, at leaft with refpect to the
manner of dividing it; for this we have the teftimony of Meibomius,
who fpeaks of a canon of Ariftides, which had been once extant, but
was perifhed, or at leaft was wanting in all the copies of his work ;
and which he his editor had happily reflored.   The following is a reprefentation of the Canon, with the numbers annexed.

* In the Canon O P is not equal to O B but to O X, and Meibomius, with all his
care, has made a miftake, which the following page, to go no farther, furnifhes the
means of rectifying ; for obferve, that in the Canon of Ariftides Quintilianus, which has
the numbers to it, Trite diezeugmenon, marked X in that of Euclid, is 3888, and Parhypate hypaton marked P in that of Euclid alfo, is 7776, which is juft double the
former number, the confequence whereof is evident.

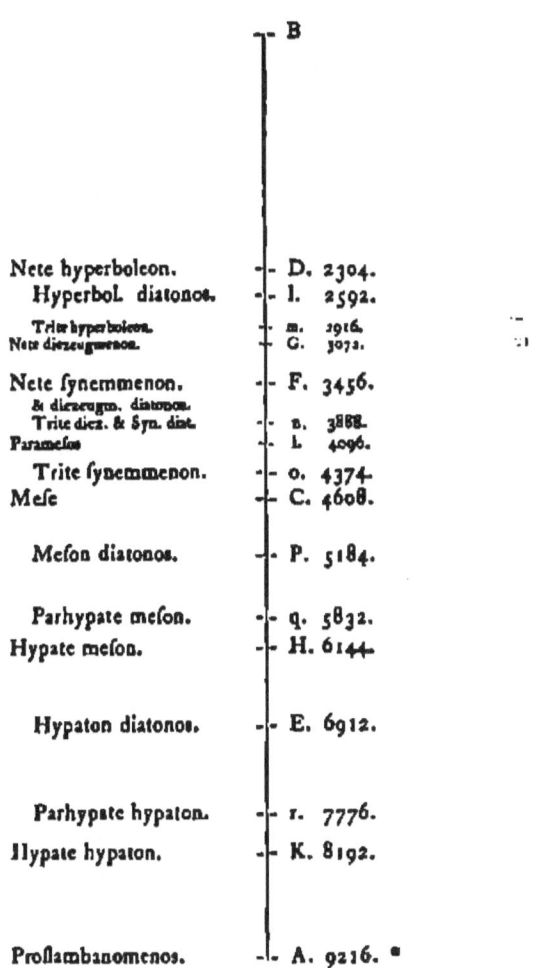

Nete hyperboleon.   D. 2304.
Hyperbol. diatonos.   l. 2592.
Trite hyperboleon.   m. 2916.
Nete diezeugmenon.   G. 3072.
Nete synemmenon.   F. 3456.
& diezeugm. diatonos.
Trite diez. & Syn. dist. n. 3888.
Paramese   L. 4096.
Trite synemmenon.   o. 4374.
Mese   C. 4608.

Meson diatonos.   P. 5184.

Parhypate meson.   q. 5832.
Hypate meson.   H. 6144.

Hypaton diatonos.   E. 6912.

Parhypate hypaton.   r. 7776.
Hypate hypaton.   K. 8192.

Proslambanomenos.   A. 9216.

It

It does not appear whether the numbers were originally part of the canon, or whether they were inserted by Meibomius. However, from several passages in Ptolemy, particularly in book I. Chap. 10, where he demonstrates the ratio of the limma, we meet with the number 2048, which is the half of 4096, 1944, the half of 3888, and others, which shew the antiquity of this method of numerical division.

The following is an explanation of the canon as given by Meibomius, in his notes on Aristides Quintilianus, page 312, et seq.

‘ The standing sounds are first set down in the division of the canon,
‘ and after them the moveable ones ; we have marked the standing
‘ sounds by capital letters, and to these are added the moveable ones.
‘ The Hypaton diatonos and the rest are marked by the small letters.
‘ They are thus to be taken.

‘ I. Proslambanomenos, A B, which is the whole length of the
‘ chord or line.

‘ II. Mese, C D, half thereof.

‘ III. Nete hyperboleon, D B, the fourth part of the whole
‘ chord.

‘ IV. Hypaton diatonos, E B, three fourths thereof.

‘ V. Nete synemmenon, F B, the said three fourths, E B, di-
‘ vided into two equal parts.

‘ VI. Nete. diezeugmenon, G B, two thirds of half the chord,
‘ that is one third of the whole chord ; but this may be perceived by
‘ multiplying an half by two thirds, thus, $\frac{1}{2}$ $\frac{1}{3}$|$\frac{1}{3}$.

* The division of Euclid agrees with that of Aristides as to the manner of obtaining the standing, but differs as to some of the moveable chords, for Euclid finds the Trite diezeugmenon, by setting off towards the grave a diatessaron from the Trite hyperboleon ; he next finds the Parhypate meson, by setting off towards the grave a diapente from the Trite diezeugmenon, which might be easier found by setting down a diapason from the Trite hyperboleon. He also finds the Parhypate hypaton by making O P equal to O X, that is by setting off a diapason towards the grave from the Trite diezeugmenon, for he had made O X equal to half X B, and consequently twice O X O P must be equal to X B. And lastly, he finds the Meson diatonos by setting off a diatessaron towards the acute from the Hypaton diatonos, whereas all the four sounds, as well as the other moveable ones, are found in Aristides, by a division into eight parts, that is by setting off sesquioctave tones. It seems, however, upon the whole, that Aristides followed the division of Euclid, but neither of these can answer to the Aristoxenian principles, for this reason, that the Sectio Canonis both of Euclid and Aristides refer to those arithmetic and harmonic ratios, which are discernible in the proportions of Pythagoras, whereas Aristoxenus rejected the criterion of ratios, and maintained that the measure of intervals was determinable by the sense of hearing only.

‘ VII.

‘ VII. Hypate mefon, H B, two thirds of the whole chord, or
‘ the two thirds, G B, of the half chord twice fet off, which chord
‘ therefore we take in the opening of the dividers, and fet off twice.

‘ VIII. Paramefos, I B, (one third I H, being taken out of the
‘ two thirds H B of the whole chord) is two thirds of two thirds
‘ of the whole.

‘ IX. Hypate hypaton, K B, two thirds I B, of the two thirds
‘ H B twice fet off.

‘ In order to affume the leffer intervals, the following method
‘ muft be made ufe of.

‘ I. The fourth part D B of the whole chord being divided into
‘ eight equal parts, I fet off I below D equal to one of thofe parts,
‘ and I B will be Paranete hyperboleon.

‘ II. Trite hyperboleon m B is affumed in the fame manner, viz.
‘ by dividing the line I D into eight equal parts, and taking I m equal
‘ to one of them out of I A.

‘ III. Trite diezeugmenon, and the following moveable founds,
‘ are eafily to be affumed in the fame manner.’

Befides the foregoing explanation of the canon, Meibomius has
given the following, which he calls a Notable Theorem, and fays
of it that it is very ufeful in facilitating the fection of the canon.

‘ The difference between two lines that are to each other in a fef-
‘ quitertia ratio, being divided into two equally, will give the eighth
‘ part of the greater line.

‘ A B is fefquitertia to D E; C B is the excefs of A B above D E,
‘ C B divided into two equally will exhibit the eighth part of A B.

‘ We fhall fee the fame in the fection of our canon. Let the line
‘ G D be divided into eight equal parts, I fay the part G D thereof
‘ will contain two eighth parts; fo that this need only be divided
‘ into two equally, as appears by this following demonftration; for
‘ as G B is fefquitertia to D B, that is, as 4 to 3, if G D be divided
‘ into twice four parts, that is eighths, D B will contain fix of thofe
‘ eighths, and confequently D G two eighths, and its half will contain
‘ one eighth. Alfo if F B is to be divided into eight equal parts, its

' part F I need be divided only into two equally, in order to have one
' eighth part, which I set off from F to n, to find the excess of the
' tone above F B. The same method may be used in the follow-
' ing ones.

' Moreover, the Mefon diatonos, and the other two moveable
' chords may also be obtained by the following method, namely,
' Mefon diatonos, by setting off the part l B, twice from B ; Parhy-
' pate mefon, by setting off the part m B, twice ; Parhypate hypa-
' ton, by setting off the part n B, twice.

' But whatsoever is here shewn in lines may, by the ingenuity of
' the intelligent reader, be easily applied in finding out the numbers.'

The canon of Ariftides Quintilianus, with the numbers affixed,
suppofes the whole chord to contain 9216 parts, and being struck
open, to produce the moft grave found of the fyftem, viz. A ; the interval then of a tone at ♭, the next found in fucceffion, as being in
the proportion of 8 to 9 to A, will require that the chord be ftopped
at 8192 ; and, fuppofing it to anfwer, we may with the utmoft propriety fay, that the ratio of a tone is as 9216 is to 8192, or in other
words, that ♭ is produced at 8192 of thofe parts whereof the chord
A, contains 9216 ; and thefe two numbers will be found to bear the
fame proportion to each other as thofe of 9 and 8. Again, for the
diapafon a, the number is 4608, which is juft the half of 9216, as 6
is the half of 12 ; for the diateffaron D, the number is 6912, which
is three fourths of 9216 ; and for the diapente E, the number is 6144,
which is two thirds of 9216. Hence it appears that the numbers
thus taken for the tone, or for the confonances of the diateffaron
and the diapente, or their replicates, as often as it may be thought
neceffary by the reiteration of an octave, or any lefs fyftem, to extend that of the bifdiapafon, anfwer in like manner to the ratios of
9 to 8, 6 to 12, 12 to 9, and 12 to 8, in the primitive fyftem.

Thefe proportions we are told will be the refult of an actual divifion of a firing, which whoever is defirous of making the experiment, is hereby enabled to try ; though, by the way, it is faid by
Meibomius that for this purpofe one of two ells in length will be
found neceffary. Neverthelefs, by the help of the principles already
laid down, namely, that the diapafon has a ratio of 2 to 1, the diapente of 3 to 2, the diateffaron of 4 to 3, and the tone of 9 to 8,
which are to be confidered as data that all harmonical writers agree

in, it is very eafy, by means of arithmetic alone, to bring out the numbers correfponding to the intervals in the diatonic bifdiapafon. Bontempi has given a very particular relation of the procefs in an account of the method taken by the ancients for that purpofe; and immediately after, an exhibition of that fyftem with the proper numbers in the following fcale.

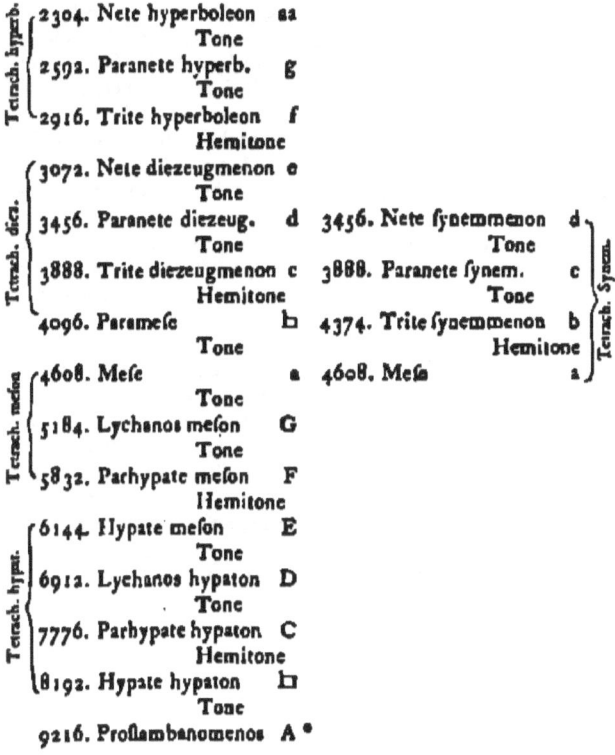

Tetrach. hyperb.	2304. Nete hyperboleon	aa			
	Tone				
	2592. Paranete hyperb.	g			
	Tone				
	2916. Trite hyperboleon	f			
	Hemitone				
Tetrach. diez.	3072. Nete diezeugmenon	e			
	Tone				
	3456. Paranete diezeug.	d	3456. Nete fynemmenon	d	Tetrach. Synem.
	Tone		Tone		
	3888. Trite diezeugmenon	c	3888. Paranete fynem.	c	
	Hemitone		Tone		
	4096. Paramefe	b	4374. Trite fynemmenon	b	
	Tone		Hemitone		
Tetrach. mefon	4608. Mefe	a	4608. Mefa	a	
	Tone				
	5184. Lychanos mefon	G			
	Tone				
	5832. Parhypate mefon	F			
	Hemitone				
Tetrach. hypat.	6144. Hypate mefon	E			
	Tone				
	6912. Lychanos hypaton	D			
	Tone				
	7776. Parhypate hypaton	C			
	Hemitone				
	8192. Hypate hypaton	Ʒ			
	Tone				
	9216. Proflambanomenos	A *			

* Bontemp. 97.

His description of the procefs is in thefe words: ' The numbers
' affixed to the feveral chords in the fyftem draw their origin from
' the fefquioctave proportion, which is the relation that the fecond
' chord bears to the firft ; and, proceeding from the acute to the
' grave, the numbers will be found to be in the ratio of fubfefqui-
' octave, fubfefquitertia, fubfefquialtera, and fubduple. But to be
' more particular :

' As the third chord was to be the fefquioctave of the fecond, and
' as the fecond had not an eighth part, the ancients multiplied by 8,
' and fet down the number produced thereby : if the fourth chord
' was to be the fefquitertia, they multiplied the numbers by 3 ; if
' it was to be fefquialtera the numbers were doubled ; and if by
' chance there were any fractions, they doubled them again to find
' even numbers, and fo they went on : but as all thefe operations
' belong to arithmetic, and of courfe muft be known, there is no
' neceffity to explain them farther.

' However, as all this is different from any practice in the modern
' mufic, in order that thofe who are not perfectly verfed in arithme-
' tic may underftand the foundation of this fcience, it will not be
' amifs here to explain it. You muft then know, that as har-
' monic mufic was fubordinate to arithmetic, the ancients fhewed
' only the intervals by numbers arifing from the meafures they
' had found out by experiments upon the monochord.

' When they wanted therefore to demonftrate in the conftitution
' of the fyftem what chord was either double, or fefquialtera, or fef-
' quitertia, or fefquioctave to another by arithmetical numbers, they
' ufed multiplication, or the doubling of the numbers, in order that
' they might rife by degrees one above the other. They began from
' the moft acute chord, which is the Nete hyperboleon, going on as
' far as the Trite fynemmenon ; which operation is demonftrated by
' the following columns of numbers.

	1	2	3	4	5	6
aa	8	64	192	576	1152	2304
g	9	72	216	648	1296	2592
f		81	243	729	1458	2916
e			256	768	1536	3072
d			288	864	1728	3456
c			324	972	1944	3888
b				1024	2048	4096
b					2187	4374 *

' The method which they ufed in thefe multiplications and redu-
' plications was this; as g was to be fefquioctave of aa, and f fefqui-
' octave of g; and as g had not an eighth part, to find it they mul-
' tiplied aa and g by 8; from which multiplication the numbers of
' the fecond order were produced, and they put down 81 fefquioctave
' of 72. As e was to be fefquitertia of aa, and had not a third part,
' they multiplied all the fecond order by 3; from which multiplica-
' tion was produced the third order, and there came out the number
' 256, fefquitertia of 192; in like manner d was found to be fefqui-
' tertia of g, and c of f.

' As b was to be fefquitertia of e, and had not a third part, they
' multiplied all the third order by 3, from which was produced the
' fourth order, and there came out 1024, fefquitertia of 768; as b
' was to be fefquialtera of f, there came out fractions, to avoid
' which all the fourth order was doubled, and fo the fifth order
' was produced; and there was the number 2187, fefquialtera of
' 1458.

' In a word, give me leave to repeat again this operation, with
' common explications for thofe who are quite unacquainted with
' the rules of arithmetic; by multiplying eight times 8 they had 64
' for aa; by multiplying nine times 8 they had 72 for g; and adding
' to 72 the number 9, they had 81 for f.

' The fefquitertia, which is nothing but the proportion 4 to 3, con-
' ftituting the diateffaron from e to aa, was produced by giving to aa
' three times 64, which made 192, and to e four times 64, which
' made 256.

* Bontemp. 98.

‘ That of d to g was produced by giving to g three times the
‘ number 72, which made 216; and to d four times the same,
‘ which made 288.

‘ That of c to f was produced by giving to g three times 81,
‘ which made 243; and to c four times the same, which made 324.

‘ That of b to e was produced by giving to e three times 256,
‘ which made 768; and to b four times the same, which made
‘ 1024.

‘ The sesquialtera, which is nothing but the proportion 3 to 2, consti-
‘ tuting the diapente from b to f, was produced by giving to f twice
‘ 729, which made 1458; and to b three times the same, which
‘ made 2187.

‘ Finally, in order that this kind of numbers might do for the
‘ chords of the chromatic and enarmonic genera; to avoid fractions
‘ they doubled all the fifth order, and thereby brought out the sixth;
‘ so that the second order is the produce of the first multiplied by 8;
‘ the third order is the produce of the second multiplied by 3: the
‘ fourth order is the produce of the third multiplied by 3; the fifth
‘ order is double the fourth, and the sixth double the fifth; and the
‘ numbers of the sixth order are the same as those of the tetrachords
‘ Hyperboleon, Diezeugmenon, and Synemmenon, in the foregoing
‘ scale.

‘ There is besides these the Mese, the number of which is 4608,
‘ which is the double of 2304, the number of the Nete hyperboleon,
‘ because there is between the one and the other chord the interval of
‘ a diapason.

‘ The number 5184 of the Lychanos meson is twice the number
‘ 2592 of the Paranete hyperboleon, because there is between them
‘ the same interval of the diapason; and so the following numbers to-
‘ wards the grave are double to the numbers belonging to the acute
‘ chords, following from the Paranete hyperboleon in succession; be-
‘ cause there is between them all, in their respective degrees, the usual
‘ interval of the diapason. As the sounds of the diatonic genus have
‘ their numbers, so likewise have the sounds of the other genera num-
‘ bers, which are peculiar to them, except the Nete hyperboleon, the
‘ Nete diezeugmenon, the Nete synemmenon, the Paramese, the
‘ Mese, the Hypate meson, the Hypate hypaton, and the Proslamba-
‘ nomenos, whose numbers are common to all the genera, as their
‘ sounds

' founds are fixed. Every thing relating to them may be seen in
' their respective systems.'

It is to be remembered, that it was for the purpose of explaining
the doctrine of the genera that the foregoing enquiry into the proportions of the intervals was entered into; this inquiry respected the
diatonic series only, and the proportions thereby ascertained are the
diapason, diapente, diatessaron, and tone; besides these, another interval, namely, that whereby the diatessaron exceeds the ditone, and
which is generally supposed to be a semitone, for now we shall use
the appellation given to it by the Latin writers, has been adjusted,
and in general shewn to have a ratio of 256 to 243.

But here it is necessary to mention, that the ratio of this interval was
a subject of great controversy with the ancient musicians. What were
the sentiments of Pythagoras about it we are no where told; though if
it be true that he constituted the diatessaron in the ratio of 4 to 3,
and made each of the tones contained in it sesquioctave, it will follow
as a consequence, that the interval necessary to complete that system
must have been in the ratio of 256 to 243: this is certain, that
Boetius, and the rest of the followers of Pythagoras, deny the possibility that it can consist in any other: but this is a method of deduction by numerical calculation, and the appeal is made to our reason,
which, in a question of this nature, say some, has nothing to do.

The first who asserted this doctrine, and he has done it in terms
the most explicit, was Aristoxenus, the disciple and successor of
Aristotle; he taught that as the ear is the ultimate judge of confonance, we are able by the sense of hearing alone to determine the
measure both of the consonants and dissonants, and that both are to
be measured or estimated, not by ratios but by intervals *. The method he took was this, he considered the diapason as consisting of the
two systems of a diatessaron and diapente; it was easy to discover the
difference between the two to be a tone, which was soon found, allowing the ear to be the judge, to be divisible into semitones. These two
latter intervals being once recognized by the ear, became a common
measure, and enabled him to determine the magnitude of any interval
whatever, which he did by various additions to, and subductions from,
those above mentioned; in like manner as is practised by the fingers of

* Wallis Appendix de Veterum Harmonica, Quarto, pg. 290.

our times, who by an inflantaneous effort of the voice, are able not only to utter a fourth, a fifth, a greater or leffer third, a tone, a femi-tone, and the reft, but by habit and practice are rendered capable of feparating and combining thefe intervals at pleafure, without the affift-ance of any arithmetical procefs or computation.

It muft be confeffed that there feems to be a kind of retrogradation in a procefs which directs the admeafurement of a part by the whole, rather than of the whole by a part, as this evidently does; but not-withftanding this feeming irregularity, the adherents to the former method are very numerous.

The principles on which thefe two very different methods of judg-ing are founded, became the fubject of great contention ; and might perhaps give rife to another queftion, as extenfive in its latitude, as important in its confequences, namely, whether the underftanding or the imagination be the ultimate judge of harmony and beauty ; or, in other words, what are the peculiar offices of reafon and fenfe in fubjects common to them both.   The confequence of this diver-fity of opinions, fo far as it related to mufic, was that, from the time of Ariftoxenus the muficians of earlier times, according as they adhered to the one or the other of thefe opinions, were denominated either Pythagoreans or Ariftoxeneans, by which appellations the two fects continued for a long time to be as much diftinguifhed as thofe of the Peripatetics and Stoics were by their refpective names[*].

But it feems that as well againft the one as the other of the pofi-tions maintained by the two parties, there lay ftrong objections; for as to that of Pythagoras, that reafon, and not the hearing, is to de-termine of confonance and diffonance, it was erroneous in this ref-pect, it accommodated harmonical proportions to incongruous inter-vals; and as to Ariftoxenus, he, by rejecting reafon, and referring all to fenfe, rendered the very fundamentals of the harmonical fcience incapable of demonftration.   The feveral offices of reafon and fenfe, by which we are here to underftand the fenfe of hearing, are very accu-rately difcriminated by Ptolemy, who undertook the tafk of review-ing this controverfy; and the method he took to reconcile thefe two militant pofitions will be fhewn at large in that extract from his trea-tife, which we mean hereafter to exhibit in its proper place; the

---

[*] Porphyrii in Ptolemæi Harmonica Commentarius, Edit. Wallifii, pag. 189.

only

only queſtion at preſent to be diſcuſſed, is that relating to the meaſure of the diateſſaron. That it exceeded two of thoſe tones one whereof conſtituted the difference between the diapente and diateſſaron, was agreed by both parties; but the meaſure of this exceſs was the point in debate : the Pythagoreans aſſerted it to be an interval in the ratio of 256 to 243, to which, for want of a better, they gave the name of Limma; the Ariſtoxeneans, on the other hand, contended that it was neither more nor leſs than a ſemitone. The queſtion then became, Whether is the ſyſtem of a diateſſaron compounded of two tones and a limma, or of two tones and a ſemitone?

Ptolemy has entered into a very minute examination of this queſtion; and though he profeſſes to be, as he certainly is, an impartial arbiter between the two ſects, and is very free in his cenſures on each; yet has he moſt irrefragably demonſtrated the Pythagorean tenet to be the true one. The method he has taken to do it may be ſeen in the firſt book of his Harmonics, chap. x. but the following proceſs will enable any one to judge of the force of his reaſoning.

Let the number 1536, which it is ſaid is the ſmalleſt that will ſerve the purpoſe, be taken, and after that 1728, its ſeſquioctave, to expreſs a tone ; and again, the ſeſquioctave of 1728, which is 1944, for another tone; the numbers 1536 and 1944 will then ſtand for the ditone. The diateſſaron is ſeſquitertian, or as 4 to 3, it is therefore neceſſary to ſeek a number that ſhall contain four of thoſe parts, of which 1536 is three, and this can be no other than 2048; ſo that the interval whereby the diateſſaron exceeds the ditone, is in the ratio of 2048 to 1944; or, in ſmaller numbers, as 256 to 243. But to judge of the magnitude of this interval, let the ſeſquioctave of 1944, 2187 be taken for a third tone ; it will then remain to enquire the difference between the two ratios 2187 to 2048, and 2048 to 1944, and the former will be found the greater; for 2187 exceeds 2048 by more than a fifteenth, and by leſs than a fourteenth part; whereas 2048 exceeds 1944 by more than a nineteenth, and by leſs than an eighteenth; and conſequently that which, together with the ditone completes the diateſſaron, is the leſſer part of the third tone.

Salinas calls this demonſtration of Ptolemy an excellent one, as moſt undoubtedly it is, and in his Treatiſe de Muſica, lib. II. cap. xx. exhibits it in the following diagram.

DIATES-

DIATESSARON.

GREATER TONE.   GREATER TONE.   GREATER TONE.

APOTOME.   LIMMA.

2187 ·   2048   1944   1728   1536

To this leffer part of the third tone 2048 to 1944, or in leffer numbers, 256 to 243, was given the name of the Limma of Pythagoras; though fome writers, and thofe of the Pythagorean fect, fcrupled not to term it a Diefis. The greater part of the tone refulting from the above divifion was termed Apotome, a word fignifying the refidue of what remains of a line after part has been cut off.

Salinas, lib. II. cap. xx. remarks, that both the theoretic and practical muficians among the moderns are deceived in thinking that the Apotome of the ancients is that interval, which, in fuch mufical inftruments as the organ, and others of the like kind, is found between ♭ and ♮; or, in other words, that the interval between ♮ and b is greater than that between ♮ and c, and than that between b and a; when, fays he, the thing is quite the reverfe, and may be proved by the ear.

Farther, lib. II. cap. x. he obferves of the Limma, that as Pythagoras had divided the diapafon into two diateffarons and a fefquioctave tone, he difcovered that the diateffaron was capable of a like method of divifion, namely, into two continued tones, and that interval which remained after a fubtraction of the ditone from the diateffaron. And this which he calls a femitone, is that which Ptolemy calls the femitone accepted and beft known; and of which Plato in Timeus makes mention; when having followed the fame proportion, he fays that all the duple ratios were to be filled up with fefquitertias and a fefquioctave, and all the fefquitertias with fefquioctaves, and the interval 256 to 243. He adds, that Cicero mentions this femitone in his book de Univerfitate, as does Boetius in all his divifions; and that there were none of the ancients to whom it was not known, for that all the philofophers embraced the Pythagorean traditions of mufic. The fame author adds, that the Pythagorean Limma was efteemed by the Greeks, particularly Bacchius and Bryennius, to be

Vol. I.   L   irrational;

irrational ; and that Plato himfelf dared not to call it a proportion, for the reafon, as he conceives, that it was not fuperparticular.

Hitherto we have fpoken of the tone in general terms, and as an interval in a fefquioctave ratio, fuch as conflitutes the difference between the diateflaron and diapente, and it is faid that the Pythagoreans acknowledged no other *; it is neverthelefs neceffary to mention that there is a leffer interval, to which the appellation of .one is alfo given; the ratio whereof is that of 10 to 9. It is not fufficiently clear who it was that firft difcovered it, but, from feveral paffages in the harmonics of Ptolemy †, it fhould feem that Didymus, an ancient mufician, whom he frequently takes occafion to mention, was the firft that adjufted its ratio.

Dr. Wallis, who feems to have founded his opinion on that of Salinas, and certainly entertained the cleareft conceptions of the fubject, has demonftrated very plainly how both the greater and leffer tone are produced; for affuming the diapente to be in the ratio of 3 to 2, or which is the fame, the numbers being doubled, 6 to 4; by the interpofition of the arithmetical mean 5, he fhews it to contain two intervals, the one in the ratio of 6 to 5, the other in that of 5 to 4 ‡.

DIAPENTE.	
Semiditone	Ditone
6 5 4	
Sefquialtera.	

The latter of thefe, which conftituted the ditone or greater third, fubtracted from the diapente, left that interval in the ratio of 6 to 5, which by the Greeks was called a Tribemitone, and by the Latins a deficient, or *femi* ditone, but by the moderns a leffer or flat third.

The confideration of the femiditone will be hereafter refumed; but as to the ditone, it had a fuperparticular ratio, and confequently would not, any more than the diapente, admit of an equal divifion‖.

* Salinas de Mufca, l b. II. cap. 17. Boet. lib. IV. cap. 5.
† Lib II. cap. 13, 14. Salinas, lib. II. cap. 17.
‡ Wallis, Append, de Vet. Harm. quarto, pag. 322.
‖ That a fuperparticular is incapable of an equal divifion is clearly demonftrated by Boetius, lib. III. cap. 1 and muft be confidered as a firft principle in harmonics. Vide. Macrobius in Somnium Scipionis, lib. II. cap. 1.

In

In order therefore to come at one that should be the nearest to equality, Dr. Wallis doubled the terms 5, 4, and thereby produced the numbers 10, 8, which have the same ratio. Nothing then was wanting but the interposition of the arithmetical mean 9,

DITONE		
Greater Tone	Lesser Tone	
8	9	10
Sesquioctave	Sesquinonal	
Sesquiquarta		

and a division was effected which produced the greater or sesquioctave tone, 9 to 8, and the lesser or sesquinonal tone, 10 to 9 *.

C H A P.   VI.

HAVING thus adjusted the proportions of the greater and lesser tone, it follows next in order to consider the several divisions of each, the first and most obvious whereof is that of the semitone; but here two things are to be remarked, the one that the adjunct *semi*, though it may seem to express, as it does in most instances, the half of any given quantity, yet in musical language has a signification the same with deficient or incomplete: the other is that although as the lesser is always contained in the greater, and consequently the tone comprehends the semitone and more, yet the semitone is not, nor can be found in, or at least cannot be extracted from, or produced by any possible division of the tone. The Aristoxeneans, who asserted that the diatessaron consisted of two tones and a half, had no other way of defining the half tone, than by taking the ditone out of the diatessaron, and the residue they pronounced to be a hemitone, as it nearly is; and the Pythagoreans, who professed the admeasurement and determination of intervals by ratios, and not by the ear, were necessitated to proceed in the same way; for after

* Wallis Append. de Vet. Harm. quarto, pag. 323. Salinas de Music. lib. II. cap. 17.

Pythagoras had adjusted the diezeuctic tone, and found its ratio to be sesquioctave, or as 9 to 8, it no where appears that he or any of his followers proceeded to a division of that interval into semitones, and indeed it is not in the nature of the thing possible to effect any such division of it by equal parts. Ptolemy, who, so far as regards the method of defining the intervals by their ratios, must be said to have been a Pythagorean, has had recourse to this method of subtracting a lesser interval from a greater for adjusting the proportion of the Limma; for after having assumed that the ratio of the diatessaron was sesquitertia, answering to the numbers 8 and 6, or which is the same, 4 to 3, he measures out three sesquioctave tones, 1536, 1728, 1944, 2187, and subtracts from them the diatessaron 2048 to 1536, and thereby leaves a ratio of 2187 to 2048, which is that of the apotome; the limma 2048 to 1944, then remains an adjunct to the two sesquioctave tones 1728 to 1536, and 1944 to 1728; and the ratio of 2048 to 1536 is 8 to 6, or 4 to 3; and would we know the ratio of 2048 to 1944, it will be found to be 256 to 243, for eight times 256 is 2048, and eight times 243 is 1944 *.

And Didymus, who after he had discovered the necessity of a distinction of tones into the greater and lesser, and found that it required an interval different in magnitude from the limma, to complete the diatessaron, had no way to ascertain the ratio of that interval, but by first adjusting that of the ditone; in the doing whereof he also determined that of the semitone, for so are we necessitated to call the interval by which the diatessaron is found to exceed the ditone.   With respect to this interval, which, in the judgment of Salinas, is of such importance, that he seems to think it the hinge on which the knowledge of all instrumental harmony turns; it seems clearly to have taken place of the limma, immediately after the discrimination of the greater and lesser tone: and there is reason to think it was investigated by Didymus in the following manner.   First he considered the ratio of the diatessaron to be, as has been shewn, sesquitertian, or as 8 to 6; or, which is the same, those numbers being doubled, 16 to 12.   The ditone he had demonstrated to be in sesquiquarta proportion, as 5 to 4.   It remained then to find out a number that should contain 5 of these parts, of which 12 contained four, and this could

* See the preceding demonstration of the ratio of the Pythagorean limma.

be no other than 15, and thefe being fet down, demonftrated the ratio of the femitone to be 16 to 15.

DIATESSARON		
Ditone	Greater Semitone	
12	15	16
Sefquiquarta	Sefquidecimaquinta	
Sefquitertia		

This interval is alfo the difference between the femiditone 6 to 5, and the fefquioctave tone 9 to 8, which, multiplying the extreme numbers by 3, is thus demonftrated.

SEMIDITONE		
Greater Semitone	Tone	
15	16	18
Sefquidecimaquinta	Sefquioctave	
Sefquiquinta		

But it feems that this interval, fo very accurately adjufted, did not anfwer all the combinations of which the greater and leffer tones were capable; nor was it adapted to any divifion of the fyftem, other than that which diftinguifhes the diatonic genus. Thefe confidera-tions gave rife to the invention of the leffer femitone, an interval fo peculiarly appropriated to the chromatic genus, that Salinas and Merfennus fcruple not to call it the Chromatic Diefis; the meafure of it is the difference between the ditone and femiditone, the former whereof is demonftrated to be in fefquiquarta proportion, or as 5 to 4; or, which is the fame, each of thofe numbers being multiplied by 5, 25 to 20. The femiditone is fefquiquinta, that is to fay, as 6 to 5; or multiplying each of thofe numbers by four, as 24 to 20; from a comparifon therefore of the femiditone with the ditone, it will ap-

---

* This and moft of the diagrams for demonftrating the other intervals are taken from Salinas, who, it is to be remarked, differs from many other writers in the order of the numbers of ratios, placing the fmalleft firft.

† Salinas, lib. II. cap. xviii.

pear

quent division of the tone into lesser parts, the name of diesis has been given sometimes to one, and at others to other parts arising from that division; and hence those different definitions which we meet with of this interval; but the general opinion touching it is that it is less than a semitone, and more than a comma. We will consider it in all its variety of significations.

Boetius, in the third book of his treatise de Musica, has related at large the method taken by Philolaus the Pythagorean for dividing the tone into nine parts, called commas, of which we shall speak more particularly hereafter; according to this division, two commas make a diaschisma, and two diaschismata a diesis. This is one of the senses in which the term diesis is used, but it is not easy to discover the use of this interval, for it does not seem to be adapted either to the tetrachord composed of sesquioctave tones, or that later one of Didymus, which supposes a distinction of a greater and lesser tone; so that in this instance the term seems to be restrained to its primitive signification, and to import nothing more than a particle; and Salinas seems to concur in this sense of the word when he says that in each of the genera of melodies the least interval is called a diesis.

In other instances we are to understand by it such an interval as, together with others, will complete the system of a diatessaron. There are required to form a diatessaron, or tetrachord in each of the genera, tones, semitones, and diesis. In the diatonic genus the diesis is clearly that, be it either a semitone, a limma, or any other interval, which, together with two tones is necessary to complete the tetrachord. If with the Pythagoreans we suppose the two tones to be sesquioctave, it will follow that the diesis and the limma 256 to 243 are one and the same interval; on the other hand, if with Didymus we assign to the two tones, the different ratios of 10 to 9, and 9 to 8, the interval necessary to complete the diatessaron will be 16 to 15; or the difference between the ditone in the ratio of 5 to 4, and the diatessaron above demonstrated. In short, this suppletory interval, whatever it be, is the only one in the diatonic genus, to which the appellation of diesis is ever given.

To the chromatic genus belong two intervals of different magnitudes, and the term diesis is common to both; the first of these is that of 25 to 24, mentioned above, and shewn to be the difference between the ditone and semiditone, and is what Salinas has appropriated

propriated to the chromatic genus. Gaudentius mentions alfo another fpecies of diefis that occurs in this genus, in quantity the third part of a tone *, in which he has followed Arifloxenus; but as all the divifions of the Arifloxeneans were regulated by the ear, and fuppofed a divifion of the tone into equal parts, which parts being equal, muft neceffarily be irrational, it would be in vain to feek a numerical ratio for the third part of a tone.

We are now to fpeak of that other diefis incident to the enarmonic genus, to which the term, in the opinion of moft writers, feems to be appropriated †; for whereas the other diefis obtained that name, only as being the fmalleft interval required in each genus, this other is the fmalleft that any kind of mufical progreffion will poffibly admit of. Ariftides Quintilianus fays, a diefis is as it were a diffolution of the voice ‡.

According to Boetius, who muft every where be underftood to fpeak the fenfe of the Pythagoreans, the two diefes contained in the tetrachord of the enarmonic genus muft have been unequal, for he makes them to arife from an arithmetical divifion of the limma, 256 to 243 ∥.

Ptolemy has exhibited §, as he has done in each of the other genera, a table of the enarmonic genus, according to five different muficians, all of whom, excepting Arifloxenus, make the diefes to be unequal, thofe of Ptolemy are 24 to 23, and 46 to 45.

Salinas ufes but one enarmonic diefis, which he makes to be the difference between the greater femitone 16 to 15, and the leffer 25 to 24.

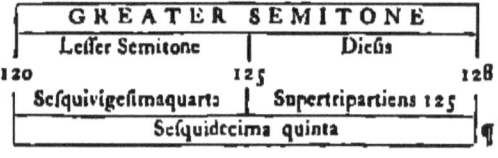

* Ex Verf. Meibom. pag. 5.
† Boetius, lib. II. cap. 23, has given diefes only to the enarmonic.
‡ Ex Verf. Meibom. pag. 13.
∥ Boetius, lib. IV. cap. 5.
§ Lib. II. cap. 14.
¶ Salinas, lib. II. cap. 21.

Which

Which numbers are thus produced, 15 and 16 each multiplied by 8 will give 120, and 128, for the greater femitone; we are then to feek for a number that bears the fame ratio to 120, as 25 does to 24, which can be no other than 125, fo that the ratio of the diefis will ftand 125 to 128.

Broffard has applied the term diefis to thofe figns or characters ufed by the moderns to denote the feveral degrees by which a found may be elevated or depreffed above or beneath its natural fituation; for the doing whereof he feems to have had no better authority than that of the practitioners of his time, who perhaps are the only perfons entitled to an excufe for having given to the fign the name of the thing fignified. He profeffes to follow Kircher, when he fays that there are three forts of diefes, namely, the leffer enarmonic or fimple diefis, containing two commas or about a quarter of a tone; the chromatic or double diefis, containing a leffer femitone, or nearly four commas, and the greater enarmonic diefis, containing nearly three fourths of a tone, or from fix to feven commas; but this definition is by much too loofe to fatisfy a fpeculative mufician.

Thefe are all the intervals that are requifite in the conftitution of a tetrachord in any of the three genera: it may not be improper however to mention a divifion of the tone, invented perhaps rather as an effay towards a temperature, than as neceffary to the perfection of the genera; namely, that afcribed by Boetius, and others to Philolaus, by which the tone was made to confift of nine parts or commas.

The account of this matter given by Boetius is long, and rather perplexed; but Glareanus[*], who has been at the pains of extracting from it the hiftory of this divifion, fpeaks of it thus. ' A tone in a
' fefquioctave ratio is divided into a greater and leffer femitone; the
' greater was by the Greeks called an apotome, the leffer a limma or
' diefis, and the difference between thefe two was a comma. The
' diefis was again divided into diafchifmata, of which it contained
' two; and the comma into fchifmata, two whereof made the comma.'
The paffage, to give it at length, is thus.

' It is demonftrated by muficians, for good reafons, that a tone
' cannot be divided into two equal parts, becaufe no fuperparticular
' ratio, fuch as is that of a tone, is capable of fuch a divifion,

‘ as Divus Severinus Boetius fully shews in his third book, chap. i.
‘ a tone which is in a sesquioctave ratio is divided into a greater and
‘ lesser semitone. The Greeks call the greater semitone an apotome,
‘ and the lesser a diesis or limma; but the lesser semitone is divided
‘ into two diaschismata. The excess whereby a greater semitone is
‘ more than a lesser one is called a comma, and this comma is divided
‘ into two parts, which are called schismata by Philolaus. This
‘ Philolaus, according to Boetius, gives us the definitions of all those
‘ parts. A diesis, he says, is that space by which a sesquialteral ratio
‘ or diatessaron exceeds two tones; and a comma is that space
‘ whereby a sesquioctave ratio is greater than two dieses, that
‘ is than two lesser semitones. A schisma is that half of a
‘ comma, and a diaschisma is the half of a diesis, that is of a lesser
‘ semitone; from which definitions and the following scheme you
‘ may easily find out into how many diaschismata, and the other
‘ smaller spaces, a tone may be divided, for the same Boetius shews
‘ that it can be done many ways in his treatise, lib. III. cap. viii.
‘ from whence we have taken these descriptions. It is to be observed
‘ that the name of diesis is proper in this place; but when, as the
‘ ancients have done, we give it to the enarmonic diaschisma it is
‘ improper.

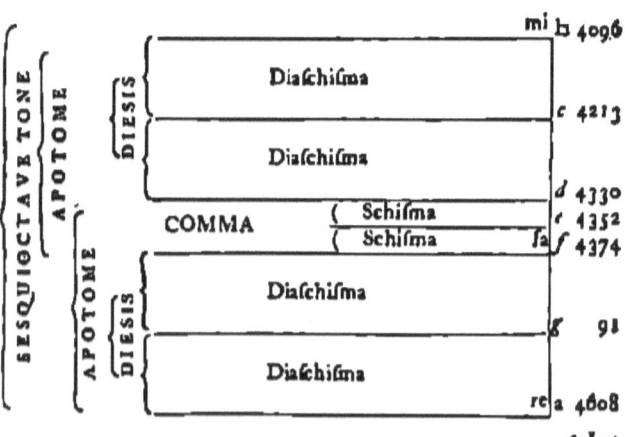

‘ Let

' Let a ♭ be a tone, ♭ d, or f a, a leſſer ſemitone, or as the Greeks
' call it, as Boetius witneſſeth lib. II. cap. xxvii, a limma or dieſis,
' ♭ f, or d a, a greater ſemitone, called by the Greeks an apotome,
' ♭ c and c d, alſo f g and g a, diaſchiſmata, or the halves of a dieſis,
' d f a comma, whoſe halves d e and e f are ſchiſmata; but it is ne-
' ceſſary for our purpoſe to obſerve this, let a be Meſe, or a la mi
' re, f Trite ſynemmenon or fa in b fa ♭ mi ♭ Parameſe or mi in b
' fa ♭ mi, therefore the note re in a la mi re is diſtant from fa in b
' fa ♭ mi by a leſſer hemitone, and from mi in the ſame key by a
' tone; from whence it follows, that the two notes in b fa ♭ mi,
' which ſeem to be of the ſame key, are farther diſtant from each
' other than from the extremes or neighbouring keys above and
' below, viz. mi from c ſol fa ut, and fa from a la mi re, for mi
' and fa are ſeparated from each other by a greater ſemitone, and
' from the extremes on either ſide by only a leſſer ſemitone, for
' which reaſon this theory is not to be deſpiſed. We muſt not omit
' what the ſame Severinus tells us in lib. III. cap. xiv. and xv. to wit
' that a leſſer ſemitone is not altogether four commas, but ſomewhat
' more than three; and that a greater ſemitone is not five commas,
' but ſomewhat more than four; from whence it comes to paſs that
' a tone exceeds eight commas, but does not quite make up nine.'

This of Philolaus is generally deemed the true diviſion of the tone,
and may ſerve to prove the truth of that poſition, which all the theoretic writers on muſic ſeem to agree in, namely, that the ſeſquioctave tone, as being in a ſuperparticular ratio, is incapable of an equal
diviſion. But unfortunately the numbers made uſe of by Glareanus
do not anſwer to the diviſion, for thoſe for the dieſis or limma ♭ d
4330, 4096 have no ſuch ratio as 256 to 243, which is what the
limma requires, and that other f a, has, and it ſeems that in his aſſertion that ♭ and b are farther diſtant from each other than from c
and a, reſpectively, he is miſtaken. This is noticed by Salinas, who
inſiſts that the converſe of the propoſition is the truth. De Muſica,
lib. II. cap. xx *.

As to the comma, it appears by the foregoing calculation to be in the
ratio of 4374 to 4330. Neverthelefs Salinas, for the purpoſe of accommodating it to practice, has aſſumed for the comma an interval in the
ratio of 81 to 80, which is different from that of Glareanus and Boe-

* See his ſentiment of it pag. 73 of the preſent work.

tius,

tius, but is clearly fhewn by Salinas to be the difference between the greater and leffer tone. Ptolemy looked upon this latter comma as an infenfible interval, and thought that therefore it was a thing indifferent whether the fefquioctave or the fefquinonal tone held the acuteft fituation in the diatonic tetrachord; but Salinas afferts, that though it is the leaft, it is yet one of the fenfible intervals, and that by means of an inftrument which he himfelf caufed to be made at Rome, he was enabled to diftinguifh, and by his ear to judge, of the difference between the one and the other of the tones.

Merfennus fays that the Pythagoreans had another comma, which was in the ratio of 531441 to 524288, and was between fefqui $\frac{1}{11}$ and fefqui $\frac{1}{12}$; and that Chriftopher Mondore, in a book inferibed by him to Margaret, the fifter of Henry III. of France, fpeaks of another between fefqui $\frac{1}{11}$, and fefqui $\frac{1}{17}$ *. As to the firft, though he does not mention it, it is clear that he took the ratio of it from Salinas, who in the nineteenth and thirty-firft chapters of his fourth book fpeaks very particularly of the Pythagorean comma, and fays that it is the difference whereby the apotome exceeds the limma.

We have now inveftigated in a regular progreffion the ratios of the feveral intervals of the greater and leffer tone, the greater and leffer femitone, the apotome and limma, the diefis, and the comma; and thereby refolved the tetrachord into its elements. It may be worth while to obferve the fingular beauties that arife in the courfe of this deduction, and how wonderfully the leffer intervals fpring out of the greater; for the difference between

The $\begin{Bmatrix} \text{Diapente and} \\ \text{Diateffaron} \end{Bmatrix}$ is   -   -   -   a fefquioctave tone.

The $\begin{Bmatrix} \text{Ditone and} \\ \text{Greater tone} \end{Bmatrix}$ is   -   -   -   a fefquinonal tone.

The $\begin{Bmatrix} \text{Semiditone and greater tone and alfo} \\ \text{between the diateffaron and ditone} \end{Bmatrix}$ is   a greater femitone.

The $\begin{Bmatrix} \text{Leffer tone and greater femitone and alfo} \\ \text{between the ditone and femiditone} \end{Bmatrix}$ is a leffer femitone.

The $\begin{Bmatrix} \text{Greater tone and} \\ \text{Leffer tone} \end{Bmatrix}$ is   -   -   a comma.

The $\begin{Bmatrix} \text{Greater femitone and} \\ \text{Leffer femitone} \end{Bmatrix}$ is   -   -   an enarmonic diefis.

* Harmonicor. lib. V. de Diffonantiis, pag. 83.

Sali-

Salinas remarks much to the same purpose on the regular order of the simple confonances in thefe words. ' It feems worthy of the ' greateft obfervation, that the differences of the fimple confonances, ' each above that which is the next under it, are found to be in the ' proportions which the firft fquare numbers hereunderwritten bear ' to thofe that are the next lefs to them : to inftance in the diapafon, ' the excefs above the diapente is the diateffaron, which is found in ' the ratio between the firft fquare number 4, and its next lefs num- ' ber 3. The excefs of the diapente above the diateffaron is the ' greater tone, which is found in the ratio between the numbers 9 ' and 8. Again, that of the diateffaron above the ditone is the ' greater femitone, found in the ratio 16 to 15; farther, the excefs ' of the ditone above the femiditone is the leffer femiditone 25 to 24. ' All thefe will appear more clearly in the following difpofition of the ' numbers.

A				
B	C	A	B	C
2	3	4	Diapafon	Diapente	Diateffaron
6	8	9	Diapente	Diateffaron	Tone Major
12	15	16	Diateffaron	Ditone	Semitone majus
20	24	25	Ditone	Semiditone	Semitone minus

' In the above difpofition, the laft numbers are fquare, the firft lon- ' gilateral, and the middle ones lefs than thofe that are fquare by ' unity, but greater than the longilateral ones by as many units as ' there are numbers of fquares above them. The greateft ratios are ' thofe between the longilaterals and the fquares, the leffer between ' the longilaterals and middle numbers, and the leaft or differences ' thofe between the fquares and the middle ones. Of the ratios the ' greateft are marked A, the leffer B, and the leaft C *.'

Obfervations of this kind are perpetually occuring in the courfe of harmonical calculations; and it cannot but be a matter of aftonifh- ment to an intelligent mind to find, that thofe combinations of mufi- cal founds which afford delight to the fenfe of hearing, have fuch a relation among themfelves, and are difpofed with fuch order and re-

* De Mufica, lib. II. cap. xx.

gularity,

gularity, that they approve themselves also to the understanding, and exhibit to the mind a new species of beauty, such as is observable in theorems, and will for ever result from design, regularity, truth, and order. It is said that the senses are arbitrary, and that too in so great a degree, as to give occasion to a well known axiom that precludes all dispute about them; but that of hearing seems to be an exception; for what the ear recognizes to be grateful, the understanding approves as true. To enquire farther into the reasons why the sense is delighted with harmony and consonance, would be vain, since all beyond what we are able to discover by numerical calculation is resolvable into the will of Him who has ordered all things in number, weight, and measure.

The genera, as has been mentioned, were three; the diatonic, the chromatic, and the enarmonic. We are farther to understand a subdivision of these into species. Gaudentius expressly says, ' The ' species or colours of the genera are many *,' and an author of much greater authority, Aristoxenus, has particularly enumerated them. According to him the diatonic genus had two species, the soft and the intense; the chromatic three, the soft, the hemiolian †, and the tonic ‡ ; as to the enarmonic, it had no subdivision. Indeed the representations of the genera and their species, as well by diagrams as in words, are almost as numerous as the writers on music. Monsieur Brossard has exhibited a view of the Aristoxenean division, taken, as he says, from Vitruvius; and the same is to be met with in an English dictionary of music, published in the year 1740, by James Grassineau ‖.

* Ex Vers. Meibom. pag. 5.
† This is but another name for sesquialtera, as Andreas Ornithoparcus asserts in his Micrologus, lib. II. on the authority of Aulus Gellius. It signifies a whole and its half, consequently the sesquialtera ratio in its smallest numbers is 3 to 2.
‡ Vide Wall. Append. de veter. Harm. quarto, pag. 299.
‖ At the time when the above book was published the world were surprized; no such person as James Grassineau being known to it as possessed of any great share of musical erudition, and the work offered to the public appeared to be the result of great study and skill in the science. But the wonder ceased when it came to be known that the basis of Grassineau's book was the Dictionaire de Musique of Monsieur Sebastian Brossard of Strasburg; though, to do him justice, Grassineau in his preface ingenuously confesses he had made a liberal use of it. For the rest of it he stood indebted to Dr. Pepusch, and perhaps in a small degree to the other masters, Dr. Greene and Mr. Galliard, who have joined in the recommendation of it.
Grassineau was an ingenious young man; he understood the Latin and French languages, the latter very well, and knew a little of music; he had been clerk to Mr. Godfrey

But this reprefentation is not near fo particular and accurate, as the Ariftoxenean Synopfis of the Genera given by Dr. Wallis in the Appendix to his edition of Ptolemy, and here inferted.

	Enarmonic Genus	Chromatic Genus			Diatonic Genus		
		Soft	Hemiolian	Toniac	Soft	Intenfe	
30	Nete	Nete	Nete	Nete	Nete	Nete	30
24						12	24
				18	15		
18	24	22	21			Paranete Lichanos	18
15					Paranete Lichanos		15
12				Paranete Lichanos		12	12
9		Paranete Lichanos	Paranete Lichanos	6	9		9
6	Paranete Lichanos	4 Trite	4½ Trite Parypate 6	Trite Parypate 6	Trite Parypate 6	Trite Parypate 6	6
3	Trite Parhypate 3	Parypate 4	Parypate 4½				3

frey the chemift in Southampton-ftreet, Covent-Garden, but being out of employ, he became the amanuenfis of Dr. Pepufch, and tranflated for him into Englifh fome of the Greek harmonicians from the Latin verfion of Meibomius. The Doctor having no far-ther occafion for him, recommended it to him to tranflate Broffard's dictionary above-mentioned, which he undertook and completed, the Doctor furnifhing him with many new articles, and with additional matter for the enlargement of thofe contained in Brof-fard; and Graffineau's dictionary would have been an ineftimable prefent to the mufical world, had due care been taken in the correction of it, but it abounds with errors, and the author is not now living to correct them in a new edition.

Although the dictionary of Broffard, and this of Graffineau contain a great variety of ufeful knowledge, it is to be wifhed that it had been communicated to the world in fome better form than that of a dictionary; for to fpeak of the latter, fome of the articles con-tained in it are complete treatifes.

2   In

In order to underſtand this ſcheme, we muſt ſuppoſe the tetrachord hypaton, though any other would have ſerved the purpoſe as well, divided into thirty equal parts: in the primitive diviſion of this ſyſtem, according to the diatonic genus, the ſtations of the two intermediate ſounds parypate and lichanos, for it is to be noted that thoſe at the extremities termed ſtabiles, or immoveables, were at 6 and 18; that is to ſay, the firſt interval in the tetrachord was 6 parts, and each of the other two 12, making together 30; ſo that the ſecond interval was the double of the firſt, and the third equal to the ſecond, anſwering preciſely to the hemitone, tone, and tone; this is ſpoken of the intenſe diatonic, for it is that ſpecies which the ancients are ſuppoſed to have meant whenever they ſpoke of the diatonic generally.

The ſoft diatonic has for its firſt interval 6, for its ſecond 9, or a hemitone and a quadrantal dieſis, or three fourths of a tone, and for its third 15, viz. a tone and a quadrantal dieſis.

We are now to ſpeak of the chromatic genus, the firſt ſpecies whereof, the tonic, had for its firſt interval 6, or a hemitone; for its ſecond alſo 6, and for its third 18, a tribemitone, or tone and a half.

In the hemiolian chromatic, called alſo the ſeſquialteral *, the firſt and alſo the ſecond interval was 4½, which is a hemiolian or ſeſquialteral dieſis; and the third 21, or a tone, a hemitone, and a quadrantal dieſis.

The ſoft chromatic makes the firſt and alſo the ſecond interval a triental dieſis or third part of a tone, by aſſigning to parypate and lichanos, the ſtations of 4 and 18; and gives to the third twenty-two twelfths of a tone, or, which is the ſame, twenty-two thirtieths of the whole tetrachord, which amount to a tone, a hemitone, and a triental dieſis.

In the enarmonic genus, which, in the opinion of moſt authors, had no diviſion into ſpecies, the firſt and ſecond intervals, being terminated by 3 and 6, were each quadrantal dieſes, or three twelfths of a tone, and the laſt a ditone. Of the dieſis in this genus it is ſaid by Ariſtoxenus and others, that it is the ſmalleſt interval that the human voice is capable of expreſſing; and it is farther to be remarked, that it is ever termed the enarmonic dieſis, as being appropriated to the enarmonic genus.

Euclid's

* Vide pag. 86, in not.

Euclid's account of the genera is not much different from this of Ariftoxenus. The diatonic, he fays, proceeds from the acute to the grave by a tone, a tone, and a hemitone; and, on the contrary, from the grave to the acute by a hemitone, a tone, and a tone. The chromatic from the acute to the grave by a trihemitone, a hemitone, and a hemitone; and, contrarywife, from the grave to the acute by a hemitone, a hemitone, and a trihemitone. The enarmonic progreffion, he fays, is a defcent to the grave by a ditone, a diefis, and a diefis; and an afcent to the acumen by a diefis, a diefis, and a ditone. He fpeaks of a commixture of the genera, as namely, the diatonic with the chromatic, the diatonic with the enarmonic, and the chromatic with the enarmonic.

He exhibits the hifdiapafon according to each of the genera, enumerating the feveral founds as they occur, from Proflambanomenos to Nete hyperboleon, and obferves that fome of them are termed Stantes or ftanding founds, and others Mobiles or moveable; the meaning of which is no more than that the extreme founds of each tetrachord are immoveable, and that the difference between the genera confifts in thofe feveral mutations of the intervals, which are made by affigning different pofitions to the two intermediate founds.

Colour he defines to be a particular divifion of a genus; and, agreeable to what is faid by Ariftoxenus, he fays that of the enarmonic there is one only; of the chromatic three, and of the diatonic two. He fays farther, that the enarmonic progreffion is by a diefis, a diefis and incompofite ditone; that the chromatic colours or fpecies are the foft, proceeding by two diefes, each being the third part of a tone, and an incompofite interval equal to a tone, and its third part; and the fefquialteral, proceeding by a diefis in a fefquialteral ratio to that in the enarmonic, another fuch diefis, and an incompofite interval confifting of feven diefes, each equal to a fourth part of a tone; and the tonic by a hemitone, a hemitone, and a trihemitone. Of the diatonic he fays there are two fpecies, namely the foft and the intenfe, by fome called alfo the fyntonous; the former proceeding by a hemitone, an interval of three quadrantal diefes, and by another of five fuch diefes; and the latter by a common divifion, with its genus, namely, a tone, a tone, and a hemitone.

And here it is to be obferved, that thefe feveral definitions of the genera are taken from fome one or other of their refpective fpecies;

thus that of the tonic chromatic is the same by which the genus itself is defined; and the definition of the syntonous or intense diatonic is what is used to denote the genus itself. From hence it should
seem that of the species some were deemed spurious, or at least that
some kind of pre-eminence among them, unknown to us, occasioned
this distinction; which amounts to no less than saying that the soft
chromatic is more truly the chromatic than either of the other two
species of that genus; and that the intense or syntonous diatonic is
more truly the diatonic than the soft diatonic: as to the enarmonic, it
cannot in strictness be said to have had any colour or species, for it
admits of no specific division.

To demonstrate the intervals in each species by numbers, Euclid
supposes a division of the tone into twelve parts. To the hemitone
he gives six, to the quadrantal diesis three, and to the triental diesis
four; and to the whole diatessaron he assigns thirty. In the application of these parts to the several species, he says first, that the intervals in the soft chromatic are four, four, and twenty-two; in the
sesquialteral four and a half, four and a half, and twenty-one; and
in the tonic six, six, and eighteen; in the soft diatonic six, nine,
and fifteen; and in the syntonous six, twelve, and twelve.

C H A P.   VII.

A RISTIDES Quintilianus, who, in the judgment of Dr.
Wallis *, seems in this respect to have been an Aristoxenean,
speaks of the genera and their species in the following manner.
‘ Genus is a certain division of the tetrachord. There are three ge-
‘ nera of modulation, namely the harmonic, chromatic, and diato-
‘ nic ; the difference between them consists in the distances of their
‘ respective intervals. The harmonic is that genus which abounds
‘ in the least intervals, and takes its name from adjoining together.
‘ The diatonic is so called because it proceeds by, or abounds in,
‘ tones. The chromatic is so termed, because, as that which is be-

---

* Append. de veter. Harm. pag. 316.

‘ tween

‘ tween white and black is called Colour, fo alfo that which holds
‘ the middle place between the two former genera as this does, is
‘ named Chroma. The enarmonic is fung by a diefis, diefis, and an
‘ incompofite ditone towards the acute; and contrarywife towards
‘ the grave. The chromatic towards the acute by a hemitone, a he-
‘ mitone, and trihemitone; and contrarywife towards the grave.
‘ The diatonic by a hemitone, a tone, and tone towards the acute;
‘ and contrarywife towards the grave. The diatonic is the moft na-
‘ tural of all, becaufe it may be fung by every one, even by fuch as
‘ are unlearned. The moft artificial is the chromatic, for only learn-
‘ ed men can modulate it; but the moft accurate is the enarmonic :
‘ it is approved of by only the moft fkilful muficians; for thofe who
‘ are otherwife look on the diefis as an interval which can by no
‘ means be fung, and to thefe, by reafon of the debility of their
‘ faculties, the ufe of this genus is impoffible. Each of the genera
‘ may be modulated both by confecutive founds and by leaps,
‘ Moreover, modulation is either direct or ftrait forward, revert-
‘ ing or turning back, or circumcurrent, running up and down:
‘ the direct is that which ftretches towards the acute from the grave;
‘ the reverting that which is contrary to the former; and the cir-
‘ cumcurrent is that which is changeable, as when we elevate by
‘ conjunction, and remit by disjunction. Again, fome of the gene-
‘ ra are divided into fpecies, others not. The enarmonic, becaufe
‘ it confifts of the fmalleft diefes, is indivifible. The chromatic may
‘ be divided into as many rational intervals as are found between the
‘ hemitone and enarmonic diefis; the third, namely the diatonic,
‘ into as many rational intervals as are found between the hemitone
‘ and tone; there are therefore three fpecies of the chromatic, and
‘ two of the diatonic. And, to fum up the whole, thefe added to
‘ the enarmonic make fix fpecies of modulation; the firft is diftin-
‘ guifhed by quadrantal diefes, and is called the enarmonic; the
‘ fecond by triental diefes, and is called the foft chromatic; the third
‘ by diefes that are fefquialteral to thofe in the enarmonic, and is
‘ therefore called the fefquialteral chromatic. The fourth has a pe-
‘ culiar conftitution of two hemitones, it is called the tonic chroma-
‘ tic : the fifth confifts of an hemitone and three diefes, and the five
‘ remaining ones, and is called the foft diatonic : the fixth has an

N 2   ‘ hemi-

' hemitone, tone, and tone, and is called the intenfe diatonic. But
' that what we have faid may be made clear, we fhall make the divi-
' fion in the numbers. Let the tetrachord be fuppofed to confift of
' fixty units, the divifion of the enarmonic is 6, 6, 48, by a qua-
' drantal diefis, a quadrantal diefis, and a ditone. The divifion of
' the foft chromatic 8, 8, 44, by a triental diefis, a triental diefis,
' and a trihemitone and triental diefis. The divifion of the fefquial-
' teral chromatic is 9. 9, 42, by a fefquialteral diefis, a fefquialteral
' diefis, and a trihemitone and quadrantal diefis. The divifion of the
' tonic chromatic is 12, 12, 36, by an hemitone, an hemitone, and
' a trihemitone. That of the foft diatonic is 12, 18, 30, by a hemi-
' tone, and three quadrantal diefes, and five quadrantal diefes. That
' of the intenfe diatonic is 12, 24, 24, by a hemitone, a tone, and a
' tone *.'

It is obfervable in this divifion of Ariftides Quintilianus, that the
numbers made ufe of by him are double thofe ufed by Euclid ; the
reafon is, that the two diefes in the fefquialteral chromatic are not fo
well defined by four parts and a half of thirty, as by 9 of 60; and
it is evident that preferving the proportions, whether we take the
number 30 or 60 for the grofs content of the tetrachord, the matter
is juft the fame.

Ptolemy, the moft copious, and one of the moft accurate of all
the ancient harmonicians, has treated very largely of the genera ; and
has, for the reafon above given, adopted the number 60 for the meafure of the tetrachord ; he has reprefented the Ariftoxenean conftitution of the fix fpecies by the following proportions.

Acute	48	44	42	36	30	24
Mean	6	8	9	12	18	24
Grave	6	8	9	12	12	12
	60	60	60	60	60	60
	Enarmonic	Chromatic foft	Chromatic fefquialteral	Chromatic tonic	Diatonic foft	Diatonic intenfe

* Ariftides Quintilianus ex verf. Meib. pag. 18, et feq. in which paffage it is obfervable that he fometimes ufes the term ápµ⊓⊓, and others iisµuuia, to fignify the enarmonic genus.

In

In which proportions he agrees both with Euclid and Ariſtides Quintilianus; though, for the purpoſe of aſcertaining them, he has preferred the numbers of the latter to thoſe uſed by Euclid.

In chapter xiv. of his ſecond book Ptolemy has given the genera, with each of their ſeveral ſpecies, according to five different muſicians, namely, Archytas *, Ariſtoxenus, Eratoſthenes †, Didymus, and himſelf. The ſum of his account, omitting the diviſion of Ariſtoxenus, for that is given above, is as follows.

Archytas	Enarmonic			
	Chromatic			
	Diatonic			
Eratoſthenes	Enarmonic			
	Chromatic			
	Diatonic			
Didymus	Enarmonic			
	Chromatic			
	Diatonic			

In his own diviſion Ptolemy ſuppoſes five ſpecies of the diatonic genus, which, together with the enarmonic, and two ſpecies of the chromatic he thus defines.

Ptolemy	Enarmonic		
	Chromatic	Soft	
		Intenſe	
	Diatonic	Soft	
		Tonic	
		Ditonic	
		Intenſe	
		Equable	

* There were two of this name, the one of Tarentum a Pythagorean, famous, an Aulus Gellius and others relate, for having conſtructed an automaton in the form of a pigeon, which had the power of flying to a conſiderable diſtance; the other a muſician of Mitylene. They are both mentioned by Diogenes Laertius, but it is not certain which of the two was the author of the diviſion here given.

† Eratoſthenes, a Cyrenean philoſopher, and a diſciple of Ariſto and Callimachus, was librarian at Alexandria to Ptolemy Evergetes. He was for his great learning eſteemed a ſecond Plato. An aſtronomical diſcourſe of his is extant in the Oxford edition of Aratus; prefixed to which is an account of many other books of his writing now loſt. He is ſaid to have lived to the age of eighty-two; and, according to Helvicus, flouriſhed about the Olympiad cxxxviii. that is to ſay about two hundred and thirty years before Chriſt.

The

Martianus Capella gives this explanation of the genera : ' The enar-
' monic abounds in small intervals, the diatonic in tones. The chromatic
' consists wholly of semitones, and is called chromatic, as partaking of
' the nature of both the others; for the same reason as we call that
' affection colour which is included between the extremes of white
' and black. The enarmonic is modulated towards the acumen, or,
' as we should now say, ascends by a diesis, diesis, and an incompo-
' site ditone; the chromatic by a semitone, semitone, and an in-
' composite trihemitone : and the diatonic, content with larger in-
' tervals, proceeds by a semitone, tone, and tone : we now chiefly
' use the diatonic.' He says farther, ' The possible divisions of the
' tetrachord are innumerable, but there are six noted ones, one of
' the enarmonic, three of the chromatic, and two of the diatonic.
' The first of the chromatic is the soft, the second is the hemiolian,
' and the third the tonian. The divisions of the diatonic are two,
' the one soft and the other robust. The enarmonic is distinguished
' by the quadrantal diesis, the soft chromatic by the triental diesis,
' and the hemiolian chromatic by the hemiolian diesis, which is
' equal to an enarmonic diesis and a half, or three eighths of a tone *.'
In all this Capella is but a copier of Aristides Quintilianus; and, in
the judgment of his editor Meibomius, and others, he is both a ser-
vile and an injudicious one.

Boetius † has treated the subject of the genera in a manner less satisfactory than could have been expected from so scientific a musician :
he mentions nothing of the species, but contents himself with an
exhibition of the enarmonic, the chromatic, and diatonic, in three several diagrams, which are here given. He says that the diatonic is
somewhat hard, but that the chromatic departs from that natural intension, and becomes somewhat more soft; and that the enarmonic
is yet better constituted through the five tetrachords. The diatonic
progression, he says, is by a semitone, tone, and tone; and that it

The abovementioned edition of Aratus is a book not unworthy the notice of a learned
musician, as containing a short but curious dissertation De Musica antiqua Græca, by the
editor Mr. Edmund Chilmead. Aratus was an eminent astronomer and poet, contemporary with Eratosthenes; and in the Oxford publication is an astronomical poem, which is
from St. Paul alludes to in his speech at Athens, Acts xvii. ver. 28, ' As certain of your
' own poets have said.' Aratus was a Cilician, and a countryman of the apostle.   Vide
Bentley's Sermons at Boyle's Lecture, sermon II.
* De Nuptiis Philologiæ et Mercurii, lib. IX. De Generibus Tetrachordorum.
† Lib. I. cap. xxi.

is

is called diatonic, as proceeding by tones. He adds that the chromatic, which takes its name from the word Chroma, signifying colour, is, as it were, the first change or inflexion from that kind of intension preferred in the diatonic : and is sung by a semitone, a semitone, and three semitones * ; and that the enarmonic, which in his judgment is the most perfect of all the genera, is sung by a diesis and a ditone ; a diesis he says is the half of a semitone. The following is his division of the tetrachord in each of the three genera.

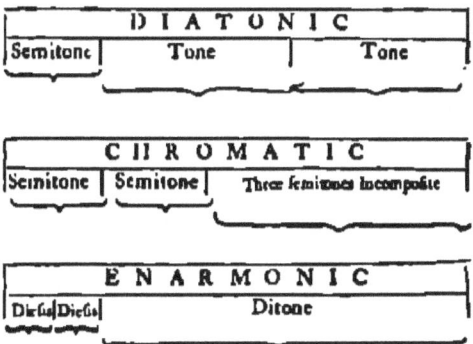

He is somewhat more particular in his fourth book, chap. v. and again in the seventh chapter, for in the chromatic tetrachord he makes the semitones to be, the one a greater and the other a lesser ; and the trihemitone he makes to consist of one greater and two lesser semitones.

* In a diagram of Glareanus, representing Boetius's division of the chromatic, the last interval is thus defined ; " tria semitonia incompofita," which epithet, as Boetius himself explains it, is not meant to signify that the semitones are incomplete, but that the interval constituted by them is to be considered as an integer, and uncompounded like the tone, without regard to its constituent parts. De Muf. lib. I. cap. xxiii.

TETRA-

TETRACHORD.

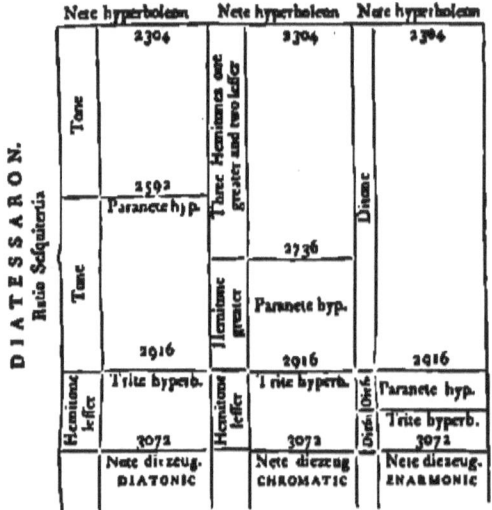

It is fomewhat remarkable that this author has faid nothing of the colours or fpecies of the genera, about which fo much is to be met with in Ptolemy and other writers, except towards the conclufion of his work, where he profeffes to deliver the fentiments of Ariftoxenus and Archytas on this head; but he feems rather to reprehend than adopt their opinions, for which it feems difficult to affign any reafon, other than that he was, as his writings abundantly prove, a moft ftrenuous affertor of the doctrines of Pythagoras.

Merfennus * has given a fcale of the fucceffion of founds in each of the three genera, as near as it could be done, in the characters of modern notation, which is here inferted, and may ferve to fhew how ill the divifion of the tetrachord in the chromatic and enarmonic genera agree with the notions at this time entertained of harmony, and the natural progreffion of mufical founds.

* Harmonie. De Generibus et Modis, pag. 97.

D I A-

Other authors there are, particularly Franchinus, Vicentino, Vincentio Galilei, and Zarlino, that profess to treat of the genera; but it is to be noted that all their intelligence is derived from the same source, namely, the writings of Aristoxenus, Euclid, Aristides Quintilianus, and more especially Ptolemy, and therefore we find no other variation among them than what seems necessarily to arise from their different conceptions of the subject. Boetius himself can in this respect be considered no otherwise than as a modern; and he himself does not pretend to an investigation of the genera, but contents himself with a bare repetition of what is to be found in the writings of the ancients respecting them: and when it is considered that in his time only the diatonic genus was in use; the other genera having been rejected for their intricacy, and other reasons, long before, it must appear next to impossible that he could contribute much to the explanation of this most abstruse part of the science; and the excessive caution with which he delivers his sentiments touching them, is a kind of proof of the difficulties he had to encounter.

If this was the case with Boetius, how little is to be expected from the writers of later times. In short, for information as to the doctrine of the genera, we are under an indispensable necessity of recurring to the ancients; and it will be much safer to acquiesce in their relations, defective and obscure as they are, than to trust to the glosses of modern authors, who in general are more likely to mislead than direct us: for this reason it has been thought proper to reject an infinitude of schemes, diagrams, and explanations, which the fertile inventions of the moderns have produced to exemplify the constitution of the chromatic and enarmonic genera, and that from a thorough persuasion that many of them are erroneous.

But it seems the considerations above suggested were not sufficient to deter a writer, who flourished in the sixteenth century, who, to say the least of him, appears to have been one of the ablest theorists of modern times, from attempting to develope the doctrine of the genera, and to deliver it free from those difficulties.

The author here meant is Franciscus Salinas, a Spaniard by birth, and who, under all the disadvantages of incurable blindness, applied himself with the most astonishing patience and perseverance to the study of the theory of music; and in many respects the success of his researches

7

researches has been equal to the degree of his resolution. His system of the genera is much too copious to be inserted here, it is therefore referred to a part of this work reserved for an account of him and his writings.

Kircher has given a compendious view of the genera *, together with the proportions of their component intervals in the tetrachord of each genus, by the help whereof we are enabled to form an idea of those various progressions that constitute the difference between the one and the other of them. But though he professes to have in his possession, and to have perused the manuscripts of Aristoxenus, Archytas, Didymus, Eratosthenes, and others †, he gives the preference to Ptolemy in respect of his division of the genera, and apparently follows the elder Galilei, not indeed in the order, but in the method of representation. According to him the species of the diatonic genus are five; namely, the ditonic or Pythagorean, the soft, the syntonous, the toniac, and the equable. The following is his definition and representation of them severally in their order, with his remarks on each.

DITONIC or PYTHAGOREAN DIATONIC I.

' The Pythagorean or ditonic diatonic consists in a progression from
' the grave to the acute, through the tetrachord, by the interval of
' a lesser semitone, and two tones, each in the ratio of 8 to 9; and
' contrarywise from the acute to the grave by two tones and a lesser
' semitone, as in the following example.

TETRACHORD		
6144	———————————————	Hypate meson
	Sesquioctave tone, 8 to 9	
6912	———————————————	Lychanos hypaton
	Sesquioctave, tone 8 to 9	
7776	———————————————	Parypate hypaton
	Lesser semitone, 243 to 256	
8192	———————————————	Hypate hypaton

* Musurg. tom. I. lib. III. cap. xiii.

† Meibomius questions the truth of this assertion, upon the supposition that Archytas, Didymus, and Eratosthenes are to be reckoned among the scriptores perditi. It is true that, excepting a small astronomical tract of Eratosthenes, there is nothing of the writing of either of them in print. But it is said that in the library of St. Mark at Venice there are even now a great number of Greek manuscripts that were brought into Italy upon the sacking of Constantinople, and among them it is not impossible that some tracts of the abovenamed writers might be found.

‘ This kind of progreffion is faid to have been held in great efti-
‘ mation by the philofophers, particularly Plato and Ariftotle, as
‘ having a conformity with the compofition of the world and with
‘ nature itfelf.

SOFT DIATONIC II.

‘ The fecond or foft fpecies of the diatonic genus proceeds from
‘ the grave to the acute by an interval, in the ratio of 20 to 21 ; the
‘ other intervals have a ratio, the one of 9 to 10, and the other of 7
‘ to 8, as is here reprefented.

```
         63 ──────────────────── Hypate mefon
TETRACHORD   Sefquifeptima, 7 to 8
         72 ──────────────────── Lychanos hypaton
             Sefquinona, 9 to 10
         80 ──────────────────── Parypate hypaton.
             Sefquivigefima, 20 to 21
         84 ──────────────────── Hypate hypaton
```

SYNTONOUS DIATONIC III.

‘ The third fpecies, diftinguifhed by the epithets fyntonum inci-
‘ tatum, or baftened, proceeds from the grave to the acute by
‘ an interval in the ratio of 15 to 16, or greater femitone, a greater
‘ tone 8 to 9, and a leffer 9 to 10; and defcends from the acute to
‘ the grave by the fame intervals.

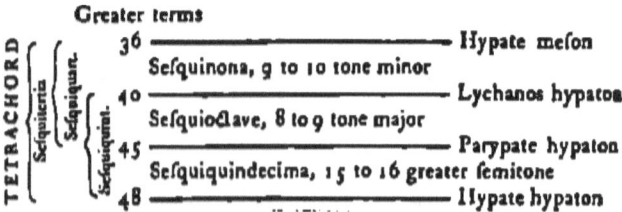

```
         Greater terms
         36 ──────────────────── Hypate mefon
             Sefquinona, 9 to 10 tone minor
         40 ──────────────────── Lychanos hypaton
             Sefquioclave, 8 to 9 tone major
         45 ──────────────────── Parypate hypaton
             Sefquiquindecima, 15 to 16 greater femitone
         48 ──────────────────── Hypate hypaton
```

TO-

TONIAC DIATONIC IV.

' The toniac, the fourth fpecies of the diatonic genus fuppofes
·' fuch a difpofition of the tetrachord as that the firft and fecond
' chords fhall include an interval of 27 to 28 ; next an interval of 7
' to 8, and laftly one of 8 to 9.   Thus adjufted it will afcend from
' the grave to the acute, and on the contrary defcend from the acute
' to the grave, as in the example.

Greater terms

D ⎰ 168 ——————————————————— Hypate mefon

TETRACHORD

        Sefquioctave, 8 to 9
    189 ——————————————————— Lychanos hypaton
        Sefquifeptima, 7 to 8
    216 ——————————————————— Parypate hypaton
        Sefquivigefimafeptima, 27 to 28
    224 ——————————————————— Hypate hypaton

EQUABLE DIATONIC V.

' The fifth and laft fpecies of this genus is the equable, proceed-
' ing in arithmetical progreffion from the grave to the acute, by the
' ratios of 11 to 12, 10 to 11, and 9 to 10; and contrarywife from
' the acute to the grave.

TETRACHORD — DIATESSARON

    9 ——————————————————— Hypate mefon
        Sefquinona
    10 ——————————————————— Lychanos hypaton
        Sefquidecima
    11 ——————————————————— Parypate hypaton
        Sefquiundecima
    12 ——————————————————— Hypate hypaton

' Ptolemy, whofe fondnefs for analogies has already been re-
' marked, refembles the tetrachord thus conftituted to Theology and
' Politics.'

'The chromatic genus, in the opinion of this author had three
fpecies, the ancient, the foft, and the fyntonous, thus feverally defcribed by him.

A N-

ANCIENT CHROMATIC I.

' This species proceeded by two semitones and a trihemitone,
' that is to say, it ascended from the grave to the acute by a lesser
' semitone; then by an interval somewhat greater, as being in the
' ratio of 81 to 76; and lastly by an incomplete trihemitone, in the
' ratio of 19 to 16.

		6144 ——————————————— Hypate meson
		Trihemitone, 16 to 19
TETRACHORD	DIATESSARON	7296 ——————————————— Lychanos hypaton
		Semitone, 76 to 81
		7776 ——————————————— Parypate hypaton
		Lesser semitone, 243 to 256
		8192 ——————————————— Hypate hypaton

SOFT CHROMATIC II.

' The chromatic molle was so disposed, as that the lowest chord
' and the next to it had a ratio of 27 to 28, the second and third 14
' to 15, and the third and fourth 5 to 6.

	105 ——————————————— Hypate meson
TETRACHORD	Sesquiquinta, 5 to 6
	126 ——————————————— Lychanos hypaton
	Sesquiquartadecima, 14 to 15
	135 ——————————————— Parypate hypaton
	Sesquivigesimaseptima, 27 to 28
	140 ——————————————— Hypate hypaton

SYNTONOUS CHROMATIC III.

' In the chromatic syntonum the first and second chords, reckon-
' ing from the lowest, were distant by an interval in the proportion
' of 22 to 21, the second was removed from the third by an interval
' in the proportion of 12 to 11, and the third from the fourth by
' one of a sesquisexta proportion, which is as 6 to 7, as here is shewn.

TETRA-

```
T E T R A C H O R D
```

66 ——————————————— Hypate meſon

Seſquiſexta, 6 to 7

77 ——————————————— Lychanos hypaton

Seſquiundecima, 11 to 12

84 ——————————————— Parypate hypaton

Seſquivigeſima prima, 21 to 22

88 ——————————————— Hypate hypaton

' Of this genus it is ſaid by Macrobius that it was deemed to be of
' an effeminate nature, and that it had a tendency to enervate the
' mind *; for which reaſon the ancients very ſeldom uſed it; Ptole-
' my reſembles this tetrachord to œconomics.'

The enarmonic, the third and laſt in order of the genera, ſeems to
have been originally ſimple or undivided into ſpecies; but the refinements of Ptolemy led to a variation in the order of the enarmonic progreſſion, which formed that ſpecies diſtinguiſhed by his name, ſo
that it may be ſaid the enarmonic contained two ſpecies, the ancient
and the Ptolemaic. Kircher thus defines it.

ANCIENT ENARMONIC I.

' In this ſpecies the tetrachord aſcended by two dieſes, and an in-
' complete ditone, the ſeveral ratios whereof were as denoted by the
' underwritten numbers.

```
T E T R A C H O R D
```

6144 ——————————————— Hypate meſon

Ditone

7776 ——————————————— Lychanos hypaton

Dieſis

7984 ——————————————— Parypate hypaton

Dieſis

8192 ——————————————— Hypate hypaton

ENARMONIC OF PTOLEMY II.

' The Ptolemaic enarmonic, which was ſcarce formed before both
' the chromatic and enarmonic grew into diſeſteem, aſcended from
' the moſt grave to the next chord by an interval in the ratio of 45
' to

* Vide Macrob. in Somn. Scipion. Lib. II. cap. iv.

' to 46, thence by one of 23 to 24, and laftly by one of 4 to 5,
' which is faid to be a true enarmonic ditone.

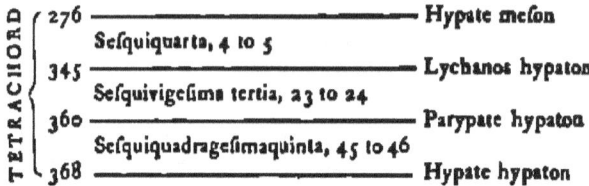

Dr. Wallis has treated this fubject of the genera in a manner
worthy of that penetration and fagacity for which he is admired.
It has been mentioned, that of all the ancients Ptolemy has entered
the moft minutely into a difcuffion of this doctrine; he has delivered
the fentiments of many writers, which but for him we fhould fcarcely have known, and has adjufted the fpecies in fuch a way as to
leave it a doubt whether even Ariftoxenus or he be the neareft the
truth : Dr. Wallis publifhed an edition of this valuable author, with
a tranflation and notes of his own; to this work he has added an appendix, wherein is contained a very elaborate and judicious difquifition on the nature of the ancient mufic, and a comparifon of the ancient fyftem with that of the moderns. In this he has taken great
pains to explain, as far as it was poffible, the genera : the enarmonic and chromatic he gives up, and fpeaks of as irrecoverably loft;
but of the diatonic genus he expreffes himfelf with great clearnefs
and precifion; for, after defining, as he does very accurately, the feveral fpecies of the diatonic, he fays, that one only of them is now
in practice; and, as touching the queftion which of them that one
is, he gives the opinions of feveral muficians, together with his own;
and laftly fhews how very fmall and inconfiderable muft have been
the difference between thofe divifions that diftinguifh the fpecies of
the diatonic genus. His words are nearly thefe.

' It now remains to difcufs one point, which we have referred to
' this place, the genera and their colours or fpecies. We have be-
' fore faid that for many years only one of them all has been received
' in practice, and this is by all allowed to be the diatonic, the enar-
' monic and all the chromatics, and the other diatonics being laid
' afide.

' afide. But it is matter of difpute whether it is the intenfe diato-
' nic of Ariftoxenus, or the ditonic diatonic of Ptolemy, or the in-
' tenfe diatonic of the fame Ptolemy ; that is to fay, when we fing
' a diateffaron from MI or LA in the grave towards the acute in the
' fyllables FA sol LA, which exprefs fo many intervals, to afcertain
' the degree of magnitude which each of thefe intervals contains.
' The firft opinion is that of Ariftoxenus, who when he made the
' diateffaron to confift of two tones and a half, would have the great-
' eft found FA, to be a hemitone, and the other two sol LA, to be
' whole tones, which is the intenfe diatonic of this author *. Ahd in
' this manner fpeak all muficians even to this day, at leaft when they
' do not profefs to fpeak with nicety. But thofe who enter more
' minutely into the matter, will have what is underftood by a hemi-
' tone to be, not exactly the half of, but fomewhat a little lefs than a
' tone ; and this is demonftrated by Euclid, who in other refpects
' was an Ariftoxenean, though I do not know whether he was the firft
' that did it. Euclid I fay, admiting the principles of the Pythago-
' reans in eftimating the intervals of founds by ratios ; and admit-
' ting alfo that a tone is in a fefquioctave ratio, in his harmonic in-
' troduction treats of the tones and hemitones in the fame manner as
' do the Ariftoxeneans ; yet in his fection of the canon he fhews
' that what remains after fubtracting two tones from a diateffaron is
' lefs than a hemitone, and is called a limma, which is in the ratio
' of ¦¦¦ ; for if a diateffaron contains two tones and a half, then a
' diapafon, which is two diateffarons and one tone, muft contain fix
' tones ; but a diapafon, which has a duple ratio, is lefs than fix
' tones, for a fefquioctave ratio fix times compounded is more than
' duple † ; a diapafon therefore is lefs than fix tones, and a diateffaron
' lefs than two tones and a half.

C H A P.   VIII.

' THE next opinion is that of thofe, who, inftead of a tone,
'   tone, and hemitone, fubftitute a tone, tone, and limma.
' And thefe, if at any time they call it a hemitone, would yet have

* See the Synopfis, p. 87, of Dr. Wallis's Appendix, herein before given.
† This is excellently demonftrated by Boetius, lib. III. cap. i.

' us underſtand them to mean a limma, which differs very little from
' a hemitone, and therefore they will have the ſyllable LA to expreſs
' a limma, and the ſyllables SOL LA two tones, that is $\frac{15}{16} \times \frac{8}{9} \times \frac{8}{9} = \frac{3}{4}$,
' and this is the ditonic diatonic of Ptolemy, but which was ſhewn
' by Euclid before Ptolemy, and it was alſo the diatonic of Eratoſ-
' thenes, as has been ſaid above; and theſe have been the ſentiments
' of muſicians almoſt as low as to our own times. Ptolemy himſelf,
' though he has given other kinds of diatonic genera, does not rejeċt
' this; and the reſt who have ſpoken of this matter in a different
' way, did it more out of compliance with cuſtom, than that they
' adhered to any contrary opinion of their own, as Ptolemy himſelf
' tells us, lib. I. cap. xvi. And thus Boetius divides the tetrachord,
' and after him Guido Aretinus, Faber Stapulenſis, Glareanus, and
' others; it is true, however, that, about the beginning of the ſix-
' teenth century, Zarlino, and alſo Kepler reſumed the intenſe diatonic
' of Ptolemy, and attempted to bring it into practice *; but for this
' they were cenſured by the elder Galileo †.

' The third opinion therefore is that of thoſe who, following Pto-
' lemy, ſubſtituted in the place of a hemitone or limma, a ſeſquide-
' cimaquinta ratio $\frac{15}{16}$, which they alſo call a hemitone; and for the
' tones, both which the others had made to be in the ratio $\frac{8}{9}$, one
' they made to be in the ratio $\frac{9}{10}$, ſo that they compounded the dia-
' teſſaron by the ratios $\frac{15}{16} \times \frac{8}{9} \times \frac{9}{10} = \frac{3}{4}$, expreſſing by the ſyllable FA the
' ratio $\frac{15}{16}$, by SOL that of $\frac{8}{9}$, and by LA $\frac{9}{10}$ $\frac{3}{4}$, which is the intenſe
' diatonic of Ptolemy, and the diatonic of Didymus, except that he,
' changing the order, has $\frac{8}{9} \times \frac{9}{10} \times \frac{15}{16} = \frac{3}{4}$.

' And as they called $\frac{15}{16}$ a greater hemitone, they made the leſſer
' $\frac{24}{25}$, which with $\frac{15}{16}$ completes the leſſer tone, as $\frac{15}{16} \times \frac{24}{25} = \frac{9}{10}$, and is
' the difference, as they ſay, between the greater and the leſſer third.

---

* Dr. Wallis has a little miſtaken Kepler in this place: it was not the intenſe diatonic
of Ptolemy, but of Didymus $\frac{8}{9} \times \frac{9}{10} \times \frac{15}{16} = \frac{3}{4}$ that he was for reſuming. Joann. Kepleri
Harm. Mundi, lib. III. cap. vii.
† Galileo did not contend for the ditonic diviſion of the diatonic, but for the intenſe of
Ariſtoxenus, defined in his ſynopſis of the genera herein before given; the reaſon whereof
was, that he was a lutaniſt, and the performers on that inſtrument unanimouſly prefer
the Ariſtoxenean diviſion.
‡ It may be proper to remark, that in this and other inſtances of ſolmiſation that occur
in the paſſage now quoting, Dr. Wallis uſes the method of ſolmiſation by the tetrachords,
in which the ſyllables UT RE are rejected, and which took place about the year 1650.
See Clifford's Collection of divine Services and Anthems, printed in the year 1664.

Mer-

' Merſennus adds two other hemitones, one in the ratio ¦¦¦, which
' with ¦¦ completes ¦ the greater tone, and the other ¦¦, which with
' ¦¦ alſo makes up ¦ the greater tone ª.'

The above is an impartial ſtate of the ſeveral opinions that at
different times have prevailed among the moderns, touching the
preference of one or other of the ſpecies of the diatonic genus to the
reſt. Dr. Wallis is certainly right in ſaying, that to the time of
Boetius, and ſo on to the end of the ſixteenth century, the ditonic
diatonic of Ptolemy prevailed, for ſo much appears by the writings
of thoſe ſeveral authors ; and as to the latter part of his aſſertion, it
is confirmed by the preſent practice, which is to conſider the tetrachord as conſiſting of a ſeſquidecimaquinta ratio, a tone major, and
a tone minor, and to this method of diviſion he gives the preference ;
but he cloſes his relation with a remark that ſhews of how very little
importance all enquiries are, which tend to adjuſt differences too minute for a determination by the ſenſes, and cognizable only by the
underſtanding, and that too not till after a laborious inveſtigation.
His words are theſe :

' But as thoſe ſpecies which we have mentioned differ ſo very
' little from one another, that the niceſt ear can ſcarcely, if at all,
' diſtinguiſh them, ſince the ratio ¦¦ from the ratio of a limma ¦¦¦,
' as alſo the ratio of a greater tone ¦ from ¦¦ differ only by the ra-
' tio ¦¦, which is ſo ſmall that the ear can with difficulty diſcriminate
' between the one and the other of the two tones; we muſt therefore
' judge not ſo much by our ſenſes, which opinion ought moſt to be
' regarded, becauſe the ſenſes would without any difficulty admit any
' of them, but reaſon greatly favours the laſt †.'

There is yet another writer, with whoſe ſentiments, and a few obſervations thereon, we ſhall conclude our account of the genera, this was
Dr. John Chriſtopher Pepuſch, a man of no ſmall eminence in his pro-
feſſion, and who for many years enjoyed, at leaſt in England, the reputation of being the ableſt theoriſt of his time. In a letter to Mr. Abra-
ham de Moivre, printed in the Philoſophical Tranſactions of the year
1746, N° 481, he propoſes to throw ſome light upon the obſcure ſubject
of the ancient ſpecies of muſic; and after premiſing that, according to
Euclid, the ancient ſcale muſt have been compoſed of tones major and

* Append. de Vet. Harm. 317, et ſeq.
† Ibid. pag. 318.

limmas,

limmas, without the intervention of tones minor, which in numbers are thus to be expreffed, ⟨...⟩, he proceeds in thefe words : ' It was ufual among the Greeks to confider a defcending as well as ' an afcending fcale, the former proceeding from acute to grave pre- ' cifely by the fame intervals as the latter did from grave to acute. ' The firft found in each was the proflambanomenos.   The not dif- ' tinguifhing thefe two fcales, has led feveral learned moderns to fup- ' pofe that the Greeks in fome centuries took the proflambanomenos ' to be the loweft note in their fyftem, and in other centuries to be ' the higheft ; but the truth of the matter is, that the proflambano- ' menos was the loweft or higheft note according as they confider- ' ed the afcending or defcending fcale.   The diftinction of thefe is con- ' ducive to the variety and perfection of melody ; but I never yet met ' with above one piece of mufic where the compofer appeared to have ' any intelligence of this kind.   The compofition is about one hundred ' and fifty or more years old, for four voices, and the words are, " Vobis datum eft nofcere myfterium regni Dei, cæteris autem in para- " bolis ; ut videntes non videant, et audientes non intelligant."   By the ' choice of the words the author feems to allude to his having per- ' formed fomething not commonly underftood.'   The doctor then exhibits an octave of the afcending and defcending fcales of the dia- tonic genus of the ancients, with the names for their feveral founds, as alfo the correfponding modern letters, in the following form.

A		Proflambanomenos		g
B	⸰	Hypate hypaton	⸰⸰	f
C	⸰⸰	Parypate hypaton	⸰	e
D	⸰	Lychanos hypaton	⸰	d
E	⸰	Hypate mefon	⸰⸰	c
F	⸰⸰	Parypate mefon	⸰	b
G	⸰	Lychanos mefon	⸰	a
a	⸰	Mefe		G

He obferves, that in the octave above given, the Proflambanome-nos, Hypate hypaton, Hypate mefon, and Mefe were called Stabiles, from their remaining fixed throughout all the genera and fpecies ; and that the other four, being the Parypate hypaton, Lychanos hypaton,

7   Par-

Parypate mefon, and Lychanos mefon, were called Mobiles, because they varied according to the different fpecies and varieties of mufic.

He then proceeds to determine the queftion what the genera and fpecies were, in this manner. ' By genus and fpecies was under-
' ftood a divifion of the diateffaron, containing four founds, into
' three intervals. The Greeks conftituted three genera, known by
' the names of Enarmonic, Chromatic, and Diatonic. The chro-
' matic was fubdivided into three fpecies, and the diatonic into two.
' The three chromatic fpecies were, the chromaticum molle, the
' fefquialterum, and the tonicum. The two diatonic fpecies were,
' the diatonicum molle,-and the intenfum ; fo that they had fix fpe-
' cies in all. Some of thefe are in ufe among the moderns, but
' others are as yet unknown in theory or practice.

' I now proceed to define all thefe fpecies by determining the in-
' tervals of which they feverally confifted, beginning by the diatoni-
' cum intenfum as the moft eafy and familiar.

' The diatonicum intenfum was compofed of two tones and a fe-
' mitone; but, to fpeak exactly, it confifts of a femitone major, a
' tone minor, and a tone major. This is in daily practice, and we
' find it accurately defined by Didymus in Ptolemy's Harmonics,
' publifhed by Dr. Wallis *.

* Dr. Wallis has remarked in the paffage above-cited, that it had long been a matter of controverfy whether the fyftem of the moderns correfponded with the intenfe diatonic of Ariftoxenus, the ditonic diatonic of Ptolemy, or rather Pythagoras, or the intenfe of Ptolemy; and though he feems to incline to the opinion of Zarlino, that the mufic now in ufe is no other than the intenfe diatonic of Ptolemy, it is far from clear that the moderns have gone farther than barely to admit in theory and in a courfe of numerical calculation the latter as the moft eligible. Salinas, lib. III. cap. xiii. contends for an equality of tones, and for the confequent neceffity of diftibuting throughout the diapafon fyftem thofe intervals by which the greater tones exceed the leffer.

Bontempi, Hift. Muf. 188. fays that that temperament which makes the intervals irra-tional, is to be looked upon as a divine thing, and afferts that no where in Italy, nor in-deed in Europe, does the practice of difcriminating between the greater and leffer tone prevail in the tuning of the organ, and that the organ of St. Mark's chapel at Venice, where he himfelf fung for feven years, continued to be tuned without regard to this dif-tinction, notwithftanding what Zarlino had written and the efforts he made to get it varied.

The practice has long been in tuning the organ, and fuch like inftruments, to make the fifths as flat and the thirds as fharp as the ear will bear, which neceffarily induces an equality in the tones.

Laftly, Dr. Smith, in his Harmonics, fecond edition, pag. 33, afferts that fince the invention of a temperament, the ancient fyftems of ditonic diatonic, intenfe diatonic, &c.

have

' The next species is the diatonicum molle, as yet undiscovered, as
' far as appears to me, by any modern author.   Its component inter-
' vals are the semitone major, an interval composed of two semi-
' tones minor, and the complement of these two to the fourth, being
' an interval equal to a tone major and an enarmonic diesis.

' The third species is the chromaticum toniæum, its component in-
' tervals are a semitone major succeeded by another semitone major;
' and lastly, the complement of these two to the fourth, commonly
' called a superfluous tone.

' The fourth species is the chromaticum sesquialterum, which is
' constituted by the progression of a semitone major, a semitone mi-
' nor, and a third minor.   This is mentioned by Ptolemy as the
' chromatic of Didymus *.   Examples among the moderns are
' frequent.

' The fifth species is the chromaticum molle.   Its intervals are
' two subsequent semitones minor, and the complements of these two
' to the fourth, that is an interval compounded of a third minor and
' an enarmonic diesis.   This species I never met with among the
' moderns.

' The sixth and last species is the enarmonic.   Salinas and others
' have determined this accurately †.   Its intervals are the semitone
' minor, the enarmonic diesis, and the third major.

' Examples of four of these species may be found in modern prac-
' tice.   But I do not know of any theorist who ever yet determined
' what the chromaticum toniæum of the ancients was; nor have any
' of them perceived the analogy between the chromaticum sesquialte-
' rum and our modern chromatic.   The enarmonic, so much admir-
' ed by the ancients, has been little in use among our musicians as
' yet.   As to the diatonicum intensum it is too obvious to be mis-
' taken.'

The above-cited letter is very far from being what the title of it
indicates, an explanation of the various genera and species of music
among the ancients.   To say the best of it, it contains very little
more than is to be met with in almost every writer on the subject of

have justly been laid aside.   So that after so many opinions to the contrary, it may very
well be doubted whether the diatonicum intensum is in daily practice or not.
* Lib. II. cap. xiv.
† Salinas de Musica, lib. III. cap. viii.

ancient

ancient mufic, except that feemingly notable difcovery, that the ancients made ufe of both an afcending and defcending fcale, the confideration whereof will be prefently refumed.   As to the fix fpecies
above enumerated, the doctor fays four are in modern practice, but
of thefe four he has thought proper to mention only two, namely, the
diatonicum intenfum, and the chromaticum fefquialterum; and it is
to be wifhed that he had referred to a few of thofe examples of the
four, which he fays are to be found, or at leaft that he had mentioned the authors in whofe works the latter two of them occur; and the
rather, becaufe Dr. Wallis afferts that the enarmonic, all the chromatics, and all but one of the diatonics, for many years, he might have
faid centuries, have been laid afide.

As to his affertion that the Greeks made ufe of both an afcending and
defcending fcale, it is to be remarked, that there are no notices of any
fuch diftinction in the writings of any of the Greek harmonicians. The
ground of it is a compofition about one hundred and fifty years old, in
the year 1746, to the words of a verfe in the gofpel of St. Mark *, fo
obfcure, if we confider them as referring to the mufic, that they
ferve more to excite, than allay curiofity; and Dr. Pepufch could not
have wifhed for a fairer opportunity of difplaying his learning and ingenuity than the folution of this mufical enigma afforded him. Nay,
had he condefcended to give this compofition in the ftate he found it,
or had he barely referred to it, the world would have been fenfible of
the obligation. The only excufe that can be alledged for that incom-
municative difpofition which the whole of this letter betrays, is, that
the author of it fubfifted for many years by teaching the precepts of
his art to young ftudents, and it was not his intereft to divulge them.
How far the compofition abovementioned, which is not yet two hundred years old, is an evidence of the practice of the ancient Greeks,
will not here be enquired into; but it may gratify the curiofity of the
reader to be told that the author of it was Coftanza Porta, a Francif-
can monk, and chapel-mafter in the church of St. Mark at Ancona,
and that it is publifhed at the end of a book printed at Venice in
1600, entitled, L' Artufi Overo delle Imperfettioni della moderna
Mufica, written by Giovanni Maria Artufi, an ecclefiaftic of Bologna,
of whom a particular account will hereafter be given.   As to the compofition, it is for four voices, and is as follows.

* Chap. iv. ver. 9.

Artufi obferves upon this compofition, which, the better to fhew
the contrivance of it, is here given in fcore, that it is a motet
for four voices, and that it may be fung two ways, that is to fay, firſt, as
the cliffs direct that are placed neareſt to the notes, and afterwards turning the top of the book downwards, from the right to the left; taking
the extreme cliff for a guide in naming the notes; the confequence
whereof will be, that the bafe will become the foprano, the tenor the
contralto, the contralto the tenor, and the foprano the bafe. Befides
this he fays that the fecond time of finging it, b muſt be affumed for
♯, and in other inſtances FA for MI. He concludes with a remark
upon the words of this motet, that they indicate that it is not given
to every one to underſtand compofitions of this kind.

Upon the example above adduced the remark is obvious, that it
falls ſhort of proving the ufe of both an afcending and defcending
fcale by the Greek harmonicians. In a word, it is evidence of nothing
more than the antiquity of a kind of compofition, of which it is probable Coſtanza Porta might be the inventor, namely that, where the
parts are fo contrived as to be fung as well backwards as forwards.
In this he has been followed by Pedro Cerone, and other Spaniſh
muficians, and by our own countryman Elway Bevin and others,
who feem to have thought that the merit of a mufical compofition
confiſted more in the intricacy of its conſtruction than in its aptitude
to produce the genuine and natural effects of fine harmony and melody on the mind of an unprejudiced hearer.

From the foregoing reprefentations of the genera, the reafons for
the early preference of the diatonic to the chromatic and enarmonic
are clearly deducible; but notwithſtanding thefe and the confequent
rejection of the latter two by Guido and all his followers, the ingenuity of a few fpeculative muficians has betrayed them into an opinion that they are yet actually exiſting, and that with the addition of
a few intervals, occafionally to be interpofed among thofe that conſtitute the diapafon, both the chromatic and enarmonic genera may
be brought into practice.

The firſt of thefe bold affertors was Don Nicola Vicentino, an
author of whom farther mention will hereafter be made. In a work
entitled L'Antica Mufica ridotta alla Moderna Prattica, publiſhed by
him at Rome in 1555, we find not only the tetrachord divided in
fuch a manner as feemingly to anfwer the generical divifion of the
ancients, but compofitions actually exhibited, not only in one and
the

the other of the genera, but in each of them feverally, and in all of them conjunctly, and this with fuch a degree of perfuafion on his part that he had accurately defined them, as feems to fet all doubt at defiance.

It is true that little lefs than this was to be expected from an author who profeffes in the very title of his book to reduce the ancient mufic to modern practice, but that he has fucceeded in his attempt fo few are difpofed to believe, that in the general eftimation of the moft fkilful profeffors of the fcience Vicentino's book has not its fellow for mufical abfurdity *. And of the juftice of this cenfure few can entertain a doubt, that fhall perufe the following account of himfelf and of his ftudies.

‘ To fhew the world that I have not grudged the labour of many
‘ years, as well for my own improvement, as to be ufeful to others,
‘ in the prefent work I fhall publifh all the three genera with their
‘ feveral fpecies and commixtures, and other inventions never given
‘ to the world by any body; and fhall fhew in how many ways it is
‘ poffible to compofe varioufly in the fharp and flat modes: though
‘ at prefent there are fome profeffors of mufic that blame me for the
‘ trouble I take in this kind of learning, not confidering the pains
‘ that many celebrated philofophers have taken to explain the doc-
‘ trine of harmonics; neverthelefs I fhall not defift from my endea-
‘ vours to reduce to practice the ancient genera with their feveral
‘ fpecies by the means of voices and inftruments; and if I fhall fail
‘ in the attempt, I fhall at leaft give fuch hints to men of genius as
‘ may tend to the improvement of mufic. We fee by a comparifon
‘ of the mufic that we ufe at prefent, with that in practice a hundred,
‘ nay ten years ago, that the fcience is much improved; and I doubt
‘ not but that thefe improvements of mine will appear ftrange in
‘ comparifon with thofe of our pofterity, and the reafon is, that im-
‘ provements are continually making of things already invented, but
‘ the invention and beginning of every thing is difficult; therefore I
‘ rejoice that God has fo far favoured me, that in thefe days for his
‘ honour and glory I am able to fhew my honourable face among the

* This is remarked by Gio Battista Doni, in his treatife entitled De Præftantia Muficæ veteris. Florent. 1647, and numberlefs other writers. Kircher however feems to entertain a different opinion of it; his fentiments are given at length in a fubfequent page of this chapter.

pro—

' profeffors of mufic. It is true that I have ftudied hard for many
' years; and as the divine goodnefs was pleafed to enlighten me, I
' began this work in the fortieth year of my age, in the year 1550,
' the jubilee year, in the happy reign of pope Julius the third; fince
' that I have gone on, and by continual ftudy have endeavoured to
' enlarge it, and to compofe according to the precepts therein con-
' tained, as likewife to teach the fame to many others, who have
' made fome progrefs therein, and particularly in this illuftrious
' town of Ferrara, where I dwell at prefent, to the inhabitants
' whereof I have explained both the theory and practice of the art;
' and many lords and gentlemen who have heard the fweetnefs of this
' harmony have been charmed therewith, and have taken pains to
' learn the fame with exquifite diligence, becaufe it really compre-
' hends what the ancient writers fhew. As to the diatonic genus, it
' was in ufe in the mufic fung at public feftivals, and in common
' places, but the chromatic and enarmonic were referved for the pri-
' vate diverfion of lords and princes, who had more refined ears than the
' vulgar, and were ufed in celebrating the praifes of great perfons and
' heroes. And, not to detract from the virtues of the ancient princes,
' the moft excellent prince of Ferrara, Alfonfo d' Efte, after having
' very much countenanced me, has with great favour and facility
' learned the fame, and thereby fhewn to the world the image of a
' perfect prince; and he, as he has a moft worthy name of eternal
' glory in arms, fo has he acquired immortal honours by his fkill in
' the fciences *.'   ·

In the profecution of this his notable defign of accommodating the
ancient mufic to modern practice, Vicentino has exhibited in the characters of modern notation a diatonic, a chromatic, and an enarmonic
fourth and fifth in all their various forms. The following is an example of their feveral varieties, taken from the third book of his
work above-cited, pages 59 a, 59 b, 62 b, et feq.

* Libro primo, cap. iv.

D I A-

Having thus adjusted the several intervals of a fourth and fifth in each of the three genera, the author proceeds to exhibit certain compositions of his own in each of them; and first we have a motet composed by himself, and sung, as he says, in his church on the day of the Resurrection, as a specimen of the true chromatic.

Al-le-lu-ia Al-le-lu-ia Al-le-lu-ia Al-le-lu-ia Al-le-lu-

-ia hæc di-es quam fecit do-mi-nus hæc di-es quam fe-cit

do-mi-nus quam fe-cit do-mi - - nus Ex-ul-te-mus et le-te-

mur ex-ul-te-mus et le-te-mur in ea et le-te-mur in ea.

Al-le-lu-ia Al-le-lu-ia Al-le-lu-ia Al-le-lu-ia Al-le-lu - ia hæc

di-es quam fe-cit do-mi-nus hæc di-es hæc di-es quam fe-cit

do-mi-nus quam fe-cit do-mi - - nus ex-ul-te-mus et le-te-mur

ex-ul-te-mus et le-te-mur in e-a et le-te-mur in e-a

VOL. I.

R

As an example of the enarmonic, he gives the following, which is the beginning of a madrigal in four parts.

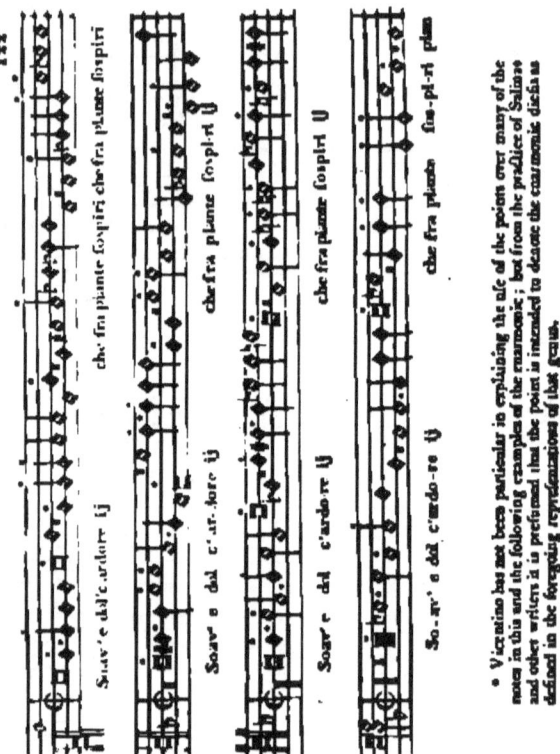

* Vicentino has not been particular in explaining the use of the points over many of the notes in this and the following examples of the enarmonic; but from the practice of Salinas and other writers it is presumed that the point is intended to denote the enarmonic diesis as defined in the foregoing representations of that genus.

And as a proof of the practicability of uniting all the genera in one composition, he exhibits the following madrigal for four voices, which he says may be sung in five ways, that is to say, as diatonic, as chromatic, as chromatic and enarmonic, as diatonic and chromatic, and lastly as diatonic, chromatic and enarmonic.

Dolce mio ben ij   fon quefti dolci lumi   dolci lu-mi   dolce mio

ben fon quefti dolci lumi   fon quefti dolci   lumi   che tanto dolce-

men-te che tanto dol-ce-men-te   mi con-fu-mi   che   tanto dal cemen-

-te fanno   che dolcemen-te   mi con-fu-mi   mi confu-mi

Dolce mio ben ij   fon quefti dolci lu-mi   dolce mio ben ij

fon quefti dolci   lu-mi   dol-ce lumi   che tanto   che tanto dol-ce-

-men-te   fanno che dolce-mente   che dolce-mente mi confumi   mi con-

-fu-mi   fanno che dolcemen te   mi con-fu-mi   mi con-fu-mi

124

Dolce mio ben fan questi dolci lumi dolce mio ben fon quef-

-ti dolci lumi fon questi dolci lumi dolci lumi che tanto

dolce-mente che tan-to dolcemente mi con-fu-mi che tan-to

dol-ce-mente mi con-fu-mi dol-ce-mente mi con-fu-mi

Dolce mio ben ij fon questi dolci lumi dol-ci

mio ben ij fon quefti dolci lumi che tanto dolce-men-te

fuum che mi con-fu-mi che dulce-mente

mi con-fu-mi mi con-fu-mi Hay-me

¹ Kircher seems to think that Vicentino has succeded in this his attempt to restore the ancient genera; and if he has, either the discovery was of no worth, or the moderns have a great deal to answer for in their not adopting It.   The following are the sentiments of Kircher touching Vicentino and his endeavours to reduce the ancient music to modern practice.   ' The first that I know of who invented the me-
' thod of composing music in the three genera, according to the
' manner of the ancients, was Nicolaus Vicentinus *; who when he
' perceived that the division of the tetrachords according to the three
' genera by Boetius could not suit a polyphonous melothesia and our
' ratio of composition, devised another method, which he treats of
' at large in an entire book.   There were however not wanting some,
' who being strenuous admirers and defenders of ancient music, ca-
' villed at him wrongfully and undeservedly for having changed the
' genera that had been wisely instituted by the ancients, and put in
' their stead I know not what spurious genera; but those who shall
' examine more closely into the affair will be obliged to confess that
' Vicentinus had very good reason for what he did, and that no other
' chromatic enarmonic polyphonous melothesia could be made than
' as he taught †.'

This declaration of Kircher is not easily to be reconciled with those positive assertions of his in the Musurgia, that the ancients were strangers to polyphonous music; and the examples above given are all of that kind.

But waving this confideration, whoever will be at the pains of examining these several compositions, will find it a matter of great difficulty to reconcile them with the accounts that are given of the manner of dividing the tetrachord in the several genera; he will not be able easily to discover the chromatic interval of three incomposite semitones; much less will he be able to make out the enarmonic diesis; and much greater will be his difficulty to persuade himself, or any one

* Kircher is mistaken in his assertion that Vicentino was the first who attempted the revival of the ancient genera; for it seems that Giovanni Spataro of Bologna, in the year 1512, made an attempt of that kind, but without success.   Storia della Musica di Giambatista Martini, tom. I. pag. 126, in not.
But notwithstanding the discouragements the two writers abovementioned met with, Domenico Mazzochi of Rome, about the year 1600, attempted a composition in all the three genera, entitled Plancts Matris Euryalis, which is printed in the Musurgia, tom. I. pag. 660.
† Musurg. tom. I. pag. 637.

else,

else, that either of the above compositions can stand the test of an ear capable of distinguishing between harmony and discord.

But all wonder at this attempt of Vicentino must cease, when it is known that he contended with some of the greatest musicians, his contemporaries, that the modern or Guidonian system was not simply of the diatonic kind, but compounded of all the three genera. He has himself, in the forty-third chapter of his fourth book, given a most curious relation of a dispute between him and a reverend father on this subject, which produced a wager, the decision whereof was referred to two very skilful professors, who gave judgment against him. An account of this dispute is contained in a subsequent chapter of the present work.

C H A P.   IX.

IT does not any where appear that the music which gave rise to the controversy between Vicentino and his opponents, was any other than what is in use at this day; which that it is the true diatonic of the ancients is more than probable; though, whether it be the diatonicum Pythagoricum, or the diatonicum intensum of Aristoxenus, of Didymus, or of Ptolemy, has been thought a matter of some difficulty to ascertain, but is of little consequence in practice.

But we are not to understand by this that the music now in use is so purely and simply diatonic, as in no degree to participate of either the enarmonic or chromatic genus, for there is in the modern scale such a comixture of tones and semitones as may serve to warrant a supposition that it partakes in some measure of the ancient chromatic; and that it does so, several eminent writers have asserted, and seems to be the general opinion. Monsieur Brossard says, that after the division of the tone between the Mese and Paramese of the ancients, which answer to our A and ♮, into two semitones, it was thought that the other tones might be divided in like manner; and that therefore the moderns have introduced the chromatic chords of the ancient scale, and thereby divided the tones major in each tetrachord into two semitones; this, he adds, was effected by raising the lowest chord a semitone by

7   means

means of this character ✻, which was placed immediately before the note so to be raised, or on its place immediately after the cliff. Again he says, that it having been found that the tones minor terminating the tetrachords upwards were no less capable of such division than the tones major, they added the chromatic chords to the system, and in like manner divided the tones minor, so that the octave then became composed of thirteen sounds and twelve intervals, eight of which sounds are diatonic or natural, distinguished in the following scheme by white notes thus ◊, and five chromatic by black ones thus ✦, with the sharp sign, which Brossard calls a double dieſis prefixed to each of the notes so elevated.

 ∘

This, though a plausible, is a mistaken account of the matter; for first it is to be observed, this introduction of the semitones into the system, was not for the purpose of a progression of sounds different from that in the diatonic genus : on the contrary, nothing more was intended by it than to render it subservient to the diatonic progression; or, in other words, to institute a progression in the diatonic series from any given chord in the diapason, and we see the design of this improvement in its effects.

For, to assume the language of the moderns, if we take the key of E, in which no fewer than four of the sharp signatures are necessary, it is evident to demonstration that in the system of the diapason the tones and semitones will arise precisely in the same order as they do in the key of C, where not one of those signatures are necessary, and the same, mutatis mutandis, may be said of all the other keys with the greater third ; and the like will be found in those with the leſser third, comparing them with that of A, the prototype of them all †.

From hence it follows, that the use of the above signatures has no effect either in the intension or remission of the intervals; but the same remain, notwithstanding the application of them the same as in the diatonic genus.

* Dictionaire de Musique, Article SYSTEMA.
† See this demonstrated in the next book.

. It

It is true, that since the invention of polyphonous or symphonical music, a species of harmony of which the ancients seem to have been totally ignorant ; among the various combinations that may occasionally occur in a variety of parts, some may arise that shall nearly answer to the chromatic intervals, and it shall sometimes happen that a given note shall have for its accompanyment those sounds that constitute a chromatic tetrachord ; and of this opinion are some of the most skilful modern organists, who are inclined to think that they sometimes use the chromatic intervals, without knowing that they do so[*]. But the question in debate can only be determined by a comparison of the melody of the moderns with that of the ancients ; and in that of the moderns we meet with no such progression as that which is characterised by three incomposite semitones and two semitones, which is the least precise division of the tetrachord that any of the antients have given us.

Our countryman Morley gives his opinion of the matter in the following words : ' The music which we now use is neither just ' diatonic, nor right chromatic. Diatonicum is that which is now ' in use, and riseth throughout the scale by a whole note, a whole ' note, and a lesser or half note. A whole note is that which the ' Latins call Integer Tonus, and is that distance which is betwixt ' any two notes, except *mi* and *fa* ; for betwixt *mi* and *fa* is not a ' full halfe note, but is lesse than halfe a note by a comma, and' ' therefore called the lesser halfe note, in this manner.

'· Chromaticum is that which riseth by semitonium minus, or the ' less halfe note, the greater halfe note, and three halfe notes thus.

* It is also said, that in passages of notes in succession the chromatic intervals sometimes occur. The following not uncommon passage is said to be an example of the hemiolian or adsquialteral chromatic.

The

' The greater halfe note betwixt *fa* and *mi* in b *fa* ♮ *mi*. Enar-
' monicum is that which riseth by diesis, diesis (diesis is the halfe of
' the lesse halfe note) and ditonus; but in our musicke I can give no
' example of it, because we have no halfe of a lesse semitonium;
' but those who would shew it set down this example

' of enarmonicum, and marke the diesis thus x as it were the halfe of
' the apotome or greater halfe note, which is marked thus ♯. This
' signe of the more halfe note we now-a-daies confound with our b
' square, or signe of *mi* in ♮ *mi*, and with good reason; for when
' *mi* is sung in b *fa* ♮ *mi*, it is in that habitude to *a la mi re*, as the
' double diesis maketh F *fa ut* (sharpe) to E *la mi*, for in both places
' the distance is a whole note; but of this enough: and by this
' which is already set downe, it may evidentlie appeare that this kind
' of musick which is usual now-a-daies, is not fully and in every ref-
' pect the ancient diatonicum; for if you begin any four notes, sing-
' ing *ut, re, mi, fa,* you shall not find either a flat in E *la mi*, or a
' sharp in F *fa ut*; so that it must needes follow that it is neither just
' diatonicum nor right chromaticum. Likewise by that which is
' said it appeareth this point, which our organists use

' is not right chromatica, but a bastard point, patched up of halfe
' chromaticke and halfe diatonick. Lastlie, it appeareth by that
' which is said, that those virginals which our unlearned musytians
' cal cromatica (and some also grammatica) be not right chroma-
' tica, but half enharmonica; and that al the chromatica may be ex-
' pressed uppon our common virginals except this

' for if you would thinke that the (sharpe) in g *sol re ut* would serve
' that turne by experiment, you shall find that it is more then halfe a
' quarter of a note too low *.'

From hence we may conclude in general, that the system as it
stands at present, is not adapted to the chromatic genus; and were

* Plaine and easie Introduction to Practicall Musicke. Annotations on Part I.

there a poſſibility, which no one can admit, of rendering the chromatic tolerable to a modern ear, the revival of it would require what has often been attempted in vain, a new and a better temperament of the ſyſtem than the preſent.

From the ſeveral hypotheſes above ſtated, and the different methods of dividing the tetrachord in each genus, it clearly appears that among the moſt ancient of the Greek harmonicians there was a great diverſity of opinions with reſpect to the conſtitution of the genera. And it alſo appears that both the chromatic and enarmonic gave way to the diatonic, as being the moſt natural, and beſt adapted to the general ſenſe of harmony; indeed it is very difficult to account for the invention and practice of the former two, or to perſuade ourſelves that they could ever be rendered grateful to a judicious ear. And after all that has been ſaid of the enarmonic and chromatic, it is highly probable that they were ſubſervient to oratory, or in ſhort that they were modes of ſpeaking and not of ſinging, the intervals in which they conſiſt not being in any of the ratios which are recognized by the ear as conſonant.

Another ſubject in harmonics, no leſs involved in obſcurity, is the doctrine of the Modes, Moods, or Tones, for ſo they are indiſcriminately termed by ſuch as have profeſſed to treat of them. The appellation of Moods has indeed been given to the various kinds of metrical combination, uſed as well in muſic as poetry, and were the word Tone leſs equivocal than Mode, it might with propriety be ſubſtituted in the place of the former. Euclid has given no fewer than four ſenſes in which the word Tone is accepted [*]; whereas that of Mode or Mood is capable of but two; and when it is ſaid that theſe appellations refer to ſubjects ſo very different from each other as ſound and duration, that is to ſay tone and time, there can be little doubt which of the two is to be preferred.

To conſider the term Mode in that which is conceived to be its moſt eligible ſenſe, it ſignifies a certain ſeries or progreſſion of ſounds. Seven in number at leaſt are neceſſary to determine the nature of the progreſſion; and the diſtinction of one mode from another ariſes from that chord in the ſyſtem from whence it is made to commence; in this reſpect the term Mode is ſtrictly ſynonymous with the word Key, which at this day is ſo well underſtood as to need no explanation.

As

[*] Introd. Harmon. ex verſ. Meibom. pag. 19. et vide Meib. in loc. citat.

As to the number of the modes, there has subsisted a great variety of opinions, some reckoning thirteen, others fifteen, others twelve, and others but seven; and, to speak with precision, it is as illimitable as the number of sounds. The sounds that compose any given series, with respect to the degree of acumen or gravity assigned to each, are capable of an innumerable variety; for as a point or a line may be removed to places more or less distant from each other ad infinitum; in like manner a series of sounds may be infinitely varied, as well with respect to the degree of acumen or gravity, as the position of each in the system *; we are therefore not to wonder at the diversity of opinions in this respect, or that while some limit the modes to seven, others contend for more than double that number.

At what time the modes were first invented does no where clearly appear. Bontempi professes himself at a loss to fix it †; but Aristides Quintilianus intimates that they were known so early as the time of Pythagoras ‡; and considering the improvements he made, and that it was he who perfected the great or immutable system, it might naturally be supposed that he was the inventor of them; but the contrary of this is to be inferred from a passage in Ptolemy, who says that the ancients supposed only three modes, the Dorian, the Phrygian, and the Lydian ‖, denominations that do but ill agree with the supposition that any of them were invented by Pythagoras, who it is well known was a Samian. But farther, Aristides Quintilianus, in the passage above referred to, has given the characteristical letters of all the fifteen modes according to Pythagoras; so that, admitting him to have been the inventor of the additional twelve, the institution of the three primitive modes is referred backwards to a period anterior to that in which the system is said to have been perfected.

Euclid relates that Aristoxenus fixed the number of the modes at thirteen, that is say, 1. the Hypermixolydian or Hyperphrygian. 2. The acuter Mixolydian, called also the Hyperiastian. 3. The graver Mixolydian, called also the Hyperdorian. 4. The acuter Lydian. 5. The graver Lydian, called also the Æolian. 6. The acuter Phrygian. 7. The graver Phrygian, called also the Iastian. 8. The Dorian. 9. The acuter Hypolydian. 10. The graver Hypolydian, called also the Hypoæolian. 11. The acuter Hypophrygian. 12. The graver Hy-

* Wallis. Append. de Ver. Harm. pag. 312.   † Histor. Muf. pag. 136.
‡ Lib. I. pag. 28, ex verf. Meibom.   ‖ Harmonicor. lib. II. cap. vi. s. ex verf. Wallis.

pophrygian, called alfo the Hypoiaftian. 13. The Hypodorian *. The moft grave of thefe was the Hypodorian ; the reft followed in a fuccef- fion towards the acute, exceeding each other refpectively by a hemitone ; and between the two extreme modes was the interval of a diapafon †.

The better opinion however feems to be, that there are in nature but feven, and as touching the diverfity between them, it is thus accounted for. The Proflambanomenos of the hypodorian, the graveft of all the modes, was, in the judgment of the ancients, the moft grave found that the human voice could utter, or that the hearing could diftinctly form a judgment of; they made the Proflambanomenos of the hypoiaftian or graver hypophrygian to be acuter by a hemitone than that of the hypodorian; and confequently the Hypate of the one more acute by a hemitone than the Hypate of the other, and fo on for the reft ; fo that the Proflambanomenos of the hypoiaftian was in the middle, or a mean between the Proflambanomenos of the hypo- dorian and its Hypate hypaton. The Proflambanomenos of the acuter hypophrygian was ftill more acute by a hemitone, and confe- quently more acute by a whole tone than the hypodorian, and there- fore it coincided with the Hypate hypaton of that mode, as is thus reprefented by Ptolemy, lib. II. cap. xi ‡.

ACUTE

——————————————————————— Hypermixolydian

    Tone

——————————————————————— Mixolydian

    Limma

——————————————————————— Lydian

    Tone

——————————————————————— Phrygian

    Tone

——————————————————————— Dorian

    Limma

——————————————————————— Hypolydian

    Tone

——————————————————————— Hypophrygian

    Tone

——————————————————————— Hypodorian

GRAVE

* Euclid. Introd. Harm. pag. xx.   † Wallis Append. de Vet. Harm. pag. 311.
‡ Ibid. pag. 313.   Thefe

Thofe who contended for fifteen modes, among whom Alypius is to be reckoned, to the thirteen above enumerated, added two others in the acute, which they termed the Hyperlydian and Hyperæolian[*].

But againſt this practice of increaſing the modes by hemitones, Ptolemy argues moſt ſtrongly in the eleventh chapter, and alſo in the four preceeding chapters of the ſecond book of his Harmonics : and indeed were it to prevail, the modes might be multiplied without end, and to no purpoſe. Notwithſtanding this, Martianus Capella contends for fifteen and Glareanus for twelve modes; but it is to be obſerved, that both theſe latter writers are, in reſpect of the Greek harmonicians, conſidered as mere moderns ; and beſides theſe there are certain other objections to their teſtimony, which will be mentioned in their proper place.

As to the two additional modes mentioned by Alypius, they ſeem to have been added to the former thirteen, more with a view to regularity in the names and poſitions of the modes, than to any particular uſe; and perhaps there is no aſſignable period of time during which it may with truth be ſaid, that more than thirteen were admitted into practice.

Ptolemy however rejects as ſpurious ſix of the thirteen allowed by the Ariſtoxeneans, and this in conſequence of the poſition he had advanced, that it was not lawful to encreaſe the modes by a hemitone. It is by no means neceſſary to give his reaſons at large for limiting the number to ſeven, as his doctrine contains in it a demonſtration that the encreaſe of them beyond that number was rather a corruption than an improvement of the harmonic ſcience. As to the three primitive modes, the Dorian, the Phrygian, and the Lydian, each of them was ſituated at the diſtance of a ſeſquioctave tone from that next to it [†], and therefore the two extremes were diſtant from each other two ſuch tones; or, in other words, the Phrygian mode was more acute than the Dorian by one tone, and the Lydian more acute than the Phrygian by one tone; conſequently the Lydian was more acute than the Dorian by two tones.

To theſe three modes Ptolemy added four others, making together ſeven, which, as he demonſtrates, are all that nature can admit of. As to the Hypermixolydian, mentioned by him in the tenth chapter of his ſecond book, it is evidently a repetition of the hypodorian.

[*] Wallis. Append. pag. 312.   [†] Ibid.

MIXO-

MIXOLYDIAN
LYDIAN
PHRYGIAN
DORIAN
HYPOLYDIAN
HYPOPHRYGIAN
HYPODORIAN *

The above is the order in which they are given by Euclid, Gaudentius, Bacchius, and Ptolemy himfelf, though the latter, in the
eleventh chapter of his fecond book, has varied it by placing the
Dorian firft, and in confequence thereof tranfpofing all the reft; but
this was for a reafon which a clofer view of the fubject will make it
unneceffary to explain.

Having proceeded thus far in the endeavour to diftinguifh between
the legitimate and the fpurious modes, it may now be proper to enter
upon a more particular inveftigation of their natures, and fee if it be
not poffible, notwithftanding that great diverfity of opinion that has
prevailed in the world, to draw from thofe valuable fources of intelligence the ancient harmonic writers, fuch a doctrine as may afford
fome degree of fatisfaction to a modern enquirer. It muft be confeffed that this has been attempted by feveral writers of diftinguifhed
abilities, and that the fuccefs of their labours has not anfwered the
expectations of the world. The Italians, particularly Franchinus, or
as he is alfo called, Gaffurius, Zaccone, Zarlino, Galilei, and others,
have been at infinite pains to explain the modes of the ancients, but
to little purpofe. Kircher has alfo undertaken to exhibit them;
but notwithftanding his great erudition and a feeming certainty in
all he advances, his teftimony is greatly to be fufpected; and, if we
may believe Meibomius, whenever he profeffes to explain the doctrines
of the ancients, he is fcarcely intitled to any degree of credit. The reafon why thefe have failed in their attempts is obvious, for it was not
till after moft of them wrote, that any accurate edition of the Greek
harmonicians was given to the world: fo lately as the time when Morley publifhed his Introduction, that is to fay in the reign of queen Elizabeth, it was doubted whether the writings of fome of the moft
valuable of them were extant even in manufcript; and it feemed
to be the opinion that they had perifhed in that general wreck of literature

* Called alfo the Lorrenfian.   Euclid Introd. Harm. pag. 16.

terature which has left us just enough to guess at the greatness of
our loss.

To the several writers above-mentioned we may add Glareanus of
Basil, a contemporary and intimate friend of Erasmus; but he confesses that he had never seen the Harmonics of Ptolemy, nor indeed
the writings of any of the Greek Harmonicians, and that for what
he knew of them he was indebted to Boetius and Franchinus. From
the perusal of these authors he entertained an opinion that the number of the modes was neither more nor less than twelve; and, confounding the ancient with the modern, or, as they are denominated,
the ecclesiastical modes, which, as originally instituted by St. Ambrose, were only four in number, but were afterwards by St. Gregory,
about the year 600, encreased to eight, he adopted the distinction of
authentic and plagal modes, and left the subject more perplexed than
he found it.

To say the truth, very few of the modern writers in the account
they give of the modes are to be depended on; and among the ancients, so great is the diversity of opinions, as well with respect to
the nature as the number of them, that it requires a great deal of attention to understand the designation of each, and to discriminate between the genuine and those that are spurious. In general it is to
be observed that the modes answer to the species of diapason, which in
nature are seven and no more, each terminating or having its final
chord in a regular succession above that of the mode next preceding:
for instance, the Dorian, which had its situation in the middle of the
lyre or system, had for its final note hypate meson or E; the Hypolydian, the next in situation towards the grave, had for its final chord
parypate meson or F; and the Hypophrygian, the next in situation
towards the grave to the Hypolydian, had for its final chord lychanos
hypaton or G; so that the differences between the modes in succession,
with respect to their degrees of gravity, corresponded with the order of
the tones and semitones in the diatonic series. But it seems that those
of the ancient harmonicians, who contended for a greater number of
modes than seven, effected an encrease of them by making the final
chord of each in succession, a semitone more acute than that of the
next preceding mode: and against this practice of augmenting the
modes by semitones Ptolemy has expresfly written in the eleventh
chapter of the second book of his Harmonics, and that with such
force

force of reason and argument, as cannot fail to convince every one that reads and underftands him, to which end nothing can fo much conduce as the attentive perufal of that learned Appendix to his Harmonics of Dr. Wallis, fo often cited in the courfe of this work.

Befides this Appendix, the world is happy in the poffeffion of a difcourfe entitled, An Explanation of the Modes or Tones in the ancient Grecian Mufic, by Sir Francis Hafkins Eyles Stiles, Bart. F. R. S. and publifhed in the Philofophical Tranfactions for the year 1760; and by the affiftance of thefe two valuable tracts it is hoped that this abftrufe part of mufical fcience may be rendered to a great degree intelligible.

C H A P. X.

TO conceive aright of the nature of the modes, it muft be underftood, that as there are in nature three different kinds of diateffaron, and alfo four different kinds of diapente; and as the diapafon is compofed of thefe two fyftems, it follows that there are in nature feven fpecies of diapafon *. The difference among thefe feveral fyftems arifes altogether from the different pofition of the femitone in each fpecies. To explain this difference in the language of the ancient writers would be very difficult, as the terms ufed by them are not fo well calculated to exprefs the place of the femitone as thofe fyllables invented by the moderns for that fole purpofe, the practice whereof is termed folmifation. We muft therefore fo far tranfgrefs againft chronological order, as, in conformity to the practice of Dr. Wallis, to affume thefe fyllables for the purpofe of diftinguifhing the feveral fpecies of diateffaron, diapente, and diapafon, referring a particular account of their invention and ufe to its proper place.

To begin with the diateffaron; it contains four chords and three intervals: its fpecies are alfo three: the firft is faid to be that which has LA, the characteriftical ratio or found of the diateffaron, as MI is of the diapente and diapafon, in the firft or more acute place; the

* Vide Prolem. Harm. lib. II. cap. ix. ex verf. Wallis. Wallis. Append. de Vet. Harm. pog. 310. Euclid. Introd. Harm. pag. 15. ex verf. Meibom. Kirch. Mufurg. tom. I. cap. xv. &c.

fecond which hath it in the fecond, and the third which hath it in the third *.

Euclid defines thefe feveral fpecies by the appellatives that denote their fituation on the lyre, viz. Βαρυπυκνοι Barypyknoi, Μεσοπυκνοι Mefopyknoi, and Οξυπυκνοι Oxypyknoi †, meaning by the firft the feries from Hypaton hypaton to Hypate mefon, which we fing in afcending from the grave to the acute by the fyllables FA, SOL, LA ; by the fecond, the feries from Parhypate hypaton to Parhypate mefon, SOL LA FA; and by the third, that from Lychanos hypaton to Lychanos mefon, FA, SOL, LA ‡. As to the other feries here under exhibited from Hypate mefon to Mefe, it is inferted to fhew that the diateffaron is capable of but three mutations; for this latter will be found to be precifely the fame as, or in truth but a bare repetition of, the firft ‖, as is evident in the following fcales, in which the extreme or grave found from which we afcend, is diftinguifhed by a difference of character; the fyllables being ever intended to exprefs the intervals or ratios, and not the chords themfelves.

SPECIES of the DIATESSARON III.

Mefe	a	la				la
	G	fol			fol	fol
	F	fa		fa	fa	fa
Hypate mefon	E	la	la	la	la	LA
	D	fol	fol	fol	SOL	t
	C	fa	fa	FA	3	
Hypate hypaton	B	MI	MI	2		
			1			

The above is the tetrachord hypaton of the great fyftem; but as a diapente contains five chords and four intervals, to explain the nature of the feveral fpecies included in that fyftem a greater feries is required; it is therefore neceffary for this purpofe to make ufe of thofe two tetrachords between which the diazeuctic tone may be properly interpofed; and thefe can be no other than the tetrachord Mefon, and the tetrachord Diezeugmenon. It has been juft faid that the characteriftic fyllable of the diapente is MI, and this will be found to occur in the firft, fecond, third, and fourth places of the following example

* Wall. Append. de Vet. Harm. pag. 310.   † Introd. Harm. pag. 15, ex verf. Meib.
‡ Wallis Append. de Vet. Harm. pag. 310.   ‖ Ibid.

of the possible variations in that syftem, the confequence whereof is, that the firft fpecies is to be fung FA, SOL, LA, MI, the fecond SOL, LA, MI, FA, the third LA, MI, FA, SOL, and the fourth MI, FA, SOL, LA, as in the following fcales.

SPECIES of the DIAPENTE IV.

Nete diezeugmenon	e	la			la	
	d	fol		fol	fol	
	c	fa		fa	fa	fa	
Paramefe	b	mi	mi	mi	mi	mi	
Mefe	a	la	la	la	la	LA	
	G	fol	fol	fol	SOL	4
	F	fa	fa	FA		3
Hypate mefon	E	LA	LA	2		
				1		

Thefe are all the mutations of which the diapente is capable; that an additional feries, namely that from b to f, was not inferted as a proof of it, agreeable to what was done in refpect to the next pre-ceeding diagram, was becaufe between b and f the diazeuctic tone marked by the fyllable MI does no where occur : or, in other words, that feries is a femidiapente or falfe fifth, containing only three tones, which is lefs by a femitone, or, to fpeak with precifion, a limma, than a true diapente. As for example:

b Semitone c Tone d Tone e Semitone f

and were another feries to be added, it muft begin from MI or b; now the diazeuctic tone is the interval between a and b, and confe-quently is out of the pentachord [*].

To diftinguifh the feven fpecies of diapafon, two conjunct diapa-fons are required; for example, from Proflambanomenos to Nete hy-perboleon, to be fung by the fyllables LA, MI, FA, SOL, LA, MI, FA, SOL, LA, FA, SOL, LA [†], in which feries will be found all the feven fpecies of the diapafon ; and that there are no more will appear by a repetition of the experiment made in the cafe of the diateffaron ; for were we to proceed farther, and after the feventh begin from a or LA, the fuc-ceffion of fyllables would be in precifely the fame order as in the firft feries, which is a demonftration that thofe two fpecies are the fame [‡].

[*] Wallis Append. de Vet. Harm. pag. 311.   [†] Ibid.   [‡] Ibid.

SPECIES of the DIAPASON VII.

Nete hyperboleon	aa	la						la
	g	fol					fol	fol
	f	fa				fa	fa	fa
	e	la			la	la	la	la
	d	fol		fol	fol	fol	fol	fol
	c	fa		fa	fa	fa	fa	fa
	b	mi	mi	mi	mi	mi	mi	mi	mi
Mefe	a	la la	la	la	la	la	la	la	LA
	G	fol fol	fol fol	fol	fol	fol	SOL
	F	fa fa	fa fa	fa	fa	FA
	E	la la	la la	la	LA
	D	fol fol	fol fol	SOL
	C	fa fa	fa	FA
	B	mi mi	MI
Proflambanomenos	A	LA LA	*

From hence it appears, that to exhibit all the various species of diapason, a lefs fyftem than the difdiapafon would have been infufficient; for though the fame founds, as 10 power, return after the fingle diapafon, yet all the fpecies are not to be found therein. Ptolemy defines a fyftem to be a confonance of confonances; adding, that a fyftem is called perfect, as it contains all the confonances with their and every of their fpecies †; for that whole can only be faid to be perfect, which contains all the parts. According therefore to the firft definition, the diapafon is a fyftem, as is alfo the diapafon and diateffaron, the diapafon and diapente, and the difdiapafon, for every of thefe is compofed of two or more confonances; but, according to the fecond definition, the only perfect fyftem is the difdiapafon; for that, which no lefs fyftem can do, it contains fix confonances, namely, the diateffaron 1, diapente 2, diapafon 3, diapafon and diateffaron 4, diapafon and diapente 5, and difdiapafon 6‡; and nature admits of no other.

The above fcales declare the fpecific difference between the feveral kinds of diateffaron, diapente, and diapafon, by fhewing the place of the femitone in each.

Salinas ||, by a difcrimination of the greater and leffer tone, has increafed the number of combinations of the diateffaron to fix in this manner.

* Wallis Append, de Vet. Harm. pag. 311. † Lib. II. cap. iv.
‡ Vide Euclid. Introd. Harm. ex verf. Meib. || Lib. IV. cap. iii.

Three

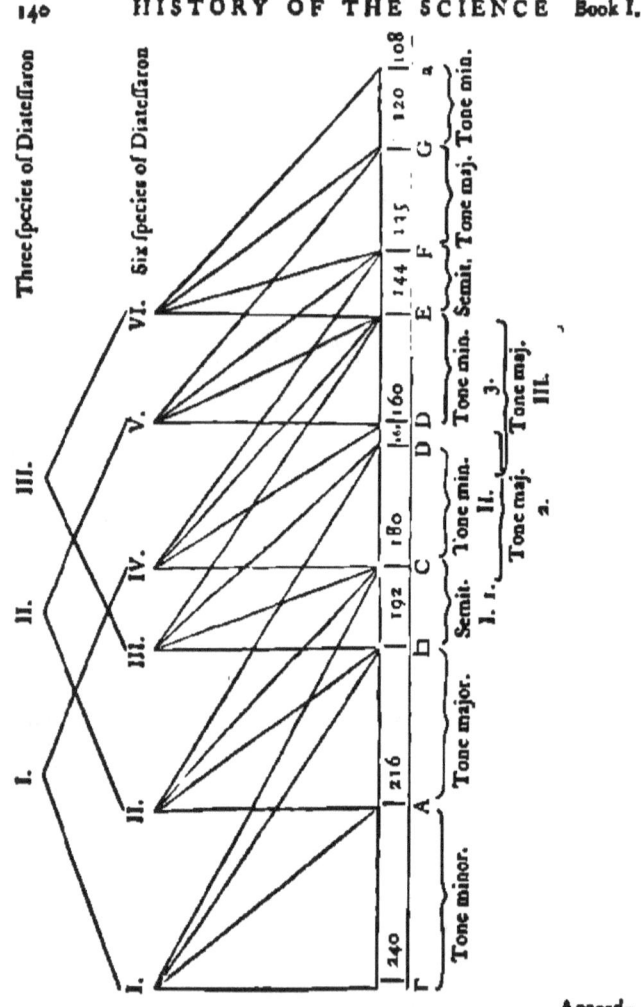

Accord-

According to which, each of the diateſſarons is made to conſiſt of a hemitone, tone, and tone; yet out of the above ſix combinations, we ſee that theſe intervals do not occur twice in the ſame order.

Beſides theſe, Salinas has ſhewn the following ſix other ſpecies of diateſſaron; in his opinion not leſs true than thoſe above exhibited.

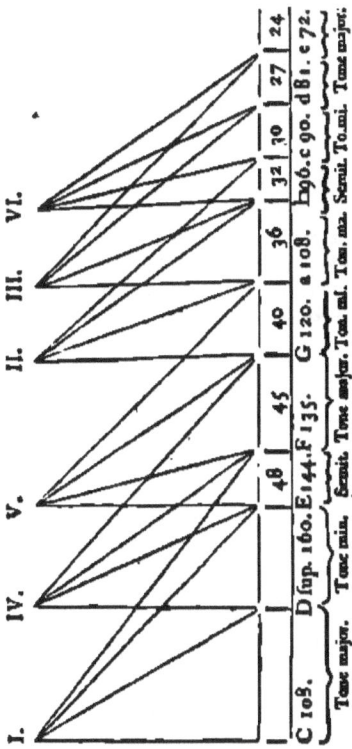

It ſeems however that he has conſidered that as a diateſſaron, which in truth is only nominally ſo, namely, the Tritonus between F and:

F and li † ; the situation whereof, in respect to the others in the
above diagram, seems to have suggested to him a motive for inferting
from Bede an account of a very curious method of divination, formerly practised, which is here, with some small variation, tranflated
from Salinas.

' It is very credible that this difpofition gave rife to that well
' known game, the defign whereof is to divine when three men
' placed in order have diftributed among themfelves three lots of
' different magnitudes, which of thofe lots each perfon has re-
' ceived; which muft be done after fix manners, and thofe the
' fame by which the diateffaron is divided, and its intervals placed
' in order as we have fhewn, that is to fay, each lot may be twice
' placed in each of the three fituations; for the three men anfwer to
' the three places, the firft to the grave, the fecond to the mean, and
' the third to the acute; and the three lots of different magnitudes to the
' three intervals alfo of different quantity; the greater to the greater
' tone, the middle to the leffer tone, and the leaft to the femitone.
' This method of divination is performed by the help of twenty-four
' little ftones, of which the diviner himfelf gives one to the firft,
' two to the fecond, and three to the third, with this injunction,
' that he who has received the greateft lot, do take up out of the
' remaining eighteen ftones as many as were at firft diftributed to
' him; he who has the lot in the middle degree of magnitude, twice
' as many as he has; and he that has the leaft lot, four times as
' many as he alfo has. By this means the diviner will be able to
' know from the number of ftones remaining, which of the things
' each perfon has; for if the diftribution be made after the firft man-
' ner, there will be one left; if after the fecond two, if after the
' third three, if after the fourth five, if after the fifth fix; and,
' laftly, if after the fixth feven; for there can never four remain,
' for which a twofold reafon may be affigned; the one from the dif-
' pofal of the inftituent, who from the truth of the thing, though
' perhaps the reafon thereof was not known by him, was impelled
' to conftitute the game in this manner.

        " Haud equidem fine mente reor, fine numine divûm."

† Salinas De Mufica, lib. IV. cap. iii.

                                                      ' The

' The other taken from the conflant and fettled order of the harmo-
' nical ratio; but four cannot poffibly remain, becaufe the firft and
' third perfons having received an uneven number of ftones, either
' of them muft, if he have the greateft lot, take up an uneven num-
' ber alfo; as by the injunction of the inftituent, he was to take up
' as many ftones as were at firft diftributed to him; and an uneven
' number being taken out of an even one, the remainder muft ne-
' ceffarily be uneven; but as each of them may have the great-
' eft lot twice, there muft be four uneven remainders of ftones
' out of the fix changes: as to the fecond, he can have it only twice;
' becaufe as he has an even number, and takes up a number
' equal thereto, there muft an even number remain; for the others
' muft alfo take up even numbers, as they are enjoined to take up
' twice, and four times as many as they had received; and the
' greateft lot may fall to the fecond perfon in two cafes, for either
' the firft may have the middling, and the third the fmalleft, and
' then the remainder will be two; or contrarywife, and then there
' will remain fix; and as the greateft lot cannot come three times to
' the fecond, it is plain that the third even number, which is four,
' cannot by any means be left.   But the other reafon taken from the
' harmonical ratio, is much truer and ftronger; for as it is fhewn in
' the feven founds of a diapafon from C to c, that a diateffaron may
' be produced towards the acute from fix of them, that is to fay, the
' firft, fecond, third, fifth, fixth, and feventh, the fourth being
' paffed over becaufe the diateffaron cannot be produced therefrom;
' fo alfo in this play the number four is paffed over as having no
' concern therein; but it does not happen fo in the compofition of
' inftrumental harmony, for though, as is fhewn in the laft example
' above, the fourth found from C makes a tritone, with its nominal
' fourth above it, it is not to be excluded from the feries.   Neither
' is the diapafon from this fourth found from C, viz. F, to be to-
' tally rejected; for though by reafon of the tritone it cannot be
' arithmetically divided as the other fix may, yet may it be divided
' harmonically.   I fhould by no means have made mention of this
' game, being apprehenfive that I may be thought to trifle on fo fe-
' rious an affair, but that I look upon it as an example very much fuited
' to explain the fubject we are treating of; and I did it the more
' willingly, becaufe I found it particularly treated of by Bede, fur-
7   ' named

' named the Venerable, a moſt grave man, and deeply learned both
' in theology and ſecular arts, from whence we may conjecture that
' it has been invented above one thouſand years *."

But, to return from this digreſſion, notwithſtanding the ſpecies
of diapaſon are manifeſtly ſeven, the modes ſeem originally to

* The paſſage on which this aſſertion is grounded, has eluded a curſory ſearch among
the writings of Bede ; nevertheleſs it may poſſibly be found in ſome one or other of thoſe
numerous little tracts on arithmetic, muſic, and other of the ſciences, contained in his
voluminous works, many whereof as yet exiſt only in manuſcript. The deſcription
given by Salinas of this method of divination is in nearly theſe words.

Ab hac etiam diſpoſitione credendum eſt, ortum habuiſſe Iuſum illum notiſſimum,
cujus propoſitum eſt, tribus hominibus ordine diſpoſitis, tres res diverſæ magnitudinis inter
ſe diſtribuentibus, quam quis eorum acceperit, divinare. Quod ſex modis fieri, neceſſe
eſt : atque eiſdem, quibus diateſſaron dividitur, et eodem ordine diſpoſitis, quo tria ipſius
intervalla, tribus in locis bis ſingula in ſingulis oſtendimus collocari. Tribus enim locis
reſpondent tres homines : primus gratiſſimo, ſecundus medio, tertius acutiſſimo. Et
tres res diverſæ magnitudinis, tribus intervallis etiam variæ quantitatis, maxima tono majori, media minori, minima ſemitonio. Conficietur autem hic luſus 24 lapillis, ex quibus
primo unum, ſecundo duos, tertio tres divinaturus ipſe tradit, ea lege, ut ex 18 reliquis, qui
rem maximam accipiet, tot, quot habet : qui mediam, bis totidem : qui minimam, totidem
quater aſſumat ; quo ex eorum, qui ſupererunt numero, quæ cuique obvenerit, poſſit cog-
noſcere. Nam ſi primo modo fiet diſtributio, relinquetur unus : ſi fiet ſecundo, duo : ſi
tertio, tres : ſi quatuor, quinque : ſi quinto, ſex : et ſi denique ſexto, ſeptem. Neque quatuor
uſquam poterunt ſupereſſe, cujus duplex ratio poteſt aſſignari. Altera, ex arbitrio inſti-
tuentis ab ipſa rei veritate forſitan illi non cognita ad luſum ſe inſtituendum impulſi,

' Haud equidem ſine mente reor, ſine numine divûm.'

Altera ex æterna rationis harmonicæ diſpoſitione deſumpta. Quod autem ad inſtituentem
attinet, quatuor id circo remanere non poſſunt, quoniam primus, et tertius lapillos impares
ſuſceperunt : et cum ea lege tot, quot habent, accipere teneantur, ſi maximam habebunt,
aſſument impares : quibus ex paribus ſublatis, impares relinqui neceſſe eſt, quod alterutri
his evenire contingit, unde quater impares reſtabunt. Et cum ſecundus etiam bis maximam poſſit accipere, quoniam habet pares, totidem aſſumptis relinquentur pares : nam re-
liquos neceſſe eſt pares aſſumere, cum duplicate, et quadruplicate lapillos, quos habent,
teneantur. Quod bis evenire contingit ; aut enim primus mediam habebit, et tertius minimam, et reſtabunt duo ; aut contra, et reſtabunt ſex. Et cum maxima ſecundo ter evenire nequeat, conſtat, tertiam rorem, qui quatuor eſt, nullo modo poſſe relinqui. Sed
multo verius, et fortior eſt, quæ ex ratione harmonica deſumitur. Nam quemadmodum
in ſeptem ſonis diapa on oſtenſum eſt, à ſex illorum diateſſaron in acutum prorabi poſſe,
qui ſunt primus, ſecundus, tertius, quintus, ſextus, ſeptimus : et quartum præteriri
neque in eo reperiri poſſe : ſic etiam in luſu ipſo præteritur quarta dictio, quæ octava eſt ;
quod non ita evenit in harmoniæ inſtrumentalis compoſitione. Quandoquidem (ut dictum
eſt) ſignificat tritonum, quod à quarto ſono inter ſeptem ſones diapaſon invenitur, eum à
ſex aliis omnibus diateſſaron inveniatur. Unde etiam in ſeptem diapaſon ſpeciebus, quæ
à ſeptem ſonis oriuntur, ſex arithmeticæ dividi poſſunt ; una verò nequaquam, quæ à C
euoi prima ſit, progrediendo in acutum, erit quarta. Hujus autem luſus nequiquam ego
mentionem feciſſem, ne in re tam ſeria ludere velle viderer, niſi ad rem, qua de agimus,
facilius explicandam, aptiſſimum eſſet exemplum. Quod eo libentius feci, quoniam cum
comperi ex profeſſo traditum à Beda, cognomento Venerabili, viro graviſſimo et in divinis
literis, ac ſecularibus diſ iplinis eruditiſſimo. Unde conjectari licet, ante mille annos ex-
cogitatum fuiſſe. Salinas de Muſica, lib. IV. cap. v.

have

have been but three in number, namely, the Dorian, the Phrygian, and the Lydian * : the firſt proceeding from E to e, the ſecond from D to d, and the third from C to c †, how theſe are generated ſhall be made appear.

And firſt it is to be remarked that the place of the diazeuctic tone is the characteriſtic of every mode. In the Dorian the diazeuctic tone was ſituated in the middle of the heptachord, that is to ſay, it was the interval between meſe or a, and parameſe b, the chords meſe and parameſe being thus ſtationed in the middle of the ſyſtem, three in the acute, namely, Trite diezeugmenon, Paranete diezeugmenon, and Nete diezeugmenon ; and three in the grave, namely, Lychanos meſon, Parhypate meſon, and Hypate meſon, determined the ſpecies of diapaſon proper to the Dorian mode. The ſeries of intervals that conſtituted the Dorian mode, had its ſtation in the middle of the lyre, which conſiſted, as has been already mentioned, of fifteen chords, comprehending the ſyſtem of a diſdiapaſon ; and to characteriſe the other modes, authors make uſe of a diapaſon with preciſely the ſame boundaries ; and that becauſe the extreme chords, both in remiſſion and intenſion, are leſs grateful to the ear than the intermediate ones.   Ptolemy takes notice of this, ſaying, that the ear is delighted to exerciſe itſelf in the middle melodies ‡ : and he therefore adviſes, for the inveſtigation of the modes, the taking the diapaſon as nearly as may be from the middle of the lyre ‖.

The Dorian Meſe being thus ſettled at a, and the poſition of the diazeuctic tone thereby determined, a method is ſuggeſted for diſcovering the conſtitution of the other ſix modes, namely, the Mixolydian, Lydian, Phrygian, Hypolydian, Hypophrygian, and Hypodorian, making together with the Dorian, ſeven, and anſwering to the ſpecies of the diapaſon ; all above which number, according to the expreſs declaration of Ptolemy, are to be rejected as ſpurious §.

But in order to render this conſtitution intelligible, it is neceſſary to take notice of a diſtinction made by Ptolemy, lib. II. cap. xi. between the natural, or, which is the ſame, the Dorian Meſe and the modal Meſe ; as alſo between every chord in the lyre or

* Ptolem. Harm. lib. II. cap. vi. Wallis Append. de Vet. Harm. p. 312.
† Vide Kirch. Muſurg. tom. 1. cap. xvi. ‡ Harmonicor. lib. II. cap. xi.
‖ Ibid. lib. II. cap. xi.   § Lib. II. cap. viii. ix. xi. ex verſ. Wallis.

great fyflem, and its correfponding found in each of the modes, which he has noted by the ufe of the two different terms Pofitions and Powers. In the Dorian mode thefe coincided, as for example, the Mefe of the lyre, that is to fay the Mefe in pofition, was alfo the Mefe in power, the Proflambanomenos in pofition was alfo the Proflambanomenos in power, and fo of the reft *.

But in the other modes the cafe was far otherwife; to inftance, in the Phrygian, there the Mefe in pofition was the Lychanos mefon in Power, and the Proflambanomenos in pofition the Paranete hyperboleon in power. In the Lydian the Mefe in pofition was the Parhypate mefon in power, and the Proflambanomenos in pofition was the Trite hyperboleon in power; and to the rule for tranfpofition of the Mefe the other intervals were in like manner fubject.

From this diftinction between the real and the nominal or potential Mefe follawed, as above is noted, a change in the name of every other chord on the lyre, which change was regulated by that relation which the feveral chords in each mode bore to their refpective Mefes, and the term Mefe not implying any thing like what we call the Pitch of the found, but only the place of the diazeuctic tone in the lyre, this change of the name became not only proper, but abfolutely neceffary: nor is it any thing more than is practifed at this day, when by the introduction of a new cliff, we give a new name, not only to One, but a feries of founds, without difturbing the order of fucceffion, or affigning to them other powers than nature has eftablifhed.

The following fcale, taken from the notes of Dr. Wallis on the eleventh chapter of the fecond book of the Harmonics of Ptolemy, exhibits the pofition on the lyre, of each of the modal Mefes.

* Vide Sir Francis Stiles on the Modes, pag. 702
By the Mefe in power is to be underftood not the actual Mefe or the middle chord of the fptenary, but that which marks the pofition of the diazeuclic tone which varies in each mode. In the Dorian, for inftance, it holds the middle or fourth, in the Phrygian the third, and in the Lydian the fecond place, reckoning from the acute towards the grave. See the diagram of the fpecies of diapafon in the feven Ptolemaic modes hereafter inferted.

as Nete-

aa Nete hyperboleon
 g Paranete hyperboleon
 f Trite hyperboleon
 e Nete diezeugmenon
 d Paranete diezeugmenon Mixolydian
 c Trite diezeugmenon   Lydian
 b Paramefe.   Phrygian
 a Mefe   Dorian   } MESE
 G Lychanos mefon   Hypolydian
 F Parhypate mefon   Hypophrygian
 E Hypate mefon   Hypodorian
 D Lychanos hypaton
 C Parypate hypaton
 b Hypate hypaton
 A Proflambanomenos *

Now that diverfity of ftations for the Mefe above reprefented, neceffarily implies the diflocation of the diazeuctic tone for every mode;
and from the rules in the tenth chapter of the fecond book of Ptolemy, for taking the modes, it follows by neceffary confequence
that in the Mixolydian mode the diazeuctic tone muft be the firft
interval, reckoning from acute to grave; in the Lydian the
fecond, in the Phrygian the third, in the Dorian the fourth, in the
Hypolydian the fifth, in the Hypophrygian the fixth, and in the
Hypodorian the laft †.

The fituation of the Mefe, and confequently of the diazeuctic tone
being thus adjufted, the component intervals of the diapafon above
and below it, follow of courfe as they arife in the order of nature; and
we are enabled to fay not only that the fpecies of diapafon anfwering
to the feveral modes in their order are as follow :

 * Ptolem. Harmonicor. ex verf. Wallis, pag. 137, in not.
 † Sir Francis Stiles on the Modes, pag. 709. And fee the diagram of the feven
Ptolemaic modes hereinafter inferted.

Mixolydian		B to b
Lydian		C to c
Phrygian		D to d
Dorian	from	E to e
Hypolydian		F to f
Hypophrygian		G to g
Hypodorian		A to a, or a to aa *

But that the following is the order in which the tones and semitones occur in each series, proceeding from grave to acute.

Mixolydian	Semitone, tone, tone, femitone, tone, tone, tone.
Lydian	Tone, tone, femitone, tone, tone, tone, femitone.
Phrygian	Tone, femitone, tone, tone, tone, femitone, tone.
Dorian	Semitone, tone, tone, tone, femitone, tone, tone.
Hypolydian	Tone, tone, tone, femitone, tone, tono, femitone.
Hypophrygian	Tone, tone, femitone, tone, tone, femitone, tone.
Hypodorian	Tone, femitone, tone, tone, femitone, tone, tone ‡.

And this, according to Ptolemy, is the conflitution of the feven
modes of the ancients.

* Sir F. S. on the Modes, 708. Kirch. Mufurg. tom. I. cap. xvi.
† Upon the conflitution of the firft of the above modes a great difficulty arifes, namely,
how to reconcile it to the rules of harmonical progreffion, for it is exprefsly laid by Kircher
and alfo by Sir Francis Stiles, in his Difcourfe on the Modes, pag. 407, and may be inferred
from what Ptolemy fays concerning them in his Harmonics, lib. II. cap. x. that the Mixolydian anfwers to the fpecies of diapafon, from Hypate hypaton to Paramefe, that is to fay,
from D to D, and that the femitones in it are the firft and fourth intervals in that feries ;
now if this be the cafe, as moft clearly it is, the interval between the chord F I and the
chord Parypate mefon or F muft be a femidiapente, which is a falfe relation, arifing from
two incommenfurous chords, and confequently is unfit for mufical practice.
Again, in the Hypolydian, from Parhypate mefon to Trite hyperboleon, or F to f, a
tritone occurs between F and b, which is a falfe relation, and renders this fpecies equally
with the former unfit for mufical practice.
Dr. Wallis feems to have been aware of this difficulty, and has attempted to folve it in
a diagram of his, containing a comparative view of the ancient modes with the feveral
keys of the moderns, by prefixing the flat fign b, to the Hypate hypaton ; agreeable to
what he fays in another place, that in the Mixolydian mi is placed in E la mi, and to get
rid of the tritone in the latter cafe he prefixes a fecond flat in E la mi, excluding thereby
mi from thence, and placing it in A la mi re.
Sir Francis Styles has done the fame, and farther both thefe writers have made ufe of the
acute fign # for fimilar purpofes. In all which inftances it is fuppofed they are juftified
by the practice of the ancients ; for it is to be noted that they had a particular tuning for
every key, which could be for no other purpofe than that of diftorting the intervals
from their refpective ftations in the feveral fpecies of diapafon, and might probably reduce them to that arrangement obfervable in the keys of the moderns, which, after all
that can be faid about them, are finally refolvable into two.

7   A

A

GENERAL HISTORY

OF THE

SCIENCE and PRACTICE

OF

M U S I C.

BOOK II. CHAP. I.

IN the foregoing enquiry touching the modes, endeavours have been ufed to demonftrate the coincidence between the feven genuine modes and the feven fpecies of diapafon. But fuppofing the relation between them to be made out, a queftion yet remains, namely, whether the progreffion in each of the modes was in the order prefcribed by nature or not. In what order of fucceffion the tones and femitones arife in each fpecies of the diapafon has already been declared; and it feems from the reprefentation above given of the fpecies, that, as the keys of the moderns are ultimately reducible to two, DO MI, and RE FA, fo the feven modes of the ancients by the diflocation of the Mefe for each, and that confequent new tuning of the diapafon for each, which is mentioned by Ptolemy in the eleventh chapter of his fecond book, are by fuch diflocation of the Mefe and new tuning reduced to two. To this purpofe Dr. Wallis feems uniformly to exprefs himfelf and particularly in this his defcription of the modes taken from Ptolemy.

' Ptolemy, in the eleventh chapter of his fecond book, and elfe-
'. where, makes the Dorian the firft of the modes, which, as having
' for its Mefe and Paramefe the Mefe and Paramefe both in pofition,
' and power, or, to fpeak with the moderns, having its *mi* in ♭,
                                                                    ' may.

' may be faid to be fituated in the midft of them all ; he therefore
' conflitutes the Dorian mode fo as that between the real and af-
' fumed names of all the chords, there is throughout a perfect coin-
' cidence : and to this mode anfwers that key of the moderns in
' which no fignature is placed at the head of the ftave to denote ei-
' ther flat or fharp.

' Secondly he takes a mode more acute than the former by a dia-
' teffaron, which therefore has for its Mefe a chord alfo more acute
' by a diateffaron, namely the Paranete diezeugmenon of the Dorian,
' and confequently its Paramefe, which is our mi, muft anfwer to
' the Nete diezeugmenon, that is as we fpeak, mi is placed in E la
' mi, and this he calls the Mixolydian. The moderns for a fimilar
' purpofe place a flat on B fa, and thereby exclude mi.

' And from hence he elfewhere, lib. II. cap. vi. concludes, that
' there is no neceffity for that which the ancients called the conjunct
' fyftem, namely, the fyftem from Proflambanomenos to Nete fy-
' nemmenon, fince that is fufficiently fupplied by the change made
' in Mefe from the Dorian to the Mixolydian mode ; for here fol-
' lows after the two conjunct tetrachords in the Dorian, from Hypato
' hypaton to the Mefe, that is from B mi to A la mi re, a third in the
' Mixolydian from its Hypate mefon, which is the Mefe in the Do-
' rian to its Mefe, that is from A la mi re to D la fol re ; fo that there
' are three conjunct tetrachords from B mi, the Hypate hypaton of
' the Dorian, to D la fol re, the Mefe of the Mixolydian.

' Thirdly, as another diateffaron above that in the acute, could not
' be taken without exceeding that diapafon in the midft whereof
' the Mefe of the Dorian was placed, Ptolemy affumes in the room
' thereof a diapente towards the grave, which may anfwer to a dia-
' teffaron taken towards the acute, in as much as the founds fo taken,
' differing from each other by a diapafon, may in a manner be ac-
' counted the fame. The Mefe therefore of this new mode muft be
' graver by a diapente than that of the Mixolydian ; that is to fay, it is
' the Lychanos hypaton of the Mixolydian, or, which is the fame, the
' Lychanos mefon of the Dorian, and confequently its Paramefe will
' be the Mefe of the Dorian ; that is as we fhould fay, mi in A la mi
' re. This is what Ptolemy calls the Hypolydian mode, to denote
' which we put befides the flat placed before in B fa b mi, a fecond

'   ' flat

' flat in E *la nu*, to exclude *mi* from thence, and thereby *mi* is re-
' moved into A *la mi re*.

' Fourthly, as he could not from hence towards the grave, take ei-
' ther a diapente or diateſſaron, without going beyond the above diapa-
' ſon, Ptolemy takes a mode more acute than the Hypolydian by a
' diateſſaron, which he calls the Lydian, the Meſe whereof is the
' Paranete diezeugmenon, and its Parameſe the Nete diezeugmenon
' of the Hypolydian ; which latter is alſo the Paranete diezeugmenon
' of the Dorian, that is as we ſpeak, *mi* in D *la ſol re*. We, to denote
' this mode, beſides the two flats already ſet in b and e, put a third
' in A *la mi re*, whereby we exclude *mi* from thence, and transfer it
' to D *la ſol re*.

' Fifthly, as the Mixolydian was taken from the Dorian, and made
' a diateſſaron more acute, ſo is the Hypodorian to be taken from the
' ſame Dorian towards the grave, and made more grave than that by
' a diateſſaron : the Meſe therefore of the Hypodorian is the Hypate
' meſon of the Dorian ; and its Parameſe, which is our *mi*, is the
' Parhypate meſon of the Dorian, that is as we ſpeak, *mi* in F *ſa ut*.
' We, to denote this mode, leaving out all the flats, place an acute
' ſignature or ſharp in F *ſa ut*, which would otherwiſe be elevated
' by a hemitone only, and called *ſa*, but is now called *mi*, and ele-
' vated by a whole tone above the next note under it; by reaſon
' whereof the next note in the acute will be diſtant only a hemitone
' from that next under it, and be called *ſa*, and *mi* will return in a
' perfect diapaſon in the F *ſa ut* next above it.

' Sixthly, as another diateſſaron towards the grave cannot be aſ-
' ſumed from the Hypodorian thus ſituated, without exceeding the
' limits of the above diapaſon, he takes the Phrygian mode a diapente
' more acute, which is the ſame thing in effect, ſince between any
' ſeries in the fifth above and in the fourth below, the diſtance is
' preciſely a diapaſon ; the Meſe therefore of this mode is the Nete
' diezeugmenon of the Hypodorian, that is the Parameſe of the
' Dorian, and conſequently its Parameſe is the Trite diezeugmenon
' of the Dorian, that is as we ſpeak, *mi* in c *ſa ut* ; to denote which,
' beſides the ſharp placed before in F *ſa ut*, we put another ſharp in
' C *ſa ut*, which would otherwiſe be elevated by only an hemitone
' above the next note under it, but is now elevated by a whole tone ;.
' and as before it would have been called *ſa*, it muſt now be called *mi*;
' and.

' and from hence to g *fol re ut* is now only a hemitone, which is
' therefore to be called *fa, mi* returning either in cc *fol fa* above, or
' in c *fa ut* below.

' Seventhly and laftly, the Hypophrygian is taken from the Phry-
' gian, as above defined, and is diftant therefrom by a diateffaron to-
' wards the grave. Its Mefe therefore is the Hypate mefon of the
' Phrygian, that is to fay the Parhypate mefon of the Dorian,
' confequently its Paramefe, which is our *mi*, is the Lychanos
' mefon of the Dorian. That is as we fpeak, *mi* in G *fol re*
' *ut*, to exprefs which, the reft ftanding as above, we place a
' third fharp in G *fol re ut*, which otherwife, by reafon that F *fa ut*
' was made fharp before, would be elevated by only a hemitone, and
' called *fa*, is now elevated by a whole tone and called *mi*, and there-
' fore A *la mi re*, diftant from G *fol re ut* by a hemitone, is called *fa*,
' and *mi* returns in g *fol re ut* above, or in Γ *ut* below.

' The modes being thus determined, we gather from thence that
' the Mixolydian mode is diftant from the Lydian as in Ptolemy,
' lib. II. cap. x. by a limma, or not to fpeak fo nicely, by a hemi-
' tone, the Lydian from the Phrygian by a tone, the Phrygian from
' the Dorian by a tone, the Dorian from the Hypolydian by a limma,
' the Hypolydian from the Hypophrygian by a tone, and the Hypo-
' phrygian from the Hypodorian alfo by a tone.

' From thefe premifes Ptolemy concludes, not only that the feven
' modes above enumerated are all that are neceffary, but even that
' there is not in nature room for any more, by reafon that all the
' chords in the diapafon are by this difpofition occupied : for fince
' all the chords, from the Hypate mefon to the Paranete diezeugme-
' non inclufively, are the Mefe of fome mode, there is no one of them
' remaining to be made the Mefe of any intermediate mode : for ex-
' ample, the Mefe in power of the Hypodorian is in pofition the
' Hypate mefon, and the Mefe in power of the Hypophrygian is the
' Parhypate mefon ; and as there is no chord lying between thefe
' two, there is none left, nor can be found to be the Mefe of any in-
' termediate mode, or which, as Ariftoxenus fuppofes, may with pro-
' priety be called the graver Hypophrygian or Hypoiaftian ; and what
' has been faid of the Mefe may with equal reafon be faid of the
' Paramefe, which is our *mi* *.'

Thus

Thus far Dr. Wallis, who has undoubtedly delivered, though in very concise terms, the sense of his author; nevertheless as the whole of the arguments for restraining the number of modes to seven is contained in the eleventh chapter of the second book of Ptolemy, and Sir Francis Stiles has bestowed his pains in an English version thereof, it may not be amiss to give it as translated by him, and his words are as follow.

' Now these being the modes which we have established, it is
' plain, that a certain sound of the diapason is appropriated to the
' Mese in power, of each, by reason of their being equal in number
' to the species. For a diapason being selected out of the middle
' parts of the perfect system, that is the parts from Hypate meson in
' position to Nete diezeugmenon, because the voice is most pleased to
' be exercised about the middle melodies, seldom running to the ex-
' tremes, because of the difficulty and constraint in immoderate in-
' tensions and remissions, the Mese in power of the Mixolydian will
' be fitted to the place of Paranete diezeugmenon, that the tone may
' in this diapason make the first species; that of the Lydian, to the
' place of Trite diezeugmenon, according to the second species; that
' of the Phrygian, to the place of Paramese, according to the third
' species; that of the Dorian, to the place of the Mese, making the
' fourth and middle species of the diapason; that of the Hypolydian,
' to the place of Lychanos meson, according to the fifth species;
' that of the Hypophrygian, to the place of Parhypate meson, accord-
' ing to the sixth species; and that of the Hypodorian, to the place
' of Hypate meson, according to the seventh species; that so it may
' be possible in the alterations required for the modes, to keep some
' of the sounds of the system unmoved, for preserving the magnitude
' of the voice, meaning the pitch of the diapason; it being impossible
' for the same powers, in different modes to fall upon the places of
' the same sounds. But should we admit more modes than these, as
' they do who augment their excesses by hemitones, the Meses of two
' modes must of necessity be applied to the place of one sound; so that
' in INTERCHANGING THE TUNINGS of those two modes, the whole
' system in each must be removed, not preserving any one of the pre-
' ceding tensions in common, by which to regulate the proper
' pitch of the voice. For the Mese in power of the Hypodorian for
' instance, being fixed to Hypate meson by position, and that of the

' Hypophrygian to Parhypate mefon, the mode taken between thefe
' two, and called by them the graver Hypophrygian, to diftinguiſh
' it from the other acuter one, muſt have its Mefe either in Hypate,
' as the Hypodorian, or in Parhypate, as the acuter Hypophry-
' gian ; which being the cafe, when we interchange the tuning of
' two fuch modes, which ufe one common found, this found is indeed
' altered an bemitone in pitch by intenfion or remiffion ; but having
' the fame power in each of the modes, viz. that of the Mefe, all the
' reſt of the founds are intended or remitted in like manner, for the
' fake of preferving the ratios to the Mefe, the fame with thofe taken·
' before the mutation, according to the genus common to both
' modes ; fo that this mode is not to be held different in fpecies from
' the former, but the Hypodorian again, or the fame Hypophrygian,.
' only fomewhat acuter or graver in pitch, that thefe feven modes
' therefore are fufficient, and fuch as the ratios require, be it thus-
' far declared *.'

Dr. Wallis continues his argument, and with a degree of perfpicuity that leaves no room to doubt but that he is right in his opinion,.
fhews that the modes of the ancients were no other than the feven·
fpecies of diapafon : for, as a confequence of what he had before laid.
down, he afferts that the fyllable *mi*, to fpeak, as he fays, with the
moderns, has occupied all the chords by the modes now determined,.
fince in the Hypodorian, *mi* is found in F, and alfo in f, which is a.
diapafon diſtant therefrom.   In the Hypophrygian it is found in G,.
and therefore alfo in Γ and in g,. which are each a diapafon diſtant·
therefrom.   In the Hypophrygian it is found in a, and therefore in·
A and aa, each diſtant a diapafon therefrom.   In the Dorian it is.
found in ♮, and therefrom in ♭ and ♭♭.   In the Phrygian *mi* is
found in c, and alfo in c and cc.   In the Lydian·it is found in d, and
therefore in D and dd.   And laftly, in the Mixolydian it is found in
e, and confequently in E and ee ; from all which it is evident that·
there can no one chord remain whereon to place *mi* for any other.
mode, which would not coincide with fome one of thefe above·
fpecified·†.

Nothing need be added to illuftrate this account of the modes but·
an obfervation, that inftead of g and c for the refpective places of *mi*
in the Hypophrygian and Phrygian modes, their. true pofitions will:
be found to be in g♯ and c♯ and their replicates.

The

The following scheme is exhibited by Dr. Wallis to shew the correspondence between the several keys as they arise in the modern system, and the modes of the ancients.

By which it should seem that the key of A with the lesser third answers to the Dorian; D with the lesser third to the Mixolydian; G with the lesser third to the Hypolydian; C with the lesser third to the Lydian; E with a lesser third to the Hypodorian; B with the lesser third to the Phrygian, and F* with the lesser third to the Hypophrygian.

These are the sentiments of those who taught that the modes were coincident with the species of diapason. Another opinion however prevailed, namely, that the word Mode or Tone signified not so properly any determinate Succession of sounds, as the Place of a sound; and indeed this is one of the definitions given by Euclid of the word Tone or Mode †; or, in other words, the difference between one tone and another consisted in the Tension, or, as we should say, the Pitch of the system ‡. The occasion of this diversity of opinion seems to be this, Aristoxenus, the father of that sect which rejected the measure by ratios, and computed it by intervals, in his treatise on Harmonics, book the second, divides the science into seven parts, 1. Of sounds. 2. Of intervals. 3. Of genera. 4. Of systems. 5. Of tones. 6. Of mutations. 7. Of melopoeïa ‖. Now had he considered the species of diapason to have been the same as, - or even connected with, the modes, it had been natural for him to have placed them under the fifth division, that is to say, of tones, or at least under the sixth, of mutations: instead of which we find them ranged under the fourth, namely, that of systems; and even there it is not expressly

* Ptolem. Harmonic. ex verf. Wallis, pag. 137, in sot.
† Introd. Harm. pag. 19, ex verf. Meibom.
‡ Sir Francis Stiles on the Modes, pag. 698.
‖ Lib. II. pag. xxiv. et seq. ex verf. Meibom.

said,

said, though from their denominations, and other circumstances it might well be inferred, that the species of diapason had a relation to the modes *. The silence of Aristoxenus, and indeed of all his followers, in this respect, has created a difficulty in admitting a connexion between the species of diapason and the modes, and has led some to suspect that they were distinct; though after all that can be said, if the modes were not the same with the species, it is extremely hard to conceive what they could be; for a definition of a mode, according to the Aristoxenians, does by no means answer to the effects ascribed by the ancient writers, such as Plutarch and others, to the modes; for instance, can it be said of the Dorian that it was grave and solemn, or of the Phrygian that it was warlike, or that the Lydian was soft and effeminate, when the difference between them consisted only in a different degree of intension or remission; or, in other words, a difference in respect of their acumen or gravity? On the other hand, the keys of the moderns, which, as already has been shewn, answer to the modes of the ancients, have each their characteristic, arising from the different measures of their component intervals; those with the minor third are all calculated to excite the mournful affections; and yet amongst these a difference is easily noted: the funereal melancholy of that of F is very distinguishable from the cloying sweetness of that of A; between those with the greater third a diversity is also apparent, for neither is the martial ardour of the key D at all allied to the hilarity that distinguishes the key E, nor the plaintive softness of E b to the masculine energy of B b; but surely no such diversity could exist, if the sole difference among them lay in the Pitch, without regard to their component intervals.

This difficulty, whether greater or less, seems however to be now removed by the industry and ingenuity of the above-named Sir Francis Stiles, who in the discourse so often above-cited, namely, his Explanation of the Modes or Tones in the ancient Grecian Music, has reconciled the two doctrines, and suggested a method for demonstrating that to adjust the pitch of any given mode is also to adjust the succession of its intervals, the consequence whereof is a discovery that the two doctrines, though seemingly repugnant, are in reality one and the same. The reasonings of this very able and accurate writer are so very close and scientific, that it

* Vide Sir Francis Stiles on the Modes, pag. 704.

is not easy to deliver his sense in other terms than his own; however it may not be amiss to give a short state of his arguments.

The two doctrines which he has undertaken thus to reconcile, he distinguishes by the epithets of Harmonic and Musical; the former of these, which he says had the Aristoxeneans for its friends, taught that the difference between one mode and another, lay in the tension or pitch of the system; the latter, and which Ptolemy with great force of reasoning contends for, teaches that this difference consisted in the manner of dividing an octave, or, as the ancients express it, in the different species of diapason: the task which this writer has undertaken is, to shew that between these two definitions of a musical mode there is a perfect agreement and coincidence.

In order to demonstrate this he shews, pag. 701, from Bacchius, pag. 12, edit. Meibom. that the Mixolydian mode was the most acute, the Lydian graver by a hemitone, the Phrygian graver than the Lydian by a tone, the Dorian graver than the Phrygian by a tone, the Hypolydian graver than the Dorian by a hemitone, the Hypophrygian graver than the Hypolydian by a tone, and the Hypodorian graver than the Hypophrygian by a tone[*]. He adds, ‘ that as
‘ the Guidonian scale answers to the system of the ancients in its na-
‘ tural situation, which was in the Dorian mode, and our A la mi re
‘ consequently answers to the pitch of the Dorian Mese, we have a
‘ plain direction for finding the absolute pitch of the Meses for all the
‘ seven in our modern notes, and they will be found to stand thus:

Mixolydian Mese in	-	-	d
Lydian in	-	-	c♯
Phrygian in	-	-	b
Dorian in	-	-	a
Hypolydian in	-	-	g♯
Hypophrygian in	-	-	f♯
Hypodorian in	-	-	e †

But to understand this doctrine as delivered by the ancients, the same author says it will be necessary to examine how the Meses of the seven modes were stationed upon the lyre; and in order to that

---

[*] Sir F. S. on the Modes, 701.

† Ibid. Dr. Wallis, in his edition of Ptolemy, pag. 137, assigns c, e, and f natural, for the positions of the Lydian, Hypolydian, and Hypophrygian Mese, but Sir Francis Stiles, ...sons mentioned in his discourse, pag. 703, places them in c♯, g♯, and f♯.

to confider the ftructure of the inftrument; this he explains in the
following words : ' The lyre, after its laft enlargement, confifted of
' fifteen ftrings, which took in the compafs of a difdiapafon or double
' octave ; thefe ftrings were called by the fame names as the fifteen
' founds of the fyftem, and when tuned for the Dorian mode corref-
' ponded exactly with them. Indeed there can be no doubt but that
' the theory of the fyftem had been originally drawn from the prac-
' tic of the lyre in this mode, which was the favourite one of the
' Greeks, as the lyre was alfo their favourite inftrument. In this
' mode then the Mefe of the fyftem was placed in the Mefe of the
' lyre, but in every one of the reft it was applied to a different ftring,
' and every found in the fyftem tranfpofed accordingly. Hence arofe
' the diftinction between a found in Power and a found in Pofition ;
' for when the fyftem was tranfpofed from the Dorian to any other
' mode, fuppofe for inftance the Phrygian, the Mefe of the lyre,
' though ftill Mefe in pofition, acquired in this cafe the power of the
' Lychanos mefon ; and the Paramefe of the lyre, though ftill Para-
' mefe in pofition, acquired the power of the Mefe. ' In thefe tranfpo-
' fitions, one or more of the ftrings always required *new tunings*, to pre-
' ferve the relations of the fyftem; but notwithftanding this alteration
' of their pitch they retained their old names when fpoken of, in ref-
' pect to their pofitions only ; for the name implied not any particu-
' lar pitch of the ftring, but only its place upon the lyre in the nume-
' rical order, reckoning the Proflambanomenos for the firft *.'

Thefe are the fentiments of the above-cited author, with refpect to
the Harmonic doctrine : the Mufical has been already explained; or if
any thing ſhould be wanting, the fcale hereinafter inferted, fhewing
the pofition of the Mefe, and the fucceffion of chords in each of the
modes in a comparative pofition with thofe in the natural fyftem, will
render it fufficiently intelligible.

C H A P.   II.

IT now remains to ſhew the method by which this author propofes
to reconcile the two doctrines. He fays that by the Harmonic
doctrine we are told the pitch of the fyftem for each mode; and by
the Mufical, in what part of the fyftem to take the fpecies of diapafon,

* Sir Francis Stiles on the Modes, pag. 702.

fon, and that by combining the two directions we gain the following plain canon for finding any mode required *.

CANON.

‘ First pitch the system for the mode, as directed by the
‘ harmonic doctrine ; then select from it the diapason, directed
‘ by the musical ; and we have the characteristic species of the
‘ mode in its true pitch †.’

To make this more plainly appear, he has annexed a diagram of the species of diapason, which is here also exhibited, and which he says will shew at what pitch of the Guidonian scale each sound of the diapason is brought out by the canon for each of the seven modes ; and that as in the construction of this diagram the directions of the canon have been strictly pursued, so it will appear that the result of it is in all respects conformable to the principles of both doctrines. ‘ Thus,’ continues he, ‘ in the Dorian, for instance, it will be seen ‘ that the Mese is placed in A la mi re, and that the rest of the sounds ‘ exhibited in that diapason, are placed at the proper distances, for pre-‘ serving the order of the system as required by the harmonic doctrine. ‘ It will also be seen that the diapason selected lies between Hypate ‘ meson and Nete diezeugmenon ; that the semitones are the first in-‘ terval in the grave, and third in the acute ; and that the Diazeuc-‘ tic tone is in the fourth interval, reckoning from the acute. All ‘ which circumstances were also required by the musical doctrine for ‘ this mode ; and in the rest of the modes all the circumstances re-‘ quired by each doctrine will in like manner be found to obtain : ‘ So that no objection can well be raised to the principles on which ‘ the diagram has been framed, by the favourers of either doctrine se-‘ parately : and the very coincidence of the two doctrines therein ‘ might furnish a probable argument in justification of the manner in ‘ which I have combined them in the canon ‡.’

Here follows the diagram of the seven species of diapason above-mentioned.

* Ibid. 710.　　　† Ibid.　　　‡ Ibid. 711.

SPECIES of the DIAPASON in the Seven Modes admitted by PTOLEMY.

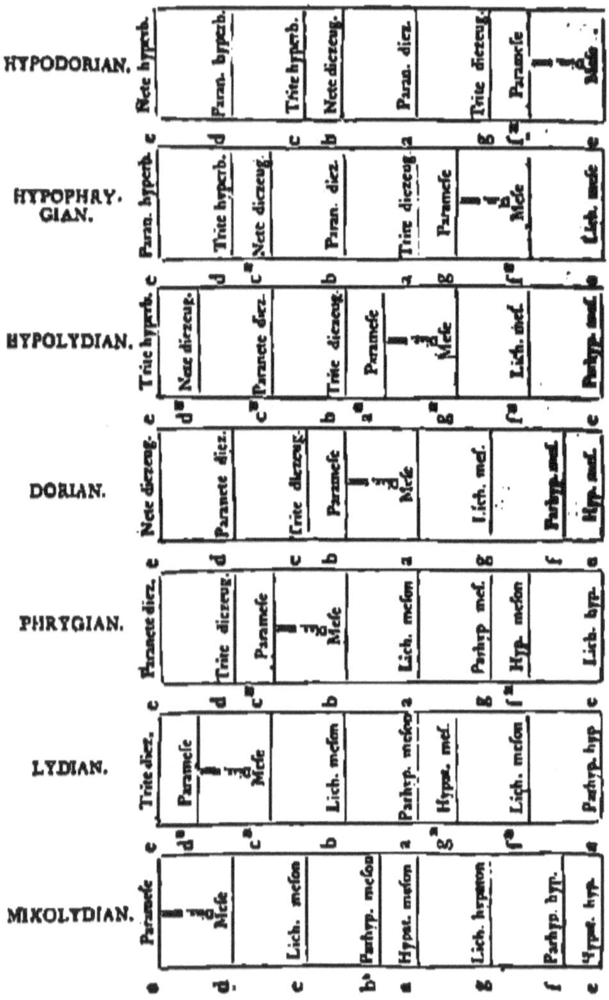

HYPODORIAN.

Nete hyperb. e — Paran. hyperb. d — Trite hyperb. c — Nete diezeug. b — Paran. diez. a — Trite diezeug. g — Paramese f♯ — Mese e

HYPOPHRY-GIAN.

Paran. hyperb. e — Trite hyperb. d — Nete diezeug. c♯ — Paran. diez. b — Trite diezeug. a — Paramese g — Mese f♯ — Lich. med. e

HYPOLYDIAN.

Trite hyperb. e — Nete diezeug. d♯ — Paranete diez. c♯ — Trite diezeug. b — Paramese a — Mese g♯ — Lich. med. f♯ — Parhyp. med. e

DORIAN.

Nete diezeug. e — Paranete diez. d — Trite diezeug. c — Paramese b — Mese a — Lich. med. g — Parhyp. med. f — Hyp. med. e

PHRYGIAN.

Paranete diez. e — Trite diezeug. d — Paramese c♯ — Mese b — Lich. mcfon a — Parhyp. mel. g — Hyp. mcfon f♯ — Lich. hyp. e

LYDIAN.

Trite diez. e — Paramese d♯ — Mese c♯ — Lich. mcfon b — Parhyp. mcfon a — Hypat. mel. g♯ — Lich. mcfon f♯ — Parhyp. hyp. e

MIXOLYDIAN.

Paramese e — Mese d — Lich. mcfon c — Parhyp. mcfon b♭ — Hypat. mcfon a — Lich. hypaton g — Parhyp. hyp. f — Hypat. hyp. e

By the help of the above diagram it is no very difficult matter to
afcertain, beyond the poffibility of doubt, the fituations of the different
modes with refpect to each other; or, in other words, to demonftrate that fix of them were but fo many tranfpofitions from the Dorian, which occupies the middle ftation : whether after fuch tranfpofition the intervals remained the fame or not, is a fubject of difpute.

With regard to this queftion it may be obferved, that throughout
the whole of Ptolemy's treatife, nothing is to be met with that leads
to a comparifon between the modes of the ancients and the keys of
the moderns; for it feems that with the former the characteriftic of
each mode was the pofition of the diazeuctic tone, and the confequent arrangement of the tones and femitones correfponding with the
feveral fpecies of diapafon, to which they refpectively anfwer.   But
the keys of the moderns are diftinguifhed by the final chord, and
therefore unlefs they could be placed in a ftate of oppofition to each
other, it is very difficult to demonftrate that this or that key anfwers
to this or that of the ancient modes, or unlefs a feveral tuning of the
lyre for each mode be fuppofed, to afcertain the conftituent intervals
of the latter.   Sir Francis Stiles feems to have been aware of this difficulty, for though in page 708 of his difcourfe, he has given a diagram in which the Mixolydian mode is made to anfwer to the feries
from ♭ to ♭, and the others in fucceffion, to the fucceeding fpecies,
he means nothing more by this than to compare them feverally with
a fpecies of diapafon felected from the middle of the lyre, without
regard to the fundamental chord or key-note.

Neither does the diagram of the feven fpecies of diapafon, given by
him and above inferted, afford any intelligence of this kind; and
but for a hint that he has dropped at the clofe of his difcourfe, that
the Hypodorian anfwers exactly to our A *mi la*, with a minor third,
and the Lydian to our A *mi la*, with a major third *, we fhould be

---

* The anonymous author of a Letter to Mr. Avifon, who by the way was the late reverend and learned Dr. Joltin, had in that letter blamed Simndon and Cerceau for affirming,
in their Obfervations on Horace, that the Dorian mode anfwered exactly to our A *mi la*
with a minor third, and the Phrygian to our A *mi la* with a major third; from hence Sir
Francis Stiles takes occafion to give the above as his opinion of the matter.   In which,
after all, it feems that he is miftaken, and that the author of the Letter was in the right :
his words are thefe, and they are well worth noting.

totally at a loss with respect to his sentiments touching the affinity between the ancient modes and the modern keys.

That there was some such affinity between the one and the other is beyond a doubt [*]; and we see Dr. Wallis's opinion of the matter in the diagram above inserted from his notes on the eleventh chapter, lib. II. of his author, containing a comparative view of the keys with the modes. And though it is to be feared that there is not that precise agreement between them which he has stated, there is good ground to suppose that, as in the keys, the succession of intervals is in the order which the sense approves, so the succession in the modes could not but have been in some degree also grateful to the ear.

This supposition is founded on a passage in the eleventh chapter of the second book of Ptolemy, importing no less than that each of the modes required a peculiar tuning, and these tunings have been severally investigated, and are given by Sir Francis Stiles; for what purpose then it may be asked, but to render the intervals grateful to the sense, was a new tuning of the lyre for every mode necessary; and what could that terminate in, but two constitutions, in the one whereof the interval between the fundamental chord and its third was a semiditone, and in the other a ditone; and when the lyre was so tuned,

---

[*] Saunders and Cereera in their observations on Horace, Carm. v. 9.

"   Sonante mixtum tibiis carmen lyra,
"   Hac Dorium, illis barbarum.

[*] affirm that the Modus Dorius answered exactly to our A mi la with a minor third, and 'the Modus Phrygius to our A mi la with a major third: but surely this is a musical 'error, and a dream from the ivory gate. Two modes, with the same tonic note, the 'one neither acuter nor graver than the other, make no part of the old system of modes.'
    This is very true; and the reason of Sir Francis Stiles for asserting was that he had deceived himself into a different opinion by placing the acute signs to f e and g in the Lydian, thereby giving to that series the appearance of the key of Aм. But upon his own principles the Lydian answers to our key of C fa ut with the major third,

    Tone, tone, semitone, tone, tone, tone, semitone.
        DO   RE   MI   FA   SOL   RE   MI

For though the acute signs require that the final chord be A, the succession of intervals is that proper to the diapason C c.
    [*] Sethus Calvisius seems to have been of this opinion in the following passage, cited by Butler in his Principles of Music, pag. 86. in note.   ' In hoc chorali cantu, diligentissime ' considera huic Arti deditus, qui sint ubique; Modulationis progressus, quod Exordium, ' et quis Finis; ut cognoscat ad quem modum referatur. Inde enim tam primariam · illius Modi clausulam, quam Secundariam, eruere, et convenientibus locis annotare, et ' inserere poterit.' Calvis, c. 17, and Butler himself adds that this is the general sentiment of musicians. Notwithstanding that Cælius Rhodiginus out of Cassiodorus distinguishes the modes by their several effects. Ibid.

what

what became of the feven fpecies of diapafon ? The anfwer to this latter demand is, that as there feem to be in nature but the two fpecies abovementioned, proceeding, as will prefently be fhewn, from A and C refpectively, the remaining five were rejected, and confidered as fubjects of mere fpeculation.

But before we proceed to refute the opinion of thofe who without knowing, or even fufpecting, that the tuning of the lyre was different in each mode, contend, that there are in nature feven, not merely nominal, but real modes, it is but juft to ftate the reafons on which it is founded.

And firft it is faid on the authority of thofe ancient writers who define a mode to be a given fpecies of diapafon, that as there are in nature feven fuch fpecies, fo are there feven modes, in each whereof the fucceffion of tones and femitones muft be in that order which nature has eftablifhed, or as they arife in the fcale, without interpofing any of thofe fignatures to denote remiffion or intenfion, which are ufed for that purpofe by the moderns. They fay farther that none of the fpecies were at any time rejected by the ancients as unfit for practice; and from thence take occafion to lament the depravity of the modern fyftem, which admits of no other diverfity of modes or keys than what arifes from the difference between the major and the minor third; for, fay they, and they fay truly, the modern fyftem admits in fact of but two, namely A and C; the firft the prototype of the flat, as the latter is of the fharp keys, all the reft being refpectively refolvable into one or the other of thefe *.

* In the Differtation for le Chant Gregorien of Monfieur Nivers, Paris 1688, chap. xii. it is faid that the eight ecclefiaftical tones, which all men know have their foundation in the ancient modes, are reducible to four, and in ftrictnefs to two, as being no otherwife effentially diftinguifhed than by the greater and leffer third; and the fame may be inferred from a well-known difcourfe, entitled a Treatife on Harmony, containing the chief rules for compofing in two, three, and four parts, which though at firft printed in 1730 by one of his difciples, was indifputably the work of Dr. Pepufch, and was afterwards publifhed by him with additions, and examples in notes. In this tract is a chapter on tranfpofition, in which the reader is referred to a plate at the end of the work, containing a table of the keys, with their characteriftics, and a ftave of mufical lines, with certain letters infcribed thereon, which, for the purpofe of refolving any tranfpofed or factitious key into its natural tone by the annihilation of the flat or fharp fignatures, he is directed to cut off and apply to the abovementioned table, by means whereof it may be difcovered that all the flat keys are tranfpofitions from that of A, and all the fharp from that of C. This is a procefs fo merely mechanical, that no one can be the wifer for having performed it, and is rather calculated to difguife than explain the true method of reducing a tranfpofition to its natural key. But in a fmall tract, entitled, Elements ou Principes de Mufique mis dans un novel Ordre, par M. Loulie, printed at Amfterdam in 1698, we meet with a notable rule or

Y 2   canon

But what, if after all, the ear will not recognize any other fucceffion of intervals than is found in the conftitution of the keys A and C?

canon for this purpofe, which fully anfwers the defign of its invention. This author premifes that the diefes, or what we fhould call the fharps, placed at the beginning of the mufical ftave, arife by fifths, beginning from F, that is to fay, C G D A E, and that the B moll or flats arife by fourths, beginning from B in this order, E A D G C. The rule or canon which he deduces from hence is this : In keys which are determined by fharp fignatures, call the laft fharp si ; or as any but a Frenchman would fay mi, and place or fuppofe fuch a cliff at the head of the ftave as in a regular courfe of folmifation, will make it fo. To give an inftance of the key of E with the major third.

Here the attentive perufer will obferve that the interval between the third and fourth, and alfo between the feventh and eighth notes, is a femitone ; and that to make the laft fharp D, mi, the tenor cliff muft be placed on the firft line of the ftave, and when this is done as here it is,

DO   RE   MI   FA   SOL   RE   MI   FA

the progreffion of tones and femitones will be exactly in the fame order as in the key of C, from which this of E is therefore faid to be a tranfpofition.

The canon farther directs in the keys with the flat fignatures, to call the laft of the flats FA, and to place or fuppofe a cliff accordingly ; and to fhew the effect of the rule in an inftance of that kind, the following example is given of the key of F with the minor third. ·

Here the intervals between the fecond and third, and alfo between the fifth and fixth notes, are femitones : and to make the laft flat, which is A, FA, it is neceffary to place the bafs cliff on the fourth line of the ftave, which annihilates the flat fignatures, and demonftrates that the above key of F is a tranfpofition from that of A with the minor third.

RE   MI   FA   RE   MI   FA   SOL   LA

Another rule for the above purpofe, and which indeed Dr. Pepufch would communicate to his favourite difciples, is, in the cafe of keys with the fharp fignatures, to call the laft fharp B, and count the lines and fpaces upwards or downwards till the ftation of a cliff is found ; and the placing that cliff accordingly annihilates the fharps, and befpeaks the natural key. In keys with the flat fignatures the rule directs to call the laft flat F, and count as before.

But amongft the keys with flat fignatures a diverfity is to be noted, that is to fay, between thofe with a major and thofe with a minor third ; for in the former the procefs muft be repeated, as in this of A b with the major third.

In

The confequence then feems to be that there are in nature no other. Now if it be true that the fenfe of hearing is averfe to thofe modulations that have no relation to any fundamental chord, and that it expects, nay longs for fome one found that fhall at ftated periods determine the nature of the progreffion, there is an end of the queftion. In fhort, a fingle experiment of the effect of the Mixolydian mode, which anfwers to the feries from ♭ to ♮, in its natural order, and gives to the diapente a femitone lefs than its true content, will offend the ear, and convince any impartial enquirer that the exiftence of feven modes is, in the fenfe contended for, nominal and not real *.

In this inftance the rule directs to call the laft flat, which is the key-note, F; and to count on to the place of a cliff: in doing this the cliff 𝄢 will fall on the firft line, and make the key-note F; by which it fhould feem that the key of A b with the major third is a tranfpofition from F alfo with a major third.

But as there is in the key of F a flat on b, it is neceffary to repeat the procefs, and fee what key this of F is a tranfpofition from; and this by the above rule is to be done by calling the flat b F, and proceeding as before directed:

and this key of F will appear to be a tranfpofition from that of C, and by confequence that of A b, from which that of F is tranfpofed, muft be a tranfpofition from the key of C alfo.

* Vide ante, pag. 162, and Dr. Wallis afferts that there are paffages in Ptolemy which plainly indicate that the ancients had a feveral tuning for every mode, which could not have been neceffary had they followed the above order. Farther, to this purpofe Malcolm expreffes himfelf in the following remarkable paffages. ‘ If every fung kept in one mode, ‘ there was need for no more than one diatonic feries; and by occafional changing the ‘ tune of certain chords thefe tranfpofitions of every mode to every chord may be eafily ‘ performed; and I have fpoken already of the way to find what chords are to be altered. ‘ in their tuning to effect this, by the various fignatures of ♯ and b: But if we fuppofe that ‘ in the courfe of any fong a new fpecies is brought in, this can only be effected by having ‘ more chords than in the fixt fyftem, fo as from any chord of that, any order or fpecies of ‘ octave may be found. On Mufic, pag. 536.
* If this be the true nature and ufe of the tones, I fhall only obferve here, that accord- ‘ ing to the notions we have at prefent of the principles and rules of melody, moft of thefe ‘ modes are imperfect and incapable of good melody, becaufe they want fome of thofe we ‘ reckon the effential and natural notes of a true mode or key, of which we reckon only two ‘ fpecies, viz that from C and A, or the Parhypate hypaton and Proflambanomenos of ‘ the ancient fixt fyftem. Ibid.

                                                                    * Again

But notwithstanding the uniformity of keys in the modern system, there is a diversity among them worth noting, arising from that surd quantity in the diapason system, which it has been the labour of ages to attemper and distribute among the several intervals that compose it, so as not to be discoverable; the consequence of which temperament is such a diversity in the several keys, as gives to each a several effect; so that upon the whole it seems that the modern constitution of the modes or keys is liable to no objection, save the want of such a division of the intervals as seems to be inconsistent with the principles of harmonics, and the established order of nature.

The several effects of the modern keys are discoverable in the tendency which each has to excite a peculiar temper or disposition of mind; for, not to mention that soothing kind of melancholy which is felt on the hearing music in keys with the minor third, and the gaiety and hilarity excited by that in keys with the greater third *, each key in the two several species is possessed of this power in a different degree, and a person endowed with a fine ear will be variously affected by the keys A and F, each with the lesser, as also by those of C and E with the greater third.

Effects like these, but to a degree of extravagance that exceeds the bounds of credibility, are ascribed to the modes of the ancients: that the Dorian was grave and solemn, and the Lydian mild and soothing †,

' Again, if the essential difference of the modes consists only in the gravity or acute-
' ness of the whole octave, then we must suppose there is one species or continuous divi-
' sion of the octave, which being applied to all the chords of the system, makes them
' true fundamentals for a certain series of successive notes. These applications may be
' made in the manner already mentioned, by changing the tone of certain chords in some
' cases, but more universally by adding new chords to the system, as the artificial or
' sharp and flat notes of the modern scale. But in this case, again, where we suppose
' they admitted only one continuous species, we must suppose it to be corresponding to
' the octave a, of what we call the natural scale; because they all state the order of the
' systema immutatum in the diagram, so as it answers to that octave.' Ibid. 537.

* Dr. Jortin has discovered a new characteristic for these two species of keys; he calls
one the male, the other the female: the thought is ingenious, and is thus expressed
by him in a letter published at the end of the later editions of Avison's Remarks on Musical Expression ' By making use of the major and minor third we have two real and
' distinct tones, a major and a minor, which may be said to divide music, as nature seems
' to have intended, into male and female. The first hath strength, the second hath soft-
' ness; and sweetness belongs to them both.'

† Milton adopts these characteristics of the Dorian and Lydian modes:

———Anon they move
In perfect phalanx to the Dorian mood
Of flutes and soft recorders; such as rais'd
To height of noblest temper heroes old
Arming to battle.   PARADISE LOST, B. L. line 549.

And

may be believed, but who can credit the relation, though of Cicero himfelf, and after him of Boetius *, that by an air in the Phrygian mode played on a folitary pipe (one of the ancient tibiæ) a drunken young man, of Tauromenium, was excited to burn down the houfe wherein a harlot had been fhut up by his rival, and that Pythagoras brought him to his reafon, by directing the tibicenift to play a fpondeus in a different mode? Or that not the fumes of wine or a difturbed imagination, rather than the flute of Timotheus, played on in the Phrygian mode, provoked Alexander to fet fire to Perfepolis.

CHAP. III.

HAVING thus collected into one point of view the fentiments of the ableft writers on thofe two moft important defiderata in the ancient mufic, the genera and the modes, in order to trace the fucceffive improvements of the fcience, it is neceffary to recur to thofe only genuine fources of intelligence, the writings of the Greek harmonicians. And here we cannot but applaud the ingenuity and induftry of thofe learned men, their remote fucceffors, who from ancient manufcripts, difperfed throughout the world, have been able to fettle the text of their feveral works; and who with a great degree of accuracy have given them to the public, together with Latin verfions, illuftrated with their own learned annotations.

Thofe whom we are moft obliged to in this refpect are, Marcus Meibomius, a German; and our countryman Dr. John Wallis: the former of thefe has given to the world feven of the ancient Greek writers, namely, Ariftoxenus, Euclid, Nicomachus, Alypius, Gaudentius, Bacchius Senioris, and Ariftides Quintilianus; as alfo a Difcourfe on Mufic, which makes the ninth book of Martianus Capella's Latin work, entitled De Nuptiis Philologiæ et Mercurii; and the

And ever againft eating cares
Lap me in faft Lydian airs.   L'ALLEGRO.
And Dryden defcribes the Lydian by its effects, in thefe words:
Softly fweet in Lydian meafures
Soon he footh'd his foul to pleafures.   ALEXANDER's FEAST.
From which paffage it is to be fufpected that the poet thought with Cornelius Agrippa and fome others, that the epithet Lydian referred to the meafure, whereas it clearly relates to the harmony. But Dryden knew little about mufic.
* De Mufica, lib. 1. cap. i.

latter

latter a complete tranflation of the harmonics of Ptolemy, with notes, and a moft valuable appendix; as alfo tranflations of Porphyry and Manuel Bryennius in like manner.

Concerning thefe writers, it is to be obferved that the Greeks are by far of the greateft authority; and that their divifion of mufic into feveral branches, as being more fcientific than that of the Latin writers, is intitled to the preference. The moft ample of thefe is the divifion of Ariftides Quintilianus, which is thus analyzed by his editor Meibomius, in his notes on that author, pag. 207.

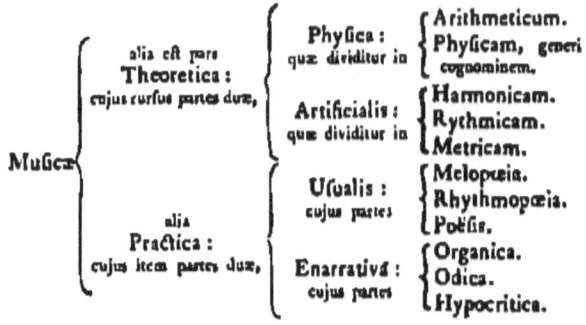

Neverthelefs, the moft general is that threefold divifion of mufic into Harmonica, Rhythmica, and Metrica; the two latter of which, as they relate chiefly to poetry, are but fuperficially treated of by the harmonic writers. Upon this divifion of mufic it is obfervable that the more ancient writers were very careful in the titles of their feveral treatifes: fuch of them as confined their difcourfes to the elementary part of the fcience, as namely, Ariftoxenus, Euclid, Nicomachus, Gaudentius, Ptolemy, and Bryennius, call the feveral treatifes written by them Harmonica; whereas Ariftides, Bacchius, and Martianus Capella entitle theirs Mufica; as does Boetius, although he was a ftrict Pythagorean. Porphyry indeed, who profeffes nothing more than to be a commentator on the harmonics of Ptolemy, inftitutes another mode of divifion, and, without diftinguifhing the fpeculative part of the fcience from the practical, divides it into fix general heads, namely, Harmonica, Rythmica, Metrica, Organica, Poetica, and Hy-

pocritica;

pocritica, Rythmica he applies to dancing, Metrica to the enonciative, and Poetica to verfes [*]. The branch of the fcience, which has been moft largely treated of by the ancients, is the Harmonica, as will appear by the extracts hereinafter given from their works.

From the relation herein before given of the invention of, and fuccesfive improvements made in, mufic, a very accurate judgment may be formed of the nature of the ancient fyftem, which, together with the ratios of the confonances, and the doctrine of the genera and the modes, conftituted the whole of the harmonical fcience as it ftood about the year of the world 3500. After which Ariftoxenus, Euclid, Nicomachus, and other Greek writers made it a fubject of philofophical enquiry, and compofed thofe treatifes on harmonics which are feverally afcribed to them, and of which, as alfo of their refpective authors, a full account will hereafter be given. What was the ftate of the fcience previous to the era abovementioned, can only be learned from thofe particulars relating to mufic, which are to be met with in the feveral accounts extant of the life and doctrines of Pythagoras, who, for any thing that can now be collected to the contrary, feems indifputably intitled to the appellation of the Father of Mufic.

PYTHAGORAS, according to the teftimony of the generality of writers, was born about the third year of the fifty-third Olympiad, which anfwers to the year of the world 3384, and to about 560 years before the birth of our Saviour; and although he was of that clafs of philofophers called the Italic fect, he is fuppofed to have been a native of Samos, and in confequence of this opinion is ufually ftiled the Samian fage or philofopher. His father, named Mnefarchus, is re-

* Malcolm has taken notice of this divifion, but prefers to it that of Quintilian, upon whofe analyfis he has given the following concife and perfpicuous commentary. ' Ariftides confiders mufic in the largeft fenfe of the word, and divides it into contemplative ' and active. 'The firft he fays is either natural or artificial; the natural is arithmetical, ' becaufe it confiders the proportion of numbers; or phyfical, which difputes of every ' thing in nature; the artificial is divided into harmonica, rythmica (comprehending the ' dumb motions) and metrica: the active, which is the application of the artificial, is ' either enunciative (as in oratory) organical, (or inftrumental performance) odical (for voice ' and finging of poems) hypocritical (in the motions of the pantomimes). To what pur- ' pofe fome add hydraulical I do not underftand, for this is but a fpecies of the organical, ' in which water is fomeway ufed, for producing or modifying the found. The mufical ' faculties, as they call them, are Melopeia, which gives rules for the tones of the voice ' or inftrument; Rythmopeia, for motions, and Poefis for making of verfe.' Treatife of Mufic. Edinb. 1721, pag. 455.

ported to have been a merchant, or, as some say, an engraver of
rings.   Of his travels into various parts of the world for the acquiring of knowledge, of the wonders related of him, or of his doctrines
in general, it is needless to give an account in this place.   It seems to
be agreed that he left not any thing behind him of his writing, and
all that is to be known of his doctrines is grounded on the testimony
of his disciples, who were very many, and were drawn to hear him
from the most distant parts of Greece and Italy.   Of these Nicomachus was one, who because he himself has written on the science of
harmonics, may well be supposed to understand the doctrines of his
master; from him therefore, as also from others, as namely, Ptolemy, Macrobius, and Porphyry, who, though they lived many years
after Pythagoras, were of his sect, we may with some degree of confidence determine as to the tenets of his school.   A summary of
these is given by his learned biographer Stanley, in the passages here
cited ; and first as to those respecting music in general, he gives them
in these words.

‘ The Pythagoreans define music an apt composition of contraries,
‘ and an union of many, and consent of differents; for it not only
‘ co-ordinates rythms and modulation, but all manner of systems.
‘ Its end is to unite and aptly conjoin.   God is the reconciler of
‘ things discordant, and this is his chiefest work, according to music
‘ and medicine, to reconcile enmities.   In music, say they, consists
‘ the agreement of all things, and aristocracy of the universe.   For
‘ what is harmony in the world, in a city is good government; in
‘ a family, temperance.’

‘ Of many sects, saith Ptolemy, that were conversant about har-
‘ mony, the most eminent were two, the Pythagoric and Aristoxe-
‘ nian : Pythagoras dijudicated it by reason, Aristoxenus by sense.
‘ The Pythagoreans, not crediting the relation of hearing, in all
‘ those things wherein it is requisite, adapted reasons to the dif-
‘ ferences of sounds, contrary to those which are perceived by the
‘ senses ; so that by this criterion (reason) they gave occasion of ca-
‘ lumny to such as were of a different opinion.

‘ Hence the Pythagoreans named that which we now call harmo-
‘ nic Canonic, not from the canon or instrument, as some imagine,
‘ but from rectitude; since reason finds out that which is right by
‘ using harmonical canons or rules even of all sorts of instru-
                                                  ‘ ments

‘ ments framed by harmonical rules, pipes, flutes, and the like.
‘ They call the exercife Canonic, which although it be not canonic,
‘ yet is fo termed, becaufe it is made according to the reafons and
‘ theorems of canonic ; the inftrument therefore feems to be rather
‘ denominated from its canonic affection.   A canonic in general is
‘ an harmonic who is converfant by ratiocination about that which
‘ confifts of harmony.   Muficians and harmonics differ ; muficians
‘ are thofe harmonics who begin from fenfe, but canonics are Pytha-
‘ goreans, who are alfo called harmonics ; both forts are termed by a
‘ general name muficians.’ *
    As touching the human voice, the fame author delivers the follow-
ing as the Pythagorean tenets.
    ‘ They who were of the Pythagorean fchool faid that there are (as of
‘ one genus) two fpecies.   One they properly named Continuous, and
‘ the other Diaftematic (intermiffive) framing appellations from the
‘ accidents pertaining to each.   The Diaftematic they conceived to
‘ be that which is fung and refts upon every note, and manifeft the
‘ mutation which is in all its parts, which is inconfufed and divided,
‘ and disjoined by the magnitudes, which are in the feveral founds as
‘ coaferved, but not commixt, the parts of the voice being applied
‘ mutually to one another, which may eafily be feparated and diftin-
‘ guifhed, and are not deftroyed together ; fuch is the mufical kind of
‘ voice, which to the knowing manifefts all founds of what magni-
‘ tude every one participates : For if a man ufe it not after this
‘ manner, he is not faid to fing but to fpeak. †
    ‘ Human voice having in this manner two parts, they conceived
‘ that there are two places, which each in paffing poffeffeth.   The
‘ place of continuous voice, which is by nature infinite in magnitude,
‘ receiveth its proper term from that wherewith the fpeaker began
‘ until he ends, that is the place from the beginning of his fpeech to
‘ his conclufive filence.   So that the variety thereof is in our power,
‘ but the place of diaftematic voice is not in our power, but natural ;
‘ and this likewife is bound by different effects.   The beginning is
‘ that which is firft heard, the end that which is laft pronounced ;
‘ for from thence we begin to perceive the magnitudes of founds, and
‘ their mutual commutations, from whence firft our hearing feems

* Hift. of Philof. by Thomas Stanley, Efq. folio edit. 1701, pag. 385.
† Ibid.

' to operate; whereas it is possible there may be some more obscure
' sounds perfected in nature which we cannot perceive or hear: as
' for instance, In things weighed there are some bodies which seem
' to have no weight, as straws, bran, and the like; but when as by
' appofition of such bodies some beginning of ponderofity appears,
' then we fay they first come within the compass of statie. So when
' a low sound increafeth by degrees, that which first of all may be
' perceived by the ear, we make the beginning of the place which
' musical voice requireth.' *

These were the sentiments of the Pythagoreans, with respect to
mufic in general, and of voice in particular. Farther, they maintained an opinion which numbers, especially the poets, have adopted,
and which seems to prevail even at this day, namely, that mufic, and
that of a kind far surpassing mortal conception, is produced by the
motion of the spheres in their several orbits. The sum of this doctrine is comprized in the following account collected by Stanley from
Nicomachus, Macrobius, Pliny, and Porphyry.

' The names of sounds in all probability were derived from the
' seven stars, which move circularly in the heavens and compass the
' earth. The circumagitation of these bodies must of necessity
' cause a sound; for air being struck, from the intervention of the
' blow sends forth a noise. Nature herself conftraining that the vio-
' lent collision of two bodies should end in sound."

' Now, say the Pythagoreans, all bodies which are carried round
' with noise, one yielding and gently receding to the other, muft ne-
' ceffarily cause sounds different from each other, in the magnitude and
' fwiftnefs of voice and in place, which (according to the reafon of
' their proper sounds, or their fwiftnefs, or the orbs of repreffions,
' in which the impetuous transportation of each is performed) are
' either more fluctuating, or, on the contrary, more reluctant. But
' thefe three differences of magnitude, celerity, and local diftance,
' are manifeftly exiftent in the planets, which are conftantly with
' found circumagitated through the ætherial diffufion; whence every
' one is called ἄσιχ, as void of στάσιχ, ftation, and ἀὶ θεῶν, always in
' courfe, whence God and Æther are called Θεὸς and Αἰθήρ.'†

' Moreover the found which is made by ftriking the air, induceth
' into the ear something sweet and mufical, or harsh and difcordant:

‘ for if a certain observation of numbers moderate the blow, it effects
‘ a harmony confonant to itſelf; but if it be temerarious, not go-
‘ verned by meaſures, there proceeds a troubled unpleaſant noiſe,
‘ which offends the ear. Now in heaven nothing is produced ca-
‘ ſually, nothing temerarious; but all things there proceed according
‘ to divine rules and ſettled proportions: whence irrefragably is in-
‘ ferred, that the ſounds which proceed from the converſion of the ce-
‘ leſtial ſpheres are muſical. For ſound neceſſarily proceeds from
‘ motion, and the proportion which is in all divine things cauſeth the
‘ harmony of this ſound. This Pythagoras, firſt of all the Greeks,
‘ conceived in his mind; and underſtood that the ſpheres ſounded
‘ ſomething concordant, becauſe of the neceſſity of proportion, which
‘ never forſakes celeſtial beings.’*

‘ From the motion of Saturn, which is the higheſt and fartheſt
‘ from us, the graveſt ſound in the diapaſon concord is called Hypate,
‘ becauſe ὕπατον ſignifieth higheſt; but from the lunary, which
‘ is the loweſt, and neareſt the earth, Neate; for νατον ſignifieth
‘ loweſt. From thoſe which are next theſe, viz. from the motion of
‘ Jupiter who is under Saturn, Parypate; and of Venus, who is
‘ above the moon, Paraneate. Again, from the middle, which is
‘ the ſun's motion, the fourth from each part Meſe, which is diſtant
‘ by a diateſſaron, in the heptachord from both extremes, according
‘ to the ancient way; as the ſun is the fourth from each extreme of
‘ the ſeven planets, being in the midſt. Again, from thoſe which
‘ are neareſt the ſun on each ſide from Mars, who is placed betwixt
‘ Jupiter and the ſun, Hypermeſe, which is likewiſe termed Licha-
‘ nus; and from Mercury, who is placed betwixt Venus and the ſun,
‘ Paramese.'†

‘ Pythagoras, by muſical proportion, calleth that a tone, by how
‘ much the moon is diſtant from the earth: from the moon to Mer-
‘ cury the half of that ſpace, and from Mercury to Venus almoſt as
‘ much; from Venus to the ſun, ſeſquiple; from the ſun to Mars, a
‘ tone, that is as far as the moon is from the earth: from Mars to
‘ Jupiter, half, and from Jupiter to Saturn, half, and thence to the
‘ zodiac ſeſquiple. Thus there are made ſeven tones, which they
‘ call a diapaſon harmony, that is an univerſal concent, in which

' Saturn moves in the Doric mood, Jupiter in the Phrygian, and in
' the reft the like.'*

' Thofe founds which the feven planets, and the fphere of fixed ftars,
' and that which is above us, termed by them Antichton, make,
' Pythagoras affirmed to be the nine Mufes ; but the compofition
' and fymphony, and as it were connexion of them all, whereof, as
' being eternal and unbegotten, each is a part and portion, he
' named Mnemofyne.'†

That the above notion of the mufic of the fpheres was firft entertained by Pythagoras feems to be agreed by moft writers. The reception it has met with has been different, according as the temper of
the times, or the different opinions of men have contributed to favour
or explode it. Cicero mentions it in fuch a way as fhews him inclined to adopt it, as does alfo Boetius, lib. I. cap. ii. Macrobius,
in his Commentary on the Somnium Scipionis, lib. II. cap. iii. fpeaks
of it as a divine and heavenly notion. Valefius, on the contrary,
treats it as an ill-grounded conceit. Sacr. Philofoph. cap. xxvi. &c.
pag. 446. edit. 1588. Notwithftanding which it has ever been favoured by the poets : Milton, who was a great admirer of mufic,
while at college compofed and red in the public fchool, a fmall tract
De Sphærarum Concentu, which with a tranflation thereof is publifhed in Peck's Memoirs of him. Mr. Fenton, in his notes on Waller,
fuggefts that Pythagoras might poffibly have grounded his opinion of
the mufic of the fpheres upon a paffage in the book of Job, the
reafons for this conjecture are very ingenious, and will be beft given
in his own words, which are thefe :

' Pythagoras was the firft that advanced this doctrine of the mufic
' of the fpheres, which he probably grounded on that text in Job,
' underftood literally, " When the morning ftars fang together,"
' &c. chap. xxix. ver. 7. For fince he ftudied twelve years in
' Babylon, under the direction of the learned impoftor Zoroaftres,
' who is allowed to have been a fervant to one of the prophets, we
' may reafonably conclude that he was converfant in the Jewifh writ-
' ings, of which the book of Job was ever efteemed of moft authen-
' tic antiquity. Jamblicus ingenuoufly confeffeth that none but
' Pythagoras ever perceived this celeftial harmony ; and as it feems
' to be a native of imagination, the poets have appropriated it to
' their

* Ibid. 386.   † Ibid.

' their own province, and our admirable Milton employs it very
' happily in the fifth book of his Paradise Loft :

> That day, as other solemn days, they spent
> In song and dance about the sacred hill ;
> Myftical dance l which yonder ftarry fphere
> Of planets and of fixt in all her wheels
> Refembles neareft, mazes intricate,
> Excentric, intervolv'd, yet regular
> Then moft, when moft irregular they feem ;
> And in their motions harmony divine
> So fmooths her charming tones, that God's own ear
> Liftens delighted———— *

Cenforinus fuggefts a notable reafon why this heavenly mufic is inaudible to mortal ears, viz. its loudnefs, which he fays is fo great as
to caufe deafnefs. De Die Natal. cap. xi. which Butler has thus
ridiculed.

> Her voice, the mufic of the fpheres,
> So loud it deafens mortal ears,
> As wife philofophers have thought,
> And that's the caufe we hear it not.
> HUDIBRAS, Part II. Cant. i. line 617.

After all, whether the above opinion be philofophically true or
not, the conception is undoubtedly very noble and poetical, and as
fuch it appears in the paffage above-cited from the Paradife Loft,
and in this other of Milton, equally beautiful and fublime.

> Ring out, ye chryftal fpheres,
> Once blefs our human ears,
> If ye have power to touch our fenfes fo ;

* One of the earlieft editors of Milton has the following note on this paffage, which
Dr. Newton has retained.
' There is a text in Job xxxviii. 37. that feems to favour the opinion of the Pythagoreans,
' concerning the mufical motion of the fpheres, though our tranflation differs therein from
' other verfions. " Concentum cæli quis dormire faciet ?" Who fhall lay afleep, or ftill
' the concert of the heaven? But this is to be underftood metaphorically of the wonderful
' proportions obferved by the heavenly bodies in their various motions.' HUME.
The above is the vulgate tranflation ; that of Beza is left to this purpofe, as is alfo that of
Tremellius.

And let your filver chime
Move in melodious time,
And let the bafe of heav'n's deep organ blow.
                        HYMN on the NATIVITY.

Touching the divifion of the diapafon, the following is the doctrine of the Pythagoreans.

'The diatonic genus feems naturally to have thefe degrees and
'progreffes, hemitone, tone and tone, (half note, whole note and
'whole note); this is the fyftem diateffaron, confifting of two tones,
'and that which is called a hemitone; and then, another tone being
'inferted, diapente is made, being a fyftem of three tones and a he-
'mitone. Then in order after this, there being another hemitone,
'tone and tone, they make another diateffaron, that is to fay, another
'Sefquitertia: fo that in the ancienter heptachord, all fourths from
'the loweft, found a diateffaron one to another, the hemitone taking
'the firft, fecond, and third place, according to the progreffion in
'the tetrachord. But in the Pythagoric octochord, which is by a
'conjunction a fyftem of the tetrachord and the pentachord, and
'that either jointly of two tetrachords, or disjointly of two tetra-
'chords feparated from one another by a tone, the proceffion will
'begin from the loweft, fo that every fifth found will make diapente,
'the hemitone paffing into four places, the firft, the fecond, the
'third, and the fourth.'*

It appears alfo that Pythagoras inftituted the canon of the Monochord, and proceeded to a fubdivifion of the diateffaron and diapente
into tones and femitones, and thereby laid the foundation for the
famous Sectio Canonis, which Euclid afterwards adjufted, and is given
in his Introduction, as alfo in a foregoing chapter of this work. Duris,
an author cited by Porphyry, mentions a brazen tablet, fet up in the
Temple of Juno by Arimneftus the fon of Pythagoras, near two cubits
in diameter, on which was engraven a mufical canon, which was afterwards taken away by Simon, a Thracian, who arrogated the canon to
himfelf, and publifhed it as his own.†

Stanley fpeaks farther of Pythagoras in thefe words : 'Pythagoras,
'faith Cenforinus, afferted that this whole world is made according
'to mufical proportion, and that the feven planets betwixt heaven

* Stanl. Hift. of Philof. pag. 387.   † Ibid. 388. 366.

'and

' and the earth, which govern the nativities of mortals, have an har-
' monious motion, and intervals correspondent to musical diastemes;
' and render various sounds, according to their several heights, so con-
' sonant that they make most sweet melody; but to us insudible, by
' reason of the greatness of the noise, which the narrow passage of our
' ears is not capable to receive. For, as Eratosthenes collected that the
' largest circumference of the earth is 252000 stadia, so Pytha-
' goras declared how many stadia there are betwixt the earth and
' every star. In this measure of the world we are to understand the
' Italick stadium, which consists of 625 feet, for there are others of a
' different length, as the Olympic of 600 feet, the Pythic of 500.
' From the Earth therefore to the Moon Pythagoras conceived it to
' be about 126000 stadia; and that distance, (according to musical
' proportion) is a tone. From the Moon to Mercury, who is called
' στίλβων, half as much, as it were a hemitone. From thence to
' Phosphorus, which is the star Venus, almost as much, that is an-
' other hemitone: from thence to the Sun twice as much, as it were
' a tone and an half. Thus the Sun is distant from the Earth three
' tones and a half, which is called Diapente; from the moon two
' and a half, which is Diatessaron. From the Sun to Mars, who is
' called Πυρόεις, there is the same interval as from the Earth to the
' Moon, which makes a tone. From thence to Jupiter, who is
' called Φαέθων, half as much, which makes a hemitone. From
' thence to the supreme heaven, where the signs are a hemitone also;
' so that the diasteme from the supreme heaven to the Sun is Diatessa-
' ron, that is two tones and a half: from the supreme heaven to the
' top of the earth six tones, a diapason concord. Moreover he refer-
' red to other stars many things which the masters of music treat of,
' and shewed that all this world is enarmonic *. Thus Censorinus:

* These positions of the Pythagoreans, that the universe is framed according to musical
proportion, and that all this world is enarmonic, refer to the general frame and contexture
of the whole. But there are arguments in favour of music, deducible from the properties
and affections of matter, discoverable in its several parts: in short, it may be said in other
words, that the whole world is in tune, inasmuch as there are few bodies but are sono-
rous. The skin of an animal may be tuned to any given note, as is observable in the
drum: a cable distended by a sufficient power is as much a musical chord as a lute string
or one of wire. And Strada somewhere mentions six great guns in a fortification at Gro-
ningen, which from the sounds uttered by them in their explosion, had the names of ut,
re, mi, fa, sol, la. The percussion of all metals, of stones, nay of timber, or of the
trunks of trees when felled, produces a musical sound: hollow vessels, as well of wood, as
earth and metal, when struck do the same. Of this fact the Indian Gong, as it is called, is
a far-

' but Pliny, delivering his opinion of Pythagoras, reckons feven
' tones from the earth to the fupreme heaven; for whereas Cenforinus
' accounts but a hemitone from Saturn to the zodiac, Pliny makes it
' Sefquiple.'

Stanley reprefents the intervals of the fpheres in the following
diagram.

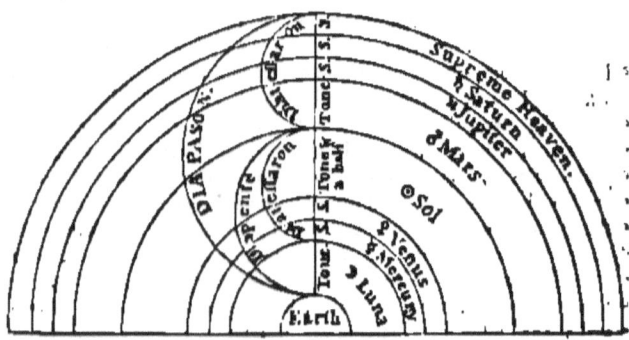

a furprizing inftance; it is an inftrument of brafs, or fome other fictitious metal, in form
like a fieve, and about two feet in diameter. The late duke of Argyle had one in his
obfervatory at Whitton near Twickenham in Middlefex, which being fufpended edgewife
by a cord, and ftruck with a ftick inclofed at the end, many times, till the quickeft vi-
bration it could make were excited, yielded not only a clear mufical found, but the
whole harmony of a diapafon, namely, the unifon third, fifth, and octave, fo clearly
and diftinctly, that each was obvious to the ear.   This inftrument is mentioned by Capt.
Dampier in one of his voyages, and is thus defcribed by him.

' In the fultan's mofque [at Mindanao] there is a great drum with but one head, called
' a Gong, which is inftead of a clock. This gong is beaten at twelve o'clock, at three,
' fix, and nine, a man being appointed for that fervice. He has a ftick as big as a man's
' arm, with a great knob at the end bigger than a man's fift, made with cotton, bound
' faft with fmall cords; with this he ftrikes the gong as hard as he can about twenty
' ftrokes, beginning to ftrike leifurely the firft five or fix ftrokes, then he ftrikes fafter,
' and at laft ftrikes as faft as he can; and then he ftrikes again flower and flower fo many
' ftrokes; thus he rifes and falls three times a-day, and then leaves off till three hours
' after.'   Dampier's Voyages, vol. I. pag. 388.

Glafs, and many other bodies, affected by the voice, or the vibrations of chords, return the founds that agitate them.   It is credibly reported of old Snitch the organ-maker,
that he could not tune a pipe in St. Paul's organ till he had broke a pane of glafs in the
fafh that inclofes it.

* Stanl. Life of Pythag. pag. 393.

C H A P.

C H A P.   IV.

IN what manner Pythagoras difcovered the confonances, and adjufted the fyftem, has already been mentioned. The particulars of his life are related by Jamblichus and other authors; and a fummary of his doctrines is contained in the account given of him by the learned Stanley, in his Hiftory of Philofophy. Pythagoras lived to the age of eighty, or, according to fome writers, ninety years. The manner of his death, which all agree was a violent one, is as varioufly reported; fome fay, that being with others at the houfe of his friend Milo, one who had been refufed admittance among them fet it on fire, and that Pythagoras, running to efcape the flames, was overtaken and killed, together with forty of his difciples, among whom was Archytas of Tarentum[*]. Others fay that he fled to the Temple of the Mufes at Metapontum, and died for want of food, having lived forty days without eating[+]. He had for one of his difciples Philolaus, a Crotonian (though he is claffed among thofe of Tarentum, his followers) whofe fyftem of a feptenary is hereinbefore inferted; and who was alfo the inventor of that divifion of the fefquioctave tone into commas, which Boetius has recognized, and is approved of even at this day. This Philolaus is faid to have been the firft that afferted the circular motion of the earth, and to have written of the doctrines of the Pythagorean fchool. One of his books was purchafed by Plato of his relations, at forty Alexandrian Minæ, an immenfe price[‡].

Among many tenets of the Pythagoreans, one was that there is a general and univerfal concent or harmony in the parts of the univerfe, and that the principles of mufic pervade the whole material world; for which reafon they fay that the whole world is enarmonic. And in the comparifon they affert that thofe proportions into which the confonances in mufic are refolvable, are alfo to be found in thofe material forms, which from the fymmetry of their parts excite pleafure

[*] Stanley in the Life of Pythagoras, chap. xix.
[+] Ibid.
[‡] Ibid. pag. 436.

in the beholder. The effect of this principle is in nothing fo difcoverable as in the works of the architects of ancient times, in
which the proportions of 2 to 1, anfwering to the diapafon; of 3 to
2, or Sefquialtera, 4 to 3, or Sefquitertia, are perpetually refulting
from a comparifon between the longitude and latitude of the whole
or conftituent parts, fuch as porticos, pediments, halls, veftibules,
and apertures of all kinds, of every regular edifice.

At a time when philofophy had derived very little affiftance from
experiment, fuch general conclufions as thefe, and that the univerfe
was founded on harmonic principles, had little to recommend them
but the bare probability that they might be well grounded ; but how
great muft have been the aftonifhment of a Pythagorean or a Plato-
nift, could he have been a witnefs to thofe improvements which a
more cultivated philofophy has produced ! And how would he who
exulted in the difcovery that the confonances had a ratio of 12. 9. 8. 6,
have been pleafed to hear the confonances at the fame inftant in a
fonorous body; or been tranfported to find, by the help of a prifm,
a fimilar coincidence of proportions among colours, and that the
principles of harmony pervaded as well the objects of fight as hearing? For Sir Ifaac Newton happily difcovered, that the breadths of
the feven primary colours in the fun's image, produced by the refrac-
tion of his rays through a prifm, are proportional to the feven differences of the lengths of the eight mufical ftrings, D, E, F, G, A, B,
C, d, when the intervals of their founds are T, H, t; T, t, H, T. *

The earlieft of the harmonic writers, whofe works are now extant,
was ARISTOXENUS; he was the fon of a mufician of Tarentum in Italy,
called alfo Spintharus. Ariftoxenus ftudied mufic firft under his father
at Mantinea, and made a confiderable proficiency therein : he had
alfo diverfe other tutors, namely, Lamprius, Erythræus, Xenophilus
the Pythagorean, and laftly Ariftotle, whom, as fome fay, he greatly
reviled after his death, for having left his fchool to Theophraftus,
which Ariftoxenus expected to have had, he being greatly applauded
by his hearers : though others on the contrary affert, that he always
mentioned Ariftotle with great refpect. He lived in the time of
Alexander the Great, viz. about the hundred and eleventh Olympiad,

* Vide Smith's Harmonics, pag. 31, in a note. And Sir Ifaac Newton's Optics,
book I. part ii. prop. 3, pag. 91 of the quarto edition.

which

which anfwers nearly to A. M. 3610. There are extant of his writing Elements of Harmonics, in three books. He is faid to have written on mufic, philofophy, hiftory, and other branches of learning, books to the number of four hundred and fifty-three, and to have expref-ly treated on the other parts of mufic, namely, the Rythmic, the Metric, and the Organic; but that abovementioned is the only work of his now remaining.

Touching the elements of Ariftoxenus, there is great diverfity of opinions : 'Cicero, who, as being a philofopher, we may fuppofe to have ftudied the work with fome degree of attention, in his Treatife de Finibus, lib. V. 19. pronounces of it that it is utterly unintelligible. Meibomius, on the other hand, fpeaks of it as a moft valuable relique of antiquity, and fcruples not to ftyle the author the Prince of Muficians. And the principal end of Euclid's Introduction is to reduce the principles of the Ariftoxeneans into form. Notwithftanding all this, a very learned writer, namely, Sir Francis Stiles, of whom mention has already been made, hefitates not to fay, that the whole three books of harmonics afcribed to Ariftoxenus are fpurious. On what authority this affertion is grounded he has forborne to mention; however, as the work is recognized by Ptolemy, and is conftantly appealed to by him, as the teft of the Ariftoxenean doctrine, its authenticity will at this day hardly bear a queftion.

In the firft book of the Elements of Harmonics of Ariftoxenus, is contained that explanation of the genera, and alfo of their colours or fpecies, which has already been given from him. The reft of that book confifts of fome general definitions of terms, particularly thofe of Sound, Interval, and Syftem, which, though in fome refpects arbitrary, all the fubfequent writers feem to have acquiefced in.

In his fecond book we meet with an affertion of the author, which at this day muft doubtlefs appear unintelligible, namely, that mufic has a tendency to improve or corrupt the morals. This notion, ftrange as it may feem, runs through the writings of all the ancient philofophers, as well thofe who did not, as thofe that did, profefs to teach mufic. Plutarch infifts very largely on it; and it is well known what effects the Spartans attributed to it, when they made it an effential in the inftitution of their youth. Ariftophanes, in his comedy of The Clouds, puts into the mouth of Juftice, whom he reprefents as engaged in a conteft with Injuftice, a fpeech fo very pertinent

tinent to this fubject, that it is here inferted at length, as Mr. Theo-
bald has tranflated it.   ' I'll tell you then what was the difcipline of
' old, whilft I flourifhed, had liberty to preach up temperance to man-
' kind, and was fupported in it by the laws; then it was not per-
' mitted for the youth to fpeech it in public, but every morning the
' young people of each borough went to their mufic fchool, marched
' with a grave compofed countenance through the ftreets, decent
' and lightly clothed, even when the fnow fell-thick. Before their
' mafter they fat with modefly, in proper ranks, at diftance from
' each other; there they were taught to fing in lofty ftrains fome
' hymn to the great and formidable Pallas, or other canto of that
' kind, in concert with the ftrong and mafculine mufic of their
' country, without pretending to alter the tones that had been de-
' rived down to them by their forefathers. And if any one were ob-
' ferved to wanton it in his performance, and fing in an effeminate
' key, like thofe that now fing your corrupted airs of Phrynis, he
' was immediately chaftifed as one that depraved and ruined mufic.
' You would not then have feen a fingle inftance of one that fhould
' dare commit the leaft immodefly, or difcover ought that honefly
' enjoined him to hide: they were fo fcrupuloufly nice in this ref-
' pect, that they never forgot to fweep up the fand on which they
' had fat. None then affumed the lawlefs minion, or defiled himfelf
' with wanton glances; none were fuffered to eat what was an incen-
' tive to luxury, or injured modefly: radifhes were banifhed from
' their meals; the anife and rock-parfley, that are proper for old
' conftitutions, were forbid them, and they were ftrangers to high
' and feafoned difhes: they fat with gravity at table, never encou-
' raged an indecent pofture, or the toffing of their legs lazily up and
' down *.'

* Polybius in his fourth book, chap. iii. has given a defcription of the ancient Arca-
dian difcipline of youth, nearly correfponding with that of the Spartans above cited, in a
paffage, which, as it is often alluded to by the writers on mufic, is here inferted in the
words of his elegant tranflator Mr. Hampton.
' All men know that Arcadia is almoft the only country in which children, even from
' their moft tender age, are taught to fing in meafure the fongs and hymns that are com-
' pofed in honour of their gods and heroes: and that afterwards when they have learned
' the mufic of Timotheus and Philoxenus, they affemble once in every year in the public
' theatres, at the feaft of Bacchus, and there dance with emulation to the found of flutes,
' and celebrate according to their proper age, the children thofe that are called the puerile,
' and the young men the manly games. And even in their private feafts and meetings
                                                                                      ' they

It has already been said that this philosopher did by no means acquiesce in the opinion of Pythagoras and his followers, that the understanding is the ultimate judge of intervals; and that in every system
there must be found a mathematical coincidence before such system
can be said to be harmonical: this position Aristoxenus and all of his
school denied. The philosopher himself, in this second book of his
Elements, expressly asserts, that ' by the hearing we judge of the mag-
' nitude of an interval, and by the understanding we consider its se-
' veral powers.' And again he says, ' that the nature of melody is
' best discovered by the perception of sense, and is retained by me-
' mory; and that there is no other way of arriving at the know-
' ledge of music;' and though, he says, ' others affirm that it is by
' the study of instruments that we attain this knowledge;' this, he
says, is talking wildly, ' for that as it is not necessary for him who
' writes an Iambic to attend to the arithmetical proportions of the
' feet of which it is composed, so it is not necessary for him who
' writes a Phrygian Cantus to attend to the ratios of the sounds proper
' thereto.' The meaning of this passage is very obvious, and may
be farther illustrated by a comparison of music with painting, the
practice whereof is so little connected with the theory of the art, that
it requires not the least skill in the former to make a painter
The laws of vision, or the theory of light and colours never suggest
themselves to him who is about to design a picture, whether it be
history, landscape, or portrait: the common places in his mind are
ideas of effect and harmony, drawn solely from experience and observation; and in like manner the musical composer adverts to those
harmonies or melodies, those combinations, which from their effect
alone he has found to be the most grateful, without recurring to the
ratios that subsist among them.

Aristoxenus then proceeds to a general division of music into seven
parts, which he makes to be 1. The Genera. 2. Intervals 3.

' they are never known to employ any hired bands of music for their entertainment, but
' each man is himself obliged to sing in turn. For though they may without shame or
' censure disown all knowledge of every other science, they dare not, on the other hand,
' dissemble or deny that they are skilled in music, since the laws require that every one
' should be instructed in it; nor can they, on the other hand, refuse to give some proofs
' of their skill when asked, because such refusal would be esteemed dishonourable. They
' are taught also to perform in order all the military steps and motions to the sound of instru-
' ments; and this is likewise practised every year in the theatres, at the public charge, and
' in sight of all the citizens.' Hampton's Polybius, pag. 359.

Sounds.

Sounds. 4. Syftems. 5. Tones or Modes. 6. Mutations. And 7. Melopœia; and in this method he is followed by Ariftides, Nicomachus, and moft other ancient writers.

The remainder of the abovementioned work, the Elements of Ariftoxenus, is taken up with a difcuffion of the feveral parts of mufic according to the order which he had prefcribed to himfelf. But it muft be owned fo great is the obfcurity in which his doctrines are involved, that very little inftruction is to be obtained from the moft attentive perufal of him; nor will the truth of this affertion be queftioned, when the reader is told that Cicero himfelf has pronounced his work unintelligible *. The ufe, however, propofed to be made of it is occafionally to refer to fuch parts of it as are leaft liable to this cenfure, and this will be done as often as it fhall appear neceffary.

The next in order of time of the writers on mufic is EUCLID, the author of the Elements of Geometry. He lived about the year of the world 3617, and wrote an Introduction to Harmonics, which he begins with fome neceffary definitions; particularly of the words Acumen and Gravitas, terms that frequently occur in the writings of the ancient harmonicians : the firft of thefe he makes to be the effect of intenfion or raifing, and the other of remiffion or falling the voice. He then proceeds to treat of the genera and the modes; what he has faid of each is herein beforementioned. His Ifagoge or Introduction is a very fmall tract, and little remains to be faid of it, except that it contains the famous Sectio Canonis, a geometrical divifion of a chord for the purpofe of afcertaining the ratios of the confonances, hereinbefore inferted. In this, and alfo in his opinion touching the diateffaron and diapente, namely, that the former is lefs than two tones and a hemitone, and the latter lefs than three tones and a hemitone he is a Pythagorean, but in other refpects he is apparently a follower of Ariftoxeaus †. The fundamental principle of Euclid's preliminary difcourfe to the Sectio Canonis is, that every concord arifes either from a multiple or fuperparticular ratio; the other neceffary premifes are, 1. That a multiple ratio twice compounded, that is multiplied by two, makes the total a multiple ratio. 2. That if any ratio twice compounded makes the total multiple, that ratio is itfelf multiple. 3. A fuper-

* De Finibus, lib V. 19.
† Wallis. Append. de Vet. Harm. pag. 307.

particu-

particular ratio admits of neither one nor more geometrical mean proportionals. 4. From the second and third propositions it follows, that a ratio not multiple, being twice compounded, the total is a ratio neither multiple nor superparticular. Again, from the second it follows that if any ratio twice composed make not a multiple ratio, itself is not multiple. 5. The multiple ratio, 2 to 1, which is that of the diapason, and is the least of the kind and the most simple, is composed of the two greatest superparticular ratios 3 to 2, and 4 to 3, and cannot be composed of any other two that are superparticular *.

The foregoing account of the nature and design of Euclid's division is contained in a series of theorems prefixed to the Sectio Canonis, and are reduced to a kind of summary by Malcolm, who appears to have been extremely well versed in the mathematical part of music.

It was not till the time of Meibomius that the world was possessed of a genuine and accurate edition of the Isagoge of Euclid ; it seems that a MS. copy of a Treatise on Harmonics in the Vatican had wrote in it ‘ Incerti Introductio Harmonica ;’ and that some person had written therein the name of Cleonidas, and some other, with as little reason, Pappus Alexandrinus. Of this MS. Georgius Valla, a physician of Placentia, published at Venice, in 1498, a Latin translation, with the title of Cleonidæ Harmonicum Introductorium ; which after all appears to be a brief compendium of Euclid, Aristides Quintilianus, and Manuel Bryennius, of very little worth : and as to Cleonidas, the reader is as much to seek for who he was, and where he lived, as he would have been had Valla never made the above translation.

* Malcolm on Music, pag. 508.
The above terms were used by the old arithmetical writers before the invention of fractional arithmetic, since which they have in a great measure been laid aside. What is to be understood by those kinds of musical proportion to which they are severally applied, will hereafter be shewn; however it may here be necessary to give a short explanation of the terms, and such a one follows.
Multiple proportion is when the antecedent being divided by the consequent, the quotient is more than unity ; as 25 being divided by 5, it gives 5 for the quotient, which is the multiple proportion.
Superparticular proportion is when one number or quantity contains another once, and an aliquot part, whose radical or least number is one ; so that the number which is so contained in the greater, is said to be so it in a superparticular proportion.
To these may be added superpartient proportion, which is when one number or quantity contains another once, and some number of aliquot parts remaining, as one ⅔, one ⅗, &c.

DIDYMUS of Alexandria, an author to be reckoned among the
scriptores perditi, inasmuch as nothing of his writing is now extant,
must nevertheless be mentioned in this place : he flourished about the
year of the world 4000, and is said to have first discovered and ascertained the difference between the greater and lesser tone. Ptolemy
takes frequent occasion to mention him, and has given his division of
the diatessaron in each of the three genera.

CHAP.   V.

MARCUS VITRUVIUS POLLIO, the architect, has usually been
ranked among the writers on music ; not so much because he
appears to have been skilled in the art, but for those chapters in his
work De Architectura, in ten books, written in Latin, and dedicated
to the emperor Augustus, in which he treats of it.   He flourished in
the time of Julius Cæsar, to whom he says he became known by his
skill in his profession, which it is agreed was superlatively great ;
though, to consider him as a writer, it is remarked that his style is
poor and vulgar.   In some editions of his work, particularly that of
Florence, 1496, and in another published at Venice the year after,
by some unaccountable mistake he is called Lucius, whereas his true
name was Marcus, and so by common consent he is called.   In the
fifth book of the abovementioned treatise, chap. iii. intitled De
Theatro, he takes occasion to treat of sound, particularly that of the
human voice, and of the methods practised by the ancients in the
construction of their theatres, to render it more audible and musical :
the various contrivances for this purpose will doubtless appear strange
to modern apprehension, and give an idea of a theatre very different
from any that can be conceived without it.   His words are as follow :
' The ancient architects having made very diligent researches into
' the nature of the voice, regulated the ascending gradations of their
' theatres accordingly, and sought, by mathematical canons and mu-
' sical ratios, how to render the voice from the stage more clear and
' grateful to the ears of the audience.'   Chap. iv. harmony, he says, is
a musical literature, very obscure and difficult to such as understand not the Greek language ; and, if we are desirous to explain it,
we.

we muſt neceſſarily uſe Greek words, ſome whereof have no Latin appellations; wherefore, ſays he, ‘ I ſhall explain it as clearly as I am able
‘ from the writings of Ariſtoxenus, whoſe diagram I ſhall give, and ſhall
‘ define the ſounds ſo as that whoever diligently attends may eaſily
‘ conceive them.’ He then proceeds, ‘ For the changes of the voices,
‘ ſome are acute and others grave. The genera of modulations are
‘ three; the firſt, named in Greek Harmonica, the ſecond Chroma,
‘ the third Diatonon; the harmonic genus is grave and ſolemn in its
‘ effect; the chromatic has a greater degree of ſweetneſs, ariſing
‘ from the delicate quickneſs and frequency of its tranſitions; the
‘ diatonic, as it is the moſt natural, is the moſt eaſy.’ He then proceeds to deſcribe the genera in a more particular manner. Chap. v.
intitled De Theatri Vaſis, he ſpeaks of the methods of aſſiſting the
voice in the manner following. ‘ Let veſſels of braſs be conſtructed
‘ agreeable to our mathematical reſearches, in proportion to the di-
‘ menſions of the theatre, and in ſuch manner, that when they ſhall
‘ be touched they may emit ſuch ſounds as ſhall be to each other a
‘ diateſſaron, diapente, and ſo on in order, to a diſdiapaſon; and let
‘ theſe be diſpoſed among the ſeats, in cells made for that purpoſe,
‘ in a muſical ratio, ſo as not to touch any wall, having round them
‘ a vacant place, with a ſpace overhead. They muſt be placed in-
‘ verſely: and, in the part that fronts the ſtage, have wedges put
‘ under them, at leaſt an half foot high; and let there be apertures
‘ left before theſe cells, oppoſite to the lower beds; theſe openings
‘ muſt be two feet long, and half a foot high, but in what places
‘ in particular they are to be fixed is thus explained. If the
‘ theatre be not very large, then let the places deſigned for the
‘ vaſes be marked quite acroſs, about half way up its height,
‘ and let thirteen cells be made therein, having twelve equal inter-
‘ vals between them. In each of theſe, at the extremes or cor-
‘ ners, let there be placed one vaſe, whoſe echo ſhall anſwer to
‘ Nete hyperbolcon; then on each ſide next the corners place an-
‘ other, anſwering to the diateſſaron of Nete ſynemmenon. In the
‘ third pair of cells, reckoning, as before, from the angles, place the
‘ diateſſaron of Nete paramefon; in the fourth pair that of Nete ſy-
‘ nemmenon; in the fifth the diateſſaron of Meſe; in the ſixth the
‘ diateſſaron of Hypate meſon; and in the middle the diateſſaron of
‘ Hypate hypaton. In this ratio, the voice, which is ſent out from

‘ the

' the stage as from a center, undulating over the whole, will strike
' the cavities of every vase, and the concords agreeing with each of
' them, will thereby return clearer and increased; but if the size of
' the theatre be larger, then let its height be divided into four parts,
' and let there be made three rows of cells acrofs the whole, one
' whereof is defigned for Harmonia, another for Chroma, and the
' other for Diatonos. In the firft or lower row, which is for Har-
' monia, let the vafes be placed in the fame manner as is above direct-
' ed for the lefler theatre; but in the middle row let thofe be placed
' in the corners whofe founds anfwer to the Chromaticon hyperbo-
' leon ; in the pair next to the corners the diateffaron to the Chro-
' maticon diezeugmenon; in the third the diateffaron to the Chro-
' maticon fynemmenon; in the fourth the diateffaron to the Chro-
' maticon mefon; in the fifth the diateffaron to the Chromaticon
' hypaton; and in the fixth the diateffaron to the Chromaticon Para-
' mefon; for the Chromaticon hyperboleon diapente has an agree-
' ment of confonancy with the Chromaticon mefon diateffaron. But
' in the middle cell nothing need be placed, by reafon that in the
' chromatic genus of fymphony no other quality of founds can have
' any concordance. As to the upper divifion or row of cells, let
' vafes be placed in the extreme corners thereof, which anfwer to the
' founds Diatonon hyperboleon; in the next pair to them the diatef-
' faron to Diatonon diezengmenon; in the third the diateffaron to
' Diatonon fynemmenon; in the fourth the diateffaron to Diatonon
' mefon; in the fifth the diateffaron to Diatonon hypaton; in the
' fixth the diateffaron to Proflambenomenon: the diapafon to Dia-
' tonon hypaton has an agreement of fymphony with the diapente.
'. But if any one would eafily arrive at perfection in thefe things, let
' him carefully infpect the diagram at the latter end of the book,
' which Ariftoxenus compofed with great care and skill, concerning
' the divifions of modulations*, from which, if any one will attend to
' his reafoning, he will the more readily be able to effect the con-
' ftructions of theatres according to the nature of the voice, and to
' the delight of the hearers.' Thus far Vitruvius.

We are too little acquainted with the nature of the ancient drama
to be able to account particularly for the effects of this fingular inven-

*. This diagram is inferted in Graffineau's Dictionary, article Genera.

tion : to fuppofe that in their theatrical reprefentations the actors
barely pronounced their fpeeches, accompanying their utterance with
correfpondent gefticulations, and a proper emphafis, as is ···ctifed
in our times, would render it of no ufe; for the vales fo particularly
defcribed and adjufted by this author, are evidently calculated to reverberate, not the tones ufed in ordinary fpeech, which have no mufical ratio, but founds abfolutely mufical : and, on the other hand,
that the actor fhoald, inftead of the leffer inflexions of the voice
proper to difcourfe, make ufe of the confonances diateffaron, diapente,
and diapafon, and confequently *fing*, as well the familiar fpeeches
proper to comedy, as thofe of the more fublime and exalted kind
which diftinguifh tragedy, is utterly impoffible for us to conceive.

If it was for the purpofe of reverberating the mufic ufed in the dramatic reprefentations of the ancient Romans, that this difpofition of
hollow veffels, directed by Vitruvius, was practifed, we may fairly
pronounce that the end was not worthy of the means ; for however
excellent the mufical theory of the ancients might be, yet in the
number and perfection of their inftruments they were greatly behind
the moderns; and were it a queftion, we need look no farther for a
proof of the fact than the comedies of Terence, where we are told that
the mufic performed at the acting of each of them was compofed by
Flaccus, a freed-man of Claudius; and that it was played in fome
inftances, as at the Andria, tibiis paribus, dextris et finiftris; and
in others, tibiis paribus generally; and at the Phormio tibiis impa-
ribus, that is to fay, by flutes or pipes right-handed and left-handed,
in pairs, or of unequal lengths. This was not at a time when the
ancient mufic was in its infancy : the fyftem had been adjufted many
ages before; and we may look on this refinement mentioned by Vitruvius as the laft that the art was thought capable of. It is not
here meant to anticipate a comparifon, which will come more properly hereafter; but let any one take a view of the ancient mufic at the
period above referred to, with even the advantage of this improvement drawn from the doctrine of Phonics, and compare it with that
of modern times ; let him reflect on the feveral improvements which
diftinguifh the modern from the ancient mufic , fuch as the multiplication of parts, the introduction of inftruments, fome to extend the
compafs of founds, others to encreafe the variety of tones, and others
more forcibly to imprefs the time and meafure, as the drum and other
inftru-

instruments of the pulsatile kind are manifestly calculated to do ; the use of a greater and lesser chorus ; that enchanting kind of symphony, known only to the moderns, called thorough bass ; and those very artful species of composition, fugue and canon.   Let this comparison be made, and the preference assigned to that æra which has the best claim to it.

Although this work of Vitruvius is professedly written on the subject of architecture, it is of a very miscellaneous nature, and treats of matters very little allied to that art, as namely, the construction of the balista, the catapulta, and other warlike engines ; clocks and dials, and the nature of colours.   In chap. xi. lib. X. intitled De Hydraulicis, he undertakes to describe an instrument called the hydraulic or water-organ, but so imperfectly has he described it, that to understand his meaning has given infinite trouble and vexation to many a learned enquirer *.

For the existence of this strange instrument we have not only the testimony of Vitruvius, but the following passage in Claudian, which cannot by any kind of construction be referred to any other.

> Vel qui magna levi detrudens murmura tactu,
> Innumeras voces segetis modulatur ahenæ ;
> Intonat erranti digito, penitusque trabali
> Vecte laborantes in carmina concitat undas.

It is said by some that the hydraulic organ was invented by Hero of Alexandria ; others assert that Ctesibus, about the year of the world 3782, invented an instrument that produced music by the compression of water on the air ; and that this instrument, which answers precisely to the hydraulic organ, was improved by Archimedes and Vitruvius, the latter of whom has given a very particular description of it.

Ctesibus the inventor of it was a native of Alexandria, and the son of a barber.   He was endowed with an excellent genius for mechanic inventions, which he soon discovered in the contrivance of a looking-glass for his father's shop, so hung as that it might be

---

* Mersennus, speaking of this machine, says it is much more complex than the common pneumatic organ, and that he has laboured to describe a thing very obscure, and the meaning of which he could not come at, though assisted by the commentary of Daniel Barbaro.   De Instrumentis Harmonicis, pag. 138.   He farther says that Politian in his Panepistemon has in vain attempted to explain it.

eafily pulled down or raifed higher by means of a hidden rope.
The manner of this invention is thus related by Vitruvius. He
put a wooden tube under a beam where he had faftened fome
pullies, over which a rope went that made an angle in afcending and
defcending into the tube, which was hollow, fo that a little leaden
ball might run along it, which ball, in paffing and repaffing in this
narrow cavity, by violent motion expelled the air that was inclofed,
and forced it againft that without; thefe oppofitions and concuffions
made an audible and diftinct found, fomething like the voice. He
therefore on this principle, invented engines which received motion
from the force of water inclofed, and others that depended upon the
power of the circle or lever; and many ingenious inventions, particularly clocks that move by water. To fet thefe engines at work he
bored a plate of gold or a precious ftone, and chofe fuch kind of materials, as not being fubject to wear by conftant paffing of the water,
or liable to contract filth and obftruct its paffage; this being done,
the water, which ran through the fmall hole, raifed a piece of cork,
or little fhip inverted, which workmen call Tympanum, upon which
was a rule and fome wheels equally divided, whofe teeth moving one
another made thefe wheels turn very leifurely. He alfo made other
rules and wheels, divided after the fame manner, which by one fingle motion in turning round produced divers effects; made feveral
fmall images move round about pyramids, threw up ftones like eggs,
made trumpets found, and performed feveral other things not effential to clock-work.   Vitruvius de Architectura, lib. IX. cap. viii.

But to return: The following is the defcription given by Vitruvius
of the hydraulic organ.

' Autem quas habeant ratiocinationes, quam breviffimè proxime
' que attingere potero: et fcriptura confequi, non prætermittam. De
' materia compacta bafi area in ea ex ære fabricata collocatur.
' Supra bafin eriguntur regulæ dextra ac finiftra fcalari forma com-
' pactæ: quibus includuntur ærei modioli fundulis ambulationibus
' ex torno fubtiliter fubactis habentibus infixos in media ferreos an-
' gones; et verticulis cum vectibus conjunctos pellibufque lanatis in-
' volutos.   Item in fumma planitie foramina circiter digitorum ter-
' num, quibus foraminibus proximè in verticulis collocati ærei del-
' phini, pendentia habent catenis cymbalia ex ore infra foramina mo-
' diorum celata.   Intra aream: quo loci aqua fuftinetur in eft in id.
                                                                     genus.

' genus uti infundibulum inverfum: quem fuper traxilli alti circiter
' digitorum ternum fuppofiti librant fpecium imum. Ima inter labra
' pliigeos et aræ fundum. Supra autem cerviculum ejus coagmenta
' arcula fuſtinet caput machinæ quæ Grecè Canon Muficos appella-
' tur : in cujus longitudine fi canalis tetrachordos eſt fiunt quatuor.
' Si exachordos fex. Si octochordos octo. Singulis autem cana-
' libus fingula epithonia funt inclufa manubriis ferreis collocata,
' Quæ manubria cum torquentur ex arca patefaciunt nares in canales.
' Ex canalibus autem canon habet ordinata in tranfverfo foramina
' refpondentia in naribus : qæ funt in tabula fumma: quæ tabula
' Græcè Pinas dicitur. Inter tabulam et canona regulæ funt interpo-
' fitæ ad eundem modum foratæ ex oleo fubactæ : ut facilitur impel-
' lantur : et rurfus introrfus reducantur : quæ obturant ea foramina :
' plinthidefque appellantur. Quarum itus et reditus alias obturat :
' alias operit terebrationes. Hæ regulæ habent ferrea choragia fixa
' et juncta cum pinnis quarum tactus motiones efficit. Regularum
' continentur fupra tabulam foramina quæ ex canalibus habent egref-
' fum fpiritus funt annuli agglutinati : quibus lingulæ omnium in-
' cluduntur organorum. E modiolis autem fiſtulæ funt continentes
' conjunctæ ligneis cervicibus : pertinentefque ad nares : quæ funt in
' arcula : in quibus axes funt ex torno fubacti : et ibi collocati. Qui
' cum recipit arcula animam fpiritum non patientur obturantes fora-
' mina rurfus redire. Ita cum vectes extolluntur ancones educunt
' fundos modiolorum ad imum. Delphinique qui funt in verticulis
' inclufi calcantes in eos cymbala replent fpatia modiolorum : at-
' que ancones extollentes fundos intra modiolos vehementi pulfus ce-
' rebritate : et obturantes foramina cymbalis fuperiora. Aera qui
' eſt ibi claufus preſſionibus coactum in fiſtulas cogunt : per quas in
' ligna concurrit : et per ejus cervices in arcam. Motione vero vec-
' tium vehementiores fpiritus frequens compreſſus epithoniorum
' aperturis iſtuit, et replet animæ canales itaque cum pinæ manibus
' tactæ propellunt et reducunt continenter regulas alterius obturant
' foramina alterius aperiendo ex muficis artibus multiplicibus modu-
' lorum varietatibus fonantes excitant voces *. Quantum potui niti,
' ut obfcura res, per fcripturam diludicè pronunciaretur ; contendi.
' Sed hæc non eſt facilis ratio : neque omnibus expedita ad Intelli-

* Vitruvius de Architectura, lib. X. cap. xi. Ibid. cap. xii.

' gendum

' gendum præter eos, qui in his generibus habent exercitationem.
' Quod fi qui parum intellexerint e scriptis cum ipfam rem cognof-
' cent : profectò invenient curiose et fubtiliter omnia ordinata.'*

This defcription, which to every modern reader muft appear unintelligible, Kircher has not only undertaken to explain, but the
ftrength of his imagination co-operating with his love of antiquity,
and his defire to inform the world, he has exhibited in the Mufurgia an inftrument which no one can contemplate ferioufly : and, after
all, he leaves it a queftion whether it was an automaton, acted upon
by that air, which by the pumping of water was forced through the
feveral pipes, or whether the hand of a fkilful mufician, fitting at the
front of it, with the quantity of fome tons of water in a refervoir
under him, was not neceffary to produce that mufic which the bigotted admirers of antiquity afcribe to this inftrument, and affect to be
fo fond of. Ifaac Voffius, in his treatife De Poematum Cantu et
Viribus Rythmi, pag. 100, has given a reprefentation of the hydraulic organ, no way refembling that of Kircher, but which he yet fays is
almoft exactly conformable to the words of Vitruvius; after which follows a defcription thereof in words not lefs obfcure than thofe of Vitruvius and Kircher : neither one nor the other of the diagrams will
bear the teft of an impartial examination, or is worthy to be inferted
in any work intended to convey information to a fober enquirer after
truth ; but the confidence with which Voffius fpeaks of his difcovery
will make it neceffary to give his delineation of the hydraulic organ,
together with a defcription of it in his own words.

Kircher indeed, after all the pains he had taken, has the modefty to
confefs the inferiority of the ancient hydraulic to the modern organ ;
for he fays that if the former be compared to the latter it muft feem
a very infignificant work, for, adds he, ' I cannot perceive what har-
' mony a difpofition of four, five, fix, or eight pipes could produce,
' and I very much wonder how Nero fhould be fo exceedingly af-
' fected by fo fmall and poor an hydraulic, for Vitruvius teftifies that
' when his life and empire were both in danger, and every thing at
' the laft hazard by a fedition of his generals and foldiers, he did not
' relinquifh his great care and affection, or defire thereof. We may
' from hence eafily form a judgment what great pleafure he muft

* Ibid. cap. xij.

'have taken in our modern organs, not compofed of four, five, fix,
'or eight pipes, but fuch as our greater organs of Germany, confift-
'ing of eleven hundred and fifty-two double pipes, animated by the
'help of twenty-four different regifters; or had he feen our auto-
'mata or engines of this kind, which move of their own accord
'without the help of any hand. Certainly thefe moft enlightned
'ages have invented feveral things to which the inventions of the
'ancients can in no manner be compared *.'

Of a very different opinion is the before-cited Voffius, who declares
himfelf not afhamed to affert, not only that the tibiæ alone of the
ancients are by very far to be preferred to all the inftruments of his
age, but that, if we except the pipes of the organs, commonly
ufed in churches, it will be found that fcarce any others are worthy
to be called by the name of tibiæ. And he adds, ' even thofe
' very organs, which now pleafe fo much, can by no means be com-
' pared to the ancient hydraulics. And the modern Organarii, to
' fpeak after the manner of the ancients, are not in reality Organarii,
' but Afcaulæ or Utricularii, that is to fay, Bag-pipers, for by that
' name were thofe called who furnifh wind to the tibiæ by the
' means of bags or wallets, and bellows, as is done in churches.'
He farther fays that ' thofe are ridiculous who fuppofe the above ap-
' pellations to belong to thofe mendicants who go about the ftreets
' with a Cornamufa, and with their arms force out continued and
' unpleafing founds.' No, fays this fagacious writer, ' the Afculæ or
' Utricularii did not in the leaft differ from our modern organifts;
' and the ancient Organarii were thofe only who played on the hy-
' draulic organ, and they were fo called from Organum, a brazen
' veffel, conftructed like a round altar, out of which the air by the
' help of the incumbent water is preffed with great force, which yet
' flows equally into the tibiæ †'. After remarking on the bad fuccefs
of many who had attempted to find out the meaning of Vitruvius in
his defcription of this inftrument, and to reftore it to practice, he fays
very confidently that he himfelf has done it, and accordingly exhibits
it in the following form.

---

* Mufurg. Univ. tom. II. pag. 333.   † Voff. de Poëmat. pag. 98.

And

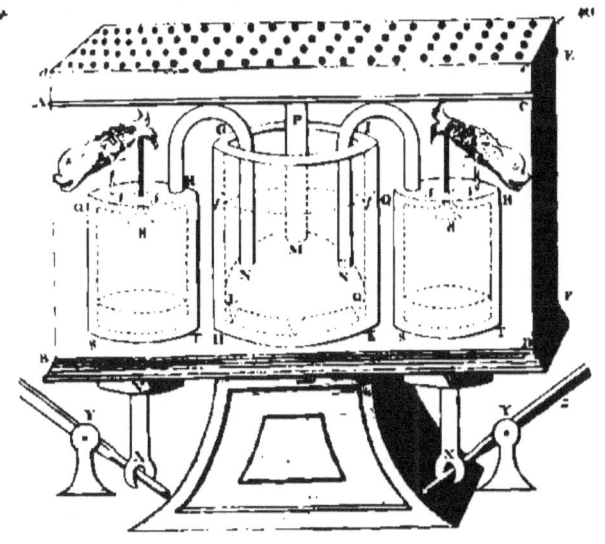

And defcribes it in thefe words : ' Fiat bafis lignea A B C D E F,
' et in ea conflituatur ara rotunda G H I K ex ære fabricata et torno
' fideliter expolita. Fiat quoque clibanus feu hemifphærium æreum
' L M N O, quam exactiffimo huic adaptatum. Sit vero in medio
' perforatus hic clibanus, et infertum habeat tubum et ipfum æreum
' et utrinque apertum M P. Habeat quoque clibanus alterum fora-
' men, cui infertus fit fiphon N I Q, cujus nares pertingunt ad mo-
' diolum æreum Q R S T. Siphon hic habeat affarium feu platyfma-
' tion ad N. Modiolo vero Q R S T aptetur embolus V cui af-
' fixa fit regula firmiter admodum compacta V X, ita ut à vecto
' X Y Z embolus V commode moveri poffit. Modiolus autem Q R
' S T habeat in fuperiori fuperficie aliud foramen 3, 4, cum platyf-
C c 2   ' matio

‘ matio per quod aër ingredi poſſit. Iſte vero ingredietur cum vecti
‘ X Y Z in Z attollitur.   Quando vero idem deprimitur, platyſma-
‘ tion hoc clauditur, et ingreſſus aër per ſiphonem Q I N, aperto pla-
‘ tyſmatio ad N, exprimitur in clibanum L M N O, unde per tubum
‘ M P influit in arcam A a Cc E e, cujus aſflatu tibiæ animantur.
‘ Clibano vero L M N O, quamvis magni ſit ponderes, veluti æneo,
‘ quo tamen fortius ſubjectum premat aërem et fidelius ne effluat cuſ-
‘ todiat, ſuperinfunditur aqua, puta ad f ſ, vel altius ſi fortiores ve-
‘ limus efficere ſonos.   Fiat itaque ex continua vectis agitatione, ut
‘ attollatur tandem clibanus L M N O, immoto interim perſtante
‘ tubo M P, et ſiphone N I Q, et notandum ſimulac vehementia in-
‘ greſſi ſpiritus attollitur clibanus, tum quoque æqualem fieri com-
‘ preſſionem aëris qui in arca continetur.   Licet enim effluente per
‘ tibias aëre clibanus deſcendat, idemque rurſus agitatione vectis at-
‘ tollatur, quamdiu tamen clibanus ſuſpenſus et à fundo ſeparatus
‘ manet, tandiu propter æqualitatem prementis ponderis, æqualis
‘ etiam mauet incluſi aëris ccnſipatio, ipſaque clibani et ſuperinfuſæ
‘ aquæ inconſtans et mobilis altitudo efficit æqualitatem flatus, quo
‘ tibiæ aſpirantur *.’

The ſame author affects to be very merry with thoſe who have
aſſerted that this organ was mounted only with ſix or eight tibiæ, and
cites the foregoing verſes of Claudian, and the following exclamation
of Tertullian to prove the contrary.   ‘ Specta portentoſam Archime-
‘ dis (Cteſibii rectius dixiſſet) munificentiam : organum hydraulicum
‘ dico, tot membra, tot partes, tot compagines, tot itinera vocum,
‘ tot compendia ſonorum, tot commercia modorum, tot acies tibia-
‘ rum, et una moles erunt omnia.   Spiritus ille qui de tormento
‘ aquæ anhelat, per partes adminiſtratur, ſubſtantia ſolidus, opera di-
‘ viſus †.’   He ſays that the uſe of the hydraulic organ ceaſed before

* De Poemat. pag. 101.
In the cabinet of Chriſtina, queen of Sweden,. was formerly a beautiful and large me-.
dallion of Valentinian : having on the reverſe one of theſe hydraulic organs, with two men,
one on the right, the other on the left ſide thereof, ſeeming to pump the water which
plays it, and to liſten to the ſound of it.   It had only eight pipes, and thoſe were placed
on a round pedeſtal ; the inſcription PLACEA SPECTAT.
† Ibid. pag. 105.   In Engliſh thus : Behold the wonderful munificence of Archimedes ! (he ſhould have ſaid of Cteſibius) I mean the hydraulie organ ; ſo many numbers,
ſo many parts, ſo many joinings, ſo many roads or paſſages for the voices, ſuch a compendium of ſounds, ſuch an intercourſe of modes, ſuch troops of tibiæ, and all com-
poſing one great whole !   The ſpirit or air which is breathed out from this engine of
water, is adminiſtered through the parts, ſolid in ſubſtance,. but divided in operation.

the

the time of Caffidorus; and that the fame appears from a paffage in
a difcourfe of that author on the hundred and fiftieth Pfalm, wherein,
without making the leaft mention of the hydraulic, he beftows the
following very high commendations on the pneumatic organ, then in
common ufe. ' An organ is as it were a tower compofed of feveral
' different fiftulæ or pipes, in which a moft copious found is furnifh-
' ed by the blowing of bellows: and that it may be compofed of a
' graceful modulation, it is conftructed with certain wooden tongues
' in the inner part, which being fkilfully preffed down by the fingers
' of the mafter, produce a great founding and moft fweet cantilena *.'

He notwithftanding afferts that the hydraulic organ continued in
ufe lower down than the time of Caffiodorus; for that in the French
annals of a certain anonymous writer, he is informed that in the year
826 a certain Venetian, called Georgius, or rather Gregorius, conftructed an hydraulic organ for Lewis the Pious, at Aix la Chapelle,
and that after the manner of the ancients †. He elfewhere fays that
the hydraulic organ of Daniel Barbaro, defcribed in his Commentary
on Vitruvius, is with great reafon exploded by all ‡; and that thofe
who in his time had in their writings concerning mufic inferted, the
conftruction of the Vitruvian organ, while they depreciate the inventions of the ancients, may ferve as an example to fhew how cuftomary
a thing it is for men to defpife what they themfelves do not underftand.
This paffage is manifeftly intended as a cenfure on Kircher's defcription of the hydraulic organ, and proves nothing but the extreme bigotry
of Voffius ‖. As to the hydraulic organs of modern Italy of which

* Organum itaque eft quafi turris diverfis fiftulis fabricata, quibus flatu follium vox
copiofiffima deftinatur, et ut eam modulatio decore componas, linguis quibufdam ligneis ab
interiore parte conftruitur, quas difciplinabiliter magiftrorum digiti reprimentes grandifo-
nem efficiunt et fuaviffimum cantilenam. De Poemat. pag. 106.
† De Poemat. 106.   ‡ Ibid. pag. 99.
‖ The enthufiaftic attachment to antiquity of this author is ftrongly evinced by
the fentiments he entertains of the energy of the ancient Tibia, which he fcruples not to
prefer to every inftrument of modern invention. His words are thefe: ' As to what belongs
' to the cantus of the Tibia which is blown upon by the mouth, I think it may be truly
' faid that the tibicinifts know no more concerning that inftrument than the ancient fhep-
' herds, and perhaps not fo much. This moft excellent art is banifhed among the men-
' dicants; and the Tibia, which was by far preferred to all ftringed inftruments, and to
' all other inftruments of mufic, is now filenced to fuch a degree, that, if you except the
' Chinefe alone, who excel in this part, you will find none in this age that can even
' pleafe a moderate ear; and the very name of the Tibia is juftly defpifed by the European
' nations. That the Tibia was formerly held in greater efteem, and accounted fweeter
' than the lyre, is not only evinced by Ariftotle, in his problems, but alfo by the very
                                                                        ' punifh-

Graffineau fays there are feveral in the grottos of vineyards, particularly one belonging to the family d'Efte, near the Tyber, defcribed by Baptifta Porta, he fays they are very different, and no way refemble the ancient hydraulic organ. Thefe perhaps will be found to be nothing more than the common organ played on by a barrel, which by a very eafy contrivance is fet in motion by a fmall ftream of water: and that thefe for more than a century paft have been in ufe in various parts of Italy there is additional evidence. In a book fuppofed to be written by one Dr. Thomas Powell, a canon of St. David's, entitled Human Induftry, or a Hiftory of the Manual Arts, it is faid that pope Sylvefter II. made an organ which was played on by warm water; and that fuch hydraulics, frequent in Italy, are founded with cold water. Oldys's Britifh Librarian, No. I. pag 51. And in an old Englifh comedy of Webfter, printed in 1623, intitled the Devil's Law-Cafe, Romelia, a wealthy merchant of Naples, fpeaking of the greatnefs of his income fays,

———————————— My factors' wives
Weare fhaperoones of velvet; and my fcriveners,
Meerely through my employment, grow fo rich
They build their palaces and belvidears
With *mufical water-workes*.

Comedy, which in general exhibits a very juft reprefentation of contemporary manners and characters, is, in cafes of this fort, authority: and the poet, in the paffage above-cited, would hardly have painted out this inflance of Italian profufion, had he not had fome example in his eye to warrant it.

‘ punifhment of Marfyas. How great the care and diligence of the ancients was in im-
‘ proving this inflrument, fufficiently appears from what both Theophraftus and
‘ Pliny have wrote concerning the reeds of the lake Orchomenius. It was not fuffi-
‘ cient that they were cut at certain periods of years, when the lake became dry;
‘ unlefs they were alfo macerated by the fun, rain, and froft, and afterwards foftened by
‘ long ufe; and, remaining without any defect, fatisfied the wifh of the artifts. He who
‘ reads and confiders thefe things, will the lefs wonder that fometimes Tibiæ have been
‘ fold for feven talents, as Lucian reflifies.' Voffius De Poemat. 107.

CHAP.

C H A P.   VI.

BUT to return to the ancient hydraulic organ, a hundred questions might be asked touching the use and application of its several parts, as also what system it was adapted to; and particularly
whether those who have undertaken to delineate it with such exactness, have not formed an idea of it from the organ of our own times,
and done a violence to historical truth by incorporating two instruments, which cannot possibly exist in a state of union.   And after all
that can be said in favour of it, the censure of Kircher above-cited,
must undoubtedly appear to be very just, and may serve to shew what
little reason there is to lament the loss of many inventions of the ancients, particularly those in which the knowledge of mechanics is any
way concerned. "The hydraulic organ is one of those ancient inventions mentioned by Pancirollus as now lost *, a misfortune which
at this day we lament perhaps with as little reason as we should
have for saying that the loss of the ancient Clepsydræ † is not amply
compensated by the invention of clocks and watches.   With respect
to this instrument, it cannot so properly be said to be lost, as to have
given way to one of a more artificial construction, and nobler in its
effects, as unquestionably the modern organ is.   It is remarkable that
those who would infer the debility of the later ages, from the few

* Guido Pancirollus De Rerum memorabilium sive deperditarum, lib. I. cap. ii.

† Clepsydra, an hour-glass made with water.   The use of Clepsydræ was very ancient,
and among the Romans there were several sorts of them; in general they resembled a
sand hour-glass, which is composed of two vessels, so joined at top and bottom, as that
what is contained in the upper may run into the under of them.   The Clepsydræ contained water, which passing through a small hole, imperceptibly raised a piece of cork
with an index fixed thereto that pointed to the hours marked on the under glass.   They
were all subject to two inconveniences: the first was that which Plutarch takes notice of,
to wit, that the water passed through with more or less difficulty, according as the air was
more or less thick, cold, or hot, far that hindered the hours from being equal; the other
was, that the water ran faster at first, when the vessel from whence the water came was
full, than at last.

These Clepsydræ were chiefly used in a city called Achanta, beyond the Nile.   In this
city there was an huge vessel of this kind, into which three hundred and sixty-five priests
daily brought water from the Nile, which running out from the vessel again, declared the
hours.   The use of the Clepsydra was to tell the hour in the night, or in cloudy weather,
when it could not be found by the sun-dial.

remaining

remaining monuments of ancient ingenuity, generally confine themselves to poefy, fculpture, and other arts, which owe their perfection rather to adventitious circumftances, than to the vigorous exertion of the powers of invention : but, with refpect to inftruments, machines, and engines of various kinds, it is not in the nature of things poffible but that mankind muft continue to improve as long as the world fhall laft.

NICOMACHUS GERASENUS, fo called from his having been born in Gerafa, a city of Arabia, lived about A. C. 60. He was a philofopher, and wrote an Introduction to Harmony, at the requeft, as it fhould feem by the beginning of it, of fome learned female contemporary. He was a follower of Pythagoras; and it is by this work alone that we know how, and by what means, his mafter difcovered the confonances. He begins his work with an addrefs to his female friend, whom he ftyles the moft virtuous of women; and reflects with fome concern on the difference in fentiment of the feveral writers on the elements of harmony. He excufes his inability to reconcile them by reafon of the long journeys he is obliged to take, and his want of leifure, which he prays the gods to vouchfafe him, and promifes to complete a work which he has in contemplation, of which what he now gives feems to be but a part. Profeffing to follow the Pythagoreans, he confiders the human voice as emitting founds, which are either commenfurable by intervals, as when we are faid to *fing*; or incommenfurable, as when we converfe by fpeech. In this latter ufe of the voice, he fays, we are not obliged by any rule; but in the former we are bound to an obfervance of thofe intervals and magnitudes in which harmony does confift.

The founds and their names, continues this author, are probably taken from the feven planets in the heavens which furround this earth; for it is faid that all bodies which are carried round with any great degree of velocity, muft neceffarily, and by reafon of their magnitude, and the celerity of their motions, caufe a found, which found will vary in proportion to the degrees of magnitude in each, the celerity of their motions, or the repreffion of the orb wherein they act. Thefe differences, he fays, are manifeft in the planets, which perpetually turn round, and produce their proper founds : for example, the motion of Saturn, the planet moft diftant from us, produces a found the moft grave, in which it refembles the confonance diapafon; as does

Hypate,

Hypate, which fignifies the fame as principal. To the motion of the moon, the loweft of the planets, and nearcft the earth, we apply the moft acute term, called Nete, for Neaton is the fame as low.

He then proceeds to declare the fuppofed analogy between the reft of the planets and the intermediate chords, as mentioned in the foregoing account of Pythagoras. But here it may be proper to take notice that the ancient writers were not unanimous in opinion that the graver founds were produced by the bodies of greateft magnitude: Cicero, in particular, is by Glareanus * faid to have maintained that the leffer bodies produce the graver founds, and the greater the more acute. And from this dictum of Cicero, Glareanus has been at the pains of forming a diagram, intended to reprefent this fanciful coincidence of revolutions and harmonies, which is given in a fubfequent page of this work.

In the Somnium Scipionis, which is what Glareanus means when he refers to Cicero de Republica, lib. VI. is a great deal concerning the mufic of the fpheres in general; and Macrobius, in his commentary on that fragment, has made the moft of it. Neverthelefs the general fentiment of mankind feems till very lately † to have been that the whole doctrine is to be regarded as a poetical fiction ; and as to the fact, that it has no foundation in reafon or philofophy.

But to return to our author Nicomachus, and his opinion of the harmony of the planets : it is true, fays he, that it is inaudible to our ears, but to our reafon it is clear.

Nicomachus proceeds to define the terms made ufe of by him, diftinguifhing, as others of the ancients do, between found and noife, Speaking of inftruments, he fays they are of two kinds, viz. fuch as are blown, as are the flute, trumpet, organ, and the like ; or fuch as are ftrung, to wit, the lute, lyre, and harp ; of the latter kind are alfo the monochord, by many called the Pandora ‡, and by the Py-

* Dodecachordon, lib. II. cap. xiii.
† See a fubfequent note, in the prefent book, containing the fentiments of Dr. Gregory and Mr. Maclaurin on this fubject.
‡ An appellative from which the Englifh word Bandore feems clearly to be derived. Meibomius gives the following note on this paffage.
* Φανδουρος. [Phandourous.] Hefychius fpeaks of it thus: " Pandura or Pandaris is a mu-
" fical inftrument ; Pandurus he who plays on that inftrument." Monochords were alfo
' by fome called Phandurus. Nicomachus here fays the fame, and feems as if he approv-
' ed of the practice. Thefe inftruments are various ; Pollux, lib. IV. cap. ix. fays, " The
" monochord was invented by the Arabians, and the trichord by the Affyrians, who gave

thagoreans the Canon, and alfo the Trigon or triangular dulcimer.
He alfo mentions crooked and other flutes made of the box-tree, of
which he propofes to fpeak again. Of the ftringed fpecies he fays
thofe with the greater tenfions exprefs the more acute founds; on the
contrary, thofe with the leffer give the more languid and grave; and
in inftruments that are blown, the more hollow and long, the more
languid and grave are their founds. Ho then proceeds to relate how
Pythagoras difcovered the confonances, and to give that account of
his fyftem which Stanley has taken into his life of that philofopher,
and is inferted in the foregoing part of this work, together with fome
remarks, the refult of late experiments, which in fome degree,
though not effentially, weaken the credit of the relation.

But without enquiring further into the weight of the hammers, and
other circumftances attending the difcovery of the confonances, we
may very fafely credit Nicomachus, fo far as to believe that Pythagoras, by the means of chords of different lengths, did difcover them;
that the philofopher to the found produced by the firft number fix,
gave the name Hypate; to eight he gave Mefe, which is fefquitertian
thereto; to nine Paramefe, which is a tone more acute, and therefore fefquioctave of the laft; and to the laft number, twelve, he gave
the name Nete; and afterwards filled up the intermediate fpaces with
founds in the fucceffion proper to the diatonic genus, and thereby
completed the fyftem of eight chords. The diatonic genus, as this
author defcribes it, is a natural progreffion to the fyftem of a diateffaron by a femitone, tone, and tone; and to a diapente by three
tones and a femitone. This is the manner in which it is faid the ancient fyftem was adjufted and extended to that of a complete octave,
an improvement fo much the more to be valued, as we are told that
in the ancient or primitive lyre, all the founds from the loweft were
fourths to each other *; whereas in the Pythagorean lyre, compofed

" it the name of Pandora." He juftly fays that Pandora was an Affyrian word. But the
" moft learned of the Hebrews do not feem fufficiently to underftand the fignification of
" it; they explain it by a twig or rod, whip, thong of leather, as appears from Buxtorf in
" the Talmudical Lexicon, from Talmud Hierofol. I imagine the true origin of
" this appellation to be this, the inftrument was mounted or ftretched with thongs
" of bull's hides, in the fame manner as the pentachord of the Scythians, concerning
" which the fame Pollux fpeaks thus: " The pentachord is an invention of the Scythians;
" it was ftretched or mounted with thongs made of the raw hides of oxen, but their plectra
" were the jaw-bones of the goats."
* Nicomach. Harmonic. Manual. pag. 5, ex verf. Meibom.

of

of a tetrachord and pentachord conjoined; or, which is the same, of two tetrachords disjoined by an intervening tone, we have a continued progression of sounds.

Nicomachus proceeds to relate that the magnitude of the scale in the diatonic genus is two diapasons, for that the voice cannot easily extend itself either upwards or downwards beyond this limit; and for this reason, to the ancient lyre formed of seven strings, by the conjunction of two tetrachords, extending from Hypate to Mese, and thence to Nete, were adjoined two tetrachords, each at the outward extremity of the former; that which began at Nete was called Hyperboleon, signifying excellent. This tetrachord, he says, consists of three adjoined sounds, whose names are worthy to be remembered; as first, Trite hyperboleon, then Paranete hyperboleon, and lastly, Nete hyperboleon. The other tetrachord was joined to the chord Hypate, and was thence called Hypaton; and each of the three adjoined sounds had the addition of Hypaton to distinguish it from the chord of the same denomination in the lower of the two primitive tetrachords; thus Hypate hypaton, Parhypate hypaton, Diatonos hypaton, or Lychanos hypaton, for it matters not which it is called; and this system from Hypate hypaton to Mese is seven chords, making two conjoint tetrachords; and that from Hypate hypaton to Nete is thirteen; so that Mese having the middle place, and conjoining two systems of a septenary each, reckoning either upwards from Hypate hypaton, or downwards from Nete hyperboleon, each system contained seven chords.

From this it is evident that the additional tetrachords were originally adapted to the system of Terpander, which did not separate Mese from Trite by a whole tone, as that of Pythagoras did. What advantages could be derived from this addition it is not easy to say; nor is it conceivable that that system could be reducible to practice which gave to a nominal diapason four tones and three hemitones, instead of five tones and two hemitones.

But the addition of the new tetrachords to the two disjunct tetrachords of Pythagoras was very natural, and made way for what this author next proceeds to mention, the tetrachord synemmenon, which took place in the middle of that interval of a tone, by which Pythagoras had divided the two primitive tetrachords. The design of introducing this tetrachord synemmenon, which placed Trite but a hemitone diftant from Mefe, was manifeftly to give to Parhypate mefon what it wanted before, a perfect diateffaron for its nominal fourth ; and this opinion of its ufe is maintained by all who have written on the fubject of mufic.

The author then proceeds to a verbal enumeration of the feveral chords, which by the disjunction made by Pythagoras, and the addition of Proflambanomenos, it appears were encreafed to fifteen, with their refpective tonical diftances : it has already been mentioned, that, contrary to the method now in ufe, the ancients gave the moft grave founds the uppermoft place in their fcale; he therefore begins with Proflambanomenos and reckons downwards to Nete hyperboleon.

He gives the fame kind of enumeration of the feveral founds that compofe the tetrachord fynemmenon, having firft Trite fynemmenon at the diftance of a hemitone from Mefe, then after a tone Paranete fynemmenon, and after another tone Nete fynemmenon of the fame tenor and found as Paranete diezeugmenon.

Mefe
　　Hemitone
Trite
　　　　Tone
Paranete
　　　　Tone
Nete

So that there exift five tetrachords, Hypaton, Mefon, Synemmenon, Diezeugmenon, and Hyperboleon; though it is to be remembered that the third of thefe is but auxiliary, and whenever it is ufed it is only in the room of the fourth, for reafons before given; and in thefe tetrachords there are two disjunctions and three conjunctions; the disjunctions are between Nete fynemmenon and Nete diezeugmenon, and between Proflambanomenos and Hypate hypaton : the conjunctions are between Hypaton and Mefon, and, which is the fame, Mefon and Synemmenon, and between Diezeugmenon and Hyperboleon.

We muft underftand that the foregoing is a reprefentation of the tetrachords as they are divided in the diatonic genus, the characteriftic whereof is a progreffion by a hemitone, tone, and tone; for as to the other genera, the chromatic and enharmonic, this author pro-
　　　　　　　　　　　　　　　　　　　　　　　　　feffes

feffes not to deliver his fentiments, but promifes to give them at large, together with a regular progreffion in all the three in his Commentaries, a work he often fpeaks of, as having undertaken it for the information of his learned correfpondent: he alfo engages to give the teftimonies of the ancients, the moft learned and eloquent of men on this fubjeQ, and an expofition of Pythagoras's feQion of the canon, not as Eratofthenes or Thrafyllus badly underftand it, but according to Locrus Timæus, the follower of Plato, although nothing of his on the fubjeQ is remaining at this day; however he has given an idea of the genera in the following words: ' The firft and moft fimple of
' confonances is the diateffaron. The diatonic tetrachord proceeds
' by a hemitone, tone, and tone, or four founds and three intervals;
' and it is called diatonic, as proceeding chiefly by tones. The chro-
' matic progreffion in the tetrachord is by a hemitone, hemitone,
' and an incompofite trihemitone, and therefore, though not confti-
' tuted as the other, it contains an equal number of intervals. The
' enharmonic progreffion is by a diefis, which is half a hemitone,
' another diefis, alfo half a hemitone, and the remainder is an in-
' compofite ditone; and thefe latter are alfo equal to a hemitone and
' two tones. Amongft thefe it is impoffible to adapt found to found,
' for it is plain that the difference of the genera does not confift in
' an interchange of the four founds, but only of the two intermediate
' ones; in the chromatic the third found is changed from the diato-
' nic, but the fecond is the fame, and it has the fame found as the
' enharmonic; and in the enharmonic the two intermediate founds
' are changed, with refpeQ to the diatonic, fo as the enharmonic is
' oppofite to the diatonic, and the chromatic is in the middle be-
' tween them both; for it differs only a hemitone from the diatonic,
' whence it is called chromatic, from Chroma, a word fignifying a
' difpofition flexible and eafy to be changed: in oppofition to this
' we call the extremes of each tetrachord Stantes, or ftanding founds,
' to denote their immovable pofition. This then is the fyftem of the
' diapafon, whether from Mefe to Proflambanomenos, or from Mefe
' to Nete hyperboleon; and as the diateffaron is two tones and a he-
' mitone, and the diapente three tones and a hemitone, the diapafon
' fhould feem to be fix whole tones; but in truth it is only five
' tones and two hemitones, which hemitones are not ftriQly com-
' plete; and therefore the diapafon is fomewhat lefs than fix complete
                                                        ' whole

' whole tones * : and with this agree the words of Philolaus when he
' says that harmony hath five superoctaves and two dieses ; now
' a diefis is the half of a hemitone, and there is another hemitone
' required to make up the number fix.'

His second book Nicomachus begins with an account of the invention of the lyre by Mercury, already related, and which has been
adopted by almost every succeeding writer on music, adding that some
among the ancients ascribed it to Cadmus the son of Agenor. He
proceeds to state the proportions, which he does in a way not easily
reconcileable with the practice of the moderns : he then reconsi-
ders the supposed relation between the sounds in the harmonical septenary and the motions of the planets ; and endeavours to account for
these different denominations, which it seems were given them in his
days. He says that the chord Hypate is applied to Saturn, as the
chief of the planets, and Nete to Luna, as the least. Mese is Sol,
Parhypate is attributed to Jove, Paramese not to Mercury but to
Venus, by a perverse order, says his editor, unless there is an error
in the manuscript. Paramese to Mars, Trite to Venus, Luna or the
Moon is said to be acute, as it answers to Nete ; and Saturn grave as
is Hypate. Those that reckon contrarywise, applying Hypate to the
Moon, and Nete to Saturn, do it, because say they the graver sounds
are produced from the lower and more profound parts of the body,
and therefore are properly adapted to the lower orbs ; whereas the
acute sounds are formed in the higher parts, and do therefore more
naturally resemble the more remote of the heavenly bodies :

Saturn	-	-	-	Nete
Jupiter	-	-	-	Paranete
Mars	-	-	-	Paramese
Sol	-	-	-	Mese
Venus	-	-	-	Lichanos
Mercury	-	-	-	Parhypate
Luna	-	-	-	Hypate

Nicomachus then proceeds to enumerate the several persons who
added to the system of the diapason, completed as it was by Pythagoras ; but as he expressly says the additional chords were not ad-

* This is demonstrated by Ptolemy, lib. I. cap. xi. of his Harmonics, and also by
Boëtius, lib. V. cap. xlii.

7   justed

jufted in any precife ratio, and as their names have already been given, it feems needlefs to be more particular about them. Speaking of the great fyftem, viz. that of the difdiapafon, he cites Ptolemy, to fhew that it muft neceffarily confift of fifteen chords; but as it is certain that Nicomachus lived A. C. 60, and that Claudius Ptolemæus flourifhed about one hundred and forty years after the commencement of the Chriftian æra, there arifes an anachronifm, which is not to be accounted for but upon a fuppofition that the manufcript is corrupted. From divers paffages in this author, and others to be met with in the Greek writers, it is evident that the ancients were not wholly unacquainted with the doctrine of the vibrations of chords: they had obferved that the acute founds were produced by quick, and the grave by flow motions, and that the confonances arofe from a coincidence of both; but it no where appears that they made any ufe of the coincidences in adjufting the ratios of the confonances; on the contrary, they feem to have referred the whole to the ratio of lengths and tenfions by weights, and a divifion of the monochord; and in this refpect it is unqueftionably true that the fpeculative part of mufic has received confiderable advantages from thofe improvements in natural philofophy which in the latter ages have been made. The inquifitive and acurate Galileo was the firft that invefligated the laws of pendulums; he found out that all the vibrations of the fame ftring, the longer and the fhorter, were made in equal time, that between the length of a chord and the number of its vibrations, there fubfifts a duplicate proportion of length to velocity; and that the length quadrupled will fubduple the velocity of the vibrations, and the length fubquadrupled will duplo the vibrations; for the proportion holds reciprocally: adding to the length will diminifh, and fhortening it will encreafe the frequency of vibrations. Thefe, and numbers of other difcoveries, the refult of repeated experiments, have been found of great ufe, as they were foon after the making of them applied to the meafure of time, and other moft valuable purpofes.

Having given an extract which contains in fubftance almoft the whole of what Nicomachus has left us on the fubject of harmony, it remains to obferve that his work is manifeftly incomplete: it appears from his own words to have been written while he was upon a journey, and for the particular information of the lady to whom he has, in

terms

terms of the greatest respect, inscribed it ; and is no other than what he himself with great modesty entitles it, a Manual ; it is however to be esteemed a very valuable fragment, as it is by much the most clear and intelligible of the works of the Greek writers now remaining. Boetius, in his treatise De Musica, cites divers passages from Nicomachus that are not to be found in this discourse of his, from whence it is highly probable that he had seen those commentaries which are promised in it, or some other tract, of which at this distance of time no account can be given.

C H A P.   VII.

PLUTARCH is also to be numbered among the ancient writers on music, for in his Symposiacs is a discourse on that subject, which is much celebrated by Meibomius, Doni, and others. A passage in the French translation, by Amyot, of the works of that philosopher, has given rise to a controversy concerning the genuineness of this tract, the merits of which will hereafter be considered. This discourse contains in it more of the history of the ancient music and musicians than is to be met with anywhere else, for which reason it is here meant to give a copious extract from it. It is written in dialogue ; the speakers are Onesicrates, Soterichus, and Lysias.

The latter of these, in answer to a request of Onesicrates, gives a relation of the origin and progress of the science, in substance as follows.

‘ According to the assertion of Heraclides, in a Compendium of
‘ Music, said to have been written by him, Amphion, the son of Ju-
‘ piter and Antiope, was the inventor of the harp and of Lyric poesy ;
‘ and in the same age Linus the Eubean composed elegies : Anthes
‘ of Anthedon in Bœotia was the first author of hymns, and Pierius of
‘ Pieria of verses in honour of the Muses ; Philamon the Delphian
‘ also wrote a poem, celebrating the nativity of Latona, Diana, and
‘ Apollo ; and was the original institutor of dancing about the tem-
‘ ple of Delphos. Thamyris, of Thracian extraction, had the finest
‘ voice, and was the best singer of his time, for which reason he is
‘ by the poets feigned to have contended with the Muses ; he wrought
‘ into

' into a poem the war of the Titans againft the Gods. Demodocus
' the Corcyrean wrote in verfe the hiftory of the deftruction of
' Troy, and the nuptials of Vulcan and Venus. To him fucceeded
' Phemius of Ithaca, who compofed a poem on the return of thofe
' who came back with Agamemnon from the fiege of Troy; and
' befides that thefe poems were feverally written by the perfons
' abovenamed, they were alfo fet to mufical notes by their refpective
' authors. The fame Heraclides alfo writes that Terpander was the
' inftitutor of thofe laws by which the metre of verfes, and confe-
' quently the mufical meafure, were regulated; and according to
' thefe rules he fet mufical notes both to his own and Homer's words,
' and fung them at the public games to the mufic of the lyre. Clo-
' nas, an epic and elegiac poet, taking Terpander for his example,
' conftituted rules which fhould adjuft and govern the tuning and
' melody of flutes or pipes, and fuch like wind-inftruments; and in
' this he was followed by Polymneftes the Colophonian.

' Timotheus is faid to have made lyric preludes to his epic poems,
' and to have firft introduced the dithyrambic, a meafure adapted to
' fongs in the praife of Bacchus, which fongs required a violent mo-
' tion of the body, and a certain irregularity in the meafure.'

' Farther of Terpander, one of the moft ancient of muficians, he
' is recorded to have been four times a victor at the Pythian games.'

' Alexander the hiftorian fays, that Olympus brought into Greece
' the practice of touching the ftrings of the lyre with a quill; for
' before his time they were touched by the fingers: and that Hyag-
' nis was the firft that fang to the pipe, and Marfyas his fon the next,
' and that both thefe were prior to Olympus. He farther fays that
' Terpander imitated Homer in his verfes, and Orpheus in his mu-
' fic; but that Orpheus imitated no one. That Clonas, who was
' fome time later than Terpander, was, as the Arcadians affirm, a
' native of Tegea, a city of Arcadia; though others contend that he
' was born in Thebes; and that after Terpander and Clonas flou-
' rifhed Archilochus: yet fome writers affirm that Ardalus the Troe-
' zenian taught wind-mufic before Clonas.'

' The mufic appropriated to the lyre under the regulations of Ter-
' pander continued without any variation, till Phrynis became fa-
' mous, who altered both the ancient rules, and the form of the in-
' ftrument to which they were adapted.'

Vol. I.   E e   Having

Having thus difcourfed concerning the ancient muficians, and ftringed and wind-inftruments in general, Lyfias proceeds, and confining himfelf to the inftruments of the latter kind, fpeaks to this effect.

' Olympus, a Phrygian, and a player on the flute, invented a certain
' meafure in honour of Apollo, which he called Polycephalus or of
' many heads. This Olympus, as it is faid, was defcended from the
' firft Olympus, the fon of Marfyas, who being taught by his father
' to play on the flute, firft brought into Greece the laws of harmony.
' Others afcribe the invention of the Polycephalus to Crates, the dif-
' ciple of Olympus. The fame Olympus was the author of the Har-
' matian mood, as Glaucus teftifies in his treatife of the ancient
' poets, and as fome think of the Orthian mood alfo *. There
' was alfo another mood in ufe among the ancients, termed Cra-
' dias, which Hipponax the Mimnermian greatly delighted in.
' Sacadas of Argos, being himfelf a good poet, compofed the mufic
' to feveral odes and elegies, and became thrice a victor at the Py-
' thian games. It is faid that this Sacadas, in conjunction with Po-
' lymneftes, invented three of the moods, the Dorian, the Phry-
' gian, and the Lydian; and that the former compofed a ftrophe,
' the mufic whereof was a commixture of all the three. The origi-
' nal conftitution of the modes was undoubtedly by Terpander, at
' Sparta ; but it was much improved by Thales the Gortynian, Xe-
' nedamus the Cytherian, Xenocritus the Locrian, and Polymneftes
' the Colophonian.'

' Ariftoxenus afcribes to Olympus the invention of the enarmonie
' genus; for before his time there were no other than the diatonic and.
' chromatic genera,'

' As to the meafures of time, they were invented at different periods
' and by different perfons. Terpander, amongft other improvements

* Thefe moods, the Harmatian and Orthian, were unqueftionably moods of time. The former, if we may truft the Englifh tranflator of Plutarch's Dialogue on Mufic, as it ftands in the firft volume of his Morals, Lond. 1684, was the meafure termed by Zarlino, La Curule, in which it is fuppofed was fung the ftory of Hector's death, and of the dragging him in a chariot round the walls of Troy : of the Orthian mood the fame tranflator gives the following defcription : ' This mood confifted of fwift and loud notes, ' and was ufed to inflame the courage of foldiers going to battle, and is mentioned by ' Homer in the feventh book of the Iliad, and defcribed by Euftathius. This mood Arion ' made ufe of when he flung himfelf into the fea, as Aulus Gellius writes, lib. XVI. ' cap. xix. the time of it was two down and four up.' Meibomius on Ariftides.

' which

‘ which he made in music, introduced thofe grave and decent meafures
‘ which are its greateft ornament; after him, befides thofe of Terpan-
‘ der, which he did not reject, Polymneftes brought into ufe other mea-
‘ fures of his own; as did alfo Thales and Sacadas, who, though of
‘ fertile inventions, kept within the bounds of decorum. Other im-
‘ provements were alfo made by Stefichorus and Alcmas, who never-
‘ thelefs receded not from the ancient forms; but Crexus, Timotheus,
‘ and Philoxenus, and others of the fame age, affecting novelty, de-
‘ parted from the plainnefs and majefly of the ancient mufic.'
    Another of the interlocutors in this dialogue of Plutarch, Soteri-
chus by name, who is reprefented as one not only fkilled in the fcience
but eminently learned, fpeaks of the invention and progrefs of mufic
to this effect.
    ‘ Mufic was not the invention of any mortal, but we owe it to the
‘ god Apollo. The fute was invented neither by Marfyas, nor
‘ Olympus, nor Hyagnis, but Apollo invented both that and the
‘ lyre, and, in a word, all manner of vocal and inftrumental mufic.
‘ This is manifeft from the dances and facrifices which were folemniz-
‘ ed in honour of Apollo. His ftatue, placed in the temple of Delos,
‘ holds in his right hand a bow, and at his left the Graces ftand with
‘ each a mufical inftrument in her hand, one bearing a lyre, another
‘ a flute, and another a fhepherd's pipe; and this ftatue is reported
‘ to be as ancient as the time of Hercules. The youth alfo that car-
‘ ries the tempic laurel into Delphos is attended by one playing on
‘ the flute; and the facred prefents of the Hyperboreans were fent of
‘ old to Delos, attended by flutes, pipes, and lyres; and fome have
‘ afferted that the God himfelf played on the flute. Venerable there-
‘ fore is mufic, as being the invention of Gods; but the artifts of
‘ thefe later times, contemning its ancient majefly, have introduced
‘ an effeminate kind of melody, mere found without energy. The
‘ Lydian mode, as firft inftituted, was very dolefut, and fuited only
‘ to lamentations; wherefore Plato in his Republic utterly rejects it.
‘ Ariftoxenus in the firft book of his Harmonics relates that Olympus
‘ fung an elegy in that mode on the death of Python, though fome
‘ attribute the invention of the Lydian mode to Menalippides, and
‘ others to Torebus. Pindar afferts that it was firft ufed at the nup-
‘ tials of Niobe; Ariftoxenus, that it was invented by Sappho, and

‘ that

' that the tragedians learned it of her, and conjoined it with the Do-
' rian; but this is denied by those who say that Pythocleides the
' player on the flute, and also Lysis the Athenian, invented this con-
' junction of the Dorian with the Lydian mode. As to the softer
' Lydian, which was of a nature contrary to the Lydian properly so
' called, and more resembling the Ionian, it is said to have been in-
' vented by Damon the Athenian. Plato deservedly rejected these
' effeminate modes, and made choice of the Dorian, as more suit-
' able to warlike tempers; not that we are to suppose him ignorant
' of what Aristoxenus has said in his second book, that in a wary
' and circumspect government advantages might be derived from the
' use of the other modes; for Plato attributed much to music, as
' having been a hearer of Draco the Athenian, and Metellus of Agri-
' gentum; but it was the consideration of its superior dignity and
' majesty that induced him to prefer the Dorian mode. He knew
' moreover that Alcmas, Pindar, Simonides, and Bacchylides, had
' composed several Parthenioi in the Dorian mode; and that suppli-
' cations and hymns to the Gods, tragical lamentations, and some-
' times love-verses were also composed in it; but he contented himself
' with such songs as were made in honour of Mars and Minerva, or
' those other that were usually sung at the solemn offerings called
' Spondalia. The Lydian and Ionian modes were chiefly used by the
' tragedians, and with these also Plato was well acquainted. As to
' the instruments of the ancients, they were in general of a narrow
' compass; the lyre used by Olympus and Terpander and their fol-
' lowers had but three chords, which is not to be imputed to ig-
' norance in them, for those musicians who made use of more were
' greatly their inferiors both in skill and practice.'
' The chromatic genus was formerly used by those who played on
' the lyre, but by the tragedians never. It is certainly of greater an-
' tiquity than the enarmonic; yet the preference given to the dia-
' tonic and enarmonic was not owing to ignorance, but was the ef-
' fect of judgment. Telephanes of Megara was so great an enemy to
' the syrinx or reed-pipe, that he would never suffer it to be joined
' to the tibia; or that other pipe made of wood, generally of the
' lote-tree, and for that reason he forbore to go to the Pythian
' games. In short, if a man is to be deemed ignorant of that which
' he makes no use of, there would be found a great number of ignorant

‘ rnot perfons in this age ; for we fee that the admirers of the Dorian
‘ mode make no ufe of the Antigenidian method of compofition : and
‘ other muficians refufe to imitate Timotheus, being bewitched with
‘ the trifles and idle poems of Polyeides.’

‘ If we compare antiquity with the prefent times, we fhall find
‘ that formerly there was great variety in mufic, and that the diverfi-
‘ ties of meafure were then more efteemed of than now. We are now
‘ lovers of learning, they were lovers of time and meafure ; plain it is
‘ therefore that the ancients did not becaufe of their ignorance, but
‘ in confequence of their judgment, refrain from broken meafures ;
‘ and if Plato preferred the Dorian to the other modes, it was only
‘ becaufe he was the better mufician; and that he was eminently
‘ fkilled in the fcience appears from what he has faid concerning the
‘ procreation of the foul in his Timæus.’

‘ Ariftotle, who was a difciple of Plato, thus labours to convince
‘ the world of the majefty and divine nature of mufic ; “ Harmony,
“ faith he, defcended from heaven, and is of a divine, noble, and
“ angelic nature ; being fourfold as to its efficacy, it has two me-
“ diums, the one arithmetical, the other harmonical. As for its
“ members, its dimenfions, and exceffes of intervals, they are beft
“ difcovered by number and equality of meafure, the whole fyftem
“ being contained in two tetrachords.”

‘ The ancient Greeks were very careful to have their children
‘ thoroughly inftructed in the principles of mufic, for they deemed it
‘ of great ufe in forming their minds, and exciting in them a love of
‘ decency, fobriety, and virtue : they alfo found it a powerful incen-
‘ tive to valour, and accordingly made ufe of pipes or flutes when
‘ they advanced to battle : the Lacedemonians and the Cretans did
‘ the fame ; and in our times the trumpet fucceeding the pipe, as
‘ being more fonorous, is ufed for the fame purpofe. The Argives
‘ indeed at their wreftling matches made ufe of fifes called Schenia,
‘ which fort of exercife was at firft inftituted in honour of Danaus,
‘ but afterwards was confecrated to Jupiter Schenius or the Mighty;
‘ and at this day it is the cuftom to ufe fifes at the games called Pen-
‘ tathla, which confift of cuffing, running, dancing, hurling the
‘ ball, and wreftling. But among the ancients, mufic in the theatres
‘ was never known ; for either they employed it in the education of
                                                        ‘ their

' their youth, or confined it within the walls of their temples; but
' now our muficians ftudy only compofitions for the ftage.'

' If it fhould be demanded, Is mufic ever to remain the fame, and
' is there not room for new inventions? The anfwer is that new in-
' ventions are allowed, fo as they be grave and decent; the ancients
' themfelves were continually adding to and improving their mufic.
' Even the whole Mixolydian mode was a new invention; fuch alfo
' were the Orthian and Trochean fongs; and, if we may believe
' Pindar, Terpander was the inventor of the Scolian fong, and Ar-
' chilocus of the iambic and divers other meafures, which the tra-
' gedians took from him, and Crexus from them. The Hypolydian
' mode was the invention of Polymneftes, who alfo was the firft that
' taught the manner of alternately foft and loud. Olympus, befides
' that he regulated in a great meafure the ancient Greek mufic,
' found out and introduced the enarmonic genus, and alfo the Pro-
' fodiac, the Chorian, and the Bacchian meafures; all which it is
' manifeft were of ancient invention. But Lafus Hermionenfis *
' applying thefe meafures to his dithyrambic compofitions, and mak-
' ing ufe of an inftrument with many holes, by an addition of tones
' and hemitones made an abfolute innovation in the ancient mufic.
' In like manner Menalippides the lyric poet, Philoxenus, and Ti-
' motheus, all forfook the ancient method. The latter until the
' time of Terpander of Antiffa ufed a lyre with only feven ftrings, but
' afterwards he added to that number. The wind-inftruments alfo
' received a great alteration; and in general the plainnefs and fimpli-
' city of the ancient mufic was loft in that affected variety which
' thefe and other muficians introduced.'

' In ancient times, when Poetry held the precedency of the other
' arts, the muficians who played on wind-inftruments were retained
' with falaries by the poets, to affift thofe who taught the actors, till
' Menalippides appeared, after which that practice ceafed.'

* Lafus Charbini from Hermione, a city of Achaia, lived about the 58th Olympiad,
in the time of Darius Hyftafpes; fome reckon him among the feven wife-men, in the
room of Periander. He was the firft who wrote a book concerning mufic, and brought
the dithyrambics into the games and exercifes, where he was a judge or moderator,
deciding contentious difputations. This Lafus was a mufician of great fame, and is
mentioned by Plutarch as the firft who changed any thing in the ancient mufic. Meibom.
on Ariftoxenus, from Suidas.

* Pherecrates

· ' Pherecrates the comic poet introduces Music in the habit of a wo-
' man with her face torn and bruised ; and alfo Juſtice, the latter of
' whom, demanding the reaſon of her appearing in that condition is
' thus anſwered by Muſic : *

" It is my part to ſpeak and yours to hear, therefore attend to my
" complaints. I have ſuffered much, and have long been oppreſſed
" by that beaſt Menalippides, who dragged me from the fountain of
" Parnaſſus, and has tormented me with twelve ſtrings: to complete
" my miſeries, Cineſias the Athenian, a pretender to poetry, com-
" poſed ſuch horrid ſtrophes and mangled verſes, that I, tortured
" with the pain of his dithyrambics, was ſo diſtorted that you would
" have ſworn that my right ſide was my left : nor did my misfortunes
" end here, for Phrynis, in whoſe brains is a whirlwind, racked me
" with ſmall wires, from which he produced twelve tireſome har-
" monies. But him I blame not ſo much, becauſe he ſoon repented
" of his errors, as I do Timotheus, who has thus furrowed my face,
" and ploughed my cheeks ; and Pyrrias the Mileſian, who as I
" walked the ſtreets met me, and with his twelve ſtrings bound and
" left me helpleſs on the earth."

* This Pherecrates the comic poet lived in the time of Alexander the Great, and attended him, as we are told, in his expeditions, (Suid. in Pherecrates) and was contemporary
with Ariſtophanes, Plato. Eupolis, and Phrynicus, all comic writers [Id. in Plato.]
Phrynis who played on the lyre was the ſon of Cabon, [Id. in Phrynis] and ſcholar of
Ariſtocleides, who pretended to be of the family of Terpander, and was a favourite with
Hiero king of Sicily, as ſome accounts tell us, which would throw him back near one hundred and fifty years in time before our poet Pherecrates ; but if we may believe Plutarch ;
he ſhould have been a contemporary with the poet at leaſt, if he perſonally contended the
muſic prize with Timotheus, with whoſe playing we are told Alexander's ſpirit was ſo
raiſed and animated to war. (Suid. in Timotheus.) But may it not be ſaid that Timotheus
did contend the prize againſt ſome piece formerly compoſed by Phrynis, as the dramatic
poets ſometimes conteſted the priority againſt a play of ſome deceaſed poet? if ſo, Phrynis
then might have lived as early as the period mentioned by Suidas.

It is true indeed Plutarch, where he gives us this point of hiſtory, does not mention
Phrynis by name, but diſtinguiſhes him only as the ſon of Cabon, and by his nick-
name Ιγναμφτης, Ionocamptes ; which farcaſtical addition he obtained, becauſe by his
effeminate modulations he had corrupted the old muſic in the like manner as the Ionic
movements had debauched the old maſculine dances.   Jul. Pollux, lib. IV. cap. ix. § 66.

The ſame Phrynis is likewiſe rallied by Ariſtophanes [in Nubibus, v. 967] and others of
the comic poets, for the levity of his compoſitions, and for overdoing every thing in his
performance. He was marked out, even to Infamy, for his innovations in muſic ; for his ſoft
and affected modulations, which were ſo abhorrent from the ſimplicity of the ancient
muſic ; for his intermingling and confounding the modes ; and for debaſing the ſcience
to paraſitiſm and ſervile offices.

' That

' That virtuous manners are in a great measure the effect of a well-
' grounded musical education, Aristoxenus has made apparent. He
' mentions Telesias the Theban, a contemporary of his, who being
' a youth, had been taught the noblest excellencies of music, and
' had studied the best Lyric poets, and withal played to perfection on
' the flute; but being past the prime of his age, he became infa-
' tuated with the corrupted music of the theatres, and the innova-
' tions of Philoxenus and Timotheus; and when he laboured to com-
' pose verses, both in the manner of Pindar and of Philoxenus, he
' could succeed only in the former, and this proceeded from the truth
' and exactness of his education; therefore if it be the aim of any
' one to excel in music, let him imitate the ancients; let him also
' study the other sciences, and make philosophy his tutor, which
' will enable him to judge of what is decent and useful in music.

' The genera of music are three, the diatonic, the chromatic, and
' enarmonic; and it concerns an understanding artist to know which
' of these three kinds is the most proper for any given subject of
' poetry.

' In musical institution the way has sometimes been for the tutor
' first to consider the genius and inclination of the learner, and then
' to instruct him in such parts of the science as he should discover
' most affection for; but the more prudent sort, as the Lacedemo-
' nians of old, the Mantinaans, and Pellenians rejected this method.'

Here the discourse of Soterichus grows very obscure, and has a reference to terms of which a modern can entertain no idea. Farther on
he resumes the consideration of the genera, which herspeaks of to this
effect.

' Now then, there being three genera of harmony, equal in the
' quantity of systems or intervals, and number of tetrachords, we
' find not that the ancients disputed about any of them except the
' enarmonic, and as to that they differed only about the interval call-
' ed the diapason.'

The speaker, by whom all this while we are to understand Soterichus, then proceeds to shew that a mere musician is an incompetent
judge of music in general; and to this purpose he asserts that Pythagoras rejected the judgment of music by the senses, and maintained
that the whole system was included in the diapason. He adds, that
the later musicians had totally exploded the most noble of the modes;

that

that they made hardly the leaft account of the enarmonic intervals; and were grown fo ignorant as to believe that the enarmonic diefis did not fall within the apprehenfion of fenfe.

He then enumerates the advantages that accrue from the ufe of mufic, and cites Homer to prove its effects on Achilles in the height of his fury againft Agamemnon : he fpeaks alfo of a fedition among the Lacedemonians, which Terpander appeafed by the power of his mufic ; and a peftilence among the fame people, which Thales the Cretan ftopped by the fame means.

Oneficrates, who hitherto appears to have acted the part of a moderator in this colloquy, after beftowing his commendations both on Lyfias and Soterichus, addreffes them in thefe terms.

' But for all this, my moft honoured friends, you feem to have ' forgotten the chief of all mufic. Pythagoras, Archytas, Plato, and ' many others of the ancient philofophers maintain that there could ' be no motion of the fpheres without mufic, fince that the fupreme ' Deity conftituted all things harmonioufly ; but now it would be un' feafonable to enter upon a difcourfe on that fubject.'

And fo finging a hymn to the Gods and the Mufes, Oneficrates difmiffes the company.

Thus ends the Dialogue of Plutarch on mufic, which though a celebrated work of antiquity, is in the judgment of fome perfons rendered ftill more valuable by the paffage from Pherecrates, which he has introduced into it. The leaft that can be faid of which is, that without a comment it is next to impoffible to underftand it : the following remarks, which were communicated to the late Dr. Pepufch by a learned but anonymous correfpondent of his, may go near to render it in fome degree intelligible.

' The poet, fpeaking of the fucceffive abufes of mufic, mentions ' firft Phrynis, and afterwards Timotheus ; fo that Phrynis fhould ' feem to have led the way to the abufes which Timotheus is repre' hended for, or rather gave into, to the prejudice of mufic ; and it is ' probable he did fo, from a fpeech of Agis made to Leonidas, which ' is tranfmitted to us by Plutarch in the life of Agis.

' What we want the explanation of, is that paffage of Pherecrates ' which relates to the five ftrings and the twelve harmonies.

' From the time of Terpander, and upwards, we know that the ' lyre had feven ftrings, and thofe adjufted to the number of the

Vol. I. F f ' feven

' feven planets, and as fome fuppofe to their motions alfo. For
' though Euphorion in Athenæus is made to fay, that the ufe of the
' inftruments with many ftrings was of very great antiquity, yet the
' lyre was reckoned complete, and to have attained the full meafure
' of perfeft harmony when it had feven ftrings; becaufe, as Ariftotle
' obferved, the harmonics confifted in the number of chords, and be-
' caufe that was the number of old ufed.

' And therefore when Timotheus added four ftrings to the former
' feven, that innovation was fo offenfive to the Lacedemonians, that
' he was formally profecuted for the prefumption; and it was one of
' the caufes for which they were faid to have banifhed him their
' ftate. The edict by which they did fo, ftill extant, is tranfmitted
' to us as a curiofity by Boetius *; fome however have faid that Ti-
' motheus cleared himfelf from this fentence by producing a very
' ancient ftatue of Apollo found at Lacedæmon, holding a lyre with
' nine ftrings†. But if he avoided this fentence of banifhment, he did
' not wholly efcape cenfure; for Paufanias, who wrote as early as
' Athenæus, tells us where the Lacedæmonians hung up his lyre pub-
' licly, having punifhed him for fuperadding four ftrings, in com-
' pofitions for that inftrument, to the ancient feven; and Plutarch
' likewife tells us that before this, when the abovementioned Phry-
' nis was playing on the lyre at fome public folemnity, one of the
' Ephori, Ecprepes by name, taking up a knife, afked him on which
' fide he fhould cut off the ftrings that exceeded the number of
' nine‡.

* Boetius, in his treatife De Mufica, lib. I. cap. i. has given it in the original Greek;
and the author of a book lately publifhed, entitled Principles and Power of Harmony, has
given the following tranflation of it.
Whereas Timotheus, the Milefian, coming to our city, has deformed the ancient mufic; and laying afide the ufe of the feven-ftringed lyre, and introducing a multiplicity of
notes, endeavours to corrupt the ears of our youth by means of thefe his novel and complicated conceits, which he calls chromatic, by him employed in the room of our eftablifhed,
orderly, and fimple mufic; and whereas, &c. It therefore feemeth good to us the King
and Ephori, after having cut off the fuperfluous ftrings of his lyre, and leaving only feven
thereon, to banifh the faid Timotheus out of our dominions, that every one beholding the
wholefome feverity of this city, may be deterred from bringing in amongft us any unbecoming cuftoms, &c.
† Cafaub. ad Athenæum, lib. VIII. cap. xi.
‡ This fact is alluded to by Agis king of Sparta, in a fpeech of his to Leonidas, thus recorded by Plutarch.
' And you that ufe to praife Ecprepes, who being Ephore, cut off two of the nine ftrings
' from the inftrument of Phrynis the mufician, and to commend thofe who did afterwards
' imitate

' But though these innovations of Timotheus were said to be so
' offensive to the Lacedæmonians, it was not the first time of their
' having been put in practice; for Phrynis had before done the like,
' and been punished, as we shall find, in the same manner.

' These accounts therefore go thus far towards an explanation of
' one part of the passage before us; that as to the five strings, we may
' be pretty certain that the lyre of Phrynis was not confined to that
' number, nay we have particular testimonies that Phrynis himself
' was noted for playing on the lyre with more than seven strings;
' the system of the lyre, from the time of Terpander to that of Phry-
' nis, had continued altogether simple and plain, but Phrynis begin-
' ning to subvert this simplicity by adding two strings to his instru-
' ment, we are told by Plutarch, in more than one passage, that Ec-
' prepes the magistrate cut of two off his nine strings *.'

' The next thing therefore to be enquired into, is what the poet
' could mean by playing twelve harmonies on five strings?

' Perhaps by Harmonies we are to understand Modes; and if so,
' Phrynis may be ridiculed for such a volubility of hand, and such an
' affectation of variety, that he extracted a dozen tones from five
' strings only, or that he played over the whole twelve modes within
' that compass. For besides the seven principal modes, it is said
' that Aristoxenus by converting five species of the diapason, intro-
' duced five other secondary modes; and that the intermingling of
' the modes is the sense of ἁρμονίας here, seems plain from another
' passage in Plutarch ‡, where he says, " That it was not allowed
" to compose for the lyre formerly, as in his time, nor to intermingle
" the modes ἁρμονίας and measures of time, for they observed one and
" the same cast peculiar to each distinct mode, which had therefore
" a name to distinguish it by'; they were called Νόμοι or rules and li-
" mitations, because the composers might not transgress or alter the
" form of time and measure appointed to each one in particular."

' imitate him in cutting the strings of Timotheus's harp, with what face can you blame me
' for designing to cut off superfluity and luxury from the commonwealth ? Do you think
' those men were so concerned only about a fiddle-string, or intended any thing else than
' by checking the voluptuousness of music, to keep out a way of living which might destroy
' the harmony of the city ? Plutarch in Vita Agidis.'
† Vide the last preceding note, and Plutarch in Laconic. Institutio.
‡ De Musica.

' For we are certain that both the Athenians and Lacedæmonians
' had their laws by which the particular species of music were de-
' signed to be preserved distinct and unconfused; and their hymns,
' threni, pæans, and dithyrambs kept each to their several sort of ode;
' and so the composers for the lyre were not permitted to blend one
' melody with another, but they who transgressed were censured and
' fined for it.'

It has already been mentioned that the genuineness of this dialogue
has been questioned, some writers affirming it to be a spurious production, and others contending it to be a genuine work of Plutarch,.
worthy of himself, and in merit not inferior to the best of the treatises contained in the Symposiacs. It is therefore necessary to take a
view of the controversy, and to state the arguments of the contending
parties in support of their several opinions. It seems that the original
ground of this dispute was a note prefixed to Amyot's French translation of this dialogue in the following words : ' Ce traité n'appartient
' point, ou bien peu à la musique de plusieurs voix accordées & entre-
' lacées ensemble, qui est aujourd'hui en usage; ainsi à la façon ancienne,
' qui consistoit en la convenance du chant avec le sens & la mesure de
' la lettre, & la bonne grace du geste; & le style ne semble point
' être de Plutarque.'

Amyot's translation bears date in 1610; notwithstanding which,
Fabricius, in his catalogue of the writings of Plutarch, has mentioned
this discourse without suggesting the least doubt of its authenticity *.
But a dispute having arisen in the French Academy of Inscriptions
and Belles Lettres, on the question, whether the ancients were acquainted with music in consonance or not, this tract of Plutarch, in
which there is not the slightest mention of any such practice, was
urged in proof that they were strangers to it. While a doubt remained
of the genuineness of this discourse, its authority could not be deemed
conclusive; those who maintained the affirmative of the principal
question, therefore insisted on the objection raised by Amyot; and
this produced an enquiry into the ground of it, or, in other words,
whether Plutarch was really the author of that discourse on music
which is generally ascribed to him or not : this enquiry is contained
in three papers written by Monsieur Burette, and inserted in the Me-

* Biblioth. Græc. lib. IV. cap. xi. pag. 364, N. 124.

moirs

moirs of the abovementioned Academy, tome onzieme, Amft. 1736, with the following titles, Examen du Traité de Plutarque fur la Mufique—Obfervations touchant l'Hiftoire litteraire du Dialogue de Plutarque fur la Mufique—Analyfe du Dialogue de Plutarque fur la Mufique, the publication whereof has put an end to a queftion, which but for Amyot had probably never been ftarted.

Meibomius, in the general preface to his edition of the mufical writers, and Doni are lavifh in their commendations of this treatife : the latter of them, in his difcourfe De Præftantia Muficæ Veteris, pag. 65, calls it a golden little work ; but whether it merits fuch an encomium muft be left to the judgment of fuch as can truly fay they underftand it. As to the hiftorical part, it is undoubtedly curious, except in fome inftances, that feem to approach too near that fpecies of hiftory which we term fabulous, to merit any great fhare of attention ; but as to that other wherein the author profeffes to explain the nature of the ancient mufic, it is to be feared he is much too obfcure for modern comprehenfion. The particulars moft worthy of obfervation in this work of Plutarch are, the perpetual propenfity to innovation, which the muficians in all ages feem to have difcovered, and the extreme rigour with which thofe in authority have endeavoured to guard againft fuch innovations : the famous decree of the Ephori againft Timotheus juft mentioned, which fome how or other was recovered by Boetius, and is inferted in a preceding note, is a proof that the ftate thought itfelf concerned in preferving the integrity of the ancient mufic ; and if it had fo great an influence over the manners of the Spartan youth, as in the above treatife is fuggefted, it was doubtlefs an object worthy their attention.

CHAP.

C H A P.   VIII.

ARISTIDES QUINTILIANUS is suppofed to have flouriſhed, A. C.
110. this is certain that he wrote after Cicero, for from his books
De Republica he has abridged all the arguments that Cicero had advanced againſt muſic, and has oppofed them to what he urged in behalf of it in his oration for Rofcius. It is farther clear that Ariſtides
moſt have been prior to Ptolemy, for he ſpeaks of Ariſtoxenus who admitted of thirteen modes, and of thoſe who after him allowed of fifteen, but he takes no notice of Ptolemy who reſtrained the number of
them to ſeven. His treatife De Muſica conſiſts of three books. The
firſt contains an ample difcuſſion of the doctrine of the modes : ſpeaking of the diagram by which the ſituation and relation of them is
explained, he ſays it may be delineated in the form of wings, to
manifeſt the difference of the tones among themſelves ; but he has
given no reprefentation of it.

All that has been hitherto faid of the modes is to be underſtood
of melody, for there is another and to us a more intelligible ſenſe of
the word, namely that, where it is applied to the proportions of
time, or the ſucceſſion and different duration of ſounds, of which
whether they are melodious, or ſuch as ariſe from the ſimple percuſſion of bodies, the modes of time, for by that appellation we
chufe to diſtinguiſh them from the modes of tone, are as ſo many
different meafures. The effect of the various metrical combinations of ſounds is undoubtedly what the ancients, more particularly this author, meant by the word Rythmus. Of time he ſays
there are two kinds, the one ſimple and indiviſible, refembling a
point in geometry ; the other compoſite, and that of different meafures, namely, duple, treble and quadruple *. The rythmic ge-

---

* This paſſage in Ariſtides Quintilianus has drawn on him a ſevere cenſure from the
late Dr. Pemberton, the Greſham profeſſor of phyſic, who ſays that he here endeavours to
make out four different meaſures of time in verſe alfo. This ſays the Dr. is talking non-
ſenſe. But, adds he, this writer is apt to amufe himfelf with fanciful refemblances; and
having fiſt imagined I know not what analogy between thefe four meaſures of time, and
the four dicſes, into which a tone was confidered as diviſible, he muſt needs try at making
out the like in relation to words. Obfervations on Poetry efpecially the Epic. Lond. 1738.
page 110.

nera

nera he makes to be three in number, namely, the equal, the ſeſquialteral, and the duple; others he ſays add the ſupertertian: theſe are conſtituted from the magnitude of the times; for one compared to itſelf begets a ratio of equality, two to one is duple, three to two is ſeſquialteral, and four to three ſupertertian: He ſpeaks of the elation and poſition of ſome part of the body, the hand or foot perhaps, as neceſſary to the rythmus, probably as a meaſure; and this correſponds with the practice of the moderns in the meaſuring of time by the tactus or beat. The remainder of the firſt book of this work of Quintilian contains a very laborious inveſtigation of meaſures, with all their various inflexions and combinations, in which the author diſcovers a profound knowledge.

The ſecond book treats of muſic as a means to regulate the external behaviour, as that of philoſophy is to improve the mind. Muſic, he ſays, by its harmony poliſhes the manners, and its rythmus renders the body more agreeable; for youth being impatient of mere admonition, and capable of inſtruction by words alone, require ſuch a diſcipline as without diſturbing the rational part of their natures ſhall familiarly and by degrees inſtruct them: he adds that it is eaſily perceived that all boys are prompt to ſing and ready for briſk motions, and that it is not in the power of their governors to hinder them from the pleaſure which they take in exerciſes of this ſort. In human things, continues this author, there is no action performed without muſic; it is certain that divine worſhip is rendered more ſolemn by it, particular feaſts and public conventions of cities rejoice with it, wars and voyages are excited by it, the moſt difficult and laborious works are rendered eaſy and delightful by it, and we are excited to the uſe of muſic by divers cauſes. Nor are its effects confined to the human ſpecies; irrational animals are affected by it, as is plain from the uſe which is made of pipes by ſhepherds, and horns by goatherds. Of the uſe of muſic in war, as practiſed by the ancients, he has the following paſſage: ‘ Numa has ſaid, that by muſic he corrected ‘ and refined the manners of the people, which before were rough ‘ and fierce: to that end he uſed it at feaſts and ſacrifices. In the ‘ wars where it is and will be uſed, is there any need to ſay how the ‘ Pyrrhic muſic is a help to martial diſcipline? certainly it is plain ‘ to every one, and that to iſſue commands by words in time of ‘ action would introduce great confuſion, and might be dangerous by

7   ‘ their

' their being made known to the enemies, if they were such as use
' the same language. To the trumpet, that martial instrument, a
' particular cantus or melody is appropriated, which varies according
' to the occasion of founding it, so as for the attack by the van or either
' wing, or for a retreat, or whether to form in this or that particular
' figure, a different cantus is requisite; and all this is so skilfully
' contrived, as to be unintelligible to the enemy, though at the
' same time by the army it is plainly understood.'

Thus much of this author is intelligible enough to a reader of this
time; but when he speaks, as he does immediately after, of the
efficacy of music in quieting tumults and appeasing an incensed
multitude, it must be owned his reasoning is not so clear: as little
can we conceive any power in music over the irascent and concupiscent affections of the mind, which he asserts are absolutely under its
dominion. The remainder of this second book consists of a chain of
very abstruse reasoning on the nature of the human soul, no way
applicable to any conception that we at this time are able to form of
music, and much too refined to admit of a place in a work, in which
it is proposed not to teach, but to deliver a history of, the science.

The third book contains a relation of some experiments made with
strings, distended by weights in given proportions, for finding out the
ratios of consonances; a method which this author seems to approve;
and to recommend this practice, he cites the authority of Pythagoras,
who he says, when he departed this life, exhorted his disciples to
strike the monochord, and thereby rather inform their understandings than trust to their ears in the measure of intervals. He speaks
also of an instrument for the demonstration of the consonances, called
a helicon, which was of a square form, and on which were stretched,
with an equal tension, four strings *. For the reason above given, it
seems no way necessary to follow this author through that series of
geometrical reasoning, which he has applied for the investigation of
his subject in the succeeding pages of his book, wherefore a passage relating to the tetrachords, remarkable enough in its kind,
shall conclude this extract from his very learned but abstruse work.
' The tetrachords are agreed to be five in number, and each
' has a relation to one or other of the senses; the tetrachord hypa-
' ton resembles the touch, which, is affected in new-born infants,

* See it in a subsequent chapter of this second book.

' when

‘ when they are impelled by the cold to cry. The tetrachord
‘ meson is like the taste, which is necessary to the preservation
‘ of life, and hath a similitude to the touch. The third, called
‘ synnemenon, is compared to the smell, because this sense is allied
‘ to the taste; and many, as the sons of art say, have been restored
‘ to life by odours. The fourth tetrachord, termed diezeugmenon, is
‘ compared to the hearing, because the ears are so remote from the
‘ other organs of sense, and are disjoined from each other. The
‘ tetrachord hyperboleon is like the sight, as it is the most acute of
‘ the systems, as the sight is of the senses.’ Farther, this author tells
us that ‘ the five tetrachords do in like manner answer to the five
‘ primary elements, that is to say, hypaton to the earth, as the most
‘ grave; meson to the water, as nearest the earth; synnemenon to
‘ the air, which passes through the water remaining in the profun-
‘ dities of the sea and the caverns of the earth, and is necessary for
‘ the respiration of animals, which could not live without it; die-
‘ zeugmenon to the fire, the motion whereof, as tending upwards,
‘ is against nature; lastly, the tetrachord hyperboleon answers to
‘ the æther, as being supreme and above the rest.’ There are, he
says, also analogies between the three several systems of diapente
and the senses; but we hasten to dismiss this fanciful doctrine.
Moreover, adds he, ‘ in discoursing of the human soul, systems are
‘ not improperly compared to the virtues. Hypaton and meson are
‘ to be attributed to temperance, the efficacy whereof is double, and
‘ consists in an abstinence from unlawful pleasures, resembling the
‘ most grave of these two systems; as also in a moderate use of law-
‘ ful enjoyments, not improperly signified by the tetrachord meson;
‘ but the tetrachord synnemenon is to be attributed to justice, which
‘ being joined with temperance, exerts itself in the discharge of pub-
‘ lic duties, and in acts of private beneficence : the diezeugmenon has
‘ the resemblance of fortitude, which virtue delivers the soul from
‘ the dominion of the body; lastly, the hyperboleon emulates the
‘ nature of prudence, for that tetrachord is the end of the acumen,
‘ and this virtue is the extremity of goodness. Again, these virtues
‘ may be assimilated to the three systems of diapente *; the two first,
‘ justice and temperance, which are always placed together as being a

* The varieties or different systems of diapente are four, and therefore it may be questioned why in this place the author has limited them to three.

‘ check to the concupiscent part of the mind, resemble the first of
‘ these systems; fortitude may be compared to the second, as that
‘ virtue denotes the irascent part and refers to each of our two na-
‘ tures; and prudence to the third, as declaring the rational essence.
‘ Add to this, that the two species of diapason answer to the twofold
‘ division of the mind; the first resembling the irrational, and the
‘ second the rational part thereof.’

It has been remarked of Quintilian that he is extremely fond of analogies, vide pag. 222, in a note; and the above passages are a proof
that this charge against him is not ill grounded.

ALYPIUS, the next in succession of the authors now remaining to
him above cited, or, as some suppose, a contemporary of his, as
flourishing about A. C. 115*, compiled a work entitled an Introduction to Music, which seems to be little else than a set of tables
explaining the order of the sounds as they arise in the several modes
of their respective genera in the ancient method of notation. The
musical characters used by the ancients were arbitrary; they were
nothing more than the Greek capitals mutilated, inverted, and variously contorted, and are estimated at no fewer than twelve hundred
and forty. A specimen of them is herein before inserted in two plates
from Kircher.

MANUEL BRYENNIUS, another of the Greek writers on music,
is supposed to have flourished under the elder Palæologus, viz. about
the year of Christ 120. He wrote three books on harmonics, the
first whereof is a kind of commentary on Euclid, as the second and
third are on Ptolemy †. He professes to have studied perspicuity for
the sake of young men, but has given very little more than is to
be found in one or other of the above authors. Meibomius had given
the public expectations of a translation of this work, but not living to
complete it, Dr. Wallis undertook it, and it now makes a part of
the third volume of his works, published at Oxford in three volumes
in folio, 1699.

BACCHIUS SENIOR was a follower of Aristoxenus; Fabricius
supposes him to have been tutor to the emperor Marcus Antoninus,
and consequently to have lived about A. C. 140‡. He wrote in Greek
a very short introduction to music in dialogue, which, with a Latin
translation thereof, Meibomius has published. It seems it was first

* Fabr. Biblioth. Græc. lib. III. cap. x.   † Ibid.   ‡ Ibid.

pub-

published in the original by Merſennus, in his Commentary on the ſix firſt chapters of Geneſis; and that afterwards he publiſhed a tranſlation of it in French, which Meibomius, in the preface to his edition of the ancient muſical authors, cenſures as being groſsly erroneous.

GAUDENTIUS the philoſopher, according to Fabricius *, ſeems to have written before Ptolemy, and treading in the ſteps of Ariſtoxenus, compoſed an introduction to harmonics, which Caſſiodorus commends as an elegant little work; though he does not pretend to ſay who he was, or where he lived; however upon his authority Caſſiodorus relates that Pythagoras found out the original precepts of the art by the ſound of hammers and the percuſſion of extended chords; and indeed as to this matter Gaudentius is very explicit. For his work in general, excepting a few definitions and a repreſentation of the muſical characters in the method of Alypius, it is little more than an abridgment of Ariſtoxenus, and that ſo very ſhort and obſcure, that little advantage can be derived from the peruſal of it.

CLAUDIUS PTOLEMÆUS was an Egyptian, born at Peluſium; not one of the Ptolemies kings of Egypt, with ſome one of whom he has been confounded; nor the ſame with Ptolemy the mathematician and aſtronomer, who, as Plutarch relates in his life of Galba, was the conſtant companion of that emperor and was alſo attendant on the emperor Otho in Spain, and foretold that he ſhould ſurvive Nero, as Tacitus tells us, lib. I. cap. xxii. The Ptolemy here ſpoken of flouriſhed in the reign of the emperor Marcus Aurelius Antoninus, as Suidas teſtifies; and alſo himſelf in his Magnæ Syntaxis, where he ſays that he drew up his aſtronomical obſervations at Alexandria, for which reaſon he is by Suidas and others called Alexandrinus, in the ſecond year of Antoninus Pius, which anſwers to the year of Chriſt 139†. He was the author of a treatiſe on harmonics in three books, a work much more copious than any of thoſe above-mentioned; and it muſt be allowed that he of all the ancient writers ſeems to have entred the moſt deeply into the ſubject of harmonics. In the firſt chapter of his firſt book, he aſsigns the criteria of harmony, which he makes to be ſenſe and reaſon: the former of theſe, he ſays, finds out what is nearly allied to truth, and approves of what is accurate, as the latter finds out what is accurate and approves of what is

* Biblioth. Græc. lib. III. cap. x.   † Ibid cap xiv.

nea:ly

nearly allied to truth.   Chap. iii. speaking of the causes of acuteness
and gravity, he takes occasion to compare the wind-pipe to a flute; and
to remark as a subject of wonder, that power or faculty which enables
a singer readily and instantaneously to hit those degrees of dilatation
and contraction as are necessary to produce sounds, grave or acute,
in any given proportion.

In the sixth chapter of the same book he condemns the method of
the Pythagoreans, and in the ninth that of the Aristoxenians, in the
adjusting of the consonances, but thinks the former the least erroneous of the two : the Pythagoreans, he says, not sufficiently attending to the ear, often gave harmonic proportions to incongruous
sounds ; on the contrary, the Aristoxenians, ascribing all to the ear,
applied numbers, the images of reason, not to the differences of
sounds, but to their intervals.   To correct the errors of these two
very different methods, he contrived an instrument very simple and
inartificial in its construction, but of singular use in the adjusting of
ratios, which though in truth but a monochord, as consisting of one
string only, he with great propriety called the Harmonic Canon, by
which appellation it is constantly distinguished in the writings of succeeding authors.   His description of the instrument and its use, as
also the reasons that led him to the invention, are contained in the
eighth chapter of the same first book, and are to the following effect:
‘ We omit to explain what is proposed, by the means of pipes or
‘ flutes, or by weights affixed to strings, because they cannot make
‘ the necessary demonstrations with sufficient accuracy, but would ra-
‘ ther occasion controversy ; for in pipes and flutes, as also in the
‘ breath which is injected into them, there is great disorder ; and as
‘ to strings with weights affixed to them, besides that of a number
‘ of such strings, we can hardly be sure that they are exactly equal
‘ in size, it is almost impossible to accommodate the ratios of the
‘ weights to the sounds intended to be produced by them ; for with
‘ the same degree of tension two strings of different thickness would
‘ produce sounds differently grave or acute: and farther, which is
‘ more to the present purpose, a string, at first of an equal length to
‘ others, by the affixing to it a greater weight than is affixed to the
‘ rest, becomes a longer string, from whence arises another difference
‘ of sound besides what might be deduced from the ratio of weight
‘ alone.   The like will happen in sounds produced from hammers or

                                                    ‘ quoits

' quoits of unequal weights; and we may obferve the fame in fome
' veffels that are firft empty, and afterwards filled; and certainly it
' is difficult in all thefe cafes to provide againft the diverfity of
' matter and figure in each; but in the canon, as I term it, the chord
' moft readily and accurately demonftrates the ratios of the feveral
' confonances.'

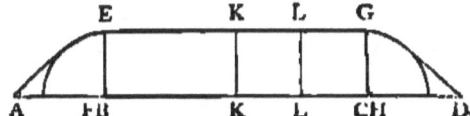

A B C D The line of the canon.
A E G D The chord.
A E, G D The ligament or place where it is faftened.
E B, G C Perpendiculars of the immoveable magades or bridges.
K K, L L The moveable magades.
B K, L C The canon or rule divided.

Suppofe A B C D to be a right line, at each end thereof apply
magades or little bridges, equal in height and having furfaces as nearly fpherical as poffible; as fuppofe the furface B, E to be defcribed
round the center F, and the furface C, G round the center H. Let
then the points E, G be taken in the middle or bifection of thefe
curved fuperficies, the magades being fo placed as that lines E, F, and
G, H, drawn from the faid bifections E and G, may be perpendicular
to the right line A B, C D. Now if from the points A D a chord
be ftrained over the middle points E and G of the faid curved fuperficies, the part E G will be parallel to the right line A B, C D, becaufe of the equal height of the magades, and will have its limits at
E and G. Transfer then the line E G to the line A B C D and
having firft bifected the whole length at K, and the half of that diftance at L, place under the chord other magades, which muft be
very thin, and fomewhat higher, but in every other refpect like the
former, fo that both the intermediate magades may be ftrait with the
middle of the external ones; now if the part of the chord E K be
found equitonal to K G, and the part K L to L G, then are we convinced that the chord is equable and perfect as to its conftitution and
make, and confequently fit for the experiment; but if it fhould not
prove fo, the trial is to be transferred to another part, or even to a new
chord,.

chord, till we obtain this condition of equability under the circum-
flances of fimilar moveable magades, and a fimilar length and tenfion
of the parts of the chord. This being done and the chord divided according to the proportions of the confonances, we fhall by the application of the moveable magades prove by our ears the ratios of correfponding founds; for giving to the diftance E K four of fuch parts
whereof K G is three, the founds on both fides will produce the
confonance diateffaron, and have a fefquitertian ratio; and giving to
E K three parts whereof K G is two, the founds on both fides will
make the confonance diapente, which is in fefquialteral ratio. Again,
if the whole length be fo divided as that E K may be two parts and
K G one of them, it fhall be the unifon diapafon, which confifts in a
duple ratio. If it be fo that E K be eight parts whereof K G is
three, it will be the confonance diapafon and diateffaron, in the ratio
of eight to three; farther if it be divided fo as that E K be three parts
and K G one of them, it will be diapente and diapafon, in a triple
ratio; and laftly if it be fo divided as that E K be four and K G one,
it will be the unifon difdiapafon in a quadruple ratio.

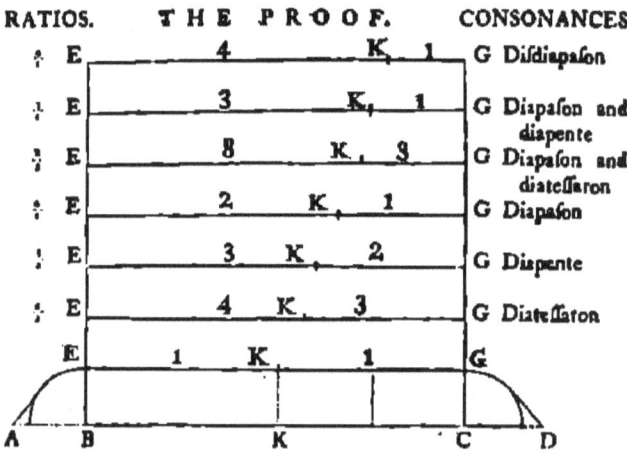

RATIOS.   THE   PROOF.   CONSONANCES

E   4   K   1   G Difdiapafon

E   3   K, 1   G Diapafon and
                                 diapente

E   8   K, 3   G Diapafon and
                                 diateffaron

E   2   K, 1   G Diapafon

E   3   K, 2   G Diapente

E   4   K, 3   G Diateffaron

E   1   K   1   G

A   B   K   C   D

How the monochord of Pythagoras was conftructed, or in what
manner he divided it, we are no where told: it feems difficult to
conceive

conceive that for producing the confonances it could be divided
in any other manner than this of Ptolemy, and yet this author
cenfures the followers of Pythagoras for not knowing how to reafon about the confonances, which one would think they could not
fail to do from principles fo clear as thofe deducible from experiments on the monochord. But as to the Ariftoxenians, he cenfures
them for rejecting the reafonings of the Pythagoreans, at the fame
time that they would not endeavour to find out better. To underftand thefe and other invectives againft this fect, it is to be obferved
that they meafured the intervals by the ear as our practical muficians
do now, that is to fay, the greater by fourths or fifths, and the lefs
by tones and femitones; thus to afcertain the meafure of an octave,
they applied that of a diateffaron or fourth above the unifon, and
another below the octave, and between the approximating extremities of thefe two intervals they found the diftance of a tone, which
furnifhed a common meafure for the lefs intervals of a fourth, a fifth,
and the reft; and enabled them to fay that a tone is the difference
between the diateffaron and the diapente: this Ptolemy calls re-
mitting one queftion to another, and he adds that the ear, when it
would judge of a tone needs not the help of a comparifon of it with
the diateffaron or any other confonance, and yet adds he, ' if we
' would afk of the Ariftoxenians what is the ratio of a tone, they
' will fay perhaps that it is two of thofe intervals, that is to fay
' hemitones, of which the diateffaron contains five, and in like man-
' ner that the diateffaron is five, of thofe of which the diapafon is
' twelve, and fo of the reft, till at laft they come to fay that the
' ratio of a tone is two, which is not defining thofe ratios.'

Ptolemy, lib. I. cap. x. farther denies the affertion of the Ariftoxenians, that the diateffaron contains two tones and half, and the
diapente three and a half; as alfo that the diapafon confifts of fix
tones, as the feveral contents of thofe two fyftems of two and a
half, and three and a half, fuppofing this eftimation of them to be
juft, would make undoubtedly fix; but by his divifion of the
monochord, he clearly demonftrates that the term by which the
diateffaron exceeds the diatone, and which he calls a limma, is lefs
than a hemitone, in the fame proportion as 1944 bears to 2048, a
difference however much too fmall for the ear to diftinguifh. His demonftration

monftration of this propofition is given in a preceding chapter of
this work.

To enter into a difcuffion of that very abftrufe fubject, the divifion
of the diapafon, would require a much more minute inveftigation of
the doctrine of ratios than is requifite in this place; it muft however
be obferved, that fuppofing the ear alone to determine the precife
limits of any fyftem, that of the diateffaron for example, and that
fuch fyftem were transferred to the monochord, a repetition of the
fyftem fo transferred would fail to produce a feries of fyftems confonant in the extremities. Thus let a given found be, as we fhould
now call it G, and let the monochord be divided by a bridge according to the rules above prefcribed, fo as to give its fourth C;
and let a tone, D, be fet on by another bridge in like manner, and
after that another fourth, which would terminate at G, and would feem
to make what we fhould call a diapafon: we fhould find upon taking
away the intermediate bridges at C and D, that the interval from G
to G would be more than a diapafon; and that were this method of
afcertaining the terms of the confonances repeated through a feries of
octaves, the diffonance would be increafed in proportion to the
number of repetitions. Ptolemy has taken another method, chap.
xi. of this his firft book, and by an accumulation of fefquioctave
tones has clearly demonftrated that fix fuch, exceed the confonance
diapafon. This deficiency, if it may be fo called, in the intervals of which the diapafon is compounded, and the difference between tuning by the ear and by numbers, has fuggefted to mathematicians what is called a temperament, which propofes a certain
number of integral parts for the limit of the diapafon, and the divifion
of the amount of the feveral limmas that occur in the progreffion to
it, in fuch a manner as to make the confonances contained in it as
nearly perfect as poffible.

The remainder of Ptolemy's firft book treats of the genera. Chap.
xii. exhibits the divifion of Ariftoxenus, which he condemns; and
chap. xiii. that of Archytas of Tarentum, whom he cenfures for defining the genera by the interjacent intervals rather than by the ratios
of the founds among themfelves, and charges him with rafhnefs and
want of thought.

The ufe and application of the genera is at this day fo little underftood, that we are greatly at a lofs to account for any other divifion of

the

the tetrachord than that which characterizes the diatonic genus: Nor does it seem possible, with the utmost strength of the imagination, to conceive how a series of sounds so extremely ungrateful to the ear as those of which the chromatic and enarmonic genera are said to be formed, could ever be received as music in the sense in which that word is now understood.

C H A P.   IX.

IN the first Chapter of his second Book Ptolemy undertakes to shew by what means the ratios of the several genera may be received by the sense, in the course of which demonstration he points out the different offices of sense or the ear, and reason, in the admeasurement of intervals, by which it should seem that the former is previously to adjust the consonances, and that these being transferred to the canon, become a subject of calculation: and this position of his is undoubtedly true; for the determination of the senses in all subjects where harmony or symmetry are concerned is arbitrary, and it is the business of reason, assisted by numbers, to enquire whether this determination has any foundation in nature or not; and if it has not, we pronounce it fantastical and capricious; for example we perceive by the ear a consonance between the unison and its octave, and we are conscious of the harmony resulting from those two sounds; but little are we aware of the wonderful relation that subsists between them, or that if an experiment be made by suspending weights to the chords that produce it, whose lengths are by the laws of harmony required to be in the proportion of 2 to 1, that the shorter would make two vibrations to one of the longer, and that the vibrations would exactly coincide in that relation as long as both chords should continue in motion. Again with respect to the forms of bodies, when we prefer that of a sphere to one less regular, we never attend to the properties of a sphere, but reason will demonstrate a perfection in that figure which is not to be found in an irregular polygon.

In the fecond chapter of his fecond book he deſcribes an inſtrument or diagram called the Helicon, invented as it ſhould ſeem by
himſelf, for demonſtrating the conſonances, ſo ſimple in its conſtruction that its very figure ſeems to ſpeak for itſelf and to render a
verbal explanation, though he has given a very long one of it, un-
neceſſary. It is of this form.

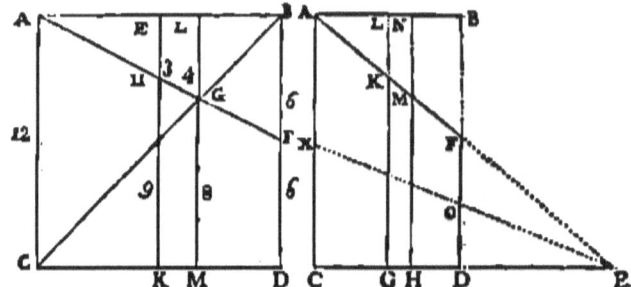

The ſide of the ſquare A C 12 ſhews the diapaſon; the half of
B D, that is to ſay B F or F D 6 the uniſon. The line G M
8, terminated by the diagonal B C, the diateſſaron. The line E K
divides the quadrangle equally, and H K 9, terminated by the line
A F, ſhews the diapente. The lines L G and E H are in the
ratio of 4 to 3, which is that of the diateſſaron; and laſtly the lines
H K 9 and G M 8 ſhew the ſeſquioctave tone.

To this diagram Ptolemy has added another not leſs eaſy to be
comprehended than the former, in which the lines B D, N H,
L G, and A C are ſuppoſed to be chords of equal lengths but
biſected by the line A F in the direction A E: this line may be
ſuppoſed to be a bridge, or ſubductorium, ſtopping the four chords
at A K M F, and thereby giving the proportions 12 9 8 6; which
proportions will alſo reſult from a ſubductorium placed in the
direction X E, for X C will be duple of O D, and the two intermediate chords ſeſquialtera and ſeſquitertia, and with reſpect to
each other, ſeſquioctave; in all agreeing with the ratios in the former
diagram.

In

In the ninth chapter of book II. Ptolemy takes occasion to say that there are only seven tones or modes, for that there are but seven species of diapason; a position that will be easily granted him by the moderns who suppose the word, tone or mode, when applied to sound, to answer to what we term the key or fundamental note. What he says farther concerning the modes has already been mentioned in a preceding chapter of this book.

Chapter xii. the same author speaks of the monochord; and here he proposes, but not for the purpose of experiments, a different method of dividing it, not, says he, according to one tone or mode only, but according to all the tones together; by which one would imagine he meant somewhat like a temperament of its imperfections, and a design to render it an instrument not of speculation but practice; and indeed besides exhibiting it in a form more adapted to practice, and more resembling a musical instrument than its primitive one *.

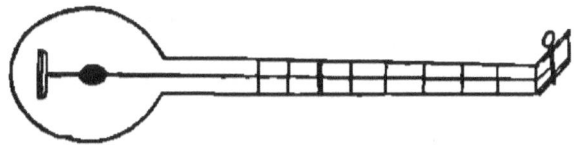

He speaks, though not very intelligibly, of the manner of performing on it, and recommends to conceal its defects the conjunction with it, either of a pipe or the voice. A little after, he speaks of Didymus a musician, who endeavoured to correct this instrument by a different application of the magades; but for the greater imperfections he says Didymus was not able to find out a cure. Towards the close of this second book he exhibits a short scheme of the three genera, according to five musicians, namely, Archytas, Aristoxenus, Eratosthenes, the same Didymus, and himself; and a little farther on, tables of the section of the canon in all the seven modes according to the several genera.

In the third book chap. iv. he speaks in general of the faculty of harmony, and of mathematical reasoning as applied to it; the use

* There is very little doubt but that the instrument here delineated is the pandura of the Arabians, mentioned in a note of Meibomius on a passage in Nicomachus, for among the Arabian and Turkish instruments described by Mersennus are many in this form.

whereof he fays is to contemplate and adjuft the ratios. In the next
enfuing chapter he proceeds, in the manner of Quintilian, to ftate the
analogy of mufic with the affections of the human mind, the fyftem
of the univerfe, and in fhort with every other fubject in which
number, proportion, or coincidence are concerned. In the courfe
of this his reafoning, he mentions that Pythagoras advifed his difciples at their rifing in the morning to ufe mufic, whereby that per-
turbation which is apt to affect the mind at the awakening from
fleep, might be prevented, and the mind be reduced to its wonted
ftate of compofure : befides which he fays, that it feems the Gods
themfelves are to be invoked with hymns and melody, fuch as that of
flutes or Egyptian trigons, to fhew that we invite them to hear and
be propitious to our prayers.

Upon a very careful review of this work of Ptolemy, it will appear that the doctrines contained in it, fo far as they are capable of
being rendered intelligible, are of fingular ufe in the determination
of ratios, and his very accurate divifion of the monochord carries demonftration with it.   It was doubtlefs for this reafon that our countryman Dr. Wallis, a man to whom the learned world are under high
obligations, undertook the publication of it from a manufcript in the
Bodleian library, in the original Greek, with a Latin tranflation of
his own, together with copious notes, and an appendix by way of
commentary, which the Doctor was the better qualified to give, as
it abundantly appears, as well by divers other of his writings in the
Philofophical Tranfactions, as the work we are now fpeaking of,
that he was very profoundly fkilled in the fcience of mufic. How far
he is to be depended on when he undertakes to render the ancient
modes in modern characters feems very queftionable, for were the
Doctor's opinion right in that matter, all that controverfy which has
fubfifted for thefe many centuries, not only touching the fpecific differences between them, but even as to their number, muft neceffarily have ended ages ago ; whereas, even at this day, the ableft
writers on the fubject do not hefitate at faying that the doctrine of
the modes is abfolutely infcrutable ; and perhaps it is for this reafon
only that fo many have imagined that with them we have loft the
moft valuable part of the art ; but on the contrary it is worth remarking that the Doctor, though he was perhaps the ableft geometer
of his time, and had all the prejudices in favour of the ancients that

2   a man

a man converfant with the beft of their writers could be fuppofed to
entertain, never intimates any fuch matter; nay, fo far is he from
adjudging a preference to the ancient mufic over that of the moderns,
that he fcruples not to afcribe the relations that are given of the effects of the former to the ignorance of mankind in the earlier ages,
the want of refinement, the charms of novelty, and other probable
caufes.   Dr. Wallis gave two editions of this work of Ptolemy, the
one publifhed in quarto at Oxford in 1682; another, as alfo the
commentary of Porphyry, and a treatife of Manuel Bryennius, makes
part of the third volume of his works, publifhed in three volumes in
folio, 1699.

CENSORINUS, a moft famous grammarian, lived at Rome about
A. C. 238 *, and wrote a book entitled De Die Natali.   It was publifhed by Erycius Puteanus at Louvain, in 1628, who ftiles it Doc-
trinæ rarioris Thefaurus; and it is by others alfo much celebrated
for the great light it has thrown on learning.   It is a very fmall
work, confifting of only twenty-four chapters; the tenth is concerning
mufic; and the fubfequent chapters, as far as the thirteenth inclufive,
relate to the fame fubject.

He profeffes to relate things not known even to muficians themfelves.   He defines mufic to be the fcience of well modulating, and
to confift in the voice or found.   He fays that found is emitted at
one time graver, at others acuter; that all fimple founds, in what
manner foever emitted, are called phthongoi; and the difference,
whereby one found is either more grave or more acute than another,
is called diaftema.

The reft of his difcourfe on mufic is here given in his own words :
' Many diaftemata may be placed in order between the loweft and the
' higheft found, fome whereof are greater, as the tone, and others
' lefs, as the hemitone; or a diaftem may confift of two, three, or more
' tones.   To produce concordant effects, founds are not joined to-
' gether capricioufly, but according to rule.   Symphony is a fweet
' concent of founds.   The fimple or primitive fymphonies are three,
' of which the reft confift; the firft, having a diaftem of two tones
' and a hemitone, is called a diateffaron ; the fecond, containing
' three tones and a hemitone,. is called a diapente ; the third is the

' diapafon, aud confifts of the two former, for it is conftituted either
' of fix tones, as Ariftoxenus and other muficians affert, or of five
' tones and two hemitones, as Pythagoras and the geometricians fay,
' who demonftrate that two hemitones do not complete the tone ;
' wherefore this interval, improperly called by Plato a hemitone,
' is truly and properly a diefis or limma.

' But to make it appear that founds, which are neither fenfible to
' the eyes, nor to the touch or feeling, have meafures, I shall relate
' the wonderful comment of Pythagoras, who, by fearching into the
' fecrets of nature, found that the founds of the muficians agreed to
' the ratio of numbers ; for he diftended chords equally thick and
' equally long, by different weights, thefe being frequently ftruck,
' and their founds not proving concordant, he changed the weights ;
' and having frequently tried them one after another, he at length
' difcovered that two chords ftruck together produced a diateffaron,
' when their weights being compared together, bore the fame ratio
' to each other as three does to four, which the Greeks call ἐπίτριτος,
' epitritos, and the Latins fupertertium. He at the fame time found
' that the fymphony, which they call diapente, was produced when
' the weights were in a fefquialtera proportion, namely, that of 2
' to 3, which they called hemiolium. But when one of the
' chords was ftretched with a weight duple to that of the other, it
' founded a diapafon.

' He alfo tried if thefe proportions would anfwer in the tibiæ, and
' found that they did ; for he prepared four tibiæ of equal cavity or
' bore, but unequal in length ; for example, the firft was fix inches
' long, the fecond eight, the third nine, and the fourth twelve ;
' thefe being blown into, and each compared with the others, he
' found that the firft and fecond produced the fymphony of the dia-
' teffaron, the firft and third a diapente, and the firft and fourth the
' diapafon : but there was this difference between the nature of the
' chords and that of the tibiæ, that the tibiæ became graver in pro-
' portion to the encreafe of their lengths, while the chords became
' acuter by an additional augmentation of their weights ; the propor-
' tion however was the fame each way.

' Thefe things being explained, though perhaps obfcurely, yet as
' clearly as I was able, I return to fhew what Pythagoras thought con-
' cerning the number of the days appertaining to the partus. Firft, he
' fays

' says there are in general two kinds of birth, the one lesser, of seven
' months, which comes forth from the womb on the two hundred
' and tenth day after conception ; the other greater, of nine months,
' which is delivered on the two hundred and seventy-fourth day.'
Censorinus then goes on to relate from Plato that in the work of
conception there are four periods, the first of six days, the second of
eight, which two numbers are the ratio of the diatessaron ; the
third of nine, which answers to the diapente, and the fourth, at
the end whereof the fœtus is formed, of twelve, answering to the
diapason in duple proportion.' After this he proceeds to declare
the relations of the above numbers in these words.

' These four numbers, six, eight, nine and twelve, being added
' together, make up thirty-five ; nor is the number six undeservedly
' deemed to relate to the birth, for the Greeks call it τικλεος, telelos,
' and we perfectum, because its three parts, a sixth, a third, and a
' half, that is one, two, three, make up itself ; but as the first stage
' in the conception is completed in this number six, so the former
' number thirty-five being multiplied by this latter six, the product is
' two hundred and ten, which is the number of days required to ma-
' turate the first kind of birth. As to the other or greater kind, it is
' contained under a greater number, namely seven, as indeed is also
' the whole of human life, as Solon writes : the practice of the Jews,
' and the ritual books of the Etruscans, seem likewise to indicate the
' predominancy of the number seven over the life of man ; and Hip-
' pocrates, and other physicians, in the diseases of the body account
' the seventh as a critical day ; therefore as the origin of the other
' birth is six days, so that of this greater birth is seven ; and as in
' the former the members of the infant are formed in thirty-five
' days, so here it is done in almost forty, and for this reason, forty
' days are a period very remarkable ; for instance, a pregnant woman
' did not go into the temple till after the fortieth day ; after the birth
' women are indisposed for forty days ; infants for the most part are
' in a morbid state for forty days ; these forty days, multiplied by the
' seven initial ones, make two hundred and eighty, or forty weeks :
' but because the birth comes forth on the first day of the fortieth
' week, six days are to be subtracted, which reduces the number of
' days to two hundred and seventy-four, which number very exactly
' corresponds to the quadrangular aspect of the Chaldeans ; for as the

' fun paffes through the zodiac in three hundred and fixty-five days
' and fome hours; if the fourth part of this number, namely ninety-
' one days and fome hours, be deducted therefrom, the remainder will
' be fomewhat fhort of two hundred and feventy-five days, by which
' time the fun will arrive at that place where the quadrature has an
' afpect to the beginning of conception. But let no man wonder
' how the human mind is able to difcover the fecrets of human na-
' ture in this refpect, for the frequent experience of phyficians
' enables them to do it.

' It is not to be doubted but that mufic has an effect on our birth;
' for whether it confifts in the voice or found only, as Socrates
' afferts, or, as Ariftoxenus fays, in the voice and the motion of the
' body, or of both thefe and the emotion of the mind, as Theophraf-
' tus thinks, it has certainly fomewhat in it of divine, and has a great
' influence on the mind. If it had not been grateful to the immor-
' tal Gods, fcenical games would never have been inftituted to appeafe
' them; neither would the tibiæ accompany our fupplications in the
' holy temples. Triumphs would not have been celebrated with the
' tibia; the cythara or lyre would not have been attributed to
' Apollo, nor the tibia, nor the reft of that kind of inftruments to
' the Mufes; neither would it have been permitted to thofe who play
' on the tibia, by whom the deities are appeafed, to exhibit public
' fhews or plays, and to eat in the Capitol, or during the leffer Quin-
' quatria *, that is on the ides of June; to range about the city, drunk,
' and difguifed in what garments they pleafed. Human minds, and
' thofe that are divine, though Epicurus cries out againft it, acknow-
' ledge their nature by fongs. Laftly, fymphony is made ufe of by
' the commanders of fhips to encourage the failors, and enable them
' to bear up under the labours and dangers of a voyage; and while
' the legions are engaged in battle the fear of death is difpelled by
' the trumpet; wherefore Pythagoras, that he might imbue his foul
' with its own divinity, before he went to fleep and after he awaked
' was accuftomed, as is reported, to fing to the cithara; and Afcle-
' piades the phyfician relieved the difturbed minds of frenetics by
' fymphony. Etophilos, a phyfician alfo, fays that the pulfes of the
' veins are moved by mufical rhythmi; fo that both the body and

* A feaft in honour of Minerva.

' the

' the mind are fubject to the power of harmony, and doubtlefs mufic
' is not a ftranger at our birth.

' To thefe things we may add what Pythagoras taught, namely,
' that this whole world was conftructed according to mufical ratio,
' and that the feven planets which move between the heavens and
' the earth, and predominate at the birth of mortals, have a rhyth-
' mical motion and diftances adapted to mufical intervals, and emit
' founds, every one different in proportion to its height, which
' founds are fo concordant as to produce a moft fweet melody, though
' inaudible to us by reafon of the greatnefs of the founds, which the
' narrow paffages of our ears are not capable of admitting.' Then
follows the paffage declaring the Pythagorean eftimate of the diftances of the planets and their fuppofed harmonical ratio, hereinbefore cited from him *.

Cenforinus concludes his Difcourfe on Mufic with faying that Pythagoras compared many other things which muficians treat of to the
other ftars, and demonftrated that the whole world is conftituted in
harmony. Agreeable to this he fays Dorylaus writes that this world
is the inftrument of God : and others, that as there are feven wandering planets, which have regular motions, that may fitly be refembled
to a dance †.

* See it in page 178, with a diagram.
† The general opinion of the learned in former ages, touching the harmony of the
fpheres, has been mentioned in a preceding page, but there appears a difpofition in the
modern philofophers to revive the notion. It feems that Dr. Gregory thought it well
founded ; and Mr. Maclaurin, in conformity with his opinion, Phil. Difcov. of Newton,
pag. 35, explains it thus : ' If we fhould fuppofe mufical chords extended from the fun to
' each planet ; that all thefe chords might become unifon, it would be requifite to en-
' creafe or diminifh their tenfions in the fame proportions as would be fufficient to render
' the gravities of the planets equal ; and from the fimilitude of thefe proportions the cele-
' brated doctrine of the harmony of the fpheres is fuppofed to have been derived.'
'The author of a book lately publifhed, entitled Principles and Power of Harmony, has
added his fuffrage in fupport of the opinion. ' Certain, fays he, as this harmonic coin-
' cidence is now become, till Sir Ifaac Newton demonftrated the laws of gravitation in
' relation to the planets, it muft have paffed for the dream of an Utopian philofopher.'
Pag. 146.
The fame author, pag. 145, agreeable to what Cenforinus above afferts, fays that ' there
' are traces of the harmonic principle fcattered up and down, fufficient to make us look
' on it as one of the great and reigning principles of the inanimate world.' Some of
thefe have hereinbefore been pointed out. Vide pag. 177, In not. To the inftances
there mentioned, the following may not improperly be added. The web of a fpider formed
of threads is of an hexangular figure, and each of the threads that divide the whole into
fix triangles, may be confidered as a beam intended to give firmnefs and ftability to the
fabric ; from one to the other of thefe beams the infect conducts lines in a parallel direc-

PORPHYRIUS, a very learned Greek philosopher, of the Platonic sect, and who wrote a commentary on the Harmonics of Ptolemy, lived about the end of the third century. His preceptors in philosophy were Plotinus and Amolius; he was a bitter enemy to the Christian religion, which perhaps is the reason why St. Jerome will have him to be a Jew; but Eunapius affirms that he was a native of Tyre, and that his true name was Malchus, which in the Syrian language signifies a king; and that Longinus the sophist, who taught him rhetoric, gave him the name of Porphyrius, in allusion to the purple usually worn by kings. Besides the Commentary on Ptolemy he wrote the lives of divers philosophers, of which only a fragment, containing the life of Pythagoras, is now remaining; a treatise of abstinence from flesh, an explication of the categories of Aristotle, and a treatise, containing fifteen books, against the Christian religion, which he once professed, as St. Augustine, Socrates, and others assert: this latter was answered by Methodius, bishop of Tyre, and afterwards by Eusebius. He died about the end of the reign of Dioclesian, and in 388 his books were burned.

With regard to his commentary, it is evidently imperfect; for whereas the treatise of Ptolemy is divided into three books, the second whereof contains fifteen chapters, Porphyry's commentary is continued no farther than to the end of chapter seven of that book, concluding with the series of sounds through each of the three genera. He seems to have been a virulent opposer of the Aristoxenians, and like his author adheres in general to the tenets of Pythagoras. Porphyry has given a description of the harmonic canon much more intelligible than that of Ptolemy, and has delineated it in the following form.

tion, which, supposing them to be ten in number, do, in consequence of their different lengths, constitute a perfect decachord. Kircher, who made this discovery, says, that were these lines or chords capable of sustaining a force sufficient to make them vibrate, it must necessarily follow from the ratio of their lengths, that between the sound of the outer and the innermost, the interval would be a diapason and semidisone; and that the rest of the chords, in proportion to their lengths, would produce the other consonances. Mufurg. tom. I. pag. 441.

By.

By which it appears that a chord A D, strained over the immoveable magades B and C, which are nothing more than two parallelograms, with a semicircular arch at the top of each, together with a movable bridge of the same form E, but somewhat higher, will be sufficient for the demonstration of the consonances, and this indeed is the representation which Dr. Wallis in his notes on Ptolemy has thought proper to give of it.

Dr. Wallis has contented himself with publishing a bare version of this author, without the addition of notes, except a few such short ones as he thought necessary to correct a vicious reading, or explain a difficult passage.

The works of the several authors above-named declare very fully the ancient Greek theory; their practice may in a great measure be judged of from the forms of the ancient instruments, and of these it may be thought necessary in this place to give some account.

The general division of musical instruments is into three classes, the pulsatile, tensile, and inflatile; and to this purpose Cardinal Bellarmine, in his Exposition of the CLth psalm, verse 3, says, ' Tria ' sunt instrumentorum genera, vox, flatus, et pulsus; omnium me- ' minit hoc loco propheta.'

Of the first are the drum, the sistrum, and bells. Of the second the lute, the harp, the clavicymbalum, and viols of all kinds. Of the third are the trumpet, flutes, and pipes, whether single or collected together, as in the organ.

And Kircher, in his Musurgia, preface to book VI. has this passage ' Omnia instrumenta musica ad tria genera, ut plurimum revocantur : ' Prioris generis dicuntur εγχορδα sive εντατα, quæ nervis, seu chordis ' constant quæque plectris, aut digitis in harmonicos motus incitantur, ' ut sunt Testudines, Psalteria, Lyræ, Sambucæ, Pandoræ, Barbita, ' Nablia, Pectides, Clavicymbala, aliaque hujus generis innumera. ' Secundi generis sunt εμφυσωμενα, πνευματικα, vel εμπνευσα, quæ inflata,

' feu

' feu fpiritu incitata fonum edunt ut Fiftulæ, Tibiæ, Cornua, Litui,
' Tubæ, Buccinæ; Claffica.   Tertii generis funt πνευσα, five pulfatilia
' uti funt Tympana, Siftra, Cymbala, Campanæ, &c.'

This divifion is adopted by a late writer, Francifcus Blanchinus of
Verona, in a very learned and curious differtation on the mufical inftruments of the ancients,* ; which upon the authority of ancient medals,
intaglias, bafs-reliefs, and other fculptures of great antiquity, exhibits
the forms of a great variety of mufical inftruments in ufe among the
ancient Greeks and Romans, many whereof are mentioned, or alluded
to, by the Latin poets in fuch terms as contain little left than a precife
defignation of their refpective forms.   He has deviated a little from
the order prefcribed by the above divifion of mufical inftruments into
claffes, by beginning with the inflatile fpecies inftead of the tenfile ;
neverthelefs his differtation is very curious and fatisfactory, and contains in it a detail to the following effect.

One of the moft fimple mufical inftruments of the ancients is the
Calamus paftoralis, made of an oaten reed ; it is mentioned by Virgil
and many others of the Latin poets, and by Martianus Capella.   See
the form of it plate I. fig. 1.

Other writers mention an inftrument of very great antiquity by the
name of Offea tibia, a pipe made of the leg-bone of a crane.   Fig. 2.

The Syringa or or pipe of Pan is defcribed by Virgil, and the ufe
of it by Lucretius, lib. V.

Et fupra calamos unco percurrere labro.

The figure of it occurs fo frequently in medals, that a particular defcription of it is unneceffary.   Fig. 3.

The Tibiæ pares, mentioned by Terence to have been played on,
the one with the right, and the other with the left hand, are di-
verfely reprefented in Merfennus De Inftrumentis harmonicis, pag. 7,
and in the Differtation of Blanchinus now citing ; in the former they
are yoked together towards the bottom, and at the top, as fig. 4.   In
the latter they are much flenderer, and are not joined. Fig. 5. †

* De tibus Generibus Inftrumentorum Muficæ veterum Organica, Differtatio ;
Romæ, 1742.

† The tibiæ of the ancients, and efpecially thofe mentioned in the titles of Terence's
comedies, have been the fubject of much learned enquiry.   Cafpar Bartholinus the ana-
tomift has written a whole volume De Tibiis Veterum. Ælius Donatus, a Latin grammarian, and the preceptor of St. Jerome, fays that the tone of the tibia dextra was grave,

and

Plate I to front page 341.

The author laſt mentioned ſpeaks alſo of other pipes, namely, the Tibia bifores, fig. 6, the Tibiæ gemine, fig. 7, inſtruments uſed in theatrical repreſentations; the latter of theſe ſeem to be the Tibiæ impares of Terence: he alſo deſcribes the Tibiæ utriculariæ, or bag-pipes, fig. 8, anciently the e·tertainment of ſhepherds and other ruſtics.

The Horn, fig. 9, was anciently uſed at funeral ſolemnities; it is alluded to by Statius, Theb. lib. VI.

The ancient Buccina or horn-trumpet, fig. 10, is mentioned by Ovid, Vegetius, Macrobius, and others.

The Tuba communis, ſeu recta, ſo called in contradiſtinction to the Tuba ductilis, is of very ancient original, it was formerly, as now, made of ſilver or braſs, of the form fig. 11. Blanchinus heſitates not to aſſert that the two trumpets of ſilver which God commanded Moſes to make in the wildernẜeſs were of this form *. It ſeems that the trumpet has retained this figure without the leaſt external diverſity, ſo low down at the year 1520; for in a very curious picture at Windſor, ſuppoſed to be of Mabuſe, repreſenting the interview between Ardres and Guiſnes, of Henry VIII. and Francis I. are trumpets preciſely correſponding in figure with the Tuba recta above referred to.

Of the inſtruments of the ſecond claſs, comprehending the tenſile ſpecies, the Monochord is the moſt ſimple. This inſtrument is mentioned by Ariſtides Quintilianus, and other ancient writers, but we have no authentic deſignation of it prior to the time of Ptolemy, it neverthelẜeſs is capable of ſo many forms, that any inſtrument of one ſtring only anſwers to the name; for which reaſon ſome have not ſcrupled to repreſent the monochord like the bow of Diana.

and adapted to the ſerious parts of the comedy; and that that of the tibiæ ſiniſtra, and alſo of the tibiæ ſarranz, or Tyrian pipes, was light and chearful. ' Dextræ tibiæ ſua gravitate
* ſeriam comediæ dictionem pronuneiabant. Siniſtræ et ſarranæ hoc eſt Tyriæ acuminis
* ſuavitate Jocum in comedia oſtendebant. Ubi autem dextrâ et ſiniſtrâ acta fabula in-
* ſcribebatur miſtim jocos et gravitatem denunciabat.' Donat. Fragm. de Traged. &
Comed.   The abbé du Bos ſays that this paſſage explains that other in Pliny, where it is
ſaid that the ancients to make left handed pipes, took the bottom of that very reed, the top
whereof they had before uſed for the right-handed.   The ſenſe of this paſſage is manifeſt;
but it does not ſtrictly agree with what Donatus ſays, unleſs it can be ſuppoſed that, contrary to the order of nature, the reeds were ſmall at bottom, and grew tapering upwards.

* ' Make thee two trumpets of ſilver; of an whole piece ſhalt thou make them, that thou
' mayeſt uſe them for the calling of the aſſembly, and for the journeying of the camps.'
Numbers, chap. x. verſe 2.

7

Figures

Figures 1, 2, plate II. are the Lyre of three and four chords, ascribed to Mercury by Nicomachus, Macrobius, Boetius, and a number of other writers, the forms whereof are here given from ancient sculptures in and about Rome, referred to by Blanchinus; as are also those fig. 3 and 4, representing the one a Lyre with seven chords, and the other one with nine.

Fig. 5. is the Lyre of Amphion, and 6. the plectrum, with which not only this, but every species of the lyre was struck, as may be collected from the following passage in Ovid.

Inflructamque fidem gemmis et dentibus Indis
Sustinet à lævâ : tenuit manus altera plectrum.
Artificis status ipse fuit, tum flamina docto
Pollice follicitat : quorum dulcedine captus
Pana jubet Tmolus citheræ submittere cannus.
　　　　　　　　　　　　　　　Met. lib. xi. l. 167. *

* It is very probable that the use of the bow, with which the viol species of instruments is founded, was borrowed from a practice of the ancients. Of the many kinds of lyre among them, it seems that they had one, in which the fingers of one hand were employed in stopping the strings, at the instant that they were stricken with a stick held in the other. Virgil intimates a practice somewhat like this in the following passage of the Æneid :

Nec non Thracius longa cum veste sacerdos
Obloquitur numeris septem discrimina vocum :
Jamque eadem digitis, jam pectine pulsat eburno.
　　　　　　　　　　　　　　Lib. VI. l. 645.

The Thracian bard, surrounded by the rest,
There stands conspicuous in his flowing vest,
His flying fingers, and harmonious quill,
Strike sev'n distinguish'd notes, and sev'n at once they fill.
　　　　　　　　　　Dryden's translation, book VI. l. 877.

From which it at least appears, that the instrument was placed in a horizontal position, and that the strings were struck, not by the fingers, but with a plectrum, which might be a quill or a bow, or almost any other thing fit for the purpose.

Plato, in his treatise De Legibus VII. 791. Ed. Serr. advises to train up children to use the right and the left hand indifferently. In some things, says he, we can do it very well, as when we use the lyre with the left hand and the stick with the right. Dr. Jortin says it may be collected from this, that the fingers of the left hand were occupied in some manner upon the strings, else barely to hold a lyre shewed no very free use of the left hand ; and it appears from Ptolemy, II. 12, that they used both hands at once in playing upon the lyre, and that the fingers of the left were employed, not in stopping, but in striking the string.

But see the figure of an ancient statue, representing Apollo playing on the lyre, fig. 10, plate III. which seems very clearly to evince the practice above spoken of.

Upon this relic of antiquity, a drawing whereof was found in the collection of the late Mr. N. Haym, it is observable that the lyre is of a form very nearly resembling the violin,

346 a

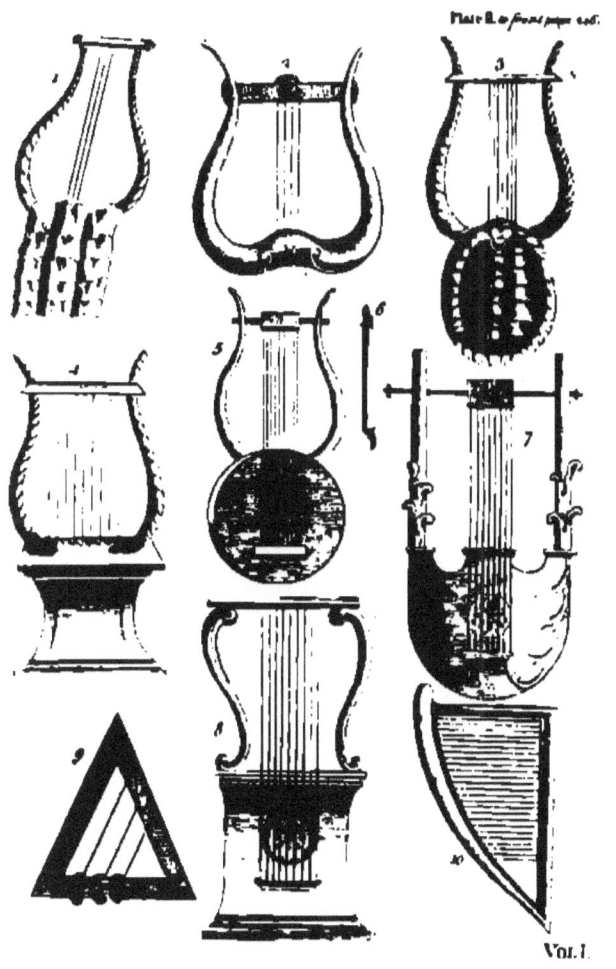

Plate II. to front page 246.

Vol. I.

Fig. 7 and 8 are other forms of the Lyre in a state of improvement.
Fig. 1 and 2, plate III. are two different representations of the Lyra triplex, the one from Blanchinus, the other from a writer of far less respectable authority; concerning this instrument it is necessary to be somewhat particular.

Athenæus, lib. XIV. cap. xv. describes an instrument of a very singular construction, being a lyre in the form of a tripod, an invention as it is said of Pythagoras Zacynthius. This person is mentioned by Aristoxenus, in his Elements, page 36; and Meibomius, in a note on the passage, says, on the authority of Diogenes Laertius, that he was the author of Arcana Philosophiæ, and adds, that it was from him that the proverbial saying, ipse dixit, had its rise; with respect to the instrument, it is exhibited, plate III. in two forms, the first taken from a sarcophagus at Rome, referred to by Blanchinus, the other from an engraving in the Histoire de la Musique of Monsieur de Blainville, for which it is to be suspected he had no other authority than the bare verbal description of Athenæus, who has said, that it comprehended three distinct sets of chords, adjusted to the three most ancient of the modes, the Dorian, the Phrygian, and the Lydian.

The Trigon, an instrument mentioned by Nicomachus, among those which were adjusted by Pythagoras, after he had discovered and settled the ratios of the consonances. It was used at feasts, and it is said, was played on by women, and struck either with a quill, or beaten with little rods of different lengths and weights, to occasion a diversity in the sounds. The figure 9, plate II. is taken from an ancient Roman anaglyph, mentioned by Blanchinus. Fig. 10. is also a Trigon, described by the same author; fig. 9, plate III. is the reverse of an ancient medal, and shews the manner of playing on it.

The Cymbals of Bacchus, plate III. fig. 3. were two small brass vessels, somewhat in the form of a shield, which being struck together by the hands, gave a sound. The well-known statue of the dancing faun has one of these in each hand.

violin, as having a body, and also a neck, which is held in the left hand; the instrument in the right, undoubtedly answers to the modern bow, with this difference, that its use was percussion and not friction, which latter is a modern and noble improvement; the position of the instrument deserves to be remarked, as it corresponds exactly with the viol di braccio.

The

The Tympanum leve, fig. 4, an inftrument yet known by the name of the Tambouret, and frequently ufed in dancing, was alfo ufed to fing to ; it is diftinguifhed by Catullus, Ovid, Suetonius, St. Auguftine, and Ifidore of Sevil, from the great brazen drum, properly fo called, this abovementioned, was covered with the fkin of fome animal, and was ftruck, either with a fhort twig or with the hand; as fig. 5, plate III.

Crotals, fig. 6. Thefe were inftruments alfo of the pulfatile kind. The Crotalum was made of a reed, divided into two by a flit from the top, extending half way downwards : the fides thus divided being ftruck one againft the other with different motions of the hands, produced a found like that which the ftork makes with her bill, wherefore the ancients gave that bird the epithet of Crotaliftria, i. e. Player upon the Crotalum *; and Ariftophanes calls a great talker a Crotalum.

Mention is made by fome writers on mufic, of an inftrument of forty chords, called, from the name of its inventor, the Epi-

* Paufanias relates, that Hercules did not kill the ftymphalides with his arrows, but that he frighted, and drove them away with the noife of the crotala, the confequence whereof, fuppofing the relation to be true, is, that the crotalum muft be a very ancient inftrument. Ovid joins the crotalum with the cymbals.

Cymbala cum crotalis prurientifque arma Priapo
Ponit, et adducit tympana pulfa manu.

It appears by an ancient poem, entitled Copa, by fome aferibed to Virgil, that thofe who played with the crotala danced at the fame time. It further appears, that in thefe dances, which were chiefly of women, fuch a variety of wanton gefticulations and indecent attitudes and poftures were practifed, that Clemens Alexandrinus fays, that the ufe of thefe inftruments ought to be banifhed from the feftivals of all chriftians. And the fame might have been faid of the cymbals. See figures 7, 8, plate III.

Some authors refemble the crotala to the caftanets of the Spaniards, or perhaps of the Moors; for caftanets are fuppofed to be of Moorifh invention; but of thefe the crumata of the ancients feem more nearly to approach. Thefe were made of bones, or the fhells of fifh. Scaliger obferves, upon the abovementioned poem, that they were very common among the Spaniards, efpecially the inhabitants of the province of Bætica [Andalufia] about Cadiz, to which Martial alludes.

Nec de Gadibus improbis puellæ
Vibrabunt fine fine prurientes
Lafcivos docili tremore lumbos.   Lib. V. epigr. lxxii.

The fame poet elfewhere fpeaks of the crumata in thefe words,

Edere lafcivos ad Bætica crufmata geftus,
Ed Gaditanis ludere docta modis.   Lib. VI. epigr. lxxi.

From which two paffages, it appears clearly, that the above cenfure of Clemens Alexandrinus was well grounded.

gonium.

Plate II.to from page xxl.

gonium. Epigonius was a native of Ambracia, a city of Epirus, and a citizen of Sicyon, a town of Peloponnesus. He is mentioned together with Lasus Hermionenfis, by Ariftoxenus, in his Elements, pag. 3. And Porphyry makes him the head of one of those many fects of muficians that formerly fubfifted, giving him the priority even of Ariftoxenus, in thefe words. ' There were many fects, fome ' indeed before Ariftoxenus, as the Epigonians, Damonians, Erato-' cleans, Agenorians, and fome others; which he himfelf, makes ' mention of; but there were fome after him, which others have ' defcribed, as the Archeftratians, Agonians, Philifcians, and Her-' mippians.'

Julius Pollux, in his Onomafticum, lib. IV. cap. ix. fpeaking of the inftruments invented by certain nations, fays, that the Epigonium obtained its name from Epigonius, who was the firft that ftruck the chords of mufical inftruments without a plectrum *. The fame author adds, that the Epigonium had forty chords, as the Simicum had thirty-five. Athenæus, lib. IV. fpeaks to the fame purpofe.

As to the Simicum, nothing more is known about it, than that it contained thirty-five chords. Vincentio Galilei, with good reafon, fuppofes it to be fomewhat more ancient than the epigonium. Of both thefe inftruments he has ventured to give a reprefentation, in his dialogue on ancient and modern mufic; but it is very much to be doubted, whether he had any authority from antiquity for fo doing. The form which he has affigned them feverally, refembles nearly that of an upright harpfichord, which feems to indicate, that when played on, it was held between the legs of the mufician, different perhaps from the harp, with the grave chords near and the acute remote from him.

The foregoing account comprehends the principal inftruments in ufe among the ancient Greeks and Romans, fo far as the refearches of learned and inquifitive men have fucceeded in their attempts to

* Plutarch in his dialogue before cited, relates that Olympus introduced the plectrum into Greece, which it is fuppofed was then deemed a ufeful invention. Certainly the lyre was originally touched by the fingers, and all that can be meant here, is, that Epigonius recurred to the primitive method, and played on his inftrument, as the harp is now played on with the fingers; between which, and the touch of a plectrum or quill, the difference is very wide, as may be difcovered by a comparifon of the lute or harp with the harpfichord.

recover them; their forms seem to be thereby ascertained beyond the possibility of a doubt, and these it may be said, declare the state of the ancient musical practice, much more satisfactorily than all the hyperbolical relations extant, of its efficacy and influence over the human passions; and leave it an unquestionable fact, that the discoveries of Pythagoras, and the improvements made by the Greeks, his successors, terminated in a theory, admirable in speculation it is true, but to which such instruments were adapted, as would have disgraced any performance, even in the least enlightened period, since the invention of that species of harmony, which has been the delight of later ages.

A

GENERAL HISTORY

OF THE

SCIENCE and PRACTICE

OF

M U S I C.

BOOK III. CHAP. I.

THE gradual declenfion of learning which had begun before
the time of Porphyry, the laft of the Greek mufical writers,
and above all, the ravages of war, and the then embroiled ftate
of the whole civilized world, put an end to all farther improvements in the fcience of harmonics; nor do we find, that after
this time it was made a fubject of philofophical enquiry: the
fucceeding writers were chiefly Latins, who, as they were for
the moft part followers of the Greeks, contributed but very little to
its advancement; and, for reafons which will hereafter be given,
the cultivation of mufic became the care of the clergy; an order of
men, in whom the little of learning then left, in a few ages after
the eftablifhment of chriftianity centered.

But before we proceed farther to trace the progrefs of the fcience,
it is proper to remark, that the writings of the Greeks not only
leave us in great uncertainty as to the ftate of mufic in other countries, but that they do not exclude the poffibility of its having
arrived at a great degree of perfection, even before that difcovery of
the confonances, which is by all of them allowed to be the very bafis
of the Greek fyftem. For let it be remembered, that Pythagoras is
fuppofed to have lived fo late as A. M. 3384, which is about 560
years before the birth of Chrift; and that long before his time, fuch

Kk 2   effects

Admitting as a fact, that Egypt, in the infancy of the world, was as well the feat of learning as of empire; and admitting also, the learning of the Perſian Magi, the Indian Brachmans, and other people of the Eaſt; not to mention the Phœnicians and the Chineſe, to be as great as ſome pretend, who have magnified it to a degree that exceeds the bounds of moderate credulity; nevertheleſs, the more ſober reſearchers into antiquity, have contented themſelves with a retroſpect limited by the time, when philoſophy began to flouriſh in Greece; and it is only on the writers of that country that we can depend.

An inveſtigation of the Jewiſh theory would be a fruitleſs attempt, but of their practice we are enabled to form ſome judgment, by the ſeveral paſſages in the Old Teſtament that declare the names and number of the Hebrew inſtruments, and mention the frequent uſe of them in ſacrifices, and other religious ſolemnities; but it is to be obſerved, that the correſpondence of the names of their inſtruments, with the names of thoſe in uſe in modern times, is a circumſtance from which no argument in their favour can be drawn, for a reaſon herein before given.

Merſennus, and after him Kircher, whoſe elaborate reſearches into the more abſtruſe parts of ancient literature, render him in ſome particulars a reſpectable authority, have exhibited the forms of many of the ancient Jewiſh muſical inſtruments: the latter of theſe authors profeſſes to have gone to the fountain head for his intelligence, and the reſult of ſo attentive peruſal of as many of the Rabbinical writers and commentators on the Talmud as he could lay his hands on he has given to the public in the Muſurgia, tom. I. pag. 47. How far the authorities adduced by him will warrant ſuch a preciſe deſignation of their reſpective forms, as verges in ſome inſtances too near our own times, is left to the deciſion of thoſe who ſhall have curioſity enough to peruſe them; but left it ſhould be ſaid that the ſubject is too important to be paſſed over in ſilence, the ſubſtance of what he has delivered on this head is here given.

He ſays that the author of a treatiſe entitled Schilte Haggiborim,. i. e. the Shield of the Mighty, who he elſewhere makes to be Rabbi Hannaſe, treats very accurately on the muſical inſtruments of the Hebrews, and reckons that they were thirty-ſix in number, and of the pulſatile kind, and that David was ſkilled in the uſe of them all.

Kircher

Kircher however does not seem to acquiesce altogether in the first of these opinions, for he proceeds to a description de instrumentis Hebreorum Polychordis sive Neghinoth; these it seems, according to his author above-named, were of wood, long and round, consisting of three strings made of the intestines of beasts; the instruments had holes bored underneath them; and, to make them sound, the strings were rubbed with a bow compofed of the hairs of a horfe's tail, well extended and compacted together. Kircher fpeaks particularly of the Pfaltery, or Nablium, the Cythara, or, which is the fame thing, the Affur, Nevel, Chinnor, the Machul, and the Minnin. He fays that no one has rightly defcribed the Pfaltery of David, and that fome have thought that the word rather denoted certain genera of harmony, or modulations of the voice, than any kind of inftrument: that according to Jofephus it had twelve founds, and was played on with the fingers; that Hilarius, Didymus, Bafilius, and Euthymius call it the ftraiteft of all mufical inftruments—that Auguftine fays it was carried in the hand of the player, and had a fhell or concave piece of wood on it that caufed the ftrings to refound—that Hieronymus defcribes this inftrument as having ten ftrings, and refembling in its form a fquare fhield—that Hilarius will have it to be the fame with the Nablium. Kircher himfelf is certain that it was a ftringed inftrument, and cites Suidas to prove that the word Pfalterium is derived from Pfallo, to ftrike the chords with the ends of the fingers. He farther fays, that many writers fuppofe it to have had a triangular form, and to refemble the harp of David, as commonly painted in pictures of him; and that fome are exprefs in the opinion that the Pfalterium and the Nablium, as being ftruck with the fingers of both hands, were one and the fame inftrument; and to this purpofe he cites the following paffage from Ovid.

Difce etiam duplici genialia Naulia palmâ
Verrere: conveniunt dulcibus illa modis.

ART. AMAT. lib. III. l. 327.

The Nevel, notwithftanding the refemblance between its name and that of the Nablium, and the confufion which Kircher has created by ufing them promifcuoufly, clearly appears to have been a different inftrument; for he fays it was in the form of a trapezium; and the Nablium, which he has taken great pains to prove to be the

fame

2542

Plate IV. to front page 357.

same with the Pſalterium, he ſhews to have been of a ſquare form. Of the Aſſur, he only ſays that it had ten chords; the Chinnor he ſuppoſes to have had thirty-two, the Machul ſix, and the Minnin three or four; and that in their form they reſembled, the one the Viol and the other the Chelys. To give a clearer idea, he has exhibited, from an old book in the Vatican library, ſeveral figures repreſenting the Pſalterium, plate IV. fig. 1; the Chinnor, fig. 2, the Machul, fig. 3, the Minnin fig. 4, and the Nevel, fig. 5 [a].

Kircher ſpeaks alſo of another inſtrument mentioned by Rabbi Hannaſe, who it ſeems was the author of the book before cited, Schilte Haggiboriim, and alſo in the Targum, called Haghniugab, conſiſting of ſix ſtrings, and reſembling the greater Chelys or Viol di Gamba, differing from it only in the number of its chords: he ſays it is often confounded with the Machul.

He next proceeds to treat of the pulſatile inſtruments of the Hebrews, in contradiſtinction to thoſe of the fidicinal or ſtringed kind, and firſt he ſpeaks of the Thoph or Tympanum, plate IV. fig. 6, an inſtrument of Egyptian original, and uſed by the prieſts of that country in their public worſhip. He relates on the authority of Rabbi Hannaſe that it had the likeneſs of a ſhip; and that by the Greeks it was alſo called Cymbalum, from cymba a boat: he adds that it was covered with the ſkin of an animal, and was beat on with a peſtle or rod of iron or braſs.

He proceeds to ſay that though the Machul is ranked among the fidicinal or ſtringed inſtruments, this name was given to an inſtrument of a very different form, and of the pulſatile kind; nay, he adds that Rabbi Hannaſe aſſerts that it was preciſely the ſame with the Siſtrum of the Egyptians, or the Krouſma of the Greeks; and that it was of a circular form, made of iron, braſs, ſilver, or gold, with little bells hung round it. Kircher corrects this deſcription, and inſtead of little bells, ſuppoſes a number of iron rings, ſtrung as it were on a rod or bar in a lateral poſition that went acroſs the circle. He ſays that a handle was affixed to it, by means whereof the in-

[a] The truth of this repreſentation, ſo far as it relates to the Machul and Minnin, is ſtrongly to be ſuſpected; they both ſeem to require the aid of the hair bow, a kind of plectrum to which the ancients ſeem to have been abſolute ſtrangers. Beſides their near reſemblance to the lute and viol, inſtruments which it is ſuppoſed had their origin in Provence, is a ſtrong argument againſt their antiquity.

ſtrument

ftrument was flung backwards and forwards, and emitted a kind of melancholy murmur, arifing from the collifion of the rings, as well againſt each other as againſt the fides, the circle, and the bar on which they moved, plate IV. fig. 7. He adds, that the Thoph, or rather Siſtrum of the Hebrews was thus conſtructed, and that the virgins every where made ufe of it in the dances of the Siſtri, as we read in the books of Exodus and Judges, that Mary the fiſter of Mofes, and the daughter of Jeptha did: and he farther fays, that according to accounts which he has received from credible witneffes, the Syrians in his time preferved the ufe of the Siſtrum in Paleſtine *.

Gneu Berufim was another of the Hebrew pulfatile inſtruments; it feems by Kircher that there was fome controverfy about the form of it, but that Rabbi Hannafe reprefents it as nothing more than a piece of fir in ſhape like a mortar. He fays there belonged to it a peſtle of the fame wood, with a knob at each end, and in the middle thereof a place for the hand to grafp it : that thofe that beat on the inſtrument held it in the left hand and ſtruck with the right on the edge and in the middle, ufing the knobs alternately. Plate IV. fig. 9, 10. Kircher compares this inſtrument to the Crotalum above defcribed, but feemingly with little propriety; and to the Gnaccari of the Italians, of which word, confidered as a technical term, it is hard to find the meaning.

Minagnhinim was the name of another of the Hebrew pulfatile inſtruments, which, according to Rabbi Hannafe, was a certain fquare table of wood, having a handle fo fitted as conveniently to be held by it. On the table were balls of wood or brafs, through which was put either an iron chain or an hempen chord, and this was ſtretched from the bottom to the top of the table. When the inſtrument was ſhook, the ſtriking of the balls occafioned a very clear found, which might be heard at a great diſtance. See the reprefentation which Kircher gives of it, plate V. fig. 1.

Magraphe Tamid, another of the pulfatile inſtruments of the Hebrews, is conjectured by Kircher to have been ufed for convoking the prieſts and Levites together in the temple : it is faid to have emitted

---

* The invention of the Siſtrum is not to be afcribed to the Jews: it is generally fuppofed to be of Egyptian original. There are fome forms of it, as that in particular, plate IV, fig. 8, which bears on it a figure of one of thofe many brute animals to which this fuperſtitious and idolatrous people paid divine honours.

a pro-

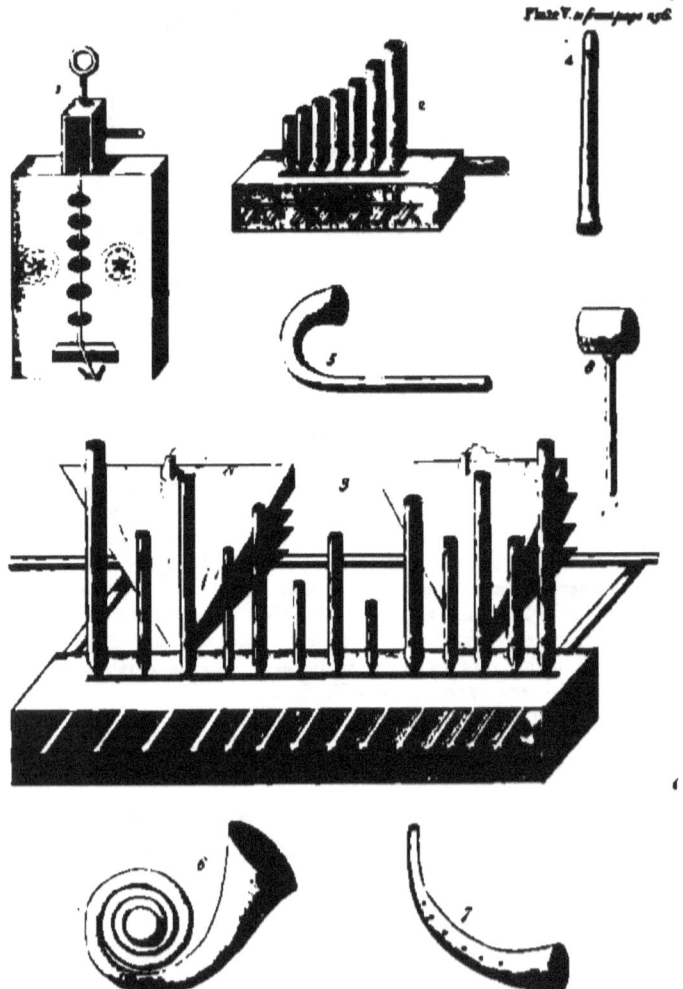

Plate V. to front page 156

prodigious found ; and though Rabbi Hannafe fays no one can deſcribe the form of it, Kircher thinks it muſt have been like one of our largeſt bells.

We are now to declare what inſtruments of the pneumatic kind were in uſe amongſt the ancient Hebrews ; and firſt we meet with the Maſrakitha, which conſiſted of pipes of various ſizes, fitted into a kind of wooden cheſt, open at the top, but at the bottom ſtopped with wood covered with a ſkin ; by means of a pipe fixed to the cheſt, wind was conveyed into it from the lips : the pipes were of lengths proportioned muſically to each other, and the melody was varied at pleaſure by the ſtopping and unſtopping with the fingers the apertures at the upper extremity. Kircher thinks it differed but little from the inſtrument which Pan is conſtantly repreſented as playing on ; there ſeems however to be a difference in the manner of uſing it. See it plate V. fig. 2.

Of the Sampunia, derived, as Kircher conjectures, from the Greek Symphonia, as alſo of the preceding inſtrument, mention is made, as Kircher aſſerts, in the Chaldaic of the book of Daniel, chap. iii. He ſays alſo that it is deſcribed in the Schilte Haggiborim, as conſiſting of a round belly, made of the ſkin of a ram or wether, into which two pipes were inſerted, one to fill the belly with wind, the other to emit the ſound ; the lower pipe had holes in it, and was played on by the fingers. In ſhort, it ſeems to have been neither more nor leſs than the Cornamuſa, or common bag-pipe ; and Kircher ſays that in Italy, even in his days, it was known by the name of the Zampugna.

The Hebrews had alſo an inſtrument, deſcribed in the Schilte Haggiborim, called Macraphe d'Aruchin, conſiſting of ſeveral orders of pipes, which were ſupplied with wind by means of bellows ; it had keys, and would at this time without heſitation be called an organ. Plate V. fig. 3*.

Of Fiſtulæ it ſeems the Hebrews had ſundry kinds ; they were chiefly the horns or bones of animals, ſtrait or contorted, as nature

* This inſtrument is delineated by Kircher, but the figure of h above referred to, is taken from the Muſica Hiſtorica of Wolfgang Gaſpar Printz, written in the German language, and printed at Dreſden in 4to. anno 1690, who cites the Collectanea Philologica of Johannes Schüterus, to juſtify his deviations from Kircher, in the form of ſome of the inſtruments deſcribed in the Muſurgia. But it is to be feared, that his author has erred in giving to the Machul and Minnin above deſcribed, the hair-bow, of which not the leaſt trace is to be found in the writings of any of the ancients.

fashioned them : the representations of sundry kinds of them, in figures 4, 5, 6, 7, plate V. are taken from Kircher.

In the account which Blanchinus has given of the Jewish musical instruments, he mentions a mallet of wood used by them in their worship, and which at certain times is beaten by the people on the beams, seats, and other parts of the synagogue, in commemoration of the tumult preceding the Crucifixion, or, as the modern Jews say, at the hanging of Haman, plate V. fig. 8. Instruments of this kind, and which produce noise rather than sound, are improperly classed among instruments of music.

Of the Hebrew musicians no very satisfactory account can be given. This of Kircher, extracted from the Rabbinical writers, is, perhaps, the best that can be expected ' Asaph, according to the ' opinion of the interpreters, was the composer of certain psalms ; ' he is said also to have been a singer, and to have sung to the cym- ' bals of brass, and to have praised the Lord, and ministred in the ' sight of the ark.

' Eman Ezraita, the singer, the son of Joel, of the children of ' Caath, was most skilful in the cymbal, and was in a manner ' equal in knowledge and wisdom to Ethan ; he is the supposed ' author of the Psalm, beginning Domine Deus salutis meæ, which, ' because he gave it to be sung by the sons of Coreh, he inscribed ' both with his own and their name.

' Ethan of Ezrachus, the son of Assaia, the son of Merari, played ' on the brass cymbal, and was endued with so much wisdom, that, ' according to the Book of Kings, no mortal, except Solomon, was ' wiser. The three sons of Coreh, Asir, Elcana, and Abiasaph, ' were famous singers and composers of Psalms.'

' Idithus was an excellent singer, and player on the cythara. ' many confound him with Orpheus.' Kircher supposes, that he and the other Hebrew musicians were inspired with the knowledge of vocal and instrumental music, and that their performance was equal to their skill. He says, he doubts not but that there were many other men, especially in the time of king Solomon, who were well skilled in divine music, for that the most excellent music was fittest for the wisest of mortals, and that of the Hebrews must have been more efficacious in exciting the affections than that of the Greeks, or of later times, but of what kind in particular it was,

and

and by what characters expressed, he says, its antiquity prevents us
from knowing [*].

A much later writer than him above cited, and who is now living,
Giambatista Martini, of Bologna, has entered very deeply into the
music of the Hebrews; and it were to be wished, that he had been
able to give a more satisfactory account of it than is to be found in
his very learned work, the Storia Musica, now publishing, but of
which, as yet [in this year 1771] the public are in possession of
only one volume. Having few other sources of intelligence than the
Talmud, and the writings of the Rabbins, we are not to expect
much information in this particular.

C H A P. II.

FROM accounts so vague, and so abounding with conjectures
as are given of the ancient Hebrew music and musicians, and
more especially of their instruments, even by writers of the best
authority, it is very difficult to collect any thing whereon an
inquisitive mind may rest. With regard to the Hebrew instruments, it is evident from the accounts of Kircher, and others,
that some of them approach so nearly to the form of those of
more modern times, as to give reason to suspect the authenticity
of the representation: others appear to have been so very inartifi-

[*] The confusion of Idithus with Orpheus, suggests a remark on the endeavours of
some, to establish the identity of eminent persons of different names and countries, and
perhaps of different ages, upon hardly any other ground, than some one particular in their
history common to them both; how far it is possible to extend an hypothesis of this kind,
the present bishop of Gloucester has shewn in his Divine Legation of Moses. In the course
of that work, the author has thought it necessary to controvert an assertion of Sir Isaac
Newton; namely, that Osiris and Sesostris, both kings of Egypt, were one and the same
person; in order to do this, he, has undertaken to prove, that the British king Arthur
and William the Conqueror were not two distinct beings, but identically one person;
and, as far as the method of reasoning usual in such kind of arguments will serve him, he
has established his proposition.

The conclusion from this correspondence of such a variety of circumstances, is much
stronger in favour of the identity of Arthur and William, than could have been imagined,
and yet, it has no other effect on the mind, than to discredit this method of reasoning,
which is fraught with fallacy, and must terminate in scepticism.

What then can we say to the opinion of those, who confound the Hebrew musician
Idithus with the ancient Orpheus; what rather can we think of him, who has attempted
to shew that this latter, and the royal prophet David, were one and the same person. See
the Life of David, by Dr. Delany.

cially

cially conftructed, that we fcarce credit the relation, given of their effects. It is clear, that Kircher and Schütterus had from the Rabbinical writers little more than the bare names of many of the inftruments defcribed by them; yet, have they both, in fome inftances, ventured to reprefent them by forms of a comparatively late invention. Who does not fee, that the Minnin, as reprefented by the former, and the lute, are one and the fame inftrument? and what difference can be difcerned between the Machul and the Spanifh Guitar? or can we believe, that the Macraphe d' Aruchin, and fuch rude effays towards melody as the Gnets Berufim, the Siftrum, or the Minagnghinim, could fubfift among the fame people, in any given period of civilization?

As to Martini's account, it fpeaks for itfelf; it is extracted from the facred writings, which, at this diftance of time, even with the affiftance of the moft learned comments, fall fhort of affording that fatisfaction, which is to be wifhed for in an enquiry of this kind.

Under thefe difadvantages, which even an enquiry into the inftruments of the Hebrews lies under, an attempt to explain their mufical theory muft feem hopelefs. Nor is it poffible to conceive any thing like a fyftem, to which foch inftruments as the Thoph, or the Gnets Berufim could be adapted: if the ftrokes of a peftle againft a mortar, like thofe of the latter, be reducible to meafure; yet, furely the rattling of a chain, like the mufic of the Minagnghinim, is not; or what if they were, would the founds produced in either cafe make mufic? To fpeak freely on this matter, whatever advantages this people might derive from the inftructions of an infpired lawgiver, and the occafional interpofitions of the Almighty, it no where appears that their attainments in literature were very great: or that they excelled in any of thofe arts that attend the refinement of human manners; the figure they made among the neighbouring nations appears to have been very inconfiderable; and with refpect to their mufic, there is but too much reafon to fuppofe it was very barbarous. The only hiftorical relation that feems to ftand in the way of this opinion, is, that the effects wrought by the mufic of David, on the mind of Saul, a man of a haughty irafcible temper, not eafily fufceptible of the emotions of pity or complacency, and, at the time when David exercifed his art on him, under the power of a demon, or, at beft, in a frenzy.

Kircher

Kircher has taken upon him to relate the whole procefs of the difpoffeffion of Saul, by David, and has done it as circumftantially as if he had been prefent at the time; his reafoning is very curious, and it is here given in his own words.

'That we may be the better able to refolve this queftion, how 'David freed Saul from the evil fpirit, I fhall firft quote the words 'of the Holy Scripture, as found in the firft book of Samuel, 'chap. xvi. ver. 23.' "And it came to pafs when the evil fpirit from "God was upon Saul, that David took an harp, and played with his "hand: fo Saul was refrefhed, and was well, and the evil fpirit "departed from him." 'The paffage in the holy text informs 'us very clearly, that the evil fpirit, whatfoever it was, was driven 'away by mufic; but how that came to pafs is differently ex-'plained. The Rabbins on this place fay, that when David cured 'Saul, he played on a cythara of ten ftrings; they fay alfo, that 'David knew that ftar, by which it was neceffary the mufic fhould 'be regulated, in order to effed the cure: thus Rabbi Abenezra. 'But Picus of Mirandola fays, that mufic fets the fpirits in motion, 'and thereby produces the like effects on the mind, as a medicine 'does on the body; from whence it may feem, that the comment 'of Abenezra, is vain and trifling, and that David regarded not the 'afpects of the ftars; but trufting to the power of his inftrument, 'ftruck it with his hand as his fancy fuggefted.

'And we, rejecting fuch aftrological fictions, affert, that David 'freed Saul, not with herbs, potions, or other medicaments, as 'fome maintain, but by the fole force and efficacy of mufic. In 'order to demonftrate which, let it be obferved, that thofe appli-'cations which unlock the pores, remove obftructions, difpel va-'pours and chear the heart, are beft calculated to cure madnefs, 'and allay the fury of the mind; now mufic produces thefe effects, 'for as it confifts in founds, generated by the motion of the air, it 'follows that it will attenuate the fpirits, which by that motion 'are rendered warmer, and more quick in their action, and fo diffi-'pate at length the melancholy humour. On the contrary, where it 'is neceffary to relax the fpirits, and prevent the wounding or af-'fecting the membranes of the brain; in that cafe, it is proper to 'ufe flow progreffions of found, that thofe fpirits and biting vapours, 'which afcend thither from the ftomach, fpleen, and hypocondria,

'may

' may be quietly difmiffed.   Therefore, the mufic of David might
' appeafe Saul, in either of thefe two ways of attenuation or difmif-
' fion : by the one, he might have expelled the melancholy from
' the cells of the brain, or he might by the other have diffolved it,
' and fent it off in thin vapours, by infenfible perfpiration.   In either
' cafe, when the melancholy had left him, he could not be mad
' until the return of it, be being terreftrial, and as it were, deftitute
' of action, unlefs moved thereto by the vital fpirits, which had
' led him here and there ; but they had left him, when for the fake
' of the harmony they had flown to the ears, abandoning, as I may
' fay, their rule over him.   And though, upon the ceffation of the
' harmony they might return, yet, the patient having been elevated,
' and rendered chearful, the melancholy might have acquired a
' more favourable habit.   From all which, it is manifeft, that this
' effect proceeded not from any cafual found of the cythara, but
' from the great art and excellent fkill of David in playing on it ;
' for, as he had a confummate and penetrating judgment, and was
' always in the prefence of Saul, as being his armour-bearer, he
' muft have been perfectly acquainted with the inclination and bent
' of his mind, and to what paffions it was moft fubject : hence,
' without doubt, be being enabled, not fo much by his own fkill,
' as impelled by a divine inftinct, knew fo dexteroufly, and with
' founds fuited to the humour and diftemper of the king, to touch
' the cythara, or indeed any other inftrument; for, as has been
' mentioned, he was fkilled in the ufe of no fewer than thirty-fix,
' of different kinds.   It might be, that at the inftant we are fpeak-
' ing of, he recited fome certain rhythmi, proper for his purpofe,
' and which Saul might delight to hear; or, that by the power of
' metrical dancing, joined to the melody of the inftrument, he
' wrought this effect : for Saul was apt to be affected in this man-
' ner, by the mufic and dancing of his armour-bearer ; as he was a
' youth of a very beautiful afpect, thefe roufed up the fpirits, and
' the words, which were rhythmically joined to the harmony, tick-
' ling the hearing, lifted up the mind, as from a dark prifon, into
' the high region of light, whereby the gloomy fpirits which op-
' preffed the heart were diffipated, and room was left for it to dilate
' itfelf, which dilatation was naturally followed by tranquility and
' gladnefs.'   Mufurgia, tom. II. pag. 214, et feq.

Whoever

Whoever will be at the pains of turning to the original from whence this very circumstantial relation is taken, will think it hardly possible for any one to compress more nonsense into an equal number of words than this passage contains, for which no better apology can be made than that Kircher, though a man of great learning, boundless curiosity, and indefatigable industry, was less happy in forming conclusions than in relating facts; his talents were calculated for the attainment of knowledge, but they did not qualify him for disquisition; in short he was no reasoner. With regard to the dispossession of Saul, supposing music to have been in any great degree of perfection among the Hebrews in his time, there is nothing incredible in it; and besides it has the evidence of sacred history to support it: it would therefore have argued more wisdom in the jesuit to have admitted the fact, without pretending to account for it, than by so ridiculous a theory as he has endeavoured to establish, to render the narration itself doubtful.

After this censure above passed on the music of the Hebrews, it would argue an unreasonable prejudice against them, were it not admitted that their poetry carries with it the signatures of a most exalted sublimity: to select instances from the prophets might be deemed unfair, as there are good reasons to believe that something more than mere human genius dictated those very energetic compositions; but if we look into those of their writings which the canon of our church has not adopted, we shall find great reason to admire their poetical abilities. It is true that the boldness of their figures, and those abrupt transitions, which distinguish the oriental compositions from those of most other countries, are not so well relished by a people with whom the false refinements on life and manners have taken place of the original simplicity of nature; but in the more regular and less enthusiastic spirit of expression, we feel and admire their excellence. Not to mention the numberless instances of this sort that occur in the Psalms, there is one poem among them, which for its truly elegiac simplicity, pathetic expression of the woes of captivity, and the lamentations for the sufferings of an afflicted people, has perhaps not its fellow in any of the dead or living languages. The poem here meant is the CXXXVIIth Psalm.

From the manner in which it appears the ancients treated music, we may observe that they reasoned very abstractedly about it; the
measure

meafure of intervals, either by their ratios, or by their ear, was in their judgment a very important branch of the fcience, and we are not to wonder at that clofe connexion, which in the writings of the Pythagoreans at leaft, is difcoverable between the three fciences mufic, arithmetic, and geometry. In this view it may perhaps be faid that the ftudy of mufic had an influence on the minds and tempers of men, as we fay that the ftudy of the mathematics has a tendency to induce a habit of thinking, to invigorate the powers of the underftanding, and to detect the fallacy of fpecious and delufive reafoning, but in what other way it could affect the manners, or indeed the mind, unlefs in that very obvious one of an addrefs to the paffions, which we at this day are all fenfible of, is utterly impoffible to determine.

And indeed the inveftigation of proportions and the properties of numbers may be faid to be very different from the art of combining founds, fo as to excite that pleafure which we afcribe to mufic; and perhaps it may not be too much to fay that the underftanding has little to do with it, nay, fome have carried this matter fo far as to queftion whether the delight we receive from mufic does not partake more of the fenfual than the intellectual kind * ; however this at leaft may be faid, that it is fome faculty, very different from the underftanding, that enables us to perceive the effects of harmony, and to diftinguifh between confonant and diffonant founds, and in this refpect, the affinity between mufic, and that other art, which for more reafons than all are aware of, has ever been deemed its fifter, is very remarkable. That painting has its foundation in mathematical principles, is certain, nay, that there is a harmony between colours, analogous to that of founds, is demonftrable; now the laws of optics, the doctrine of light and colours, and the principles of perfpective, connected as they are with geometry, all of which painting has more or lefs to do with, are things fo different from the reprefentation of corporeal objects, from the felection and artful arrangement of beautiful forms, from the expreffions of character and paffion as they appear in the human countenance, and, laftly, from that creative faculty in which we fuppofe the perfection of painting to confift, that we fcruple not to fay that a man may be an excellent painter with a gen-

* This metaphyfical queftion is difcuffed and determined in the negative, i. e. that mufic is an intellectual pleafure, by the ingenious Mr. John Norris of Bemerton. See his Mifcellanies, pag. 309, 12mo.

der

der knowledge of the mathematics; and the examples of the most eminent professors of the art, are a proof the assertion.

But the reason why the ancient writers treated the subject in this manner is, that they used the word Harmony to express relation and coincidence in general; nay, so extensively was this appellation used, that many authors of treatises on this subject have thought it previously necessary to a discussion of music in its three most obvious divisions of rythmic, metric, and harmonic, to treat of mundane, humane, and political music; the three last of which species, if at all intitled to the name of music *, must owe it to a metaphor, and that a very bold one: Aristides Quintilianus uses another method of division, which it must be confessed is the more natural of the two, and says that music is of two kinds, the contemplative and the active; the first of these he subdivides into natural and artificial; which latter he again divides into the harmonic, the rhythmic, and the metric; the the active he divides into the usual and the enunciative; the usual,

* Aristoxenus's division is rythmic, metric, organic, lib. II. That of Boetius, mundane, humane, and instrumental. By the first is to be understood the harmony of the spheres, before spoken of; by the second, the harmony subsisting between the body and the rational soul as united together, each being actuated by the other; and also that other kind of harmony, consent, relation, or whatever else it may be called, between the parts of the body, with respect to each; and again between those affections of the human mind, which, opposed to, or counterbalancing each other, and aided by reason, produce a kind of moral harmony, the effects whereof are visible in an orderly and well-regulated conduct.

To these Kircher and others have added musica politica, which, say they, consists in that harmonical proportion, which in every well-regulated government subsists between the three several orders of the people, the high, the low, and the middle state.

Kircher, whose inventive faculty never fails him, has given scales demonstrating each of these supposed kinds of harmony; but whoever would be farther informed as to the nature of mundane music, as it is above called, or is desirous of knowing to what extravagant lengths the human imagination may be led, may consult the writings of our countryman Dr. Robert Fludd, or de Fluctibus, a physician, and a Rosicrusian philosopher; and who, though highly esteemed for his learning by Selden, was perhaps one of the greatest mystics that ever lived. In a work of his intitled, Utriusque Cosmi majores scilicet et minoris metaphysica, physica, atque technica Historia, printed at Oppenheim 1617, folio, is one book intitled De Musica mundana, wherein the author exhibits the form of what he calls Monochordium mundanum, an instrument representing a monochord, with the string screwed up by a hand that issues from the clouds. Fludd supposes the sound of the chord, when open, to answer to terra or the earth, and to correspond with the note gamut in the scale of music: from thence he ascends by tones and semitones, in regular order, to water; and the other elements, through the planets, and so to the empyrean, answering to g g in the ratio of the disdiapason.

Mersennus has thought this diagram worthy of a place in his Latin work; and, to say the truth, most of the places in this and other of Fludd's works, and by the way they abound with them, are to the last degree curious and diverting. There will be farther occasion to speak of this extraordinary man, Fludd, in the course of this work.

containing melopœia, rhythmopœia, and poesia; and the enunciative the organic, the otliae; the hypocrite *: . . .

Thus we fee that the ancients, when they treated of mufic, ufed the word Harmony in a fenfe very different from that in which it is underflood at this day; for there is doubtlefs a harmony between founds emitted in fucceffion, which is difcernible as long as the impreffion of thofe already ftruck remains uneffaced; yet we choofe to diftinguifh this kind of relation by the word Melody, and that of Harmony is appropriated to the coincidence of different founds produced at the fame inftant: if it be afked why the ancients ufed the word Harmony in a fenfe fo very reftrained, as is above reprefented, the anfwer is eafy, if that pofition be true which many writers have advanced, namely, that their mufic was folitary, and that they were utter ftrangers to fymphoniac harmony. This the admirers of antiquity will by no means allow; and, to fay the truth, there are very few queftions which have more divided the learned world than this. In order that the reader may be able to form a judgment on a matter of fo great curiofity, the authorities on both fides fhall now be produced, and fubmitted to his confideration.

To avoid confufion, it will be neceffary firft to reduce the propofition to the form of a queftion, which, to take it in the fenfe in which it has generally been difcuffed, feems to be, Whether the ancients had the knowledge of mufic in fymphony or confonance, or not?

The advocates for the affirmative are Franchinus, or, as he is frequently named, Gaffurius, Zarlino, Gio. Battifta Doni, Ifaac Voffius, and Zaccaria Tevo, all, excepting Voffius, muficians, and he confeffedly a man of learning, but a great bigot, and of little judgment: the fum of their arguments is, that it appears by the writings of the ancients that their fkill in harmony was very profound, and that they reafoned upon it with all the accuracy and precifion which became philofophers; that the very firft difcoveries of the nature of mufical confonance, namely, thofe made by Pythagoras, tended much more naturally to eftablifh a theory of harmony than of mere melody or harmony in fucceffion, that fuppofing Pythagoras never to have lived, it could not have happened, but that the innumerable coincidences of founds produced by the voice or by the

* See the Analyfis of Quintilian, in chap. iii. of the next preceding book.

percussion of different bodies at the same instant, which must necessarily occur in the course of a very few years, could not fail to suggest a trial of the effects of concordant sounds uttered together, or at one and the same point of time; that those passages of sacred writ that mention commemoration of remarkable events, or the celebration of public festivals, as that of the dedication of Solomon's temple, with a great number of voices and instruments, hardly allow of the supposition that the music upon these occasions was unisonous.

All this it may be said is mere conjecture, let us therefore see what farther evidence there is to countenance the belief that the ancients were acquainted with the use of different parts in music; Aristotle in his treatise concerning the world, lib. V. has this question, ‘ If the ‘ world is made of contrary principles, how comes it that it was not ‘ long ago dissolved?’ In answer to this he shews that its beauty, perfection, and duration are owing to the admirable mixture and temperament of its parts, and the general order and harmony of nature. In his illustration of this argument he introduces music, concerning which he has this passage: Μουσικὴ δὲ ὀξεῖς ἅμα καὶ βαρεῖς, μακροὺς τε καὶ βραχεῖς φθόγγους μίξασα, ἐν διαφόροις φωναῖς, μίαν ἀπετέλεσεν ἁρμονίαν. ‘ Music, ‘ by a mixture of acute and grave, and of long and short sounds of ‘ different voices, yields an absolute or perfect concentus or concert.’——— Again, lib. VI. explaining the harmony of the celestial motions, he says, that ‘ though each orb has a motion proper to itself, yet is it ‘ such a motion as tends to one general end, proceeding from a prin- ‘ ciple common to all the orbs, which produce, by the concord arising ‘ from their motions, a choir in the heavens:’ and he pursues the comparison in these words: Καθάπερ δὲ ἐν χορῷ κορυφαίου κατάρξαντος, συνεπηχεῖ πᾶς ὁ χορὸς ἀνδρῶν ἔσθ᾽ ὅτι καὶ γυναικῶν ἐν διαφόροις φωναῖς ὀξυτέραις καὶ βαρυτέραις μίαν ἁρμονίαν ἐμμελῆ κεραννύντων.

Seneca, in his Epistles, has this passage. ‘ Do you not see of how ‘ many voices the chorus consists, yet they make but one sound? In ‘ it some are acute, others grave, and others in a mean between both; ‘ women are joined with men, and pipes are also interposed among ‘ them, yet is each single voice concealed, and it is the whole that is ‘ manifest [*].’

* Non vides quam multorum vocibus chorus constet? unus tamen ex omnibus sonus redditur. Aliqua illic acuta est, aliqua gravis, aliqua media. Accedunt viris feminæ, interponuntur tibiæ, singulorum latent voces, omnium apparent'. Seneca Epist. 84.

Cassiodo-

Caſſiodorous has the following paſſage, which may ſeem ſomewhat ſtranger : ' Symphony is the adjuſtment of a grave ſound to an acute, ' or an acute to a grave ſound, making a melody.'

From the ſeveral paſſages above-cited it appears, that the ancients were acquainted with ſymphonetic muſic of a certain kind, and that they employed therein voices differing in degrees of acuteneſs and gravity ; and thus far the affirmative of the queſtion in debate may ſeem to be proved.

But in ſupport of the negative we have the authorities of Glareanus, Salinas, Bottrigari, Artuſi, Cerone, Kircher, Meibomius, Kepler, Bontempi, our countrymen Morley, Wallis, and others, a numerous band, who infer an abſolute ignorance among the ancients of harmony produced by different and concordant ſounds, affecting the ſenſe at the ſame inſtant, from the general ſilence of their writers about it, for the exceeding ſkill and accuracy with which they diſcuſſed the other parts of muſic, leave no room to imagine but that they would have treated this in the ſame manner had they been acquainted with it : what diſcoveries accident might produce in that long ſeries of years prior to the time of Pythagoras no one can ſay ; hiſtory mentions none, nor does it pretend that even he made any uſe of his diſcovery, other than to calculate the ratios of ſounds, regulate the ſyſtem, and improve the melody of his time.

That voices and inſtruments, to a very great number, were employed at public ſolemnities is not denied, but it is by no means a conſequence that therefore the muſic produced by them conſiſted of different parts ; at this day among the reformed churches ſinging by a thouſand different voices of men, women, and children, in divine worſhip is no very unuſual thing ; and yet the reſult of all this variety of ſound is hardly ever any thing more than mere melody, and that of the ſimpleſt and moſt artleſs kind. Thus much in anſwer to the arguments founded on the improbability that the ancients could be ignorant of ſymphonetic harmony, in the ſenſe wherein at this day the term is underſtood.

With reſpect to the ſeveral paſſages above-cited, they ſeem each to admit of an anſwer ; to the firſt, produced from Ariſtotle, it is ſaid that the word Symphony, by which we ſhould underſtand the harmony of different ſounds uttered at one given inſtant, is uſed by him to expreſs two different kinds of conſonance, ſymphony and antiphony ; the

ſirſt,

firſt, according to him, is the conſonance of the uniſon, the other of the octave. In his Problems, § xix. prob. 16. he aſks why ſymphony is not as agreeable as antiphony? the anſwer is, becauſe in ſymphony the one voice being altogether like the other, they eclipſe each other; the ſymphony can therefore in this place ſignify nothing but uniſonous or integral harmony: and he elſewhere explains it to be ſo, by calling that ſpecies of conſonance, Omophony; as to Antiphony, it is clear that he means by it the harmony of an octave, for he conſtantly uſes the word in that ſenſe; and left there ſhould any doubt remain about it, he ſays that it is the conſonance between ſounds produced by the different voices of a boy and a man, that are as Nete and Hypate; and that thoſe ſounds form a preciſe octave is evident from all the repreſentations of the ancient ſyſtem that have ever been given. The ſum of Ariſtotle's teſtimony is, that in his time there was a commixture of ſounds, which produced a concinnous harmony: no doubt there was, but what is meant by that concinnous harmony his own words ſufficiently explain.

As to Seneca, it muſt be confeſſed that the vox media muſt imply two extremes; but what if in the chorus which he ſpeaks of, the ſhrill tibiæ were a biſdiapaſon above the voices of the men, and that the women ſung, as they ever do, an octave above them, would not theſe different ſounds produce harmony? Certainly they would, but of what kind? Why the very kind deſcribed by him, ſuch as ſeems to make but one ſound, which can be ſaid of no harmony but that of the uniſon or octave.

Laſtly, as to Caſſiodorus, his words are 'Symphonia eſt temperamentum ſonitus gravis ad acutum vel acuti ad gravem, modulamen efficiens, five in voce, five in percuſſione, five in flatu *:' as to the word Temperamentum, it can mean only an adjuſtment; and Modulamen was never yet applied to ſounds but as they followed each other in ſucceſſion: to modulate is to paſs, to proceed from one key or ſeries to another; the very idea of modulation is motion: the amount then of this definition is, that the attemperament or adjuſtment of a grave to an acute ſound, or of an acute to a grave one, conſtitutes ſuch a kind of ſymphony as nothing will anſwer to but melody; which is above ſhewn to be not inſtantaneous, but ſucceſſive ſymphony or conſonance.

* M. Aur. Caſſiodor. Oper. De Muſica.

There

There is yet another argument to the purpose. The ancients did not reckon the third and fixth among the confonances; this is taken notice of by a very celebrated Italian writer Giov. Maria Artufi of Bologna, who, though he has written expresfly on the imperfections of modern music, fcruples not therefore, and becaufe the third and fixth are the beauty of fymphonic mufic, to pronounce that the ancients muft have been unacquainted with the harmony of mufic in parts, in the fenfe in which the term is now underftood *: and an author whom we fhall prefently have occafion to cite more at large, fays exprefsly that they acknowledged no other confonances than the diapafon, diapente, and diateffaron, and fuch as were compofed of them †; nor does it any where appear that they were in the leaft acquainted with the ufe of difcords, or with the pleafing effects produced by the preparation and refolution of the diffonances; and if none of thefe were admitted into the ancient fyftem, let any one judge of its fitnefs for compofition in different parts.

In Morley's Introduction is a paffage from whence his opinion on this queftion may be collected; and, as he was one of the moft learned muficians that this nation ever produced, fome deference is due to it; fpeaking of Defcant ‡, he ufes thefe words: ' When defcant did begin, ' by whom, and where it was invented, is vncertaine; for it is a great ' controuerfie amongft the learned if it were knowne to the antiquitie, ' or no; and diuers do bring arguments to proue, and others to dif-' proue the antiquitie of it; and for difprouing of it, they fay that in all ' the workes of them who haue written of muficke before Franchinus, ' there is no mention of any more parts then one; and that if any did ' fing to the harpe (which was their moft vfuall inftrument) they fung ' the fame which they plaied. But thofe who would affirme that the ' ancients knew it, faie, That if they did not know it, to what ende ' ferued all thofe long and tedious difcourfes and difputations of the ' confonantes, wherein the mofte part of their workes are confumed; ' but whether they knew it or not, this I will fay, that they had it ' not in halfe that variety wherein we now haue it, though we read ' of much more ftrange effects of their muficke then of ours.' Annotations on Morley's Introduction, part II.

* Artufi delle Imperfettioni della Moderna Mufica. Ragionam. primo, Cap. 14.
† Mofurg. tom. I. pag. 540.
‡ Defcant, as ufed by this author, has two fignifications; the one anfwers precifely to mufic in confonance, the other will be explained hereafter.

CHAP.

C H A P. III.

THE fuffrage of Kircher, in a queftion of this nature, will be thought to carry fome weight: this author, whofe learning and fkill in the fcienc are univerfally acknowledged, poffeffed every advantage that could lead to fatisfaction in a queftion of this nature, as namely, a profound fkill in languages, an extenfive correfpondence, and an inquifitive difpofition; and for the purpofe had been indulged with the liberty of accefs to the moft celebrated repofitories of literature, and the ufe of the moft valuable manufcripts there to be met with; and who, to fum up all, was at once a philofopher, an antiquary, an hiftorian, a fcholar, and a mufician, has given his opinion very much at large in nearly the following words.

'It has for fome time been a queftion among muficians whether
'the ancients made ufe of feveral parts in their harmony or not: in
'order to determine which, we are to confider their polyodia as
'threefold, natural, artificial, and unifonous; I call that natural
'which is not regulated by any certain rules or precepts, but is per-
'formed by an extemporary and arbitrary fymphony of many voices,
'intermixing acute and grave founds together; fuch as we obferve
'even at this time, happens amongft a company of failors or reapers,
'and fuch people, who no fooner hear any certain melody begun
'by any one of them, than fome other immediately invent a bafs or
'tenor, and thus is produced an harmony extemporary, and not
'confined by any certain laws, and which is very rude and imper-
'fect, as it is almoft always unifon, containing nothing of harmony,
'except in the clofes, and therefore of no worth: that the Greeks
'had fuch a kind of mufic none can doubt. But the queftion is not
'concerning this kind of polyodia, but whether they had compofitions
'for feveral voices, framed according to the rules of art. I have
'taken great pains to be fatisfied in this matter; and as in none of
'the Greek and Latin writers I have met with, any mention is made
'of this kind of mufic, it feems to me that either they were ignorant
'of it, or that they did not make ufe of it, as imagining perhaps that

'it

' it interrupted the melody, and took away from the energy of the
' words; as to the term Harmonici concentus, it is only to be under-
' derstood of the agreement between the voice and the sound of the
' instrument.

' Those who attempt to prove from Euclid that the ancients did
' compose music in really different parts, do not seem to understand
' his meaning; for when he mentions the four parts of a song, ἀγωγή,
' τονή, πετ]εία, πλοκή, he does not thereby mean the four polyodical
' parts of cantus, altus, tenor, and bass, but so many different affec-
' tions of the voice, certain harmonical figures or tropes, whereby
' the song acquired a particular beauty and grace; for what else can
' the word Ἀγωγή mean than a certain transition of the voice from
' some given sound to another that is related to it. Τονή signifies a
' certain stay or dwelling on a found; Πλοκή, or implication, is a
' particular species or colour of the Ἀγωγή, as Πετ]εία, frisking or play-
' ing on, is of Τονή: what the Ἀγωγή is to Τονή, such is the Πλοκή
' to the Πετ]εία.

' Some imagine that the ancients had a polyodical instrumental
' music from the diversity of their pipes; and are of opinion that at
' least an organical or instrumental harmony or symphony, regulated
' by art, was in use among the ancients, because their authors make
' mention of certain pipes, some of which were termed Παρθενικοί, or
' fit for girls; some Παιδικοι, or fit for boys; some Τέλειοι, as being in a
' mean between the acute and grave sounds; and others Τέσσαρες, as
' agreeing with the grave. The better to clear up this doubt, we
' must consider the organical polyodia as twofold, natural and arti-
' ficial; and both these I make no doubt were in use as well as
' the vocal polyodia; for it is very probable that such as played on
' those pipes, becoming skilful by such practice, invented certain
' symphonies adapted to their purpose, and which they played on
' their public festivals, distributing themselves into certain chorusses.
' Symphonies of this sort are at this time to be heard among the coun-
' try people, who, though ignorant of the musical art, exhibit a
' symphony, such a one as it is, on their flutes and pipes of different
' sizes, and this merely through the judgment of their ear; and it is
' also probable that the ancient Hebrews by this means alone became
' enabled to celebrate the praises of God on so many Cornua, Fistulæ,

7 ' Litui,

' Litui, Tubæ, Buccinæ, as they are said to have been used at once
' in their temple; and I remember to have heard the Mahometan
' slaves in the island of Malta exhibit symphonies of this kind. An
' affection therefore of the polyodia is implanted in the nature of
' man; and I doubt not but that the ancients knew and practised it
' in the manner above related: but though I have taken great pains
' in my researches, I could never find the least sign of their having
' any artificial organical Melothesis of many parts; which, had they
' been acquainted with it, they would doubtless have mentioned, it
' being so remarkable a thing. What Boetius, Ptolemy, and others
' speak concerning harmony, is to be understood only as to a single
' voice, to which an instrument was joined; add to this that the
' ancients acknowledged no other concords than the diapason, the
' diapente, and the diatessaron, and such as were composed of them;
' for they did not reckon as now, the ditone, semiditone, and hexa-
' chord among the consonances. It therefore follows that the an-
' cient Greeks acknowledged nothing more than the Monodia,
' adapted, it must be confessed, with much care and the greatest art
' to the sound of the lyre or the tibia; so that nothing was deficient
' either in the variety of the modulation, the sweetness of the singing,
' the justness of the pronunciation, or the gracefulness of the body in
' all its gestures and motions: and I imagine that the lyre of many
' strings was founded in a harmonical concentus to the voice, in
' no other manner than is used in our days *.'

Dr. Wallis has given his opinion on this important question in
terms that seem decisive; for speaking of the music of the ancients
he makes use of these words:

' We are to consider that their music, even after it came to some
' good degree of perfection, was much more plain and simple than ours
' now-a-days. They had not concerts of two, three, four, or more
' parts or voices, but one single voice, or single instrument a-part,
' which to a rude ear is much more taking than more compounded
' music; for that is at a pitch not above their capacity, whereas this
' other confounds it with a great noise, but nothing distinguishable
' to their capacity †.' And again in the same paper he says: ' I do not

* Musurg. tom. I. pag. 537, et seq.
† Abridgment of Philosoph. Translations by Lowthorp and Jones, vol. I. pag. 618.

' find among the ancients any footſteps of what we call ſeveral parts
' or voices, (as baſs, treble, mean, &c. ſung in concert) anſwering
' to each other to complete the muſic.' And in the Appendix to
his edition of Ptolemy, pag. 317, he expreſſes himſelf on the ſame
ſubject to this purpoſe : ' But that agreement which we find in the
' modern muſic, of parts (as they term it) or of two, three, four, or
' more voices (ſinging together ſounds which are heard all together)
' was intirely unknown to the ancients, as far as I can ſee.'

From the ſeveral paſſages above-cited, it appears that the queſtion,
whether the ancients were acquainted with muſic in conſonance or
not, has been frequently, and not unſucceſsfully agitated, and that
the arguments for the negative ſeem to preponderate, Neverthelefs
the author of a book lately publiſhed, entitled, ' Principles and Power
' of Harmony,' after taking notice that Dr. Wallis, and ſome others,
maintained that the ancients were ſtrangers to ſymphoniac muſic,
has, upon the ſtrength of a ſingle paſſage in Plato, been hardy enough
to aſſert the contrary : his words are theſe.

' The ſtrongeſt paſſage which I have met with in relation to this
' long-diſputed point, is in Plato ; a paſſage which I have never ſeen
' quoted, and which I ſhall tranſlate : " Young men ſhould be
" taught to ſing to the lyre, on account of the clearnefs and preciſion
" of the ſounds, ſo that they may learn to render tone for tone.
" But to make uſe of different ſimultaneous notes, and all the variety
" belonging to the lyre, this ſounding one kind of melody, and the
" poet another—to mix a few notes with many, ſwift with ſlow,
" grave with acute, conſonant with diſſonant, &c. muſt not be
" thought of, as the time allotted for this part of education is too
" ſhort for ſuch a work." Plat. 895. I am ſenſible that objections
' may be made to ſome parts of this tranſlation, as of the words
' πυκνοτης, μανοτης, and ανιφωνσις, but I have not deſignedly diſguiſed
' what I took to be the true ſenſe of them, after due conſideration.
' It appears then upon the whole, that the ancients were acquainted
' with muſic in parts, but did not generally make uſe of it *.'

* Princip'es and Power of Harmony, p. 133. The ſpeech in the original, containing
the paſſage of which it is pretended that above is a tranſlation, is here given at length, as it
ſtands in the edition of Plato, by Marſilius Ficinus ; which is what this author appears to
have made uſe of : Τετων τοινυν δει χαριν τοις φθιγγοι τας λιρας προςχρισθαι, ſapſ-
τετας

1

Whoever will be at the pains of comparing the discourse of Dr
Wallis, above-cited, and his appendix to Ptolemy, with the several
paragraphs in the Principles and Power of Harmony, relating to the
question in debate, and calculated, as the author professes, to vindi-
cate the Greek music, will discover in the one the modesty of a philosopher, and in the other the arrogance of a dogmatist.

Opinions delivered in terms so positive, and indeed so contemptu-
ous, as this latter writer has chosen to make use of *, are an affront to
the understandings of mankind, who are not to be supposed ready to
acquiesce in the notions of others merely because they are propagated
with an unbecoming confidence : and as to the judgment of this author on the question in debate, the least that can be said of it is, that it
is founded in mistake and ignorance of his subject ; for, first, it is very
strange, seeing how much the powers of harmony exceed those of
mere melody, that the ancients, when once they had found themselves in possession of so valuable an improvement as symphoniac
music, should ever forego it.   The moderns in this respect were wiser
than their teachers, for no sooner did they discover the excellence
of music in parts than they studied to improve it, and have cultivated it with great care ever since.   Secondly, this writer, in support
of his opinion, has been driven to the necessity of translating those
words of his author which he thinks make most for his purpose,
in a manner which he confesses is liable to objections, and into
such English phrase as, in the opinion of many, is not intelligible.
Thirdly and lastly, this very passage of Plato, upon which he lays
so much stress, was discovered above fifty years ago, and adduced

ὑίας ἴσικα τῶν χερδῶν, τόι τε αἰλαριζὰ ἢ τὸ παιδευύμπον, ἀπακλέίσται περέχορία τὰ
Φθέγματα τοῖς Φθέγμασι· τὰς δ' ἐντερεΦωνίας ἢ ποικιλίαν τῆς λύρας, ἄλλα μὲν μέλη τῶν
χερδῶν ἱτσεῖν, ἄλλα δὲ τὰ τῆς μελχδίας ξυνθέντο· ποιεῖ· ἢ δὲ ἡ πυκνότητα μανότητι, ἢ
τάχος βραδυτῆτι, ἢ ἐξύτητα βαρύτητι, σύμφωνον ἢ ἀντίφωνον παρεχόμενος, ἢ τῶν ῥυθμῶν
ὡσαύτως παντοδαπὰ ποικιλματα προσαρμόττοντας τοῖσι Φθόγγοις τῆς λύρας· παντα δὲ τὰ
τοιαῦτα μὴ προσφέρειν τοῖς μέλλουσιν ἐν τριοὶ ἔτεσι τὸ τῆς μουσῆς χρήσιμον ἐκλήψεσθαι διὰ
τάχος. τὰ γὰρ ἐναντία, ἄλληλα ταράττοντα δυσμαθίαν παρέχει. δεῖ δὲ ὅτι μάλιστα εὐμα-
θεῖς ἴσθαι τοὺς ἐων.
   * As where he insinuates a resemblance between those who doubt the truth of his assertions and the most ignorant of mankind, in these words : ' If all these circumstances are
' not sufficient to gain our belief, merely because we moderns have not the same musical
' power, then have the Kamschatcans a right to decide that it is impossible to foretel an
' eclipse, or to represent all the elements of speech by about twenty four marks.'

for the very purpofe for which he has cited it, by Monf. l'Abbé Fraguier, a member of the Academy of Inscriptions and Belles Lettres,
and occasioned a controversy, the result whereof will presently be
related.

Monfieur Fraguier had entertained a high opinion of the Greek
music, and a belief that the ancients were acquainted with music in
confonance; in fupport of which latter opinion he produced to the
academy the paffage above-cited, which is to be found in Plato de
Legibus, lib. VII *. He alfo produced for the fame purpofe a paffage
in Cicero de Republica, and another from Macrobius, both which
are given in the note fubjoined †.

The arguments deduced by Monf. Fraguier from thefe feveral paffages, were learnedly refuted by Monf. Burette, a member alfo of
the academy : and as to the interpretations which Monf. Fraguier
had put upon them, the fame Monf. Burette demonftrated that they
were forced and unwarranted, either by the context or the practice
of the ancients.

The fubftance of thefe arguments is contained in a paper or me-
moir entitled Examen d'un Paffage de Platon fur la Mufique, which
may be feen in the Hiftory of the Academy of Infcriptions, tom. III.
pag. 118. This queftion was farther profecuted by the fame parties,
as appears by fundry papers in the fubfequent volumes of the Hiftory
and Memoirs of the above Academy; and in the courfe of the controverfy the paffages above-cited from Ariftotle, Seneca, Caffidorus,
and others, were feverally infifted on. As to thofe from Cicero and
Macrobius, and this from Horace,

> Sonante miftum tibiis carmen lyra,
> Hac Dorium, illis Barbarum.
>
> Ad Mecænat. Epod. ix.

---

* In Stephens's edition It is pag. 812, and in that of Marfilius Ficinus 895.

† ' Ut in fidibus, ac tibiis atque cantu ipfo, ac vocibus concentus eft quidam tenendus
' ex diftinctis fonis, quem immutatum ac difcrepantem aures eruditæ ferre non poffunt;
' ifque concentus ex diffimilimarum vocum moderatione concors tamen efficitur et con-
' gruens: fic ex fummis, et infimis, et mediis interjectis ordinibus, ut fonis, moderata
' ratione civitas, confenfu diffimilimorum concinit, et quæ harmonia a muficis dicitur in
' cantu, ea eft in civitate concordia.' Cicer. lib. ii. de Repub. Fragm pag. 527, tom. III.

* Vides quam multorum vocibus chorus conftet una tamen ex omnibus redditur. Ali-
' qua eft illic acuta, aliqua gravis, aliqua media: accedunt viris feminæ: interponuntur
' fiftula Ita fingulorum illic latent voces, omnium apparent, et fit concentus ex diffonis.'
Macrob. Saturnalior. Proem.

                                                                    which

which had formerly been adduced for the same purpose, they went but a very little way towards proving the affirmative of the question in debate. Monf. Burette took all these into confideration; he admits, that the ancients made ufe of the octave and the fifteenth, the former in a manner refembling the drone of a bag-pipe; and he allows that they might accidentally, and without any rule, ufe the fourth and fifth; but this is the fartheft advance he will allow the ancients to have made towards the practice of fymphoniac mufic; for as to the imperfect confonances and the diffonances, he fays they were ignorant of the ufe and application of all of them in harmony: and finally demonftrates, by a variety of arguments, that the ancients were abfolute ftrangers to mufic in parts.

Martini, in his Storia Mufica, vol. I. pag. 172, has given an abridgment of this controverfy, as it lies difperfed in the feveral volumes of the Memoirs of the Academy of Infcriptions, and acquiefces in the opinion of Monf. Burette, who, upon the whole, appears to have fo much the advantage of his opponents, that it it is highly probable this difpute will never be revived.

To fpeak of the ancient Greek mufic in general, thofe who reflect on it will be inclined to acquiefce in the opinion of Dr. Wallis, who fays, he takes it for granted, ' that much of the reports concerning ' the great effects of mufic in former times, beyond what is to be ' found in latter ages, is highly hyperbolical, and next door to fabu- ' lous; and therefore, he adds, great abatements muft be allowed to ' the elogies of their mufic.' Certainly many of the relations of the effects of mufic are either fabulous or to be interpreted allegorically, as this in Horace:

* The learned Dr. Jortin, who, with the character of a very worthy man and a profound fcholar, poffeffed that of a learned mufician, has delivered his fentiments on this queftion in the following terms: ' One would think that an ancient mufician, ' who was well acquainted with concords and difcords, who had an inftrument of many ' ftrings or many keys to play upon, and two hands and ten fingers to make ufe of, ' would try experiments, and would fall into fomething like counterpoint and compofition ' in parts. In fpeculation nothing feems more probable, and it feemed more than probable ' to our fkilful mufician Dr. Pepufch, when I once converfed with him upon the fubject; ' but in fact it doth not appear that the ancients had this kind of compofition, or rather it ' appears that they had not; and it is certain, that a man fhall overlook difcoveries which ' ftand at his elbow, and in a manner intrude themfelves upon him.' Letter to Mr. Avifon, ' publifhed in the fecond edition of his Effay on Mufical Expreffion, pag. 36.

Silveftres

Silveſtres homines ſacer interpreſque Deorum,
Cædibus & victu fœdo deterruit Orpheus;
Dictus ob hoc lenire tigres rabidoſque leones.
Dictus & Amphion, Thebanæ conditor Arcis,
Saxa movere ſono teſtudinis, & prece blanda
Ducere quo vellet.

ARTE POETICA, lib. II. l. 391.

The wood-born race of men, when Orpheus tam'd,
From acorns and from mutual blood reclaim'd,
This prieſt divine was fabled to aſſuage
The tiger's fiercenefs, and the lion's rage.
Thus rofe the Theban wall; Amphion's lyre
And foothing voice the liſt'ning ſtones inſpire.

FRANCIS.

Hyperbolical expreſſions of the power and efficacy of mufic ſignify but little; for thefe convey nothing more than the ideas of the relator: and every man ſpeaks in the higheſt terms he can invent of that, whatever it be, that has adminiſtered to him the greateſt delight. How has the poet, in the Proluſions of Strada, laboured in defcribing the conteſt between the nightingale and the luteniſt! and what does that celebrated poem contain, but a profuſion of words without a meaning?

To conclude, every one that underſtands mufic is enabled to judge of the utmoſt effects of a ſingle pipe, by hearing the flute, or any other ſingle ſtop, finely touched on the organ: and as to the lyre, whether of three, four, ſeven, or ten ſtrings, it is impoſſible but that it muſt have been greatly inferior to the harp, the lute, and many other inſtruments in ufe among the moderns.

Having taken a view of the ſtate of mufic in the earlier ages of the world, and traced the ancient ſyſtem from its rudiments to its per-fection, and thereby brought it down to nearly the cloſe of the third century, we ſhall proceed to relate the feveral fubfequent improve-ments that have from time to time been made of it, in the order in which they occurred; and ſhew to whom we owe that ſyſtem, which for its excellence is now univerſally adopted by the civilized world.

We have feen that hitherto the fcience of mufic, as being a fubject of very abſtracted ſpeculation, and as having a near affinity with

7

arithme-

arithmetic and geometry, had been ftudied and taught by fuch only as were eminent for their fkill in thofe fciences : of thefe the far greater number were Greeks, who, in the general eftimation of mankind, held the rank of philofophers. The accounts hereafter given of the Latin writers, fuch as Martianus Capella, Macrobius, Caffiodorus, and others, will fhew how little the Romans contributed to the improvement of mufic; and in general their writings are very little more than abridgments of, or fhort commentaries on the works of Nicomachus, Euclid, Ariftides, Quintilianus, Ariftoxenus, and others of the ancient Greeks. As to Boetius, of whom we fhall fpeak hereafter, it is clear that his intention was only to reftore to thofe barbarous times in which he lived, the knowledge of the true principles of harmony, and to demonftrate, by the force of mathematical reafoning, the proportions and various relations to each other, of founds; in the doing whereof he evidently fhews himfelf to have been a Pythagorean. As this was the defign of his treatife De Mufica, we are not to wonder that the author has faid fo little of the changes that mufic underwent among the Latins, or that he does but juft hint at the difufe of the enarmonic and chromatic genera, and the introduction of the Roman characters in the room of the Greek.

It muft however be admitted, that for one improvement of the fyftem we are indebted to the Latins, namely, the application of the Roman capital letters to the feveral founds that compofe the fcale, whereby they got rid of that perplexed method of notation invented by the Greeks: we have feen, by the treatife of Alypius, written profeffedly to explain the Greek mufical characters, to what an amazing number they amounted, 1240 at the loweft computation; and after all, they were no better than fo many arbitrary marks or figns placed on a line over the words of the fong, and, having no real inherent or analogical fignification, muft have been an intolerable burthen on the memory. Thefe the Latins rejected, and in their ftead introduced the letters of their own alphabet, A, B, C, D, E, F, G, H, I, K, L, M, N, O, P, fifteen in number, and fufficient to exprefs every found contained in the bifdiapafon. If it be afked, how could this fmall number ferve the purpofe of more than 1200? the anfwer is, that this amazing multiplicity of characters arofe from the neceffity of diftinguifhing each found with refpect to the genus, and alfo the mode in which it was ufed; and before this innovation of the

Romans,

Romans, we are assured, that both the enarmonic and chromatic
genera were grown out of use, and that the diatonic genus, on account
of its sweetness and conformity to nature, was retained amongst
them : and as to the modes, there is great reason to suspect, that
even at the time when Ptolemy wrote, the doctrine of them was but
ill understood ; fifteen characters, we know, are at this time sufficient
to denote all the sounds in a diatonic bisdiapason, and consequently
must have been so then.

It has already been observed, that the science of harmony was anciently a subject of philosophical enquiry ; and it is manifest, from the
account herein before given of them and their writings, that the Greeks
treated it as a subject of very abstract speculation, and that they neither attended to the physical properties of sound, nor concerned themselves with the practice of music, whether vocal or instrumental.
Ptolemy was one of the last of the Greek harmonicians ; and from
his time it may be observed, that the cultivation of music became
the care of a set of men, who, then at least, made no pretensions to
the character of philosophers. This may be accounted for either by
the decline of philosophy about this period, or by the not improbable
supposition, that the subject itself was exhausted, and that nothing
remained but an improvement in practice on that foundation which
the ancient writers, by their theory, had so well laid.   But whatever
may have been the cause, it is certain, that after the establishment
of Christianity the cultivation of music became the concern of the
church : to this the Christians were probably excited by the example
of the Jews, among whom music made a considerable part of divine
worship, and the countenance given to it in the writings of St. Paul.
Nor is it to be wondered at by those who consider the effects of music,
its influence on the passions, and its power to inspire sentiments of
the most devout and affecting kind, if it easily found admittance into
the worship of the primitive Christians: as to the state of it in the
three first centuries, we are very much at a loss ; yet it should seem
from the information of St. Augustine, that in his time it had arrived
at some degree of perfection ; possibly it had been cultivating, both
in the Eastern and Western empire, from the first propagation of
Christianity.   The great number of men who were drawn off from
secular pursuits by their religious profession, amidst the barbarism of
the times, thought themselves laudably employed in the study of a
science

science which was found to be subservient to religion : while some
were engaged in the oppugning heretical opinions, others were taken
up in compofing forms of devotions, framing liturgies ; and others in
adapting fuitable melodies to fuch pfalms and hymns as had been received into the fervice of the church, and which made a very confiderable part of the divine offices : all which is the more probable, as
the progrefs of human learning was then in a great meafure at a ftand.

But as the introduction of mufic into the fervice of the church
feems to be a new æra, it is neceffary to be a little more particular, and relate the opinions of the moft authentic writers, as
well as to the reception it at firft met with, as its fubfequent progrefs among the converts to Chriftianity. If among the accounts
to be given of thefe matters, fome fhould carry the appearance of
improbability, or fhould even verge towards the regions of fable,
let it be remembered, that very little credit would be due to hiftory, were the writer to fupprefs every relation againft the credibility whereof there lay an objection. Hiftory does not propofe to
tranfmit barely matters of real fact, or opinions abfolutely irrefragable; falfehood and error may very innocently be propagated, nay the
general belief of falfehood, or the exiftence of any erroneous opinion,
may be confidered as facts ; and then it becomes the duty of an
hiftorian to relate them. Whoever is converfant with the ecclefiaftical hiftorians muft allow that the fuperftition of fome, and the enthufiafm of others of them, have fomewhat abated the reverence due
to their teftimony. But notwithftanding this, the characters of Eufebius, Socrates, Sozomen, Theodoret, and Evagrius, for veracity
and good intelligence, ftand fo high in the opinion of all fober and
impartial men, that it is impoffible to with-hold our affent from the
far greater part of what they have written on this fubject.

The advocates for the high antiquity of church-mufic urge the
authority of Saint Paul in its favour, who, in his Epiftle to the Ephe-
fians, charges them to fpeak to themfelves in pfalms, and hymns, and
fpiritual fongs, finging and making melody in their hearts to the Lord *;
and who exhorts the Coloffians to teach and admonifh one another in
pfalms, hymns, and fpiritual fongs †. Cardinal Bona is one of thefe ;
and he fcruples not to affert, on the authority of thefe two paffages,

* Chap. v. verfe 19.   † Chap. iii. verfe 16.
VOL. I.   O o   that

that fongs and hymns were, from the very eftablifhment of the church, fung in the affemblies of the faithful. Johannes Damafcenus goes further back; and relates, that at the funeral of the Blefed Virgin, which was celebrated at Gethfemane, the apoftles, affifted by angels, continued finging her requiem for three whole days inceffantly. The fame author, fpeaking of the ancient hymn called the Trifagion, dates its original from a miracle that was performed in the time of Proclus, the archbifhop: his account is, that the people of Conftantinople being terrified with fome portentous figns that had appeared, made folemn proceffions and applications to the Almighty, befeeching him to avert the calamities that feemed to threaten their city, in the midft whereof a boy was caught from among them, and taken up to heaven; who, upon his return, related, that he had been taught by angels to fing the hymn, in Greek,

Αγιος ο Θεος, αγιος ιχυρος, αγιος αθανατος, ελπισον ημας.

Holy God, holy and ftrong, holy and immortal, have mercy upon us.

The truth of this relation is queftioned by fome, who yet credit a vifion of St. Ignatius; of which Socrates, the ecclefiaftical hiftorian, gives the following account: ' St. Ignatius, the third bifhop of An-
' tioch, in Syria, after the apoftle Peter, who alfo converfed familiarly
' with the apoftles, faw the blefed fpirits above finging hymns to the
' Sacred Trinity alternately, which method of finging, fays the fame
' hiftorian, Ignatius taught to his church; and this, together with an
' account of the miracle which gave rife to it, was communicated
' to all the churches of the Eaft *.' Nicephorus, St. Chryfoftom,
Amalarius, and fundry others, acquiefce in this account of the origin
of antiphonal finging; as do our countrymen, Hooker, Hammond,
Beveridge, and Dr. Comber.

By the Apoftolical Conftitutions, faid to have been, if not compiled
by the apoftles themfelves, at leaft collected by Clement, a difciple of
theirs, the order of divine worfhip is prefcribed; wherein it is exprefly required, that after the reading the two leffons, one of the
prefbyters fhould fing a pfalm or hymn of David; and that the people fhould join in finging at the end of each verfe. It would be too
little to fay of this collection, that the authority of it is doubted, fince
it is agreed, that it did not appear in the world till the fourth century;

* Hift. Ecclef. lib. VI. cap. viii.

7

and the opinions of authors are, that either it is so interpolated as to deserve no credit, or that the whole of it is an absolute forgery.

Hitherto, then, the high antiquity of church-music stands on no better a foundation than tradition, backed with written evidence of such a kind as to have scarce a pretence to authenticity: there are, however, accounts to be met with among the writers of ecclesiastical history, that go near to fix it at about the middle of the fourth century.

In short the æra from whence we may reasonably date the introduction of music into the service of the church, is that period during which Leontius governed the church of Antioch; that is to say, between the years of Christ 347 and 356, when Flavianus and Diodorus, afterwards bishops, the one of Antioch and the other of Tarsus, divided the choristers into two parts, and made them sing the Psalms of David alternately, Theodoret. Hist. Eccl. lib. II. cap. xxiv.; a practice, says the same author, which began first at Antioch, and afterwards spread itself to the end of the world. Valesius acquiesces in this account, and professes to wonder whence Socrates had the story of Ignatius's vision, Valef. in Socrat. lib. VI. cap. viii. The occasion of antiphonal singing seems to have been this: Flavianus and Diodorus, although then laymen, but engaged in a monastic life, were in great repute for their sanctity; and Leontius, their bishop, was an avowed Arian, whom they zealously opposed: in order to draw off the people from an attendance on the bishop, who, in the opinion of Flavianus and Diodorus, was a preacher of heresy, they set up a separate assembly for religious worship, in which they introduced antiphonal singing, which so captivated the people, that the bishop, to call them back again, made use of it also in his church. Flavianus, it seems, had an high opinion of the efficacy of this kind of music; for it is reported, that the city of Antioch having, by a popular sedition, incurred the displeasure of the emperor Theodosius, sent Flavianus to appease him, and implore forgiveness; who, upon his first audience, though in the imperial palace, directed the usual church-service, to be sung before him: the emperor melted into pity, wept, and the city was restored to his favour. Other instances are to be met with in history, that shew the fondness of the people of Antioch for this kind of music; and which favour the supposition, that amongst them it took its rise.

Antioch

Antioch was the metropolis of Syria; the example of its inhabitants was soon followed by the other churches of the east; and in a very few ages after its introduction into the divine service, the practice of singing in churches not only received the sanction of public authority, but those were forbid to join in it who were ignorant of music. For at the council of Laodicea, held between the years of Christ 360, and 370, a canon was made, by which it was ordained, 'That none but the canons, or singing-men of the church, which ascend the Ambo *, or singing-desk, and sing out of the parchment, [so the words are] should presume to sing in the church. Balsamon seems to think that the fathers intended nothing more than to forbid the setting or giving out the hymn or psalm by the laity: but the reason assigned by Baronius for the making this canon, shews that it was meant to exclude them totally from singing in the church-service; for he says that when the people and the clergy sang promiscuously, the former, for want of skill, destroyed the harmony, and occasioned such discord as was very inconsistent with the order and decency requisite in divine worship. Zonaras confirms this account, and adds, that these canonical singers were reckoned a part of the clergy †. Balsamon, in his scholia on this canon, says, that before the Laodicean council, the laity were wont, in contempt of the clergy, to sing, in a very rude and inartificial mannner, hymns and songs of their own invention; to obviate which practice, it was ordained by this canon that none should sing but those whose office it was. Our learned countryman Bingham declares himself of the same opinion in his Antiquities of the Christian Church, book III. chap. vii. and adds, that from the time of the council of Laodicea the psalmistæ, or singers, were called κανονικοι ψαλται, or canonical singers, though he is inclined to think the provision in the canon only temporary.

---

* The Ambo was what we now call the Reading desk, a place made on purpo'e for the readers and singers, and such of the clergy as ministred in the first service called Missa Catechumenorum. It had the name of Ambo, not as Walafridus Strabo imagines, 'ab ambiendo,' because it surrounded them that were in it, but from αναβαινειν, because it was a place of eminency, to which they went up by degrees or steps. Bingham's Antiquities of the Christian Church, book VIII. chap v. § 4.

† It seems they were one of the many orders in the primitive church, and that they received ordination at the hands, not of the bishop or choriepiscopus, but of a presbyter, using this form of words, preferibed by the canon of the fourth council of Carthage. 'See ' that thou believe in thy heart what thou singest with thy mouth; and approve in thy ' works what thou believest in thy heart.' Bingh. Antiq. book III. chap. vii. § 4.

CHAP.

C H A P.   IV.

GREAT ſtreſs is alſo laid on the patronage given to church-muſic by St. Baſil, St. Ambroſe, and St. Chryſoſtom; as to the firſt, he had part of his education at Antioch, where he was a continual ſpectator of that pompous worſhip which prevailed there. He was firſt made a deacon by Meletius, and afterwards, that is to ſay about the year 371, was promoted to the biſhoprick of Cæſarea in Cappadocia, his own country; and in this exalted ſtation he contracted ſuch a love for church-muſic, as drove him to the neceſſity of apologizing for it *. In his epiſtle to the Neocæſarian clergy, ſtill extant, he juſtifies the practice, ſaying, that the new method of ſinging, at which they were ſo offended, was now become common in the Chriſtian church, the people riſing before day and going to church, where, having made their confeſſions and prayers, they proceeded to the ſinging of pſalms : and, he adds, that in this holy exerciſe, the choir being divided into two parts, mutually anſwered each other, the precentor beginning, and the reſt following him. He farther tells them, that if to do thus be a fault, they muſt blame many pious and good men in Egypt, Lybia, Paleſtine, Arabia, Phœnicia, and Syria, and ſundry other places. To this they urged that the practice was otherwiſe in the time of their biſhop Gregory Thaumaturgus; in anſwer to which Baſil tells them, that neither was the Litany uſed in his time; and that in objecting to muſic, while they admitted the Litany, they ſtrained at a gnat and ſwallowed a camel.

St. Chryſoſtom, whoſe primitive name was John, was a native of Antioch, and received his education there, he was ordained a deacon by Meletius, and preſbyter by Flavianus; and having been accuſtomed to the pompous ſervice introduced by the latter into the church of Antioch, he conceived a fondneſs for it. When he became biſhop of Conſtantinople, which was about A. C. 380, he found occaſion to introduce muſic among his people : the manner of his doing it is thus related. The Arians in that city were grown very inſolent : they held conventicles at a ſmall diſtance without the walls; but on Saturdays and Sundays, which were ſet apart for the

* Valeſ. in Socrat. lib. IV. cap. xxvi.

public

public affemblies, they were wont to come within the city, where, dividing themfelves into feveral companies, they walked about the porticos, finging fuch words as thefe : ' Where are they who affirm ' three to be one power ?' and hymns compofed in defence of their tenets, adding petulant reflexions on the orthodox * ; this they continued for the greateft part of the night ; in the morning they marched ed through the heart of the city, finging in the fame manner, and fo proceeded to the place of their affembly. In oppofition to thefe people, St. Chryfoftom caufed hymns to be fung in the night ; and to give his performance a pomp and folemnity, which the other wanted, he procured croffes of filver to be made at the charge of the emprefs Eudoxia, which, with lighted torches thereon, were borne in a procef- fion, at which Brifo, the emprefs's eunuch officiated as precentor ; this was the occafion of a great tumult, in which Brifo received a wound in the forehead with a ftone, and fome on both fides were flain †. This was followed by a fedition, which ended in the expulfion of the Arians. This manner of finging, thus introduced by them, was, as Sozomen relates ‡, ufed in Conftantinople from that time forwards ; however, in a fhort time it was performed in fuch an unfeemly way as gave great offence ; for the fingers, affecting ftrange geftures and boifterous clamours, converted the church into a

* It feems that the orthodox could in their turns not only be petulant, but induftrious in provoking their enemies to wrath, as may be collected from the following relation of Theodoret.

' Publia, the deaconefs, a woman admired and celebrated for her piety, was the mother ' of the famous John, who for many years was firft prefbyter of the church of the Antioch, ' and though often and unanimoufly elected to the apoftolic throne, refufed that dignity. ' She, and a chorus of confecrated virgins with her, fpent great part of their time in finging ' anthems and divine fongs ; and once when the emperor (Julian) had occafion to pafs by ' them, they fung pfalms chofen purpofely to expofe and ridicule the extravagancies of hea- ' thenifm and idolatry, finging them with an exalted voice ; and among the reft they ap- ' plied, very properly to the occafion, the hundred and fifteenth, from the fourth to the ' eighth verfe, " Their idols are filver and gold, even the work of men's hands, &c." " Let " thofe that make them be like unto them, and alfo all fuch as put their truft in them." ' This fo difturbed the emperor, that he commanded filence fhould be kept whenever he ' came by that place, but to fo little purpofe, that upon his returning, at the motion of Pub- ' lia they gave him another welcome in thefe words : " Let God arife, and let his enemies " be fcattered." And now his anger was raifed fo high, that he ordered the chantrefs to ' be brought before him, and bad her beat on the face till her cheeks were ftained with ' blood ; which efforts of the tyrant's unmanly paffion the aged good woman received with ' pleafure, went home, and, as often as an opportunity offered, entertained him ftill with ' the very fame fort of difagreeable compofitions.' Hift. Ecclef.
† Sociat. Hift. Ecclef. lib. VI. cap. viii.
‡ Hift. Ecclef. lib. VIII. cap. viii.

mere

mere theatre; for which Chryfoſtom reproved them, by telling his people that their rude voices and diſorderly behaviour were very improper for a place of worſhip, in which all things were to be done with reverence to that Being who obſerves the behaviour of every one there.

St. Ambroſe, who had entertained a ſingular veneration for St. Baſil, like him was a great lover of the church-ſervice: it is true he was not originally an ecclefiaſtic, but having been unexpectedly elected biſhop of Milan, he applied himſelf to the duties of the epiſcopal function. Juſtina, whom the emperor Valentinian had married, proving an Arian, commenced a profecution againſt Ambroſe and the orthodox; during which the people watched all night in the church, and Ambroſe appointed that pſalms and hymns ſhould be ſung there after the manner of the oriental churches, left the people ſhould pine away with the tedioufnefs of ſorrow; and from this event, which happened about 374, we may date the introduction of ſinging into weſtern churches.

But the zeal of St. Ambroſe to promote this practice, is in nothing more confpicuous than in his endeavours to reduce it into form and method; as a proof whereof, it is ſaid that he, jointly with St. Auguſtine, upon occaſion of the converſion and baptiſm of the latter, compoſed the hymn Te Deum laudamus, which even now makes a part of the liturgy of our church, and cauſed it to be ſung in his church at Milan; but this has been diſcovered to be a miſtake* : this however is certain, that he inſtituted that method of ſinging, known by the name of the Cantus Ambroſianus, or Ambroſian Chant, a name, for ought that now appears, not applicable to any determined ſeries of notes, but invented to expreſs in general a method of ſinging agreeable to ſome rule given or taught by him. This method, whatever it was, is ſaid to have had a reference to the modes of the ancients, or rather to thoſe of Ptolemy, which we have ſhewn to have been precifely coin-

* The very learned Dr. Uſher, upon the authority of two ancient manuſcripts, afferts the Te Deum to have been made by a biſhop of Triers, named Nicetius or Nicetius, and that not till about the year 500, which was almoſt a century after the death both of St. Ambroſe and St. Auguſtine. L'Eſtrange's Alliance of Divine Offices, 79. The Bene-dictines, who publiſhed the works of St. Ambroſe, judge him not to have been the author of it; and Dr. Cave, though at one time he was of a different judgment, and biſhop Stillingfleet concur in the opinion that the Te Deum was not the compoſition of St. Ambroſe, or of him and St. Auguſtine jointly. Bingham's Antiquities of the Chriſtian Church, book XIV. chap. ii. § 9.

cident

cident with the feven fpecies of the diapafon ; but St. Ambrofe conceiving all above four to be fuperfluous, reduced them to that
number, retaining only the Dorian, the Phrygian, the Lydian, and
the Mixolydian *, which names he rejected, chufing rather to diftinguifh them by epithets of number, as protos, deuteros, tritos,
tetrartos. His defign in this was to introduce a kind of melody
founded on the rules of art, and yet fo plain and fimple in its nature,
that not only thofe whofe immediate duty it was to perform the divine fervice, but even the whole congregation might fing it ; accordingly in the Romifh countries the people now join with the choir in
chanting the divine offices ; and if we may credit the relations of
travellers in this refpect, this diftinguifhed fimplicity of the Ambrofian Chant is even at this day to be remarked in the fervice of the
church of Milan, where it was firft inftituted.

A particular account of the ecclefiaftical modes, as originally conftituted by St. Ambrofe, with the fubfequent improvement of them
by Gregory the Great, is referved for another place : in the interim
it is to be noted that the ecclefiaftical modes are alfo called tropes,
but more frequently tones ; which latter appellation was firft given
to them by Martianus Capella, as we are informed by Sir Henry Spelman, in his Gloffary, voce FRIGDORÆ. The following fcheme reprefents the progreffion in each.

d	c	f	g
c	d	e	f
b	c	d	e
a	b	c	d
G	a	b	c
F	G	a	b
E	F	G	a
D	E	F	G

And this was the original inftitution of what are called, in contradif-
tinction to the modes or moods of the ancients, the ecclefiaftical modes
or tones. Thefe of St. Ambrofe, however well calculated for ufe and
practice, were yet found to be too much reftrained, and not to admit of
all that variety of modulation which the feveral offices in the church-

* Sir Henry Spelman in his Gloffary, voce FRIGDORÆ, in the place of the Mixolydian puts the Æolian.

fervice

ſervice ſeemed to require ; and accordingly St. Gregory, ſurnamed the Great, the firſt pope of that name, with the aſſiſtance of the moſt learned and ſkilful in the muſic of that day, ſet about an amendment of the Cantus Ambroſianus, and inſtituted what became known to later times by the name of the Cantus Gregorianus, or, the Gregorian Chant : but as this was not till near two hundred and thirty years after the time of St. Ambroſe, the account of this, and the other improvements made in muſic by St. Gregory, muſt be referred to another place.

With reſpect to the muſic of the primitive church, though it con-ſiſted in the ſinging of pſalms and hymns, yet was it performed in ſundry different manners, that is to ſay, ſometimes the pſalms were ſung by one perſon alone, the reſt hearing with attention ; ſometimes they were ſung by the whole aſſembly; ſometimes alternately, the congregation being for that purpoſe divided into ſeparate choirs ; and, laſtly, by one perſon, who repeated the firſt part of the verſe, the reſt joining in the cloſe thereof *.

Of the four different methods of ſinging above enumerated, the ſecond and third were very properly diſtinguiſhed by the names of ſymphony and antiphony, and the latter was ſometimes called re-ſponſaria † ; and in this, it ſeems, women were allowed to join, not-withſtanding the apoſtle's injunction on them to keep ſilence.

The method of ſinging in the laſt place above mentioned, clearly ſuggeſts the origin of the office of precentor of a choir, whoſe duty, even at this day, it is to govern the choir, and ſee that the choral ſer-vice be reverently and juſtly performed.

It farther appears, that almoſt from the time when muſic was firſt in-troduced into the ſervice of the church, it was of two kinds, and conſiſt-ed in a gentle inflection of the voice, which they termed plain-ſong, and a more artificial and elaborate kind of muſic, adapted to the hymns and ſolemn offices contained in its ritual ; and this diſtinction has been maintained through all the ſucceeding ages, even to this time.

* Bingham's Antiq. book XIV. chap. I.

† In this diſtinction between ſymphoniac and antiphonal pſalmody, we may diſcern the origin of the two different methods of ſinging practiſed in the Romiſh and Lutheran churches, and of thoſe that follow the rule of Calvin, and others of the reformers; in the former the ſinging is antiphonal, in the latter it is a plain metrical pſalmody, in which all join ; ſo that for each practice the authority of the primitive church may be appealed to.

Befides the reverend fathers of the church above mentioned, we are told, and indeed it appears from many paffages in his writings, that SAINT AUGUSTINE was a paffionate lover of mufic ; this which follows, taken from his Confeffions, lib. IX. cap. vi. is the moft commonly produced as an evidence of his approbation of mufic in the church-fervice, though, it muft be owned, he lived to recant it: 'How abundantly did I weep before God, to hear thofe hymns of 'thine ; being touched to the very quick, by the voices of thy fweet 'church-fong. The voices flowed into my ears, and thy truth 'pleafingly diftilled into my heart; which caufed the affections of 'my devotion to overflow, and my tears to run over; and happy 'did I find myfelf therein.' From hence there is little reafon to doubt, that he enjoined the ufe of it to the clergy of his diocefe. He wrote a treatife De Mufica, in fix books, chiefly, indeed, on the fubject of metre and the laws of verfification, but interfperfed with fuch obfervations on the nature of the confonances, as fhew him to have been very well fkilled in the fcience of mufic.

It is not neceffary to enter into a particular character, either of St. Auguftine or of this his work : thofe who are acquainted with ecclefiaftical hiftory need not to be told, that he was a man of great learning, for the time he lived in, of lively parts, and of exemplary piety. To fuch, however, whofe curiofity is greater than their reading, the following fhort account of this eminent father of the church may not be unpleafing.

He was born at Thagafte, a city of Numidia, on the 13th of November, 354. His father, a burgefs of that city, was called Patricius; and his mother, Monica, who being a woman of great virtue, inftructed him in the principles of the Chriftian religion. In his early youth he was in the rank of the catechumens, and falling dangeroufly ill, earneftly defired to be baptized ; but the violence of the diftemper ceafing, his baptifm was delayed. His father, who was not yet baptized, made him ftudy at Thagafte, Madaura, and afterwards at Carthage. St. Auguftine, having read Cicero's books of philofophy, began to entertain a love for wifdom, and applied himfelf to the ftudy of the Holy Scriptures; neverthelefs, he fuffered himfelf to be feduced by the Manicheans. At the age of nineteen, he returned to Thagafte,

gufte, and taught grammar, and alſo frequented the bar : he afterwards taught rhetoric at Carthage, with applauſe. The inſolence of
the ſcholars at Carthage made him take a reſolution to go to Rome,
though againſt his mother's will. Here alſo he had many ſcholars ;
but diſliking them, he quitted Rome, and ſettled at Milan, and was
choſen public profeſſor of rhetoric in that city. Here he had opportunities of hearing the ſermons of St. Ambroſe, which, together with the ſtudy of St. Paul's Epiſtles, and the converſion of two
of his friends, determined him to retract his errors, and quit the ſect
of the Manicheans : this was in the thirty-ſecond year of his age. In
the vacation of the year 386, he retired to the houſe of a friend of his,
named Verecundus, where he ſeriouſly applied himſelf to the ſtudy of
the Chriſtian religion, in order to prepare himſelf for baptiſm, which
he received at Eaſter, in the year 387. Soon after this, his mother
came to ſee him at Milan, and invite him back to Carthage ; but at
Oſtia, whither he went to embark, in order to his return, ſhe died.
He arrived in Africa about the end of the year 388, and having obtained a garden-plot without the walls of the city of Hippo, he aſſo-
ciated himſelf with eleven other perſons of eminent ſanctity, who
diſtinguiſhed themſelves by wearing leathern girdles, and lived there
in a monaſtic way for the ſpace of three years, exerciſing themſelves
in faſting, prayer, ſtudy, and meditation, day and night : from hence
ſprung up the Auguſtine friars, or eremites of St. Auguſtine, being
the firſt order of mendicants ; thoſe of St. Jerome, the Carmelites, and
others, being but branches of this of St. Auguſtine. About this time,
or as ſome ſay before, Valerius, biſhop of Hippo, againſt his will, ordained him prieſt : neverthelefs, he continued to reſide in his little
monaſtery, with his brethren, who, renouncing all property, poſſeſſed their goods in common. Valerius, who had appointed St. Auguſtine to preach in his place, allowed him to do it in his preſence,
contrary to the cuſtom of the churches in Africa. He explained the
creed, in a general council of Africa, held in 393. Two years after,
Valerius, fearing he might be preferred to be biſhop of another
church, appointed him his coadjutor or colleague, and cauſed him to
be ordained biſhop of Hippo, by Megalius, biſhop of Calame, then
primate of Numidia. St. Auguſtine died the 28th day of Auguſt,
430, aged ſeventy-ſix years, having had the misfortune to ſee his
country invaded by the Vandals, and the city where he was biſhop
beſieged for ſeven months.

The works of St. Augustine make ten tomes; the best edition of them is that of Maurin, printed at Antwerp, in 1700: they are but little read at this time, except by the clergy of the Greek church and in the Spanish universities; our bookfellers in London receive frequent commissions for them, and indeed for most of the fathers, from Russia, and also from Spain.

About this time flourished AMBROSIUS AURELIUS THEODOSIUS MACROBIUS, an author whose name appears in almost every catalogue of musical writers extant; but whose works scarcely entitle him to a place among them. He lived in the time of Theodosius the younger, who was proclaimed emperor of the East anno 402. He was a man of consular dignity, and held the office of chamberlain to the emperor. Fabricius makes it a question whether he was a Christian or a Pagan. His works are a Commentary on the Somnium Scipionis of Cicero, in two books, and Saturnaliorum Conviviorum, in seven books; in both which he takes occasion to treat of music, and more especially the harmony of the spheres. The chief of what he says concerning music in general is contained in his Commentary on the Somnium Scipionis, and is taken from Nicomachus, and others of the followers of Pythagoras. Martini mentions also a discourse on mundane music of his, which was translated into Italian by Ercole Bottrigari, with notes; but he speaks of it as a manuscript, and by the list of the works of Macrobius, it does not appear to have ever been printed.

Of such writers as Macrobius, and a few other of the Latins who will shortly be mentioned, that have written not professedly on music, but have briefly or transiently taken notice of it in the course of a work written with some other view than to explain it, little is to be said. There is nevertheless a Greek writer of this class, who lived some considerable time before Macrobius, and indeed was prior to Porphyry, the last of the Greek musical writers that deserves to be taken notice of, not so much because he has contributed to the improvement of the science, as because in a voluminous work of his there are interspersed a great variety of curious particulars relating to it, not to be found elsewhere. The author here meant is Athenæus the grammarian, called, by way of eminence, the Grecian Varro; he was born at Naucratis in Egypt, and flourished in the third century; of many works that he wrote, one only remains, intitled The Deipnosophists, that is to say, the Sophists at

7   Table,

Table, where he introduces a number of learned men of all pro-
feſſions, who converſe upon various ſubjects at the table of a Roman
citizen named Larenſius. In this work there are many very pleaſant
ſtories, and an infinite variety of facts, citations, and alluſions, which
make the reading of it extremely delightful. The little that he has
ſaid of muſic lies ſcattered up and down in this work, which, with
the Latin tranſlation of it, makes a large folio volume.

In his fourth book, pag. 174, he gives the names of the ſuppoſed
inventors of the ancient muſical inſtruments, and, among others, of
Creſibius, and of the hydraulic organ conſtructed by him ; and it is
ſuppoſed that this is the moſt ancient and authentic account of that
inſtrument now extant. He ſays, pag. 175, that the Barbiton or
lyre, or, as Merſennus will have it, the viol, was the invention of
Anacreon ; and the Monaulon, or ſingle pipe, of the Egyptian
Oſiris.

Elſewhere, viz. in his fourteenth book, he ſpeaks of the power
of muſic, and of the fondneſs which the Arcadians, above all other
people, entertained for it : and in the ſame book, pag. 637, he deſcribes that ſtrange inſtrument, invented by Pythagoras Zacynthius,
called the tripod lyre, correſponding in every particular with the deſcription of it hereinbefore given from Blanchinus; to which may be
added, that Athenæus expreſsly ſays that the three ſeveral ſets of
chords between the legs, were in their tuning adjuſted to the three
primitive modes, the Dorian, the Lydian,° and the Phrygian.

Of this learned, curious, and moſt entertaining work, the beſt
edition is that of Dalechamp, with the Greek original and Latin
tranſlation in oppoſite columns. To this are added the animadver-
ſions of Iſaac Caſaubon, which are very curious, and make another
volume. In theſe it is ſaid that the Muſicorum διαγράμματα, or Tab-
latura, i. e. the art of writing or noting down of muſic, was invented by Stratonicus of Rhodes. If. Caſaub. Animadverſ. in Athenæum,
lib. VIII. cap. xii.

MARTIANUS MINEUS FELIX CAPELLA was born, as Caſſiodorus teſtifies, at Madaura, a town in Africa, ſituated between the
countries of Getulia and Numidia, lived at Rome under Leo the Thracian, viz. about the year of Chriſt 437; he was the author of a work intitled, De Nuptiis Philologiæ et Mercurii, the ſtyle whereof, in the
opinion of ſome, is harſh, and rather barbarous, though others, and Fabricius

bricius in particular, who terms it a delightful fable [*], think it in nowise deserves such a character: this work, which consists of prose and verse intermixed, is in fact a treatise on the seven liberal sciences, and consequently includes a discourse on music, which makes the ninth book thereof, and is introduced in the following manner: the author supposes the marriage of Philologia, a virgin, to Mercury, and that Venus and the other deities, as also Orpheus, Amphion, and Arion, are assembled to honour the solemnity; the Sciences, who, to render the work as poetical as may be, are represented as persons, also attend, among whom is Harmonia, described as having her head decked with variety of ornaments, and bearing symbols of the faculty over which she is feigned to preside. She is made to exhibit the power of sounds by such melody as Jupiter himself commends, which is succeeded by a request of Apollo and Minerva to unfold the mysteries of harmony. She first craves leave to relate that she formerly was an inhabitant of the earth, and that through the inspirations of Pythagoras, Aristoxenus, and others, she had taught men the use of the lyre and the pipe; and by the singing of birds, the whistling of the winds, and the murmuring of water-falls, had instructed even the artless shepherds in the rudiments of melody. That by the power of her art she had cured diseases, quieted seditions, and composed and attempered the irregular affections of mankind; notwithstanding all which, she had been contemned and reviled by those sons of earth, and had therefore sought the heavens, where she found the motions of the orbs regulated by her own principles. She then proceeds to explain the precepts of harmony in a short discourse, which, if we consider the substance and method rather than the style of it, must be allowed to be a very elegant composition, and by much the most intelligible of any ancient treatise on the science of music now extant.

Capella concludes this ninth book of his treatise De Nuptiis thus: ' When Harmonia had run over these things concerning songs, and the ' sweetness of verse, in a manner both august and persuasive, to the ' gods and heroes, who were very intent, she decently withdrew; ' then Jupiter rose up, and Cymesis modulating in divine sympho- ' nies, came to the chamber of the virgin, to the great delight of all.'

[*] Biblioth. Lat. Art. CAPELLA.

The

The above difcourfe of Martianus Capella is manifeftly taken from Ariftides Quintilianus, of which, to fay the truth, it is very little more than an abridgment, but it is fuch a one as renders it in fome refpects preferable to the original ; for neither is it fo prolix as Quintilian's treatife, nor does it partake of that obfcurity which difcourages fo many from the ftudy of his work ; and when it is faid, as it has been by fome, that the ftyle of Capella is barbarous, this muft be taken as the opinion of grammarians, who, without regarding the intrinfic merit of any work, eftimate it by certain rules of claffical elegance, which they themfelves have eftablifhed as the teft of perfection. It is by thefe men, and for this reafon, and perhaps becaufe he had not the good fortune to be born at Rome, that Capella is termed a femi-barbarian, and his writings reprobated as unworthy the perufal of men of fcience *. But, notwithftanding thefe opinions, one of the beft grammarians of the prefent age, the learned and ingenious author of Hermes, or a Philofophical Inquiry concerning Univerfal Grammar, has forborne to pafs a cenfure of barbarity on the ftyle of this author: his fentiment of him is, that he was rather a philologift than a philofopher ; a teftimony that leaves him a better character than fome of thofe deferve who have been fo liberal in their cenfures of him. It has been faid above, that Fabricius has given to the treatife De Nuptiis the character of a delightful fable; and Gregory of Tours delivers his opinion of it at large in the following words : ' In grammatices docent legere, in ' dialecticis altercationum propofitiones advertere, in rhetoricis per' fuadere, in geometricis terrarum linearumque menfuras colligere, in ' aftrologicis curfus fiderum contemplari, in arithmeticis numerorum

---

* The learned bifhop of Avranches is fomewhat lefs fevere in his cenfure. He gives the following character of Capella and his work. ' Martianus Capella has given the name ' of fatire to his work becaufe it is written in verfe and profe, and the profitable and enter' taining parts are agreeably interwoven. His defign is to treat of the arts, which have ' the appellation of liberal ; and thefe he reprefents by certain allegorical perfonages, with ' attributes proper to each. The principal action in this fable is the marriage of Mercury ' and Philology, a feigned being, intended to fignify the love of literature. The artifice ' of this allegory is not very fubtle, and as to the ftyle it is barbarifm itfelf; and for the ' figures, they are unpardonably bold and extravagant; befides all which it is fo obfcure ' as hardly to be intelligible; otherwife it is learned, and full of notions not common. ' Some write that the author was an African ; if he was not, his harfh and forced ftyle ' would induce one to believe he was of that country. The time he lived in is unknown ; ' it only appears that he was more ancient than Juftinian.' Huetius de l'Origine des Romaines.

' partes

' partes colligere, in harmoniis fonorum modulationes fuavium ac-
' centuum carminibus concrepare.' ·Hence it may feem that Mr.
Malcolm was rather too hafty in condemning this work ; and that in
pronouncing of its author as he has done in his Treatife on Mufic,
pag. 498, that he was but a forry copier from Ariftides, he has done
him injuftice.   Of Capella's work, De Nuptiis Philologiæ et Mercurii, there have been many editions; that of Meibomius is the
moft ufeful to a mufician ; but there is a very good one, with corrections and notes, by Grotius, in octavo, publifhed in 1559, when he
was but fourteen years of age.

C H A P.   V.

THE feveral works hereinbefore enumerated contain the whole
of what, in the ftrict fenfe of the term, we are to underftand by
the ancient fyftem of mufic; and as many of them appear to be of very
great antiquity, we are to efteem it a fingular inftance of good fortune that they are yet remaining; that they are fo, is owing to the
care and induftry of very many learned men, who, from public libraries, and other repofitories, have fought out the moft correct manufcripts of the refpective authors, and given them to the world in
print ; as to Ariftoxenus, the firft in the lift of the harmonical writers, it is doubtful whether his Elements ever appeared in print, till
near the middle of the feventeeth century, inafmuch as Morley, who
lived in the reign of our queen Elizabeth, and was a very learned and
inquifitive man in all matters relating to mufical fcience, profeffes never
to have feen the Elements of Ariftoxenus; Euclid indeed had been
publifhed in the year 1498, in a Latin tranflation of Georgius Valla,
of Placentia, but under the name of Cleonidas.   It was alfo, in 1557,
publifhed at Paris in Greek, with a new Latin tranflation by Johannes Pena, mathematician to the French king, but in a very incor-
rect manner ; other editions were alfo publifhed of it, in which the
errors of the former were multiplied.   At length, with the affiftance
of our countrymen Selden, Gerard Langbaine, Marcus Meibomius,
a man well acquainted with the fcience, and well fkilled in Greek
literature, publifhed it, together with Ariftoxenus Nicomachus, Alypius, Gaudentius, Bacchius Senioris, Ariftides Quintilianus, and the

ninth

ninth book of the fable de Nupriis Philologiæ et Mercurii of Martianus Capella, with a Latin translation of the first seven of the above-named writers, a general preface replete with excellent learning, and copious notes on them all.

Besides the general preface, Meibomius has given a particular one to each author as they stand in his edition, which prefaces, as they contain a variety of patticulars relating to the respective authors and their works, and are otherwise curious, are well worthy of attention. The Manual of Nicomachus was first published and translated into Latin by Meibomius, who gives the author a very great character, and with great ingenuity fixes the time when he lived; for he observes that Nicomachus in the course of his work mentions Thrasyllus, who he says he thinks to be the same with one of that name mentioned frequently by Suetonius in Augustus and Tiberius, and by the old commentator on Juvenal, Sat. VI. as a famous mathematician; and from hence he infers that he lived after the time of Augustus.

To the Isagoge of Alypius the preface is but very short, but in that to Gaudentius, which follows it next in order Meibomius cites a passage from Cassiodorus, a Latin writer on music, who flourished in the fifth century, and will presently be spoken of, from whence he thinks the age when Alypius lived may in some measure be learned. He observes also that it appears from the same passage of Cassiodorus that Gaudentius had been translated into Latin by a Roman, a friend of his, named Mutianus *; the whole passage, to give it together as it stands in Cassiodorus, is in these words : ' Gratissima ergo
' nimia utilisque cognitio, quæ et sensum nostrum ad superna erigit,
' et aures modulatione permulcet : quam apud Græcos Alypius, Eu-
' clydes, Ptolomæus, et cæteri probabili institutione docuerunt.
' Apud Latinos autem vir magnificus Albinus librum de hac re, com-
' pendio, sub brevitate conscripsit, quem in bibliotheca Romæ non
' habuisse atque studiose legisse retinemus. Qui si forte gentili in-
' cursione sublatus est, habetis hic Gaudentium Mutiani Latinum :
' quem si solicita intensione legitis, hujus scientiæ vobis atria pate-
' facit. Fertur etiam latio sermone et Apuleium Madaurensem insti-
' tuta hujus operis effecisse, scripsit etiam et pater Augustinus de
' Musica sex libros, in quibus humanam vocem, rhythmicos sonos, et

* Mutianus also translated the Homilies of St. Chrysostom. Fabr. Biblioth. Græc. lib. III. cap. x.

' har-

' harmoniam modulabilem in longis fyllabis atque brevibus natura-
' liter habere monftravit.   Cenforinus quoque de accentibus voci
' noftræ ad neceffariis fubtiliter difputavit, pertinere dicens ad mufi-
' cam difciplinam : quem vobis inter cæteros tranfcriptum reliqui.'
Caffiod. de Mufica.

Gaudentius is publifhed from a manufcript, which the editor procured of his friends Selden and Langbaine, who collated it for him,
with two others which had been prefented to the Bodleian library,
the one by Sir Henry Savil, and the other by William earl of Pem-
broke, formerly chancellor of the univerfity of Oxford.   It feems
that our countryman Chilmead had undertaken to publifh an edition
of Gaudentius, but being informed that Meibomius had entertained
a defign of giving it to the world, he generoufly fent him his papers,
and remitted the care of publifhing them to him.

Bacchius Senior was firft publifhed in the original Greek, and
with a French tranflation by Merfennus, in a commentary on certain
chapters in the book of Genefis, written by him to explain the mufic
of the ancient Hebrews and Greeks, intitled ' Queftiones et Expli-
' catio in fex priora capita Genefeos, quibus etiam Græcorum et He-
' bræorum Mufica inflauratur.'   Of this tranflation Meibomius, in his
general preface, fpeaks in very fevere terms ; he fays he did not know
that any fuch was extant, till he was informed thereof by his friend
Ifmael Bullialdus ; he fays that he then had it brought to him from
Paris by the courier, and that if he had feen it before he had publifhed his notes on that author, they would have been made much
fuller by obfervations on his errors.   However the only error that
Meibomius here charges Merfennus with, is that of having confounded the Stantes with the Mobiles in his reprefentation of the Syftema
maxima.

Ariftides Quintilianus is taken from a manufcript which Meibomius frequently mentions as belonging to Jofeph Scaliger, in which
was contained Alypius, Nicomachus, Ariftoxenos, Ariftides, and
Bacchius.   This manufcript was depofited in the library of Leyden,
and communicated to him by Daniel Heinfius, together with two
manufcripts of Martianus Capella.

With the affiftance of the feveral manufcripts above mentioned,
and a correfpondence with the moft learned men of his time, namely, Selden, Langbaine, Salmafius, Leo Allatius, and many others,
                                                        Meibomius

Meibomius completed his edition of the ancient musical authors, and published it at Amsterdam in the year 1652, with a dedication to Christina queen of Sweden.

With respect to the other Greek writers, namely, Ptolemy, Manuel Bryennius, and Porphyry, the former of these was published, together with Porphyry's Commentary, by Antonius Gogavinus, at Venice, with a Latin version in 1562, but, as it should seem from Dr. Wallis's censure of it, in a very inaccurate manner: Meibomius somewhere says that he had intended to publish both Porphyry and Manuel Bryennius, but he not having done it, Dr. Wallis undertook it, and has given it to the world in the third volume of his works. Most of the manuscripts that were made use of for the above publications, had been carried to Constantinople upon the erection of the eastern empire, to preserve them from the ravages of the northern invaders: and as that city continued to be the seat of learning for some centuries, they, together with an immense collection of Greek and Latin manuscripts, containing the works of the most valuable of the Greek and Roman writers, were preserved there with great care. But the taking and sacking of Constantinople by the Turks, in the year 1452, was followed by an emigration of learning and learned men, who, escaping from the destruction that threatened them, settled chiefly in Italy, and became the revivers of literature in the western parts of Europe.

These men upon their removal from Constantinople brought with them into Italy an immense treasure of learning, consisting of ancient manuscripts in all the several branches thereof, which they disseminated by lectures in the public schools: many of these manuscripts have at different periods been printed and dispersed throughout Europe, and others of them remain unpublished, either in public libraries, or in the collections of princes and other great persons *.

These men are also said to have introduced into Italy the knowledge of ancient music, which they could no otherwise do than by public lectures, and by giving to the world copies of the several treatises of the Greek harmonicians, hereinbefore particularly men-

* The manuscripts relating to music which Kircher procured access to for the purpose of compiling his Musurgia, are by him said to be extant in the library of the Roman College; and he speaks of one huge tome in particular, in which he says are the several works of Aristides Quintilianus, Bryennius, Plutarch, Aristotle, Callimachus, Aristoxenus, Alypius, Ptolemy, Euclid, Nicomachus, Boetius, Martianus Capella, Valla, and some others.

tioned ; and the effects of these their labours to cultivate that kind of knowledge were made apparent by Gaffurius, or Franchinus, as he is otherwise called, who, before the end of the fifteenth century, published those several works of his, which have justly entitled him to the appellation of the Father of Music among the moderns.

Before the migration of learning from the East, all that was known of the ancient music in the western parts of Europe was contained in the writings of Censorinus, Macrobius, Martianus Capella, Boetius, Cassiodorus, and a few other Latin writers, who, as Meibomius says of Capella, might very justly be termed Pedarians, inasmuch as they were strict followers of the ancient harmonicians ; or else in the works of a very learned and excellent man, to whom this censure cannot be extended, namely, Boetius, of whom, and of whose inestimable work De Musica a very particular account will shortly be given ; in the interim it will be necessary to mention some innovations that had been made in music subsequent to Ptolemy, and before Boetius, of whom we are about to speak ; and first it is to be noted that in this interval, if not before the commencement of it, the genera, at least in practice, were reduced to one, namely, the diatonic : and next it is to be remarked, that the method of notation used by the ancients, the explanation whereof is almost the sole purpose of Alypius's book, was totally changed by the Romans, who to the great system, which consisted, as has been shewn, of a bisdiapason, containing fifteen sounds, applied as many letters of their own alphabet ; so that assigning to Proslambanomeuos the letter A, the system terminated at P. It does not appear that at this time, nor indeed till a long time after, any marks or characters had been invented to denote the length or duration of musical sounds ; nor, notwithstanding all that has been said about the rhythmus of the ancients, does it in the least appear that they had any rule for determining the length of the sounds, other than that which constituted the

In the account of the late discoveries in the ruins of Herculaneum, given by the abbé Winckelman, mention is made of an ancient Greek treatise on music found there, written by one Philodemus, an author who has escaped the researches of the industrious Fabricius. Nevertheless, a philosopher of that name occurs amongst the Locrians, in Stanley's list of the Pythagorean school. Hist. of Philosophy, Pythagoras. chap. xxiv. This manuscript the antiquaries employed by the king of Naples, though it is burned to a crust, have begun to unroll ; but the condition of it, and the nature of the process made use of for developing it, render it almost impossible that the world can ever be the better for its contents. See the Letter of the Abbé Winckelman to Count Brohl on this subject.

measure

meafure of the verfes * to which thofe founds were feverally applied ; which confideration leaves it in fome fort a queftion whether among the ancients there was any fuch thing as merely inftrumental mufic.

In this method of notation by the firft fifteen letters of the Latin alphabet, a modern will difcover a great defect ; for, being in a lineal pofition, they by their fituation inferred no diverfity between grave and acute, whereas in the ftave of the moderns the characters by a judicious analogy are made to exprefs, according to their different fituations in the ftave, all the differences of acute and grave from one extremity of the fyftem to the other.

ANITIUS MANLIUS TORQUATUS SEVERINUS BOETIUS, was the moft confiderable of all the Latin writers on mufic ; indeed his treatife on the fubject fupplied for fome centuries the want of thofe Greek manufcripts which were fuppofed to have been loft ; for this reafon, as alfo on account of his fuperior eminence in literature, he merits to be very particularly fpoken of. He was by birth a Roman, defcended of an ancient family, many of whom had been fenators, and fome advanced to the dignity of the confulate : the time of his birth is related to have been about that period in the Roman hiftory when Auguftulus, whofe fears had induced him to a refignation of the empire, was banifhed, and Odoacer king of the Herulians began to reign in Italy, viz. in the year of Chrift 476, or fomewhat after. The father of Boetius dying while he was yet an infant, his relations undertook the care of his education and the direction of his ftudies ; his excellent parts were foon difcovered, and, as well. to enrich his mind with the ftudy of philofophy, as to perfect himfelf in the Greek language, he was fent to Athens. Returning young to Rome, he was foon diftinguifhed for his learning and virtue, and promoted to *

* In the Chronology of Sir Ifaac Newton, pag. 14. is the following paffage. ' In ' the year 1035 [before Chrift] the Idæi Dactyli [a people fuppofed to have come from ' Numidia, vide fteyl. Cofm. pag. 555. edit. 1703] find out iron in mount Ida in Crete, ' and work it into armour and iron tools, and thereby give a beginning to the trades of ' fmiths and armourers in Europe ; and by finging and dancing in their armour, and ' keeping time by ftriking upon one another's armours with their fwords, they bring in ' mufic and poetry, and at the fame time they nurfe up the Cretan Jupiter in a cave of ' the fame mountain, dancing about him in their armour.'

The origin of metrical numbers, and of the rhythmus, as is called, is by fome referred to this event ; but admitting this as a fact, it does not afcertain the time when the characters declaring the length or duration of founds were firft invented ; and the truth is that thefe are, comparatively fpeaking, a modern improvement in mufic.

the

the principal dignities in the state, and at length to the consulate. Living in great affluence and splendour, he addicted himself to the study of theology, mathematics, ethics, and logic ; and how great a master he became in each of these branches of learning appears from those works of his now extant. The great offices which he bore in the state, and his consummate wisdom and inflexible integrity, procured him such a share in the public councils, as proved in the end his destruction ; for as he ever employed his interest in the king for the protection and encouragement of deserving men, so he exerted his utmost efforts in the detection of fraud, the repressing of violence, and the defence of the state against invaders. At this time Theodoric the Goth had attempted to ravage the Campania ; and it was owing to the vigilance and resolution of Boetius that that country was preserved from destruction. At length, having murdered Odoacer, Theodoric became king of Italy, where he governed thirty-three years with prudence and moderation, during which time Boetius possessed a large share of his esteem and confidence. It happened about this time that Justin, the emperor of the East, upon his succeeding to Anastasius, made an edict condemning all the Arians, except the Goths, to perpetual banishment from the eastern empire ; in this edict Hormisda bishop of Rome, and also the senate concurred ; but Theodoric, who, as being a Goth, was an Arian, was extremely troubled at it, and conceived an aversion against the senate for the share they had borne in this proscription. Of this disposition in the king, three men of profligate lives and desperate fortunes, Gaudentius, Opilio, and Basilius, took advantage ; for having entertained a secret desire of revenge against Boetius, for having been instrumental in the dismission of the latter from a lucrative employment under the king, they accused him of several crimes, such as the stifling a charge, the end whereof was to involve the whole senate in the guilt of treason; and an attempt, by dethroning the king, to restore the liberty of Italy ; and, lastly, they suggested that, to acquire the honours he was in possession of, Boetius had had recourse to magical arts.

Boetius was at this time at a great distance from Rome ; however Theodoric transmitted the complaint to the senate, enforcing it with a suggestion that the safety, as well of the people as the prince, was rendered very precarious by this supposed design to exterminate the Goths : the senate perhaps fearing the resentment of the king, and

having

having nothing to hope from the fucceſs of an enterprize, which, ſuppoſing it ever to have been meditated, was now rendered abortive, without ſummoning him to his defence, condemned Boetius to death. The king however, apprehending ſome bad conſequence from the execution of a ſentence ſo flagrantly unjuſt, mitigated it to baniſhment. The place of his exile was Ticinum, now the city of Pavia, in Italy: being in that place ſeparated from his relations, who had not been permitted to follow him into his retirement, he endeavoured to derive from philoſophy thoſe comforts which that alone was capable of affording to one in his forlorn ſituation, ſequeſtered from his friends, in the power of his enemies, and at the mercy of a capricious tyrant; and accordingly he there compoſed that valuable diſcourſe, entitled De Conſolatione Philoſophiæ. To give a more particular account of this book would be needleſs, it being well known in the learned world: one remarkable circumſtance relating to it is, that, by thoſe under affliction it has in various times been applied to, as the means of fortifying their minds and reconciling them to the diſpenſations of Providence, almoſt as conſtantly as the ſcriptures themſelves. Our Saxon king Alfred, whoſe reign, though happy upon the whole, was attended with great viciſſitudes of fortune, had recourſe to this book of Boetius, at a time when his diſtreſſes compelled him to ſeek retirement; and, that he might the better impreſs upon his mind the noble ſentiments inculcated in it, he made a complete tranſlation of it into the Saxon language, which, within theſe few years, has been given to the world in its proper character: Chaucer made a tranſlation of it into Engliſh, which is printed among his works, and is alluded to in theſe verſes of his:

> Adam Scrivenir, yf ever it the befalle
> Boece or Croiles for to write new,
> Under thy longe lockes thou muſt have the ſcalle:
> But aftir my makynge thou write more true;
> So ofte a daye I mote thy werke renewe,
> It to corrette, and eke to rubbe and ſcrape,
> And al is thorow thy negligence and rape.

And Camden relates, that queen Elizabeth, during the time of her confinement by her ſiſter Mary, to mitigate her grief, red and afterwards tranſlated it into very elegant Engliſh.

It

It is more than probable that Boetius would have ended his
exile by a natural death, had it not been for an event that happened about two years after the pronouncing his fentence; for,
in the year 524. Juftin, the emperor, thought fit to promulgate
an edict againft the Arians, whereby he commanded, without excepting the Goths, as he had done lately, on another occafion,
that all bifhops who maintained that herefy fhould be depofed, and
their churches confecrated after the true Chriftian form. To avert
this decree, Theodoric fent an embaffy to the emperor, which, to
render it the more fplendid and refpectable, confifted of the bifhop or
pope himfelf, who at that time was John the Second, the immediate fucceffor of Hormifda, and four others, of the confular and
patrician orders, who were inftructed to folicit with the emperor
the repeal of this decree, with threats, in cafe of a refufal, that
the king would deftroy Italy with fire and fword. Upon the arrival of the ambaffadors at Conftantinople, the emperor very art-
fully contrived to receive them in fuch a manner as naturally
tended to detach them from their mafter, and make them flight the
bufinefs they were fent to negociate, and he fucceeded accordingly;
for as foon as they approached the city, the emperor, the clergy, and
a great number of the people, went in proceffion to meet them. In
their way to the church, the upper hand of the emperor was given to
the bifhop; and upon their arrival there, the holy father, to fhew his
gratitude for the honour done him of fitting on the right of the imperial throne, celebrated the day of the Refurrection after the Roman ufe,
and crowned Juftin emperor. Of the infufferable pride and arrogance
of this John fo many inftances are related, that no one who reads
them can lament the fate which afterwards befel him, viz. that he died
in a dungeon. It is recorded, that upon his arrival at Corinth, in his
way to Conftantinople, great enquiry was made for a gentle horfe for
him to ride on; upon which, a nobleman of that city fent him one
that, for the goodnefs of its temper, had been referved for the ufe of
his lady; the bifhop accepted the favour, and, after travelling as far as
he thought fit, returned the beaft to the owner: but behold what followed, the fagacious animal, confcious of the merit of having once
borne the fucceffor of St. Peter, refufed ever after to let the lady mount
him; upon which the hufband fent him again to the pope, with a
requeft that he would accept of that which was no longer of any ufe

to

to the owner. This event, it is to be noted, is recorded as a miracle; but if we allow it the credit due to one, it will reflect but little honour on the worker of it, since the utmost it proves is, that the pope had the power of communicating to a horse a quality which had rendered the primitive possessor of it to the last degree odious.

It is not easy to see how, with any degree of propriety, or consistent with justice, the misbehaviour of the ambassadors could be imputed to Boetius, who, all this while, was confined to the place of his exile, and seemed to be employing his time in a way much more suited to his circumstances and character than in the abetting the misguided and malevolent zeal of either of two enthusiastic princes; nevertheless, we are told, that Theodoric no sooner heard of the behaviour of John and his colleagues, than he began to meditate the death of Boetius : he however suppressed his resentment, till he had received a formal complaint from his people of the infidelity of those entrusted by him. Immediately on his arrival, he committed the bishop to close confinement, wherein he shortly after ended his days. Had his revenge stopped here, his conduct might have escaped censure, but he completed the ruin of his character by sentencing Boetius, to death, who, together with Symmachus, the father of his wife, was beheaded in prison on the tenth of the kalends of November, 705. In order to palliate the cruelty of the king, it has been insinuated, that the treachery of his ambassadors was a kind of evidence that the conspiracy had a foundation in truth; and that fact once established, the intimacy which had subsisted for several years between Boetius and the bishop, before the banishment of the former, furnished a ground for suspicion that he was at least not ignorant of it. It is farther said, that, as if he believed the conspiracy to be real, the king sent to Boetius, in prison, offers of pardon, if he would disclose the whole treason; but the protestations which he made upon that occasion of his innocence, afford the strongest evidence that could be given that he was not privy to it.

But the causes of this severe resolution of Theodoric are elsewhere to be sought for : he was arrived at the age of seventy-two, and for some years had been infected with the vices usually imputed to old age : he had reigned more than thirty-three years ; and though the mildness and prudence of his government, and that paternal tenderness with which he had ruled his people, were greater than could be expected from a prince who had made his way to dominion by the mur-der of the rightful fovereign, the difappointments he had met with, the infults that had been offered him, one particularly in the perfon of his fifter, who had received fome indignities from the African Vandals, the contempt that had been fhewn him in this late embaffy, and, above all, his utter inability to refent thefe injuries in the way he moft defired, thefe misfortunes concurring, deprived him of that quanimity of temper which had been the charaƈteriſtic of his reign: in fhort, he grew jealous, timid, vindiƈtive, and cruel; and after this, nothing he did was to be wondered at .   But to return to Boetius.

The extenfive learning and eloquence of this great man are confpicuous in his works; and his fingular merits have been celebrated by the ableft writers that have lived fince the reftoration of learning. His firft wife, for he was twice married, was named Helpes, a Sicilian lady of great beauty and fortune, but more eminently diftinguifhed by the endowments of her mind, and her inviolable affection for fo excellent a man. She had a genius for poetry, and wrote with a degree of judgment and correƈtnefs not common to her fex. He defired much to have iffue by her; but fhe dying young, he embalmed her memory in the following elegant verfes:

Helpes diƈta fui, Siculæ regionis alumna,
   Quam procùl à patria, conjugis egit amor.
Quo fine, mœfta dies, nox anxia, flebilis hora
   Nec folum caro, fed fpiritus unus erat.
Lux mea non claufa eft, tali remanente marito,
   Majorique animæ, parte fuperftes ero.
Porticibus facris nam nunc peregrina quiefco,
   Judicis eterni teftificata thronum.

* Procopius relates that he was frighted to death; the following is his account of that ſtrange accident:
' Symmachus and his fon-in-law, Boetius, juſt men and great relievers of the poor,
' fenators and confuls, had many enemies, by whofe falfe accufations Theodoric being
' perfuaded that they plotted againſt him, put them to death, and confifcated their eſtates.
' Not long after, his waiters fet before him at fupper the head of a great fifh, which feemed
' to him to be the head of Symmachus, lately murthered; and with his teeth ſticking out,
' and fierce glaring eyes, to threaten him. Being frighted, he grew chill, went to bed
' lamenting what he had done to Symmachus and Boetius, and foon after died.' De Bello
Gothico, lib L

Ne

Ne qua manus buftum violet, nifi fortè jugalis,
Hæc iterum cupiat jungere membra fuis.
Ut Thalami cumuliq; comes, nec morte revellar,
Et focios vitæ nectat uterque cinis.

His other wife, Rufticiana, was the daughter of Quintus Aurelius Menius Symmachus, a chief of the fenate, and conful in the year 485 : with her he received a confiderable acceffion to his fortune. He had feveral children by her; two of whom arrived to the dignity of the confulate. His conjugal tendernefs was very exemplary; and it may be truly faid, that, for his public and private virtues, he was one of the great ornaments of that degenerate age in which it was his misfortune to be born.

The tomb of Boetius is to be feen in the church of St. Auguftine, at Pavia, near the fteps of the chancel, with the following epitaph :

Mœonia et Latia lingua clariffimus, et qui
Conful eram, hic perii, miffus in exilium;
Et quia mors rapuit? Probitas me vexit ad auras,
Et nunc fama viget maxima vivit opus.

Many ages after his death the emperor Otho the Third enclofed his bones, then lying neglected amongft the rubbifh, in a marble cheft; upon which occafion Gerbert, an eminent fcholar of that time, and who was afterwards advanced to the papal chair by the name of Sylvefter the Second, did honour to his memory in the following lines:

Roma potens, dum jura fuo declarat in orbe,
Tu pater, et patriæ lumen, Severine Boeti,
Confulis officio, rerum difponis habenas,
Infundis lumen ftudiis, et cedere nefcis
Græcorum ingeniis, fed mens divina coercet
Imperium mundi. Gladio bacchante Gothorum
Libertas Romana perit: tu conful et exul,
Infignes titulos præclara morte relinquis,

Tunc decus Imperii, fummas qui pragravat artes,
Tertius Otho fua dignum te judicat aula ;
Æternumque tui flatuit monumenta laboris,
Et bene promeritum, meritis exornat honeftis.

The writings of Boetius, the titles whereof are given below *, feem to have been collected with great care : an edition of them was printed at Venice, in one volume in folio, 1499. In 1570, Glareanus, of Bafil, collated that with feveral manufcripts, and publifhed it, with a few various readings in the margin. To render his author more intelligible, the editor has inferted fundry diagrams of his own ; but has been careful not to confound them with the original ones of Boetius.

But before thefe, or indeed the doctrines of Boetius, can be rendered intelligible, it is neceffary firft to ftate the general drift and tendency of the author, in his treatife De Mufica ; and next to explain the feveral terms made ufe of by him in the demonftration of the proportions of the confonances and other intervals, as alfo the proportions themfelves, diftinguifhing between the feveral fpecies of arithmetical, geometrical, and harmonical proportion.

The defign of Boetius in the above mentioned treatife was, by the aid of arithmetic, to demonftrate thofe ratios which thofe of the Py-

* In Porphyrium à Victorino tranflatum, lib. II. In Porphyrium à fe Latinum factum, lib. V. In Prædicamenta Ariftotelis, lib. IV. In librum de Interpretatione Commentaria minora, lib II. In eundem de Interpretatione Commentaria majora, lib. VI. Analyticorum priorum Ariftotelis, Anitio Manlio Severino Boethio interprete, lib. II. Analyticorum pofteriorum Ariftotelis, Anitio Manlio Severino Boethio Interprete, lib. II. Introductio ad categoricos Syllogifmos, lib I. De Syllogifmo categorico, lib. II. De Syllogifmo hypothetico, lib. II De Divifione, lib. I. De Diffinitione, lib. I. Topicorum Ariftotelis, Anitio Manlio Severino, Interprete, lib. VII. Elenchorum Sophifticorum Ariftotelis, Anitio Manlio Severino Boethio interprete, lib. II. In Topica Ciceronis, lib. VI. De Differentiis Topicis, lib. IV. De Confulatione Philofophiæ, lucenlentiffimis Johannis Murmelli (partim etiam Rodolphi Agricolæ) Commentariis illuftrati, lib. V. De Sancta Trinitate, cum Gilberti epifopi Pictavienfis, cognemento poritæ doctiffimi olim viri commentariis, jam primum ex vetuftiffimo fcripto codice in lucem editis, lib. IV. Quorum primus continet excellentem & piam doctrinam, de Trinitate & Unitate Dei: quomodo Trinitas fit Unus Deus, & non Tres Dii, lib. I. Secundus ractae Quæftionem An Pater, & Filius, & Spiritus Sanctus fubftantialiter prædicentur, lib. I. Tertius compleditur Hebdomades : An omne quod fit, bonum fit, lib. I. Quartus evidenter & pie docet, in Chrifto duas effe Naturas, & unam Perfonam, adverfus Eutychen & Neftorium, lib. I. De Unitate & Uno, lib. I. De Difciplina Scholarium, lib. I. De Arithtica, lib. II. De Mufica, lib. V. De Geometria, lib. II.

thagorean

thagorean school had afferted fubfifted between the confonances. Thefe ratios are either of equality, as 1 : 1, 2 : 2, 8 : 8, or of inequality, as 4 : 2, becaufe the firft contains the latter once, with a remainder : and of thefe ratios, or proportions of inequality, there are five kinds, as, namely, multiplex, fuperparticular, fuperpartient, multiplex fuperparticular, and multiplex fuperpartient ; all which will hereafter be explained. Thefe terms are made ufe of by Euclid, and others of the Greek writers, and were adopted by Boetius, and through him have been continued down to the Italian writers, in whofe works they are perpetually occurring ; and though the modern arithmeticians have rejected them, and fubftituted in their places, or a much fhorter and more intelligible method of defignation, the numbers that conftitute the feveral proportions, it is neceffary to the underftanding of the ancient writers, that the terms ufed by them fhould alfo be underftood.

Another thing neceffary to be known, in order to the underftanding not only of Boetius and his followers, but all who have written on thofe abftrufe parts of mufic the ancient modes, the ecclefiaftical tones, and their divifions into authentic and plagal, is the nature of the three different kinds of proportion, namely, arithmetical, geometrical, and harmonical ; an explanation whereof, as alfo of the feveral kinds of proportion of inequality can hardly be given in terms more accurate, precife, and inelligible, than thofe of Dr. Holder, in his treatife on the Natural Grounds and Principles of Harmony, chap. v. wherein, after premifing that all harmonic bodies and founds fall under numerical calculations, he fpeaks thus of proportion in general :

' We may compare (i. e. amongft themfelves) either (1) magni-
' tudes (fo they be of the fame kind) ; or (2) the gravitations, mo-
' tions, velocities, durations, founds, &c. from thence arifing ; or, far-
' ther, the numbers themfelves, by which the things compared are
' explicated ; and if thefe fhall be unequal, we may then confider
' either, firft, how much one of them exceeds the other ; or, fe-
' condly, after what manner one of them ftands related to the other,
' as to the quotient of the antecedent (or former term) divided by the
' confequent (or latter term) which quotient doth expound, denomi-
' nate, or fhew, how many times, or how much of a time or times, one
' of them doth contain the other : and this by the Greeks is called
' λόγος,

‘ λόγΟ-, ratio, as they are wont to call the fimilitude or equality of
‘ ratios αναλογία, analogie, proportion, or proportionality ; but cuftom,
‘ and the fenfe affifting, will render any over-corious application of
‘ thefe terms unneceffary.’

From thefe two confiderations laft mentioned, the fame author fays,
there are wont to be deduced three forts of proportion, arithmetical,
geometrical, and a mixed proportion, refulting from thefe two, called
harmonical. Thefe are thus explained by him :

‘ 1. Arithmetical, when three or more numbers in progreffion
‘ have the fame difference ; as 2, 4, 6, 8, &c. or difcontinued, as
‘ 2, 4, 6; 14, 16, 18.’

‘ 2. Geometrical, when three or more numbers have the fame
‘ ration, as 2, 4, 8, 16, 32 ; or difcontinued, as 2, 4; 64, 128.’

‘ Laftly, Harmonical, (partaking of both the other) when three
‘ numbers are fo ordered, that there be the fame ration of the greateft
‘ to the leaft, as there is of the difference of the two greater to the
‘ difference of the two lefs numbers, as in thefe three terms, 3, 4, 6,
‘ the ration of 6 to 3, (being the greateft and leaft terms) is duple ; fo
‘ is 2, the difference of 6 and 4 (the two greater numbers) to 1, the
‘ difference of 4 and 3 (the two lefs numbers) duplo alfo. This is
‘ proportion harmonical, which diapafon, 6 to 3, bears to diapente,
‘ 6 to 4, and diatefferon, 4 to 3, as its mean proportionals.’

‘ Now for the kinds of rations moft properly fo called ; i. e. geo-
‘ metrical : firft obferve, that in all rations, the former term or
‘ number, (whether greater or lefs) is always called the antecedent ;
‘ and the other following number, is called the confequent. If there-
‘ fore, the antecedent be the greater term, then the ration is either
‘ multiplex, foperparticular, fuperpartient, or (what is compounded
‘ of thefe) multiplex fuperparticular, or muliplex fuperpartient.’

‘ 1. Multiplex ; as duple, 4 to 2 ; triple, 6 to 2 ; quadruple,
‘ 8 to 2.’ -

‘ 2. Superparticular ; as 3 to 2, 4 to 3, 5 to 4 ; exceeding but by
‘ one aliquot part, and in their radical, or leaft numbers, always
‘ but by one ; and thefe rations are termed fefqoialtera, fefquitertia,
‘ (or fupertertia) fefquiquarta, (or fuperquarta) &c. Note, that num-
‘ bers exceeding more than by one, and but by one aliquot part, may
‘ yet be fuperparticular, if they be not expreffed in their radical, i. e.

‘ leaft

' leaſt numbers, as 12 to 8, hath the ſame ratio as 3 to 2; i, o-
' ſuperparticular; though it ſeem not ſo till it be reduced by the
' greateſt common divisor to its radical numbers, 3 to 2. And the
' common divisor, (i. e. the number by which both the terms may
' ſeverally be divided) is often the difference between the two
' numbers; as in 12 to 8, the difference is 4, which is the common
' divisor. Divide 12 by 4, the quotient is 3; divide 8 by 4, the
' quotient is 2; ſo the radical is 3 to 2. Thus alſo, 15 to 10, divided
' by the difference, 5, gives 3 to 2; yet in 16 to 10, 2 is the common
' divisor, and gives 8 to 5, being ſuperpartient. But in all ſuper-
' particular rations, whoſe terms are thus made larger by being
' multiplied, the difference between the terms is always the greateſt
' common divisor; as in the foregoing examples.'
    ' The third kind of ration is ſuperpartient, exceeding by more than
' one as 5 to 3; which is called ſuperbipartiens tertias, (or tria)
' containing 3 and ⅖ to 5, ſupertripartiens quintas, 5 and ⅗.'
    ' The fourth is multiplex ſuperparticular, as 9 to 4, which is du-
' ple, and ſeſquiquarta; 13 to 4, which is triple and ſeſquiquarta.'
    ' The fifth and laſt is multiplex ſuperpartient, as 11 to 4; duple,
' and ſupertripartiens quartas *.'
    ' When the antecedant is leſs than the conſequent, viz. when a
' leſs is compared to a greater; then the ſame terms ſerve to expreſs
' the rations, only prefixing ſub to them; as, ſubmultiplex, ſubſuper-
' particular, (or ſubparticular) ſubſuperpartient, (or ſubpartient) &c.
' 4 to 2 is duple; 2 to 4 is ſubduple, 4 to 3 is ſeſquitertia; 3 to 4 is
' ſubſeſquitertia, 5 to 3 is ſuperbipartiens tertias; 3 to 5 is ſubſuper-
' bipartiens tertias, &c.'
    The ſame author proceeds to find how the habitudes of rations are
found in theſe words :
    ' All the habitudes of rations to each other, are found by multipli-
' cation or diviſion of their terms, by which any ration is added to or
' ſubtracted from another; and there may be uſe of progreſſion of
' rations or proportions, and of finding a medium, or mediety, be-

* The above terms were uſed by the ancient geometers and arithmeticians; and therefore, for the underſtanding of ſuch, and of Boetius in particular, it is very neceſſary that
their meaning ſhould be aſcertained; but the manner now is to expreſs the proportions
by the numbers themſelves, rather than by the terms; and briefly to ſay, as 31 is to 7, or
as 7 is to 31, rather than to ſay, quadrupla ſuperbipartiens ſeptimas, or ſubquadrupla ſuper-
ui partiens ſeptimas. Vide Harris's Lex. Tecb. vol I. PROPORTION.

tween-

' tween the terms of any ration ; but the main work is done by
' addition and fubtraction of rations, which, though they are not
' performed like addition and fubtraction of fimple numbers in arith-
' metic, but upon algebraic grounds, yet the praxis is moft eafy.'

' One ration is added to another ration, by multiplying the two
' antecedent terms together, i. e. the antecedent of one of the ra-
' tions, by the antecedent of the other. (For the more eafe, they
' fhould be reduced into their leaft numbers or terms) ; and then the
' two confequent terms, in like manner. The ration of the product
' of the antecedents to that of the product of the confequents, is equal
' to the other two, added or joined together. Thus, for example,
' add the ration of 8 to 6 ; i. e. (in radical numbers) 4 to 3, to the
' ratio of 12 to 10, i. e. 6 to 5 ; the product will be 24
' and 15, i. e. 8 to 5 ; you may fet them thus, and
' multiply 4 by 6, they make 24 ; which fet at the
' bottom ; then multiply 3 by 5, they make 15 ; which
' likewife fet under, and you have 24 to 15 : which is
' a ration compounded of the other two, and equal to
' them both. Reduce thefe products, 24 and 15, to their leaft ra-
' dical numbers, which is by dividing as far as you can find a com-
' mon divifor to them both (which is here done by 3), and that
' brings them to the ration of 8 to 5. By this you fee that a third
' minor, 6 to 5, added to a fourth, 4 to 3, makes a fixth minor, 8
' to 5. If more rations are to be added, fet them all under each
' other, and multiply the firft antecedent by the fecond, and that pro-
' duct by the third ; and again that product by the fourth, and fo
' on ; and in like manner the confequents.'

' This operation depends upon the fifth propofition of the eighth
' book of Euclid ; where he fhews that the ration of plain num-
' bers is compounded of their fides. See thefe diagrams.'

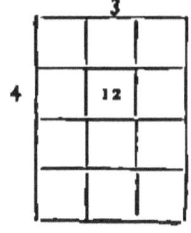

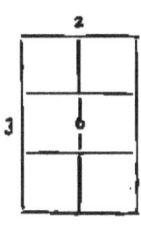

' Now

' Now compound thefe fides. Take for the antecedents, 4, the
' greater fide of the greater plane, and 3, the greater fide of the lefs
' plane, and they multiplied give 12. Then take the remaining two
' numbers, 3 and 2, being the lefs fides of the planes (for confequents),
' and they give 6. So the fides of 4 and 3, and of 3 and 2, com-
' pounded (by multiplying the antecedent terms by themfelves and
' the confequents by themfelves) make 12 to 6 ; i. e. 2 to 1, which
' being applied, amounts to this ; ratio fefquialtera 3 to 2, added to
' ration fefquitertia 4 to 3, makes duple ration, 2 to 1. There-
' fore, diapente added to diatefferon, makes diapafon.'

' Subtraction of one ration from another greater, is performed in
' like manner, by multiplying the terms ; but this is done not late-
' rally, as in addition, but croffwife ; by multiplying the antecedent
' of the former (i. e. of the greater) by the confequent of the latter,
' which produceth a new antecedent ; and the confequent of the
' former by the antecedent of the latter, which gives a new confe-
' quent ; and therefore, it is ufually done by an oblique
' decuffation of the lines. For example, if you would take
' 6 to 5 out of 4 to 3, you may fet them down thus :
' Then 4, multiplied by 5, makes 20 ; and 3, by 6, gives
' 18 ; fo 20 to 18, i. e. 10 to 9, is the remainder. That
' is, fubtract a third minor out of a fourth, and there will
' remain a tone minor.

4 . 3
X
6 . 5
20 . 18
10 . 9

' Multiplication of rations is the fame with their addition ; only
' it is not wont to be of divers rations, but of the fame, being taken
' twice, thrice, or oftener, as you pleafe. And as before, in addition,
' you added divers rations, by multiplying them ; fo here, in multi-
' plication, you add the fame ration to itfelf, after the fame manner,
' viz. by multiplying the terms of the fame ratio by themfelves ;
' i. e. the antecedent by itfelf, and the confequent by itfelf, (which
' in other words, is to multiply the fame by 2) and will in the ope-
' ration be to fquare the ration firft propounded (or give the fecond
' ordinal power ; the ration firft given being the firft power or fide)
' and to this product, if the fimple ration fhall again be added, (after
' the fame manner as before) the aggregate will be the triple of the
' ration firft given ; or the product of that ration, multiplied by 3,
' viz. the cube, or third ordinal power. Its biquadrate, or fourth

' power, proceeds from multiplying it by 4 1. and fo fucceffively in
' order, as far as you pleafe you may advance the powers. For in-
' ftance, the duple ration, 2 to 1, being added to itfelf, dupled or
' multiplied by 2, produceth 4 to 1, (the ration quadruple) ; and if
· to this, the firſt again be added, (which is equivalent to multiply-
' ing that ſaid firſt by 3), there will arife' the ration octuple, or
' 8 to 1. Whence the ration, 2 to 1, being taken for a root, 'its du-
' ple, 4 to 1, will be the ſquare ; its triple, 8 to 1, the cube thereof,
' &c. as hath been ſaid above. And to ufe another inſtance ; to du-
' ple the ration of 3 to 2, it muſt be thus ſquared : 3 by 3 gives 9 ;
' 2 by 2 gives 4, fo the duple or ſquare of 3 to 2 is 9 to 4. Again,
' 9 by 3 is 27, and 4 by 2 is 8 ; fo the cubic ration of 3 to 2 is 27 to 8.
' Again, to find the fourth power or biquadrate, (i. e. ſquared ſquare,)
' 27 by 3 is 81, 8 by 2 is 16 ; fo 81 to 16 is the ration of 3 to 2
' quadrupled ; as it is dupled by the ſquare, tripled by the cube, &c.
' To apply this inſtance to our prefent purpofe, 3 to 2 is the ration of
' diapente, or a fifth in harmony ; 9 to 4 is the ratio of twice dia-
' pente, (or a ninth, viz. diapafon, with tone major ;) 27 to 8 is the
' ration of thrice diapente, or three fifths, which is diapafon, with
' fixth major, viz. 13 major ; the ration of 81 to 16 makes four
' fifths, i. e. difdiapafon, with two tones major, i. e. a feventeenth
' major, and a comma of 81 to 80.'
    ' To divide any ration, the contrary way muſt be taken ; and by
' extracting of thefe roots refpectively, divifion by their indices will
' be performed. E. gr. to divide it by 2, is to take the ſquare root
' of it ; by 3, the cube root ; by 4, the biquadratic, &c. Thus, to
' divide 9 to 4 by 2, the ſquare root of 9 is 3, the ſquare root of 4 is
' 2 ; then 3 to 2 is a ration juſt half fo much as 9 to 4.'

C H A P.   VI.

THE nature of proportion being thus explained, without a
    competent knowledge whereof it would be in vain to attempt
the reading of Duetius, it remains to give ſuch an account of his

treatife

treatife De Mufica as is confiftent with a general hiftory of the fcience, and may be fufficient to invite the ftudious inquirer to an attentive perufal of this moft valuable work. Here therefore follow, in regular order, the titles of the feveral chapters contained in the five books of Boetius's treatife De Mufica, with an abridgment of fuch of them as feem moft worthy of remark.

Chap. i.   Muficam naturaliter nobis effe conjunctam, et mores vel honeftare vel evertere.

Boetius in this chapter obferves, that the fenfitive power of perception is natural to all living creatures, but that knowledge is attained by contemplation. All mortals, he fays, are endued with fight, but whether the perception be effected by the coming of the object to the fight, or by rays fent forth to it, is a doubt. When any one, continues he, beholds a triangle or a fquare, he readily acknowledges what he difcovers by his eyes, but he muft be a mathematician to inveftigate the nature of a triangle or a fquare. Having eftablifhed this propofition, he applies it to the other liberal arts, and to mufic in particular; which he undertakes to fhew is connected with morality, inafmuch as it difpofes the mind to good or evil actions; to this purpofe he expreffes himfelf in thefe terms : ' The power or ' faculty of hearing enables us not only to form a judgment of ' founds, and to difcover their differences, but to receive delight, if ' they are fweet and adapted to each other; whence it comes to pafs ' that, as there are four mathematical fciences *, the reft labour at ' the inveftigation of truth; but this, befides that it requires fpecula- ' tion, is connected with morality; for there is nothing that more ' peculiarly diftinguifhes human nature, than that difpofition ob- ' fervable in mankind to be one way affected by fweet, and another ' by contrary founds; and this affection is not peculiar to particular ' tempers or certain ages, but is common to all; and infants, ' young, and even old men, are by a natural inftinct rendered fuf- ' ceptible of pleafure or difguft from confonant or difcordant founds. ' From hence we may difcern that it was not without reafon that

* The four mathematical arts are arithmetic, geometry, mufic, and aftronomy; thefe were anciently termed the quadrivium, or fourfold way to knowledge; the other three, grammar, rhetoric, and logic, completing the number of the feven liberal fciences, were termed the trivium or threefold way to eloquence. Vide Du Cange, voce QUADRIVIUM. This fcholaftic divifion is recognized in an ancient monumental infcription in Weftminfter abbey, in memory of Gilbert Crifpin, who died abbot of Weftminfter in 1117.

' Plato ſaid, that the ſoul of the world was conjoined with muſical
' proportion : and ſuch is the effect of muſic on the human man-
' ners, that a laſcivious mind is delighted with laſcivious modes, and
' a ſober mind is more diſpoſed to ſobriety by thoſe of a contrary
' kind : and hence it is that the muſical modes, for inſtance the Ly-
' dian and Phrygian, take their names from the tempers or diſtin-
' guiſhing characteriſtics of thoſe nations that reſpectively delight in
' them : for it cannot be that things, in their nature ſoft, ſhould
' agree with ſuch as are harſh, or contrarywiſe ; for it is ſimilitude
' that conciliates love ; wherefore Plato held that the greateſt cau-
' tion was to be taken not to ſuffer any change in a well-moraled
' muſic, there being no corruption of manners in a republic ſo great
' as that which follows a gradual declination from a prudent and
' modeſt muſic ; for, whatever corruptions are made in muſic, the
' minds of the hearers will immediately ſuffer the ſame, it being
' certain that there is no way to the affections more open than that
' of the hearing : and theſe effects of muſic are diſcernible among
' different nations, for the more fierce, as the Getæ, are delighted
' with the harder modes, and the more gentle and civilized with
' ſuch as are moderate ; although in theſe days few of the latter are
' to be found.'

Boetius then proceeds to relate that the Lacedæmonians, ſenſible
of the great advantages reſulting to a ſtate from a ſober, modeſt, and
well-regulated muſic, invited, by a great reward, Taletas the Cretan to
ſettle among them, and inſtruct their youth in muſic. And he relates
that the Spartans were ſo jealous of innovations in their muſic, that, for
adding only a ſingle chord to thoſe he found, they baniſhed Timotheus from Sparta by a decree ; which, however he could come by ſo
great a curioſity, he gives in the original Greek, and is as follows :

Mitis eras juſtus prudens fortis moderatus
Doctus quadrivio nec minus in trivio.
Widmore's Hiſt. of Weſtminſter Abbey.

And theſe are the arts underſtood in the academical degrees of bachelor and maſter of arts,
for the ancient courſe of ſcholaſtic inſtitution required a proficiency in each. The ſatire,
as it is called, of Martianus Capella, De Nuptiis Philologiæ et Mercurii, is a treatiſe on
the ſeven liberal ſciences: Caſhodorus, who lived about half a century after him, wrote
alſo De ſeptem Diſciplinis ; and others of the learned in like manner have written profeſſedly on them all.

ΕΠΕΙ ΔΕ ΤΙΜΟΘΕΟΣ Ο ΜΙΛΕΣΙΟΣ ΠΑΡΑΓΙΜΕΝΟΣ ΕΝ ΤΑΝ ΑΜΕΤΕΡΑΝ ΠΟΛΙΝ,
ΤΑΝ ΠΑΛΑΙΑΝ ΜΟΛΠΗΝ ΑΤΙΜΑΣΑΣ ΚΑΙ ΤΑΝ ΔΙΑ ΠΑΝ ΕΠΤΑ ΧΟΡΔΑΝ
ΚΙΘΑΡΙΖΕΙ, ΑΠΟΣΤΡΕΦΟΜΕΝΟΣ ΠΟΛΤΦΩΝΙΑΝ ΕΙΣΑΓΩΝ, ΑΤΜΑΙΝΕΤΑΙ
ΤΑΣ ΑΚΟΑΣ ΤΩΝ ΝΕΩΝ ΔΙΑ ΤΕ ΤΑΣ ΠΟΛΥΧΟΡΔΑΣ, ΚΑΙ ΤΑΣ ΚΑΙΝΟΤΑ-
ΤΑΣ ΤΟΤΤΩΝ ΜΕΛΕΟΣ ΑΓΕΝΝΕ ΚΑΙ ΠΟΙΚΙΛΑΝ ΑΝΤΙΑΠΛΟΑΝ, ΚΑΙ ΤΕ-
ΤΑΓΜΕΝΑΝ ΑΜΦΙΑΤΙΑΝ ΜΟΛΠΗΝ ΕΠΙ ΧΡΩΜΑΤΟΣ ΣΤΝΕΙΣΤΑΜΕΝ ΤΟΤΤΟΤ
ΜΕΛΕΟΣ, ΔΙΑΣΤΑΣΙΝ. ΑΝΤΙ ΓΑΡ ΕΝΑΡΜΟΝΙΩ ΠΟΛΑΝ ΑΝΤΙΣΤΡΕΦΟΝ
ΑΜΟΙΒΑΝ. ΠΑΡΑΚΑΛΑΘΕΙΣ ΔΕ ΕΝ ΤΟΝ ΑΓΩΝΑ ΤΑΣ ΕΛΕΤΕΙΝΙΑΣ ΔΑΜΑ-
ΤΡΟΣ ΑΙΧΟΣ ΔΙΕΘΗΜΙΣΑΤΟ ΤΑΝ ΤΩ ΜΤΘΩ ΧΙΔΝΗΣΙΝ: ΤΑΝ ΓΑΡ ΣΕΜΕΛΑ
ΩΔΤΝΑΝ ΟΤΕ ΕΝΔΕΚΑΤΟΣ ΝΕΟΣ ΔΙΔΑΧΗΝ ΕΔΙΔΑΞΕ. ΕΙΤΑ ΠΕΡΙ ΤΟΤΤΩΝ
ΤΟΝ ΒΑΣΙΛΕΑΝ ΚΑΙ ΤΟΤ ΡΗΤΟΡΟΣ ΜΕΜΨΑΤΑΙ ΤΙΜΟΘΕΟΝ, ΕΠΑΝΑΤΙΘΕΤΑΙ
ΔΕ ΚΑΙ ΤΑΝ ΕΝΔΕΚΑ ΧΟΡΔΑΝ ΕΚΤΑΝΩΝ ΤΑΣ ΠΕΡΙΑΣΤΑΣ ΕΠΙΛΕΙΠΟΜΕ-
ΝΟΣ ΤΑΝ ΕΠΤΑΚΟΡΔΟΝ ΑΕΤΟΣ. ΤΟ ΓΑΡ ΠΟΛΙΟΣ ΒΑΡΟΣ ΑΠΤΟΝ ΤΕΤΑΡ
ΒΙΙΤΑΙ ΕΣ ΤΑΝ ΣΠΑΡΤΑΝ ΕΠΙΦΕΡΕΙΝ: ΤΙΘΩΝ ΜΗ ΚΑΛΩΝ ΝΙΙΤΩΝ
ΜΗΠΟΤΕ ΤΑΡΑΤΤΗΤΑΙ ΚΛΕΟΣ ΑΓΟΡΩΝ.

He then proceeds to declare the power of mufic in thefe words :
' It is well known that many wonderful effects have been wrought
' by the power of mufic over the mind; oftentimes a fong has re-
' prefled anger ; and who is ignorant that a certain drunken young
' man of Taurominiutn being incited to violence by the found of the
' Phrygian mode, was by the finging of a fpondeus appeafed ; for
' when a harlot was fhut up in the houfe of his rival, and the young
' man, raging with madnefs, would have fet the houfe on fire, Py-
' thagoras, who, agreeable to his nightly cuftom, was employed in
' obferving the motions of the celeftial bodies, as foon as he was in-
' formed that the young man had been incited to this outrage by the
' Phrygian mode, and found that he would not defift from his wick-
' ed attempt, though his friends repeated their admonitions to him
' for that purpofe, ordered them to change the mode, and thereby
' attemperated the difpofition of the raging youth to a moft tranquil
' ftate of mind.   Cicero relates the fame ftory in different words, but
' in nearly the fame manner. " When, (fays he) certain drunken
" men, ftirred up, as is often the cafe, by the found of the tibia,
" would have broke open the doors of a modeft woman, Pythagoras
" is faid to have admonifhed the tibicinift to play a fpondeus, which
" he had no fooner done than the luftfulnefs of thefe men was ap-
" peafed by the flownefs of the mode and the gravity of the per-
" former." But, to gather fome fimilar examples in few words, Ter-
' pander and Arion of Methymne, the next city in Lefbos to Mity-

* lene

‘ lene for grandeur, cured the Lesbians and Ionians of most grievous
‘ diseases by the means of music; Ilismenias, the Theban, by his
‘ music is reported to have freed from their torments divers Beotians,
‘ who were sorely afflicted with sciatic pains *. Empedocles also,
‘ when a certain person in a fury would have attacked his guest, for
‘ having accused and procured the condemnation of his father, is said
‘ to have diverted him by a particular mode in music, and by that
‘ means to have appeased the anger of the young man. And so well
‘ was the power of music known to the ancient philosophers, that
‘ the Pythagoreans, when they had a mind to refresh themselves by
‘ sleep after the labours and cares of the day, made use of certain
‘ songs to procure them an easy and quiet rest; and when they
‘ awaked they also dispelled the dulness and confusion occa-
‘ sioned by sleep by others, knowing full well that the mind and
‘ the body were conjoined in a musical fitness, and that whatever
‘ affects the body will also produce a similar effect on the mind;
‘ which observation it is reported Democritus, whom his fellow-
‘ citizens had confined, supposing him mad, made to Hippo-
‘ crates the physician, who had been sent for to cure him. To what
‘ purpose then are all these things ? we cannot doubt but that our
‘ body and mind are in manner constituted in the same proportions
‘ by which harmonical modulations are joined and compacted, as
‘ the following argument shall shew; for hence it is that even in-
‘ fants are delighted with a sweet, or disgusted with a harsh soug:
‘ every age and either sex are affected by music, and though they are
‘ different in their actions, yet do they agree in their love of music.
‘ Nay, such as are under the influence of sorrow, even modulate
‘ their complaints, which is chiefly the case with women, who by
‘ the sweetness of their songs find means to alleviate their sorrows †;

---

* There are many relations in history of the efficacy of music in the cure of bodily
diseases. It is reported that Thales the Cretan being by the advice of the Oracle called
to Sparta, cured a raging pestilence by the power of music alone. The assertion of Boetius with respect to the Sciatica seems to be founded on a passage in Aulus Gellius, lib. IV.
chap. xiii. who reports that persons afflicted with that disease were eased of their pains by
certain gentle modulations of the tibia; and that by the same means many had been cured
who had been bitten by serpents and other venemous creatures.

† Modern history furnishes a curious fact to prove the truth of this observation; for it
is related of the princess of Navarre, mother of Henry IV. of France, that at the instant
when she was delivered of him she sung a song in the Bearnois language. Life of Henry
le Grand by the bishop of Rodez.

‘ and

‘ and it was for this reason that the ancients had a custom for the
‘ tibia to precede in their funeral processions.   Papinius Statius testi-
‘ fies as much in the following verse.

    ‘ Cornu grave mugit adjunco,
    ‘ Tibia cui teneros fuctum producere manes.

‘ And though a man cannot fing fweetly, yet while he fings to
‘ himfelf he draws forth an innate fweetnefs from his heart.   Is it
‘ not manifeft that the found of the trumpet fires the minds of the
‘ combatants, and impels them to battle; why then is it not proba-
‘ ble that a perfon may be incited to fury and anger from a peaceful
‘ ftate of mind?   There is no doubt but that a mode may reftrain
‘ anger or other inordinate defires; for what is the reafon that when
‘ a perfon receives into his ears any fong with pleafure, that he fhould
‘ not alfo be fpontaneoufly converted to it, or that the body fhould
‘ not form or fafhion fome motion fimilar to what he hears: from all
‘ thefe things it is clear beyond doubt that mufic is naturally joined
‘ to us, and that if we would we cannot deprive ourfelves of it;
‘ wherefore the power of the mind is to be exerted, that what is
‘ implanted in us by nature fhould alfo be comprehended by fcience.
‘ For as in fight it is not fufficient for learned men barely to behold
‘ colours and forms, unlefs they alfo invefligate their properties;
‘ fo alfo is it not fufficient to be delighted with mufical fongs, un-
‘ lefs we alfo learn by what proportion of voices or founds they are
‘ joined together.’

    Cap. ii.   Tres effe muficas, in quibus de vi muficæ narratur.

    The three kinds of mufic here meant are, mundane, humane, and
inftrumental; and of each of thefe mention has been made in a preceding page.

    Cap. iii.   De vocibus ac de muficæ elementis.

    Cap. iv.   De fpeciebus inequalitatis.

    Cap. v.   Quæ inequalitatis fpecies confonantiis aptentur.

    Cap. vi.   Cur multiplicitas, et fuperparticularitas confonantiis
        deputentur.

    Cap. vii.   Quæ proportiones quibus confonantiis muficis ap-
        tentor.

    Cap. viii.   Quid fit fonus, quid intervallum, quid concinentia.

                                                        Cap.

Cap. ix. Non omne judicium dandum esse sensibus, sed amplius rationi esse credendum, in quo de sensuum fallacia.

It is the business of this chapter to shew, that though the first principles of harmony are taken from the sense of hearing, for this reason, that were it otherwise there could be no dispute about sounds; yet, in this case, the sense is not the sole arbiter. Boëtius to this purpose expresses himself very rationally in the following terms: 'Hearing is as it were but a monitor, but the last perfection and 'power of judging about it depends upon reason. What need is 'there for many words to point out the error which the senses are 'liable to, since we know that neither is the same power of percep-'tion given to every one alike, nor is it always equal in the same 'man; on the other hand, it is vain to commit the examination of 'truth to an uncertain judgment. The Pythagoreans for this rea-'son took as it were a middle way; for though they did not make 'the hearing the sole arbiter, yet did they search after and try some 'things by the ears only: they measured the consonants themselves 'by the ears, but the distances by which these consonants differed 'from each other they did not trust to the ears, the judgment where-'of is inaccurate, but committed them to the examination of reason, 'thereby making the sense subservient to reason, which acted as a 'judge and a master. For though the moments of all arts, and of 'life itself, depend upon our senses, yet no sure judgment can be 'formed concerning them, no comprehension of the truth can 'exist, if the decision of reason be wanting; for the senses themselves 'are equally deceived in things that are very great or very little: and 'with respect of that of hearing, it with great difficulty perceives 'those intervals which are very small, and is deafened by those which 'are very great.'

Cap. x. Quemadmodum Pythagoras proportiones consonan-tiarum investigaverit.

Cap. xi. Quibus modis varië à Pythagora proportiones conso-nantiarum perpensæ sint.

The account delivered in the two preceding chapters, and which is mentioned in almost every treatise on the subject of music extant, is evidently taken from Nicomachus, whose relation of this supposed discovery of Pythagoras is herein before given at length.

Cap. xii. De divisione vocum, earumque explanatione.

Cap.

Cap. xiii. Quod infinitatem vocum humana natura finierit.
Cap. xiv. Quis fit modus audiendi.
Cap. xv. De ordine theorematum, id eft fpeculationum.
Cap. xvi. De confonantiis proportionum, et tonu et femitonio.
Cap. xvii. In quibus primis numeris femitonium conftet.
Cap. xviii. Diatefaron a diapente tono diftare.
Cap. xix. Diapafon quinque tonis, et duobus femitoniis jungi.
Cap. xx. De additione chordarum, earunique nominibus.

The fubftance of this chapter has already been given.

Cap. xxi. De generibus cantilenarum.
Cap. xxii. De ordine chordarum nominibufque in tribus generibus.
Cap. xxiii. Quæ fint inter voces in fingulis generibus proportiones.

Thefe three chapters give a brief and but a very fuperficial account of the genera.

Cap. xxiv. Quid fit fynaphe.
Cap. xxv. Quid fit diezeuxis.

In thefe two chapters the difference between the conjunct and dif-
junct tetrachords is explained.

Cap. xxvi. Quibus nominibus nervos appellaverit Albinus.

Albinus is faid by Cafliodorus to have been a great man, and to
have written a brief difcourfe on mufic, which he himfelf had feen
and attentively perufed in one of the public libraries at Rome ; and
Cafliodorus feems to prophecy that fome time or other it would be
taken away in an incurfion of the Barbarians: it has accordingly fuftained that fate; for Meibomius, in his preface to Gaudentius,
fpeaks of that manufcript as irrecoverably loft.

Cap. xxvii. Qui nervi quibus fyderibus comparentur.

The fubftance of this chapter is for the moft part an extract from
Cicero de Repub. lib. VI. and is a declaration of the fuppofed analogy between the planets and the founds in the feptenary.

Cap. xxviii. Quæ fit natura confonantiarum.
Cap. xxix. Ubi confonantiæ reperiuntur.
Cap. xxx. Quemadmodum Plato dicat fieri confonantias.
Cap. xxxi. Quid contra Platonem Nicomachus fentiat.
Cap. xxxii. Quæ confonantia quam merito præcedat.
Cap. xxxiii. Quo fint modo accipienda quæ dicta fuut.

Cap. xxxiv. Quid fit muficus.

In this, which is a very curious chapter, the author obferves that
the theoretic branch of every fcience is more honourable than the
practical, for ' that practice attends like a fervant, but reafon com-
' mands like a miftrefs; and unlefs the head executes what reafon
' dictates, its labour is vain.' He adds, ' the fpeculations of reafon
' borrow no aid of the executive part; but contrarywife, the opera-
' tions of the hand without the guidance of reafon are of no avail;'
' —that the greatnefs of the merit and glory of reafon may be col-
' lected from this; corporeal artifts in mufic receive their appella-
' tions, not from the fcience itfelf, but rather from the inftruments,
' as the citharift from the cithara; the tibicen, or player on the pipe,
' from the tibia; but he only is the true mufician, who, weighing
' every thing in the balance of reafon, profeffes the fcience of mufic,
' not in the flavery of execution, but in the authority of fpeculation.
' In like manner he fays thofe who are employed in the erection of
' public ftructures, or in the operations of war, receive no praife
' except what is due to induftry and obedience; but to thofe by
' whofe fkill and conduct buildings are erected, or victory at-
' chieved, the honours of infcriptions and triumphs are decreed.'
He then proceeds to declare that three faculties are employed
in the mufical art; one which is exercifed in the playing on inftruments, another that of the poet, which directs the compofition
of verfes, and a third which judges of the former two; and touching thefe, and that which he makes the principal queftion in this
chapter, he delivers his opinion thus: ' As to the firft, the per-
' formance of inftruments, it is evident that the artifts obey as fer-
' vants, and as to poets, they are not led to verfe fo much by reafon
' as by a certain inftinct which we call genius. But that which
' affumes to itfelf the power of judging of thefe two, that can exa-
' mine into rhythmus, fongs, and their verfe, as it is the exercife of
' reafon and judgment, is moft properly to be accounted mufic; and
' he only is a mufician who has the faculty of judging according to
' fpeculation and the approved ratios of founds, of the modes, ge-
' nera, and rhythmi of fongs, and their various commixtures, and of
' the verfes of the poets.'

    Lib. II. cap. i. Proemium.
    Cap. ii. Quid Pythagoras effe philofophiam conftituerit.

                        I   Cap.

Cap. iii.   De differentiis quantitatis, et quæ cuique disciplinæ
fit deputata.

Cap. iv.   De Relatæ quantitatis differentiis.

Cap. v.   Cur multiplicitas antecellat.

Cap. vi.   Qui sint quadrati numeri deque his speculatio.

Cap. vii.   Omnem inequalitatem ex equalitate procedere, ejusque
demonstratio.

Cap. viii.   Regula quotlibet continuas proportiones superparticulares inveniendi.

Cap. ix.   De proportione numerorum qui ab alias metiunter.

Cap. x.   Quæ ex multiplicibus et superparticularibus multipli-
citates fiant.

Cap. xi.   Qui superparticulares quos multiplices efficiant.

The nine foregoing chapters contain demonstrations of the five
several species of proportion of inequality; of these an explanation
may be seen in that extract from Dr. Holder's Treatise on the Natural Grounds and Principles of Harmony, hereinbefore inserted,
with a view to facilitate the study of Boetius, and to render this very
abstruse part of his work intelligible.

Cap. xii.   De arithmetica, geometrica, harmonica, medietate.

The three several kinds of proportionality, that is to say, arithmetical, geometrical, and harmonical, are also explained in the extract
from Dr. Holder's book above referred to.

Cap. xiii.   De continuis medietatibus et disjunctis.

Cap. xiv.   Cur ita appellatæ sint digestæ superius medietates.

Cap. xv.   Quemadmodum ab æqualitate supradictæ procefferant
medietates.

Cap. xvi.   Quemadmodum inter duos terminos supradictæ medietates viciffim collocentur.

Cap. xvii.   De consonantiarum modo secundum Nicomachum.

Cap. xviii.   De ordine consonantiarum sententia Eubulidis et
Hippasi.

Two ancient musicians, of whose writings we have nothing now
remaining.

Cap. xix.   Sententia Nicomachi quæ quibus consonantiis appo-
nantur.

Cap. xx.   Quid oporteat præmitti, ut diapason in multiplici genere demonstretur.

Cap.

Cap. xxi. Demonſtratio per impoſſibile, diapaſon in multiplici genere eſſe.

Cap. xxii. Demonſtratio per impoſſibile, diapente, diateſſaron, et tonum in ſuperparticulari eſſe.

Cap. xxiii. Demonſtratio diapente et diateſſaron in maximis ſuperparticularibus collocari.

Cap. xxiv. Diapente in ſeſquialtera, diateſſaron, in ſeſquitertia eſſe, tonum in ſeſquioctava.

Cap. xxv. Diapaſon ac diapente in tripla proportione eſſe; biſdiapaſon in quadrupla.

Cap. xxvi. Diateſſaron ac diapaſon non eſſe conſonantiam, ſecundum Pythagoricos.

The two foregoing chapters have an immediate connection with each other; in the firſt it is demonſtrated that the diapaſon and diapente conjoined, making together the conſonant interval of a twelfth, are in triple proportion; and that the biſdiapaſon is in quadruple proportion, the ratios whereof are ſeverally 3 to 1 and 4 to 1; but with reſpect to the diapaſon and diateſſaron conjoined, the ratio whereof is 8 to 3, the interval ariſing from ſuch conjunction is clearly demonſtrated by Boetius to be diſſonant : from hence ariſes an evident diſcrimination between the diateſſaron and the other perfect conſonances; for whereas not only they but their replicates are conſonant, this of the diateſſaron is ſimply a conſonance itſelf, its replicates being diſſonant. It is true that the modern muſicians do not reckon the diateſſaron in the number of the conſonances; and whether it be a concord or a diſcord has been a matter of controverſy; nevertheleſs it is certain that among the ancients it was always looked upon as a conſonance, and that with ſo good reaſon, that Lord Verulam * profeſſes to entertain the ſame opinion; and yet after all, the imperfection which Boetius has pointed out in this chapter, ſeems to ſuggeſt a very good reaſon for diſtinguiſhing between the diateſſaron and thoſe other intervals, which, whether taken ſingly, or in conjunction with the diapaſon, are conſonant.

Cap. xxvii. De ſemitonio in quibus minimis numeris conſtet.

The arguments in this chapter are of ſuch a kind, that it behoves every muſician to be maſter of them. The ratios of the limma and apotome have already been demonſtrated in thoſe larger numbers

* Nat. Hiſt. Cent. II. Numb. 107.

which

which Ptolemy had made choice of for the purpofe. In this chapter Boetius gives the ratio of the limma in the fmalleft numbers in which it can poffibly confift, that is to fay, 256 to 243 ; and as this is the moft ufual defignation of the Pythagorean limma, or the interval, which, being added to two fefquioctave tones, completes the interval of a diateffaron, it is a matter of fome confequence to know how thefe numbers are brought out ; and this will beft be declared in the words of Boetius himfelf, which are as follow :

‘ The femitones feem to be fo called not that they are exact-
’ ly the halves of tones, but becaufe they are not whole tones.
’ The interval which we now call a femitone was by the ancients
‘ called a limma, or diefis ; and it is thus found : if from the fefqui-
‘ tertia proportion, which is the diateffaron, two fefquioctave ratios,
‘ be taken away, there will be left an interval, called a femitone.
‘ To prove this, let us find out two confecutive tones ; but becaufe
‘ thefe, as has been faid, are conftituted in fefquioctave proportion,
‘ we cannot find two fuch, until that multiple from whence they are
‘ derived be firft found : let therefore unity be firft fet down, and
’ then 8, which is its octuple : from this we derive one multiple ;
‘ but becaufe we want to find two, multiply 8 by 8, to produce 64,
‘ which will be a fecond multiple, from which we may bring out
’ two fequioctave ratios; for if 8, which is the eighth part of 64,
‘ be added thereto, the fum will be 72 ; and if the eighth part of
’ this, which is 9, be added to it, the fum will be 81 ; and thefe will
‘ be the two confecutive tones, in their loweft terms. Thus, fet
‘ down 64, 72, 81.

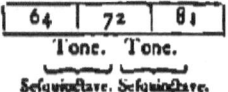

64	72	81

Tone.   Tone.

Sefquioctave. Sefquioctave.

‘ We are now therefore to feek a fefquitertia to 64 ; but it is found
‘ not to have a third part : wherefore, all thefe numbers muft be
‘ multiplied by 3, and all remain in the fame proportion as they were
‘ in before this multiplication by 3. Then three times 64 makes
‘ 192, to which if we add its third part, 64, the fum will be 256 ;
‘ which gives the fefquitertia ratio, containing the diateffaron. Then
‘ fet down the two fefquioctaves to 192, in their proper order,
‘ that is, three times 72, which is 216, and three times 81, which is
‘ that

‘ that 243 : thefe two being fet between the terms of the fefquitertia,
‘ the whole will ftand thus :

Tone	Tone	Semit.
192	216	243	256

Diateffaron.

‘ In this difpofition of the numbers, the firft conftitutes a diatef-
‘ faron with the laft, and the firft with the fecond, and alfo the
‘ fecond with the third, do each conftitute a tone ; therefore the
‘ remaining intervals 243 and 256, is a femitone in its leaft terms.’

　Cap. xxviii.　Demonftrationes non effe, 243, ad 256, toni me-
　dietatem.

That the limma in the ratio 256 to 243 is lefs than a true femitone, has been already demonftrated in the courfe of this work.

　Cap. xxix.　De majore parte toni in quibus minimis numeris
conftet.

The apotome has no place in the fyftem, nor can it in any way be
confidered as a muficel interval ; in fhort, it is nothing more than that
portion of a fefquioctave tone that remains after the limma has been
taken therefrom.　For this reafon, its ratio is a matter of mere curiofity ; and it feems from this chapter of Boetius, that the fmalleft
numbers in which it can be found to confift, are thofe which Ptolemy
makes ufe of, that is to fay, 2187 to 2048.

　Cap. xxx.　Quibus proportionibus diapente, diapafon, conftent,
et quoniam diapafon fex tonis non conftet.

The demonftrations contained in this chapter are levelled againft
the Ariftoxenians, and declare fo fully the fentiments of the Pythagoreans, with refpect to the meafure of the confonant intervals, that
they are worthy of particular attention, and cannot be better given
than in the words of Boetius himfelf.

‘ The diapente confifts of three tones and a femitone, that is, of a
‘ diateffaron and a tone : for let the numbers 192, 216, 243, 256,
‘ comprehended in the above fcheme, be fet down thus :

DIATESSARON			
192	216	243	256

Tone　Tone　Semitone.

‘ In

' In this difpofition, the firft number to the fecond and the fecond
' to the third, bear the proportions of tones, and the third to the
' fourth that of a leffer femitone, as has been fhewn above. If then
' for the purpofe of afcertaining the contents of the diapente, 32 be
' added to 256, the fum will be 288, which is another fefquioctave
' tone ; for 32 is the eighth part of 259, and 256 to 288 is 8 to 9.
' The extreme numbers will then be 192 to 288, which is fefquialtera,
' the ratio of the diapente.

DIAPENTE
Sefquialtera.

' Finally, by comparing the firft number with the fecond, the fe-
' cond with the third, and the fourth with the fifth, i. e. 288, it
' will plainly appear, firft, that in the diapente are three tones, and
' a leffer femitone. If then the diateffaron confifts of two tones and
' a leffer femitone, and the diapente of three tones and a leffer femi-
' tone ; and if the diateffaron and diapente make up together the dia-
' pafon, it will follow, that in the diapafon are five tones and two
' leffer femitones, which joined together do not make up a full and
' complete tone, and therefore that the diapafon does not confift of
' fix tones, as Ariftoxenus imagined, which alfo will evidently appear
' when thefe intervals are properly difpofed in numbers. For let fix
' octuples be thus produced :

          1, 8, 64, 512, 4096, 32768, 262144.

' From this laft number fix tones, conftituted in fefquioctave pro-
' portion, may be fet down, with the octuple terms and their feveral
' eighth parts, in the order following :

                    Octuples.
        1, 8, 64, 512, 4096, 32768, 262144.

	262144		32768
	294912		36864
	331776		41472
Sefquioctaves.	373248	Eighth parts.	46656
	419904		52488
	472392		59049
	531441		

                                             The

' The nature of the above difpofition is this : the firft line con-
' tains the octuple numbers ; and the fefquioctave proportions in tho'
' firft column are deduced from the laft of them. The numbers con-
' tained in the fecond column are the eighth parts of thofe to'
' which they are refpectively oppofite ; and if each of thefe be added
' to the number againft it, the fum will be the number of the next
' fefquioctave, in fucceffion. Thus, if to the number 262144
' 32768 be added, the fum will be 294912 ; and the reft are
' found in the fame manner. And were the laft number, 531441,
' duple to the firft, 262144, then would the diapafon truly confift
' of fix tones ; but here it is found to be more ; for the duple of
' 262144 is 524288, and the number of the fixth tone is 531441.
' Hence it appears, that the confonant diapafon is lefs than fix tones ;
' and the excefs of the fix tones above the diapafon is called a com-
' ma, which in its loweft terms is 524288 to 531441.

	7153
524288	531441

COMMA, or the in-
terval by which fix
tones exceed a diapafon*

Six Octuples.

1	8	64	512	4096	32768	262144
9	72	576	4608	36864	294912
81	648	5184	41472	331776
729	5832	46656	373248
6561	52488	419904
59049	472392
531441

All the diagonals are ninefold.

The numbers in the upper
row make fix octuples, and
thefe placed under them are
fefquioctaves to each other
in fucceffion.

---

* This is called the Pythagorean comma, and is taken notice of by Merfennus, vide
Harmonicor. de Diffonantiis, pag. 88. It is lefs than that of 81 to 80, called the comma
majus, or fchifma, and is the difference between the greater and leffer tone.

In

In the third book Boetius continues his controversy with the Aristoxenians, who, as they assert that the diatessaron contains two tones and an half, and the diapente three tones and an half, must be supposed to believe that the tone is capable of a division into two equal parts, contrary to that maxim of Euclid, that ' inter superparticulare non ' cadit medium,' a superparticular ration cannot have a mediety. And Boetius, in the first chapter of his third book, with great clearness and precision demonstrates, that no such division of the tone can be made, as that which Aristoxenus and his followers contend for.

Lib. III. cap. i.   Adversus Aristoxenum demonstratio, superparticularem proportionem dividi in æqua non posse, atque ideo nec tonum.

Cap. ii.   Ex sesquitertia proportione sublatis duobus tonis, toni dimidium non relinqui.

Cap. iii.   Adversum Aristoxenum demonstrationes, diatessaron consonantiam ex duobus tonis et semitonio non constare, nec diapason sex tonis.

Cap. iv.   Diapason consonantiam à sex tonis commate excedi, et qui fit minimus numerus commatis.

Cap. v.   Quemadmodum Philolaus tonum dividat.

Pythagoras found out the tone by the difference of a fourth and fifth, subtracting one from the other; Philolaus, who was of his school, proceeded farther, and effected a division of the tone into commas. The manner of his doing it is thus related by Boetius :

' Philolaus the Pythagorean tried to divide the tone, by taking the ' original of the tone from that number which among the Pythagoreans was esteemed very honourable : for as the number 3 is the ' first uneven number, that multiplied by 3 will give 9, which being ' multiplied by 3 will necessarily produce 27, which is distant from ' the number 24 by a tone, and preserves the same difference of 3 ; ' for 3 is the eighth part of 24, and being added thereto completes the ' cube of the number 3, viz. 27. Philolaus therefore divided this into ' two parts ; one whereof was greater than the half, which he called ' the apotome; and the other less, which he termed the diesis, and ' those that came after him denominated a lesser semitone ; and their ' difference he termed a comma. The diesis he supposed to consist of ' 13 unities, because he supposed that to be the difference between ' 243 and 256, and because the number 13 consisted of 9, 3, and

Vol. I.   U u   ' unity ,

' unity ; which unity be confidered as a punctum. 3 he confidered as
' the firft uneven number, and 9 as the firft uneven fquare : for this
' reafon, when he fixed the diefis or femitone at 13, he made the re-
' maining part of the number 27, containing 14 unities to be the apo-
' tome. But becaufe unity is the difference between 13 and 14, he
' imagined unity ought to be affigned to the place of the comma ; but
' the whole tone he made to be 27 unities, that number being the dif-
' ference between 216 and 243, which are diftant from each other by
' a tone.'

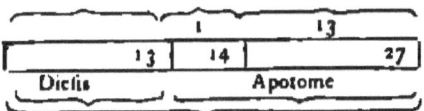

		1	13
	13	14	27
Diefis		Apotome	

Cap. vi.   Tonum ex duobus femitoniis ac commate conftare.
Cap. vii.   Demonftratio, tonum duobus femitoniis commate
   diftare.
Cap. viii. De minoribus femitonii intervallis.
Cap. ix.   De toni partibus per confonantias fumendis.
Cap. x.   Regula fumendi femitonii.
Cap. xi.   Demonftratio Archytæ, fuperparticularem in equa di-
vidi non poffe ejufque : reprehenfio.

It feems by this chapter, that this Archytas, who it is fuppofed was
he of Tarentum, mentioned in the account herein before given of the
genera and their fpecies, was a Pythagorean. He it feems had undertaken to demonftrate that propofition of the Pythagorean fchool,
that a fuperparticular ratio cannot be divided into two equally ; but
Boetius fays he has done it in a loofe manner, and for this be repre-
hends him. It may be inferred from this chapter, that fome of the
writings of Archytas on mufic were in being in the time of Boetius ;
but that there are none now remaining is agreed by all.

Cap. xii.   In qua numerorum proportione fit comma, et quoniam in ea quæ major fit quam 75 ad 74 minor quam, 74
ad 73.
Cap. xiii. Quod femitonium minus majus quidem fit quam 20
ad 19, minus quam 19½ ad 18½.
Cap. xiv.   Semitonium minus, majus quidem effe tribus coma-
tibus ; minus vero quatuor.

7   Cap. xv.

Cap. xv. Apotome majorem effe quam 4 commata, minorem quam 5. Tonum majorem quam 8, minorem quam 9.
Cap. xvi. Superius dictorum per numeros demonstratio.
Lib. IV. cap. i. Vocum differentias in quantitate confistere.
Cap. ii. Diverfæ de intervallis fpeculationes.

This, as its title imports, is a chapter of a mifcellaneous kind. Among other things, it contains a demonftration fomewhat different from that which he had given before, that fix fefquioctave tones are greater than a duple interval. That they are fo will appear upon a bare infpection of the following diagram.

Six fefquioctave proportions greater than a duple interval.

Sefqui-octave.	Sefqui-octave.	Sefqui-octave.	Sefqui-octave.	Sefqui-octave.	Sefqui-octave.	Sefqui-octave.
A	B	C	D	E	G	K
262144.	294912.	331776.	373248.	419904.	472392.	531441.

The number A 262144. is half the underwritten number; and therefore the diapafon is deficient of the number K by 7153.

The duple interval reaches to 524288.

Cap. iii. Muficarum per Græcas ac Latinas literas notarum nuncupatio.

In this chapter are contained fome of the principal characters ufed by the Greeks in their mufical notation. It feems, that at the time when Glareanus publifhed his edition of Boetius, they had been corrupted, which, confidering they were arbitrary, or at beft that they were the letters of the Greek alphabet reduced to a ftate of deformity, is not to be wondered at. Meibomius had the good fortune to get intelligence of an ancient manufcript here in England, in which this chapter was found, in a ftate of great purity. He had intereft enough with Mr. Selden to get him to collate his own by it; and the whole is

very

very correctly published, and prefixed to the Isagoge of Alypius, in his edition of the ancient musical authors.

Cap. iv.   Monochordi regularis partitio in genere diatonico.
Cap. v.   Monochordi netarum hyperboleon per tria genera partitio.
Cap. vi.   Ratio superius digeſtæ deſcriptionis.
Cap. vii.   Monochordi netarum diezeugmenon per tria genera partitio.
Cap. viii.   Monochordi netarum ſynemmenon per tria genera partitio.
Cap. ix.   Monochordi meſon per tria genera partitio.
Cap. x.   Monochordi hypaton per tria genera partitio, et totius diſpoſitio deſcriptionis.
Cap. xi.   Ratio superius diſpoſitæ deſcriptionis.
Cap. xii.   De ſtantibus et mobilibus vocibus.
Cap. xiii.   De conſonantiarum ſpeciebus.
Cap. xiv.   De modorum exordiis, in quo diſpoſitio notarum per ſingulos modos ac voces.
Cap. xv.   Deſcriptio continens modorum ordinem ac differentias.
Cap. xvi.   Superius diſpoſitæ modorum deſcriptiones.
Cap. xvii.   Ratio superius diſpoſitæ modorum deſcriptionis.
Cap. xviii.   Quemadmodum indubitanter muſicæ conſonantiæ aure dijudicari poſſint.
Lib. V.   Proemium.

In this Boetius gives the form of the monochord, little differing from that of Ptolemy and Porphyry herein before deſcribed.

Cap. i.   De vi harmonicæ, et quæ ſint ejus inſtrumenta judicii, et quo nam uſque ſenſibus oporteat credi.
Cap. ii.   Quid ſit harmonica regula, vel quam intentionem harmonici Pythagorici, vel Ariſtoxenus, vel Ptolemæus eſſe dixere.
Cap. iii.   In quo Ariſtoxenus, vel Pythagorici, vel Ptolemæus gravitatem atque acumen conſtare poſuerint.
Cap. iv.   De ſonorum differentiis Ptolemæi ſententia.
Cap. v.   Quæ voces enharmoniæ ſunt aptæ.
Cap. vi.   Quem numerum proportionum Pythogarici ſtatuunt.

Cap.

Cap. vii. Quod reprehendat Ptolemæus Pythagoricos in numero proportionum.

Cap. viii. Demonstratio secundum Ptolemæum diapason et diatessaron consonantiæ.

Cap. ix. Quæ sit proprietas diapason consonantiæ.

Cap. x. Quibus modis Ptolemæus consonantias statuat.

Cap. xi. Quæ sunt equisonæ, vel quæ consonæ, vel quæ emmelis.

Cap. xii. Quemadmodum Aristoxenus intervallum consideret.

Cap. xiii. Descriptio octochordi, qua ostenditur diapason consonantiam minorum esse sex tonis.

Cap. xiv. Distessaron consonantiam tetrachordo contineri.

Cap. xv. Quomodo Aristoxenus vel tonum dividat vel genera ejusque divisionis dispositio.

Cap. xvi. Quomodo Archytas tetrachordo dividat, eorumque descriptio.

Cap. xvii. Quemadmodum Ptolemæus et Aristoxeni et Archytæ, tetrachordorum divisiones reprehendat.

Cap. xviii. Quemadmodum tetrachordorum divisionem fieri dicat oportere.

C H A P. VII.

FROM the foregoing extracts a judgment may be formed, not only of the work from which they are made, but also of the manner in which the ancients, more especially the followers of Pythagoras, thought of music. Well might they deem it a subject of philosophical speculation, when such abstruse reasoning was employed about it. To speak of Boetius in particular, it is clear that he was upon the whole a Pythagorean, though he has not spared to detect many of the errors imputed to that sect; and his work is so truly theoretic, that in reading him we never think of practice: the mention of instruments, nor of the voice, as employed in singing, never occurs; no allusions to the music of his time, but all abstracted speculation, tending doubtless to the perfection of the art, but seemingly little connected with it. Here then the twofold nature of music is apparent: it has its foundation in number and proportion; like geometry,

metry, it affords that kind of pleasure to the mind which results from the contemplation of order, of regularity, of truth, the love whereof is connatural with human nature; like that too, its principles are applicable to use and practice. View it in another light, and if it be possible, consider music as mechanical, as an arbitrary constitution, as having no foundation in reason: but how exquisite is the pleasure it affords! how subservient are the passions to its influence! and how much is the wisdom and goodness of God manifested in that relation which, in the case of music, he has established between the cause and the effect!

That Boetius is an obscure writer must be allowed; the very terms used by him, and his names for the proportions, though they are the common language of the ancient arithmeticians, are difficult to be understood at this time. Guido, who lived about five hundred years after him, scruples not to say, that ' his work is fit only for philoso-' phers.' It was, nevertheless, held in great estimation for many centuries, and to this its reputation many causes co-operated; to which may be added that the Greek language was little understood, even by the learned, for a much longer period than that above mentioned; and to those few that were masters of it, all that treasure of musical erudition contained in the writings of Aristoxenus, Euclid, Nicomachus, Ptolemy, and the rest of the Greek harmonicians, was inaccessible. So late as the time of our queen Elizabeth, it was doubted whether the writings of some of them were any where extant in the world *.

For these reasons, we are not to wonder that the Treatise de Musica of Boetius was for many ages looked upon as the grand repository of harmonical science. To go no farther than our own country for proofs, the writings of all who treated on the subject before the beginning of the fourteenth century, and whose names are preserved in the collections of Leland, Bale, Pits, and Tanner, are but so many commentaries on him: nay, an admission to the first degree in music, in the universities of Oxford and Cambridge, was but a kind of manuduction to the study of his writings †; and in the latter the exercise for a doctor's degree was generally a lecture on Boetius ‡.

* Morley, in the Peroratio to his Introduction.
† Wood, in the Fasti. Oxon. pag. 5 & 8. says, of bachelors of music, that they were such who were admitted to the reading any of the musical books of Boetius; and in his account of John Nendus, a secular priest, who, anno 1535, supplicated for that degree, he says, he obtained it with the privilege of reading Boetius. Fasti Oxon. pag. 56.
‡ Athen. Oxon. passim.
                                                                          And

And, to come nearer to our own times, Salinas and Zarlino have purfued the fame train of reafoning that Boetius firft introduced. If it be afked how has this contributed to the improvement of mufic, the anfwer is not eafy, if the queftion refers to the practice of it; fince what Merfennus and others have faid is very true, that in the divifion of founds we are determined wholly by the ear, and not by ratios; and therefore the makers and tuners of inftruments are in fact, though they know it not, Ariftoxenians; but if by Mufic we are to underftand the Theory of the fcience, this method of treating it has contributed greatly to its improvement. This is enough to fatisfy fuch as are aware of the importance of theory in every fcience: thofe whofe minds are too illiberal to conceive any thing beyond practice and mere manual operation or energy, might perhaps demand, What has theory, what have the ratios of numbers to do with an art, the end whereof is to move the paffions, and not convince the underftanding; were thefe confidered, or even underftood, by the ableft profeffors of the fcience; did Paleftrina, Stradella, did Corelli adjuft their harmonies by the monochord, or confult Euclid or Ptolemy when they compofed refpectively their motets, madrigals, and concertos; or is it neceffary in the performance of them that the fingers, or any of thofe who perform on an inftrument, the tuning whereof is not adjufted to their hands, perpetually bear in mind the true harmonic canon, and be aware of the difference between the greater and leffer tone, and the greater and leffer femitone; and that what in common practice is called a femitone, is in fact an interval in the ratio of 256 to 243, and unlefs fo prolated is a diffonance? And after all it may perhaps be argued that this kind of knowledge adds nothing to the pleafure we receive from mufic.

To fuch as are difpofed to reafon in this manner it may be faid, We all know that the dog who treads the fpit-wheel; or, to go higher, the labourer that drives a wedge, or adds the ftrength of his arms to a lever, are ignorant of all but the effects of their labour; but we alfo know that the ignorance of the brute and of the uninftructed rational in this refpect afford no reafon why others are to remain ignorant too; much lefs does it prove it fruitlefs and vain for men of a philofophical and liberal turn of mind to attempt an inveftigation of the principles upon which thefe machines act *.

* The reader will find this argument much better enforced by the learned and ingenious author of a treatife intitled Hermes or a Philofophical Inquiry concerning Univerfal Grammar.

Farther, as a motive to the study of the ratios and coincidences of harmonic intervals, it may be said that the noblest of our faculties are exercised in it; and that the pleasure arising from the contemplation of that truth and certainty which are found in them, is little inferior to what we receive from hearing the most excellent music. And to this purpose the learned and ingenious Dr. Holder expresses himself in a passage which is inserted in a note subjoined *.

After all, we ought not to estimate the works of learned men by the consideration of their immediate utility: to investigate is one thing; to apply, another; and the love of science includes in it a degree of enthusiasm, which whoever is without, will want the strongest motive to emulation and improvement that the mind is susceptible of. Is it to be conceived that those who are employed in mathematical researches attend to the consequences of their own discoveries, or that their pursuits are not extended beyond the prospect of bare utility? In short, no considerable progress, no improvement in any science can be expected, unless it be beloved for its own sake: as well might we expect the continuation of our species from principles of reason

---

Grammar. Here it was necessary to vary it, in order to adapt it to the present subject; but the author applies it to that of speech; the whole passage is very beautiful, and is as follows: ' Methinks I hear some objector, demanding with an air of pleasantry and ridicule—Is there no speaking then without all this trouble? Do we not talk every one ' of us, as well unlearned as learned, as well poor peasants as profound philosophers? ' We may answer by interrogating on our part—Do not those same poor peasants use the ' lever and the wedge, and many other instruments, with much habitual readiness? And ' yet have they any conception of those geometrical principles from which those machines ' derive their efficacy and force? And is the ignorance of these peasants a reason for ' others to remain ignorant, or to render the subject a less becoming enquiry? Think ' of animals and vegetables that occur every day—of time, of place, and of motion—of ' light, of colours, and of gravitation—of our senses and intellects by which we perceive ' every thing else—That they are, we all know and are perfectly satisfied—What they are, ' is a subject of much obscurity and doubt; were we to reject this last question because ' we are certain of the first, we should banish all philosophy at once out of the world.' Hermes, pag. 293.

* ' And in searching, stating, and comparing the ratios of those intervals of sounds ' by which harmony is made, there is found so much variety and certainty, and facility ' of calculation, that the contemplation of them may seem not much less delightful than ' the very hearing the good music itself, which springs from this fountain; and those ' who have already an affection for music cannot but find it improved and much enhanced ' by this pleasant and recreating chace, as I may call it, in the large field of harmonic ' rations and proportions, where they will find, to their great pleasure and satisfaction, the ' hidden causes of harmony (hidden to most, even to practitioners themselves) so amply ' discovered and laid plain before them.' Natural Grounds and Principles of Harmony, chap. v.

and

and duty, abſtracted from that paſſion which holds the animal world in ſubjection, and to which humane nature itſelf owes its exiſtence *.

Taking this for granted, the merit of Boetius will appear to conſiſt in the having communicated to the world ſuch a knowledge of the fundamental principles of the ancient muſic, as is abſolutely neceſſary to the right underſtanding even of our own ſyſtem : and this too at a period when there was little or no ground to hope for any other intelligence, and therefore Morley has done him but juſtice in the eulogium which he has given of him in the following words.

‘ Boetius being by birth noble, and moſt excellent well uerſed in di-
‘ uinity, philoſophy, law, mathematicks, poetry, and matters of
‘ eſtate, did notwithſtanding write more of muſick than of al the
‘ other mathematical ſciences, ſo that it may be juſtly ſaid, that if it
‘ had not beene for him the knowledge of muſicke had not yet come
‘ into our weſterne part of the world. The Greek tongue lying as it
‘ were dead under the barbariſme of the Gothes and Hunnes, and
‘ muſicke buried in the bowels of the Greeke works of Ptolemæus

* For the farther illuſtration of this propoſition, viz. that knowledge is an object worthy to be purſued for its own ſake, we muſt be indebted to the author above-cited, who to this purpoſe thus expreſſes himſelf : ‘ But a graver objector now accoſts us. What (ſays he) ‘ is the utility, whence the profit, where the gain ? Every ſcience whatever (we may ‘ anſwer) has its uſe. Arithmetic is excellent for gauging of liquors ; geometry for mea- ‘ ſuring of eſtates ; aſtronomy for making of almanacks ; and grammar perhaps for draw- ‘ ing of bonds and conveyances.
‘ Thus much to the ſordid—If the liberal aſk for ſomething better than this, we may ‘ anſwer, and aſſure them from the beſt authorities, that every exerciſe of the mind upon ‘ theorems of ſcience, like generous and manly exerciſe of the body, tends to call forth ‘ and ſtrengthen nature's original vigour. Be the ſubject itſelf immediately lucrative or ‘ not, the nerves of reaſon are braced by the mere employ, and we become abler actors in ‘ the drama of life, whether our part be of the buſier, or of the ſedater kind.
‘ Perhaps too there is a pleaſure even in ſcience itſelf, diſtinct from any end to which ‘ it may be farther conducive. Are not health and ſtrength of body deſirable for their ‘ own ſakes, though we happen not to be fated either for porters or draymen ? And have ‘ not health and ſtrength of mind their intrinſic worth alſo, though not condemned to the ‘ low drudgery of ſordid emolument ? Why ſhould there not be a good (could we have ‘ the grace to recognize it) in the mere energy of our intellect, as much as in ener- ‘ gies of lower degree ? The ſportſman believes there is good in his chace ; the man of ‘ gaiety, in his intrigue ; even the glutton, in his meal. We may juſtly aſk of theſe, why ‘ they purſue ſuch things ; but If they anſwer they purſue them becauſe they are good, ‘ 'twould be folly to aſk them farther, why they purſue what is good. It might well in ‘ ſuch eaſe he replied on their behalf (how ſtrange ſoever is may at firſt appear) that if there ‘ was not ſomething good, which was in no reſpect uſeful, even things uſeful themſelves ‘ could not poſſibly have exiſtence. For this is in fact no more than to aſſert, that ſome ‘ things are ends, ſome things are means ; and that if there were no ends, there could be ‘ of courſe no means.' Hermes, pag. 294.

' and Ariftoxenus, the one of which as yet hath never come to light,
' but lies in written copies in fome bibliotheke of Italy, the other
' hath been fet out in print; but the copies are every where fo fcant
' and hard to come by, that many doubt if he have beene fet out
' or no *.'

Other improvements were referved for a more enlightened age,
when the ftudy of phyfics began to be cultivated, when the hypo-
thefes of the ancients were brought to the teft of experiment; and
the doctrine of pendulums became another medium for demonftrating
the truth of thofe ratios which the ancient harmonicians had inveftigated merely by the power of numbers.

To the reafons above adduced in favour of the writings of Boetius,
another may be added, which every learned reader will acquiefce in,
namely, that he was the laft of the Latin writers whofe works
have any pretence to purity, or to intitle them to the epithet of
claffical.

It muft however be confeffed that the treatife De Mufica of Boetius is but part of a much larger difcourfe which he intended on that
fubject: moft authors fpeak of it as of a fragment, and the very abrupt
manner in which it concludes fhews that he had not put the finifhing
hand to it. The whole of the five books extant are little more than
an inveftigation of the ratios of the confonances, the nature of the
feveral kinds of proportionality, and a declaration of the opinions of
the feveral fects with refpect to the divifion of the monochord and
the general laws of harmony: thefe are, it is true, the foundations
of the fcience, but there remained a great deal more to be faid in
order to render this work of Boetius complete; and that it was his
defign to make it fo, there is not the leaft reafon to doubt.

The defiderata of the ancient mufic feem to be the genera and the
modes, and to thefe may be added the meafure of founds in refpect of
their duration, or, in other words, the laws of metre. It is to be obferved that mufic was originally vocal, and in that fpecies of it the
voice was employed, not in the bare utterance of inarticulate founds,
but of poetry, to the words whereof correfpondent founds in an harmonical ratio were adopted, and therefore the duration of thofe founds
might be, and probably was determined by the meafure of the verfe, yet
both were fubject to metrical laws, which had been largely difcuffed

* See the Peroratio to his Introduction, towards the end.

before

before the time of Boetius, and thefe it became a writer like him to have reduced to fome ftandard.

Had Boetius lived to complete his work, it is more than probable that he would have entered into a difcuffion of the modes of the ancients, and not left it a queftion, as it is at this day, whether they regarded only the fituation of the final or dominant note in refpect of the fcale, or whether they confifted in the different pofition of the tones and femitones in the fyftem of a diapafon. For the fame reafon we may conclude that, had not his untimely death prevented it, Boetius would have treated very largely on the ecclefiaftical tones : he was a Chriftian, and, though not an enthufiaft, a devout man ; mufic had been introduced into the church-fervice for above a century before the time when he lived ; St. Ambrofe had eftablifhed the chant which is diftinguifhed by his name, and the ecclefiaftical tones, then but four in number, were evidently derived from the modes of the ancients.

Thefe are but conjectures, and may perhaps be thought to include rather what was to be wifhed than expected from a writer of fo philofophical a turn as Boetius ; we have neverthelefs great reafon to lament his filence in thefe particulars, and muft impute the prefent darknefs in which the fcience is unhappily involved, to the want of that information which he of all men of his time feems to have been the moft able to communicate.

MAGNUS AURELIUS CASSIODORUS, fenator, a chriftian, born at Brutium, on the confines of Calabria, flourifhed about the middle of the fixth century. He had a very liberal education confidering the growing barbarifm of the age he lived in, and by his wifdom, learning, and eloquence, recommended himfelf to the protection of the Gothic kings Theodoric and Athalaric, Amalafuentha the daughter of the former, Theodohadus her hufband, and Vitiges his fucceffor. Theodoric appointed him to the government of Sicily, in which province he gave fuch proofs of his abilities, that in the year 490 he made him his chancellor, and admitted him to his councils. After having filled feveral important and honourable pofts in the ftate, he was advanced to the confulate, the duties of which office he difcharged without any colleague in the year 514. He was continued in the fame degree of confidence and favour by Athalaric, who fucceeded Theodoric about the year 526 ; but in the year 537, being

difmiffed

dismissed from all his employments by Vitiges, he betook himself to a religious life. Trithemius says he became a monk, and afterwards abbot of the monastery of Ravenna; after which it seems he retired to the monastery of Viviers, in the extreme parts of Calabria, which he had built and endowed himself. In his retirement from the business of the world he led the life of a scholar, a philosopher, and a Christian, amusing himself at intervals in the invention and framing of mechanical curiosities, such as sun-dials, water hour-glasses, perpetual lamps, &c. He collected a very noble and curious library, and wrote many books himself, particularly Commentaries on the Psalms, Canticles, the Acts of the Apostles, the Epistles of St. Paul, and the Apocalypse, and a Chronology: farther he framed, or drew into one body, the tripartite history of Socrates, Sozomen, and Theodoret, translated by Epiphanius the scholastic. He wrote also Institutionem Divinarum Lectionum, in two books, which Du Pin says abounds with fine remarks on the Holy Scriptures, and a treatise De Ratione Animæ, which the same writer also highly commends. There are extant of his, twelve books of Letters, ten of which are written in the names of Theodoric and Athalaric, he being it seems secretary to them both; the other two are in his own name, and they all abound with a variety of curious and interesting particulars. He was also the author of a treatise De septem Disciplinis, or of the Arts of Grammar, Rhetoric, Logic, Arithmetic, Geometry, Music, and Astronomy * ; what he says of music is contained in one chapter or

---

* This arrangement of the liberal sciences had been made before the time of Cassiodorus, as appears by the fable De Nuptiis Philologiæ et Mercurii of Martianus Capella, which contains a separate discourse on each of them. This division comprehends both the trivium and the quadrivium described in a preceding page. Mosheim censures the professors, or scholastics, as they were called, of that day, for teaching the sciences in a barbarous and illiberal manner.

' The whole circle of sciences was composed of what they called the seven liberal arts,
' viz. grammar, rhetoric, logic, arithmetic, music, geometry, and astronomy; the three
' former of which they distinguished by the title of trivium, and the four latter by that of
' quadrivium. Nothing can be conceived more wretchedly barbarous than the manner in
' which these sciences were taught, as we may easily perceive from Alcuin's treatise con-
' cerning them; and the dissertations of St. Augustin on the same subject, which were in
' the highest repute at this time. In the greatest part of the schools the public teachers
' ventured no farther than the trivium, and confined their instructions to grammar, rhetoric,
' and logic; they, however, who, after passing the trivium, and also the quadrivium,
' were desirous of rising yet higher in their literary pursuits, were exhorted to apply them-
' selves to the study of Cassiodorus and Boethius, as if the progress of human knowledge
' was bounded by the discoveries of those two learned writers.' Ecclesiast. Hist. Cent.
VIII. part ii. cap. 1.

fection of four quarto pages; in this he is very brief, referring very often to Gaudentius, Cenforinus, and other writers. His general divifion of mufic is into three parts, harmonic, rhythmic, and metric. His divifion of inftrumental mufic is alfo into three parts, namely, percuffional, tenfile, and inflatile, agreeing in this refpect with other writers of the beft authority.

One thing worthy of remark in the treatife of Caffiodorus De Mufica is, that he makes the confonances to be fix, namely, the diatefaron, diapente, diapafon, diapafon and diatefaron, or eleventh, diapafon and diapente, or twelfth, and, laftly, the bifdiapafon; in which he manifeftly differs from Boetius, whom he muft have known and been intimate with, for Boetius has beftowed a whole chapter in demonftrating that the diapafon cum diatefaron is not a confonant but a diffonant. Caffiodorus makes the number of the modes, or, as he calls them the tones, to be fifteen; from which circumftance, as alfo becaufe he here prefers the word Tone to Mode, it may be concluded that he writes after Martianus Capella.

Caffiodorus died at his monaftery of Viviers, about the year 560, aged above ninety. Father Simon has given a very high character of his theological writings; they, together with his other works, have been feveral times printed, but the beft edition of them is that of Rohan, in the year 1679, in two volumes folio, with the notes and differtations of Johannes Garetius, a Benedictine monk *.

The feveral improvements of mufic hereinbefore enumerated, regarded chiefly the theory of the fcience, thofe that followed were for the moft part confined to practice: among the latter none have a greater title to our attention than thofe made about the end of the

* Upon the writings of the Latins the remark is obvious, that they added nothing to mufical fcience; and indeed their inferiority to the Greeks, both in philofophy and the more elegant arts, feems to be allowed by the beft judges of ancient literature.

Indeed in their practice of mufic they feem to have fomewhat improved on that of their predeceffors, as is evident from Vitruvius's defcription of the hydraulic organ, an inftrument which Sidonius Apollinaris takes notice of in one of his epiftles, where he fpeaks of the amufements of Theodoric, and particularly adds that he was wont to be entertained with the mufic of the hydraulic organ while he fat at dinner: and it is in the hiftory of the period in which Boetius and Caffiodorus flourifhed, that we meet with the firft intimation of fuch a profeffion as that of a teacher of mufic. The following is an epitaph in the epiftles of the fame Sidonius Apollinaris on one of this profeffion.

Orator Dialecticus Poeta
Traditor, Geometra, Muficus
Pfalmorum Modulator, Phonafcus
Inftructas docuit fonare claffes. Lib. IV. pag. 143.

fixth

fixth century, by St. Gregory the Great, the firft pope of that name, a man not more remarkable for his virtues than for his learning and profound fkill in the fcience of mufic.

The firft improvement of mufic made by this father confifted in the invention of that kind of notation by the Roman letters, which is ufed at this day. It is true that before his time the ufe of the Greek characters had been rejected; and as the enarmonic and chromatic genera, with all the various fpecies of the latter, had given way to the diatonic genus, the firft fifteen letters of the Roman alphabet had even before the time of Boetius been found fufficient to denote all the feveral founds in the perfect fyftem; and accordingly we find in his treatife De Mufica all the founds from Proflambanomenos to Nete hyperboleon characterifed by the Roman letters, from A to P inclufive; but Gregory reflecting that the founds after Lychanos mefon were but a repetition of thofe before it, and that every feptenary in progreffion was precifely the fame, reduced the number of letters to feven, which were A, B, C, D, E, F, G; but, to diftinguifh the fecond feptenary from the firft, the fecond was denoted by the fmall, and not the capital, Roman letters; and when it became neceffary to extend the fyftem farther, the fmall letters were doubled thus, aa, bb, cc, dd, ee, ff, gg.

But the encreafing the number of tones from four to eight, and the inftitution of what is called the Gregorian Chant, or plain fong, is the improvement for which of all others this father is moft celebrated. It has already been mentioned that St. Ambrofe when he introduced finging into the church-fervice, felected from the ancient modes four, which he appropriated to the feveral offices: farther it is to be obferved, that to thefe modes the appellation of Tones was given, probably on the authority of Martianus Capella, who, as Sir Henry Spelman remarks, was the firft that fubftituted the termTones in the room of Modes. But we are much at a lofs to difcover more of the nature of the tones inftituted by St. Ambrofe, than that they confifted in certain progreffions, correfponding with different fpecies of the diapafon; and that under fome kind of regulation, of which we are now ignorant, the divine offices were alternately chanted, and this by the exprefs inftitution of St. Ambrofe himfelf, who all agree was the firft that introduced the practice of alternate or antiphonal finging, at leaft into the weftern church; but it was fuch a
kind

kind of recitation as in his own opinion came nearer to the tone of reading than singing *.

Cardinal Bona † cites Theodoret, lib. IV. to prove that the method of singing introduced by St. Ambrose was alternate; and proceeds to relate that as the vigour of the clerical discipline, and the majesty of the Christian religion eminently shone forth in the ecclesiastical song, the Roman pontiffs and the bishops of other churches took care that the clerks from their tender years should learn the rudiments of singing under proper masters; and that accordingly a music-school was instituted at Rome by pope Hilary, or, as others contend, by Gregory the Great, to whom also we are indebted for restoring the ecclesiastical song to a better form; for though the practice of singing was from the very foundation of the Christian church used at Rome, yet are we ignorant of what kind the ecclesiastical modes were, before the time of Gregory, or what was the discipline of the singers. In fact the whole service seems to have been of a very irregular kind, for we are told that in the primitive church the people sung each as his inclination led him, with hardly any other restriction than that what they sung should be to the praise of God. Indeed some certain offices, such as the Lord's Prayer and the Apostle's Creed, had been used in the church-service almost from the first establishment of Christianity ‡; but these were too few in number to prevent the introduction of hymns and spiritual songs at the pleasure of the heresiarchs, who began to be very numerous about the middle of the sixth century, and that to a degree that called aloud for reformation. The evil increasing, the emperor Theodosius requested the then pope, Damasus, to frame such a service as should consist with the solemnity and decency of divine worship; the pope readily assented, and employed for this purpose a presbyter named Hieronymus, a man of learning, gravity, and discretion, who formed a new ritual, into which he introduced the Epistles, Gospels, and the Psalms ‖, with the Gloria Patri and Alleluiah; and these, together with certain hymns which he thought proper to retain, made up the whole of the service.

* Vossius De Scientiis mathematicis, cap. xxi. § 11.
† De Rebus Liturgicis.
‡ Nivers sur le Chant Gregorien, chap. I.
‖ Ibid. Damasus is said to have first introduced the Psalms into the service. Platina in Damasus, Useef. Chron. anno 371.

It

It is very doubtful whether any thing like an antiphonary exifted at this time, or indeed whether St. Ambrofe did any thing more than inftitute the tones, leaving it to the fingers, under the regulations thereby prefcribed, to adapt fuch mufical founds to the feveral offices as they fhould from time to time think fit; and to this the confufion that had arifen in the church-fervice was in a great meafure owing. What methods were taken by Gregory to remedy this evil will be related in the following account of him.

C H A P. VIII.

GREGORY the Firft, furnamed the Great, was born at Rome of an illuftrious family, about the year 550. He ftudied with great fuccefs, and his quality and merit fo recommended him, that the emperor Juftin the younger made him prefeft of that city. After he had held this high office for fome time, he difcovered that it made him too fond of the world, and thereupon he retired to a convent which he had founded in his own houfe at Rome; but he was foon called out of this retirement by pope Pelagius II. who, in 582, made him one of his deacons, and fent him to Conftantinople, there to refide in the court of the emperor Tiberius, in quality of his nuncio or furrogate, though his immediate bufinefs there was to follicit fuccours againft the Lombards. Upon the death of Tiberius in 586, Gregory returned to Rome, and was there employed as fecretary to Pelagius; but at length he obtained of him leave to retire again to his monaftery, the government whereof he had formerly beftowed on an ecclefiaftic named Valentius, whom for his great merit he had taken from a monaftery in the country. Here he thought to indulge himfelf in the pleafures of a ftudious and contemplative life, but was foon drawn from his retirement by a contagious difeafe, which at that time raged with fuch violence, that eight hundred perfons died of it in one hour *. To avert this calamity Gregory quitted his retreat, came forth into the city, and inftituted litanies and a fevenfold proceffion, confifting of feveral orders of the people, upon whofe arrival

* One of the fymptoms of this difeafe was a violent fneezing, which was looked upon as mortal, and upon this occafion gave rife to the ejaculation ' God blefs you !' in favour of fuch as were fuddenly taken with that convulfion. Ifaacfon's Chronology, anno 590.

at

at the great church it is said the diftemper ceafed. Of this difeafe
Pelagius himfelf died, and by the joint fuffrage of the clergy, the
fenate, and people of Rome, Gregory was chofen for his fucceffor;
but he was fo little difpofed to accept this dignity, that he got himfelf fecretly conveyed out of the city in a bafket, thereby deceiving
the guards that were fet at the gates to hinder his efcape, and
went and hid himfelf in a cave in the middle of a wood; but being
difcovered, he was prevailed on to return, and was confecrated on
the third of September 590, and was the firft of the popes that ufed
the ftyle ' Servus fervorum Dei.' He was of a very infirm and
weakly conftitution, but had a vigorous mind, and difcharged the
duties of his ftation with equanimity and firmnefs. He poffeffed a
great fhare of learning, and was fo well fkilled in the tempers and
difpofitions of mankind, that he made even the private interefts and
ambitious views of princes fubfervient to the ends of religion. One
of the greateft events which by his prudence and good management
he brought about during his pontificate, was the converfion of the
Englifh to Chriftianity, which, as related by Bede, makes one of
the prettieft ftories in our hiftory. But what gives him a title to a
place in this work is his having effected a reformation in the mufic
of the church *.

Maimbourg in his Hiftoire du Pontificat de St. Gregoire has collected from Johannes Diaconus and others, all that he could find on
this fubject. The account given by him is as follows.

' He efpecially applied himfelf to regulate the office and the fing-
' ing of the church, to which end he compofed his antiphonary—
' nothing can be more admirable than what he did on this occafion.
' Though he had upon his hands all the affairs of the univerfal
' church, and was ftill more burthened with diftempers than with
' that multitude of bufinefs which he was neceffarily to take care of
' in all parts of the world, yet he took time to examine with what

---

* Johannes Diaconus, who wrote the life of this pope, fays that he imitated the moft
wife Solomon in this refpect; and that he with infinite labour and great ingenuity compofed an antiphonary; and other writers add a gradual alfo, not in the way of compilation, or by collecting the offices therein contained, but that he dictated or pointed, and
actually neum-mized the mufical cantus both to the antiphonary and gradual. Neuma is
a word poffibly derived from the Greek πνευμα, and, as explained by Sir Henry Spelman,
fignifies an aggregation of fo many founds as may be uttered in one fingle refpiration.
Spelm. Gloff. voce NEUMA: and in this fenfe it is ufed by Guido himfelf, Franchinus, and other writers.

' tunes the pfalms, hymns, oraifons, verfes, refponfes, canticles,.
' leffons, epiftles, the gofpel, the prefaces, and the Lord's Prayer
' were to be fung; what were the tones, meafures, notes, moods
' moft fuitable to the majefty of the church, and moft proper to in-
' fpire devotion; and he formed that ecclefiaftical mufic fo grave and
' edifying, which at prefent is called the Gregorian mufic. He
' moreover inftituted an academy of fingers for all the clerks to the
' deaconfhip exclufively, becaufe the deacons were only to be em-
' ployed in preaching the Gofpel and the diftributing the alms of the
' church to the poor; and he would have the fingers to perfect them-
' felves in the art of true finging according to the true mufic,.
' and to bring their voices to fing fweetly and devoutly; which, ac-
' cording to St. Ifidore, is not to be obtained but by fafting and ab-
' ftinence: for, fays he, the ancients fafted the day before they were
' to fing, and lived for their ordinary diet upon pulfe, to make their
' voices clearer and finer; whence it is, that the heathens called
' thofe fingers bean-eaters*. ***** However, St. Gregory took
' care to inftruct them himfelf, as much a pope as he was,.and to.
' teach them to fing well. Joannes Diaconus fays, that in his time,
' this pope's bed was preferved with great veneration, in the palace
' of St. John of Lateran, in which he fung, though fick, to teach the.
' fingers; as alfo the whip, wherewith he threatened the young clerks
' and the finging boys, when they were out, and failed in the notes.'
    The account given by Johannes Diaconus is fomewhat more parti-
cular than that of Malmbourg, and is to this effect: ' Gregory infti-
' tuted a finging fchool, and built two houfes for the habitation of the
' fcholars, and endowed them with ample revenues; one of thefe
' houfes was near the ftairs of the church of St. Peter, and the other.
' near the Lateran palace. For many ages after his death, the bed
' on which he modulated as he lay, and the whip which he ufed to
' terrify the younger fcholars, were preferved with a becoming vene-
' ration, together with the authentic antiphonary, above faid to have
' been compiled by him †.'

* ' Pridie quam cantandum erat cibis abftinebant pfallentes, legumine in enafi vocis
' affidue utebantur, unde et cantores apud gentiles Fabarii dicti funt.' Ifid. de Eccl.
Offic. lib. II. cap. xii.
† ' Deinde in domo Domini (Divus Gregorius) more fapientiffimi Salamonis propter
' mufice compunctionem dulcedinis, antiphonarium centonem cantorum ftudiofiffimus
' nimis utiliter compilavit. Scholam quoque cantorum, quæ hactenus ejufdem inftitutioni-
                                                                                    ' bus

Other additions to and improvements of the service are attributed to St. Gregory. It is said, that he added the prayers, particularly this, ' Diefque noftros in pace difponas,' and the Kyrie Eleefon, and the Alleluia, both which he took from the Greek liturgy; and that he introduced many hymns, and adopted the refponfaria to the leffons and gofpels: nay, fome have gone fo far as to affert that he invented the ftave. Kircher fpeaks of a MS. eight hundred years old, which he had feen, containing mufic, written on a ftave of eight lines; but Vincentio Galilei, in his Dialogo della Mufica, fhews that it was in ufe before Gregory's time † : this is a matter of fome uncertainty; but the merit of fubftituting the Roman letters in the room of the Greek characters, the reformation of the antiphonary, the foundation and endowment of feminaries for the ftudy of mufic and the introduction of four additional tones, are certainly his due; and thefe are the chief particulars which hiftorians have infifted on, to fhew Gregory's affection for mufic. The augmentation of the tones muft doubtlefs be confidered as a great improvement; the tones, as they ftood adjufted by Saint Ambrofe, were only four, and are defined by a feries of eight founds, in the natural or diatonic order of progreffion, afcending from D, from E, from F, and from G, in the grave, to the fame founds in the acute.

But before the nature of this improvement can be underftood, it muft be premifed, that although the ecclefiaftical tones, confifting merely of a varied fucceffion of tones and femitones, in a gradual afcent from the lower note to its octave, anfwer exactly to the feveral

‡ bus in Sancta Romana Ecclefia modulatur conftitult; eique cum nonnullis prædiis duo ° habitacula; fcilicet, alterum fub gradibus Bafilicæ B. Petri Apoftoli, alterum verò fub ° Lateranenfis Ecclefiæ Patriorchii domibus fabricavit; ubi ufque hodie lectus ejus, in ‡ quo recubans modulabatur, et flagellam ipfius, quo pueris ruinabatur veneratione con° gnra, cum authentico antiphonario refervatur.' Johann. Diacon. in Vita Greg. lib. II. cap. vi.
Johannes Diaconus flourifhed about the year 880; fo that thefe relics might have been two hundred and feventy years old at the time when he wrote the life of Gregory.
† It is worthy of remark, that the mufical ftave has varied in its limits fince it was firft invented. By the paffage in Galilei above referred to, it feems to have been originally contrived to include the fyftem of a diapafon, as containing eight lines; on which only, and not in the fpaces, the points or notes were originally placed. Guido Aretinus, by making ufe of the fpaces, reduced it to five lines. After his time, that is to fay in the thirteenth century, the ftave was finally fetled at four lines, in confequence, it is fuppofed, of that correction of the antiphonary of the Ciftercian order, which St. Bernard undertook and perfected fome years before; and this number has ever fince been found fufficient for the notation of the Cantus Gregorianus.

keys,

keys, as they are called by modern muficians; yet in this refpect they differ; for in modern compofitions the key-note is the principal, and the whole of the harmony has a relation to it; but the modes of the church fuppofe another note, to which that of the key feems to be but fubordinate, which is termed the Dominant, as prevailing, and being moft frequently heard of any in the tone; the other, from whence the feries afcends, is called the Final †.

Farther, to underftand the nature and ufe of this diftinction between the dominant and final note of every tone, it is to be obferved, that at the introduction of mufic into the fervice of the Chriftian church, it was the intent of the fathers that the whole fhould be fung, and no part thereof faid or uttered in the tone or manner of ordinary reading or praying. It feemed therefore neceffary, in the inftitution of a mufical fervice, fo to connect the feveral parts of it as to keep it within the bounds of the human voice; and this could only be done by reftraining it to fome one certain found, as a medium for adjufting the limits of each tone, and which fhould pervade the whole of the fervice, as well the pfalms and thofe portions of fcripture that were ordinarily read to the people, as the hymns, canticles, fpiritual fongs, and other parts thereof, which, in their own nature, were proper to be fung.

Hence it will appear, that in each of the tones it was neceffary not only that the concords, as, namely, the fourth, the fifth, and the octave, fhould be well defined; but that the key-note fhould fo predominate as that the fingers fhould never be in danger of miffing the pitch, or departing from the mode in which the fervice fhould be directed to be fung; this diftinction, therefore, between the dominant and final, muft have exifted at the very time of inftituting the Cantus Ambrofianus, and the fame prevails at this day.

The characteriftics of the four primitive modes were thefe: in each of them the diateffaron was placed above the diapente, which is but one of the two kinds of divifion of which the diapafon is fufceptible. Gregory was aware of this, and interpofed four other tones between the four inftituted by St. Ambrofe, in which the diapente held the uppermoft place in the diapafon: in fhort, the tones of St. Ambrofe arife from the arithmetical, and thofe of St. Gregory from the har-

† Niv. fur le Chant Gregorien, chap. xii.

7   monical,

monical, divifion of the diapafon *. The addition of the four new tones gave rife to a diftinction which all the writers on the fubject have adopted; and accordingly thofe of the firft clafs have the epithet of Authentic, and the latter that of Plagal: the following diagram may ferve to fhew the difference between the one and the other of them.

	1		3		5		7	
Diateffaron.	d		e		f		g	
	c		d		e		f	
	b		c		d		e	
Diapente.	a		b		c		d	Diateffaron.
	G		a		b		c	
	F		G		a		b	
	E		F		G		a	
	D		E		F		G	Diapente.
	C		D		E		F	
	b		C		D		E	
	A		b		C		D	
	2		4		6		8	

Occafion has already been taken to remark, that there are three different fpecies of diateffaron, and four of diapente; and that from the conjunction of thefe two, there arifes feven fpecies of diapafon. Authors have differed in their manner of charactering thefe feveral fyftems, as may be feen in Bontempi, who calls the comparifon of them an unprofitable operation †. That of Gaffurius feems beft to correfpond with the notions of thofe who have written profeffedly on the Cantus Gregorianus, particularly of Erculeo, who, in his treatife, intitled Il Canto Ecclefiaftico, has thus defined them:

---

* We have no authentic formula of the tones in mufical characters more ancient than what is to be found in the writings of Franchinus: there is indeed one in MS. in the Britifh Mufeum, which was part of the Cotton library, Nero, A. xii. 13. beginning ' Si vis ' fcire artem muficam;' but the notes, which were written in red ink, are effaced by time.

† Hift. Muf. pag. 177.

350

THREE Species of DIATESSARON.
I.   II.   III.

Re   Sol Mi   La Fa   Fa

FOUR Species of DIAPENTE.
I.   II.   III.   IV.

Re   La Mi   Mi Fa   Fa Do   Sol

SEVEN Species of DIAPASON.
I.   II.   III.   IV.

Re   La Mi   Mi Fa   Fa Re   Sol

V.   VI.   VII.

Mi   La Fa   Fa Do   Sol

I.   II.   III.   IV.   V.   VI.   VII.   VIII.
Sentenziofe. Mefte. Difdegno. Parifiche. Allegre. Flebile. Divote. Mifteriofe.

D.   E.   F.   G.

It now remains to shew how the tones correspond with the seven species of diapason ; and this will most clearly appear from the description which Gaffurius has given of them in his Practica Musicæ utriusque Cantus, lib. 1. wherein he says,

' The first tone is formed of the first species of diapente, between ' D sol re and A la mi re, and the first species of diatessaron from ' the same A la mi re to D la sol re in the acute, constituting ' the fourth species of diapason, D d.

' The second is formed of the same species of diapente and dia- ' tessaron ; but so disposed as to form the first species of diapason, ' A a.

' The third is formed of the second species of diapente, between ' E la mi, grave, and ♮ mi ; and the second species of diatessa- ' ron from the same ♮ mi, to E la mi, acute, constituting the ' fifth species of diapason, E e.

' The fourth is formed of the same species of diapente and dia- ' tessaron ; but so disposed as to form the second species of dia- ' pason, ♮ ♭.

' The fifth is formed of the third species of diapente, between ' F fa ut, grave, and C sol fa ut ; and the third species of ' diatessaron, from the same C sol fa ut to F fa ut, acute ; ' constituting the sixth species of diapason, F f.

The sixth is formed of the same species of diapente and dia- ' tessaron ; but so disposed as to form the third species of dia- ' pason, C c.

' The seventh is formed of the fourth species of diapente, between ' G sol re ut, grave, and D la sol re ; and the first species ' of diatessaron from the same D la sol re, to G sol re ut, acute ; ' constituting the seventh species of diapason, G g.

' The eighth is formed of the same species of diapente and diatesf- ' faron ; but so disposed as to form the fourth species of diapason, ' D d, which is the characteristic of the first tone : but the dominant ' of the one being A, and that of the other G, there is an essential ' difference between them.'

Hence it appears, that the difference between the Authentic and Plagal Modes, arises from the different division of the diapason in each ; the Authentics being divided in harmonical, and the Plagals in arithmetical proportion. The nature of these is fully explained in the treatise De Musica of Boetius, lib. II. cap. xii. ; and by Dr.

Holder,

352 HISTORY OF THE SCIENCE Book III.

Holder, in his treatise of the Natural Grounds and Principles of Harmony, chap. v. *

From the principles laid down by the latter of these writers †, it will follow, that taking the numbers 12, 9, 8, 6, to express the proportion of the diapason, and its component intervals, the diatessaron and diapente; when the division of the diapason is thus, 12, 9, 6, or A D a, giving to the diatessaron the lowest position, the proportion is arithmetical: When it is 12, 8, 6, or A E a, in which the diapente holds the lowest place, it is harmonical ‡.

Having adjusted the number and limits of the tones, Gregory proceeded to the invention of a Cantus, such as he thought would be confident with the gravity and dignity of the service to which it was to be applied. A plain unisonous kind of melody, frequently inflected to the concords of its key, seemed to him the fittest for this purpose; and having prescribed a rule to himself, as well as to others, he proceeded to apply to the divine offices that kind of Cantilena which prevails in the Roman church even at this day; and which is known in Italy by the name of Canto Fermo, in France by that of Plain Chant, and in Germany and most other countries by that of the Cantus Gregorianus. Cardinal Bona gives this description of it: ' The cantus ' instituted by Saint Gregory was plain and unisonous, proceeding by ' certain limits and bounds of tones, which the musicians term ' Modes or Tropes, and define by the octonary number, according to ' the natural disposition of the diatonic genus.'

Considering that the right understanding of the ecclesiastical tones is essential to the regular performance of choral service, it is not to be wondered at, that almost every writer on music, who professes to treat the subject at large, has taken them under his consideration; and though it may seem, that after they were first established and promulgated through the church, they ceased to be an object worthy the attention of theorists in musical science, yet there is no assignable period

* See an extract from it, supra, chap. v.   † Vide Hold. pag. 86.
‡ Malcolm, in his Treatise of Musick, page 167, says that the arithmetical division puts the 5th next the lesser extreme, and the harmonical next the greater, as in the numbers 6, 8, 9, 12, as they certainly do. Again he says, page 563, that the harmonical division places the 5th lowest, which is also true; hence it appears that he looks upon the lesser extreme to be the lowest position, but in this he errs; for if six parts give a, twelve must give the octave below it, i. e. A. Bontempi is also grossly erroneous in pages 70 and 173, et seq. of his history, and has made strange confusion by giving the smaller number to the graves, and the larger to the acutes, and in the consequent misapplication of the adverbs *sotto* and *sopra*.

in

in which it was not neceſſary to review them, and purge them from
thoſe errors which the levity and inattention of the ſingers were
from time to time, introducing ; for, for near a century after Gregory's
time, innovations of this kind were ſo frequent, that it ſeemed hardly
poſſible to preſerve the Cantus Gregorianus in any degree of purity ;
and, therefore, the court of Rome was continually troubled with applications from the princes of Europe, expreſſing their fears that the
Cantus Gregorianus was in danger of being loſt, and praying its in-
terpoſition in order to its reſtoration.

A more particular account of theſe applications, and the ſucceſs
they met with will ſhortly follow ; they are mentioned in this place
to ſhew that the Cantus Gregorianus was eſteemed a matter of great
importance in divine worſhip, and to account in ſome meaſure for the
numerous tracts that are extant in the world concerning it.

C H A P. IX.

IN the earlier ages the treatiſes written with a view to preſerve the
integrity of the eccleſiaſtical tones, were compoſed in monaſteries :
Guido Aretinus, a Benedictine monk, in a tract entitled Micrologus, a very particular account whereof will hereafter be given,
has beſtowed three chapters on the explanation of the modes or tropes,
which are no other than the eight eccleſiaſtic tones. Many other
diſcourſes on the ſame ſubject are alſo extant in manuſcript ; and in
print they are innumerable.

Of manuſcripts none can pretend to greater authority than the
Micrologus of Guido Aretinus, the twelfth, thirteenth, and fourteenth chapters whereof contain a general deſcription of the eight
eccleſiaſtical modes, tropes, or tones, but without any diſtinction of
their reſpective finals and dominants. In a manuſcript in the library
of Baliol college, containing the Micrologus of Guido, and ſeveral
other muſical tracts, is a dialogue beginning with theſe words ' Quid
eſt Muſica ?' in which the tones are treated with a ſomewhat leſs degree of obſcurity ; but this alſo is defective in that it contains no Formula to aſcertain the relation between the Dominant and the Final
in each of them. But the manuſcript of greateſt value and curioſity,
in reſpect of its copiouſneſs and perſpicuity, of any now extant, is

one on vellum with the following title, ' Hunc Librum vocitatum
' Muficam Guidonis fcripfit Dominus Johannes Wylde, quondam
' exempti Monafterii Sancta Crucis de Waltham Præcentor,' the property of Mr. Weft now prefident of the Royal Society, and which
formerly belonged to Tallys, as appears by his hand-writing on a blank
leaf thereof *. In this book, of which a more particular account will
be given hereafter, are contained a great number of difcourfes on the
fubject of mufic, compofed by fundry perfons, as namely, the above-
mentioned Johannes Wylde,   Kendale, Johannes Torke-
fey, Thomas Walfyngham, Lyonell Power,   Chillfon,
and others ; and among thefe are feveral fhort tracts on the tones or
tropes as they are called. The firft in the book, which feems to
have been not barely copied, but compofed by Wylde, is on the fubject of what he calls Guidonian mufic. It is divided into two parts,
the one treating of Manual, i. e. elementary mufic, from the figure
of the left hand, which Guido is faid to have made ufe of for explaining his fyftem ; and the other of Tonal mufic, containing the
doctrine of the ecclefiaftical tones.

   In the thirteenth chapter of this fecond part of Wylde's tract it is
faid that all the tones are produced from the feven fpecies of diapafon ; but as there are eight of the former, and only feven of the latter, the author firft takes upon him to explain how the eighth
tone was generated : he fays that Ptolemy confidered the feventh
fpecies as produced from the third, and thought that the fourth was
alfo capable of producing another tone, which he added to the
feven, making thereby an eighth : he adds, that he difpofed one after
another, the fifteen letters, which comprehended the bifdiapafon ; conftituting A for the firft note thereof, and P for the laft ; and having
drawn feven femicircles, which pointed out feven fpecies or tones,
he added the eighth, extending from the middle letter □ or H to the
laft letter P, which was the only eighth that wanted a femicircle ;

* This manufcript paft through the hands of Morley, and was of great ufe to him in
the annotations on his Introduction ; many years after his death it had for its owner Mr.
Powle, fpeaker of the houfe of commons in the reign of king William ; from him it came
to lord Somers ; and after his decreafe to Sir Jofeph Jekyll, at an auction of whofe books it
was bought by a country organift, and he in gratitude for fome kindneffes done him, preft
the acceptance of it on his prefent worthy poffeffor. A copy of it was found in the library
of Dr. Pepufch upon his deceafe, but it is from the original that this and the fubfequent
extracts from it are taken.   2

                                                                        point-

pointing out thereby the fourth species, which has its mediation in
C, in which the eighth tone is terminated : and this, says he, Boetius
afferted to be the eighth mode or tone which Ptolemy fuperadded.
The fame author obferves that though the fpecies are Eight, yet the
genera of tones are in truth but Four, each being divided into authentic and plagal; and that each genus is by fome writers termed a
Maniera, which appellation he rejects, as coming from the French.
He fays that no cantus in any of the tones can with propriety exceed
the limits of a tenth; and fo indeed do all the writers on this
fubject *.

In the fame manufcript are feveral other tracts, one in particular
compofed by a certain monk of Sherborne, in metre, tending to explain the precepts of what was then called tonal mufic.

Many other manufcripts on this fubject there are, which, by the
affiftance of the printed catalogues may be found ; but as a comparifon of the feveral definitions therein contained, might introduce a degree of confufion which no diligent enquirer would wifh to encounter, it is fafeft to rely on thofe authors who have written fince the
invention of printing, and whofe works have ftood the teft of ages.

Of thefe Gaffurius, as he is of the greateft antiquity, fo is he of
unqueftionable authority.   In his book intitled Practica Muficæ
utriufque Cantus, printed in the year 1502, he has entered into a
large difcuffion of the ecclefiaftical tones, and has exhibited them
feverally in the following forms.

* This rule muft be underftood as referring only to that unifonous cantus which is ufed
in the intonation of the pfalms and other parts of the fervice, and not to that of the antiphons and hymns; for to thefe a double, triple, and frequently a quadruple cantus is
adapted; and in thefe the interior parts have often anomalous initials and finals; and in
the extreme parts the ambit of the grave and acute founds will often neceffarily exceed the
interval of a tenth.

356

TONE I.

Primus tonus fic incipit fic mediatur & fic fi ni

Seculo rum a men Euouae   Euouae

TONE II.

Secundus tonus fic in ci pit fic me di a tur

& fic fi ni tur   Euouae

TONE III.

Tertius tonus fic incipit fic me di a tur & fic

fi ni tur   Euouae   Euouae

TONE IV.

Quartus tonus fic incipit fic me di a tur & fic

fi ni tur   Euouae   Euouae

TONE V. 357

Quintus tonus fic in-ci-pit fic me-di-a-tur

& fic fi ni tur   Euouae

TONE VI.

Sextus tonus fic in-ci-pit fic me-di-a-tur

& fic fi ni tur

TONE VII.

Vel fic

Septimus tonus fic incipit fic media-tur & fic

fi ni tur   Euoun e   Euouae   Euoun e

TONE VIII.

Vel fic folennis

Octauus tonus fic   incipit fic me-di-a-tur

& fic fi ni tur   Euouae

The above characters exhibit the essential parts of each of the tones, that is to say, the beginning, the mediation, and the close, which is generally contained in the Euouae, a word, or rather a compages of letters, that requires but little explanation, being nothing more than the vowels contained in the words Seculorum Amen; and which whenever it occurs, as it does almost in every page of the antiphonary, is meant as a direction for singing those words to the notes of the Euouae.

From Gaffurius the tones have been continued down to this time, through all the books that have been written on the subject of music at large, in almost every country in Europe. Of those written professedly on the ecclesiastical tones, there are two that merit a particular attention, the one entitled Armonia Gregoriana, by Gerolamo Cantone, Master of the Novices, and vicar of the convent of St. Francis, at Turin, published in 1678, oblong quarto. The other has the title of Il Canto Ecclesiastico, the author D. Marzio Ercukeo, printed at Modena in 1686, in small folio.

The first of these books contains the rudiments of singing, and the most important rules for the Canto Fermo, which for the most part are comprized in short memorial verses. The author has given a brief designation of the eight tones, but in his twenty-second chapter, entitled De' Toni Misti, he has assumed a licence which seems unwarranted by any precedent, at least in ancient practice, of combining together the first and second, the third and fourth, the fifth and sixth, and the seventh and eighth tones, and thereby exceeded the limits prescribed by the ancient writers, who all concur in restraining the canto fermo to the ambit of a tenth.

The latter of these books gives very ample directions for the singing of all the offices in the Roman service, and a representation of the tones in the following order.

The firſt Tone has its final in D. and its dominant in A. [359]
the fifth above its final and is intonated by RE. LA.

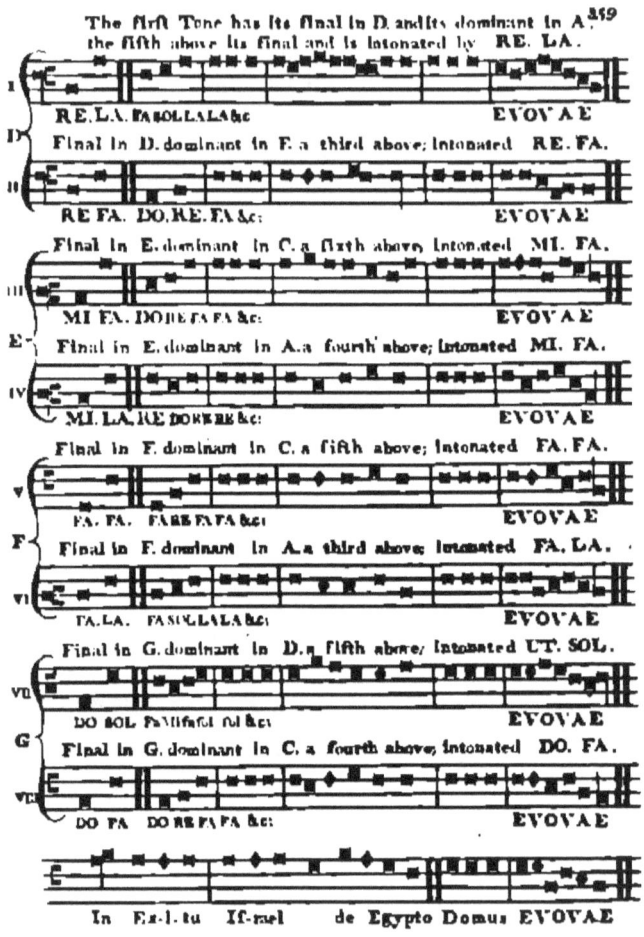

I
RE. LA. FA SOL LA LA &c.   EVOVAE

II)
Final in D. dominant in F. a third above; Intonated RE. FA.

II
RE FA. DO. RE. FA &c.   EVOVAE

III
Final in E. dominant in C. a ſixth above; Intonated MI. FA.

III
MI FA. DO RE FA FA &c.   EVOVAE

E⁻}
Final in E. dominant in A. a fourth above; Intonated MI. FA.

IV
MI. LA. RE DO RE RE &c.   EVOVAE

Final in F. dominant in C. a fifth above; Intonated FA. FA.

V
FA. FA.   FA RE FA FA &c.   EVOVAE

F{
Final in F. dominant in A. a third above; Intonated FA. LA.

VI
FA. LA.   FA SOL LA LA &c.   EVOVAE

Final in G. dominant in D. a fifth above; Intonated UT. SOL.

VII
DO SOL FA SOL FA SOL &c.   EVOVAE

G{
Final in G. dominant in C. a fourth above; Intonated DO. FA.

VIII
DO FA   DO RE FA FA &c.   EVOVAE

In Ex-l-tu Iſ-rael   de Egypto Domus EVOVAE

There is alſo another tone uſed in the Romiſh ſervice, called by ſome of the writers on the Cantus Gregorianus, Il Tuono Pellegrino, i. e. the Wandering Tone; and by others Tuono Miſto, or mixed; the manner in which it is intonated appears by the laſt ſtave in the preceding plate.

The writers on the Cantus Gregorianus have aſſigned to each of the eight eccleſiaſtical tones a peculiar character, ſuppoſing that each is calculated to excite different affections of the mind : this notion is to the laſt degree fanciful, as will appear from what Bontempi and Kircher ſeverally ſay touching the power and efficacy of each *. Erculeo has diſtinguiſhed them in the manner repreſented at the end of his ſcheme of the ſpecies of diateſſaron, diapente, and diapaſon, herein before inſerted †.

The conſequence of theſe and other publications of the ſame im- port, was that the doctrine of the Cantus Gregorianus was rendered ſo perſpicuous, and the forms of the tones ſo well eſtabliſhed, that they became familiar even to children; but the ſtability they had ac- quired was not ſo great, but that about the beginning of the ſeven- teenth century the levity and wantonneſs of the ſingers gave reaſon to fear the corruption of them ‡. It was about this time that the theatric ſtyle of muſic began to be formed, in the performance whereof Caſtrati, and others with flexible and extenſive voices, were principally employed; theſe ſingers, for very obvious reaſons, made uſe of diviſions and all the other uſual artifices to excite applauſe; and theſe were ſo grateful to the ears of the vulgar, that the ſingers em- ployed in the choral ſervice became infected with the like paſſion, and ſo mutilated and diſtorted the Cantus Gregorianus, that the dig- nity and ſimplicity of it was almoſt loſt. This gave occaſion in the year 1683 to an excellent French muſician, Guillaume Gabriel

---

* Vide Bontemp. pag. 241. Kirch. Muſurg. lib. VIII. pag. 142.

† Doctor Pepuſch, in his ſhort Introduction to Harmony, pag. 63, has remarked of the key E that it differs from all others, as in truth it does; for it has for its ſecond a ſe- mitone, for which reaſon, and becauſe of certain peculiarities in the modulation of it, and which render it very ſolemn; be ſays it is as it were appropriated to church-muſic, and called by the Italians Tuono di Chieſa.
This aſſertion of the Doctor may poſſibly be well grounded, but it is to be remarked that no ſuch diſtinction occurs in the writings of Guido or Franchinus, or any of the other authors who have been conſulted in the courſe of this work, for the purpoſe of explaining the Cantus Gregorianus, and the nature of the eccleſiaſtical tones.

‡ Erculeo, pag. 51.

Nivers

Nivers, organist of the chapel of Lewis XIV. and master of music to his queen *, to publish a book entitled Differtation fur le Chant Gregorien. In the composition of this learned and judicious work, the author appears to have derived great affistance from the writings of Amalarius Fortunatus and St. Bernard, and from Cardinal Bona's book De Rebus Liturgicis, Durandus's Rationale Divinorum Officiorum, and, above all, from a more modern author, named Peytat, who wrote a history of the chapel of the king of France, a book abounding with a great variety of curious particulars.

Nivers succeeded so well in his endeavours to reform the cantus ecclefiasticus, that he was employed by the king to correct the Roman antiphonary, for the ufe of the churches in France; and the editions of that great volume fince his time, bear testimony to the fkill and industry which he must have exercised in fo laborious and important a reformation. In short, he has not only reduced the tones to the standard of primitive purity, but has given such directions for the performance of the Cantus Gregorianus, and guarded fo well against innovations in it, that there is very little reafon to fear the lofs of this precious relic of antiquity.

* Nivers was also organist of the church of St. Sulpice, in Paris. He was the author of a book, entitled, Traite de la Composition de Musique, printed at Amsterdam, in octavo, 1697, and of fome motets and pieces for the organ, which are also in print.

A

GENERAL HISTORY

OF THE

SCIENCE and PRACTICE

OF

M U S I C.

BOOK IV.   CHAP. I.

THE firſt eight chapters of Nivers's Diſſertation ſur le Chant Gregorien, contain a hiſtory of the primitive inſtitution of it, and a vindication of the practice of antiphonal ſinging in general, from Socrates, Theodoret, and other eccleſiaſtical writers, with anſwers to the objections of ſuch as either denied its authority or had contributed to the increaſe of thoſe errors in the practice of it which it is the purpoſe of his book to detect and reform.

In the ninth chapter the author enumerates the ſeveral characters neceſſary in the notation of it, and deſcribes them thus :

‘ Twelve characters are ſufficient for the plain-ſong ; the firſt con-
‘ ſiſts of four lines, upon which, and in the ſpaces between them,
‘ all the notes are ſituate ; the fifth line, which certain innovators
‘ have added, is uſeleſs and embaraſſing.

‘ The ſecond character is the key of C ſol ut fa, or elſe by the

‘ method of the si ; the key of C ſol ut made thus ▒ or thus ▒

‘ cannot be ſituate but on the firſt, the ſecond, or the third, and
‘ never or very rarely on the fourth, becauſe the key on the ſecond
‘ line with a b ſoft commonly in B, has altogether the ſame effect
‘ as the ſame key on the fourth line without b ſoft ; for it is always
ſaid the note on this fourth line is always ſung ut, and the other
‘ notes,

' notes confecutively in order.   This is to be underftood of the fong,
' but not of the organ or other inftruments.

' The third character is the key of F UT FA, made thus 🎵 or

' thus 🎵 which is generally fituated on the fecond line, and fome-
' time, but very rarely, upon the firft.

' The fourth and fifth characters are the two notes, the long and
' the breve, made thus ■ ◆, but as the number of characters necef-
' fary in it is one of the grand queftions relating to the cantus, we
' defer fpeaking of it till in the next chapter, to confute the opinion
' of thofe who admit but one of them, namely, the long ■.

' The fixth and feventh characters are the two bars ; the great and
' the lefs, made thus 🎵 which are ufed to denote the place
' where all the choir together ought to take breath and make
' a little paufe.   Thefe are the fame in a fong as ftops are to words,
' wherefore we always at two points or a colon, and fometimes at
' commas, put a great bar to make the fong complete, anfwering to
' a full ftop.   The principal ufe of the leffer bar is to give time for
' the whole choir together to draw breath, to the end that none of the'
' fingers may go on fafter than the reft, and that the uniformity of the
' cantus may be preferved by all, and in all with an equal meafure.
' At the end of every piece there are put two great bars to mark the end
' of the fong ; thefe bars are the moft efficacious contrivance that can

* Nivers, in the fubfequent chapter, undertakes the difcuffion of a queftion which it feems
had fubfifted for a long time, namely, how many characters or marks of time were neceffary in the cantus ecclefiafticus ? He contends that no more than two, namely, the long
and the breve, are admiffible into it ; for this he cites the acts of the council of Rheims
in 1564, in which it was decreed that the cantus fhould contain but one note on a fyllable, and that the quantities of each fhould be obferved in the notation.   He feems to think
that this was the very reformation intended by the council of Trent, in that decree of it
which is mentioned by Father Paul, pag. 559 of his hiftory, to have been made in 1562,
againft over-curious and wanton finging.   He alfo cites Rabanus Maurus to prove
that all clerks fhould perfectly underftand the nature of the accents, and accommodate
their notation to it.   Farther he afferts, on the authority of Radulphus, that in the gradual of the bleffed Gregory at Rome there are but few notes, and that there is reafon to
believe that many characters in thofe of an hundred years after him have no warrant for
their admiffion.
    In the courfe of this difquifition Nivers feems not to be in the leaft aware of a reforma-
tion of the cantus ecclefiafticus made by Paleftrina and Francefco Buriano, about the year
1580, which confifted in the reduction of the characters to three, namely, the long, the
breve, and the femibreve ; and is expref́sly mentioned by Marzio Erculeo, in his Difcourfe
on the Cantus Ecclefiafticus above-cited.

' be thought on to remedy all the cacophonies and contrarieties
' the voices of the fingers, who, without them, could not guefs
' when to reft ; but the abufe of thefe bars is become almoft general,
' for the markers or writers of notes and the printers imagine
' there muft be one at every word; fo that if there are four, five, fix, or
' feven monofyllables following one another, they put as many bars
' as there are notes, as if all the notes were not of themfelves as well
' feparated, without bars, as the words are. St. Bernard fpeaks of
' this confufion in thefe words : " What fort of liberty is this
" which introduces the confufion of uncertainty, &c." And in effect
' this confufion of bars is of no fervice, fince all the notes are of
' themfelves as diftinct as the words ; and all thefe bars are not
' only ufelefs and embarraffing, but they yet (which is remarkable)
' deftroy the benefit of their inftitution, becaufe the fingers, no
' longer knowing where to repofe themfelves, fome flop while others
' advance, which occafions the greateft diforders in the fong ; and the
' excefs of bars puts the fong again into its former abufe, when it
' had no bars, which we fee in the more ancient manufcripts.

' The eighth character is the guidon, made upon the line, or
' in the fpace thus ⸬ or thus ⸻ to mark where
' the following note will be fituate in the other line.

' The ninth character is the bemol, made thus in a fpace, but
' rarely on a line ♭♭ which is always marked in B, and very rarely
' in E.

' The tenth is the point ● between two fhort notes : the ufe of it is
' to augment the precedent one, and diminifh that following it, to ob-
' ferve a certain regulated meafure, for example, that of two times.
' Sometimes the point is alfo put between a long note and a fhort
' one ; and in fuch cafe it only augments the long note with the half
' of its own value, fo that the point and the following breve con-
' fidered together complete the juft meafure of a long note.

' The eleventh character is the bond or joining, made thus ‿,
' or thus ⁀, which ferves to tie two or more notes, or long ones and
' breves on one and the fame fyllable, to keep the regulated meafure.

* This is the form of the guidon in ancient miffals, and other books written or printed
with mufical notes : it is an indication of the firft note in a fucceeding ftave, and is that
note in a fmaller character. This kind of guidon is now difufed, and has given place to
that other above defcribed.

' The

' The laſt character is the dieſis, made thus ✷, or thus x ; the uſe
' of it is to ſoften the following note, or that above or under which it
' is placed ; the dieſes are rarely marked in the plain-ſong, becauſe
' the voice itſelf naturally leads to it *.

Having thus explained the characters, Nivers, in his twelfth book,
proceeds to a diſcrimination of the tones by the finals and dominants of each in their reſpective order, in the words following :

' The firſt has its final in D, and its dominant in A, the fifth to.
' its final ; RE LA.'

* The following directions of Nivers contain the principal rules to be obſerved in the
performance of the cantus ecclefiaſticus.

' To begin to ſing or intonate an anthem, or any other part of the office whatſoever,
' the rule is to attend particularly to the dominant of the choir, which ought to be regu-
' lated according to the voices which compoſe it ; for it would be acting quite contrary to
' nature and reaſon to pretend to eſtabliſh the ſame dominant for the low, the middle, and
' the higheſt voices.

' To arrive at a perfect knowledge of theſe things, it ought to be known that the whole
' ſong conſiſts in eight modes or tones, which may be reduced to four by their finals, and
' even to two, by only the difference of the greater third and the leſſer third.

' The uneven tones, which are only ſo termed, as being diſtinguiſhed by the odd num-
' bers 1, 3, 5, 7, are called authentics or principals : the others are named plagals or de-
' pendents, becauſe they have one and the ſame final each with their authentic, and thus
' the firſt and ſecond have one and the ſame final, ſo the third and fourth, the fifth and
' ſixth, the ſeventh and eighth ; all their difference conſiſts only in the extent, which in
' the authentics is above, and in the plagals below.

' Every tone has two eſſential chords, called the final and the dominant, upon which all
' ſorts of ſongs turn and are founded. The final is that by which the tone ought for the moſt
' part to begin, but always to end The dominant is that which rules or prevails the often-
' eſt in the ſong, and upon which the tenor of the pſalms, oraiſons, and all that is to be
' be ſung ſtrait forward, or nearly ſtrait forward, is made. Wherefore this dominant
' on,   > be a little higher than the middle of the natural voice, and not lower, becauſe
' that in all the tones the extent of the notes is greater below than above the dominant ;
' but it is not a ſmall difficulty to take it juſt and in a good pitch.

' For the common and ordinary voices they put the dominant of the choir in A of the
' organ ; I mean the organs which have the tone of the king's chapel, which all the famous
' organs of Paris and elſewhere have, wherefore this tone is called the tone of the chapel,
' to diſtinguiſh it from the tone of the king's chamber, which is a ſeminone higher. and
' ſo commonly put, or ought to be, the organs in numeries ; the nuns having generally
' an extent of voice higher by an octave than the common voices of men.

' For the low voices they put the dominant in G of the organ.

' For the high voices they put the dominant in B of the organ.

' For the voices of religious women they put the dominant in C, or even in D of the
' organ, according to the quality of the voices.

' The firſt thing therefore that ought to be known is the dominant of the choir, which
' is only a generical ſound, or tone if you will, and not fiſed to any note or degree, that
' is to any rule or interval on which this dominant can be placed.

' The ſecond thing to be obſerved is the mode or tone of the anthem which is to be
' ſung, and to regulate the dominant of the anthem to the uniſon of the dominant of the
' choir which performs it, and then to proceed from this dominant regularly, and paſs
' through

' The fecond has its final in D, and its dominant in F, a third to
' its final ; RE FA.'

' The third has its final in E, and its dominant in C, a fixth to its
' final ; MI UT *.'

' The fourth has its final in E, and its dominant in A, a fourth to
' its final ; MI LA.'

' The fifth has its final in F, and its dominant in C, a fifth to its
' final ; UT SOL, or elfe FA UT with B ♭, not ♭.'

' The fixth has its final in F, and its dominant in A, a third to
' its final; UT MI, or elfe FA LA, with B ♭, not ♭. '

' The feventh has its final in G, and its dominant in A, a fifth
' to its final ; SOL RE.'

' The eighth has its final in G, and its dominant in C, a fourth to
' its final ; SOL UT.'

The differtation of Nivers contains alfo Formulæ Cantus Ordinarii
Officii Divini. Thefe he has given in Latin, together with the mufical notes : they contain directions for finging the oraifons and refponfes, and for reading the prophets, the epiftles, and gofpels, and
for the intonation of the pfalms. There are alfo feveral litanies and
antiphons, and that famous lamentation of the Virgin, in monkifh
rhyme,

                Stabat mater dolorofa
                Juxta crucem lachrymofa.

The formula of the tones intitled Tabula tonorum, is alfo given
in mufical characters, and contains the following examples :

' through all the degrees as far as the note by which the anthem ought to begin ; for ex-
' ample, if I would intonate the firft authem of the Feaft of the Holy Sacrament, " Sa-
' cerdos in æternum," I fing flowly the dominant of this anthem, which is LA,
' to the unifon of the dominant of the choir, and defcend by degrees to the final
' of the anthem, by which it begins, finging LA, SOL, FA, MI, RE, to find the
' juft tone of the firft note of the faid anthem, " Sacerdos in æternum," and after the
' fame manner in other anthems and tones. But one fhould not be ignorant of the effen-
' tial chords of every tone.'

It fhould feem by thefe feveral tracts of Erculeo and Nivers, and other authors who
might be named, that thé doctrine of the tones is now fo well eftablifhed, that there is not
the leaft reafon to fear any corruption of them. In England the little book entitled A pious
Affociation, publifhed for the inftruction of perfons of the Romifh perfuafion in the true
church plain-fong, contains a formula of the eight tones, exactly correfponding with that
of Nivers above given ; and it further appears, that in the feminaries throughout Italy it is
taught to children in a way that admits of no variation. In fhort, its principles feem to be
as well underftood as thofe of arithmetic, or any other mathem·tical fcience.

* According to the French method of folmifation ; but Erculeo makes it LA.

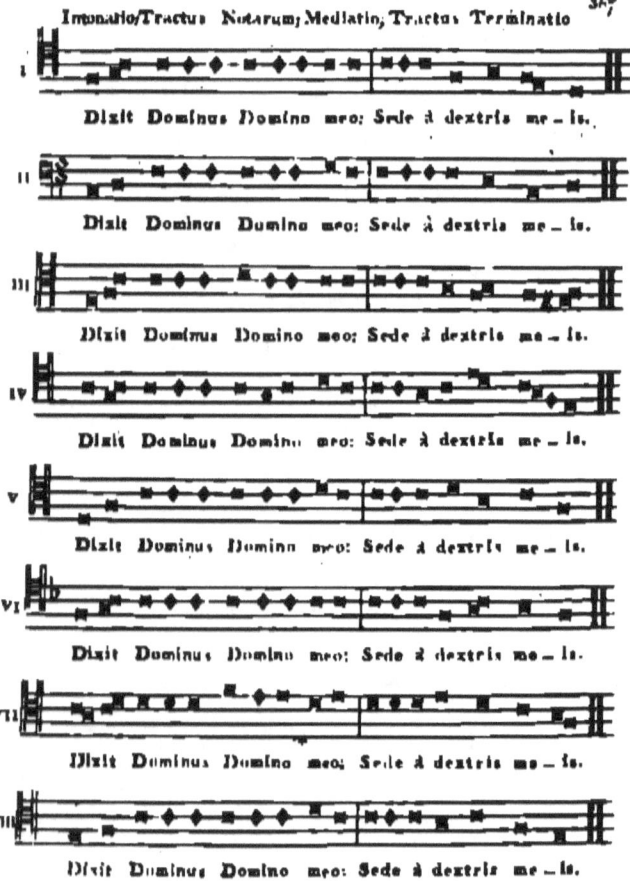

I

Dixit Dominus Domino meo: Sede à dextris me _ is.

II

Dixit Dominus Domino meo: Sede à dextris me _ is.

III

Dixit Dominus Domino meo: Sede à dextris me _ is.

IV

Dixit Dominus Domino meo: Sede à dextris me _ is.

V

Dixit Dominus Domino meo: Sede à dextris me _ is.

VI

Dixit Dominus Domino meo: Sede à dextris me _ is.

VII

Dixit Dominus Domino meo: Sede à dextris me _ is.

VIII

Dixit Dominus Domino meo: Sede à dextris me _ is.

To facilitate the remembrance of the formula of each of the tones, and particularly to imprefs upon the minds of children the finals and dominants that charaéterife them, memorial verfes have been compofed, of which the following are a fpecimen.

Primus habet tonus F sol la, fextus et idem :
Ut re fa oétavus : fit tertius, atque fecundus :
La sol la quartus : dant ut mi sol tibi quintum :
Septimus at tonus fa mi fa sol tibi monftrat.

Septimus et fextus, dant fa mi re mi quoque primus.
Quintus et oétavus, dant fa sol fa ficque fecundus.
Sol fa mi re fa tertius, re ut re mi reque quartus.

Primus cum quarto dant A la mi re, quoque fextus
E fa ut fecundus: C sol fa ut tertius tibi notat,
Cum eo quintus, oétavufque fignat ibidem :
Septimus in D la sol re fuum ponit euouae.

By the foregoing deduétion of the nature of the Cantus Gregorianus, nothing more is intended than to explain its original form, for it will be obferved that none of the authors abovecited prefume to make any additions to, or amendments of it, on the contrary they labour to reprefent it in its purity, and to preferve it from corruption. This was evidently the defign of Nivers; and his book, which is of the controverfial kind, is calculated to correét certain abufes in the fervice that arofe from the wantonnefs and levity of the fingers, and were peculiar to his time ; but the Cantus Gregorianus fuffered greatly from corruptions that were the effeét of ignorance, and which took place within a century after its inftitution ; and thefe corruptions, their nature and caufes, and the methods taken to remove them by the feveral princes of Europe, efpecially thofe of Germany, France, and England, make a very confiderable part of the Hiftory of Mufic, and therefore require to be particularly mentioned ; and if the foregoing digreffion may feem to deviate from the rule which chronology prefcribes in the relation of events, let it be remembered that in this cafe a ftriét adherence to it would have been abfurd ; for who can underftand a relation of the feveral corruptions of the Cantus Gregorianus, who is not firft made

fenfible

senfible of its nature and application ; in fhort, who has not a clear conception of the thing itfelf, in its original ftate of purity and perfection.

That the Cantus Gregorianus became corrupt in a fhort time after its inflitution, may be gathered from the ecclefiaftical and other writers, from the feventh century downwards. Saint Bernard, in a preface to the antiphonary of the Ciftercians, has enumerated many abufes, diforders, and irregularities which had crept into the church-fervice before his time, and this even at Rome itfelf: he fpeaks of the fingers of his time as ignorant and obftinate to a degree that is fcarce to be credited ; for he reprefents them as confounding the rules, and preferring error to truth ; and referring to an Antiphon, ' Nos ' qui vivimus,' the proper termination whereof is in D, he adds, that thofe unjuft prevaricators, the fingers of his time, would terminate it in G; and affert with an oath or wager, that it was of the eighth tone.

Sir Henry Spelman (whom Gerard Voffius has followed, in an account given by him of this matter)* upon the authority of an anonymous commentator on Hugo Reutlingenfis, relates that the Cantus Gregorianus was very much corrupted by the Germans. The words of the author thus referred to are, ' Certain Germans, and particular-
' ly the clergy of the order of St. Benedict, who had learned perfect-
' ly and by heart the mufical cantus, not only theoretically, but alfo
' by practice and exercife, leaving out the keys and lines which are
' required in the mufical Neuma,† note or character, began to note
' them down fimply in their books ; and after that, their fucceffors
' fung in the fame manner, and taught their fcholars, not theoreti-
' cally, but by frequent practice and long exercife ; which cantus
' thus learned by practice, became various in different places,
' wherefore it was then termed practice, ufus ‡, and not mufic.
' In this cantus however the fcholars afterwards began to differ
' in many things from their mafters, and the mafters from their
' fcholars ; from which difference, and the ignorance of the theory,

* Voci Frigdorae. Sed vide Ger. Voff. De Scientiis Mathematicis, cap xxi §. 12.
† This word, which Sir Henry Spelman has elfewhere faid is fynonymous with the noun Note, has two fignifications ; that which Gaffurius has given of it is its primitive and true one ; and he fays it is an aggregation of as many founds or notes as may be conveniently uttered in one fingle refpiration. Vide Spelman's Gloff. voce NEUMA ; and Gaffurius, Pract. Muf. lib. 1 cap. viii Probably it is derived from the Greek Πνευμα.
‡ For which reafon, the terms Salifbury ufe, Hereford ufe, the ufe of Bangor, York, Lincoln, are taken to defcribe the ritual of thofe feveral cathedrals in the preface to the book of Common Prayer.

VOL. I. Bbb ' the

' the practice was said to be confused, which confused practice being
' despised, almost all the Germans, who were hitherto miserably se-
' duced by that cantus, are returned to the true art.'

These corruptions, according to the author above-cited, seem to
have been peculiar to Germany; but there were others of an earlier
date which prevailed in France and also in Britain, for the latter of
which countries Gregory seems to have entertained such a degree of
affection, as makes it highly probable that the inhabitants of it were
some of the first people to whom the knowledge of the Cantus Gregorianus was communicated, and that they became Christians and
singers at one and the same period.

The history of the conversion of the Saxon inhabitants of this
island to christianity in the year 585, is related by all our historians,
particularly by Bede, whose account of it, as exhibiting a very natural representation of the simplicity of manners which then prevailed, is here inserted.

' It is reported that merchants arriving at Rome, when on a
' certain day many things were to be sold in the market-place,
' abundance of people reforted thither to buy, and Gregory himself
' with the rest, where, among other things, boys were set to sale,
' for slaves, their bodies white, their countenance beautiful, and
' their hair very fine: having viewed them, he asked, as. is said,
' from what country or nation they were brought, and was told,
' from the island of Britain, whose inhabitants were of such a pre-
' sence *. He again enquired whether those islanders were Christians,
' or still involved in the errors of paganism, and was informed that
' they were pagans. Then fetching deep sighs from the bottom of
' his heart, " Alas! what pity said he, that the author of darkness,
" is possessed of men of such fair countenances, and that being re-
" markable for such graceful aspects, their minds should be void of
" inward grace." He therefore again asked what was the name of
' that nation, and was answered, that they were called Angles:
' Right, said he, for they have an angelical face, and it becomes
' such to be coheirs with the angels in heaven. What is the name,
' proceeded he, of the province from which they are brought?"
' It was replied, that the natives of that province were called Deiri†,

---

* William Thorn, a monk of St. Augustine's Canterbury, says there were three of
these boys: ' Vidit in foro Romano tres pueros Anglicos lactei candoris.' Decem Scriptores, pag. 1757.
† i.e. of Deirham, or Durham.

2   " Truly

"Truly Deiri, faid he, withdrawn from wrath and called to the
" mercy of Chrift.   How is the king of that province called?"
' They told him his name was Elle; and he, alluding to the name,
' faid, " Hallelujah, the praife of God the creator muft be fung in
' thofe parts." Then repairing to the bifhop of the Roman and
' apoftolical fee (for he was not himfelf then made pope) he intreated
' him to fend fome minifters of the word into Britain, to the nation
' of the Englifh, by whom it might be converted to Chrift *.'

The above relation is very characteriftic of the humanity and fimplicity of the reverend father. Fuller, who labours hard to make all
mankind as merry as himfelf, thinks that in his ready application of
the anfwers of the merchants to his purpofe, his wit kept pace with
his benevolence, and having a mind to try whether he could not be
as witty as the father, he has given the whole converfation a dramatic
turn, by putting it into the form of a dialogue †.

The fight of thefe children, and the knowledge which Gregory
thereby acquired of this country and its inhabitants, were the motives for fending Auguftine the monk hither, with whom, as we
are exprefsly told by Johannes Diaconus, who wrote the Life of
St. Gregory, fingers were alfo fent with Auguftine, then going
to Britain, and afterwards difperfed through the weft, who thoroughly inftructed the barbarians in the Roman inftitution.   The
fame author proceeds to relate that after the death of thefe men ‡ the

* Fcd. Hift. Ecclefaft. lib. II. cap. i.
† Church Hift. of Britain, Cent. VI. book ii.
‡ The names of the fingers who came into Britain with Auguftine are no where particularly mentioned. We learn however from Bede that the church fong was at firft only
known in Kent; that afterwards, that in fay about the year 620, when Paulinus became
bifhop of the Northumbrians, a deacon of his, named James, had rendered himfelf very famous for his fkill in the church fong; and that Willfrid, a fucceeding bifhop of the fame
fee, about the year 664 invited out of Kent Eddi, furnamed Stephen, for the purpofe of
teaching the fame in the feveral churches of the Northumbrians.   Farther, Bede gives a particular account of John the finger above-mentioned, whom he ftiles archchanter or precentor
of the church of the holy apoftle Peter, and abbot of the monaftery of St. Martin, and elfewhere finger of the apoftolic fee: he fays he was fent into Britain by pope Agatho, that
he might teach the method of finging throughout the year, as it was practifed at St. Peter's
at Rome; and that he fettled in a monaftery which Egfrid king of the Northumbrians
had founded at the mouth of the river Wire.   He farther fays that John did as he had
been commanded by the pope, teaching the fingers of this monaftery the order and manner of finging and reading aloud, and committing to writing all that was required
throughout the whole courfe of the year for celebrating feftivals, all which were in Bede's
time obferved in that monaftery, and tranfcribed by many others elfewhere: he fays farther that the faid John did not only teach the brethren of that monaftery, but that fuch as

modulation of the weſtern churches became very corrupt, and continued ſo till pope Vitalianus the Firſt, who introduced the organ into the choral ſervice, ſent John, a famous Roman ſinger, together with Theodore, afterwards archbiſhop of Canterbury, by the way of

had ſkill in ſinging reſorted from almoſt all the monaſteries of the ſame province to hear him.

The reverend Mr. Johnſon, late of Cranbrook in Kent, has given a ſummary of this relation, with his own ſentiments thereon, in a book which hardly any one now looks into, but which abounds with a great variety of curious learning, his Collection of Eccleſiaſtical laws ; in the general preface to which he ſays, upon the authority of Bede, that pope Agatho, above eighty years after Auguſtine's coming over, ſent John, the precentor of St. Peter's church in Rome, to inſtruct the monks of Wirmuth in the annual courſe of ſinging ; and that he did accordingly teach them the order and rite of ſinging and reading in the celebration of feaſts through the circle of the whole year, and that he wrote down and left behind him whatever was requiſite to this purpoſe. And that the ſum of what he taught them conſiſted in new tunes or modes of muſic, ſome variations of habit, geſture, and perhaps of the ſeries of performing religious offices according as the faſhions had been altered at Rome ſince Auguſtine's coming hither—that he taught them viva voce, and what he wrote down concerned only the celebration of the feſtivals—that John was ſent to one monaſtery only, and is not ſaid to have taught any but the Northumbrians.—That upon Theodore's firſt coming to Canterbury, which was ten or twelve years before this, the Roman way of ſinging was well known in Kent, and then began to be taught in other churches—that Wilfrid ſoon after invited Eddi, otherwiſe called Stephan, out of Kent into the North, to teach this practice there.—But thirty-five years before Theodore's arrival, James the Kentiſh deacon had been left at York by Paulinus when he retired to Rocheſter, on purpoſe to teach them the way of ſinging uſed by the Romans and the Kentiſh. The ſame author adds as a conjecture of his own, that it is probable that neither of theſe Kentiſh ſinging-maſters went farther than Hexham, however not to Wirmuth.

The ſame Collection contains a decree of the Rman council, which as it relates to muſic, and was made to reform an abuſe of it that prevailed about this time, it may not be improper here to mention. By this act it is decreed that biſhops, and all whoſoever that profeſs the religious life of the eccleſiaſtical order, do not uſe weapons, nor keep muſicians of the female ſex, nor any muſical concerts whatſoever, nor do allow of any buffooneries or plays in their preſence.

Of James, the deacon of Paulinus above-mentioned, he ſays that he lived to his [Bede's] time. If ſo, and conſidering that Paulinus was biſhop of Northumbria, in which province Bede's monaſtery was ſituate, it is more than probable that Bede and James were intimately acquainted.

Bede alſo mentions as living in the time of Theodore, Putta, a man of great ſimplicity in his manners, extremely well verſed in eccleſiaſtical diſcipline, and remarkably ſkilful in church-muſic, and who, on account of theſe his excellencies, was preferred to the ſee of Rocheſter. Mention will be made of this perſon hereafter, in the interim it is to be obſerved, that the teſtimony of Bede is of great weight in all matters that relate to church diſcipline, and that hardly any man of his time was better acquainted with the muſic of the church than himſelf : in a ſummary of his own life, at the end of his Eccleſiaſtical Hiſtory, he mentions his being a prieſt of the monaſtery of Wiremouth, the very monaſtery where John the precentor ſettled upon his arrival in Britain ; and that he there applied himſelf to the meditation of ſcripture, the obſervance of regular diſcipline, and the daily care of ſinging in the church ; and that he always delighted in learning, teaching, and writing.

France

France into Britain, who corrected the abuses that had crept into the church-service of this, as it should seem, favourite people.

Farther he says, that afterwards the Gregorian chant became again corrupt, particularly in France, for which reason Charlemagne sent two clerks to Rome with a request to Adrian, the then pope, that they might be instructed in the rudiments of the genuine Roman song; these brought back the metropolis of Metz to its original purity of singing, and that city communicated its example to all France. The same author adds that the death of these two men produced the same effect, though in a less degree, in France, as that of the others had done in Britain; wherefore the king wrote again to Adrian; who sent him two singers, who found that the church of Metz had deviated a little from the true rule of singing, but the other churches a great deal. The same author adds, that this diversity was remarkable in his time, for that the rest of the French and all the German churches were then as much inferior in the purity of their choral service to that of Metz, as the latter were to the Roman; but for the present he says these men reduced the church of Metz to order.

Monsieur Nivers, from Peytat, a modern writer, and a countryman of his, who it seems wrote an ecclesiastical history of the chapel of the king of France, cites the following passage:

Pope Stephen II. being constrained to seek to Pepin king of France for protection of the holy see against the Lombards, arrived in that kingdom so soon after Pepin's ascent to the throne, as to perform the ceremony of his consecration in the abbey-church of St. Denys. From Rome the pope had brought with him chaplains and singers, who first made it their business to instruct the choir of St. Denys in the Roman office; and afterwards, for the pope made a considerable stay in France, assisted in communicating the knowledge of it to the other churches in that kingdom. At that time the chapel of Pepin consisted of the very flower of the clergy, and, with the assistance of the Romans, not only the plain-chant but the use of instruments was spread throughout the realm. This reformation it is true did not last long, for upon the death of Pepin his son Charlemagne found the choral service in as great disorder as ever, which, says the monk of St. Cibard of Angoulesme, was the reason that induced this emperor to apply to Adrian for assistance from Rome.

CHAP.

C H A P. II.

THE account given of this matter by another ancient writer, a monk of St. Gal, is that the pope sent to France, at the request of the emperor Charlemagne, twelve excellent singers, answering to the number of the apostles, whose instructions were to reform the music of the French churches, and regulate the service, so as that there might be an uniformity in this respect throughout the kingdom ; but that these men, jealous of the glory of France, in their way thither plotted to corrupt and diversify the plain-chant in such a manner as to increase the confusion in which it was involved, and thereby render the people for ever incapable of performing it correctly. As soon as they arrived in France, where they were received with great honour, they were, by order of the emperor, dispersed to different parts of the kingdom ; but how well they answered the purpose of sending for them, the event soon shewed ; for every man teaching a different chant for the true one of St. Gregory, which they were sent for to restore to its original purity and propagate, the confusion was greater than ever *.

The emperor it seems was too well skilled in music for this deceit to pass upon him unnoticed : he had, in the life-time of his father, heard the true Roman chant at Treves, where he had passed the Christmas, and at Metz also he had been present when it was sung in its perfection ; but after the arrival of these people, spending part of that festival at Paris and the rest at Tours, he was surprised to hear a melody different from that which before he had so much admired ; his disappointment excited in him a curiosity to hear the service as it was performed in the other churches ; but among the singers he found such a disagreement, that he complained to the pope of the behaviour of those whom he had sent ; the pope recalled them to Rome, and condemned some of them to banishment, and the rest to perpetual imprisonment. After this it was that Adrian sent to France the two singers who reformed the French church-music, as above is related.

* Vid. Niv. sur le Chant. Greg. chap iv. pg. 33.

None

None of the historians who relate the transactions of this period, except Baronius, assign the reason of the emperor's application to pope Adrian for affistance in the reformation of choral music in his kingdom of France. It seems that that pope had established the ufe of the Cantus Gregorianus by the decree of a council, which he had fummoned for that purpose, and that his zeal to render it univerfal was the effect of a miracle, which, if we may believe the writers of thofe times, had then lately been wrought in its favour. It is faid, that after the death of Gregory the method of finging inflituted by him began to decline, and the Ambrofian cantus to revive. Adrian had entertained an opinion of the fuperior excellence of the former, and was determined to establish the ufe of it throughout the church; for this purpofe he fummoned a council above-mentioned; who being unable to determine the preference between the one and the other of the offices, referred the decifion of the matter to God, and a miracle announced that the preference was due to the Gregorian office.

Durandus has given a very circumftantial relation of this extraordinary event in the following words *.

' We read in the life of St. Eugenius that till his time the ' Ambrofian office was more ufed by the church than the Gre- ' gorian : pope Adrian fummoned a council, by which it was ' decreed that the Gregorian ought to be univerfally obferved. ' Moreover St. Eugenius coming to a certain council, fummoned ' for this purpofe, and finding that it had been already diffolved ' three days, he perfuaded the lord pope to recall all the prelates who ' had been prefent thereat. The council, therefore, being reaffem- ' bled, it was the unanimous opinion of all the fathers, that the Am- ' brofian and Gregorian miffals fhould be laid upon the altar of St. ' Peter the apoftle, fecured by the feals of moft of the bifhops, and ' the doors of the church fhut, and that all perfons prefent fhould ' fpend the night in prayer that God would fhew by fome fign which ' of thefe miffals he chofe to have ufed by the church; and this was ' done in every refpect. Accordingly, in the morning, when they en- ' tered the church they found the Gregorian miffal turn to pieces, ' and fcattered here and there, but they found the Ambrofian only

---

* Afterwards pope; the fecond of that name. Du Pin, Hift. Eccl. vol. III. pag. 6.

' open

‘ open upon the altar, in the fame place where it had been laid.
‘ By which fign they were taught from heaven that the Gregorian
‘ office ought to be difperfed throughout the whole world, and that
‘ the Ambrofian fhould be obferved only in that church in which it
‘ was firft inftituted. And this regulation prevails to the prefent day ;
‘ for in the time of the emperor Charles, the Ambrofian office was
‘ very much laid afide, and the Gregorian, by the imperial
‘ authority, was brought into common ufe. Ambrofe inftituted
‘ many things according to the ritual of the Greeks.’ Gulielm. Durandus Rationale Divinorum Officiorum. Lugd. 1574, lib. II. cap. ii.
numb. 5.

The hiftorians of the time take notice, that in the year 787 a violent conteft arofe between the Roman and French fingers, concerning
the true method of finging divine fervice, which was carried on with
fo much heat and bitternefs, that neither fide could be made to yield.
At length, the matter was brought before the emperor ; who, after
hearing the reafons and arguments of each party, determined in favour
of the Roman practice, by declaring, that the French fingers had corrupted the Cantus Gregorianus. Baronius has related the tranfaction
at length in thefe words :

‘ In the ancient chronicle of Charles king of France, which Pi-
‘ thoeus publifhed, thefe things then done at Rome are recorded.
‘ The moft pious king Charles returned, and celebrated Eafter at
‘ Rome with the apoftollical lord. Behold a contention arofe, during
‘ the time of the pafchal feaft, between the Roman and French
‘ fingers : the French faid that they fung better and more gracefully
‘ than the Romans ; the Romans faid they performed the ecclefiafti-
‘ cal cantus more learnedly, as they had been taught by St. Gregory,
‘ the pope ; and that the French fung corruptly, and debafed and
‘ ruined the true cantilena. This contention came before the em-
‘ peror Charles ; and the Gauls, relying on his favour, violently ex-
‘ claimed againft the Roman fingers ; and the Romans, upon the
‘ authority of their great learning, affirmed that the Gauls were fools
‘ and ruftics, and as unlearned as brute beafts, and preferred the learning
‘ of St Gregory to their rufticity : and the altercation ceafing on
‘ neither fide, the emperor faid to his fingers, “ Tell me plainly,
“ which is the purer, and which the better, the living fountain, or its
“ rivulets running at a diftance.” They all, with one voice, anfwered,

I　　　　　　　　　　　　　　　‘ the

‘ the fountain ; as the head and origin is the purer, and the rivulets,
‘ the farther they depart from the fountain, are by so much the more
‘ muddy, foul, and corrupted with impurities. “ Then, said the
“ emperor, return ye to the fountain of St. Gregory, for ye have
“ manifestedly corrupted the ecclesiastical cantus.”

‘ The emperor, therefore, soon after desired singers of pope Adrian,
‘ who might reform the French singing ; and he sent to him Theo-
‘ dore and Benedict, two of the most learned singers of the Roman
‘ church, who had been taught by St. Gregory ; and he sent by
‘ them the antiphonary of St. Gregory, which he had marked with
‘ the Roman note. The emperor returning into France, sent a singer
‘ of the city of Metz, with orders that the masters of schools
‘ throughout all the provinces of France should deliver their anti-
‘ phonaries to them to be corrected, and that they should learn to sing
‘ of them. Upon this, the antiphonaries of the French were correct-
‘ ed, which every one had corrupted, by adding or diminishing ac-
‘ cording to his own fancy, and all the singers of France learned the
‘ Roman note ; except that the French who with their voices, which
‘ are naturally barbarous, could not perfectly express the delicate or
‘ tremulous, or divided sounds, in music, but broke the sounds in
‘ their throats, rather than expressed them : but the greatest singing
‘ school was that in the city of Metz ; and as much as the
‘ Roman school excels the Metensian in the practice of singing, by
‘ so much does the Metensian excel the other schools of France.
‘ In like manner, the aforesaid Roman singers instructed the singers
‘ of the French in the art of instrumental music ; and the emperor
‘ Charles again brought with him from Rome into France, masters
‘ of grammar and mathematics, and ordered the study of letters to
‘ be every where pursued ; for before his time, there was no atten-
‘ tion paid to the liberal arts in Gaul. This account is given of these
‘ affairs in that chronicle. Moreover, there is an ordinance of
‘ Charles the Great himself concerning the performance of the Ro-
‘ man music in Gaul, in these words : “ That the monks fully and
“ regularly perform the Roman singing in the nocturnal stated ser-
“ vice, according to what our father king Pepin, of blessed memory,
“ decreed should be done, when he introduced the Gallican singing
“ for the sake of unanimity in the Apostolic See, and the peaceful
‘‘ concord of the Holy Church *.”

* Baron. Annal. Ecclesiast. tom. IX. pag. 415.

The zeal which this prince difcovered through the courfe of a long reign, in favour of the church, and for the re-eftablifhment of ecclefiaftical difcipline, has procured him a place among thofe ecclefiaftical writers enumerated in Du Pin's voluminous hiftory. It was the good fortune of this emperor to have in his fervice a fecretary, named Eginhart, a man not more eminent for his knowledge of the world, than celebrated for his fkill in the literature of thofe times. To him we are indebted for a life of this great prince, one of the moft curious and entertaining works of the kind at this day extant : in this are recorded, not only the great events of Charlemagne's reign, but the particulars of his life and character, a very exact defcription of his perfon, his ftudies, his recreations, and, in fhort, all that can gratify curiofity, or tend to exhibit a lively portrait of a great man. Not to enter into a minute detail of his wars and negociations, or the other important tranfactions during his government, let this fhort fketch of his perfonal and mental endowments, and his labours to reftore the fervice of the church to its original purity, fuffice, as having a more immediate relation to the fubject of this work.

CHARLEMAGNE was born in the year of Chrift 769, at Ingelheim, a town in the neighbourhood of the city of Liege, in Germany. His father was Pepin, king of France, furnamed the Little, by reafon of the lownefs of his ftature ; who, upon his deceafe, made a partition of his dominions between his two fons, bequeathing to Charlemagne, the elder, France, Burgundy, and Aquitain, and to Carloman, Auftria, Soiffons, and other territories ; but Carloman furviving his father a very fhort time, Charlemagne became the heir of all his dominions, and at length emperor of the Weft.

The ftature and perfon of Charlemagne are very particularly taken notice of and defcribed by the writers of his hiftory, by which it appears, that he was as much above the ordinary fize of men, as his father Pepin was below it. Turpin, the archbifhop of Rheims, relates, that he was eight feet high, that his face was a fpan and an half long, and his forehead one foot in breadth, and that his body and limbs were well proportioned. He had a great propenfity to learning, having had fome of the moft celebrated fcholars of the age in which he was born, for his tutors; and it is to the honour of this country that Alcuin, an Englifhman, and a difciple of Bede, furnamed the Venerable, was his inftructor in rhetoric, logic, aftronomy, and

the

the other liberal fciences *, notwithftanding which, there is a very curious particular recorded of him, namely, that he never could, though he took infinite pains for the purpofe, acquire the manual art of writing or delineating the letters of the alphabet † ; fo that whatever books or collections are afcribed to him, muft be fuppofed either to have been dictated by him, or written by others under his immediate infpection : indeed, the works attributed to him are of fuch a kind as neceffarily to imply the affiftance of others, and that they are to be deemed his in no other fenfe than as they received his fanction or approbation ; for they are chiefly either capitularies, as they are called, relating to ecclefiaftical matters, as the government of the church, the order of divine fervice, the obfervance of rites and ceremonies, and the regulation of the feveral orders of the clergy ; or they are letters to the feveral princes and popes, his contemporaries, and to bifhops, abbots, and other ecclefiaftical perfons ‡. Two works in particular are afcribed to him, and the opinion that they were of his compofition is generally acquiefced in ; thefe are letters written in his name to Elipandus, bifhop of Toledo, and other bifhops of Spain, on certain points of doctrine ; and four books againft the worfhip of images : and it is with a view to thefe, and fome other compofitions that paffed for his, that Sigebert, Du Pin, and others, give him a place among the ecclefiaftical writers of the eighth century.

The zeal of this emperor to introduce the Cantus Gregorianus into his dominions, and to preferve it in a ftate of purity, has drawn upon him an imputation of feverity ; and upon the authority of that fingle paffage in the Rationale of Durandus, above-cited, he is cenfured as having forced it upon the French with great cruelty. But there is nothing either in his relation of the fuppofed miracle in its favour, or in that of Baronius touching the contention at Rome, which will warrant this charge ; for in that difpute at which Eugenius was pre-

---

* Alcuin was well verfed in the liberal fciences, particularly in mufic, as appears by a tract of his on the ufe of the Pfalms, and by the preface to Caffiodorus De feptem Difciplinis, firft printed in Garetius's edition of that author, and which is expreffly faid by Du Pin, Fabricius, and others, to have been written by Alcuin. It was at the inftance of Alcuin that Charlemagne, in the year 790, founded the univerfity of Paris.

† Tentabat et fcribere, tabulafque et codicellos ad hoc in lectulo fub cervicalibus circumferre folebat, ut cum vacuum tempus effet, manum effingendis literis affuefaceret. Sed parum profpere fucceffit labor praepofterus ac fero inchoatus. Eginhart De Vita Caroli Magni, cap. xxv. edit. Beffelii.

‡ Du Pin, Nouv. Biblioth. de Auteurs Ecclefiaft. Siec. VIII.

fent,

sent, it does not appear that he at all intermeddled ; and in the other, the question which he put to his own clergy, is manifestly an appeal to reason, and no way indicates a disposition to coercive measures. ' Tell me, said the emperor, which is the purer, the living fountain, ' or its rivulets ?' They answered, ' the former.' Then said the emperor, ' Return ye to the fountain of St. Gregory ; for in the ri- ' vulets the ecclesiastical cantus is manifestly corrupted.' Eginhart has mentioned in general that Charlemagne laboured to rectify the disorderly manner of singing in the church * ; but he mentions no circumstances of bloodshed, or cruelty, to enforce a reformation ; and the fact is, that several churches in his dominions, particularly those of Milan and Corbetta, were suffered to retain either the Am- brosian or a worse use, notwithstanding his wishes and efforts to the contrary †. In short, it seems that his behaviour upon this occasion was that of a wise man, or, at least, of one whose zeal had a sufficient

---

* Eginhart, De Vita Caroli Magni, cap. xxvi. edit. Besselii.
† Mosh. Eccl. Hist. 8vo. vol. II pag. 98.

The notes of Besselius and others upon this passage of Eginhart [Legendi atque psal- lendi disciplinam diligentissime emendavit] are very curious, as they declare what were the abuses in singing which Charlemagne laboured to reform.   Quantum veteres sono vocum distincto studuerint, vel illud argumento est, quod plurusque sedulam dederint operam, teste etiam de Augusto Sueton. cap. lxxxiv. Caeterum de suffetieris cantionibus et affuis Ambrosiano à Carolo correctis, prolixe Sigebertus, ad an. 774 & 790. Gobelin. Person- erat. 6. Cosmodrom cap. al. p. 193. Gislel. Durendus, lib. V. Rationel. Divin. Offic. cap. ii. Frid. Lindenbrogius Glossar. L L. Antiq. fol. 1369, & Goldast. in Ekke- hardi Junioris rebus, pag. 114. tom. I. Rer. Alemannic. Besselius. Carolus dissonantia cantus inter Romanos & Francos offensus, cum conciliare & emendare omnibus viribus studuit ; ideo a papa cantores Romanos sibi mitti petiit, qui Francos vera psalleudi ra- tione imbuerent.   Horum duos accepit, ex quibus unum palatio suo praefecit, alterum mense misit, qui etiam ejus urbis incolas ita in canendi scientia erudivit, ut seu Roma inter omnes cantu, sic mens inter Francos emineret, & seminarium quasi cantorum Cisal- pinorum esset.   Ab hac igitur urbe cantilena ecclesiastica Germanice tunc temporis mote dicebatur, quia hic praecipue cantus excolebatur, cujus denominationis vestigia adhuc ho- die in vulgari locutione, die Frish metts fingen, deprehenduntur.   Horisonus maxime majorum nostrorum erat cantus, quem Monach. Egolism. in Vita Karoli M. ita describit : Tremulas vel vinnulas, seu collisibiles, seu secabiles voces in cantu non poterant perfecte exprimere Franci, naturali voce barbarica frangentes in gutture voces potius, quam experi- mentes.   Clarius Ekkehard. Minim. in vit. Notkeri, cap. viii.   Alpina siquidem cor- pora, ait, vocum suarum tonitruis altisone perstrepentia, susceptae modulationis dulcedinem proprie non resultant, quia bibuli gutturis barbara prosecas, dum inflexionibus et repercus- sionibus et diaphonanrium diphtongis mitem nititur edere cantilenam, naturali quodam fragore, quasi plaustra per gradus confusa sonantia, rigidas voces jactat, sique audientium animos, quos mulcere deberant, tales consperrando magis et obstrependo conturbent.   Nemo haec opinor, mirabitur, qui fragmenta antiquae Germanorum linguae legit, ex quibus satis aestimari potest, quam difficilis fuerit Teutonicae linguae pronunciatio, ac proin modulatio. Schmincke.

allay

allay of difcretion * ; and that he was poſſeſſed of a very confiderable portion of this latter quality, and entertained a mild and for-
giving difpofition towards thofe who had offended him, may be inferred from that very pretty ſtory related by Mr. Addiſon, in the
Spectator, Nº 181, of the princeſs Imma, his daughter, and his fecretary Eginhart, and her ingenious device, by carrying him on her
back through the ſnow, to prevent the difcovery of an amour which
terminated in their marriage.

The purity to which the Gregorian chant was reſtored by the zeal of
Charlemagne, fubfiſted no longer in France than to the time of Lewis
the Debonnaire, his fon and immediate heir, who fucceeded to the empire of the Weſt in 814 ; for in his reign the muſic of the church was
again corrupted to that degree, that the Gregorian chant fubfiſted only
in the memory of certain Romans, who had been accuſtomed to the
finging it ; for neither were there in France or at Rome, any books
wherein it had been written.   This ſtrange circumſtance is related
by Amalarius Fortunatus, a principal eccleſiaſtic in the chapel of
Lewis le Debonnaire, who himſelf was fent by Lewis to requeſt of
Gregory IV. then pope, a fufficient number of fingers, to inſtruct the

* His behaviour in this refpect ſeems to have been widely different from that of Al-
phonſus, king of Spain, who, in the year 1080, baniſhed the Gothic liturgy out of his kingdom, and introduced the Roman office, though miracles were pleaded in favour of the
former.   Talent. ann. 1080. col. I. and vide Mariana, in his Hiſtory of Spain, book IX.
pag. 152.   The circumſtances of this extraordinary event, and the miracles that preceded
it, are more particularly related by other hiſtorians, who ſpeak to this purpoſe : Alexander
II. had proceeded ſo far in the year 1068, as to perſuade the inhabitants of Arragon into
his meaſures, and to conquer the averſion which the Catalonians had difcovered for the
Roman worſhip.   But the honour of finiſhing this difficult work, and bringing it to perfection was reſerved for Gregory VII. who, without interruption, exhorted, threatened,
admoniſhed, and intreated Sancius and Alphonſo, the kings of Arragon and Caſtile,
until, fatigued with the importunity of this reſtleſs pontiff, they conſented to aboliſh the
Gothic ſervice in their churches, and to introduce the Roman in its place ; Sancius was
the firſt who ſubmitted to this innovation, and in the year 1080 his example was
followed by Alphonſo.   The methods which the nobles of Caſtile employed to decide
the matter were very extraordinary.   Firſt, they choſe two champions, who were to determine the controverſy by fingle combat, the one fighting for the Roman liturgy, the other
for the Gothic.   The fiery trial was next made uſe of to terminate the difpute; the Roman and Gothic liturgies were committed to the flames, which, as the ſtory goes, confumed the former, while the latter remained unblemiſhed and entire.   Thus were the
Gothic rites crowned with a double victory, which however was not fufficient to maintain
them againſt the authority of the pope, and the influence of the queen Conſtantia, who
determined Alphonſo in favour of the Roman ſervice.   Vide Bona De Rebus Liturg.
lib. I. cap. ii. pag. 216.   Le Brun, loc. cum. pag. 292.   Jo. de Ferreras, Hiſt. de
l' Eſpagne, tom. III. pag. 237. 241. 246.   Nuſh. Eccl. Hiſt. vol. II. pag. 341.

people ; by whom the pope fent to the emperor for anfwer, that he could not comply with his requeſt, for that the laſt of thoſe men remaining at Rome had been fent into France with Walla, who had formerly been ambaſſador from Charlemagne on the fame errand. The words of Amalarius, in the preface to his book De Ordine Antiphonarii, are theſe : ‘ When I had been a long while affected with ‘ anxiety, on account of the difference among the fingers of antiphons ‘ in our province, and did not know what fhould be rejected and ‘ what retained, it pleafed him who is bountiful to all, to eafe me of ‘ my fcruples ; for there having been found in the monaſtery of ‘ Corbie, in Picardy, four books, three whereof contained the noc- ‘ turnal, and the other the diurnal, office, I ſtrove to make all the ‘ fail I could out of this fea of error, and to make a port of quiet ; ‘ for when I was fent to Rome by the holy and moſt chriſtian em- ‘ peror, to the holy and moſt reverend father Gregory, concerning ‘ thefe books, it pleafed his holinefs to give me the following anfwer : ‘‘ I have no fingers of antiphons, whom I can fend to my fon and ‘‘ lord the emperor ; the only remaining ones that we had, were ‘‘ fent from hence into France with Walla, who was here on an em- ‘‘ baſſy.” By means of thefe books, I difcovered a great difference ‘ between the antiphons of our fingers and thofe formerly in ufe ; ‘ the books contained a multitude of refponfaria and antiphons, ‘ which they could not fing : among them I found one of thofe ‘ which were ordained by the apoſtolic Adrian. I knew that thefe ‘ books were older than that which remained in the Roman city, ‘ and though in fome refpects better inſtituted, yet they ſtood in need ‘ of fome corrections, which, by the affiſtance of the Roman book, ‘ might made of them : I therefore took the middle way, and cor- ‘ rected one by the other.’ Notwithſtanding this labour of Amalarius to reform the antiphonary, Nivers afferts, that the corruptions of mufic were then fo great, that it was very difficult to fay where the Gregorian Chant lay * ; and, after all, the corrections of it by

* The true caufes of the firſt corruptions of the Cantus Gregorianus are plainly printed out by the interpreter of Hugo Reutlingenfis, who, in the paſſage cited by Sir Henry Spelman, afcribes it to the difufe of the flave, the cliffs, and other characters, neceſſary in the notation of mufic. To the fame purpofe Nivers relates, that they were not marked by notes, but by little points and irregular characters ; which account is confirmed by fome manufcripts, in which the corrupt method of notation above hinted at does moſt evidently appear. Martini of Bologna has exhibited fome curious examples of this kind, and has,

I

with

Amalarius Fortunatus were very ill received, as will appear by the following account of him.

SYMPHOSIUS AMALARIUS, or, as he is called by most writers, AMALARIUS FORTUNATUS was a deacon of Metz, and, as some ancient manuscripts assert, also an abbot.   There seems to have been another of the latter name, archbishop of Treves, with whom he is often confounded; they both flourished about the middle of the ninth century.   This of whom it is meant here to speak was a great ritualist, and wrote four books on the ancient ecclesiastical offices, which he dedicated to Lewis the Debonnaire, by whom he seems to have been greatly favoured.   In these books he gives mystical reasons for those rites and ceremonies in divine worship, which wiser men look on as mere human inventions.   To give a specimen of his manner of treating this subject, speaking of the habits of the priests, he says, ' The ' priest's vest signifies the right management of the voice; his albe, ' the subduing of the passions; his shoes, upright walking; his ' cope, good works; his stole, the yoke of Jesus Christ; the sur- ' plice, readiness to serve his neighbour; his handkerchief, good ' thoughts; and the pallium, preaching *.

with no less ingenuity than industry, from characters the most barbarous that can be conceived, and which were intended to express the initial clauses, and also the cæsurae of sundry antiphons, as used in particular churches, extracted a meaning, and reconciled them to the true method of notation.

* An opinion something like this, touching the mystical signification of habits and the manner of wearing them, seems to have been entertained by the common-law judges in the reign of king James, as appears by a solemn decree or rule, made by all the judges of the courts at Westminster, on the fourth day of June, 1635, for the purpose of appointing what robes they should thenceforth wear, upon ordinary and special occasions.   In this decree mention is made of the scarlet casting-hood, which is by the decree directed to be put above the tippet, for which it is given as a reason that ' justice Walmesley and ' justice Warburton, and all the judges before, did wear them in that manner, and did ' declare, " that by wearing the hood on the right side and above the tippet, was signified " mere temporal dignity; and by the tippet on the left side only, the judges did resemble " priests." Dugd. Origines Juridiciales, pag. 102.

The author from whom the above passage is cited, craves leave to mention a word or two concerning the collar of S S, worn by the chief justices and chief baron, some orders of knights, the kings at arms, and others.   Touching this badge of distinction, he, upon the authority of Georgius Wicelius, relates, that it has a reference to two brethren, Roman senators, named Simplicius and Faustinus, who suffered martyrdom under the emperor Dioclesian; and gives the following description of it from his author: ' It was the custom ' of those persons (the society of St. Simplicius) to wear about their necks silver collars, ' composed of double S S, which noted the name of St. Simplicius.   Between these dou- ' ble S S the collar contained twelve small plates of silver, in which were engraved the ' twelve articles of the creed, together with a single trefoyle.   The image of St. Sim-
' plicius

But the book of Amalarius Fortunatus which more immediately relates to choral fervice, or the mufic of the church, is intitled, De Ordine Antiphonarii. In this he vindicates the difpofition of the anthems, refponfes, and pfalms, which he had made in the antiphonary, for the ufe of the churches in France. It feems, that in this and other of his works, he had cenfured the ufage of the church of Lyons : this drew on him the refentment of two very able men, Agobard, archbifhop of that city, and Florus, a deacon of the fame church; the former of thefe wrote three treatifes againft his book of offices, and his correction of the antiphonary ; and the latter accufed him, in the councils of Quierci and Thionville, of maintaining erroneous opinions touching the moral and myftical fignifications of the ceremonies, and of infifting too ftrenuoufly on the ufe of the Roman ritual, which, notwithftanding its authority, had never been generally acquiefced in.

Agobard himfelf had corrected the antiphonary of his own church ; and the treatifes which he wrote againft Amalarius, were not only a defence of thofe corrections, but a cenfure of his adverfary. He fays, that the poetical compofitions of vain and fantaftical men are not to be admitted into divine fervice, the whole of which ought to be taken from the fcriptures : he complains, that the clergy fpent more time in the practice of finging than in the ftudy of the holy fcriptures, and the difcharge of their duty in the miniftry of the gofpel.

The writings of Amalarius upon the offices had given rife to many very captious queftions ; and to this in particular, Whether it be lawful to fpit immediately after receiving the euchariſt ? His opinion on this point of theology is contained in one of his letters, wherein, after premifing that he himfelf was very much troubled with phlegm, he holds it lawful to fpit, when the communicant can no longer forbear that evacuation*.

From the time of the attack on him by Agobard, and Florus, his deacon, we hear no more of Amalarius Fortunatus ; and there is good

* platius hung at the collar, and from it feven plates, reprefenting the feven gifts of
‘ the Holy Ghoft.'
Dugdale adds, ‘ that the reafon of wearing this chain was in regard that thefe two
‘ brethren were martyred, by tying a ftone with a chain about their necks, and cafting
‘ their bodies into the river Tiber.'
• Du Pin, Nouv. Biblioth. des Aut. Ecclefiaff. Siec IX.

reafon to believe, that immediately after it, his memory funk into oblivion.

Before we difmifs this fubject of the Cantus Gregorianus, it may not be improper to mention, that it has ever been held in fuch high eftimation, that the moft celebrated muficians in every age fince its firft inftitution, have occafionally exercifed themfelves in compofing harmonies upon it; and numberlefs are the antiphons, hymns, mifereres, and other offices, which have one or other of the ecclefiaftical tones for their fundamental harmony. In a collection of madrigals, intitled Mufica Divina, publifhed by Pietro Phalefio, at Antwerp, in 1595, is one compofed by Gianetto Paleftina, beginning ' Vefliva ' i Colli,' in five parts, which is evidently a praxis on the foorth tone ; and in 1694, Giov. Paolo Colonna, of Bologna, publifhed certain of the pfalms, for eight voices, ' Ad rifum ecclefiafticæ muficei con- ' cinendi.'

C H A P.   III.

IT is highly probable that from the time of its original inftitution the cantus ecclefiafticus pervaded the whole of the fervice ; but this at leaft is certain, that after the final improvement of it by St. Gregory, all the accounts of the Romifh ritual, and the manner of celebrating divine fervice in the weftern church, lead to the belief that, excepting the epiftles and gofpels, and certain portions of fcripture, and the paffional or martyrology, the whole of the fervice, nay that even the prayers and penitential offices, were fung. Among the canons of Elfric, made anno 957 *, is the following.

' Now it concerns mafs-priefts and all God's fervants to keep ' their churches employed with divine fervice. Let them fing ' therein the feven tide-fongs that are appointed them, as the fynod ' earneftly requires, viz. the uht-fong, the prime-fong, the undern-

---

* Elfric is fuppofed to have been archbifhop of York about the time above mentioned, and Wulfin, to whom they are directed, bifhop of one of the ancient fees of Dorchefter or Shirburn, but which of the two is rather uncertain. This, as alfo fome other collections of ecclefiaftical laws here cited, are to be found in Sir Henry Spelman's Councils ; but the extracts above given are from Mr. Johnfon's valuable and ufeful work, which in fome refpects is preferable to the former.

' fong, the midday-fong *, the noon-fong, the even-fong, the fe-
' venth [or night] fong.' Can. xix. What thefe feverally are, may
be feen in a collection of ecclefiaftical laws by the reverend and learned Mr. Johnfon of Cranbrook who has beftowed a note on the
paffage.

The twenty-firft of the fame canons is in thefe words : ' The prieft
' fhall have the furniture for his ghoftly work before he be ordained,
' that is the holy books, the pfalter, and the piftol-book, gofpel-
' book, and mafs-book, the fong-book, and the hand-book, the
' kalendar, the pafconal †, the penetential, and the leffon-book. It
' is neceffary that the mafs-prieft have thefe books; and he cannot
' be without them if he will rightly exercife his function, and duly
' inform the people that belongeth to him.'

Thefe injunctions may feem to regard the celebration of mafs, as
well on feftivals as on ordinary occafions, in cathedral and other
churches ; neverthelefs the practice of finging, by which in this
place nothing can poffibly be underftood but the Cantus Gregorianus,
was not reftrained either to the folemn choral fervice, or to that in
parifh-churches, but in fhort it was ufed in the leffer offices. In the
Englifh-Saxon homily for the birth-day of St. Gregory, the people
are told that it was one of the injunctions of that father that the litany
fhould be fung, and upon certain occafions to the number of feven
times a-day. Among the ecclefiaftical laws of king Canute, who
reigned from 1016 to 1035, is one whereby the people are required to learn the Lord's prayer and the creed, becaufe, fays
the law, ' Chrift himfelf firft *fang* pater-nofter, and taught that
' prayer to his difciples.' Mrs. Elftob in her preface to the tranflation of the above homily, pag. 36, has inferted this law, and on
the words Criʃt ƿealf ɽunʒe Paten Noʃter, has the following note:
' Singing the fervice was fo much in practice in thefe times, [i. e.
' about the fixth century, when Auftin the monk was fent by Gre-

* Midday-fong was certainly at twelve o'clock, which we call noon ; and the canon
above mentions both a midday and a noon-fong ; this noon was the hora nona with the
Latins, and our three o'clock. In the Shepherd's Almanac noon is midday, high noon
three. Vide Johnfon's C. aoms, title King Edgar's Laws Ecclefiaftical, in a note on law V.
High noon is expressly mentioned in the old ballad of Chevy-Chafe.

Anh long before highe noone they hah.
An hundrede fat buckes flaine ;

† I. e. The Paffional or Martyrology.

' gory

' gory into Britain] that we find the fame word ꝼingau to fignify
' both to pray and fing, as in the prefent inftance.'

Farther, among the canons of Elfric above-cited is one containing
directions for vifiting the fick, wherein that rule of St. James, ' And
' they fhall pray over him,' is expreffed in thefe words, ꝶ hi him oꝼeꝼ
ꝼinᵹon, that is, ' they fhall fing over them.' The paffage
above-cited is part of the thirty-firft of Elfric's canons, and is in
truth a paraphrafe on the words of St. James in his General Epiftle,
chap. v. ver. 13, 14, and, to give it at length, is as follows.

' If any of you be afflicted, let him pray for himfelf with an even
' mind, and praife his Lord.   If any be fick among you, let him
' fetch the mafs-priefts of the congregation, and let them fing over
' him, and pray for him, and anoint him with oil in the name of the
' Lord.   And the prayer of faith fhall heal the fick, and the Lord
' fhall raife him up ; and if he be in fins, they fhall be forgiven him :
' confefs your fins among yourfelves, and pray for yourfelves among
' yourfelves that ye be healed.'

The feveral paffages above-cited, as they fhew in fome meafure the
ancient manner of celebrating divine fervice, and prove that almoft
the whole of it, particularly the leffer offices, was fung to mufical
notes ; fo do they account for that care and affiduity with which the
ftudy of mufic appears to have been cultivated in the feveral monafteries, fchools, and univerfities throughout Europe, more efpecially
in France and England.   That the knowledge of mufic was confined
to the clergy, and that monks and prefbyters were the authors of
moft of the treatifes on mufic now extant, is not fo well accounted
for by the general courfe of their lives, and the opportunities they
had for ftudy, as by this confideration, it was their profeffion ; and to
fing was their employment, and in a great meafure their livelihood *.
The works of Chaucer and other old poets abound with allufions to
the practice of finging divine fervice, and with evidences that a
knowledge of the rudiments of finging was effential in every cleric,
indeed little lefs fo than for fuch a one to be able to read.   In the
Vifions of Pierce Plowman, Sloth, in the character of a prieft,
among other Inftances of lazinefs and ignorance, confeffes that he

* The ftatutes of All-Souls college in Oxford, which are but declaratory of the ufage
of ancient times, require that thofe elected to fellowfhips fhould be ' bene nati, bene vef-
titi, et mediocriter docti in plano cantu.'

cannot

cannot perfectly repeat his Pater-noster as the priest singeth it; and
that though he had been in orders above thirty years, he can neither fol-fa, nor fing, nor read the lives of faints : the whole of his
speech, which is exceedingly humourous and characteristic, is here
inserted.

Than came Sloth, al beslabred, with two slimy eyne,
I must fit faid the seg, or els I must nedes nap,
I mai not stond ne stoupe, ne without mp stole kncle,
Wer I brought a bed, but if mp talend it made,
Should no ringing do me rise, or I were ripe to dine,
He began benedicite with a belke, and on his breast knoked
And raskled and rored, and rut at the last.
A wah, renk quod Repentaunce, and rape thee to the shrift.
If I should die by this day, me lyst not to looke :
I can not perfitlp mp pater noster, as the prist it singeth,
But I can rimes of Robenhod, and Randal of Chester
But of our lord or our ladp, I lerne nothing at all;
I have made vows xl, and forgotten hem on the morow:
I' performed never penance, as the priest me hight,
Ne right sorp for mp sinnes, yet was I never ;
And if I did anp beades, but it be of wrathe
That I tel with mp tong, is two mile from mp hart ;
I am occupied every day, holp day and other
With idle tales at the ale, and other while in churches.
Gods pepne and his passion, ful selde I thinke thereon,
I visited never seble men, ne fettred folk in pittes
I have lever hear an harlotrp, or a sommers game
Or lessinges to laugh at, and belpe mp neighbours
Than al that ever Marke made, Mathew Jhon and Lucas,
And vigiles and fasting daies, all these I let passe,
And lie in bed in lent, and mp lemman in mine armes
Till matttens and masse be done, & than go I to the freres,
Com I to ' Ite missa est *' I hold me serbed
I am not shriben sometime, but if sickenes it make

* i. e. See an explanation of these words in a subsequent note. The meaning of
the above passage is, ' If I come before the instant the people are dismissed from mass, I
' hold it sufficient.'

Dot

Not twice in two yeer, and than up guesse I shribe me
I habe been peiest and person passing thirty winter
Yet can I neither solfe nor sing, ne saintes libes read
But I can finde in a fielde, or a furloug an hare
Better than in Beatus bir, or in Beati omnes
Construe one clause, and ken it to my parishens
I con hold loue daies, and heare a rebeues rekening
And in canuon and in deeretals I cannot read a line
Yf I bugge and borow ought, but if it be tailed
I forget it as fonne, and if men me it aske
Sir sithes or seben, I forsake it with othes
And thus tene I true men, ten hundred times,
And my serbauntes salary sometimes is behind,
Ruth is to hear the rekening, when we shal mak accoune ;
So with wicked wil and with wrath my workmen I pai.
Yf any man do me benefite, or helpe me at nede
I am unkind against his curtesi, & cannot understand ie
For I habe & habe had some deale haulees manees
I am not kured with lobe, but if ought be under the thumbe
That kindnes that mine eben christen, kid me serther
Sixe sithes I sloth, habe forgotten it sithe.
In speeh and in sparing of spence, I spile many a time
Both flesh and fish, and many other bitailes
Both bread and ale, butter, milke, and chese
For slouth in my serbice til it might serbe no man.
I can about in youth, and gabe me not to learning
And ever sith habe ben a beggar for my foule slouth *.

The foregoing account, as it relates solely to the Cantus Gregorianus, muſt be ſuppoſed to contain only the hiſtory of the choral
muſic of the weſtern church ; for it is to be remembered that antiphonal ſinging was introduced by the Greek fathers, and was firſt
practiſed in the churches of the Eaſt ; and that the cantus of the
Greek church, whatever it was, was not near ſo well cultivated and
refined as that of the Roman ; this conſideration, together with the

* Viſions of Pierce Plowman, Paſſus quintus.

ſhort duration of the eaſtern empire, may ſerve to ſhew how little is to be expected from an enquiry into the nature of the ancient Greek choral muſic. Voſſius ſays in general, that the Greek church made uſe of modulations different from thoſe of the weſtern *; but for a formula of them we are very much to ſeek. As to the method of notation made uſe of by the Greeks in after-times, it did not in the leaſt reſemble that of the Latins, and was widely different from that of the ancient Greeks. Montfaucon, in his Palæographia Græca, lib. V. cap. iii. gives the following curious ſpecimen of Greek muſical notation from a manuſcript of the eleventh century.

---

* Ger. Voſſ. De Scientiis Mathematicis, cap. xii. § 12.

Dr. Wallis had once in his hands a manuscript, which upon examination proved to be a Greek ritual; it had formerly been part of
the famous library founded at Buda by Matthæus Corvinus, king of
Hungary, in 1485. In 1529 the city of Buda was taken by the
Turks, and in 1686 retaken, after a long siege, by the forces of the
emperor Leopold.

A description of this manuscript, and a general account of its contents is extant in a letter of Dr. Wallis to some person, probably the
owner of it, who seems to have referred to the Doctor as being well
skilled in music; the doctor's opinion of it may be seen in the copy
of his letter inserted at length at the bottom of the page. It has
lately been discovered that the MS. abovementioned was the property
of Mr. Humfrey Wanley, as appears by a letter of his to Dr. Arthur
Charlett, inserted also in the note, in which he offers to part with
it to the university of Oxford. It is to be conjectured that the university declined purchasing it, and that Mr. Wanley disposed of it to
the earl of Oxford, for in the printed Catalogue of the Harleian manuscripts in the British Museum, No. 1613, is the following article.

' ' Sir, I have seen and cursorily perused that ancient Greek manuscript which is said
' to have been found in Buda, at the taking of that place from the Turks in the present
' war between the German emperor and the Turk.
' It is elegantly written in a small Greek hand, and is judged to be at least three hundred
' years old. The form of the letter is much different from that of those which we now
' use, and not easy to be read by those who are not acquainted with the Greek hand used
' in the manuscripts of that age.
' It bears, after the first three leaves, this title Ἀρχὴ σὺν Θεῷ ἁγίῳ τῆς κανονικῆς Τέχνης,
' which I take to intimate thus much: Here begins, with the assistance of the sacred Deity,
' the patriarchal art; for I take πάππας then to signify as much as pope or patriarch, which
' is farther thus explained: ἀκολουθίαι ἢ ἀλλόμεναι ἢ Κωνσταντινουπόλει, εὐτεθείσαι παρὰ τῶν
' κατὰ χώραν εὑρισκομένων ἢ αὐτῶν ποιητῶν πολλῶν τε καὶ μων. That is, the order of
' services in Constantinople composed by poets, such as from time to time have been there
' found, as well ancient as modern; so that it seems to be a masdect or general collection
' of all the musical church-services there used, as well the more ancient, as those which
' were then more modern; after which it thus follows: εἶ ἡ ἀρχὴ ἀρμοδία καὶ αἱ τάξεις
' Ὠδαι, beginning with the musical notes and their sounds.
' After which title we have accordingly for about five leaves, an account of the musical
' notes then in use, their figures, names, and significations; without which the rest of the
' book would not be intelligible, and even as it is, it will require some sagacity and study
' to find out the full import of it, and to be able to compare it with our modern music.
' The rest of the book consists of anthems, church services for particular times, and
' other compositions, according to the music of that age, near a thousand I guess of one
' sort or other, or perhaps more.
' The whole consists of four hundred and thirteen leaves, close written on both sides in a
' small Greek hand, in the shape or form of what we would now call a very large octavo,
' on a sort of thick paper used in the eastern countries at that time.
' There is for the most part about twenty eight lines in each page, that is fourteen lines
' of Greek text, according to which it is to be sung; not such as those which we now use,
' not

'Codex chartaceus in 8vo, ut ajunt, majori, diverfis manibus ſcrip-
'tus, et Græcorum more compactus; quem Dño Henrico Worſlejo in-

'nor like thoſe of the more ancient Greeks, which they called   of which Mai-
'bomius gives us a large account out of Alypius. But a new ſort of notes, later than thoſe
'of the ancient Greeks, but before thoſe of Guido Aretinus, which we now uſe; and com-
'monly two or three compoſitions in one leaf, with the author's name for the moſt part.

'I do not find in it any footſteps of what is now common in our preſent muſic; I mean
'compoſitions in two, three, four, or more parts; all theſe, for ought I find, being only
'ſingle compoſitions.

'That which renders it moſt valuable is this; we have of the more ancient Greek muſi-
'cians ſeven publiſhed by Marcus Meibomius in the year 1652, Ariſtoxenus, Euclid, Ni-
'comachus, Alypius, Gaudentius, Bacchius, and Ariſtides Quintilianus, before that of
'Martianus Capella in Latin. I have ſince publiſhed Ptolemy's Harmonics in the year
'1682, and I have now cauſed to be printed Porphyry's Commentary on Ptolemy and
'Bryennius, which are both finiſhed ſome while ſince, and they will thereby come abroad;
'as ſoon as ſome other things are finiſhed which are to bear them company. All theſe,
'except Martianus Capella, in Greek and Latin, and theſe are thought to be all the Greek
'muſicians now extant.

'But all thoſe concern only the theoretical part of muſic, of the practical part of it,
'that is, muſical compoſitions of the ancient Greeks, it hath been thought till that, there
'was not one extant at this day, whereby we have been at a loſs what kind of compoſi-
'tions theirs were, and how theirs did agree or diſagree with what we now have, and it
'is a ſurprize to light at once upon ſo many of them.

''Tis true that all thoſe are more modern than thoſe of Ariſtoxenus, Euclid, Nicoma-
'chus, and others of the more ancient Greeks, being all ſince the times of Chriſtianity,
'and ſuch as were uſed in the Greek church of Conſtantinople: but they are much more
'ancient than any were thought to be extant.   Your's
                                                       'JOHN WALLIS.'

Copy of Mr. Wanley's letter to Dr. Charlett.

'Honoured Sir,   London, June 13, 1698.
'I cannot forbear ſending you word of the good fortune I have lately had to compaſs a
'Greek manuſcript, which contains the art of ſinging, with the names, powers, and cha-
'racters of their muſical notes, in great variety. And a collection of anthems, hymns,
'&c. ſet to their muſick by the beſt maſters of Conſtantinople, as intended and uſed to be
'ſung in their churches upon all the chief feſtivals of the year. It has likewiſe the muſi-
'cal part of their common liturgy with the notes; and both theſe, not only of the later
'muſic of the ſaid maſters, but very often the more antient too, uſed before their times.
'The names of theſe maſters prefixed to their compoſitions, are about threeſcore in num-
'ber, ſome of which I here ſet down: [Here follows a long liſt of Greek names, which
'it is needleſs to inſert, as the MS. is yet in being and acceſſible.]
'I believe many of their names, and much more their works, might have been long
'enough unknown to us without the help of this book. Here is likewiſe a ſprinkling of
'the muſic uſed in the churches of Anatolia, Theſſalonica, Thebes, and Rhodes, beſides
'that piece called Hyporchema, and other traſh.
'The MS. was taken from the Turks in plundering Buda, about the year 1686, and
'was afterwards bought by an Engliſh gentleman for 4l. but I lying here at great charges,
'cannot afford to ſell it ſo cheap. It is about 300 years old, fairly written upon cotton
'paper, taking up above four hundred leaves in a large 8vo
'The book ought to be placed in the publick library; and if, Sir, you are willing to
'think that the univerſity will conſider me for it, I will bring it along with me the next
'week: If not, I can be counted to part with it here upon my own terms.
'For the Rev. Dr. Charlett,   I am reverend and honoured Sir,
'Maſter of Univerſity college,   Your moſt faithful and obedient ſervant,
'in Oxford.   HUMFREY WANLEY.'

'Terra.

' Terra Sancta peregrinanti dono dedet Notara (Νοταρᾶ an Νοταρίος ι)
' tunc Metropolita Cæsariensis, qui exinde, de mortuo doctissimo suo
' avunculo, factus est Patriarcha Hierosolymitanus; adhuc, ni fallor,
' superstes.   In illo habentur varia Ecclesiæ Grecæ Officia, Cantica,
' &c. Græcè descripta, Notulisq; Græcis Musicalibus insignita.   Non
' iis dico, quæ priscis seculis apud Ethnicos Poetas et Philosophos in
' usu fuerunt; quarum etiamnum nonnullæ restant quasi e Naufragio
' Tabulæ: sed alterius planè formæ, quas ante plurima secula intro-
' ductas adhuc retinet hodierna Græcorum Ecclesia.'

Mr. Wanley has inserted the rubrics in the order in which they
occur; these are to be considered as so many distinct heads, and
give occasion for an explanation of many difficult words made use of
in them, and also in the offices *; in which he discovers great learning and sagacity.

* To give a few instances.   195. Τροπάριον. Vox generica, et Cantica in Ecclesia
Græca receptis communis; MODULUM semper verus, et ANTIPHONAS Latinorum qua-
damtenus respondere observat Goarus.   Du Cang.
In Ecclesia Orientali, canebantur certis diebus certi CANONES, quas in TROPARIA di-
videbant plerumque 30. et nonnumquam plura: excepto uno MAGNO CANONE, qui 250
complectebatur.   Suicer. ex Triodio.
CANONES in ODAS dividuntur; ODÆ in TROPARIA, ex quibus componuntur.
Singula namque Troparia continent aut plura aut pauciora, cum eorum Numerus determi-
natus non sit.   Troparia quandoque Libera ac Vaga relinquuntur; quandoque primis
Litteris quasi Annulis in Verbis veluti Catenula inseruntur, quam Aerostichida autores
vocant.   Du Cang. ex Allatio de Georgiis.
378. Antiphona. Fœminium ANTIPHONA à Neutrio ANTIPHONUM discrimen apud
nos obtinet maximum: quamvis ab uno Græco vocabulo; utrumque fuerint Latini mutuati:
ANTIPHONA namque est Sententia vel Modulus cuilibet Psalmo decantato adjunctus, et
quasi ex OPPOSITO RESPONDENS, inquit Honorius Solitarius, lib. ii cap. 17.   ANTI-
PHONUM autem ut hic usurpatur Psalmi sunt plures Versus, ad quorum singulos, una et
eadem sit semper ab alteroChoro Responsio: et propter hanc Unam et Reciprocam Senten-
tiam semper illatam, αντίφωνι, quasi Vox OPPOSITA, seu Vocis oppositio vocatur.   Ejus
forma qualis sit, ex his Mysallibus Antiphonis (i. e. Liturgia S. Chrysostomi) fol. 105,
et seq. positis innotescit.   Extat enim ibi Psalmus ἀγαθὸν τὸ ἐξομολογεῖσθαι τῷ κυρίῳ,
cujus singulis versibus respondet αντιφωνον Τοῖς μισοῦσίν σε Σωτὴρ ᾗ τὰ εξῆς, illis
Eccpius OPPONENDUM.   Quamvis fatear rem potius in adversum sensum trahendam: cum
enim Psalmus ipse vocatur αντιφωνον, ejus Versus sunt qui uni et eidem dicto, i. e. resumpto
(ἰσοφωνον ejus frequentius repetito) OPPONUNTUR.   Vel certe, quia mutua et utriusque
Chori ad invicem Responsio: et voces jam audice, rursum vel ex toto, vel ex parte, iteran-
tur prout quoque in Latinis RESPONSORIIS contingit) αντιφωνα appellatur.   Unde, tum
propter Vocis Significationem, tum propter Compositionis formam, Latine RESPONSORIUM
congrue reddi posset.   Vetus tamen Usus loquendi antiquus, ut Missæ Introitum alio quam
ANTIPHONI vel ANTIPHONA Nomine dicatur, &c.   Goar.
428. Τρισάγιον, TRISANCTUM, Hymni genus, cujus hæc erant Verba. Ἅγιος ὁ Θεὸς,
ἅγιος ἰσχυρὸς, ἅγιος ἀθάνατος, ἐλέησον ἡμᾶς in quo, ἅγιος ὁ Θεὸς, referebatur ad Deum
Patrem; ἅγιος ἰσχυρὸς ad Deum Filium; ἅγιος ἀθάνατος ad Spiritum sanctum.   Vocatur etiam τρισαγία ὑμνολογία, χερθιμικὴ ὑμνὸς, ἀγγελικον ὑμνολογία, τρισαγία ἀυθ,

But as a mere verbal defcription of this MS. would fail to convey an adequate idea of the charaćter in which it is written, or of the mufical notes, which are the principal objećt of the prefent enquiry, the initial and final pages of the volume are here given in that kind of tranfcript which the curious diftinguifh by the appellation of fac-fimile.

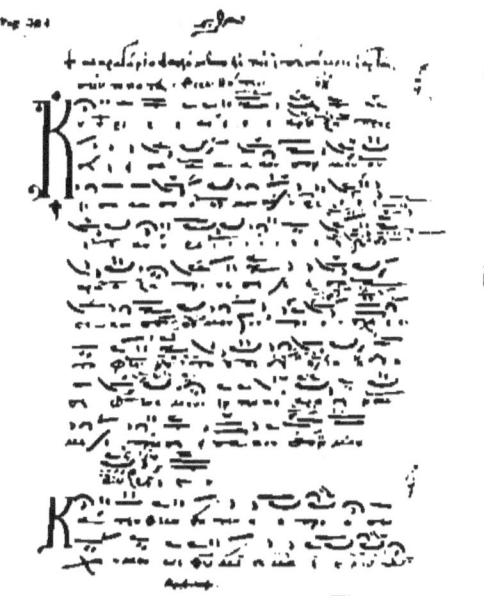

a7γ8λw 'Tµrad'ia et τρικαγιε sam. Anno enim Theodofii Junioris quinto (vel trigefi-mo fecundum Cedrenum, &c.) magno exiftente Terre Motu, et Muris corruentibus, quia Amalechitæ intra Urbem inhabitarent, et adverfus Hymnum hanc Blafphemias pro-loquerentur: Preces et Supplicationes in Campo Tribunalis, 1 heodofius cum Proclo Pa-triarcha inftituit. Cum vero Κύρι ιαλεσω clamarent Horis aliquot continuis, Adolefcen-tulus quidam in confpectu omnium in aerem fublatus eft, audivitque Angelos clamantes, ΑγιΘ ὁ Θεὸς, ἀγιΘ· ἰσχυρὸς, ἀγιΘ· ἀθάνατος, ἐλεησον ἡμᾶς. Quod cum mox demiffus narraffet, omnes eodem modo ΤΡΙΣΑΓΙΟΝ canere cœperont, et ceffavit Terre Motus. Huic Hymno Imperator Anaftafius poft illa ἀγιΘ· ἀθάνατος addi voluit ὁ σταυρωθεὶς ὑπὲρ ἡμῶν, verum id cum magno Malo et fuo, et Conftantinopolitanorum.—Obfervandum autem difcrimen quod eft inter τὸ Τρισάγιον et ΗΥΜΝΥΜ ΕΠΙΝΙCΙΟΝ, in quo fimiliter 'Αγ:Θ·

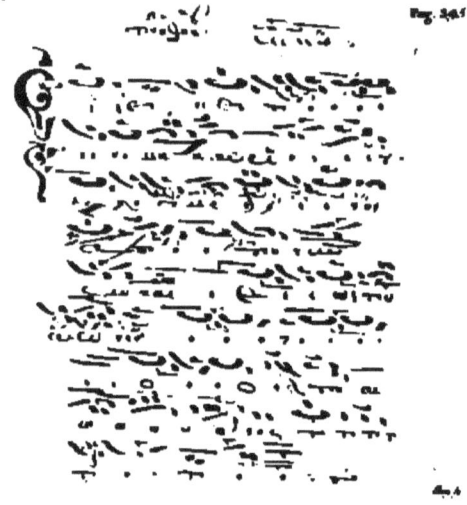

It is very clear from the above-mentioned letter that Dr. Wallis looked upon manuscripts of this kind as a very great curiosity; and this judgment of his is founded upon an opinion which he says prevailed at the time of giving it, that there was no such thing as an ancient Greek musical composition extant.

Ἄγιθ- canebatur, hunc in modum, ἄγιθ-, ἄγιθ-, ἄγιθ- κύριθ- ἐλέησθ.—Ergo τριάγιω Initio Liturgiæ ante Epistolæ Lectionem canebatur. Hymnus vero CHERUBICUS et Ἰσαΐσϑ, post Catechumenorum et Pœnitentium dimissionem. Τριάγιω quoque usurpabant pro Sacrosancta Trinitate. Suicer

441. Κωϑ᾽, proprie notat Canentium atque Saltantium collectam Multitudinem, notum est in Ecclesia hodie Psalmodiam retineri, et quidem CHORO, quibusdam in Locis, bifariam diviso. Improprie notat Multitudinem amice conspirantium in doctrina, &c. Suicer.

Χορὸς dividelantur χϑδ in Ἰεξιὸν, DEXTRUM, et ἀρίστρον, SINISTRUM. Tricinium in Sabbato Sancto αρχιται δυθι μέϑα μιᾶς ὶ ᾶεξᾶς ἄγω ὶ πρῶτος χορὶς, in quo quidem DEXTRO ac PRIMO CHORO consistit Sacerdos qui sacræ Liturgiæ præst Du Cang.

The practice of dividing the chorus into two parts, and disposing the singers on both sides of the choir, seems best of any method to correspond with the intention of antiphonal or responsive singing. But it is to be remarked that in the Romish service there are many offices composed for four, and even eight choirs as they are termed. These are in fact not distinct choirs, but rather so many smaller chorusses, singing alternately with each other, and together at stated intervals; and these are also divided according to the

choral

The caufes of this fcarcity of Greek ritual mufic are to be fought in the hiftory of that church. It has already been related that choral fervice was firft introduced by the Greek fathers, and that as the pomp and fplendent of the Greek worfhip was very great, and calculated to engage the affections of the people, the greater part of the offices were fung. The confequence thereof was, that the clerks employed for that purpofe were of little lefs eftimation than thofe that exercifed the facerdotal function. This appears from a paffage in the liturgy of St. Mark, wherein is a prayer for priefts, deacons, and fingers *. We may hence conclude that a ritual of fome kind or other fubfifted in that very early age; and it is very probable that that kind of melody which St. Ambrofe inftituted in his church at Milan, was no other than what was ufed by St. Bafil and Chryfoftom in their feveral churches in Afia, fince it is apparently founded on the ancient Greek modes. The mufic of the Greek church might in all probability continue to flourifh until the tranflation of the imperial feat from the Eaft to the Weft; and as after that important event that church loft the protection of an emperor, and was left in a great meafure to fhift for itfelf, its fplendor, its magnificence and difcipline declined apace, and it was not the authority of a patriarch that was fufficient to fupport it.

But the ruin of the Greek church was completed in the taking and facking of Conftantinople by the Turks in the year 1453, when their libraries and public repofitories of archives and manufcripts were deftroyed, and the inhabitants driven to feek fhelter in the neighbouring iflands, and fuch other places as their conquerors would permit them to abide in.

From that time the Greek Chriftians, excepting thofe who inhabit the empire of Ruffia, have lived in a ftate of the moft abfolute fubjection to the enemies of true religion and literature, and this to

choral order, and ftationed on both fides of the choir. In our Englifh fervice-books the two different fides are diftinguifhed by the names of the officers that fuperintend them refpectively; for inftance, as the feat of the Dean is on the right, thofe on that fide are directed when to fing by the word Decani; and as the ftation of the praecentor or chanter is on the left, thofe on that fide are directed by the word Cantoris.

242. Κανονάρχης, PRÆFECTUS CANONUM, qui Monachos ad pfalleudos in Vigiliis Canones excit-bat. Suicer.

509. Πρωτοψάλτης, PRIMICERIUS CANTORUM; qui dictos etiam Απίερας τῶν Λαῶν. Verum non habebant Ecclefiae PROTO-PSALTAE, fed DOMESTICOS Cantorum; cum PROTO-PSALTAE proprie effent Cleri Palatini, &c. Du Cang.

* See a collection of the principal liturgies ufed in the celebration of the holy euchariſt, by Dr. Thomas Brett, pag. 34.

fo

fo great a degree, that the exercife of public worfhip is not permitted them but upon conditions fo truly humiliating, as to excite the compaffion of many who have been fpectators of it. Maundrell in his Journey from Aleppo to Jerufalem, mentions his vifiting a Greek church at a village called Bellulca, where he faw an altar of no better materials than dirt, and a crucifix of two bits of lath faftened crofs-wife together *.

A modern traveller, Dr. Frederic Haffelquift, who vifited the Levant in the year 1749, indeed mentions that in the church at Beihlehem he faw an organ, but it feems that it belonged to the Latin convent: as to the Greek Chriftians he reprefents them as living in a ftate of abfolute poverty and dejection in almoft all the places that he vifited.

Laying all thefe circumftances together, it will ceafe to be a wonder that fo few vefliges of the Greek church-mufic are now remaining, whatever others there are may poffibly be found in the Ruffian ritual; but as no one can fay how far that may have deviated from the primitive one, it is to be feared that an enquiry of this kind would elude the utmoft efforts of induftry †.

* ' Being informed that here were feveral Chriftian inhabitants in this place, we went ' to vifit their church, which we found fo poor and pitiful a ftructure, that here Chrifti-
' anity feemed to be brought to its humbleft ftate, and Chrift to be laid again in a man-
' ger. It was only a room of about four or five yards fquare, walled with dirt, having
' nothing but the uneven ground for its pavement; and for its ceiling only fome rude
' traves laid athwart it, and covered with bafhes to keep out the weather. On the eaft
' fide was an altar built of the fame materials with the wall; only it was paved at top with
' pot-fherds and flates, to give it the face of a table. In the middle of the altar ftood a
' fmall crofs compofed of two laths nailed together in the middle: on each fide of which
' enfign were faftened to the wa'l two or three old prints, reprefenting our bleffed Lord and
' the bleffed Virgin, &c. the venerable prefents of fome itinerant friars, that had paffed
' this way. On the fourth fide was a piece of plank fupported by a poft, which we under-
' ftood was the reading-defk, juft by which was a little hole commodioufly broke through
' the wall to give light to the reader. A very mean habitation this for the God of hea-
' ven! but yet held in great efteem and reverence by the poor people; who not only come
' with all devotion hither themfelves, but alfo depofite here whatever is moft valuable to
' them in order to derive upon it a bleffing. When we were there the whole room was
' hanged about with bags of filk-worms eggs; to the end that by remaining in fo holy a
' place, they might attract a benediction and a virtue of encreafing.' Maundrell's Journey
from Aleppo to Jerufalem, pag. 7.

† A gentleman, who has lately obliged the world with an account of the Greek church, in Ruffia, fpeaking of the ritual of the Ruffians, takes notice that the mufic of their fervice books is written on a ftave of five lines, from which he rightly infers that the ecclefiaftical notes as fung by them are either corrupted, or have widely deviated from their original inftitution. The Rites and Ceremonies of the Greek Church in Ruffia, by Dr. John Glen King, pag. 43. in not.

C H A P. IV.

ISIDORE, bishop of Seville, is frequently ranked among the writers on music, for this reason, as it seems, that he was the author of Originum, five Etymologiarum, a kind of epitome of all arts and sciences, in which are several chapters with the following titles, as Cap. i. De Musica et ejus Nomine. Cap. ii. De Inventoribus ejus. Cap. iii. Quid fit Musica. Cap. iv. De tribus Partibus Musicæ. Cap. v. De triformi Musicæ Divisione. Cap. vi. De prima Divisione Musicæ harmonica. Cap. vii. De secunda Divisione organica. Cap. viii. De tertia Divisione rythmica. Cap. ix. De Musicis Numeris, and also a Treatise on the Ecclesiastical Offices, in both of which there are many things relating to music, and in the former especially, many etymologies of musical terms, and names of musical instruments. His father was Severianus, a son of Theodoric king of Italy ; he succeeded his brother Leander in the bishopric of Seville about the year 595, and governed that church near forty years : he was very learned in all subjects, more especially in geometry, music, and astrology; his book on the Offices contains the principal points of discipline and ecclesiastical polity. Mosheim in his chronological tables makes him the principal compiler of the Mosarabic liturgy, which is the ancient liturgy of Spain. He died in the year 636, and has a place in the calendar of Romish saints.

Of the introduction of music into the church-service, of the institution of the four tones by St. Ambrose, and of the extension of that number to eight by St. Gregory, mention has been made ; we are now to speak of another very considerable improvement of church-music, namely, the introduction of that noble instrument the organ, which we are told took place about the middle of the seventh century. Authors in general ascribe the introduction of organs into churches to pope Vitalianus, who, as Du Pin, Platina, and others relate, was advanced to the pontificate in A. C. 663 : the enemies of church-music, among whom the Magdeburg commentators are to be numbered, invidiously insinuate that it was in the year 666 that organs were first used in churches, from whence they infer the unlawful-

nefs

nefs of this innovation, as commencing from an era that correfponds with the number of the beaft in the Apocalypfe: but the wit of this farcafm is founded on a fuppofition that, upon enquiry, will appear to be falfe in fact; for though it is oncontroverted that Vitalianus introduced the organ into the fervice of the Romifh church, yet the ufe of inftruments in churches was much earlier; for we are told that St. Ambrofe joined inftruments of mufic with the public fervice in the cathedral church of Milan, which example of his was fo well approved of, that by degrees it became the general practice of other churches, and has fince obtained in almoft all the Chriftian world befides.   Nay, the antiquity of inftrumental church-mufic is ftill higher, if we may credit the teftimony of Juftin Martyr and Eufebius, the latter of whom lived fifty, and the former two hundred years before the time of St. Ambrofe.   But to return:

Sigebert relates that in the year 766 the emperor Conftantine * fent an organ as a prefent to Pepin, then king of France, though the annals of Metz refer to the year 757; from hence fome with good reafon date the firft introduction of the organ into that kingdom, but it was not till about the year 826 that organs became common in Europe.

Whoever is acquainted with the exquifite mechanifm of this inftrument, and confiders the very low ftate of the manual arts at that time, will hardly be perfuaded that the organ of the eighth century bore any very near refemblance to that now in ufe.   Zarlino, in his Sopplimenti Muficali, libro VIII. pag. 290, has beftowed great pains in a difquifition on the ftructure of the ancient organ; the occafion of it he fays was this, a lady of quality, Madonna Laura d'Efte, in the year 1571, required of Zarlino, by his friend Francefco Viola, his fentiments of the organ in general, and whether he took the modern and the ancient inftrument of that name to be alike or different: in giving his opinion on this queftion he attempts a defcription of the hydraulic organ from Vitruvius, which he leaves juft as he found it; he then cites a Greek epigram of Julian the Apoftate, who lived about the year 364, in which au organ is defcribed.   A tranfla-

---

* Surnamed Copronymus, becaufe he is faid to have defiled the font at his baptifm. Mofh. vol. II pag. 92. in not.
Other writers fpeak particularly, and fay that the firft ufe of organs in the weftern church was at Aeon. Ifaef. Chron. Anno Chrifti 826. Church Story.

I   tion

tion of this epigram in the following words is to be found in Merfennus, lib. III. De Organis, pag. 113.

Quam cerno, alterius naturæ eſt fiſtula : nempe
Altera produxit fortaſſe hæc ænea tollus.
Horrendum ſtridet, nec noſtris illa movetur
Flatibus, et miſſus taurino e carcere ventus
Subtus agit læves calamos, perque ima vagatur.
Mox aliquis velox digitis, inſignis et arte
Adſtat, concordes calamis pulſatque tabellas :
Aſt illæ ſubito exiliunt, et carmina miſcent.

As to the organ of the moderns, he ſays the common opinion is
that it was firſt uſed in Greece, and from thence introduced into
Hungary, and afterwards into Bavaria ; but this he refutes, as he does
alſo the ſuppoſed antiquity of an organ in the cathedral church of
Munich, pretended to be the moſt ancient in the world, with pipes
of one entire piece of box, equal in magnitude to thoſe of the modern church organ : he then ſpeaks of the ſommiero of an organ in
his poſſeſſion that belonged to a church of the nuns in the moſt ancient city of Grado, the ſeat of a patriarch before the ſacking of it by
Pepo the patriarch of Aquileia, in the year 580.   This ſommiero he
deſcribes as being about two feet long, and a fourth of that meaſure
broad, and containing only thirty pipes and fifteen keys, but without
any ſtop ; the pipes he ſays were ranged in two orders, each containing fifteen, but whether they were tuned in the uniſon or octave, as
alſo whether they were of wood or metal, he ſays is hard to gueſs :
he ſays farther that this inſtrument had bellows in the back part,
ſuch as are to be ſeen in the modern regali, and exhibits a draft of
this inſtrument in the following form.

Zarlino

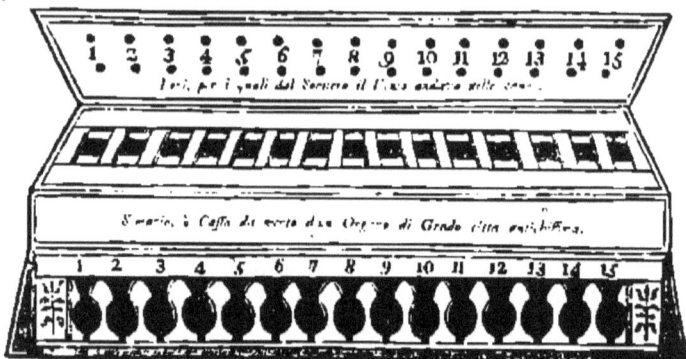

Zarlino speaks also of an ancient organ in the church of St. Anthony of Padua, of a convenient bigness, which had many orders of pipes, but no stops; and both these instruments he makes to be much more ancient than that of Munich in Bavaria; concerning the accounts of which he seems to be dissatisfied; for as to the pipes, he says there are no box-trees, except such as grow in the country of Prester John, of a size sufficient to make pipes of one piece so large as those are said to be; and that, after such were found, an organ so constructed as that a single pipe should require a whole tree, is not easily to be conceived of.

He farther takes some pains to shew the error of those who imagine that the organ mentioned by Dante, in the ninth canto of his Purgatory, was different in many respects from that of the ancients. The passage in Dante is an imitation of Lucan, lib. III.
' Tune rupes tarpeia sonat.'

> Non ruggiò sì, ne sì mostro sì acra
> Tarpea; come tolto le su' il buono
> Metello; donde poi rimase maca.
> I mi rivolsi attento al primo tuono;
> Et Te Deum laudamus mi parea,
> Udir in voce mista al dolce suono.

Tal imagin a punto mi rendea
Ciò, ch' i udia, qual prender fi fuole,
Quand' a cantar con organi fi ftea:
C' hor fi hor, non s' intendon le parole.

But upon the whole, he is clearly of opinion that the hydraulic
organ of Vitruvius, that other mentioned in the epigram of Julian
above cited, the Bavarian organ, and that in the city of Grado, were
effentially the fame with the organ of his time *.

That choral mufic had its rife in the church of Antioch, the metropolis of Syria, and that from thence it fpred through Greece, and
was afterwards brought into Italy, the feveral teftimonies above adduced fufficiently fhew : from thence it made its way into France,
Britain, Spain, and Germany, and at length was received throughout
Chriftendom. As to the time and manner of its introduction into
Britain, hiftory has afcertained it beyond a poffibility of doubt; for
we are exprefsly told, that at the time when Auftin the monk arrived here, charged with a commiffion to convert the inhabitants of
Britain to Chriftianity, fingers attended him : and fo watchful were
the Roman pontiffs over its progrefs in this ifland, that in little more
than half a century, one of the moft excellent chanters that Rome
afforded was fent hither, by Agatho, to reform fuch abufes as in that
fhort period he might find to have crept into it. That it was received
with great eagernefs by the people of this country, there are many
reafons for thinking ; for, firft, their fondnefs for mufic of all kinds

* Merfennus feems to carry the antiquity of the organ farther back than Zarlino has
done in the paffage above cited, and to think that not only the hydraulic but the pneumatic organ, was in ufe among the Romans, though he has left it to the antiquaries to afcertain the precife time; for fpeaking of the epigram made in its praife by the emperor
Julian, and which is inferted in his [Merfennus's] Latin work, he relates ' that the Sieur
' Naudè had fent him from the Matthei gardens at Rome, the form of a little cabinet of
' an organ, with bellows like thofe made ufe of to kindle a fire, and a reprefentation of a
' man placed behind the cabinet blowing the bellows, and of a woman touching the keys.'
He fays, ' that on the bottom of the cabinet was the following infcription : L. APISIUS
' C. F. SCAPTIA CAPITOLINUS EX TESTAMENTO FIERI MONUMEN.
' JUSSIT ARBITRATU HEREDUM MEORUM SIBI ET SUIS; concerning
' which, he adds, the antiquarians may conjecture what they can ; for that it is fufficient
' that he has given the practice of his own age, which, he fays, by far furpaffes any thing
' that the ancients have left behind on this fubject.' Harm. Univer. lib. Vh pag. 387.
The monument above fpoken of has been recovered. Probably it is extant in fome one
or other of the collections of antiquities, publifhed fince the time of Merfennus, but the
following reprefentation of it was found among the papers of Nicola Francefco Haym, the
                                                                                        author

was remarkably great ; Giraldus Cambrenſis aſſerts, almoſt in poſitive terms, that the natives of Wales and the northern parts of Great Britain were born muſicians.

author of Il Teſoro Britannico delle Medaglie Antiche, and as it correſponds exactly with the deſcription of it by Merſennus, it is here inſerted.

I. APISIUS C. F. SCAPTIA CAPITOLINUS EX TESTAMENTO FIERI MONUMEN. JUSSIT ARBITRATU HEREDUM MEORUM SIBI ET SUIS,

The ſame author takes occaſion to mention an organ deſcribed in an epiſtle to Dardanus, in the fourth volume of the works of St. Jerome, which, from the many barbariſms that appear in it, he ſays, ought not to be attributed to that excellent man. This organ, he ſays, is repreſented as having twelve pair of bellows and fifteen pipes, and a wind-cheſt, made of two elephant ſkins ; and as yielding a ſound as loud as thunder, which might be heard at more than a thouſand paces diſtance. Merſennus adds, that in the ſame epiſtle mention is made of an organ at Jeruſalem, which was heard at the Mount of Olives. He ſays, there are many other Inſtruments deſcribed in the ſame epiſtle ; but he remarks, that if the elephant ſkins above mentioned were ſewed together, and were fined by bellows, the inſtrument was more properly a cornamuſa, or bagpipe, than an organ.

To this account of organs of a ſingular conſtruction, the following may be added of ſome leſs ancient. Fuller, in his Worthies of Denbighſhire, pag. 33, mentions an organ with golden pipes. Leander Alberti, in his Deſcription of Italy, ſays, he ſaw one, in the court of the duke of Mantua, of alabaſter ; and another at Venice, made all of glaſs ; and Pope Sylveſter the Second made an organ that was played on by warm water. See Oldys's Britiſh Librarian, Nº 1. pag. 51.

F f f 2   Beſides

Befides this, there are proofs in hiftory that in a very fhort time after its firft planting amongft us, mufic was obferved to flourifh; and that, in fhort, it loved the foil, and therefore could not fail to grow.

It was in the cathedral church of Canterbury that the choral fervice was firft introduced; and till the arrival of Theodore, and his fettlement in that fee, the practice of it feems to have been confined to the churches of Kent; but after that, it fpred over the whole kingdom. The clergy made mufic their ftudy, they became proficients in it, and, differing perhaps in that refpect from thofe of other countries, they diffeminated the knowledge of it among the laity. Hollinfhed, after Bede, defcribes the progrefs of finging in churches in thefe words :

' Alfo, whereas before-time there was in a manner no finging in
' the Englifhe churches, except it were in Kent, now they began in
' every church to ufe finging of divine fervice, after the ryte of the
' church of Rome. The archbifhop Theodore, finding the church of
' Rochefter void by the death of the laft bifhop, named Damian, he
' ordeyned one Putta, a fimple man in worldly matters, but well in-
' ftructed in ecclefiaftical difcipline, and namely well feene in fong,
' and muficke to be ufed in the church, after the manner as he had
' learned of Pope Gregories difciples *.'

After this, viz. in 677, Ethelred, king of the Mercians, invaded the kingdom of Kent with a great army, deftroying the country before him, and amongft other places the city of Rochefter; the cathedral church thereof was alfo fpoiled and defaced, and Putta driven from his refidence; upon which, as the fame hiftorian relates, ' he wente unto
' Scroulfe, the bifhop of Mercia, and there obteyning of him a fmall
' cure, and a portion of ground, remayned in that country; not once
' labouring to reftore his church of Rochefter to the former ftate,
' but went aboute in Mercia to teach fong, and inftruct fuch as
' would learne muficke, wherefoever he was required, or could get
' entertainment.' †

* Firft volume of the Chronicles of England, Scotland, and Ireland, pag. 78, col. ii. edit. 1577.
† Ibid. pag. 181.

CHAP.

C H A P. V.

THE several improvements herein before enumerated, related solely to that branch of music which those who affect to use the terms of the ancients, called the Melopœia ; what related to the measures of time, which, as has been shewn, were regulated solely by the metrical laws, as they stood connected with poetry, or, to use another ancient term, the rhythmopœia was suffered to remain without innovation till the beginning of the fourteenth century, as it is said, when John De Muris, a doctor of the Sorbonne, and a native of England, though the generality of writers suppose him to have been a Norman, invented characters to signify the different lengths of sounds, and, in short, instituted a system of metrical music.

It has already been mentioned, that till within these few years it was a dispute among the writers on music, whether the ancients, by whom we are to understand the Greek harmonicians and their followers, were acquainted with music in consonance, or not : the several arguments of each party have been stated, and, upon a comparison of one with the other, it does most clearly come out, that music in consonance, though as to us it be of great antiquity, is, with respect to those of whom we are now speaking, a modern improvement.

In fixing the æra of this invention, those who deny that it was known to the ancients are almost unanimous in ascribing it, as indeed they do the invention of the polyplectral species of instruments, which are those adapted to the performance of it, to Guido Aretinus. Kircher was the first propagator of this opinion *, which he confesses is founded on a bare hint of Guido ; but in this he is mistaken, both in his opinion and in the fact which he assigns as a reason for it ; for neither in the Micrologus nor in the other tract of Guido, intituled, . Argumentum novi Cantus inveniendi, of both which a very particular account will be given hereafter, is there the least intimation of . a claim to either of the above inventions.

* Musurg. tom. 1. pag. 215.

Not:

Not to infift farther on this miftake, the fact is, that fymphoniac
mufic was known in the eighth century, and that Bede does very particularly mention a well-known fpecies of it, termed Defcant : and
this alone might fuffice to fhew that mufic in confonance, though
unknown to the ancient Greeks, was yet in ufe and practice before
the time of Guido, who flourifhed not till the beginning of the eleventh century ; for what are we to underfland by the word Defcant,
but mufic in confonance ?

But left a doubt fhould remain touching the nature of the practice
which the word Defcant is intended to fignify, let us attend to a very
particular defcription of it, contained in an ancient manufcript, formerly part of the Cotton library, but which was deftroyed by the accident of fire which happened fome years ago at Afhburnham-houfe,
where it was depofited.   The paffage above mentioned may be thus
tranflated *.

' If two or three defcant upon a plain-fong, they muft ufe their
' beft endeavours to begin and proceed by different concordances ;
' for if one of them fhould concur with another, and fing the fame
' concord to the plain-fong, then ought they immediately to confti-
' tute another. If you would defcant under the plain-fong, in the
' duple, [i. e. octave] in the fixth, the fifth, the third, the twelfth,
' or in the fifteenth, you ought to proceed in the fame manner as you
' would were you to defcant above the plain-fong ; whoever fings
' above it muft be experienced in the grave founds, their na-
' ture and fituation ; for on this the goodnefs of the harmony in a
' great meafure depends. Another method of defcanting is practifed,
' which, if it be well pronounced, will, though eafy, appear very ar-
' tificial, and feveral will feem to defcant on the plain-fong, when in
' reality one only fhall defcant, and the others modulate the plain-fong
' in different concordances : it is this, let there be four or five
' fingers, and let one begin the plain-fung in the tenor ; let the fe-
' cond pitch his voice in the fifth above, the third in the eighth, and
' the fourth, if there be four befides him who fings the tenor or plain-
' fong, in the twelfth, and all begin and continue in thefe con-
' cordances to the end ; only let thofe who fing in the eighth and

' twelfth

' twelfth break and flower the notes in fuch manner as may beft grace
' the meafure; and note well, that whofoever fings the tenor muft
' pronounce the notes full in their meafure, and that he who defcants
' muft avoid the perfect, and take only the imperfect concords,
' namely, the third, fixth, and tenth, both afcending and defcending;
' and thus a perfon who is fkilled in the practice of defcant, and
' having a proper ductility of voice, may make great melody with
' others, finging according to the above directions; and for this kind
' of finging four perfons are fufficient, provided there be one to
' defcant continually, in a twelfth above the plain-fong.'

Morley, in his Introduction, pag. 70, fpeaking of the word Defcant,
indeed fays, that ' it is a word ufurped of the mufitions in divers
' fignifications;' yet he adds, ' that it is generally taken for finging a
' part extempore, on a playne-fong; fo that when a man talketh of a
' defcanter, it muft be one that can extempore fing a part upon a
' playne-fong.'

The practice of defcant, in whichfoever of thefe two fenfes the
word is accepted, may reafonably be fuppofed to have taken its rife
from the choral fervice, which, whether we confider it in its primitive
ftate, as introduced by St. Ambrofe, or as improved by pope Gregory, confifted either of that plain and fimple melody which is underftood when we fpeak of the Ambrofian or Gregorian chant, or of
compofitions of the hymnal kind, differing from the former, in that
they were not fubject to the tonic laws which at different periods had
been laid down by thofe fathers of the church.

Continual practice and obfervation fuggefted to thofe whofe duty
obliged them to a conftant and regular attendance at divine fervice,
the idea of a polyphonous harmony; by means whereof, without difturbing the melody, the ear might be gratified with a variety of concordant founds, uttered by a number of voices; and indeed little lefs
than a difcovery of this nature was to be expected from the introduction of mufic into the church, confidering the great number of perfons whofe duty it became to ftudy and practife it; confidering alfo,
the great difference, in refpect of acutenefs and gravity, between the
voices of men and boys; and, above all, that nice difcriminating
fenfe of harmony and difcord, refulting from an attention to the
found of that noble inftrument the organ. Platina has fixed the

æra when the organ was first introduced into churches at the year 660, and gives the honour of it to Vitalianus; and in less than half a century afterwards, we discover the advantages arising from it, in that which is the subject of the present enquiry, the invention of a kind of music consisting of a variety of parts, called descant, the nature whereof is explained above, and is mentioned by Bede, who flourished at the beginning of the eighth century, and not only was extremely well skilled in the science of music, but spent the far greater part of his life in the study and practice of it.

An Italian writer of good authority *, whose prejudices, if he had any, did not lead him to favour the moderns, has gone farther, and ascribed the use of the term to our countryman; and there is extant, in the Cambriæ Descriptio of Giraldus Cambrensis, a relation of a practice that prevailed in his time among the inhabitants of this country, not inconsistent with the supposition that either Bede himself, or some of the brethren of the monastery where he resided, might be the inventors of music in consonance.

The relation of Giraldus Cambrensis above referred to is to the following effect :

‘ In the northern parts of Britain, beyond the Humber and on the
‘ borders of Yorkshire, the people there inhabiting, make use of a
‘ kind of symphoniac harmony in singing, but with only two dif-
‘ ferences or varieties of tones or voices. In this kind of modulation,
‘ one person [submurmurante] sings the under part in a low voice,
‘ while another sings the upper, in a voice equally soft and pleasing.
‘ This they do, not so much by art as by a habit, which long practice
‘ has rendered almost natural ; and this method of singing is become
‘ so prevalent amongst these people, that hardly any melody is ac-
‘ customed to be uttered simply, or otherwise than variously, or in
‘ this twofold manner *.’

* Gio. Tut. Doni, in his treatise De Generi e de Modi della Musica, pag. 97.
* In mustico modulamine non unformiter ut alibi, sed multipliciter multisque ; modis & modulis cantilenas emittunt, adeo ut in tirba cinentium, sicut huic genti mos est, quot vides capita, tot audias carmina discrimina que voxum, varia in unam denique sub B. Mollis dulcedine blanda consonantiam & organicam convenientia melodiam. In borealibus quoque majoris Britanniæ partibus trans Humbrum, Eboracique finibus Anglorum populi qui partes illas inhabitant simili canendo symphoniaca utuntur harmonia ; binis tantum solummodo tonorum differentiis & vocum modulando varietatibus, una inferius sub murmurante altera vero superne demulcente pariter & delectante. Nec arte tantum sed usu
longius

As this method of finging feems by the account above given of it to have been fubfervient to the laws of harmony, an enquiry into its origin may lead to a difcovery when and where mufic in confonance was firſt practifed. The author above cited would infinuate that the inhabitants of this country might receive it from the Dacians, or Norwegians; but he has not fhewn, nor is there the leaſt reafon to think that any fuch practice prevailed among either of thofe people; and till evidence to that purpofe fhall be produced, we may furely fufpend our belief, and refer the honour of the invention to thofe who are admitted to have been in poſſeſſion of the practice. It will be remembered, that in the foregoing pages it has been related that the monaſtery of Wiremouth, in the kingdom of Northumbria, was famous for the refidence of John the arch-chanter, and other the moſt ſkilful muficians in Britain. It is therefore not improbable that ſymphoniac muſic might have its rife there, and from thence it might have been diſſeminated among the common people inhabiting that part of the kingdom; nay, it is next to impoſſible that a practice fo very delightful, and to a certain degree fo eafily attainable, could be confined within the walls of a cloiſter.

It is true, that the reafons above adduced will warrant nothing more than a bare conjecture that mufic in confonance had its rife in this iſland; but it may be worth confidering whether any better evidence than that it was known and practifed in England fo early as the eighth century, can be produced to the contrary.

But without purfuing an enquiry touching the particular country where ſymphoniac muſic had its rife, enough has been faid to afcertain, within a few years, the time of its origin; it remains to account for the error of thofe writers who afcribe the invention of it to Guido.

longævo & quaſi in naturam mora diutina jam converfo, hæc vel illa fibi gens hanc fpecialitatem comparavit. Qui adeò apud otramque invaluit & altas jam radices pofuit, ut nihil his ſimpliciter, ubi multipliciter et apud priores, vel faltem dupliciter et apud fequentes, mellitè proferri confueverit. Pueris etiam (quod magis admirandum) & fere infantibus, (cum primum à fletibus in cantus erumpunt) eandem modulationem obferuantibus. Angli verò quoniam non generaliter omnes fed boreales folùm hujufmodi vocum utuntor modulationibus, credo quòd a Dacis & Norwagienfibus qui partes illas infulæ frequentiùs occupare ac diutiùs obtinere fo'ebant, ficut loquendi affimilatem, fic canendi proprietatem contraxerunt. Cambriæ Deferiptio, cap. xiii.

Befides the application of the fyllables UT, RE, MI, FA, SOL, LA, to the firft fix notes of the feptenary, it is univerfally allowed that he improved, if not invented the flave; and that if he was not the firft who made ufe of points placed upon one or other of the lines to fignify certain notes, he was the firft that placed points in the fpaces between the lines, and by the invention of the keys or cliffs, comprefled, as it were, the whole fyftem of the double diapafon into the narrow limits of a few lines.

After he had thus adjufted the flave, and had either invented or adopted, it matters not which, the method of notation by points inftead of letters, it was but a confequénce that the notation of mufic of more points than one fhould be by points placed one under another : and as in his time, the refpective notes contained in the feveral parts, being regulated by one common meafure, viz. that of the feet or fyllables to which they were to be fung, they flood in need of no other kind of difcrimination than what arofe from their different fituations on the fame flave, or on different flaves, and, by confequence, the points muft have been placed in a vertical fituation, and in oppofition to each other; and this method of notation fuggefted for mufic of more than one part the name of Counterpoint, a term in the opinion of fome favouring of the barbarity of the age in which it was invented, but which is too expreffive of the idea intended to be conveyed by it to be quarrelled with.

What has been faid above refpecting the improvements of Guido, will furnifh a rule for judging of the credibility of the affertion which it is here propofed to refute, namely, that he was the inventor of polyphonous or fymphoniac mufic, and lead to the fource of that, which by this time, cannot but be thought an error. The writers who maintain this pufition, and they are not a few, have miftaken the fign for the thing fignified, that is to fay, Counterpoint, for Mufic in Confonance, the thing characterifed by counterpoint. The fact in fhort is, that mufic in confonance was in ufe before Guido's time ; he invented a method of notation, calculated to define it, called Counterpoint : this is the whole relating to the invention now under confideration that can be afcribed to him; and it muft have been the effect of ftrange inattention that a different opinion has prevailed fo long in the world.

Towards the end of the eighth century flourifhed BEDE, well known to the world by the epithet of VENERABLE. He was born
about

about the year 672, and was educated in the monastery situate at Weremouth, near the mouth of the river Tyne, in the bishopric of Durham. He studied with incredible diligence, and, in the opinion of the famous Alcuin, was, for learning, humility, and piety, a pattern for all other monks. He wrote an Ecclesiastical History of Britain, at the end whereof are some memoirs of his own life, from which it appears that he was very assiduous in acquiring a knowledge of music, and punctual in the performance of choral duty in the church of his monastery. He had the good fortune to be very intimately acquainted with some of the singers whom pope Agatho had sent into Britain to teach the method of singing, as it was practised at Rome; and was, in a word, one of the greatest men of his time. He died in the year 735. His works have been many times printed, and in the latter editions make eight volumes in folio; the last is that of Cologne, in 1688. The first volume contains a great number of small tracts on arithmetic, grammar, rhetoric, astronomy, chronology, music, the means of measuring time, and other subjects. On that of music, in particular, there is a tract intitled De Musica Theorica; and another, De Musica Quadrata, Mensurata, seu Practica *. It is said, that he had no fewer than six hundred pupils; and that Alcuin, the preceptor to Charlemagne, was one of them. There is a well written life of him in the Biographia Britannica, and an accurate catalogue of his works in the Bibliotheca Britannico-Hibernica of bishop Tanner.

NOTGERUS, or NOTKER, surnamed LE BEGUE, a monk of St. Gal, flourished about the year 845, under the emperor Lotharius, son of Lewis the Pious. Among other things, he is famed for his book De Musica et Symphonia. He is supposed to have been the inventor of the Sequentiæ, which are those parts of the office in which the people answer to the priest, and which pope Nicolas I. ordained to be sung at mass. He died in 912. Innocent III. had taken order for his canonization, but his design was never carried into execution. There was another of the name, bishop of Liege: Trithemius has confounded them together.

RABANUS MAURUS, a Moor, as his surname imports, is reckoned in the number of those who have written on music. He was born at

* Vide Tan. Biblioth. pag. 89. in not. col. ii.

Mentz,

Mentz, in 788, and bred up in the monastery of Fulda. He studied at Tours, under Alcuin, and returning to his monastery, was chosen abbot thereof, in 822. Having enjoyed that dignity twenty years, he laid it down to please the monks, who said he applied himself too much to study, and too little to the affairs of the monastery. He retired to Mount St. Pierre; and was at last chosen archbishop of Mentz, in 847. In a treatise of the universe, consisting of twenty-two books, which he wrote and sent to Lewis le Debonnaire *, he has comprised an infinite number of common places, amongst which, it is supposed, are many relating to music, since Brossard has ranked him in his second class of writers on that subject. In a commentary of his upon the liturgy, he expatiates on the sacrifice, as it is called of the mass †, which latter word he supposes to be derived from the ' Ite missa est,' Go, ye are dismissed, the form used for the dismission of the catechumens, and to signify that the service was ended.

WALAFRIDUS STRABO, so surnamed because he squinted, was first a monk of Fulda, and afterwards abbot of Richenou, in the diocese of Constance. He is reckoned among the musical writers, and had been a disciple of Rabanus Maurus. He flourished about the year 842, and wrote De Officiis Divinis, the twenty-fifth chapter of which tract is intitled De Hymnis & Cantilenis eorumque incrementis, &c. ‡ The Benedictines, compilers of

* Du Pin. Nouv. Biblioth. des Auteurs Ecclef. fiec. ix.

† As the word Mass will frequently occur in the course of this work, the following note of the translator of Du Pin's Bibliotheque, vol. VI. pag 3, may ferve for an explanation of that rite.

' The word Missa, or Mass, is an old Latin word, and signifies generally the whole ser-
' vice of the church, but more especially the holy sacrament of Christ's body and blood.
' It was called Missa, or Dimissio, because no man was suffered to remain in the church
' that could not or would not receive the sacrament; and therefore such persons as had a
' mind to see and hear, but not receive, were all, without exception, dismissed by the dea-
' con, after the sermon was ended, with these words, " Ite, missa est; Go, ye are dif-
' missed;" and if any delayed, they were urged to depart by the deacons and exorcists,
' saying aloud, " Si quis non communicat det locum; Whoever will not receive, let
' him go out." The Roman church puts a different sense upon this word Mass, under-
' standing by it that solemn service wherein they do pretend to offer unto God the
' body and blood of his Son, as a propitiatory sacrifice for the sins, both of the quick and
' dead. Isidore here takes it in the first sense, calling it Ordo Precum, i. e. the Form of
' Prayers. But Du Pin, by joining it with the word Canon, (a word of a much later use,
' and which signifies, in the Roman church, the rule or form of celebrating their mass)
' seems to bring it over to the latter, but against the sense of St. Isidore of Seville.'

‡ Vide Du Pin. Biblioth. cent. i. cap. xiii.

the

the Hiftoire Litteraire de la France, have difcovered that there was another of his name, dean of the abbey of St. Gal, in the preceding century, with whom he is often confounded. Hift. Lit. de la France, tom. IV. pag. 59, in not.

BRISTAN, or BRICSTAN, a native of England, a Benedicline monk, and precentor in the monaftery of Croyland, is celebrated by Pits as an excellent mathematician, poet, and mufician [*]. Ingulphus, pag. 867, fpeaks thus of him : ' Briftanus, quondam cantor monafterii, ' muficus peritiffimus et poeta facundiffimus.' He lived about 870, at the time when, in one of the invafions of the Danes, his monaftery was burned, and the monks flain : he had, however, the good fortune to efcape, aud compofed certain elegiac verfes, wherein he relates the cruelties exercifed by the invaders, the fufferings of his brethren, and the misfortunes attending this difaftrous event.

As it is propofed in this work to give an account as well of practical as theoretical muficians, there will need little apology for inferting in this place a few particulars of our own king ALFRED, who is celebrated by Bale, and other writers, for his fkill in mufic, and his performance on the harp : that he was very fedulous in his endeavours to promote the ftudy of mufic in his kingdom, we are told by Sir John Spelman, in his life of this great monarch, pag. 135 ; and particularly that he procured to be fent from France one Grimbald [†], a man very fkilful in mufic, of a fingular good life, great learning, and who befides was an excellent churchman. Sir John Spelman adds, that the king firft came to the knowledge of this perfon by his courtefy, he having made very much of him in his childhood, at Rheims, when he was in his paffage towards Rome.

<hr/>

[†] Pits. De Reb. Angl. pag. 167. Tann. 124.

[‡] Of this Grimbald very honourable mention is made in the Hiftoire Litteraire de la France, tom. V. pag. 694. Alfred had written to Fulk, archbifhop of Rheims, intreating him to fend to England a perfon fkilled in the liberal fciences, particularly mufic. The archbifhop wrote the king a long letter In anfwer, recommending Grimbald, a monk of St. Bertin, the perfon above mentioned. This was about the year 880 ; and had Grimbald been a much greater man than he was, the French would have been bound in gratitude to have fpared him to us ; for a few years before, they had from us Alcuin, the tutor of Charlemagne. It appears that Grimbald behaved very well whilft he was here. In the chronicle of Nic. Harpsfield are the heads of a fpeech of his, in a fyned at London, before king Alfred and archbifhop Æthelred, wherein he difcourfed gravely aud wifely of the primitive dignity of human nature, and of its corruption by the fall of Adam. The whole is faid to be in the Annals of Winchefter. Vide Spelm. Life of Alfred, pag. 135, in not.

Again,

Again, the same author relates, that among the rest of his attendants, he is noted, Solomon like, to have provided himself of muficians, not common, or fuch as knew but the practic part; but men fkilful in the art itfelf, whofe fkill and fervice yet farther improved with his own inftruction, and fo ordered the manner of their fervice as beft befitted the royalty of a king. Spelm. Life of Alfred, pag. 199.

That he himfelf was alfo a confiderable proficient on the harp, were other evidences wanting, the well-known ftory related by Ingulphus, William of Malmefbury, and fucceeding hiftorians, of his entering the Danifh camp, difguifed like a harper or minftrel, is a proof.

The fubftance of which relation is, that being defirous to know the ftrength and circumftances of the Danifh army, then in Somerfetfhire, he difguifed himfelf like a minftrel, and taking with him a harp, and one only confidant, he went into the Danifh camp, the privilege of his difguife intitling him to free admittance every where, even into the king's tent; and there, for many days, he fo employed himfelf as that, while he entertained his enemies with his mirth and mufic, he obtained the fulleft fatisfaction touching their ability to refift the attac on them, which he had for fome time been meditating. This was in the year 378 *.

HUCBALD, HUCBALDUS, or HUBALDUS, for by all thefe names is he called, is fpoken of as the moft celebrated doctor in France at the clofe of the ninth century. He was a Benedictine monk, of the abbey of St. Amand, in the diocefe of Tournay, and flourifhed about the year 880, under Charles the Bald. He is celebrated for his profound fkill in the learning of thofe days, and particularly for his excellence in poetry and mufic †. He is faid to have invented a divifion of the monochord, by means whereof mufic might be learned without the help of a mafter; and to have invented certain figns, independent of lines and letters, to mark the founds in the octave. Martini, who fometimes calls him Ubaldo, has given a fpecimen of this his method

* Vide Spelman's Life of Alfred, pag. 63.
† Hift. Litteraire de la France, tom. VI. pag. 210.
Sigebert, Tritbemius, and others, mention a poem of Hugbald's compofing, and of a very fingular kind. It is an encomium on Baldnefs, in heroic verfe, infcribed to the emperor Charles the Bald, in which every word begins with the initial letter of the emperor's name, as in the following line.
Carmina clarifona clavis cantate Camenæ.
2   of

of punctuation from a manuscript of his, intitled De Harmonica Institutione, in the following form :

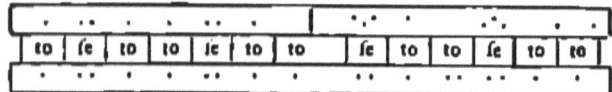

Which he renders thus in modern characters :

The authors of the Histoire Litteraire de la France also speak in general terms of a method of musical punctuation invented by him, doubtless the same with that above ; and add, that he composed and noted offices in honour of many of the saints. He died at the age of ninety, in the year 930, and was buried in the church of St. Peter, in his own abbey. The merits of Hucbald, his learning and virtues, were celebrated by many of his surviving friends, in epitaphs, and other metrical compositions ; the two which follow are extant in the work above cited, and are here inserted, not so much on account of their elegance, as to shew the degree of estimation in which he stood with his contemporaries.

EPITAPH I.

Dormit in hac tumba simplex sine felle Columba
Doctor, flos, & honos tam cleri quàm monachorum
Hucbaldus, famam cujus per climata mundi
Edita sanctorum modulamina, gestaque clamant.
Hic Cyrici membra pretiosa, reperta Nivernis.
Nostris invexit oris, scripsitque triumphum. .

EPITAPH II.

Praecluis orator sudans opobalsama cosmo
Archas mellifluus rhetor super æthera notus,
En Huncbalde pater salve per secla verenter
Tu lampas monachis, tu flos & donu peritis :

* Storia della Musica, pag. 183.

Te plebs æternùm lugens fibi deflet ademtum.
Vige juge, fophifta, vale, Theophile care.
Ediderat ftylo examuffim certamen honeflo
Matris Julitæ, Cirici prolifque venuftæ,
Ceu doctor, celeber gnavus per cuncta magifter.
Laudetur, vigeat, quod quæfo legatur, ametur.
Hæc quifquis legis, requiem die det Deus illi,
Palmam cum fuperis geftet fuper aftra choreis
Gloria pauper hæc peregit, metra clienter.

The above Hucbald is ufually ftyled Hucbald de Saint Amand; notwithftanding which he is fometimes confounded with two other writers of the fame name, the one a monk of Orbais, the other a clerk in the church of Liege, neither of whom feem to ftand in any degree of competition with him *.

AURELIANUS, a clerk in the church of Rheims, lived in the year 890, under the emperor Arnulphus, and on to the reign of Lewis IV. He was in great eftimation for his learning, and author of a treatife on the tones, intitled, Tonarius regularis, which he compofed for the ufe of his church, and infcribed to Bernard, the precentor of the choir. He is placed by Trithemius among the ecclefiaftical writers †.

C H A P.   VI.

WE are now arrived at a period, namely the commencement of the tenth century, when learning began to flourifh throughout Europe. In France, particularly, not only mathematics, but the arts of painting, fculpture, and architecture, were cultivated with great affiduity. The abbies of Corbie, of Rheims, and Cluni, were the great feminaries of that country, and produced a fucceffion of men eminent in all faculties : the former of thefe was fo famous for mufical inftitution, that young monks from England were ufually fent thither to be taught the true method of finging in divine fervice. Letald, Remi de Auxerre, Notker le Begue, Wigeric bifhop of Metz,

* Storia della Mufica, pag. 214.
† Voffius De Scientiis Mathem. cap. ix. § 6.

and

and Hucbald de St. Amand, before-mentioned, were all skilled in music, and are some of the most celebrated names that occur in the literary history of those times *.

Odo, abbot of Cluni, in the province of Burgundy, a Frenchman of noble descent, also flourished in this age, that is to say, about the year 920. He is highly celebrated by the writers of those times, for his learning, his piety, and his zeal to reform the manners of the clergy. The authors of the Histoire Litteraire de la France speak of him as one of the great luminaries of that kingdom. As to his skill in music, they represent him as surpassing most of his cotemporaries : they speak also of a manuscript of his, which is no other than the Enchiridion, mentioned by Gerard Vossius, and commended by Guido himself, beginning ' Quid est musica ?' as a great curiosity, and being extant only in the Vatican library, and in that of the queen of Sweden ; nevertheless, it is to be found in the library of Baliol college, and makes part of a volume, that contains the Micrologus, and other tracts of Guido, with some others on the subject of music, of great value ; and Martini refers to another, in the conventual library at Cesana, near Ravenna, in Italy.

The Enchiridion of Odo is in the form of a dialogue between a teacher and his disciple : it begins with directions for the making and dividing of the monochord, and contains a general definition of the consonances, the method of notation by the Roman letters, as instituted by Gregory, a formula of the tones, and concludes with general directions for antiphonal singing.

It is to be remarked, that all the tracts written about this time, which profess to teach the knowledge of music, and there are innumerable of them extant, begin, as this does, with directions for making and dividing the monochord : the reason of this is, that the method of ascertaining the places of the semitones in the diapason, by the syllables, was not then discovered ; and hardly any instrument then in use, excepting the organ, would answer the end of impressing upon the memory of a child, the difference between the greater and lesser intervals ; the teachers of music therefore invariably directed their pupils to find out the intervals themselves, and lay

---

* Hist. Litteraire de la France, tom. VI. pag. 71.

the foundation of their studies in the knowledge of the monochord.

SILVESTER, the second pope of that name, is justly celebrated as
one of the great ornaments of the tenth century. He was a monk
of Aurillac, in the province of Auvergne, a monastery which had
been founded at the latter end of the preceding age. His pursuits were so various, and his excellence in all branches of learning so great, that it is difficult to say in what class of learned
men he merits most to be placed; or whether we should consider
him as a divine, a mathematician, or a philosopher at large. It
is certain that he wrote upon geometry, particularly on the quadrature of the circle, on astronomy, logic, and rhetoric; that he
was deeply skilled in the science of music, as a proof whereof it
is said that he made some considerable improvements of the organ,
on which he was an excellent proficient: William of Malmesbury
speaks, with admiration, of an improvement made by him in the
hydraulic organ *. He was born of obscure parents, in the neighbourhood of Aurillac: his name of baptism was Gerbert, or Girbert:
his great merit, and a disposition to communicate to the world the
discoveries he made in the course of his studies, facilitated his pro-
motion to the highest dignities of the church; for he was succes-
sively archbishop of Rheims and Ravenna, and at last pope. While
he was archbishop of Rheims, he had the misfortune to see that
city sustain a close siege, which obliged him to seek refuge in the
court of the emperor Otho III. who had been his disciple. During
his residence there, he invented an instrument for the measuring of
time by the motion of the polar star, which some writers have confounded with the astrolabe. By the interest of his patron Otho, in
the year 998, he was promoted to the archbishopric of Ravenna,
and the following year to the papacy on the death of Gregory V.
which he held but four years, for he died in 1003.

Mosheim has bestowed an eulogium on Gerbert as characteristic of
the age in which he lived, as of the person he means to celebrate.
He relates that he derived his learning in a great measure from the

---

* Said to have been played on by warm water. See the History of the Manual Arts, by
Dr. Thomas Powell, octavo, 1661, abridged in Oldys's British Librarian, N° I. pag. 51.

2   Arabians,

Arabians, among whom at that time there were many very confiderable men ; though it is remarkable that we meet with the name of
but one writer on mufic of that country, viz. Alfarabius, who is
barely mentioned in a note in the life of Hai Ebn Yokdhan, an ingenious fiction tranflated from the original Arabic by Simon Ockley,
8vo. 1708. A treatife of his on mufic is referred to in the Marga-
rita Philofophica of Georgius Reifchius, printed at Bafil in 1517.
Mofheim fpeaks thus of the ftate of learning in Gerbert's time.

‘ It was not however to the fecundity of his genius alone that Ger-
‘ bert was indebted for the knowledge with which he now began to
‘ enlighten the European provinces ; he had derived a part of his
‘ erudition, particularly in phyfic, mathematics, and philofophy,
‘ from the writings and inftructions of the Arabians, who were fet-
‘ tled in Spain. Thither he had repaired in purfuit of knowledge, and
‘ had fpent fome time in the feminaries of learning at Cordoua and
‘ Seville, with a view to hear the Arabian doctors ; and it was, per-
‘ haps, by his example, that the Europeans were directed and engaged
‘ to have recourfe to this fource of inftruction in after-times. For it
‘ is undeniably certain, that, from the time of Gerbert, fuch of the
‘ Europeans as were ambitious of making any confiderable progrefs in
‘ phyfic, arithmetic, geometry, or philofophy, entertained the moft
‘ eager and impatient defire of receiving inftruction either from the
‘ academical leffons, or from the writings of the Arabian philofo-
‘ phers, who had founded fchools in feveral parts of Spain and Italy.
‘ Hence it was that the moft celebrated productions of thefe doctors
‘ were tranflated into Latin, their tenets and fyftems adopted with
‘ zeal in the European fchools, and that numbers went over to Spain
‘ and Italy to receive inftruction from the mouths of thefe famous
‘ teachers, which were fuppofed to utter nothing but the deepeft
‘ myfteries of wifdom and knowledge. However exceffive this vene-
‘ ration for the Arabian doctors may have been, it muft be owned ne-
‘ verthelefs that all the knowledge, whether of phyfic, aftronomy,
‘ philofophy, or mathematics, which flourifhed in Europe from the
‘ tenth century, was originally derived from them, and that the
‘ Spanifh Saracens in a more particular manner may be looked upon
‘ as the fathers of European philofophy.’   Mofh. Ecclef. Hift.
vol. II. pag. 199.

The

The diligence with which Gerbert purfued his ftudies, and his proficiency in fo many various branches of learning, raifed in the vulgar a fufpicion of his being addicted to magic, which Platina has without hefitation adopted ; for he fays he obtained the papacy by ill arts, and that he left his monaftery to follow the devil. He however allows him the merit of a fincere repentance, but mentions fome prodigies at his death, which few can believe on the authority of fuch a writer. Naddeus has written a juftification of a great number of learned men who have undergone the fame cenfure, and has included Silvefter among them ; but long before his time a certain poet had done him that good office in the following epigram.

Ne mirare Magum fatui quod inertia vulgi
    Me (veri minime gnara) fuiffe putat.
Archimedis ftudium quod eram fophiæque fequutus
    Tum, cum magna fuit gloria fcire nihil.
Credebant Magicum effe rudes, fed bufta loquuntur
    Quam pius, integer & religiofus erant.

The following epitaph befpeaks his character, and is an epitome of his hiftory.

Ille locus mundi Silveftri membra fepulti
    ' Venturo Domino conferet ad fonitum.
Quem dederat mundo celebrem doctiffima virgo.
    Atque caput mundi culmina Romulea.
Primum Gerbertus meruit Francigena fede
    Remenfis populi metropolim patriæ.
Inde Ravennatis meruit confcendere fummum
    Ecclefiæ regimen nobile, ficque potens
Poft annum Romam mutato nomine fumfit,
    Ut toto paftor fieret orbe novus.
Cui nimium placuit fociali mente fidelis.
    Obtulit hoc Cæfar tertius Otho fibi.
Tempus uterque comit clara virtute fophiæ ;
    Gaudet, & omne feclum frangitur omne reum
Clavigeri inftar erat cælorum fede potitus,
    Terna fuffectus cui vice paftor erat.

Ille

Iſte vicem Petri poſtquam ſuſcepit, abegit
Luſtrali ſpatio ſæcula morte ſui.
Obriguit mundus diſcuſſa pace triumphus
Eccleſiæ mutans, dedidicit requiem.
Sergius hunc loculum miti pietate ſacerdos,
Succeſſorque ſuus comſit amore ſui.
Quiſquis ad hunc tumulum devexa lumina vertis,
Omnipotens Domine, dic, miſere ſui.

Berno, abbot of Richenou, in the diocese of Conſtance, who flouriſhed about the year 1008, is celebrated as a poet, rhetor, muſician,
philoſopher and divine. He was the author of ſeveral treatiſes on
muſic, particularly of one De Inſtrumentis Muſicalibus, beginning
with the words ' Muſicam non eſſe contem l' which he dedicated to
Aribon, archbiſhop of Mentz. He alſo wrote De Menſura Monochordi : but the moſt celebrated of his works is a treatiſe De Muſica ſeu Tonis, which he wrote and dedicated to Pelegrinus, archbiſhop of Cologne, beginning ' Vero mundi iſti advenæ et Peregrino':
this latter tract is part of the Baliol manuſcript, and follows the Enchiridion of Odo, above referred to : it contains a ſummary of the
doctrines delivered by Boetius, an explanation of the eccleſiaſtical
tones, intermixed with frequent exhortations to piety, and the application of muſic to religious purpoſes. He was highly favoured by
the emperor Henry II. for his great learning and piety, and ſucceed-
ed ſo well in his endeavours to promote learning, that his abbey of
Richenou was as famous in his time as thoſe of St. Gal and Cluni,
then the moſt celebrated in France. He died in 1048, and was in-
terred in the church of his monaſtery, which but a ſhort time before
he had dedicated to St. Mark.

From the account herein before given of the riſe and progreſs of
choral ſervice, and of the inſtitution of the eccleſiaſtical tones, modes,
tropes, or whatever elſe they may be termed, it is clear that before
the eleventh century they were in number eight, beſides which, the
actual exiſtence at this day of manuſcripts, ſuch as thoſe of Aurelianus, Odo of Cluni, and this of Berno above-mentioned, in which
not only eight tones are ſpoken of, but a formula of each is given
in words at length, are indiſputable evidence of the fact. A learned
gentleman, Dr. King, the author of a book lately publiſhed, intitled
the Rites and Ceremonies of the Greek Church in Ruſſia, has intimated

mated, pag. 43, that the addition of the four plagal tones, as they are called, to the four authentic of St. Ambrofe, is by fome afcribed to Guido Aretinus, who, by the way, in his Micrologus lays not the leaft claim to this improvement, but fpeaks of the eight ecclefiftical tones as an ancient eftablifhment. We are therefore neceffitated to conclude that the contrary opinion is without foundation, and the rather, as no writer of authority among the many that have been confulted in the courfe of this work, has intimated the leaft doubt but that the Cantus Gregorianus confifted of eight tones.

Through all the variations that attended mufic, the ancient fyftem of a bifdiapafon, conftituted of tetrachords, retained its authority; we do not find that even in the time of Boetius the fyftem itfelf had received any alteration ; the Latins it is true had rejected the ancient Greek characters, and introduced the Roman capital letters in their ftead ; and pope Gregory reduced thofe letters to the firft feven of the Roman alphabet, which, by repeating them in each feptenary, he made to ferve the purpofe of a great number, calling the firft feries graves, the fecond acutes, and the third, diftinguifhed by double fmall letters, fuper-acutes ; but the tetrachord fyftem, faid to be immutable, as alfo the Greek names anciently appropriated to the feveral chords, continued in ufe till the clofe of the tenth century, foon after which fuch a reformation of the ancient fcale was made, as was thought worthy of commemoration, not only by chronologers, but by the graveft hiftorians. The perfon to whofe ingenuity and induftry we owe this ineftimable improvement was an ecclefiaftic, GUIDO ARETINUS, a Benedictine monk. The relation given by Cardinal Baronius of this event is to the following effect ; viz. That in the pontificate of Benedict VIII. Guido Aretinus, a monk, and an excellent mufician, to the admiration of all, invented a method of teaching mufic, fo that a boy in a few months* might learn what no man, though of great ingenuity, could before that attain in feveral years.— That the fame of this invention procured him the favour of the pope, who invited him to Rome, as did afterwards John XX. his fucceffor.—That in the thirty-fourth year of his age he compofed a treatife, which he called Micrologus, and dedicated to Theodald, bifhop of Arezzo. Annal. Eccl. tom. XI. pag. 73, et feq.

* Guido in the prologue to the Micrologus fays, in the fpace of one month, ' anius ' menfis fpatium.'

To

To this account Baronius has fubjoined the epiftle from Guido to a friend of his Michael of Pompofa, beginning, ' Clariffimo atque dul-
' ciffimo fratri Michaéli,' containing the hiftory of his invention, and of his invitation to Rome and reception by the pope; the particulars whereof are referred to an extract from the epiftle itfelf, which is given in a fubfequent page of this work *.   General accounts of the reformation of the fcale made by Guido are to be met with in almoft every treatife on the fubject compofed fince his time; yet among thefe fome improvements are attributed to him, as namely, the in-vention of the ftave, and of the figure of a hand, to explain his me-thod of notation, to the merit whereof, if we are to judge from his own writings, he does not appear to have made the leaft claim.

It has been related that the method of notation among the Greeks was by the letters of their alphabet, as alfo that the Latins in their ftead made ufe of the Roman capital letters, A, B, C, D, E, F, G, and fo on to P, as is mentioned by Boetius in his fourth book; and that afterwards Gregory rejected all but the firft feven, which he made to ferve for the whole fcale, diftinguifhing the grave feries by the capitals and the acute by the fmall letters.   Their manner of finging was from A to B, a tone; from B to C, a femitone; from C to D, a tone; from D to E, a tone; from E to F, a femitone; from F to G, a tone; fo that, to fpeak of the diapafon only, the feven capital letters ferved to exprefs, afcending and defcending, either gradually or by leaps, the feven notes *; but fo difficult was it ac-

* By the epiftle above referred to, it appears, that Baronius has been guilty of an error in faying that Guido was lurized to Rome both by Benedict and John; for it was from John only that he received this mark of favour.   Neither does he clearly diftinguifh between the Argumentam novi Cantus inveniendi and the Micrologus; the former contained his method of finging by the fyllables, and procured him a general reputation, and the favour of Benedict: the latter, his reformation of the fcale, and, as Guido himfelf exprefly fays, was compofed in the thirty-fourth year of his age, John XX. being then pope.   Befides this, he adds, that the Micrologus was written at the monaftery of Pompofa, whither he retired not, till after his interview with the pope.

* Zarlino has been guilty of a grofs miftake in afferting, as he does in his Inftitutions, part ii. chap. 30. that Guido firft made ufe of the method of notation by the capital and fmall Roman letters: the current opinion is, that Gregory introduced it; but fuppofing that matter doubtful, there is fufficient evidence to prove that the practice in queftion pre-vailed before Guido's time; for the Enchiridion of Odo, abbot of Cluni, contains direc-tions for dividing the monochord, and marking the firft feptenary with the capital, and the fecond with the fmall Roman letters; and Vincentio Galilei, in his Dialogo della Mufica, pag. 96, has given the following fpecimen of Canto Fermo.

```
      d   c   b   c   d   e   d   c   b   a   b   c   d   a   G   F   G   G
      Sit  nomen Do       mi      ni  bene   dictum in fa       cula
      F   O   a   G   F   F   G   F   F   E   F   G   F   E   D   C   D   D
      Adju to     rium noftrum  la  po           mine  Do    mi  ni
```

Sit

cording to this method to know and to hit precisely the place of the
two femitones, that before the pupils were able to acquire a knowledge of the Canto Fermo, ten years were usually confumed. Guido
studied with great diligence to remove this obstruction; and the current account of this invention is, that being at vespers, and singing
the hymn to St. John, ' Ut queant laxis,' it by chance came into his
head to apply, as being of easy pronunciation, certain syllables of
that hymn to as many sounds in a regular succession, and thereby he
removed those difficulties that had a long time retarded the improvement of practical music.

UT queant laxis REsonare fibris
MIra gestorum FAmuli tuorum
SOLve polluti LAbii reatum,
Sancte Joannes *.

This is the substance of what is related, by Gaffurius, Glareanus,
Vicentino, Galilei, Zarlino, Kircher, Merfennus, Bontempi, and
other writers, touching the invention of the syllables; but the scale,

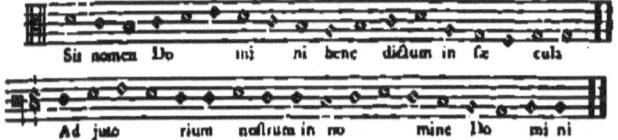

Sii nomen Do   mi   ni bene dictum in fæ   cula

Ad justo   rium noftrum in no   mine Do   mi ni

which he afferts was compofed many years before Guido was born.
The perufal of the Enchiridion of Odo has furnifhed the means of refuting a vulgar
error, namely, that Guido, to perpetuate the memory of his reformation of the fcale, prefixed to it the Greek Γ, the initial letter of his name; the contrary of th s is manifeft in the
directions of Odo for dividing the monochord, in which he affumes that very character.
* The words of the above hymn were compofed by Paulus Diaconus, Paul, a deacon of
the church of Aquilea, about the year 770, and in the reign of Charlemagne, as Poffevin
relates. Dr. Wallis, from Alftedius, in the room of the Adonic, Sancte Joannes, has inferted O Pater Alme. Droffard, and others after him fay, that Angelo Berardi has very
prettily comprifed the fix fyllables in this line.

Ut relevet miferum fatum folitofque Labores.

But Gerard Voffius, De quatuor Artibus Popularibus, pag. 93, without taking notice of
Berardi, fays it is only part of the following verfe compofed by fome perfon who lived after
Guido,

Cur adhibes trifti numeros cantumque labori ?
Ut relevet miferum fatum folitofque Labores.

as it ſtood in the time of Guido, was not adapted for the reception of ſix ſyllables, and therefore the application which he made of them does neceſſarily imply ſome previous improvement of the ſcale, either actually made by him, or which he had at that time under conſideration. It is pretty certain that this improvement could be no other than the converting the ancient tetrachords into hexachords, which, to begin with the tetrachord Hypaton, he effected in this manner: that tetrachord was terminated in the grave by Hypate hypaton, or ♭; for though the Proſlambanomenos A, carried the ſyſtem a tone lower, it was always conſidered, as its name imports to be, acquiſitus, ſupernumerary, or redundant; the addition therefore of a tone below A immediately converted the tetrachord Hypaton into a hexachord, and drove the ſemitone into a ſituation that divided the hexachord into two equal parts. To this additional tone Guido, as ſome ſay, in honour of the Greeks, the fathers of muſic, or, as others ſuggeſt, to perpetuate the memory of his invention, and thereby acquire honour to himſelf, affixed the Greek gamma Γ, which fortunately for ſuch a ſuppoſition, was the initial letter of his name *.

By this conſtitution the poſition of the ſemitone was clearly pointed out to every theoriſt; but the thing in purſuit was a method of hitting it in practice, the want whereof rendered the ſinging extempore ſo very difficult, that few could attain to it without great labour; but the accidental hearing of the hymn above-mentioned ſuggeſted to Guido a thought that the ſix ſyllables therein contained might be ſo fitted to the ſix ſounds in his newly-formed hexachord, as to furniſh a rule for this purpoſe; accordingly he made the experiment, and applying the ſyllable UT to the firſt note of the hexa-

* Meibomius denies that Guido extended the ancient Greek ſyſtem either upwards or downwards, or that he even made any addition to the tetrachord Hypaton; for he aſſerts, with an unwarrantable degree of confidence, that though the Proſlambanomenos was generally underſtood as the loweſt ſound in the ancient ſyſtem, yet that the Greeks in truth recognized another, which was a tone below it, but that as it profited a confuſed and undiſtinguiſhable ſound, it was neglected. He ſays that when Guido determined to reaſſume this tone, he was neceſſitated to mark it with the Grecian gamma, Γ; for that otherwiſe, as he had given the Latin G to its diapaſon Lychanos meſon, he muſt either have introduced a ſtrange character, or doubled the letter G, which latter method could not pleaſe him ſo well. Meibomius alſo ſays that the Greek ſyſtem proceeded even farther in the acutes than that of Guido; but the truth of this aſſertion will be beſt judged of by a compariſon of the ancient ſyſtem with that of Guido, as they ſtand oppoſſed to each other in a ſubſequent page of this volume.

chord, and the reſt to the others in ſucceſſion, he gave to every note an articulate ſound.

The view of Guido in this contrivance was to impreſs upon the minds of learners an idea of the powers of the ſeveral ſounds, as they ſtood related to the firſt ſound in the hexachord; for he ſaw that from an habitual application of the ſyllables to their reſpective notes, it muſt follow that the former would become a common meaſure for the five intervals included within the limits of the hexachord, and that in a ſhort time the idea of aſſociation between the ſyllables and the notes would become ſo ſtrong as to make it almoſt impoſſible to miſ-apply them.

Finding that this invention was likely to ſucceed, he added two tones to the tetrachord Meſon, thereby making that alſo a hexachord, and to this alſo he applied the ſyllables.

Laſtly, he made a like addition of two tones to the tetrachord Synemmenon, and thereby formed a third tetrachord.

The ſeveral combinations and conjunctions of theſe tetrachords for the purpoſe of aſcertaining the intervals in any given ſyſtem, exceeding the limits of the hexachord, will be hereafter explained ; the reſult of the invention was clearly this, that in a regular ſucceſſion of ſix ſounds in their natural order, beginning either from Γ, from C, or from F, taking in B b, the progreſſion with reſpect to the tones and ſemitone in each was preciſely the ſame : and ſuppoſing the learner to have acquired by conſtant practice a habit of expreſſing with his voice the interval G C, which is an exact fourth, by the ſyllables UT FA, the two ſounds proper to the interval G C would become a kind of tune, which he muſt neceſſarily apply to UT FA, wherever thoſe . ſyllables ſhould occur; and in what other ſituation they occur the above conſtitution of the different hexachords ſhews ; for as in the hexachord from G to E the ſyllables UT FA expreſs the fourth G C, ſo in that from C to A do they expreſs a fourth C F, and in the hexachord from F to D the fourth F B b.

The introduction of B b to avoid the Tritonus has been related at large ; and here it may be proper to add that the exceeding diſcordancy or hardneſs of B ♮, when taken as a fourth, gave occaſion to the epithet ſoft, which for the ſake of diſtinction was given to B b ; for this reaſon the hexachord from F is called the molle or ſoft hexachord, as that from G is called durum or hard ; theſe appellatives

begot

begot another, namely, that of the natural hexachord, which is given to the hexachord from C. The method of finging each is termed a property in finging, and is thus defcribed in the following diftich.

C Naturum dat, f b molle nunc tibi fignat,
g quoque b durum tu femper habes caniturum *.

The intervals thus adjufted in the feveral hexachords, became alike commenfurable in each by the fyllables; and UT MI would as truly exprefs the ditone C E or F A as G B, to which they were originally adapted: the fame may be faid of every other interval in each of the hexachords, and their exact uniformity is vifible in this, that the femitone has the fame fituation in them all, and divides them into two equal parts.

C H A P. VII.

THE writers on mufic, as has been mentioned above, have alfo attributed to Guido another very confiderable improvement of the mufical fcale, which they fuppofe to be coeval with the formation of the hexachords, namely the Stave, confifting of parallel lines in a horizontal pofition, fuch as is now ufed in the writing of mufic: in this they feem to have been miftaken, for all the examples made ufe of by him to illuftrate his doctrine, are given in the Roman capital and fmall letters, agreeable to the method of St. Gregory. Befides which it is demonftrable that the ftave was of a much earlier invention than this opinion fuppofes. The proof of this affertion is to be found in the Dialogo della Mufica of Vincentio Galilei, pag. 37, which contains a diagram of mufical punctuation on a ftave confifting of no lefs than feven lines, which he fays was in ufe long before the time of Guido †.

* Morley in the Annotations on book I. of his Introduction to Practicall Muficke.
† By an unaccountable accident the examples here referred to, are in fome copies of Galilei's book defective, as giving only the ftave, and not the points; but they are here fupplied from Martini, who has rendered them into the characters of modern notation. Vid. Stor. della Mufica, pag. 185.

And

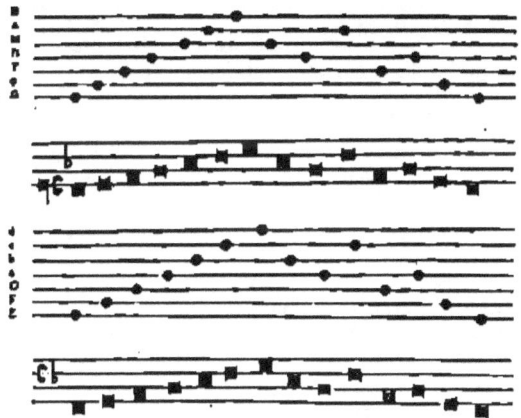

And immediately after he exhibits an example of notation on a
stave of ten lines, concerning which he thus expresses himself:
‘ Eccovi l' essempio d' una Cantilena tra le altre, che mi sono capi-
‘ tate in mano, la quale mi fu gia da un gentiluomo nostro Fioren-
‘ tino donata, ritrovata da lui in un antichissimo suo libro : ed è delle
‘ pui intere, è meglio conservata d' altra che io abbia mai veduta.’

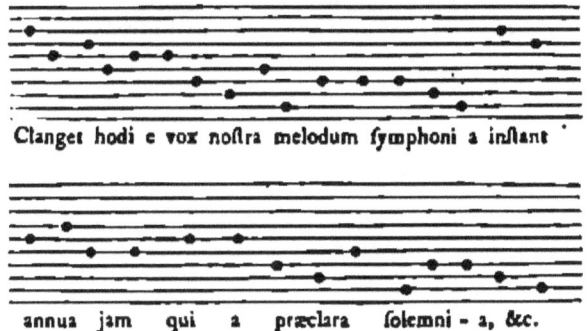

Clanget hodi e vox nostra melodum symphoni a instant

annua jam   qui   a   præclara   solemni - a, &c.

Clanget

Clanget ho die vox, noſtra melodum ſymphoni a inſtant

annua   jam   quia   præclara   ſolemni   a.

To theſe examples of lineal punctuation another may be adduced
from the Muſurgia, tome 1. pag. 213, wherein the points are
placed on a ſtave of eight lines.   We owe this diſcovery to Kircher,
who relates that being on a voyage to Malta he went to viſit the library of S. Salvator in Meſſana, which is well furniſhed with Greek
manuſcripts; and that one of the monks there produced to him a
manuſcript book of hymns, which had been written about ſeven hundred years, in which was contained the following.

Παρθι ει ε μὶ γα χορὶ ἱος ἰ ὶ ει ἰωτὲ ιαα τ μιτις ατιμι τνὶιις

Kircher mentions that while he was writing the Muſurgia, he received from a friend of his, the reverend abbot Didacus De Fran-
chis, an extract from a very ancient antiphonary in the monaſtery of
Vallombroſa, containing an example of interlineary punctuation in
the following form.

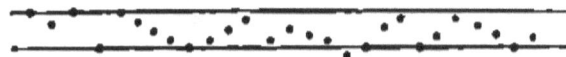

In which he ſays the points correſpond with the notes of a well-
known antiphon, beginning with the words ' Salve Regina.'
These evidences ſufficiently prove that the ſtave is more ancient
than is generally ſuppoſed; for it is agreed that the Micrologus was
written between the years 1020 and 1030; and a period of ſeven hundred

dred years before the publication of the Mufurgia, in 1650, will carry the ufe of the ftave back to the year 950, which is more than forty years before Guido was born, and fhew the error of thofe who afcribe the invention of the ftave to him.

Indeed Guido has intimated that in his method of notation, points may be placed as well in the fpaces as on the lines; and for this, as alfo for the confequent reduction of the ftave from eight to five, or rather, for the purpofe of ecclefiaftical notation, to four lines, pofterity are undoubtedly obliged to him.

It will be remembered that the ancient Greek fcale was compofed of tetrachords, and that it exhibits a fucceffion of chords from Proflambanomenos, or A, to Nete hyperboleon, or aa. As to the Proflambanomenos, it was termed Acquifitus or Affumed, and therefore made no part of the tetrachord Hypaton. In profecution of his fcheme of converting the tetrachords into hexachords, with refpect to the loweft tetrachord in the fcale Guido had nothing more to do than to add to it a fingle chord, to which he affixed the Greek letter Γ, and this he termed the durum hexachord, to diftinguifh it from that other beginning at F, in which B is flat, and which therefore is called the molle hexachord: but of this, and alfo of the natural hexachord beginning at C, mention is made before.

The hexachords, conftituted in the manner above defcribed, with the additional improvement of the ftave, and before they were incorporated into the fcale affumed the following form.

DURUM HEXACHORD.

G' A B C D E

NATURAL HEXACHORD.

C D E F G A

MOLLE

MOLLE HEXACHORD.

F G A Bb C D

UT RE MI FA SOL LA

The power or fituation in the fcale, of each of thefe points is fignified by the letters refpectively placed above them : but the intention
of the ftave was to fuperfede the literal fcheme of notation ; it may
therefore be faid, fuppofing the letters away, that each hexachord
is but a repetition of the other two, and that the power of each point
in all the three is fimilar : but the cafe is far otherwife ; for by a contrivance, which fhews the admirable fagacity of the inventor, the
ftave of four lines is rendered capable of expreffing every one of
the three different hexachords which the reformed mufical fcale
requires.

To manifeft this diverfity Guido invented certain characters called
Cliffs, in number three, whereof the firft was Γ, the other two
were the letters C and F : the firft of thefe indicated a progreffion of
founds from the loweft note in the fcale upwards to E : the fecond
denoted a feries from C to A, and the third another feries from F
through Bb to D : thefe cliffs, which were alfo termed claves or
keys, were placed by Guido on the lower line at the head of his
ftave. It is evident from hence, that by the application of the characters Γ, C, F, the power of the fix points ufed to denote the hexachord, were, without the leaft change of their fituation in refpect of
the ftave, made capable of a threefold variety, and confequently required different denominations.

That Guido invented fome method for afcertaining the initial chords
of each of the hexachords is certain, but that he made ufe of the letters, or cliffs, Γ, C, F, for that purpofe, is rather conjecture than fact.
Indeed the contrary feems to be clear from his own words, and that
his method of difcriminating the hexachords was not by the cliffs,
but by making thofe lines of the ftave, which were their proper ftations, of a different colour from the reft. In the Micrologus we
meet with thefe verfes.

> Quafdam lineas fignamus variis coloribus
> Ut quo loco fit fonus mox difcernat oculus ;

i

Ordine

Ordine terciæ vocis fplendens crocus radiat,
Sexta ejus, fed affinis flavo rubet minio.

To underftand which, it is neceffary to obferve that the third
and fixth notes here mentioned are the third and fixth from A ; for
Γ, as has been frequently faid, was an affumed chord : Hypo-
Proflambanomenos is the appellation given to it even by modern
muficians, and for fome ages after its introduction it was not in
ftrictnefs confidered as part of the fcale.   That this is Guido's meaning is clear from the following paffage in the Micrologus : ' We
' make ufe of two colours, viz. yellow and red, which furnifh a
' very ufeful rule for finding the tone and letter of the monochord to
' which every Neuma and note belongs.   There are feven letters
' in the monochord, and wherefoever you fee yellow it is the third,
' and wherever red it is the fixth letter.'   The third and fixth letters
here mentioned are moft evidently the third and fixth from A, the
firft of the feven letters on the monochord, that is to fay C and F,
which are the ftations of two of the cliffs ; and the above citations
inconteftibly prove that to indicate the key of C, Guido made ufe of
a yellow, and for that of F, a red line *.

Hitherto we have confidered the hexachords as the integral parts
of Guido's fyftem, and as independent of each other ; but their ufe,
and indeed the ingenuity and excellence of his invention,' can only
be difcerned in that methodical arrangement of them by means
whereof they are made to coincide with the great or immutable
fyftem : this, as has been fhewn, was comprehended in the Hypaton, Mefon, Diezeugmenon, and Hyperbolcon tetrachords ; for the
tetrachord to which they gave the name Synemmenon was merely
auxiliary, as being fuited to that kind of progreffion only, which
leads through what we now call b flat.   The fyftem of Guido, fuppofing it to terminate as that of the ancients did at aa, and exclufive
of the chord Γ added by him, to contain the bifdiapafon, includes five
hexachords differently conflituted, the molle hexachord being auxiliary, and anfwering to the tetrachord fynemmenon, which five hexachords refpectively have their commencement from Γ, from C, from
F, from G, and from C: but he found it capable of extenfion, and by
adding four chords above aa, and a confequent repetition of the molle

* See an example of this kind in a fubfequent page of this book.

and

and durum hexachords from f and from g, he carried it up to ee, beyond which it was so seldom extended, as to give occasion to a proverbial exclamation, by which even at this day we reprehend the use of hyperbolical modes of speech, viz. ' that was a note above ' e la.' By this addition of chords the hexachords were encreased to seven, that is to say, so many as are necessary for the conjugation of the system included within Γ and ee.

But between the tetrachords of the ancients, and the hexachords of Guido, this difference is most apparent : the former were simply measures of the diatessaron system ; they succeeded each other in an orderly progression through the whole bisdiapason : the hexachord is also, at least in the opinion of the moderns, the measure of a system; but their collateral situation, and the being made as it were to grow the one out of the other, varies the nature of their progression, and points out, in the compass of twenty-two notes, seven gradations or deductions, for so they are termed by the monkish writers, of six notes, each beginning at a different place in the diapason, and yet in all other respects precisely the same. Add to this that the hexachords with the syllables thus adapted to them, become as it were, so many different conjugations, by which we are able to measure and try the musical truth of the several intervals of which they are composed.

The chords contained in the enlarged system of Guido are twenty-two in number, reckoning b in the acutes, and bb in the superacutes : otherwise in strictness they are but twenty, seeing that b and ♮ can never occur in one and the same hexachord : for the designation of them two staves of five lines each are necessary ; and in that conjoint position which the ascending scale requires, the hexachords will have this appearance *.

---

* The representations of Guido's system are many and various ; for he not having exhibited it by way of diagram, succeeding writers have thought themselves at liberty to exercise their several inventions in schemes and figures to explain it. Franchinus, and others after him, have enclosed each column of syllables, as they apply to Γ, and the letters above it, in two parallel lines, with a point at bottom, exactly like an organ-pipe ; but as there is not the least analogy to warrant this form, others have rejected it. Peter Aron and others have placed the hexachords in a collateral situation, resembling the

tables of the decalogue. Bontempi makes use of the following scheme of the hexachords
to represent their mutations, and dependence on each other. Hist. Muf. pag. 183.

1536	ee	.	.	.	la
1728	dd	.	.	.	la fol
1944	cc	.	.	.	fol fa
2048	bb♭	.	.	.	mi
2187	bb	.	.	.	fa
2304	aa	.	.	.	la mi re
2592	g	.	.	.	fol re ut
2916	f	.	.	.	fa ut
3972	e	.	.	.	la mi
3456	d	.	.	.	la fol re
3888	c	.	.	.	fol fa ut
4096	♭	.	.	.	mi
4374	♮	.	.	.	fa
4608	a	.	.	.	la mi re
5184	G	.	.	.	fol re ut
5832	F	.	.	.	fa ut
6144	E	.	.	.	la mi
6912	D	.	.	.	fol re
7776	C	.	.	.	fa ut
8192	◻	.	.	.	mi
9216	A	.	.	.	re
10368	Γ	.	.	.	ut

It may seem strange, as Guido has characterised the durum hexachord by the key Γ, that
that of F should be the first that occurs in the scale; but the reason of this is, that the
placing of F on the fourth line of the stave, does as much determine the series as Γ on the
last would have done; the same reason may serve for postponing the clisf C to F. As to

3

The above scheme is intended to shew the situation of the notes on the lines and spaces, and the relation which the hexachords bear each

g. It occurs as soon as is necessary, and not before; and here it may be remarked that g is situated on the third line above C, as C is on the third line above F. Farther, a stave of five lines, with the cliff F on the fourth, is supposed to signify the five lower lines of the scale. One with C on the third, the five above F inclusive, and one with g on the second, the five above C. All this will most clearly appear from the two foregoing schemes, which exhibit an example of ingenuity and sagacity that has stood the test of ages, and is worthy the admiration of all men.

Many have thought Guido's scheme defective in that it gives no syllable to F. Dr. Wallis was of this opinion, and says what a wonder it is that he did not apply to it the syllable sa, from the first word of the Adonic verse Sancte Joannes? Mersennus, Harmonie Universelle, pag. 183, seems to have thought much in the same manner, by his adding the syllable si, which is used by the French at this day. The original introduction of this syllable is by him and other writers attributed to one Le Maire, a French musician, who says he laboured for thirty years in vain to bring it into practice; but that he was no sooner dead than all the musicians of his country made use of it. Notwithstanding which the general opinion is that the syllable si was introduced into the scale by Ericius Puteanus of Lion, who lived about the year 1580, and wrote a treatise on music entitled Musathena.

This is in substance the account which Monf. Brossard has given of the introduction of the syllable si; but another writer, Monf. Bourdelot, has given a very different account of this matter; for he relates that about the year 1675 a certain Cordelier introduced the syllable si into the scale. He seems however to doubt the fact, as being founded only on tradition; and goes on to relate that the abbé de la Louette, master of the choir of the cathedral church of Paris, had assured him that the syllable in question was invented, or perhaps a second time brought into practice, by one Metru, a famous singing-master in Paris about the year 1676. Bourdelot adds that Le Moine, an excellent lutenist, of sixty years practice, had assured him that he knew Metru very well, and that he introduced the syllable si; and that he remembered also a Cordelier of the convent of Ave Maria, who had made some variation in the ancient scale about the latter end of the last century. For these reasons Bonet inclines to think that the honour of the invention might be due to the Cordelier, but that the merit of reviving it is to be ascribed to Metru. But whichsoever of the above relations is true, it is pretty certain that both Mersennus and Brossard are mistaken in what they say respecting the invention of the syllable si by Le Maire.

The same author, Bourdelot, insinuates, that notwithstanding the use of the syllable si is much approved of by the French musicians, yet in Italy they disdain to make use of it, as being the invention of a Frenchman. Histoire de la Musique et de ses Effets, par Bourdelot, Amsterd. 1725, tom. I. pag. 17.

It seems that the musicians of other countries have been aware of the necessity of a seventh syllable in order to get rid of the difficulties which the mutations, as they are called, are attended with in the practice of singing; for in the Musica de la Musica of Andrea Lorente of Alcala, published in 1672, we find the syllable si applied to b in the progression from C to c.

And here it may not be improper to observe, that the Italians at this day make use of the syllable po instead of ut, as being more easy of pronunciation; this variation may be traced back to the year 1678, and is to be found in a treatise herein before cited, entitled Armonia Gregoriani, written by Girolamo Cantone, and printed at Turin in that year.

Mersennus, Harm. Univers. pag. 183, intimates that for expressing the semitone between A and B b, some of the musicians of his country made use of the syllable za, that of si being appropriated to B b; but this distinction seems not to prevail at this day. Monf. Loulie, the author of Elements ou Principes de Musique, printed at Amsterdam, 1698, rejecting the syllable za, has retained only si; and this method of solmisation is practised throughout France.

to the others : this that follows, compounded of two schemes, the one
of Bontempi, and the other of Doctor Wallis, contains the reformed
scale of Guido in a collateral situation with that of the ancients.

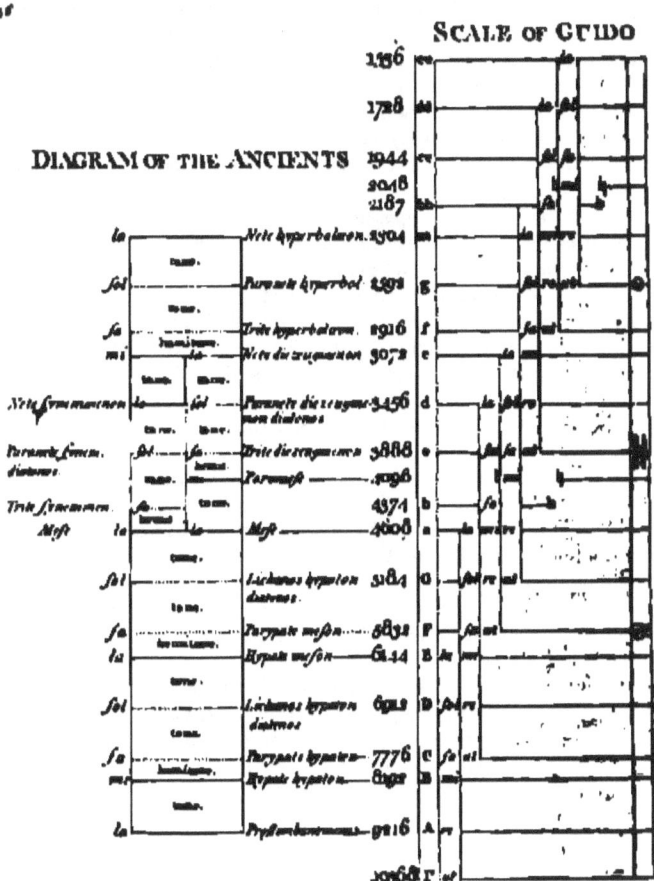

SCALE OF GUIDO

DIAGRAM OF THE ANCIENTS

To the lower chord the moderns have given the name Hypo-Prof-lambanomenos; the number assigned to it may, by the rule herein before given, be easily found, it being nine of those parts of which 9216 is eight, and shews the ratio of Γ to A to be sesquioctave, in the proportion of 9 to 8. The same rule will also suggest the means of bringing out the numbers proper to the notes added to the scale by Guido, which are those from a a upwards; for, to begin with b h, it is in a subduplicate ratio to b, its number therefore will be the half of 4374, that is to say 2187. The next note b h having the same ratio to b, will in like manner require the subduplicate of 4096, which is 2048.

From the foregoing disposition of the tetrachords we learn the true names of the several sounds that compose the system; for it is observable that though in fact each septenary contained in it is but a repetition of the former, and that therefore the generical name of each chord is repeated, yet their specific differences in respect of situation are admirably distinguished by the different names assigned to each: thus, for instance, the lower chords is Γ ut, or Gamut, but its replicate is for a very obvious reason termed g sol re ut ; the replicates of A re are a la mi re, those of C fa ut are c sol fa ut and c sol fa; those of D sol re, d la sol re, and d la sol ; and here it is to be remarked that as well the recision as the addition of a syllable expresses the situation of a note ; for the last of the seven hexachords cuts off a syllable from the names of the three upper chords, leaving to the uppermost one only, e la, as may be seen in the example.

As a farther improvement of his system, and to facilitate the practice of solmisation, for so we are to call the conjugation of any given cantilena by means of the syllables ut, re, mi, fa, sol, la, most authors relate that he made use of the left hand, calling the top of the thumb Γ, and applying the names of the rest of the notes to the joints of each finger, giving to the top of the middle finger, as being the highest situation, the note e la, as in the following page is shewn.

But

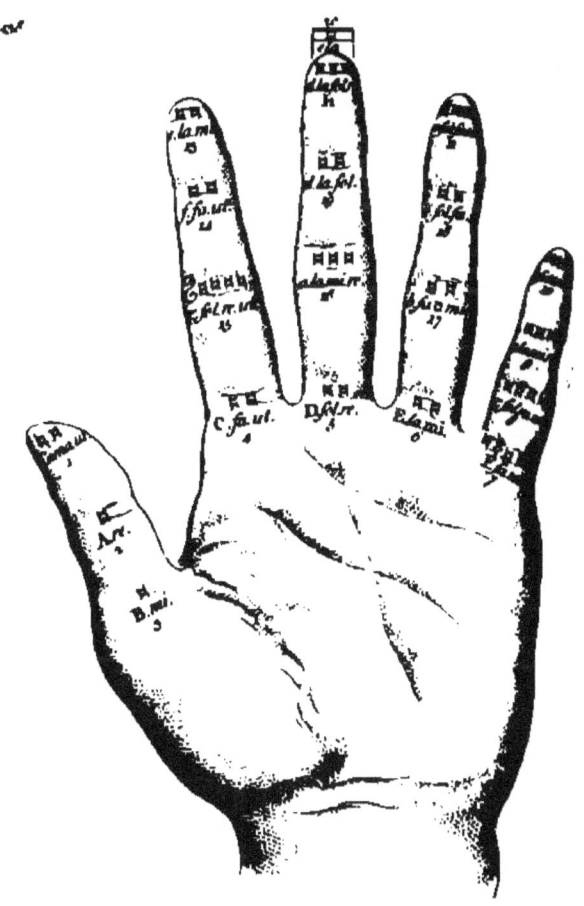

But to warrant this opinion there seems to be no better authority than bare tradition; for in no part of Guido's writings does the mention of the hand occur: nay it seems from a passage in the manuscript of Waltham Holy Cross, herein before cited, that the hand was an invention posterior in time to that when Guido is supposed to have lived *; its use was to instruct boys in the names and respective situations of the notes of his scale; and for choosing the left hand rather than the right this notable reason is given, ' that it being ' nearest the heart, the instruction derived from thence is likely to ' make the deeper impression on the minds of learners.'

As to the precise time when he lived, authors are very much divided.   Zaccone and others assert it to have been about the year of Christ 960; Baronius, that it was about 1022; Alstedius, and after him Bontempi, place him under pope Leo IX. and the emperor Henry III. in the year 1049; but Sigebert testifies that he flourished in the time of the emperor Conrade the younger, and that 1028 was the precise year when the reformation of Guido took place; and for this opinion we have also the authority of Trithemius †. But Guido has decided this question in a relation given by him of his invitation to Rome by John XX. and he it is agreed began his pontificate in the year 1024.

C H A P.   VIII.

SOME account of Guido is to be gathered from his writings, particularly an epistle from him to his friend Michael, a monk of Pomposa, and the tract to which that is an introduction, entitled Argumentum novi Cantus inveniendi : from these, and some scattered passages to be met with in ancient manuscripts, the following memoirs are collected.

He was a native of Arezzo, a city in Tuscany, and having been taught the practice of music in his youth, and probably retained as a chorister in the service of the Benedictine monastery founded in that city, he became a monk professed, and a brother of the order of St. Benedict :' the state of learning was in those times very low, and the

* Kircher, in the Musurgia, tome I. pag. 115, says this expressly.
† De Viris illustr. ord. Bened. lib. II. cap. 74.

l   eccle-

ecclefiaftics had very few fubjects for ftudy, if we except theological controverfy, church hiftory, logic, and aftrology, which was
looked on by them as the moft confiderable of the mathematical
fciences : thefe engaged the attention of fuch members of thofe fra-
ternities as were endued with the moft active, not to fay contentious,
fpirits ; while the exercifes of devotion, the contemplating the lives
of faints, and the qualifying themfelves for the due difcharge of the
choral duty, employed thofe of a more afcetic and ingenuous turn of
mind. Voffius makes Guido to have been at firft a monk in the monaftery of St. Leufred in Normandy *; but this is by a miftake,
which will be accounted for hereafter ; fo that the only places of his
fettlement, of which we can fpeak with certainty, are the Benedictine monaftery of Arezzo, the city where he was born, and that of
Pompofa in the duchy of Ferrara.

In this retirement he feems to have devoted himfelf to the ftudy of
mufic, particularly the fyftem of the ancients, and above all to reform
their method of notation. The difficulties that attended the inftruction
of youth in the church-offices were fo great, that, as he himfelf fays,
ten years were generally confumed barely in acquiring the knowledge
of the plain-fong ; and this confideration induced him to labour after
fome amendment, fome method that might facilitate inftruction, and
enable thofe employed in the choral office to perform the duties of it
in a correct and decent manner. If we may credit thofe legendary
accounts that are extant in old monkifh manufcripts, we fhould believe he was affifted in his pious intention by immediate communications from heaven : fome fpeak of the invention of the fyllables as the
effect of infpiration ; and Guido himfelf feems to have been of the
fame opinion, by his faying it was revealed to him by the Lord ; or
as fome interpret his words, in a dream ; but graver hiftorians fay, that
being at vefpers in the chapel of his monaftery, it happened that one
of the offices appointed for that day was the above-mentioned hymn
to St. John Baptift, written by Paulus Diaconus, and that the hearing
thereof fuggefted this notable improvement.

We muft fuppofe that the converting the tetrachords into hexachords had been the fubject of frequent contemplation with Guido,
and that a method of difcriminating the tones and femitones was the

* De Scient. Mathem. cap. xxli. § 7.

one thing wanting to complete his invention. During the performance of the hymn he remarked the iteration of the words, and the frequent returns of UT, RE, MI, FA, SOL, LA : he obferved likewife a diffimilarity between the clofenefs of the fyllable MI, and the broad open found of FA, which he thought could not fail to imprefs upon the mind a lafting idea of their congruity, and immediately conceived a thought of applying thefe fix fyllables to his new formed hexachord.

Struck with the difcovery, he retired to his ftudy, and having perfected his fyftem, began to introduce it into practice : the perfons to whom he communicated it were the brethren of his own monaftery, from whom it met with but a cold reception, which in the Epiftle to his friend, above-mentioned, he afcribes undoubtedly to its true caufe, envy; however, his intereft with the abbot, and his employment in the chapel, gave him an opportunity of trying the efficacy of his method on the boys who were training up for the choral fervice, and it exceeded the moft fanguine expectation.

The fame of Guido's invention foon fpred abroad, and his method of inftruction was adopted by the clergy of other countries : we are told by Kircher that Hermannus, bifhop of Hamburg, and Elvericus, bifhop of Ofnabrug made ufe of it ; and by the authors of the Hiftoire Litteraire de la France *, that it was received in that country, and taught in all the monafteries in the kingdom. It is certain that the reputation of his great fkill in mufic had excited in the pope a defire to fee and converfe with him, of which, and of his going to Rome for that purpofe, and the reception he met with from the pontiff, himfelf has given a circumftantial account of in the epiftle before cited,

The particulars of this relation are very curious, and as we have his own authority, there is no room to doubt the truth of it. It feems that John XX. or, as fome writers compute, the nineteenth pope of that name, having heard of the fame of Guido's fchool, and conceiving a defire to fee him, fent three meffengers to invite him to Rome ; upon their arrival it was refolved by the brethren of the monaftery that he fhould go thither attended by Grimaldo the abbot, and Peter the chief of the canons of the church of

* Tum. VII. pag. 143. 144.

Arezzo. Arriving at Rome he was prefented to the holy father, and by him received with great kindnefs. The pope had feveral converfations with him, in all which he interrogated him as to his knowledge in mufic; and upon fight of an antiphonary which Guido had brought with him, marked with the fyllables agreeable to his new invention, the pope looked on it as a kind of prodigy, and ruminating on the doctrines delivered by Guido, would not ftir from his feat till he had learned perfectly to fing off a verfe; upon which he declared that he could not have believed the efficacy of the method if he had not been convinced by the experiment he had himfelf made of it. The pope would have detained him at Rome, but labouring under a bodily diforder, and fearing an injury to his health from the air of the place, and the heats of the fummer, which was then approaching, Guido left that city upon a promife to revifit it, and explain to his holinefs the principles of his new fyftem. On his return homewards he made a vifit to the abbot of Pompofa, a town in the duchy of Ferrara, who was very earneft to have Guido fettle in the monaftery of that place, to which invitation it feems he yielded, being, as he fays, defirous of rendering fo great a monaftery ftill more famous by his ftudies there.

Here it was that he compofed a tract on mufic, intitled Micrologus, i. e. a fhort difcourfe, which he dedicated to Theodald, bifhop of Arezzo, and finifhed, as he himfelf at the end of it tells us, under the pontificate of John XX. and in the thirty-fourth year of his age. Voffius fpeaks alfo of another mufical treatife written by him, and dedicated to the fame perfon.

Divers others mention alfo his being engaged in the controverfy with Berenger about the Euchariſt, particularly Merfennus and Voffius; the latter of whom, who, by the manner in which he has fpoken of Guido elfewhere, can hardly be fuppofed to have miſtaken another perfon for him, fays exprefsly that in the year 1070, namely, in the time of Gregory VII. flourifhed Guido, or Guidmundus, by country an Aretine, firft a monk of the monaftery of St. Leufred, and afterwards a cardinal of the church of Rome, and archbifhop of Averfa; that while he was a monk he wrote two books on mufic to the bifhop Theodald, the firft in profe, the other partly in heroic verfe, and partly in rhythmical trochaics; and that he is the fame who
who

who wrote againſt Berengarius three books concerning the body and blood of our Lord in the ſacrament of the Euchariſt *. Trithemius refers him to the year 1330, and Sigebert to 1028, which latter ſpeaks alſo of the muſical notes found out by him.

Du Pin, who in his Eccleſiaſtical Hiſtory has given an account of Berenger and his errors, has enumerated the ſeveral authors that have written againſt him ; among theſe he mentions Guimond or Guitmond, biſhop of Averſa, as one who, in oppoſition to Berenger, maintained the real preſence of the body and blood of Jeſus Chriſt in the Euchariſt. Nay, he goes ſo far as to cite ſeveral books of his writing in the controverſy with Berenger, as namely, a treatiſe De Veritate Euchariſtiæ, wherein he charges him with maintaining, among other errors, the nullity of infant baptiſm, and the lawfulneſs of promiſcuous embraces.

Suppoſing this to be true, and Guimond and Guido to be one and the ſame perſon, the generality of writers have done his memory an injury in repreſenting Guido as ſimply a monk, who was not only a dignitary of the church, but an archbiſhop, and a member of the ſacred college. But it ſeems that Voſſius and thoſe whom he has followed are miſtaken in theſe particulars : Bayle has detected this error, and has ſet the matter right, by relating that Guido and Guitmond were nearly contemporaries, but that it was the latter who was the monk of St. Leufred, in the dioceſs of Evreux in Normandy, afterwards biſhop of Averſa in Italy, and at length a cardinal, and who wrote three books De Veritate Corporis et Sanguinis Chriſti in Euchariſtia adverſus Berengarium, which, he adds, have been printed ſeparately, and in the Bibliotheca Patrum †.

Moſt of the authors who have taken occaſion to mention Guido, ſpeak of the Micrologus as containing the ſum of his doctrine : what are the contents of the Micrologus will hereafter be related ; but if is in a ſmall tract, intitled Argumentum novi Cantus inveniendi, that his declaration of the uſe of the ſyllables, with their ſeveral mutations, and, in ſhort, his whole doctrine of ſolmiſation, is to be found. This tract makes part of an epiſtle to a very dear and intimate friend of

* De Scientiis Mathem. cap. xxii. § 7.
† Art. Aretin [Guy] in not. Vide alſo Hiſt. Litter. de France, tom. VIII. Guimond Evèque d'Averſe, pag. 561, where this error is taken notice of, and rectified.

Guido, whom he addreſſes thus, ' Beatiſſimo atque dulciſſimo fratri
' Michaëli ;' * and at whoſe requeſt the tract itſelf ſeems to have been
compoſed.   In this epiſtle, after lamenting very pathetically the exceeding envy that his fame had excited, and the oppoſition that his
method of inſtruction met with, he relates the motives of his journey
to Rome, and the reception he met with there, and then proceeds
to an explanation of his doctrine.

It ſeems that in the time of Guido, muſical inſtruments were either
ſcarce or ill tuned, and that the only method of acquiring a true
knowledge of the intervals was by means of the monochord ; for both
in the Micrologus, and in this ſhorter work, of which we are now
ſpeaking, the author gives directions how to conſtruct and divide
properly this inſtrument ; but upon the whole he ſeems to condemn
the uſe of it, comparing thoſe who depend on it to blind men ; for
this reaſon he diſcovers to his friend a method of finding out an
unknown cantus, which he ſays he tried on the boys under his care,
who thereby became able to ſing in no greater a ſpace of time than
three days what they could not have maſtered by any other method in
leſs than many weeks : and this method is no other than the applying
the ſyllables to the hexachords in the manner before directed.   But
here perhaps it may be fitting that he ſhould ſpeak for himſelf, and
the following is a tranſlation of his own words.

' I have known many acute philoſophers, not only Italians, but
' French, Germans, and even Greeks themſelves, who, though they
' have been ſought out for as maſters in this art, have truſted to this
' rule, the monochord alone ; but yet I cannot ſay that I think ei-
' ther muſicians or ſingers can be made by the help of it.   A ſinger
' ought to find out and retain in memory the elevations and depreſ-
' ſions of notes, with their ſeveral diverſities and properties ; and
' this by our method you may attain to do, and alſo be able to com-
' municate the means of doing it to others; for if you commit to
' memory any Neuma, ſo as that it may immediately occur to you
' when you find it in any cantus, then you will directly and without
' heſitation be able to ſound it : and this Neuma, whatever it be,
' being retained in your memory, may with eaſe be applied to any
' new cantus of the ſame kind.   The following is what I made uſe
' of in teaching the boys.

* The copy inſerted in Baronius reads, ' Chariſſimo atque dulciſſimo, &c.

' UT

UT queant laxis REfonare fibris
MIra geftorum FAmuli tuorum,
SOLve polluti LAbii reatum
Sancte Joannes *

* Martini, in his Storia della Mufica, vol. I. pag. 180, from a manufcript in his pofseffion, written in praise of Guido, and, as he conjectures, in the fixteenth century, has given the notes to this hymn in the Gregorian characters in the following order.

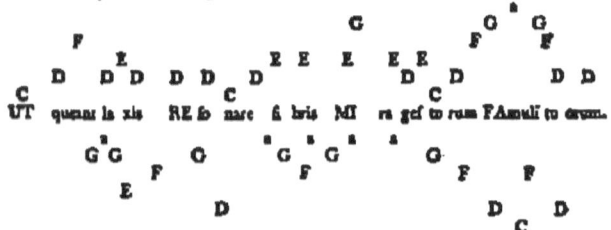

which he has rendered them in modern characters:

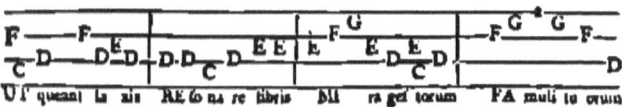

Pedro Cerone and Berardi, the one in his treatife De la Mufica, lib. II. cap. 44, and the other in his Mifcellanea Muficale, part II. pag. 55, give it in this form.

which they both render thus;

UT

' In the above fymphony you fee fix different particles, which are
' to be applied to as many different notes ; and whenever the finger
' is able to apply thefe to fuch of the fix notes as they properly be-
' long to, he will be able to fing his devotions with eafe. When
' you hear any Neuma, examine in your own mind which of thefe
' particles does beft agree with its ending, fo as that the final note
' of the Neuma, and the principal particles may be equifonous,
' whereby you will be certain that the Neuma ends in that note with
' which the particle agreeing therewith begins: but if you under-
' take any written cantus which you never faw before, you muft
' fing it often over, that you may be able to end every Neuma por-
' perly, fo that the end of each Neuma may in the fame manner be
' joined with the beginning of the particle which begins by the fame
' note in which the Neuma ends. By this method you will pre-
' fently be able to fing any new cantus by the notes; and
' when you hear any that is not noted, you will foon perceive
' how it is to be written down, in the doing whereof this rule
' will greatly affift you. I have fet down fome fhort fymphonies
' through every note of thefe particles, and when you fhall carefully
' have looked them over, you will be glad to find out the depref-
' fions and elevations of every note in order in the beginnings of
' thefe particles: but if you fhould have a mind to attemperate cer-
' tain particles of different fymphonies by connexion, you may by a
' very fhort and eafy rule learn all the difficult and manifold varieties
' of Neumas ; but thefe cannot all be fo well explained by letter,
' and would be more plainly opened in a familiar colloquy.

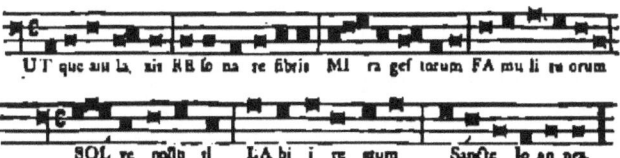

UT que au la, xit RB fo na re fibris MI ra gef torum FA mu li re orum

SOL ve poffu tl LA bi i re atum Sanfte Jo an nea.

Berardi adds, that the method of notation by the letters of Gregory, as in the above
example, was ufed in his time in Hungary, and other parts of Germany. He alfo cites as
paffage from the Practica Mufica of Hermann Finck, or Fink, to prove that thefe were the
notes which Guido applied to the hymn ' Ut queant laxis.' Fink has afferted this fact on
the authority of Albertus Magnus, who wrote on mufic, and lived in the thirteenth
century.

A

A
F Alme rector mores nobis facrato ; Summe pater fer-
D

A
F vis tuis miferere ; Salus noftra honor nofter efto Deus.
D

A
F Deus, judex juftus fortis, et patiens : Tibi totus fer-
D

A
F vit mundus uni, Deus.   Stabunt jufti ante dominum
D

A
F Semper læti : Domino laudes omnis creatura dicat *.

He then proceeds thus : ' In writing we have twenty-three letters,
' but in every cantus we have only feven notes ; for as there are
' feven days in a week, fo are there feven notes in mufic, for all that
' are added above are the fame, and are fung alike through the
' whole, differing in nothing but that they are founded doubly
' higher.   We fay there are feven grave and feven acute, and that
' the fecond order of feven letters is written different from the other
' in this manner.

    a   b   c   d   e   f   g
    A   B   C   D   E   F   G

Towards the end of this tract Guido directs the manner of conftructing and dividing the monochord, which becaufe he has done it
more at large in the Micrologus, we forbear to fpeak of here ; the
reft of the epiftle is taken up with a fhort difquifition on the ecclefiaftical tones, at the clofe whereof he recommends the perufal of his
Micrologus, and alfo a Manual, written with great perfpicuity by the

   * It is fuppofed that the above are the initial fentences of fome hymns or other offices
anciently ufed in the church, and which were part of the choral fervice.   Guido has intimated that thefe examples can hardly be rendered intelligible without a verbal explanation ;
but it is conjectured by the letters D F A, that they are to be fung in the firft of the ecclefiaftical tones, that having A for its dominant, and D for its final.

most

moſt reverend abbot Obdo *, from whoſe example he owns he has
ſomewhat deviated, chooſing, as he ſays, to follow Boetius, though he
gives it as his opinion that his work is fitter for Philoſophers than
Singers.

The Micrologus, though, as its title imports, a ſhort diſcourſe, is
conſiderably longer than the former tract. The title of it, as given
by ſome tranſcriber of his manuſcript, is, Micrologus, id eſt brevis
Sermo in Muſica, editus a Domine Guidone piiſſimo Monacho et peri-
tiſſimo Muſico.

In this tract too the author complains very feelingly of the envy of
the times, and the malignity of his detractors.

In the dedication of the Micrologus to Theodald, the biſhop of
Arezzo, his dioceſan, Guido confeſſes the goodneſs of his patron in
vouchſafing to become his aſſociate in the ſtudy of the Holy Scriptures,
which he attributes to a deſire to comfort and ſupport him under the
weight of his bodily and mental infirmities, and acknowledges, that
if his endeavours are productive of any good to mankind, the merit of
it is due to his patron, and not to him. He ſays that when muſic
was employed in the ſervice of the church, he laboured in the art not
in vain, ſeeing that his diſcoveries in it were made public by the authority, and under the protection of his patron, who as be had regulated the church of St. Donatus, over which it was his office to pre-
ſide, ſo had he rendered the ſervants thereof, by thoſe privileges by
him conferred on them, reſpectable amongſt the clergy. He adds,
that it is matter of ſurprize to him to find that the boys of the church
of Arezzo ſhould, in the art of modulation, excel the old men of other
churches ; and profeſſes to explain the rules of the art for the honour
of their houſe, not in the manner of the philoſophers, but ſo as to be
a ſervice to their church, and a help to their boys, for that the art
had a long time lain hid, and, though very difficult, had never been
ſufficiently explained.

The dedication is followed by a prologue, in which the author attributes to the grace of God the ſucceſs of his endeavours to facilitate the practice of muſic ; which ſucceſs he ſays was ſo great, that
the boys taught by his rules, and exerciſed therein for the ſpace of a
month, were able to ſing at firſt ſight, and without heſitation, muſic

* Ono of Cluni, of whom, and alſo of his Enchiridion, ſee an account in chap. 6.
of this book.

they had never heard before, in such a manner as to surprise most people.

It appears, as well from the epistle to his friend Michael, as from the Micrologus, that in the opinion of Guido the only way of coming at a knowledge of the intervals so as to sing them truly, was by means of the monochord; for which reason, though he condemns the use of it for any other purpose than the bare initiation of learners in the rudiments of singing, he constantly recommends the study of it to young people. In the very beginning of the Micrologus he says,
' Whoever desires to be acquainted with our exercise, must learn
' such songs as are set down in our notes, and practise his hand in
' the use of the monochord, and often meditate on our rules, until
' he is perfect in the power and nature of the notes, and is able to
' sing well at first sight; for the notes, which are the foundation of
' this art, are best to be discerned in the monochord, by which also
' we are taught how art, imitating nature, has distinguished them.'
Guido proposes that the monochord shall contain twenty-one notes, concerning the disposition whereof he speaks thus.

' First set down Γ Greek, which is added by the moderns, then
' let follow the first seven letters of the alphabet, in capitals, in this
' manner, A, B, C, D, E, F, G; and after these the same seven let-
' ters in the smaller characters; the first series denotes the graver,
' and the latter the acuter sounds. Nevertheless, among the smaller
' letters we insert occasionally ♭ or ♮, the one character being round,
' the other square, thus a, b, ♮, c, d, e, f, g; to these add the tetra-
' chord of superacutes, in which b is doubled in the same manner,
' aa, bb, ♮♮, cc, dd, ee. These letters make in all twenty-two,
' Γ, A, B, C, D, E, F, G, a, b, ♮, c, d, e, f, g, aa, bb, ♮♮, cc, dd,
' ee, the disposition whereof has hitherto been so perplexed as not to
' be intelligible, but it shall here be made most clear and plain, even
' to boys.'

For the division of the monochord he gives the following directions.

' Gamma Γ being placed at one extremity of the monochord, di-
' vide the space between that and the end of the chord into nine
' parts, and at the end of the first ninth part place A, from whence
' the ancients fixed their beginning; then from A divide the space
' to the end of the chord into nine parts, and in the same manner

VOL. I.   M m m   ' place

' place B ; then returning to Γ, divide the whole space to the end
' into four parts, and at the end of the first fourth part place C. In
' the same manner as from Γ you found C, by a division of four
' parts, you will from A find D ; from B, E ; from C, F ; from D,
' G ; from E, a acute ; from F, b round ; the rest that follow are
' easily found by a bisection of the remaining parts of the line in
' the manner above directed, as for example, in the middle be-
' tween B and the end place ♭. In like manner from C you
' will find a new c ; from D a new d ; from E another e ; from
' F another f ; and from G another g ; and the rest in the same
' manner, proceeding upwards or downwards, ad infinitum, un-
' less the precepts of the art should by their authority restrain it.
' Out of the many and divers divisions of the monochord, I have set
' down this in particular, it being easily to be understood, and when
' once understood is hardly to be forgotten.—Here follows another
' method of dividing the monochord, which, though not so easily to
' be retained, is more expeditiously performed. Divide the whole
' into nine parts, the first part will terminate in A, the second is va-
' cant ; the third in D, the fourth vacant ; the fifth a, the sixth d,
' the seventh aa, the rest vacant. Again, divide from A to the end
' into nine parts ; the first part will terminate in B, the second will be
' vacant, the third E, the fourth vacant, the fifth ♭, the sixth e, the
' seventh ♭♭, the rest vacant : again, divide the whole from Γ to the
' end into four parts, the first will terminate in C, the second in G,
' the third in g, and the fourth finishes. Divide from C to the end
' likewise into four parts, the first part will end in F, the second in
' c, the third in cc, and the fourth finishes. Divide from F into
' four parts, the first will end in b round, the second in f : divide
' from b round into four parts, in the second you will find bb round,
' the rest are vacant. Divide from aa into four parts, the first will
' be dd, the rest are vacant. For the disposition of the notes these
' two methods of division are sufficient ; the first is the more easy to
' be remembered, the second the more expeditious.'

Upon this division of the monochord he observes, that there appears a greater distance between some of the notes, as Γ, A, and A,
B, than between others, as B, C : he says the greater distance is called a tone, and the lesser a semitone, from semis an half ; that a ditone is an interval consisting of two tones, as C, D, E, and that
that is called a semiditone which contains only a tone and half, as
from

from D to F. He says that when between any two notes there occurs in any order whatever, two tones and a semitone, as from A to D, from B to E, and from C to F, the extreme sounds make a diateſſaron, but that a diapente is greater by a tone; as when between any two notes there occur three tones and a semitone, as from A to E, or from C to G. He reckons up six conſonances, that is to ſay, the tone, semitone, ditone, semiditone, diateſſaron, and diapente, to which number he ſays may alſo be added the diapaſon as a ſeventh; but that as it is ſeldom introduced, it is not ſo commonly ranked among them [*].

In the ſeventh chapter of the Micrologus the author treats of the affinity of notes, or, in other words, of the conſonances; thoſe of the diateſſaron and diapente he explains by the following figure.

A   B   C   D   E   F   G   a   ♭   c

In the eighth he ſhews the affinity between ♭ and ♮, and diſtinguiſhes between the diateſſaron and diapente in this diagram.

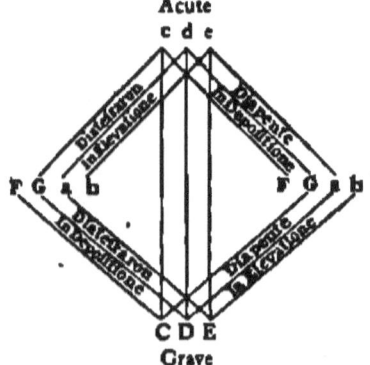

Acute
c d e

F G a ♭   F G a ♭

C D E
Grave

* The manuſcript moſt certainly be erroneous in this place, for the ſemitone can in no ſenſe whatever be deemed a conſonance; and as to the diapaſon, it is ſo far from being ſeldom introduced, that it is the moſt uſual and perfect of all the conſonances.

In the twelfth and thirteenth chapters he speaks of the division of
the four modes into eight, and says that as there are eight parts of
speech, and eight forms of blessedness, i. e. beatitudes, so ought
there to be eight modes in music.   In the fourteenth chapter
he treats more particularly of the modes, which he calls Tropes,
and of the effects of music : of these he says their properties are so
different, that in the same manner as a person accustomed to different
countries is able out of several men placed before him, to say ' this
' is a Spaniard, this an Italian, this a German, and this other a
' Frenchman ;' so may one that is skilled in music by their diversi-
ties distinguish the tropes.   Farther he ascribes to the tropes different
properties, for ' one person,' says he, ' delights in the broken leaps
' of the second authentic ; another in the softness of the third plagal ;
' a third shall be delighted with the garrulity of the fourth authen-
' tic, and another shall approve the mellifluous sweetness of the
' fourth plagal.'   As to the power of music, he says it is so great as
to cure many diseases of the human body ; he cites a relation of a
frantic person who was restored to reason by the music of Asclepiades
the physician ; and mentions also that a certain other person was by
the sound of the lyre, so stirred up to lust, that he attempted to force
into the chamber of a young woman with intent to violate her
chastity, but that the musician, immediately changing the mode,
caused him to desist from his purpose.

C H A P.   IX.

ACCORDING to Guido, cap. xv. four things are required in every
    cantus, sounds, consonances, neumas, and distinctions : from
sounds proceed consonances, from consonances neumas, and from
neumas distinctions : this it seems was the ancient scholastic division
of vocal music, and it is adopted by all the monkish writers on the art.
A Neuma is the smallest particle of a cantus, and is elsewhere said
to signify as many notes as can be sung in one respiration.   By
distinctions the author seems to mean nothing more than the different

ferent meafures of time, which, for ought that any where appears to
the contrary, were regulated folely by the metre of the verfe to
which the notes were fung. Speaking of neumas, he fays they may
be reciprocated, or return by the fame fleps as they proceeded by;
and adds that a cantus is faid to be metrical when it fcans truly,
which, if it be right, it will do even if fung by itfelf. Neumas, he
fays, fhould correfpond to neumas, and diflinctions to diflinctions,
according to the perfectly fweet method of Ambrofius. Farther he
fays that the refemblance between metres and fongs is not fmall, for
that neumas anfwer to feet, and diflinctions to verfes; the neuma
anfwers to the dactyl, fpondee, or iambic; the diflinction to the
tetrameter, the pentameter, or the hexameter, and the like. He
adds, ' Every cantus fhould agree with the fubject to which it is
' adapted, whether it be grave, tranquil, jocund, or exulting; and
' that towards the end of every diflinction the notes fhould be thinly
' difpofed, that being the place of refpiration; for we fee that when
' race-horfes approach the end of the courfe they abate of their fpeed,
' and move as if wearied.'

Cap. xvi. he treats of the manifold variety of founds and neumas,
and fays that it ought not to feem wonderful that fuch a variety
fhould arife from fo few notes, fince from a few letters fyllables are
formed, which, though not innumerable, do yet produce an infinite
number of parts. ' How many kinds of metre' adds he, 'arife out of a
' few feet, and by how many varieties is each capable of diverfifica-
' tion? but this he fays is the province of the grammarians.' He
proceeds to fhew what different neumas may be formed from the fix
confonances; he affumes that every neuma, or, as we fhould now fay,
every paffage, muft neceffarily either afcend or defcend; an afcending neuma he terms Arfis, a defcending, Thefis; thefe he fays may
be conjoined: and farther he fays that by means of a total or partial
elevation or depreffion of any neuma, different combinations may be
formed, and a great variety of melody produced.

In cap. xvii. he lays it down as a rule, that as whatever is fpoken
may be written, fo there can be no cantus formed but what may be
defigned by letters; and here he exhibits a rule for a kind of extem-
poraneous mufical compofition, which muft doubtlefs appear very
ftrange to a modern: he fays in finging no found can be uttered but
by

by means of one or other of the five vowels, and that from their
changes a sweet concord will enfue; he therefore firft directs the
placing the letters of the monochord, and the vowels under them in
this order :

     Γ   A   B   C   D   E   F   g   a   b   c   d   e   f   g   a

     a   e   i   o   u   a   e   i   o   u   a   e   i   o   u   a

And, to exemplify their ufe, recommends the taking fome fuch
known fentence as this :

Sancte Joannes, meritorum tuorum copias, nequeo digne canere.

In this example the vowels determine the mufic; for as in the
above fcheme the power of each found is transferred to its correfpondent vowel, the fucceflion of the vowels will exhibit a feries of
founds to which every fyllable may be fung.

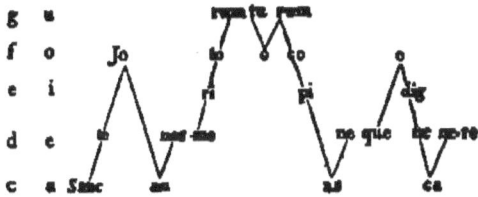

It is clear from the connection between the vowels and the letters
of the monochord, that the diapente here made ufe of is taken from
among the acutes; becaufe in the difpofition above made, the vowel
a anfwers to Γ; but had he chofen the graves for an example, the
progreffion of the cantus had been precifely the fame; for as d is to
c, fo is A to Γ, and as f is to c, fo is C to Γ; as g is to c, fo is D to
Γ, and fo of the reft.

This it muft be confeffed is but a fortuitous kind of melody; it feems
however to have fuited well enough with the fimplicity of the times,
which affords us no reafon to believe that the art of compofing mufic

6   was

was arrived at any great degree of perfection. By the rule here given the above cantus may eafily be rendered into modern notes, in which it will have this appearance.

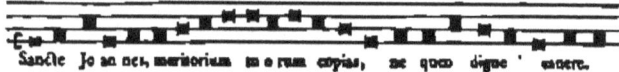

Sancte Jo an nes, meritorium in e rum copias, ae quo digue * eanere.

The eighteenth chapter of the Micrologus is an explanation of the Diaphonia, by which term we are to underftand thofe precepts that teach the ufe of the organ, and its application to vocal melody ; concerning which Guido fays, that fuppofing the finger to utter any given found, as for inftance A, if the organ proceeds to the acutes, the A may be doubled, as A D' a, in which cafe it will found from A to D, a diateffaron, from D to a, diapente, and from A to a, a diapafon : he farther fays, that thefe three kinds, when uttered by the organ, commix together with great fweetnefs, and that the apt copulation of notes is called Symphony. He gives this which follows as an example of the diaphonia.

		c	d	e	d	c	d	e	d	c	c	h
	Diapente											a
												G
Diapafon		F	G	A	G	F	G	A	G	F	F	E
												D
	Diateffaron											F
		C	D	E	D	C	D	E	D	C	C	B A
												Γ

And adds that a cantus may be doubled by the organ, and the organ itfelf in the diapafon, as much as the organift pleafes. He fays that having made the doubling of founds fufficiently clear, he will explain the method of adapting grave founds to a cantus, in the doing whereof he premifes that the Diaphonia admits not of the femitone nor diapente, but that it accepts of the tone, ditone, femiditone, and diateffaron, among which confonances the diateffaron holds the principal place. Of the modes, which he calls Tropes, he fays that fome are fit, fome more fit, and others moft fit, for the Diaphonia ; and

thefe

thefe degrees of fitnefs feem to bear a proportion to the number of concordant intervals in each. As an inftance of the higheft degree of this kind of perfection, he mentions the third and fourth tones, which he fays follow kindly and fweetly, with a tone, ditone, and diateffaron.

In the nineteenth chapter are contained fundry examples to illuf- trate the precepts delivered in the chapter preceding, among which are the following.

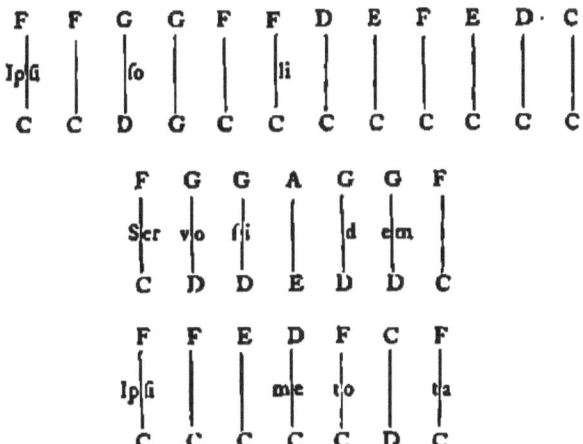

The feveral precepts contained in the Micrologus, together with the examples above given, may ferve to fhew the inartificial contexture of the mufic in thofe early days: they farther tend to confirm thofe accounts which carry the antiquity of the organ back to a time, when, from the uncultivated ftate of the mechanic arts, it would hardly be fuppofed that an inftrument fo wonderfully conftructed could have been fabricated *.

* The ftate of the mechanic arts, fo far as they relate to the conftructing and making the feveral utenfils and conveniences for domeftic life, would, were it poffible to come at it, afford great fatisfaction to a curious enquirer, as it would enable him, by a comparifon of two very remote periods, to eftimate the degree of perfection at which we are now arrived. Few of thofe perfons, who are curious enough to attend to the manual operations of our
                                                                      Englifh

After delivering the precepts of the Diaphonia, the author from Boetius relates the difcovery of the confonances by Pythagoras. He exhorts fuch as mean to become excellent in mufic to take the mo- nochord for their guide, and repeats his inftructions for making and dividing it.

A little farther on he refumes the confideration of the tones, and is fomewhat precife in afcertaining their refpective limits, and diftin- guifhing between the authentic and the plagal. He fays that the fame antiphon may be fung in different founds without changing the harmony : or, in other words, that it may be fo tranfpofed, as that the founds may bear the fame relation to each other as if not tranfpofed. He fays that the fecond letter, by which we are to underftand ♭, is rejected as ignoble, and unfit to be the principal of any tone : the reafon of this is, that its fifth is defective, as being lefs than a true diapente by a femitone.

The refidue of this tract, the Micrologus, confifts of mifcellane- ous reflections on the ufe and efficacy of mufic : towards the clofe of it is the following tetraftic.

> Quafdam lineas fignamus variis coloribus
> Ut quo loco fit fonus mox difcernat oculus ;
> Ordine terciæ vocis fplendens crocus radiat,
> Sexta ejus, fed affinis flavo rubet minio.

Upon which he obferves, that if a letter and colour be not affixed to a Neuma, it will be ' like a well without a rope.' Thefe verfes are an abfolute enigma, and it would be a vain attempt to explain them, did not a paffage in another part of this author's writings afford fome intimation that by the red line he intended to denote the F, and by the yellow the C cliff: however we are not to lock on this method of diftinguifhing the cliffs by lines of different colours as

Englifh artificers, are ignorant that they work with an amazing degree of truth and accu- racy. A very curious book, now extant, called the Book of St Alban's, written by dame Julyans Bernes, priorefs of the nunnery of Sopwell, near St. Alban's, defcribes the method of making an angling rod in the year 1496; and gives us to underftand that the mechanics of that time thought the neateft method of hollowing a ftick for that purpofe was the burn- ing it through with a hot fpit; and it is not unlikely but that four hundred years before that, an organ-pipe was perforated in no better a manner : and if we fuppofe the fame want of neatnefs in the various other parts of that complicated machine of which we are now fpeaking, we may fairly conclude that both the organ and the mufic of the eleventh cen- tury were equally rude and inartificial.

the invention of Guido, fince it appears to have been in ufe fo early as the year 900, which is at leaft an hundred years before the time when he wrote.

He feems to clofe his tract with an affurance that he has made the rules clear, and laid open to fingers the regular and perfect manner of finging, in a method unknown to former times. But he immediately refumes his fubject in thefe words, ' Temporibus noftris ' fuper omnes homines fatui funt cantores;' and goes on to explain fome particulars that are before but obfcurely treated of; in the doing whereof Guido takes occafion to reprefent the woful ftate of mufic, and the deplorable ignorance of fingers at the time when he wrote; the whole is curious, and will be beft underftood if given in his own words, which are nearly thefe.

' In thefe our times no fet of men are fo infatuated as fingers; in
' every other art we improve, and in time attain to a greater degree
' of knowledge than we derived from our teachers : thus by reading
' over the fimple pfalter, boys are enabled to read other books; the
' countryman by ufe and exercife acquires the knowledge of agricul-
' ture; he who has pruned one vine, planted one fhrub, or loaded
' one afs, is able not only to do the fame again, but to do it better;
' but, miferable difciples of fingers, they, though they fhould practice
' every day for an hundred years, would never be able to fing even
' one little antiphon themfelves, nor without the help of a mafter,
' but lofe as much time in attaining to fing, as would have enabled
' them fully to underftand the divine writ. And what is more to
' be lamented is, that many clerks of the religious orders, and
' monks too, neglect the pfalms, the nocturnals, and vigils, and
' other leffons of piety, by which we are led to everlafting glory,
' while they with a moft foolifh and affiduous labour profecute the
' art of finging, which they are never able to attain. Who then can
' refrain from tears to fee fuch an evil creep into the church ? from
' whence fuch difcord enfues, that we are unable to celebrate the di-
' vine offices. Nor is this all, for this ignorance of their duty begets
' reproach, from whence proceeds contention; fcarce the fcholar
' with the mafter can agree, and much lefs one fellow fcholar with
' another. Neither is there any uniformity of mufic at this day in
' the churches; for there are as many kinds of antiphons as there are
' mafters; infomuch that no one can fay as heretofore, this is the
' antiphon

' antiphon of Gregory, of Leo, or Albert, or any other; but every
' one either varies these, or forms others at his pleasure. It ought
' not therefore to give offence if I contend with the corruptions of the
' times, and endeavour to render the practice of music conformable
' to the rules of the art : and as all these corruptions have arisen from
' the ignorance of musicians, I must earnestly request that no one
' will presume to make antiphons, unless he be well skilled in the
' art of forming them according to the known and established rules
' of music ; it being most certain that he who is not the disciple of
' truth will be a teacher of error. And for these reasons I intend,
' with the help of God, to note down a book of antiphons, by means
' whereof any assiduous person may attain to sing truly, and without
' hesitation ; and if any one doubts the efficacy of our method, let
' him come and see what our little boys can do, who labouring un-
' der their ignorance, as not being able to read the common pfalter,
' are yet capable of singing the music to it, and can without the
' help of a master sing the notes, though they cannot pronounce
' the words.'

The letters of Gregory, he says, ' are so disposed, that if a note be
' repeated ever so often it will always have the same character; but the
' better to distinguish the order of notes, lines are drawn near to each
' other, and notes are placed on these lines, and also on the spaces be-
' tween the lines.' He adds, ' we make use of two colours, yellow
' and red, by means whereof I give a rule very useful and convenient
' for finding out the tone and the letter of the monochord, to which
' any given neuma is to be referred. There are seven letters in the
' monochord ; and wherever you see the yellow it is the sign of the
' third letter, and wherever red it denotes the sixth, whether the
' colours are drawn in the lines or over them.'

This is the passage above hinted at as containing a solution of the
enigmatical tetrastic at the latter end of the Micrologus : the author
has said that the letters of the monochord are seven ; it is supposed
that he means to exclude Γ from the number, as the chord of which
that letter is a sign is assumed ; if so, the letters must be A, B, C, D,
E, F, G, and then the yellow line will denote the place of C, and
the red that of F. Father Martini, who had an opportunity of con-
sulting a greater variety of missals and other manuscripts than are to
be found in this country, makes no scruple to assert that this is Guido's

meaning,

meaning, and produces divers fragments from ancient books of the
church-offices, which have both a yellow and a red line, the first
ever with the letter C, and the other with F, in the usual place of
the cliff.

The examples of the use of the yellow and red lines produced by
Martini are very many, but as the lines do all stand single, and as
upon, above, and below them divers characters are placed, which
bear not the least resemblance to the points used by Guido and his
successors, it may be questioned whether this variety of colours was
not originally adapted to a method of notation in use before his time,
notwithstanding that it coincides so well with the stave. But Kircher,
in the Musurgia, tome I. pag. 555, has reduced this question to a certainty; and, notwithstanding the general opinion, that before the time
of Guido the only method of notation in use was by the Roman capital
and small letters, which St. Gregory introduced, Martini proves that
the notators, as they are called, of that time, made use of certain marks
in this form)) Π w •• ⌡ : * and as to lines of different colours, Kircher relates that he had found in the monastery of Vallom-
brosa sundry very ancient books, written for the use of the choir there,
before the time of Guido; and that the method of notation in those
books was by a red line, with certain notes or points placed in different
situations above and below, according to the intervals intended to be
marked by them †.   Nivers speaks also to the same purpose; for enquiring into the causes of the corruption of the Cantus Gregorianus,
he assigns for one, the uncertainty of the method of notation before
the time of Guido; for he says till his reformation of the scale, the
characters were only small points, commas, accents, and certain little
oblique strokes, occasionally interposed; which great variety of minute
figures he says was very difficult to comprehend, still more to retain,
and impossible to reduce to practice without the assistance of a master.
In proof of this assertion he waves the authority of Kircher, who has
mentioned the same fact, and says that he engaged in an exact and

* Stor. della Musica, pag. 183.
† What Guido has said respecting the stations of the cliffs, and the practice of distinguishing them by red and yellow lines, is confirmed by the specimens above inserted from
Kircher; but it may here be remarked that they were also distinguished by lines of a different thickness from the others in the stave, as appears by the following example, taken
from the Lexicon Diplomaticum of Johannes Ludolphus Walther, fol. Ulm. 1756.

laborious

Laborious refearch among the moſt ancient manuſcripts in the library of the king of France, and in that of St. Germain De Prez, and others. Nay, he ſays that he had cauſed the Vatican to be ſearched, and

Pag. 461.

Benedicta ᳵ ᳵet uenerabilis es uirgo mari

a que fine tactu pudoris inuen· ta es

mater faluato ris ᷎Ꝟ uirgo ᳵ ᳵ

ᳵ ᳵ dei genetrix quem to tus non capit

or ᳵ bis in tua fe claufit fit uif' tera

factus homo· Alleln ᳵ ᳵ ya ᳵ ᳵ ᳵ

and had received from thence, memoirs and extracts from manuscript
antiphonaries, and graduals, many of which were above nine hundred years old, in which these characters appear. He farther says,
that in this method of notation, by points and other marks, it was
impossible to ascertain the difference between the tone and semitone,
which is in effect saying that the whole contrivance was inartificial,
productive of error, and of very little worth. Dissertation sur le Chant
Gregorien, chap. vi.   Specimens of this method of notation, taken
from Martini, vol. I. pag. 184, are inserted in the following plate *.

* There has lately been discovered in the library of Bennet college in Cambridge, a
manuscript containing examples of the method of notation by irregular points above
                                                                          spoken

From what has been said some idea may be formed of the nature and tendency of the Micrologus, and other tracts of Guido. Whether he was the author of any other than have been mentioned, is not easy to determine; but it seems that those from which the foregoing extracts are taken, contain as much of his doctrine as he thought communicable by writing; for it is to be remarked that he frequently takes occasion to say that some particulars of it are not to be underftood but by a familiar converfation, and it is to be feared that moft of his readers muft entertain the fame opinion.

It no where appears that any of his works were ever printed, except that Baronius, in his Annales Ecclefiaftici, tom. XI. pag. 73, has given at length the epiftle from him to his friend Michael of Pompofa, and that to Theodald bifhop of Arezzo, prefixed to the Micrologus, and yet the writers on mufic fpeak of the Micrologus as of a book in the hands of every one. Martini cites feveral manufcripts of Guido, as namely, two in the Ambrofian library at Milan, the one written about the twelfth century, the other lefs ancient: another among the archives of the chapter of Piftoja, a city in Tufcany; and a third in the Mediceo-Laurenziano library at Florence, of the fifteenth century, thefe are clearly the Micrologus. Of the Epiftle to Michael of Pompofa, together with the Argumentum novi Cantus inveniendi, he mentions only one, which he fays is fomewhere at Ratifbon [*].

Of the feveral tracts above-mentioned, the laft excepted, a manufcript is extant in the library of Baliol college in Oxford. Several fragments of the two firft, in one volume, are alfo among the Harleian manufcripts now in the Britifh Mufeum, Numb. 3199, but fo very much mutilated, that they afford but fmall fatisfaction to a curious enquirer. The Baliol manufcript contains alfo the Enchiridion of Odo, which Guido, at the clofe of the Argumentum novi Cantus inveniendi, highly commends; as alfo the tract of Berno abbot of Richenou before mentioned.

fpoken of; and a learned and ingenious gentleman of that college has furnifhed this work with the following article from the catalogue of that collection.
473. N. xxxviii. Codex membranaceus minoris formæ, ante Conquifitionem exaratus. Hymni (five ut fæpius in hoc Codice nominantur Tropi) recitandi diebus Dominicis et feftis inter facra celebranda cum notis muficis.
The laft fpecimen in the above place is inferted from the manufcript thus defcribed.
[*] Storia della Mufica, paffim, et pag. 457, Guido.

2   The

The above particulars of the life and labours of Guido, which have indeed the merit of being immediately collected from his own writings, are poffibly all that we fhall ever be able to learn about him ; for by a kind of fatality, very difficult to account for, his memory lives only in his inventions, and though there is fcarce a dictionary, not to mention the innumerable tracts that direct the practice of vocal mufic, but mention him as having taken the fyllables UT, RE, MI, FA, SOL, LA from a hymn of St. John the Baptist, and applied them to certain notes in the fcale of mufic, yet no one author of credit, if we except cardinal Baronius, and he feems more defirous of recording the Invention, than perpetuating the Memory of its author, has thought him worthy of a more honourable teftimony than is every day given by the writers of Biliotheques, Memoirs, and Anecdotes, to any fcribbling profeffor of the Belles Lettres.

This fupinenefs, or ignorance, or whatever elfe it may deferve to be called, with refpect to Guido and his improvements, has been the fource of many miftakes, as namely, that he was the inventor of mufic in confonance, and of the organ and harpfichord ; and that he was the firft that introduced the practice of defcant in finging. In the courfe of the prefent work fome of thefe inventions have been, and the others feverally will be, fixed at periods very remote from that in which Guido lived : at prefent it fhall fuffice to refute them by faying, that as to the organ, it was invented probably about the middle of the eighth century ; for that in 797 the emperor Conftantine Copronymus fent one as a curious and valuable prefent to Pepin king of France ; and in 828 pope Vitalianus introduced the organ into the fervice of the church ; and farther, Guido himfelf in his Micrologus frequently mentions the organ as an inftrument in common ufe in his time. As to the harpfichord, the name of it, or of the fpinnet, of which it is manifeftly but an improvement, does not once occur in the writings of the monkifh muficians who wrote after Guido, nor in the works of Chaucer, who feems to have occafionally mentioned all the various inftruments in ufe in his time. Gower indeed fpeaks of an inftrument called the citole, in thefe verfes :

He taught hir, till fhe was certeyne
Of harpe, citole, and of riote,
With manp a tetune, and manp a note.
Confeffio Amantis, fol. 178, b.
And

And by an ancient lift of the domeſtic eſtabliſhment of Edward III.
it appears that he had in his ſervice a muſician called a cyteller, or
cyſteller: the citole or ciſtole, derived from ciſtella, a little cheſt,
might probably be an inſtrument reſembling a box with ſtrings on the
top or belly, which by the application of the taſtatura or key-board,
borrowed from the organ, and jacks, became a ſpinnet. But as to the
harpſichord, the earlieſt deſcription of it which, after a careful re-
ſearch, could be found, is, that of Ottomarus Luſcinius, in his Muſurgia, publiſhed at Straſburg, in 1536. As to deſcant, it was
the invention, as ſome imagine, of Bede, and he lived under the
Saxon heptarchy, about the year 673; and laſtly, whether the
common uſe of the organ and the practice of deſcant, do not pre-
ſuppoſe muſic in conſonance, is ſubmitted to the judgment of all who
profeſs to know any thing of the ſcience.

As Guido made no pretenſions to great learning, or ſkill in philoſophy, but ſeems indeed to have been abſorbed in the ſtudy of his
pſalter and the church offices, no one of the many writers who have
occaſionally mentioned him, has entered into the particulars either
of his character or his inſtitution; but his reformation of the ſcale,
his improvement of the ſtave, and the method of notation invented
by him, which has introduced into the world a kind of univerſal
character [*], beſpeak his merit more than the moſt laboured encomium could do, and have procured him a reputation that muſt in
all probability endure as long as the love of muſic ſhall ſubſiſt.

[*] It is literally true, that for the purpoſe of repreſenting muſical ſounds by writing,
the ſyſtem of Guido is an univerſal character; and every day's experience informs us
that men of different countries, and who ſpeak different languages, and therefore are incapable of verbal communication, have yet the ſame idea of the power of the muſical characters, which they diſcover by their readineſs in performing compoſitions that they
have never ſtudied. And this conſideration has induced ſome men to aſſert that the ſcale
of muſic might be made to ſerve the purpoſe of an alphabet. Biſhop Wilkins firſt ſtarted
this notion, and it is very ingeniouſly proſecuted in his tract entitled The ſecret and ſwift
Meſſenger, chap. xviii. and by Mr. Oldys in the life of Peter Bales, the famous penman,
in the Biographia Britannica.

END OF THE FIRST VOLUME.